Introduction

Never has a highway been so symbolic as Route 66. Snaking across the belly of America, this fragile ribbon of concrete first connected the prairie capital of Chicago with the California dreamin' of Los Angeles in 1926. Along the way, lightning-bug towns sprouted up with neon signposts, motor courts and drive-ins, all providing the simple camaraderie of the road.

History credits Oklahoma entrepreneur Cyrus Avery with pushing through the new national highway linking the Great Lakes with the greater Pacific Ocean. But Route 66 was not built on a surveyor's straight-lined course like other transnational highways. Instead the new highway linked existing roads, many of them through rural areas, earning itself the moniker 'The Main Street of America.'

Called the 'Mother Road' in John Steinbeck's novel *Grapes of Wrath,* Route 66 came into its own during the Depression years, when hundreds of thousands of migrants escaping the Dust Bowl slogged westward in beat-up old jalopies painted with 'California or Bust' signs. Meanwhile unemployed young men were hired to pave the final stretches of muddy road. They completed the job, as it turns out, just in time for WWII.

Hitchhiking soldiers and factory workers rode the road next. Then amid the jubilant post-war boom, Americans took their newfound optimism and wealth on the road, essentially inventing the modern driving vacation. And so the era of 'getting your kicks on Route 66' was born. Traffic flowed busily in both directions.

But just as the Mother Road hit her stride, President Dwight Eisenhower, a US army general who had been inspired by Germany's *autobahn,* proposed a new interstate system for the USA. Slowly but surely, each of Route 66's more than 2200 miles was bypassed. Towns became ghosts and traffic ground nearly to a halt. The highway was officially decommissioned in 1984.

Yet individuals and small towns struggled on. A movement for preservation of the Mother Road resulted in the **National Historic Route 66 Association** (w *www.national66.com*), a nonprofit alliance of federal, state and private interests. Every year another landmark goes up for sale, but more are rescued from ruin.

Today this phoenix-like highway relies on travelers just like you, who are daring enough to leave the interstate behind for a combination of blue-line highways and gravel frontage roads. You can still spy relics of the original road, stay in a jewel of a 1930s motor court, revel in sunsets over the Painted Desert or splash in the Pacific Ocean. This is not just your mother's Mother Road. It's yours.

Getting There

Chicago's **O'Hare International Airport** *(ORD; ☎ 800-832-6352)*, 18 miles northwest of downtown, is the nation's busiest airport. Other domestic flights land at **Midway Airport** *(MDW; ☎ 773-838-0600)*. There are taxi stands and shuttle services *($12-20 to downtown)* waiting curbside at both. **Chicago Transit Authority** (CTA) trains depart for 'The Loop' (downtown) from O'Hare *(Blue Line; $1.50; 45 min)* and Midway *(Orange Line; $1.50; 30 min)* around the clock.

Los Angeles International Airport *(LAX;* ☎ *310-646-5252)*, 13 miles southeast of Santa Monica, can be reached by direct domestic and international flights. Airport transport and shared van services *($15 to Santa Monica)* depart outside the arrivals level. Shuttle C connects to LA's county bus center, **Big Blue Bus No 3** *(75¢; 45 min)* departs for Santa Monica until midnight daily.

Chicago and LA are served by **Amtrak** *(*☎ *800-872-7245;* |W| *www .amtrak.com)* trains, which arrive at Union Station in both cities, and by **Greyhound** *(*☎ *800-229-9424;* |W| *www.greyhound.com)* buses.

When & How to Drive Route 66

Peak season for traveling Route 66 is Memorial Day to Labor Day. If you want to do it right, plan on two weeks, though it'd be easy to spend up to a month, taking detours that tickle your fancy. In a hurry? Zoom on the interstate through most of southern Illinois, Missouri and Texas, and concentrate on New Mexico and Arizona. As long as the weather holds, the shoulder months (April, May and September) can be good, especially for avoiding crowds, but most events happen in summer. Also, some attractions are closed (or at least keep shorter hours) during the off-season.

If you're going to drive your own car, joining the **American Automobile Association** *(AAA;* ☎ *800-922-8228;* |W| *www.aaa.com; annual membership $50)* makes sense. AAA provides minor breakdown service, short-distance towing and free driving maps.

National car rental chains like **Alamo** *(*|W| *www.alamo.com)* usually charge $120 to $200 per week, plus $400 for one-way rentals (ie, pick-up in Chicago, return in LA). Renting an RV or motorhome runs $850 to $1100 per week, plus excess mileage and return fees; try **El Monte** *(*☎ *562-483-4941, 800-367-3687;* |W| *www.elmonterv.com)*, **Road Bear RV** *(*☎ *818-865-2925, 866-491-9853;* |W| *www.roadbearrv.com)* or **Cruise America** *(*☎ *480-464-7300, 800-327-7799;* |W| *www.cruiseamerica.com)*.

Visions of *Easy Rider?* It's tempting to rent a motorcycle. **Eagle Rider** *(Chicago* ☎ *708-749-1500, 888-966-1500; 1301 S Harlem Ave, Berwyn; Los Angeles* ☎ *310-536-6777, 800-501-8687; 11860 S La Cienega Blvd)* charges $750 weekly (plus requires a hefty deposit) for borrowing its hogs.

HOW TO USE THIS BOOK

Opening hours for places listed in this book apply during summer, except where otherwise noted. When entry fees are not listed, sites are free (although some may request a small donation). Price gradings (eg $10/7/5) indicate admission for adults/students & seniors/children. As a rule of thumb, diner and cafe meals cost $5 to $10, while motel doubles start from $25 to $35.

This guide follows the classic route from Chicago to LA. Those driving eastbound should look out for the ⟨east⟩ icon, which indicates where driving instructions differ from simply 'going the other way.'

In Route 66's gateway cities, rely on Lonely Planet's condensed *Best of Chicago* and *Best of LA* guides. Lonely Planet's *Southwest USA* explores New Mexico and Arizona in depth. Buying a Rand McNally USA road atlas (priced from $12) isn't a bad idea either.

ONELY PLANET
)AD TRIP
OUTE 66

Sara Benson

Lonely Planet Publications
Melbourne • Oakland • London • Paris

Road Trip Route 66
1st edition – October 2003

**Published by Lonely Planet
Publications Pty Ltd**
ABN 36 005 607 983
90 Maribyrnong St, Footscray, Victoria
3011, Australia

Lonely Planet Offices
Australia Locked Bag 1, Footscray,
Victoria 3011
USA 150 Linden St, Oakland, CA 94607
UK 72-82 Rosebery Ave, Clerkenwell
London EC1R-4RW
France 1 rue du Dahomey, 75011 Paris

Photographs
The cover image is available for licensing
from Lonely Planet Images.
e lpi@lonelyplanet.com.au
W www.lonelyplanetimages.com

Cover photograph by
Oliver Strewe

ISBN 1 74059 580 7

text & maps © Lonely Planet Publications
Pty Ltd 2003
photos © photographers as indicated
2003

Printed through The Bookmaker
International Ltd.
Printed in China

Contents

Introduction 3
Getting There.......................................3
When & How to Drive
Route 66 4
Highlights...5
Illinois 7
   Chicago 7
   Springfield 11
Missouri 14
   St Louis.......................................14
   Springfield 18
Kansas 20
Oklahoma 21
   Tulsa 22
   Oklahoma City.........................24
Texas 28
   Amarillo 29
New Mexico 32
   Santa Fe 35
   Albuquerque.............................37
   Gallup 41
Arizona..42
   Petrified Forest &
   Painted Desert.........................43
   Winslow 43
   Flagstaff 45
   Kingman 49
California...51
   Barstow 53
   Pasadena 56
   Hollywood 57
   End of the Road -
   Santa Monica 59
Index 62

BEST ROUTE 66 BOOKSTORES

Whether you're wondering about the history of the Mother Road or looking for a bestseller to read en route, these local independents will hook you up.

57th Street Books ☎ 773-684-1300; 1301 E 57th St, Chicago, IL

Savvy Traveller ☎ 312-913-9800; 310 S Michigan Ave, Chicago, IL

Left Bank Books ☎ 314-367-6731; 399 N Euclid, St Louis, MO

Full Circle Bookstore ☎ 405-272-9321; 50 Penn Pl, Oklahoma City, OK

Travelers Pack ☎ 405-755-2924; 9427 N May Ave, Oklahoma City, OK

Collected Works Bookshop ☎ 505-988-4226; 208B W San Francisco St, Santa Fe, NM

Travel Bug ☎ 505-992-0418; 328 S Guadalupe Suite E, Santa Fe, NM

Bookworks NM ☎ 505-344-8139; 4022 Rio Grande Blvd NW, Albuquerque, NM

Page One Inc ☎ 505-294-2026; 11018 Montgomery NE, Albuquerque, NM

University of New Mexico Bookstore ☎ 505-277-5451; University of New Mexico, Albuquerque, NM

Northern Arizona University Bookstore ☎ 928-523-6673; San Francisco St, Flagstaff, AZ

Distant Lands ☎ 626-449-3220; 56 S Raymond Ave, Pasadena, CA

Duttons Brentwood ☎ 310-476-6263; 11975 San Vicente Blvd, Los Angeles, CA

Book Soup-West Hollywood ☎ 310-659-3110; 8818 Sunset Blvd, West Hollywood, CA

Travelers Bookcase ☎ 323-655-0575; 8375 W Third St, Los Angeles, CA

Highlights

SWEET SLEEPS

The flavor of the Mother Road is often strongest in small towns, where the vintage neon signs flicker on after sunset and there's only one bar to kick it at with the locals (and of course, a diner for breakfast the morning after). You can still feel a blast from the past in: McLean, TX (p28); Tucumcari, NM (p32); Santa Rosa, NM (p33); Grants, NM (p40); Holbrook, AZ (p43); Winslow, AZ (p43); Williams, AZ (p46); Kingman, AZ (p49); Oatman, AZ (p50) and Needles, CA (p51).

CHICAGO ARCHITECTURE FOUNDATION

See Chicago's finest buildings – minimalist skyscrapers to Prairie School designs – on foot or bike, or by bus, train or boat. Book ahead.

☎ 312-922-8687, tickets ☎ 312-902-1500; **W** www.architecture.org; ArchiCenter shop, Santa Fe Bldg, 224 S Michigan Ave; open 9am-7pm Mon-Sat, 9:30am-6pm Sun

SLEEPING

You'll pay through the nose to stay in the Loop. The well-run **Hostelling International (HI) Chicago** *(☎ 312-360-0300, 800-909-4776 code 244; 24 E Congress Pkwy; dorm beds $30-33)* is ideally placed.

OHIO HOUSE MOTEL

Exhibiting an astounding 1960s-style exterior, this motel's rooms are clean, if not quite inspiring, and rates are rock-bottom for the location.

☎ 312-943-6000; 600 N LaSalle Dr; doubles from $85

RED ROOF INN

Only a block off the glittering 'Miracle Mile' of Michigan Ave, this high-rise version of the motel chain is a bargain. Small pets allowed.

☎ 312-787-3580, 800-733-7663; 162 E Ontario St; doubles from $75, off-site parking $22

HOTEL BURNHAM

As lavish as its sister Allegro and Monaco hotels, this living architectural landmark boasts luxury boutique rooms, sensational views and evening wine service in the lobby.

☎ 312-782-1111, 866-690-1986; 1 W Washington St; double room/suite from $165/215

EATING & ENTERTAINMENT

Free weeklies *New City* and the *Chicago Reader* cover dining, nightlife and entertainment; pick them up to see what's on.

LOU MITCHELL'S

Near Union Station, Lou's coffee shop is *the* place to get breakfast before hitting the road. Choose fluffy omelettes or the French toast stacked sky-high.

☎ 321-939-3111; 565 W Jackson Blvd; open 5:30am-3pm Mon-Sat, 7am-3pm Sun

PIZZERIAS

Chicagoans get fired up about the rivalry between deep-dish pizza joints. Sample the inimitable pies of the original **Pizzeria Uno** *(☎ 312-321-1000; 29 E Ohio St)* or its stepchild, **Pizzeria Due** *(☎ 312-943-2400; 619 N Wabash Ave)*. Another favorite is **Gino's East** *(☎ 312-943-1124; 633 N Wells St)*.

BILLY GOAT TAVERN

'Butt In Any Time' is the motto at this underground haunt of hard-nosed journalists and other big-shouldered types. Double cheeseburgers were made famous by the *Saturday Night Live* skit.

☎ 312-222-1525; 430 N Michigan Ave; open 6am-2am Mon-Fri, 10am-3am Sat, 11am-2am Sun

LIVE JAZZ & BLUES

In the Loop, **Buddy Guy's Legends** *(☎ 312-427-0333; 754 S Wabash Ave)* blues club also serves Southern soul food. **Andy's Jazz Club** *(☎ 312-642-6805; 11 E Hubbard St)* has acts at noon and again at night. Around since the Prohibition-era speakeasy days, the **Green Mill** *(☎ 773-878-5552; 4802 N Broadway)* is worth the drive. Show up on Wednesdays when Kurt Elling works his vocal magic.

THE CHAIN GANG

Tired of the motel crapshoot along Route 66? Some vintage motor courts are great for snapping photos in front of – and yet not so nice to stay in. Chain motels along the interstate cloverleaves are characterless, but standards are usually guaranteed. Some offer special deals for Internet-only bookings. Also try online travel discounters (such as w *www.orbitz.com*). An outdoors(-ish) alternative, **Kampgrounds of America (KOA)** (☎ *406-248-7444;* w *www.koacampgrounds.com*) offer 'kamping kabins' (bring a sleeping bag and cooking equipment).

Best Western ☎ 800-780-7234, w www.bestwestern.com
Days Inn ☎ 800-329-7466, w www.daysinn.com
Microtel Inn ☎ 888-771-7171, w www.microtelinn.com
Motel 6 ☎ 800-466-8356, w www.motel6.com
Travelodge ☎ 800-578-7878, w www.travelodge.com
Super 8 Motels ☎ 800-800-8000, w www.super8.com
Howard Johnson ☎ 800-446-4656, w www.hojo.com

WRIGLEY FIELD
As the sun shines on the ivy-covered walls of 'The Friendly Confines,' the outfield bleachers are the place to be. No matter that the underdog Chicago Cubs last won the World Series baseball championship in 1908!

information & tours ☎ 773-404-2827, tickets ☎ 800-843-2827; 1060 W Addison St, at N Clark St

SOUTHPORT LANES & BILLIARDS
The 1920s are preserved here, and attendants still reset the pins on all four lanes by hand. Microbrews and stained-glass windows dandify the bar.

☎ 773-472-6600; 3325 N Southport Ave, north of Belmont Ave; bowling $17 per game; open until 1am

On the Road

Getting out of Chicago is simple. From Michigan Ave drive west on Adams St (east▷: one-way traffic follows Jackson Blvd) past Greektown, then turn left on Ogden Ave and drive through the suburbs of Cicero and Berwyn. At Harlem Ave, detour north to Cermak Rd, where **'The Spindle'** (*Cermak Plaza Shopping Center*) impales a tower of cars on a steel spike. Farther north is the turn-of-the-20th-century **Frank Lloyd Wright Home & Studio** (☎ *708-848-1976; 951 Chicago Ave, Oak Park; admission $9/7; tours at 11am, 1pm & 3pm Mon-Fri, every 20mins 11am-3:30pm Sat-Sun*).

Backtrack south of Ogden Ave, turning west onto Joliet Rd. Join southbound I-55 (exit 277). Timeless **Dell Rhea's Chicken Basket** (*645 Joliet Rd; open 11am-9pm Mon-Thu, 11am-10pm Fri-Sat, 11am-8pm Sun*), east of exit 274 on the north frontage road, started off as a 1930s gas station lunch counter; there's live music some weekends. At exit 269, take Joliet Rd, which merges onto IL53 south in **Romeoville**. Lockport's lovely **Illinois & Michigan (I&M) Canal Visitor Center** (☎ *815-838-4830; 8th & State Sts; open 10am-5pm Tue-Sat*), which has a historical museum and recreational trail, is a short drive east.

Stay on US53 south to **Joliet**. Its prison was parodied in *The Blues Brothers* with John Belushi and Dan Aykroyd. These days Joliet is known for its riverboat casinos. Turn left at Ruby St, cross over the bridge, then turn right onto Chicago St. Downtown is the **Rialto Square Theatre** (☎ 815-726-6600; 102 N Chicago St), an old vaudeville movie palace, and the brand-spanking-new **Joliet Historical Museum** (204 Ottawa St; admission $5/4/3; open 10am-5pm Tue-Sat, noon-5pm Sun).

Drive south on Clinton St, turn left on Ottawa St, then veer left onto Martin Luther King Jr Dr (east▷: turn right at the T-intersection, left onto Scott St, another left onto Van Buren St, then right onto Chicago St) and follow IL53 out of Joliet. NASCAR stock car races, drag races and demolition derbies happen at the **Route 66 Raceway** (☎ 815-727-7223; 500 Speedway Blvd). Pass by **Elwood** and the antiques shops of **Wilmington**, before which the **Launching Pad Drive-In** (810 E Baltimore St; open 10am-10pm) is towered over by the 1960s **Gemini Giant**, a fiberglass astronaut with a rocket in his hand. Farther on in **Braidwood** is the **Polka Dot Drive-In** (☎ 815-458-3377; 222 N Front St), and in **Godley**, look for reproduced **Burma Shave signs**.

After **Braceville**, take a right on Main St in **Gardner**, then join the frontage road south. In downtown **Dwight**, by the old rail depot, is a Frank Lloyd Wright–designed **bank** (122 W Main St), next to the Fox Development Center, which boasts Tiffany stained-glass windows. Back on the frontage road, drive south through **Odell** past the restored **Standard Gas Station**. On the outskirts of **Pontiac**, look for the **Old Log Cabin Inn** (18700 Old Route 66; 5am-4pm Mon-Tue, 5am-8pm Wed-Sat); when Route 66 was re-aligned, the restaurant was jacked up and rotated 180° to face the new road.

A string of nondescript small towns – Chenoa, Lexington and Towanda – leads into the university cities of **Bloomington-Normal**. Route 66 zigzags through Normal by turning left on Henry St, right on Pine St, left on Linden St, right on Willow St and finally meeting Main St. Follow Business 51 through downtown Bloomington all the way south to Veterans Pkwy (Business 55). En route, detour east on Washington St to the **Beer Nuts Factory Outlet Shop** (☎ *800-233-7688; 103 N Robinson St; open 8am-5pm Mon-Fri*) or out west to the **Upper Limits** (☎ *309-829-8255; 1304 W Washington St*), one of North America's biggest climbing and rappelling venues, inside an old grain elevator.

On Veterans Parkway drive west past Morris Ave, then go right on Cabintown Rd, left onto Fox Creek Rd and angle onto Beich Rd, which passes under I-55. Take the west frontage road lazily south, stopping off in Shirley at **Funk's Grove** *(open 9am-5pm)*, a 19th-century farm justifiably famous for its 'maple sirup.' Enter **McLean**, taking a left onto Main St, then right onto US136 by the **Dixie Trucker's Home** *(open 24hrs)*, a truck stop that stakes its reputation on good food and hospitality. Inside is the diverting Illinois Route 66 Hall of Fame.

Before crossing the railroad tracks, turn left onto the west frontage road. At **Atlanta**, future home of a 'Tall Paul' Bunyan statue, follow Arch St through town. Back on the frontage road, motor south to **Lincoln**, renamed in 1853 after a circuit judge of such integrity that he was called 'Honest Abe.' Mr Lincoln allegedly christened the town by spitting watermelon seeds on the ground. Take Lincoln Parkway west, then south through town.

Eventually turn left back onto the east frontage road. Drive south by turning left again toward **Broadwell**, where the legendary 1930s-era **Pig-Hip Restaurant** has been renovated as a museum. In **Elkhart**, the **Under the Prairie Frontier Archaeological Museum** (☎ *217-947-2522; 109 Governor Oglesby St; admission $3; open 10am-4pm Wed-Sun*) exhibits frontier relics from pre–Civil War days. The museum's **Route 66 Drive-In** *(open 9am-4pm Mon-Fri)* serves up soups and sandwiches. At **Williamsville** (exit 109), rejoin I-55 to exit 105. Take Business 55 into Springfield, driving south onto Peoria Rd. Turn right onto Taintor Rd, which becomes 5th St.

Springfield

The capital of Illinois is a perfect overnight stop. Its obsession with Abe Lincoln, the prairie lawyer who practiced here before serving as US president during the Civil War, does not detract from the quieter pleasures of simply ambling its old-fashioned streets.

Take 5th St south (〈east〉 : one-way northbound traffic follows 6th St) through downtown. The **Springfield Illinois Convention & Visitors Bureau** (☎ *800-545-7300; ⓦ www.visit-springfieldillinois.com; 109 N 7th St; open 8am-5pm Mon-Fri*) has maps and brochures.

SIGHTS & ACTIVITIES

The **Illinois state fair** takes over the fairgrounds in mid-August. In September, the **International Route 66 Mother Road Festival** (☎ *866-783-6645; ⓦ www.route66fest.com*) features a '50s sock hop, live entertainment, classic car shows and a nighttime parade cruise.

LINCOLN'S HOME NATIONAL HISTORIC SITE
Pedestrian-only 'Mr Lincoln's Neighborhood' covers four square city blocks. Abe and Mary Lincoln lived here until 1861, before moving into the White House. Lines for tours can be long.

☎ 217-492-4241; visitor center: 426 S 7th St; open 8:30am-5pm, extended hours in summer

LINCOLN'S TOMB

It's majestically situated in **Oak Ridge Cemetery** *(open 9am-5pm)*, where poet Vachel Lindsay lies. A full-sized reproduction of Lincoln's casket is found nearby at the curious **Museum of Funeral Customs** *(1440 Monument Ave; admission $3; open 10am-4pm Mon-Sat, 1-4pm Sun)*.

MUSEUMS

An early Frank Lloyd Wright prairie-style design, the 1902 **Dana-Thomas House** *(☎ 217-782-6776; 301 E Lawrence St; tours $3/1; open 9am-4pm Wed-Sun)* has an impressive interior collection of architect-designed furniture and fixtures. With over five decades of memorabilia collected from alongside Route 66, **Shea's Gas Station Museum** *(2075 Peoria Rd; open 7am-4pm Tue-Fri, 7am-noon Sat)* is delightful. So is the **Oliver Parks Telephone Museum** *(529 S 7th St; open 9am-4:30pm Mon-Fri)*.

SLEEPING, EATING & ENTERTAINMENT

There are a few campgrounds on the outskirts of town. Overlooking Mr Lincoln's neighborhood, the **Henry Mischler House B&B** *(☎ 217-525-2660; 802 E Edwards St; doubles/suites $75/95)* has antique furnishings. Decent chain motels cluster near interstate exits.

Cozy Dog Drive In *(2935 S 6th St; open 8am-8pm Mon-Sat)* is run by the family who invented the corn dog (a hot dog deep-fried in cornmeal batter and served on a stick, you know). Another vintage 1940s sign hangs outside **Coney Island Restaurant** *(210 S 5th St; open 7am-2pm Mon-Sat)*, a tasty greasy spoon. Near the Lincoln home, **Route 66 Sandwich Shop** *(727 Cook St)* also sells souvenirs.

Southwest of downtown, **Route 66 Drive-In** *(☎ 217-698-0066; 1700 Recreation Dr, off Chatham Rd; open in summer & Oct weekends)*, at Knight's Action Park and Caribbean Water Adventure, has been recently reincarnated.

On the Road

Leaving Springfield, join southbound I-55 (exit 92A/B) past Lake Springfield. At exit 88, take the west frontage road, driving south through **Glenarm**. A few miles west, the red **Sugar Creek Covered Bridge** is a well-signposted diversion. Rejoin I-55 (exit 82) to **Divernon** (exit 80). On the west frontage road, drive south by **Farmersville**. Three

DETOUR: LINCOLN'S NEW SALEM	

So you've been to Springfield, Illinois. Now step back 150 years in time to Honest Abe's childhood home, completely restored as an outdoor living history museum with live blacksmithing, rail-splitting and even a country store. The outdoor amphitheater stages musicals on summer nights and during the off-season, traditional Chautauqua entertainment. A state historic site, **Lincoln's New Salem** *(☎ 217-632-4000; tent/RV campsites $8/11; open 9am-5pm Wed-Sun)* is about 25 miles northwest of Springfield on IL97.

IN THE MIX

Where would the Great American Road Trip be without a mix tape of travelin' tunes? You'd have to include Bobby Troup's original 'Route 66' song that told us to 'get our kicks' here (note: Nat King Cole did a sweet cover version; for a more ominous interpretation, try Depeche Mode). Then throw in some folk music by Woody Guthrie, Chuck Berry rock 'n roll, country swing by Bob Wills and California surf songs to complete the time warp.

In California, **Route 66 Records** (☎ 760-241-2005; *Victorville Auction House, 15538 7th St, Victorville; open 10am-5pm Mon-Sat, 11am-4pm Sun*) can customize CDs with selections from their own handpicked vinyl collections. Otherwise Texas' **Lazy SOB Recordings** (☎ 512-480-0765; w *www.lazysob.com*) sells *Songs of Route 66: All-American Highway* and *More Songs of Route 66: Roadside Attractions* (featuring 'Albuquerque – Asleep at the Wheel') online.

miles beyond **Waggoner** is **Our Lady of the Highways**, a 1950s Italian marble replica of the Virgin of Lourdes.

A few miles past IL108, the route turns left over I-55 on N 16th Ave. Take the east frontage road south toward **Litchfield**, which has classic car shows during summer. Hook left onto Old Route 66 (1938–46 alignment), passing the **SkyView Drive-In Theatre** (☎ 217-324-4451; *entry $1 per person; open in summer*) and the 1924 **Ariston Cafe** (☎ 217-324-2023; *open 11am-10pm*), serving some of the best food on Route 66, south of IL16 (Union St). Leaving Litchfield, rejoin the east frontage road (1940–77 alignment) by turning left (east⟩: turn right onto N 10th Ave).

Take Old Route 66 south to **Mt Olive**. At the Union Miners Cemetery is the **Mother Jones Memorial**, where Mary Harris Jones, the early labor activist who organized protests against local mine bosses before her death in 1930, lies buried. Farther south the 1926 **Soulsby Shell Station** may be the oldest of its kind on Route 66. After the railroad trestle, turn left onto US Hwy 66, then right on Old Route 66 to cross back west over I-55 and keep going past **Staunton**, home of **Henry's Route 66 Rabbit Ranch** (☎ 618-635-5655; *cnr Old Route 66 & Madison Ave; open 9am-4pm Mon-Fri*), a souvenir shop and information center. Staunton's **Crystal Ballroom** (☎ 618-635-3506; *20631 Staunton Rd*) has live big bands and dancing.

Drive past **Williamson**, turning left onto IL4 to head back toward I-55, where you pick up IL157 south toward **Hamel**. A few lonely farmhouses and grain silos appear on the horizon before you enter **Edwardsville**. Follow IL157 as it twists through town. Outside town, where IL157 turns off left toward the interstate, instead drive straight onto Chain of Rocks Rd and into **Mitchell**. Follow IL203 south onto I-270 (exit 204), but before driving west over the Mississippi River, detour at exit 3. Follow IL203 south again, then turn right at the first stoplight and drive west to the 1929 **Chain of Rocks Bridge** (*open to pedestrians & cyclists sunrise-sunset*). A mile long, this bridge has a 22-degree angled bend, a well-known hazard until the 1960s, when it was closed to automobiles.

MISSOURI

Beyond southern Illinois' cornfields, Route 66 lands across the mighty Mississippi in St Louis, where the Gateway Arch stands. Explorers Lewis and Clark started their journey west in nearby St Charles. The Mother Road gathers momentum as it speeds over the Ozark Plateau, dipping in a rich vein of Civil War history across the state. Although a handful of Route 66 icons can still be seen in Missouri – the Black Madonna shrine, Meramec Caverns and the ruins of John's Modern Cabins – this 300-mile stretch of highway doesn't have as much to catch your eye as states farther west. In addition to publishing a quarterly magazine, the **Route 66 Association of Missouri** (☎ *417-865-1318;* |w| *www.missouri66.org; 1602 E Dale St, St Louis, MO 65803)* has a nifty website and organizes an annual motor tour every September.

St Louis

St Louis may be seriously underrated. With its leafy tree-lined neighborhoods, a thriving music scene, university life and not least of all, professional sports, what's not to like? Get the lowdown at the **St Louis Visitors Center** (☎ *800-916-0092;* |w| *www.explorestlouis.com; Kiener Plaza, 6th & Chestnut Sts; open 9am-5pm Mon-Fri, 9am-2pm Sat)* or grab a free weekly *Riverfront Times*.

Route 66 passes through some of the city's prettiest and most impoverished neighborhoods. After crossing the Mississippi bridge on I-270, exit immediately onto Riverview Blvd. Turn left at Broadway, then right at Calvary Ave, winding uphill through a historic cemetery. Turn left onto Florissant Ave, veer onto Mullanphy St, then right at 13th Ave and left onto Tucker Ave. Parking lots at Laclede's Landing, a short walk north of the Arch, charge $5. Leaving downtown, make two rights – first on Gravois Ave, then on Chippewa St heading west.

SIGHTS & ACTIVITIES

Near Washington University, St Louis' **Walk of Fame** *(6200-6600 Delmar Blvd)* salutes hometown stars Betty Grable, Chuck Berry and Miles Davis, as well as poet TS Eliot. Family-friendly **Forest Park**, site of the 1904 World's Fair, has free art and history museums and an Art Deco greenhouse.

GATEWAY ARCH
The Eiffel Tower of the Great Plains, this stainless-steel icon rises 600 feet tall (and it's an unnerving four-minute tram ride to the top). Also part of the Jefferson National Expansion Memorial, visit the subterranean **Museum of Western Expansion** and nearby 1839 **courthouse**, where the Dred Scott slavery case was tried.

☎ 877-982-1410; |w| www.stlouisarch.com; tram ride $8/5/3, plus movie $11/8/5.50; open 9am-5pm, to 9pm in summer

ANHEUSER-BUSCH BREWERY
On tours of the Bud 'King of Beers' bottling plant, visit the famous Clydesdale horse stables. Bring ID for free draft beers from the bar afterwards.

☎ 314-577-2626; 12th & Lynch Sts; tours 9am-4pm Mon-Sat & 11:30am-4pm Sun, to 5pm Jun-Aug

INTERNATIONAL BOWLING MUSEUM & CARDINALS HALL OF FAME

Bowl on a 1922 attendant-sets-up-the-pins lane and pay tribute to the city's beloved baseball team here.

☎ 314-231-6340; 111 Stadium Plaza; admission $6/4; open 9am-5pm Apr-Sep, 11am-4pm Tue-Sat Oct-Mar

MUSEUM OF TRANSPORTATION

A railroad and classic car haven, this one displays pieces of the Route 66's Coral Court motel, a Streamline Moderne landmark demolished in 1995.

☎ 314-965-7998; 3015 Barrett Station Rd, off I-270 exit 8; admission $4/1.50; open 9am-5pm Tue-Sun

SLEEPING & EATING

Chain motels hide around outlying interstate cloverleaves. If you're hoping for a room with a view of the Arch, it's gonna cost you. On the Illinois side of the river, **Casino Queen** (☎ 800-777-0777; |w| www.casinoqueen .com; Sun-Thu doubles from $49) offers complimentary breakfast and an RV park.

Imo's (☎ 314-421-4667; 742 S 4th St) serves up fresh, tasty thin-crusted St Louis pizza. Farther south in Soulard, **John D McGurk's Irish Pub** (☎ 314-776-8309; 1200 Russell Blvd) has Irish country cooking and Bailey's cheesecake. The **Soulard farmers market** (Lafayette Ave & 7th St; open 8am-5:30pm Wed-Fri, 6am-5:30pm Sat) dates from 1779.

On warm summer evenings, lines outside **Ted Drewes Frozen Custard** (6726 Chippewa St; open from 11am Feb-Dec) get incredibly long. Other neighborhoods with good grazing are **Grand South Grand**, north of Chippewa St, and **'The Loop'** on Delmar Ave near Washington University.

ENTERTAINMENT

The city's Latin quarter, **Soulard**, is known for its blues music. In a red-brick townhouse, **1860s Hard Shell Cafe & Bar** (☎ 314-231-1860; 1860 S 9th St) is one of many clubs. The **Big Muddy Blues Festival** happens over Labor Day weekend at Laclede's Landing.

University-area **Blueberry Hill** (tickets ☎ 314-534-1111; 6504 Delmar Blvd; open from 11am), a burger joint filled with rock memorabilia and dart boards, hosts Chuck Berry shows monthly ($25).

Inside Union Station, **Route 66 Brewery & Restaurant** (☎ 314-231-4677; 1820 Market St) has touristy American food, but also microbrews and memorabilia. **Busch Stadium** (☎ 314-421-2400; tickets from $9) is the shrine to the Cardinals major-league baseball team.

On the Road

From Watson Rd, take I-44 west of I-270. On the former site of the later infamous 1920s Times Beach housing development, **Route 66 State Park** (open 7am-30mins after sunset) offers hiking, cycling and bird-watching, with a visitor center inside a 1930s roadhouse.

At Eureka (exit 264), drive south on Hwy W, turn right on Hwy FF, left on Hwy F and after another half-mile, right onto St Joseph Rd for the **Black Madonna Shrine** (open 9am-4pm, to 7pm May-Sep, Sun mass 10am), built by a Polish émigré Franciscan monk. A series of folk-art grottoes hand-decorated with shells, glass and statuary surround an open-air chapel. Inside hangs a copy of the 'Black Madonna' painting, associated with miracles in the Old World. Downtown Eureka has fetching antiques shops.

Back on I-44 drive west to **Allenton** (exit 261), the turn-off for **Six Flags** (☎ *636-938-4800)* theme park, and follow the south frontage road past the **Red Cedar Inn** (☎ *636-257-5414; 1047 E Osage St; meals $5-25; open 4-10pm Mon-Sat, 1-9pm Sun)*, made with logs from the family's farm in 1934. Continue through **Pacific** on Business 44. Before reaching Diamonds truck stop restaurant, **Shaw Nature Reserve** (☎ *636-451-3512; admission $3/2/free; open 7am-30mins before sunset)* has tallgrass prairie and a wetlands boardwalk

Cross over I-44 on MO100, then cruise west on the north frontage road past US50. Beyond the concrete wigwam selling curios and jerky, turn back south over exit 242. Head west through **St Clair** on the frontage road, watching for the MO30 intersection, then move back to the north frontage road of I-44 (exit 239) and continue westbound. Take Hwy JJ back south over the interstate at **Stanton** (exit 230). Famous as a childhood vacation destination since 1935, **Meramec Caverns** (☎ *573-468-3166, 800-676-6105; admission $14/7, tent/RV sites $12/16, motel doubles $45-55; open 9am-4pm, extended hours in summer)* pioneered the bumper sticker, and painted advertisements on barns across Midwest. The stalactites are remarkable, but the experience pure kitsch.

Closer to I-44 is the **Riverside Reptile Ranch** (☎ *573-927-6253; admission $4.50/3.50)*. Drive west on the south frontage road, gawking at the conspiracy-crazy **Jesse James Wax Museum** (☎ *573-927-5233; admission $5/2.50; open 9am-6pm Jun-Aug, 9am-5pm Sat-Sun May & Sep)*, which insists that the outlaw was alive until 1951. Next door the **Antique Toy Museum** (☎ *573-927-5555; admission $5/2; open 10am-4pm in summer)* displays 20th-century toys in the windows. Farther west in **Sullivan**, after passing the two-story **White House Grill** (☎ *573-468-8565; 960 E Springfield Rd)*, jog right on Elmont Rd, then left at the stop sign.

HIGH POINTS

Route 66 has miles of flat highway for cruisin'. To achieve a bird's-eye perspective over the landscape, visit:

Sears Tower (p7; Chicago, IL)
Gateway Arch (p14; St Louis, MO)
Oral Roberts University Prayer Tower (p22; Tulsa, OK)
Cross of the Martyrs walk (p35; Santa Fe, NM)
Acoma Pueblo, nicknamed 'Sky City' (p38; NM)
Sandia Tramway (p37; Flagstaff, AZ)
Grand Canyon's Desert View Watchtower (p47; AZ)
Sitgreaves Pass (p50; AZ)
Griffith Observatory (p57; Hollywood, CA)
Pacific Park's oceanfront Ferris wheel (p59; Santa Monica, CA)

Keep going through **St Cloud** and **Bourbon**. In **Cuba**, the quaint **Wagon Wheel Motel** (☎ 573-885-3411; 901 E Washington St) often has its 'No Vacancy' sign lit. It's next door to the **Missouri 'Hick'-ory Barbecue** restaurant. The **Route 66 Cafe** (510 W Washington St) is on the way to **Rosati**, where the vineyards at **Rosati Winery** (☎ 573-265-6892; 22050 State Rd KK; B&B doubles $70-75) were planted in the 1920s. Drive west into downtown **St James**, with its antiques shops, a popcorn company and **Johnnie's Bar** (225 N Jefferson St). Turn right, taking MO68 north across the interstate. Drive almost 9 miles west toward **Rolla**, turning south onto US63 and entering town after passing **Memoryville USA** (☎ 573-364-1810; 1008 W 12th St; open 8am-6pm Mon-Fri, 9am-5:30pm Sat-Sun), an antique car museum and full-fledged automobile restoration shop. Follow Business 44 through town, looking for the **Stonehenge replica** on the University of Missouri campus. On Kingshighway St, avoid the interstate on-ramp by turning left on the south frontage road. Hungry? En route to **Doolittle**, stop off at the **Sirloin Stockade** (1401 Martin Springs Ave) buffet and bakery or the pink 'faux'-dobe **Pinga's Tortilla Flat** (14775 County Road 7100) for Southwest cuisine.

Rejoin I-44 westbound (exit 176), but first detour west on the north frontage road to see the ruins of the 1950s **John's Modern Cabins**. An homage to Burma Shave signs advises, 'Photograph these / While You're Here / The Wrecking Ball / Is Looming Near.' Back on I-44, take exit 172 onto the north frontage road, then turn left onto Hwy J to cross over to the south side of the interstate again. Drive on the divided road and turn left before the Big Piney River onto an older loop by **Devil's Elbow**, a river bend that once created logjams for lumberjacks and road accidents for Route 66ers. The **Elbow Inn Bar & Barbecue Pit** has live music, dartboards and canoe rentals.

Rejoin the south frontage road by turning left near **Judy's Place** (Teardrop Rd), another roadhouse. Drive west through **St Robert** and follow MO17 into **Waynesville**, which has a town square. Its old stagecoach stop, which later served as a Civil War hospital, is now a **historical museum** (open 10am-4pm Sat Apr-Sep). Breakfast and lunch are served at **Paradise German Deli & Sidewalk Café** (219 W Historic 66), or stop by **Big Will's Bar-B-Que** (326 E Historic 66; closed Sun).

Refreshed, drive west on MO17. Cross back south over I-44 (exit 153) for **Buckhorn**. Turn right onto Hwy P, then left onto Hwy AA in **Laquey**. Hang a right onto Hwy AB and drive over a steel-truss bridge above the Gasconade River toward **Hazelgreen**. Route 66 rolls in perfect harmony with the Ozark's green hills, in contrast to the straight, dull cut of interstate superslab nearby. Watch carefully for Hwy F, then turn right and cross I-44. Take the north frontage road into **Lebanon**, turning right onto Mill Creek Rd, then left onto Business 44. The landmark 1940s **Munger Moss Motel** (☎ 417-532-3111; 1336 Route 66) has a rich history – its motto is 'here yesterday, today and tomorrow.' You can bowl across the street at purple-painted **Starlite Lanes**. Driving west out of town, **Dowd's Catfish House** (☎ 417-532-1777; 1760 W Elm St) has fishing nets with plastic starfish in the window. At Hwy W (I-44 exit 127) jog onto the north frontage road to **Phillipsburg** (exit 118). Cross back over to the south side of I-44, then cruise Hwy CC west through **Conway** and **Marshfield**. Take Hwy OO through **Strafford** and MO744 (Kearney St) into Springfield.

Springfield

Springfield is a natural stopping point – on the map, that is. But it's not a pretty place to spend the night.

Through town, Route 66 follows two alignments. Either stay on Kearney St all the way to US160 south, or turn left earlier onto Glenstone Ave south, then right onto St Louis St, which becomes College St near downtown. Either way, end up driving west on the Chestnut Expressway (Business 44) out of Springfield.

SIGHTS & ACTIVITIES

The **Ozark Empire Fair** happens in late July or early August. In downtown, the 1923 **Shrine Mosque auditorium** *(601 E St Louis St)* and **Landers Theater**, a restored 1909 playhouse, are worth seeing.

A mecca for fishers, hunters and others with macho pursuits, **BASS Pro Shops Outdoor World** *(☎ 417-887-7334; 1935 S Campbell Ave)* has its own artificial waterfalls, aquariums and stuffed game animals mounted on the walls. The **PFI Western Store** *(☎ 417-889-2668; 2816 S Ingram Mill Rd, near Hwy 65 & Battlefield Rd)* stocks over 8000 pairs of cowboy boots and boasts a 16-screen wall playing country music videos.

Twelve miles southwest of Springfield, rural **Wilson's Creek National Battlefield** *(☎ 417-732-2662; 6424 W Farm Road 182; admission $3; open 8am-5pm)* is near **General Sweeney's Museum** *(☎ 417-732-1224; 5228 S Hwy ZZ; admission $3.50/2.50; open 10am-5pm Wed-Sun Mar-Oct)* of trans-Mississippi regional Civil War history.

SLEEPING, EATING & ENTERTAINMENT

The renovated **Best Western Route 66 Rail Haven** *(☎ 417-866-1963, 800-304-0021; 203 S Glenstone Ave; doubles from $55)* still has that old motor court feel. Other budget motels on S Glenstone Blvd charge from $20.

Steak & Shake *(1158 E St Louis St; open 24hrs)* restaurant, the chain that urged Americans to 'Takhomasak' (ie, take home a sack of steakburgers), has an early vintage outlet here. Do the time warp again at **Anton's Coffee Shop** *(S Glenstone Ave, at Grand St; open 7am-2pm)*. Arty eateries and nightlife spots line **Walnut St** downtown. Elsewhere, **Cowboys 2000** *(☎ 417-866-5577; 2929 E Kearney St)* advertises live bull riding on Friday and Saturday nights.

On the Road

Follow Business 44 toward **Halltown**, joining MO266. Where the road splits, don't veer left on MO96. Instead go straight on an old section of highway, past where it meets MO96 again. After another half-mile, turn right over a steel-truss bridge through the ruins of **Spencer** and on the other side of town, finally turn left onto westbound MO96. The highway passes through **Heatonville**, **Albatross**, **Phelps**, **Rescue** and **Avilla**. Follow MO96 (a detour left onto CR118 for an older highway loop) over the Spring River bridge. Closer to Carthage near the Conoco station is the turn-off to **Red Oak II** (look for folk artist Lowell Davis' metal sculpture signs). This oddball town was moved here from over

DETOUR: BRANSON

An hour's drive south of Springfield on US65, Branson is the Disneyland of country music. On the neon-lit '76 Strip' (MO76), it's an Ozark Vegas with miles of motels, restaurants, wax museums and dozens of music and comedy theaters putting on three shows daily ('Baldknobbers Jamboree,' anyone?). Helping to spur the Branson boom, **Silver Dollar City** (☎ 800-475-9370; 399 Indian Point Rd) is an amusement park simulating the Mark Twain era. The **Roy Rogers & Dale Evans Museum** (☎ 417-339-1900; 3950 Green Mountain Dr; admission $14.50/9; open 9am-6pm) was recently moved here lock, stock and Trigger from California. Outside town, **Table Rock State Park** (reservations ☎ 877-422-6766; tent/RVsites $8/14) has beautiful lakeside camping.

20 miles away. It's part rural history museum, part art installation – but 100 percent wacky.

Take Central Ave into **Carthage**, burned down by Confederate forces in 1864. Belle Starr, aka the 'Bandit Queen,' grew up in her father's hotel here on the town square, presided over by the Neoclassical Revival–style **Jasper County Courthouse** (open 8:30am-4:30pm Mon-Fri). Belle later achieved infamy as a horse thief and Civil War guerrilla. Learn about her and the 1861 Battle of Carthage at the **Civil War Museum** (205 S Grant St; open 8:30am-5pm Mon-Sat, 1-5pm Sun). For walking and driving tour booklets, ask at the **visitors bureau** (☎ 417-359-8181; 335 S Main St; open 8am-5pm Mon-Fri). On the square, **Carthage Deli & Ice Cream** (301 S Main St) has a soda fountain.

Drive south on Garrison Ave, then right onto Oak St and over the bridge. On the site of the old Park Cafe and Motor Court, the small **Powers Museum** (☎ 417-358-2667; 1617 W Oak St; open 11am-4pm Tue-Sat, extended & Sun hours Jun-Oct, closed Jan & Feb) delves into Missouri history. Continue west on Oak St, veering left at the Y-intersection. Past the **66 Drive-In Theatre** (☎ 417-359-5959; 17231 Old 66 Boulevard; admission $5/2), take US71 southbound to **Webb City**. Historic Route 66 signs point the way into a charmingly old-fashioned downtown, but to see the giant 1970s **praying hands sculpture** ('Hands in Prayer – World in Peace'), stay on US71.

Then turn left at Madison Ave (Business 71), follow Rangeline Rd and turn left onto 7th St for the vintage **Ko Ko Motel** (☎ 417-624-6493; 3102 E 7th St; rooms $35) or right into downtown **Joplin**, where the **Red Onion Cafe** (203 E 4th St; open 8am-9pm) flavors its fried chicken with coconut and hangs chalkboard dessert menus on the walls. One of Joplin's most fascinating sights, the **Crystal Cave**, can't be seen; find out why at the **Tri-State Mineral Museum & Dorothea B Hoover Historical Museum** (☎ 417-623-1180; 4th St & Schifferdecker Ave; open 10am-4pm Mon-Sat, 1-4pm Sun) in Schifferdecker Park. Then drive west on MO66, cutting off right onto old Route 66 before the state line.

KANSAS

Today the Sunflower State is known more for its tornadoes and the *Wizard of Oz* movie than its Route 66 heritage. Just over 13 miles – less than 1 percent of the Mother Road – pass through this southeast corner of Kansas. But the roadside relics seen here are impeccably preserved, making it well worth driving. The **Kansas Historic Route 66 Association** (☎ *316-848-3330;* |w| *www.route66.itgo.com/ks66.html; PO Box 66, Riverton, KS 66770)* is headquartered at Eisler Bros General Store.

On the Road

Pass over the state line on old Route 66. **Hell's Half Acre**, where the land has been left ravaged by lead and zinc mining, saw violent miner strikes in the mid-1930s. Enter **Galena** on Front St, then turn left at Main St. **Up in Smoke** (☎ *620-783-5106; 418 S Main St)* claims an original Route 66–style barbecue recipe.

Turn right a few blocks later on KS66, following 7th St west. In an old train depot, the **Galena Mining and Historical Museum** (☎ *620-783-2192; 319 W 7th St; open hours vary)* was the pet project of Howard Litch, a Route 66 garage owner. Mr Litch has passed on, but the museum lives with photo exhibits and precious metals on display. Volunteers show off some odd gadgets, like the hand-operated razor sharpener.

Drive past the spooky **cemetery** with its wrought-iron gates and out of Galena. Elm and maple trees shade the route over the Spring River into **Riverton**. The 1920s **Eisler Brothers General Store** sells Route 66 souvenirs, deli picnic food, groceries and even greenhouse plants.

Keep driving old Route 66 (go straight across the four-lane highway) toward the 1923 **Marsh Rainbow Arch Bridge**, the last of its kind. From here, it's less than 4 miles south to **Baxter Springs**, the site of a Civil War massacre. Veer left off Willow Ave onto 3rd St toward downtown, turning right onto Military Ave. Nearby, the **Heritage Center & Historical Museum** *(8th & East Aves; open 10:30am-4:30pm Tue-Sat, 1-4:30pm Sun)* is a comprehensive place.

Old-timers gossip over morning coffee at circa-1940 **Murphey's Restaurant** *(1046 Military Ave; open 6:30am-1pm)*, famed for its pies. Catty-corner stands the **Cafe on the Route & Little Brick Inn** (☎ *620-856-5646; 1101 Military Ave; singles/doubles/suites $55/65/70)*, in a Victorian-era bank. Take Military Ave south to the comfy **Baxter Inn** (☎ *620-856-2106, 866-856-9820; 2451 Military Ave; singles/doubles $40/45)* motel. Briefly detour here on a signposted older loop, then rejoin US69A and roll into Oklahoma.

Oklahoma rightly touts itself as 'Native America' – referring both to its natural beauty and cultural roots. Oil discovery in the early 20th century brought the state wealth, but a severe Depression-era drought caused the 'Dust Bowl,' in which the western half of Oklahoma's topsoil literally blew away. Thousands of 'Okies' migrated west hoping for a better future, the subject of John Steinbeck's *Grapes of Wrath*.

At the gateway to the American West, Oklahoma claims nearly 400 miles of the Mother Road. Both favored stopovers – the cultural oasis of Tulsa and cowboy-proud Oklahoma City – are worth exploring. In between those cities, lazy stretches of highway dip into local history, ranging from pioneer battlefields to a motel where Elvis once slept. The **Oklahoma Route 66 Association** (☎ *918-712-7229, 405-258-0008;* [w] *www.oklahomaroute66.com; PO Box 21382, Oklahoma City, OK 73156*) sponsors a statewide cruise in June and publishes an invaluable and comprehensive trip guide ($4.95).

On the Road

Slip into Oklahoma on Alt US69, and notice the downtown murals of **Quapaw**. Ask around for directions to the Devil's Promenade east of town, where fans of the mysterious can glimpse the 'Spooklight' phenomenon (maps are available at Waylan's in Miami; see below). In **Commerce**, follow US69 (aka Mickey Mantle Blvd) past the **'Rock Shop.'** Drive into **Miami** on Main St. **Waylan's Ku-Ku Hamburgers** *(915 N Main; open 10am-11pm)* has an adorable cuckoo sign, mushroom burgers and sells the Oklahoma Route 66 Association's trip guide. Farther along, the Spanish Revival–style **Coleman Theater** (☎ *918-540-2425; 103 N Main St; tours 10am-4pm Tue-Fri, 10am-noon Sat)* was on the 1930s vaudeville circuit. The **Dobson Museum** *(110 'A' St SW; open 1-4pm Wed, Fri & Sun)* has Native American and pioneer artifacts. At the main intersection, turn right onto OK10 (Steve Owens Blvd).

Drive over the Neosho River bridge. Stay with US69 through **Narcissa** and **Afton**, past the ruins of the Rest Haven Motel and an old **DX gas station**, now undergoing restorations (sneak a peek at the Packards inside). US69 leads past pecan groves into **Vinita**, home to the **Will Rogers Memorial Rodeo** in August and a **Calf Fry Festival** (ie, cooked bull testicles) in September. The 70-year-old **Eastern Trails Museum** (☎ *918-256-2115; 215 W Illinois St; open 1:30-4pm Mon-Sat)* is respected. Across town, a sharp-looking exterior cloaks an inexpensive menu at fourth-generation **Clanton's Cafe** *(319 E Illinois St; open 5:30am-8pm Mon-Sat, 11am-2pm Sun)*.

Take Wilson Ave past a few mom-and-pop motels out of town, following US60 onto OK66. Drive through **White Oak**, **Chelsea** and **Foyil**. Turn right by the **Top Hat Dairy Bar** *(open 8am-9:30pm)* onto Hwy 28A for 4 miles to **Totem Pole Park** *(open dawn-dusk)*, a pinnacle of kitschy folk art dating from 1948. Foyil was also the home of Andy Payne, winner of the 1928 Bunion Derby, a transcontinental foot race.

Continue on OK66 into **Claremore**, a worthwhile stop for Old West memorabilia. At the **Will Rogers Memorial Museum** (☎ *918-341-0719;*

1720 W Will Rogers Blvd; open 8am-5pm), the vaudevillian, who famously never met a man he didn't like, is buried on a hillside. Downtown **JM Davis Arms & Historical Museum** *(☎ 918-341-5707; 333 N Lynn Riggs Blvd; open 8:30am-5pm Mon-Sat & 1-5pm Sun)* holds the world's largest privately owned gun collection. **Will Rogers Stampede Rodeo** saddles up in June. A circa-1900 home, **Carriage House Bed & Breakfast Inn** *(☎ 918-342-2693, 800-634-8541; 109 E 4th St; doubles $50-100)* provides guests with cookies for late-night snacking. Family-owned **Swan Brothers Dairy Farm** *(☎ 918-341-2298; 938 E 5th St)* sells all-natural cheese. Continue on Lynn Riggs Blvd past a few motels and **Cotton-Eyed Joe's Barbeque** *(☎ 918-342-0855; 715 S Moretz Ave)*.

West of the Verdigris River bridge, the first turn-off is to **Molly's Landing** *(☎ 918-266-7853; 3700 N Hwy 66; open noon-9pm Mon-Sat)*, a charmingly backwoods restaurant serving steaks and seafood. Farther west sits the defunct Arrowhead Trading Post. Opposite is a 1970s water park, the **Blue Whale**. It may still be the leviathan's king of the road, but swimming and sliding down the water slides is forbidden. Closer to central **Catoosa**, take a right onto Ford St after crossing Spunkey Creek, then left at Cherokee St and left again onto 193rd Ave. Drive south under I-44 to 11th St, which cruises west into Tulsa.

Tulsa

Oklahoma's second-largest city is also its nicest. 'Oil Capital of the World' in the early to mid-20th century, Tulsa reaped the rewards of statewide wells. Cyrus Avery, godfather of the Mother Road, made his home here. Follow 11th St west into downtown. At Elgin Ave, curve left onto 10th St briefly, then follow onto 11th St at Boulder Ave. Cross Denver Ave and curve onto 12th St, heading toward the river. At the bridge, turn left onto Southwest Blvd out of town (east⟩ : after bridge, take 2nd right onto 12th St).

SIGHTS & ACTIVITIES

Tulsa is famed for its downtown **Art Deco buildings**, mainly between 2nd, 6th, Cheyenne and Cincinnati Sts. After dark the spires of the **Boston Union Methodist Church** *(1301 S Boston Ave)* are lighted.

The 76-foot-tall **Golden Driller** *(21st St & Pittsburg Ave)* stands guard over the International Petroleum Exhibition (IPE) fairgrounds.

GILCREASE MUSEUM
Fine arts and artifacts depict the American West, Native American and Mexican culture, all endowed by an oil baron of Creek ancestry.

☎ 888-655-2278; 1400 Gilcrease Museum Rd; admission $3; open 10am-4pm Tue-Sun

MAC'S ANTIQUE CAR MUSEUM
Down by the railroad tracks, explore a cavalcade of old-time automobiles, even a 1912 Model T Ford.

☎ 918-583-7400; 1319 E 4th St; admission $3.75/2; open 10am-5pm Sat-Sun

ORAL ROBERTS UNIVERSITY
Named for the TV evangelist, this retro-futuristic campus is where the Jetsons meet Jesus. To prompt funds, Oral once camped out in the 200-foot-tall glass Prayer Tower, east of the huge, bronze praying hands.

☎ 918-495-6807; 7777 S Lewis Ave

SLEEPING & EATING

West of the Arkansas River on I-44 and along E 11th Ave are budget **motels**, some a bit haggard. Chain motels may be a better bet. The 1929 **Nelson's Buffeteria** (☎ 918-584-9969; 514 S Boston Ave), downtown, is popular for its chicken-fried steaks. The faux-retro **Metro Diner** (3001 E 11th St; open 7am-10pm Sun-Fri, 7am-midnight Sat) isn't far from the Bama Pie factory. Railroad-themed **Ollie's Station Restaurant** (☎ 918-446-0524; 4070 Southwest Blvd; open 11am-9pm Mon-Fri, 7am-3pm Sat-Sun) is west of the river. Other neighborhoods for good grazing are **Brookside** (Peoria Ave, south of 33rd St) and **Cherry St** (15th St, east of Peoria Ave).

ENTERTAINMENT

Free *Urban Tulsa Weekly* covers the surprisingly hip scene. With luck, catch a show at the 1920s **Cain's Ballroom** (☎ 918-584-2306; 423 N Main St), which has seen everyone from Patsy Cline to the Sex Pistols. **Caravan Cattle Company** (☎ 918-663-5468; 7901 E 41st St, at Memorial Dr; open Thu-Sat; cover free-$3) has free two-step lessons on Friday nights.

In summer, there's a dandy production of *Oklahoma!* at **Discoveryland!** (☎ 918-245-6552; tickets $16), in Sand Springs, 10 miles west of Tulsa. The **Admiral Twin Drive-In** (☎ 918-835-5181; 7355 E Easton Ave, north of I-244) made an appearance in the Coppola film of SE Hinton's The Outsiders. Bowl at **Rose Bowl** (☎ 918-836-4605; 7419 E 11th St).

On the Road

Southwest Blvd is easy to follow into Sapulpa, becoming Frankoma Rd by **Frankoma Pottery** (☎ 800-331-3650; 2400 Frankoma Rd), established in the 1930s. At OK66, turn right and continue on Mission St past the landmark Norma's Diamond Cafe. Follow OK66 by turning toward downtown, passing the restored 'ghost signs' on historic buildings. **Mr Indian's Cowboy Store** (☎ 918-224-6511; 1000 S Main St; open 10am-5pm Tue-Sat) sells Western and Native American goods.

Heading out of Sapulpa, look for the old highway turning off to the right after the Rock Creek Bridge. Follow this tree-lined stretch for a little over 3 miles to the OK33/I-44 intersection. Hook back onto OK66 through **Kellyville** to **Bristow**, entering on Main St. For barbecue and hot buttered corn-on-the-cob, stop at **Russ' Ribs** (223 S Main St; open 10:30am-7pm Mon-Thu, 10:30am-8pm Fri-Sat). Otherwise, take a right onto 4th St out of town. OK66 passes **Depew** and then **Stroud**, a simple town that hosts an International Brick & Rolling Pin competition on July 4th. The fetching **Rock Cafe** (114 W Main St; open 11am-9pm Mon-Sat) was built in 1939 with stones left over from building Route 66. The **Skyliner Motel** (717 W Main St) has quite a sign.

Drive west to **Davenport** for stomach satisfaction, including **Dan's Bar-B-Que Pit** (706 Broadway) or Indian tacos at **Gar Wooly's 66 Cafe** (☎ 918-377-2230; 1023 Broadway). Next, the road arrives in **Chandler**, the self-proclaimed 'pecan capital of the world.' The **Museum of Pioneer History** (☎ 405-258-2425; 717 Manvel Ave; open 10am-5pm Mon-Fri), with its original brick outhouse, is near the restored cottage-style **Phillips 66 Station** (707 Manvel Ave). With its red-brick buildings, the **Lincoln Motel**

DETOUR: GUTHRIE

Oklahoma's first capital, 30 miles north of Oklahoma City via I-35, is one of the Great Plains' best-preserved towns. Next to the frontier drugstore museum, Guthrie's helpful **visitor center** (☎ 800-299-1889; 212 W Oklahoma Ave) has dozens of B&B brochures. Around the historic 12-square-block downtown are the Scottish Rite Temple, National Four-String Banjo Museum, Oklahoma Territorial Museum and **Vic's Place** (123 N 2nd St), selling gas pump memorabilia. Most places are closed Sunday. A mile south on US77, the **Beacon Drive-in Theater** (☎ 405-282-4512; 2404 S Division St) is open nightly in summer. Look for April's '89er Celebration, the Jazz Banjo Festival in late May and International Bluegrass Festival in October.

(☎ 405-248-0200; 740 E 1st St) has been operating since 1939. **PJ's BBQ** (☎ 405-258-1167; 1423 S Manvel Ave) is open weekends only.

Keep going on OK66 – look for a Meramec Caverns barn – past **Warwick** and **Pioneer Camp BBQ** (☎ 405-356-9409) in **Wellston**. An older alignment of Route 66 here cuts back and forth across OK66, which continues to **Luther**. In **Arcadia**, the settlement where Washington Irving camped in 1832 during his *Tour of the Prairies,* pause at the 1898 **Round Barn** (open 10am-5pm), lovingly restored by volunteers. Inside is a museum of oddly shaped barns around the world. Chow down at **Hillbillee's Cafe** (☎ 405-396-2982; 208 E Hwy 66; B&B rooms $55), where on weekends bands play foot-stompin' tunes. Snap a photo of the old tourist cabins out back, then continue west. Enter **Edmond** on 2nd St, turning left at Broadway onto US77. At Memorial Rd head west, then right onto Kelly Ave for Oklahoma City.

Oklahoma City

Oklahoma's capital is like a four-door 1976 Coup de Ville with broken bumpers and bullhorns on the front: It's big and brawny, but with a style all its own. Enter on Kelly Ave, driving south onto I-44 westbound. Exit at Lincoln Blvd, then head south toward the capitol. Turn right onto 23rd St, bypassing downtown, then head north on May Ave. Enter I-44 west briefly, then follow OK66 out of town.

The **Oklahoma City Convention & Visitors Bureau** (☎ 800-225-5652; w www.okccvb.org; 189 W Sheridan Ave; open 8:30am-5pm Mon-Fri) is downtown.

SIGHTS & ACTIVITIES

Oklahoma City hosts **rodeo events** throughout the year. In late May, the **Red Earth Festival** celebrates Native American culture. Jazz greats like Isaac Hayes and Branford Marsalis turn up for the **Charlie Christian Jazz Festival** in June.

OKLAHOMA CITY NATIONAL MEMORIAL

In April 1995 the terrorist bomb that destroyed the Murrah Federal Building also tore up an entire city block. Self-guided tour booklets of the eloquent memorial are free.

☎ 405-235-3313; 620 N Harvey Ave; museum admission $7/6/5; last tickets sold 5pm

NATIONAL COWBOY & WESTERN HERITAGE MUSEUM

Devoted to cowboy and Native American rodeo traditions, art and popular culture, this big-time museum even contains an entire turn-of-the-century town. Sadly, most cowgirls are left in the dust.

☎ 405-478-2250; 1700 NE 63rd St; admission $8.50/7/4; open 9am-5pm

OKLAHOMA NATIONAL STOCKYARDS

Wake up to the sounds (and smells) of a real-live, whip-cracking stock auction. Bidding starts at 8am. Afterwards walk the Stockyards City district and shop for Western shirts, cowboy boots and Stetson hats.

☎ 405-235-8675; Exchange Ave, south of I-40 exit 148B/149A; admission free; auctions Mon & Tue

SLEEPING & EATING

The **Carlyle Motel** *(☎ 405-946-3355; 3600 NW 39th St; doubles $35)* is one of a precious few mom-and-pop motels, mostly found on the northwest side of town.

Nostalgic eateries abound: try drive-in **Charcoal Oven** *(2701 NW Expressway; open 11am-10:30pm)*, **Beverly's Pancake Corner** *(2115 NW Expressway)* and **Ann's Chicken Fry House** *(4106 NW 39th St; open 11am-9pm Tue-Sat)*, where a *Dragnet*-style police cruiser is parked. Near the famous Milk Bottle building in central OKC, **Kamp's Market & Café** *(☎ 405-524-2251; 1310 NW 25th St; open 8am-7pm)* has delicious deli fare, fruity smoothies and salads fit for a king.

The neon sign outside **County Line Barbecue** *(☎ 405-478-4955; 1226 NE 63rd St; open 11am-9pm Sun-Thu, 11am-10pm Fri-Sat)* handily flashes for 'Immediate Seating.' Inside this former speakeasy, look for jukeboxes, trap doors once used by gangsters, margaritas and sinful desserts. The **Stockyards City District** across town has places to get hearty breakfasts, steaks at night and knock back a drink with real ranchers.

ENTERTAINMENT

Oklahoma Gazette is the free arts and entertainment weekly. The **66 Bowl** *(☎ 405-946-3966; 3810 NW 39th St Expressway)* often hosts Saturday night rockabilly shows. In the Paseo arts district, **Galileo Bar & Grill** *(☎ 405-415-7827; 3009 Paseo Dr; open 11am-2am Tue-Sat, 4pm-midnight Sun)* is a hipster hangout for live open-mic and music events. Sports bars and brewpubs stand near the **Bricktown** stadium.

On the Road

West of Warr Acres and Bethany, turn off OK66 by veering left before Lake Overholser onto an old steel-truss bridge. On the west side of the lake, veer right onto 36th St/Lakeshore Dr. At Mustang Rd turn right, then left onto OK66 toward **Yukon**, country singer Garth Brooks' hometown. An annual Czech festival is held the first Saturday in

October. Look for the famous 'Yukon's Best Flour' sign, opposite a railroad museum.

Farther west in **El Reno**, grab a bite of a 750lb whopper at the **Fried Onion Burger Festival** each May. **Johnnie's Grill** *(301 S Rock Island; open 6am-9pm Mon-Sat, 11am-8pm Sun)* serves 'em year-round. Stay with Business 40 as it zigzags, eventually onto Sunset Dr. A few blocks east at the old Rock Island depot, the **Canadian County Historical Museum** *(☎ 405-262-5121; 300 S Grand; open 10am-5pm Wed-Sat, 1-5pm Sun)* gives trolley tours during summer. Back on Sunset Dr, **Jobe's Charcoal Burgers** *(1220 Sunset Dr; open 9am-6pm)* is a classic drive-in.

Heading west out of El Reno, turn off right by **Fort Reno** *(☎ 405-262-3987; 7107 W Cheyenne St; open 10am-5pm Mon-Fri, 10am-4pm Sat-Sun)*, an old military camp and cemetery, now an agricultural research station. Almost 5 miles farther, at the four-way stop sign, turn north onto US270 for solitary **Calumet**. Curve left before the railroad tracks into **Geary**, where an old log jail sits by the historical museum. Drive south on US281 for 4 miles, then branch right onto a road marked 'South US281.' Here the old two-lane concrete highway crosses the **Pony Bridge** over the Canadian River during its journey toward **Bridgeport**, veering right at the Y-junction by the park.

Follow the north frontage road past **Hydro**. Old downtown is a short detour north, with rooftop dining at the **Graffiti Grill** *(206 W Main; open 11am-8pm)*, which has an old Texaco gas pump, and **Route 66 Soda Fountain** *(125 W Main)* at North Side Drug. Back on the frontage road,

---

PERFECTLY LAZY

Route 66 has plenty of wide open spaces to kick back and do nothing, or take a break by:

- Drinking with the bleacher bums at **Wrigley Field** (p9; Chicago, IL)

- Cycling along the **Illinois & Michigan canal** (p9; Lockport, IL)

- Ambling around eccentric **Red Oak II** village (p18; MO)

- Picnicking beside the **Rainbow Arch Bridge** (p20; KS)

- Getting lost in the **Corn Maize** (p27; Hydro, OK)

- Watching flicks at the **Route 66 Twin Drive-In** (p27; Weatherford, OK)

- Soaking up scenery in the **Painted Desert** (p43; Petrified Forest NP, AZ)

- Catching a perfect desert sunrise over **Death Valley** or **Joshua Tree National Park** (p52; CA)

- Betting on the thoroughbred races at **Santa Anita Park** (p55; CA)

- Splashing in the surf by **Santa Monica Pier** (p59; CA)

drive west past the walk-through **Corn Maize** (☎ 580-772-4401; open Sep & Oct only) and outside **Weatherford**, veer left at the fork to stay on the frontage road. At Washington Ave, jog left, then ride Main St west through downtown, which has a turn-of-the-20th-century **blacksmith shop** (208 W Rainey Ave). Take a left onto 4th St, then right back onto the north frontage road.

Cruise the **Route 66 Twin Drive-In** (☎ 580-772-2432; admission $5/3.50; open Fri-Sun) and several miles later, turn left at the T-intersection to cross over I-40. Take the south frontage road, then before it dead ends, cross back over to the north side of the interstate. Enter **Clinton** by veering right at the stop sign onto Business 40 (Gary Blvd), just east of the Cheyenne Cultural Center. On the west side of town, truly get your kicks at the **Route 66 Museum** (☎ 580-323-7866; 2229 W Gary Blvd; self-guided audio tours $3/2.50/1; open 9am-7pm Mon-Sat, 1-6pm Sun in summer), full of wonderfully esoteric Mother Road memorabilia. The **Best Western Trade Winds & Route 66 Restaurant** (☎ 580-323-2610; 2128 Gary Blvd; doubles from $55) has a shrine to Elvis, who stayed in Room 215. Down the road, the **Dairy Best Drive-In** mixes limeades and chicken-and-potato dinners. **Jiggs Smoke House** (open 9am-5pm Tue-Fri, 9am-7pm Sat), a little log cabin west of town on the north frontage road, sells jerky.

Back in downtown Clinton, take 10th St south past the WPA-built **McLain Rogers Park**. Pass under the interstate, veering right at the Y-intersection and heading west onto the south frontage road. Zigzag back and forth across I-40, reaching **Canute**. Next to its Route 66 Park is a Catholic cemetery with a Depression vintage **grotto**. Drive west on the south frontage road for a mile, then jog north over I-40. Continue west into **Elk City**, turning left onto OK34, then follow Business 40. Heading west, the **Old Town Museum** (☎ 580-225-6266; 2717 W Hwy 66; admission $5; open 9am-7pm Mon-Sat & 1-5pm Sun in summer), a life-sized museum of pioneer, farm and ranch life, has Route 66 exhibits.

West of the OK34 intersection, veer right and at the next T-junction, drive back over I-40. Motor west, then cross back to the north side of the interstate immediately. Follow the frontage road into **Sayre**, where scenes from the movie The Grapes of Wrath were filmed.

Follow Business 40, turning left onto 4th St (US283) and south into downtown. It's hard to resist the **Western Motel** (☎ 580-928-3353; 315 NE Hwy 66; doubles $35) and the **Picket Fence Sandwich & Spud Shop** (1416 N 4th St). Enthusiasts can inspect the privately owned **RS&K Railroad Museum** (☎ 580-928-3525; 411 N 6th St). In downtown, drop by **Owl Drug Store** (101 W Main St) for thick milkshakes or have dinner at the **River Bend Steakhouse** (☎ 580-928-5446; 313 W Main St).

Leaving Sayre, drive over the Red River, then veer right onto the frontage road before reaching the interstate. Cruise west through **Hext**. In the one-stoplight town of **Erick**, there's the quirky **100th Meridian Museum** (☎ 580-526-3221; tours by appt) and a work-in-progress **Roger Miller Museum**, dedicated to the musician who composed 'King of the Road.' Finally, drive into the ghost town of **Texola**.

TEXAS

Texas takes pride in its size, yet Route 66 swallows only a 178-mile slice of highway as it zips across the hard-baked plains of the Panhandle. It's a place of sprawling cattle ranches and endlessly flat landscape, punctuated only by utility poles and windmills. Tumbleweeds and cowboys make it clear this is the American West, but the provincial attitudes are 100 percent Texan. Summers can be stiflingly hot. Some folks hustle as fast as they can to Adrian, the mid-point of Route 66, and drive on. But it's worth slowing down for offbeat attractions and restored relics, maybe stopping overnight in Amarillo. The **Texas Old Route 66 Association** (☎ 860-779-2225; PO Box 66, McLean, TX 79057) makes its home at the Devil's Rope Museum.

On the Road

West of Texola, veer left onto the south frontage road, which follows Business 40 into **Shamrock**, its name an homage to early Irish immigrant settlers. At the intersection with US 83, the **Tower Conoco Station & U-Drop-Inn Cafe** (207 N Main St) is a restored 1930s Art Deco masterpiece. Beside an ancient-looking Magnolia filling station, the **Pioneer West Museum** (206 N Madden St; open 1-5pm Tue-Sat) has a few wacky gadgets, such as an early permanent-wave machine that would suit Medusa. Leaving Shamrock, stay on the south frontage road past **Lela**, then pass over I-40 (exit 146) onto the north frontage road.

Drive west following the divided highway into nostalgia-filled **McLean**, a town established by a rancher who perished on the *Titanic*. One-way traffic west follows First St. (east> : take Railroad St.). The **Devil's Rope Museum** (☎ 806-779-2225; w www.barbwiremuseum.com; 100 Kingsley St; open 10am-4pm Tue-Sat & 1-4pm Sun) has an encyclopedia of barbed-wire fencing and cattle brands. Check out the antiques stores downtown and the vintage **Phillips Service Station** (First St), the first of its kind in Texas. Farther west is the down-home **Red River Cafe** (☎ 806-779-8940; 101 W Hwy 66), serving steaks and catfish.

If good weather allows when you leave McLean, a mile west of TX273, turn south to avoid entering I-40. Hang a right instead and drive east beside I-40, then abruptly turn with the road under the interstate and start driving west on the south frontage road. Entering quiet **Alanreed**, you'll pass the 1890 cemetery, an antique **66 Super Service Station** and church. Back at the interstate, ask at **Crockett's Post Office Motel & Cafe** (☎ 806-779-2202) to see the old Alanreed jail. Then head west on the south frontage road again, getting back on I-40 at exit 132. West of Alanreed, heading toward Groom, once was the most notoriously muddy part of the Mother Road, the **Jericho Gap**. The Gap wasn't paved until the 1930s.

Drive westbound on the interstate to exit 124, then keep to the south frontage road (do not veer back onto I-40) heading west into **Groom**. This one-road town could be completely ignored, except for the so-called 'Leaning Tower of Texas' (a water tower built at an angle) and the 'Tallest Cross in the Western Hemisphere,' erected by a local farmer in

1995. (These days an even taller cross has stands in Effingham, IL.) Want more evidence that Texas stands staunchly in the Bible Belt? Follow the signs to **Blessed Mary's Amer-Tex-Mex Restaurant** (☎ 806-248-0170; *701 Front St).*

Back on the south frontage road, head west toward **Conway**, where a quick detour north on Hwy 207 leads to the **Bug Ranch**, an homage to Amarillo's Cadillac Ranch done with VW Beetles buried in the dirt. Drive west of Conway, then cross over I-40 (exit 89) and pick up the north frontage road. Continue across the first intersection with Business 40, then turn right onto FM1912 and left (west) at the US60 intersection to take Business 40 (Amarillo Rd) past the airport and **English Field Air & Space Museum** (☎ 806-335-1812; *2014 English Rd; open noon-5pm Sat-Sun)* into Amarillo.

Amarillo

Boot-stompin' Amarillo is a real live cattle town. Bizarrely, it also produces 90 percent of the world's helium supply. The **Amarillo Convention & Visitors Council** (☎ 800-692-1338; [w] *www.amarillo-cvb.org; Civic Center, 401 S Buchanan St; open 9am-6pm Mon-Fri, 10am-4pm Sat-Sun)* is a handy point.

On Amarillo's north side, Route 66 turns south near US287 onto Pierce St ([east] : take Buchanan St north). Through downtown, take 6th St west and curve left onto Bushland Blvd, then right onto 9th St at Western Ave. Where 9th St intersects Amarillo Blvd., turn west and follow Business 40 out of town.

SIGHTS & ACTIVITIES

Amarillo's most famous sight is the **Cadillac Ranch**, an experimental art installation of tailfin-bearing Cadillacs buried hood-down in a wheat field. It's south of I-40, between exits 60 and 62. Another brainchild of eccentric helium tycoon Stanley Marsh 3 is the **Dynamite Museum**, a collection of farcical roadside signs placed randomly around town.

Amarillo's **livestock auction** (☎ 806-373-7464; *100 S Manhattan St, off E 3rd Ave)* happens every Tuesday morning at the Western Stockyards. The action starts at 10am sharp. Show up early to breakfast at the Stockyard Cafe. Rodeos take place in summer and autumn.

SLEEPING & EATING

Some RV parks are found off I-40 East. Far outside town are **Lake Meredith National Recreation Area** (☎ 806-857-3151; *tent & RV campsites free)* or, to the south, **Palo Duro Canyon** (☎ 806-488-2227, *reservations* ☎ 512-389-8900; *entry $3, tent sites $9-12, cabins $65).*

Mostly chain motels stand along I-40 on the outskirts of town. On Amarillo Blvd sit a few vintage motel holdouts such as the red-brick **Bronco Motel** (☎ 806-355-3321; *6005 W Amarillo Blvd; rates $35)* near the 9th Ave intersection. B&Bs cost from $75 per night; ask at the visitor center.

BIG TEXAN STEAK RANCH & MOTEL

Win a 72oz steak if you can eat the entire meal within an hour. Be fore-warned – five out of every six people fail to do so! Across the parking lot from the false-front Old West motel, look for the 'Texas Tornado Museum.'

☎ 806-372-5000, 800-657-7177; 7700 I-40 E, exit 74; doubles from $55 in summer, meals from $5; restaurant open 7am-10:30pm

GOLDEN LIGHT CAFE

At a 1940s San Jacinto roadhouse, chomp on burgers and Route 66 chili. Equally popular are the blues-jammin' **Blue Gator Bar & Grill** *(2903 W 6th Ave)* and Caribbean-style **The Shack** *(3020 W 6th Ave)*.

☎ 806-374-9237; 2908 W 6th Ave; open 11am-10pm Mon-Sat

BLUE FRONT CAFE

Eavesdropping on locals' conversations inside this greasy spoon gives a real taste of Panhandle attitude, especially from the gum-smacking waitresses.

801 W 6th Ave; open 6am-3pm Mon-Fri, 6am-2pm Sat

ENTERTAINMENT & SHOPPING

Ride the Texas Tornado, a double-loop wooden roller coaster, at **Wonderland Park** *(☎ 800-383-4712; 2601 Dumas Dr, off Hwy 87)* or cool off at **Firewater Water Park** *(☎ 866-234-3473; 1415 Sunrise Dr, off I-40 exit 73)*. The **Amarillo Dillas** *(☎ 806-342-3455; 3000 E 3rd St; tickets $5-8)* play minor-league baseball at Dilla Villa stadium from May to August.

The **Big Texan Steak Ranch** has an old-time Opry show every Tuesday night, and the Golden Light's **cantina** *(open 4pm-2am Tue-Sat)* hosts live acoustic music almost nightly. The **Midnight Rodeo** *(☎ 806-358-7083; 4400 S Georgia St; open Thu-Sat)* is a brash honky-tonk dance club inside a converted supermarket.

Antiques fans should set aside an hour or two to peruse the **antiques shops** *(W 6th St)* in the San Jacinto district. **Cavender's Boot City** *(☎ 806-358-1400; 7920 I-40 W, btwn exits 64 & 65)*, a warehouse-sized Western-wear emporium, is among the biggest in Texas.

MEMORABLE MEALS

After a few days of burgers, fries and shakes, you'll be ready for something more exciting. These spots are worth the splurge:

Dell Rhea's Chicken Basket (p9; IL)
Molly's Landing (p22; Catoosa, OK)
County Line Barbecue (p25; Oklahoma City, OK)
Big Texan Steak Ranch (p30; Amarillo, TX)
Café Pasqual's (p36; Santa Fe, NM)
Artichoke Cafe (p38; Albuquerque, NM)
La Posada's Turquoise Room (p44; Winslow, AZ)
El Tovar Hotel dining room (p47; Grand Canyon, AZ)
Hotel Brunswick's Hubbs Café (p49; Kingman, AZ)
Sycamore Inn (p55; CA)

On the Road

Head west on Business 40 (Amarillo Blvd) through Soncy to Indian Hill Rd, turning right before the interstate overpass. Jog left at the T-intersection, then right onto the north frontage road, driving west through **Bushland** and **Wildorado** over the 'staked plains' *(llano estacado)*, named for the markers left by early pioneers to compensate for the absence of natural landmarks.

Scattered along the road are a few ruined motels, cafes and service stations en route to **Vega**, where Route 66 follows Business 40 once again. North of the route on a signposted dead-end street, **Dot's Mini Museum** *(105 N 12th St)* showcases one collector's memorabilia of Western life and the Mother Road. Another Route 66 landmark is the **Vega Motel** (☎ 806-267-2205; 1005 Vega Blvd), offering cozily furnished rooms and covered carports, opposite the hearty **Hickory Inn Cafe** *(1004 Vega Blvd)*.

The oft-disputed midpoint of Route 66 resides in **Adrian**, though some still vote for Vega. Approaching the halfway mark, the **Antique Ranch** (☎ 806-538-9944; 106 E Hwy 66) makes real Texas barbecue. Farther west is the **Midpoint Café** (☎ 806-538-6379; breakfast & lunch $4-13; open 7am-2pm, to 9pm summer). The gift shop, with Burma Shave shaving kits and Spam thermometers, is more of a draw than the food (but don't knock that pie!). Next door stands the red brick **Fabulous 40 Motel** (☎ 806-538-6215; 605 W Hwy 66).

Keep driving west of Adrian almost to where the frontage road ends. Rejoin I-40 at Gruhlkey (exit 18) westbound to the poetically named 'Exit 0.' Get back on the south frontage road and motor out of Deaf Smith County at the ghost town of **Glenrio**, where a broken-down sign for the **Last Motel in Texas** still stands. (On the reverse, it reads 'First Motel in Texas.') With tall Stetsons and tumbleweeds in the rearview mirror, drive west over the state line. Remember to set your watch back an hour.

NEW MEXICO

Dropping off the vast Texas plains, New Mexico comes as electric shock to the senses. Obviously this is the Southwest, where timeless adobe houses, canyons painted with pastel palettes, and a rich mix of ethnicities – from Native American nations to the Mexican-born descendants of Spanish *conquistadores* – all burn lasting images into the heart and memory.

New Mexico revels in all 475 miles of its Route 66 legacy. On the way to Santa Fe are historic monuments, ruins and natural wonders. Cruise through the yesteryear towns of Tucumcari, Las Vegas and hard-edged Gallup, the unofficial capital of Indian country. Save time for quirky Albuquerque and a detour to Acoma Pueblo (Sky City) or the Navajo Nation, just across the border in Arizona. The active **New Mexico Route 66 Association** (☎ 505-224-2802; w www.rt66nm.org; 1415 Central Ave NE, Albuquerque, NM 87106) publishes a quarterly magazine. Check online for archives, news and event calendars.

On the Road

Exhaling as it leaves Texas, the old road takes (weather permitting) a mostly gravel road straight west, driving over bridges and gulches around **Endee** and **Bard**, both farming communities, into **San Jon**. On the south side of I-40, keep heading west into **Tucumcari**. Billboards used to advertise 'Tucumcari Tonite – 2000 rooms' for miles. Today this strip of vintage establishments still makes for a convenient break in the journey.

Tucumcari's modern **Mesalands Dinosaur Museum** (☎ 505-461-3466; 222 E Laughlin St; admission $5/2.50; open noon-5pm Tue-Sat, until 8pm mid-Mar–mid-Nov) holds the bones of the world's only *Torvosaurus*, a Jurassic-era carnivore. Inside a 1903 schoolhouse, the **Tucumcari Historical Museum** (☎ 505-461-4201; 416 S Adams Ave; admission $2/50¢; open 9am-5pm Mon-Sat, until 6pm May-Sep) has an eclectic Western collection and a free Route 66 exhibit. **Tepee Curios** (☎ 505-461-3773; 924 E Tucumcari Blvd; open 10am-6pm) is a must-see.

The 1940s-era **Blue Swallow Motel** (☎ 505-461-9849; 815 E Tucumcari Blvd; singles/doubles $34/39), sitting under a blinking neon sign, has spic-and-span lodgings, cozy furnishings and individual garages. The **Safari Motel** (☎ 505-461-3642; 722 E Tucumcari Blvd) is one of dozens of convenient motels where rooms cost from $25. Endearing **Redwood Lodge** (☎ 505-461-3635; 1502 W Tucumcari Blvd; rooms from $24) was once a youth hostel, RV park and motel, but its future is uncertain.

A sombrero-shaped roof marks **La Cita** (☎ 505-461-1740; 812 S 1st St; open 11am-10pm), earning praise for its fajitas. No-fuss **Del's Restaurant** (1202 E Tucumcari Blvd; open 6am-9pm Mon-Sat) serves full steak dinners. Vegetarians rejoice in the **Mediterranean Cafe & Cheese Store** (☎ 505-461-3755; 1804 E Tucumcari Blvd), next to Dean's diner. After dark on Friday or Saturday, take up two-steppin' at **Trails West Lounge** (508 E Tucumcari Blvd) or the restaurant lounge at the **Best Western Pow Wow Inn** (801 W Tucumcari Blvd). The 1936 **Odeon Theater** (☎ 505-461-0100; 123 S 2nd St), by the railroad tracks, shows movies.

West of Tucumcari, rejoin I-40 (exit 329). RVs and other high-overhead vehicles should stay on the interstate west to exit 311. Otherwise, get off at **Paloma** (exit 321), then drive west on the south frontage road, cross under I-40 via a tunnel and take the north frontage road into **Montoya**, where old-fashioned gas pumps stand outside Richardson's store, now abandoned. Cross back onto the south frontage road, carefully running over cattle guards while the road curves back north and shadows the railroad tracks through **Newkirk** – look for a Phillips 66 station – and orphaned **Cuervo**. Rejoin I-40 (exit 291) westbound to exit 277.

Roll into **Santa Rosa**, scuba capital of the Southwest. Its bell-shaped, 80-foot-deep **Blue Hole** is cooled by natural springs. For diving permits and information, call **city hall** (☎ 505-472-3404, 141 S 5th St). Stop by the **Route 66 Auto Museum** (☎ 505-472-1966; 3766 Route 66; admission $5/ free; open 8am-6pm, to 8pm Apr-Aug), which has a snack shop, to ogle nearly three dozen classic cars. With a tin-roofed church and weathered adobe buildings, **Puerto de Luna** dates from the mid-19th century. It's south of town, via beautiful winding Hwy 91. **Santa Rosa Lake State Park** (☎ 505-472-3110; day-use fee $4, tent/RV sites $10/14), 8 miles north of downtown on NM91, has swimming by an artificial dam.

A SACKFUL OF SOUVENIRS

From tempting kitsch to top-notch art, it's all sold along the Mother Road. Some of the most unique items include:

- Maple 'sirup' at **Funk's Grove** (p11; Shirley, IL)

- Retro bowling goods from the **International Bowling Museum** (p15; St Louis, MO)

- Cowgirl and cowboy duds sold at **PFI Western Store** (p18; Springfield, MO), the **Tockyards City District** (p24; Oklahoma City, OK) or **Cavender's Boot City** (p30; Amarillo, TX)

- Barbed wire art from the **Devil's Rope Museum** (p28; McLean, TX)

- Burma Shave kits and other nostalgia from the **Midpoint Café** (p31; Adrian, TX)

- Textiles woven at **Taepetes de Lana Weaving Center** (p34; Las Vegas, NM)

- Arts and crafts sold by Gallup's authentic **trading posts** (p41; New Mexico)

- Navajo rugs at the **Lorenzo Hubbell Trading Post** (p42; Navajo Nation, AZ)

- Jewelry from **AIAC Gallery** (p44; Winslow, AZ) or **Turquoise Teepee** (p46; Williams, AZ)

- Second-hand TV celebrity clothes at **It's a Wrap!** (p58; Hollywood, CA)

A short drive west of Santa Rosa, **Rocking J Ranch** (☎ 505-472-5127, 505-472-4215; W *www.rocking-j.com; tepee rentals $10, 2-bedroom cabins $75/double*) serves complimentary breakfast. In town are the modest **Motel La Loma** (☎ 505-472-4379; 761 Route 66) and mom-and-pop **La Mesa Motel** (☎ 505-472-3021; 2415 Route 66). The **Sun 'n Sand Motel & Restaurant** (☎ 505-472-5268; 1120 Route 66) is famous for sourdough biscuits and cherry dump cake. With the historic 'Fat Man' sign that once graced the swanky Club Cafe (now defunct), **Joseph's Bar & Grill** (865 Route 66; open 6am-10pm) serves steaks, seafood and inexpensive Mexican-American fare. The circa-1950s **Silver Moon Cafe** (3501 Route 66; open 6am) and **Comet II Drive-in** (217 Route 66) are classics.

West of Santa Rosa, rejoin I-40 (exit 273). From I-40, take exit 256. Ease north on US84 through sun-baked country to Romeroville. It's worth taking the 4-mile detour east along I-25, then onto NM329 toward **Las Vegas**, where outlaw Butch Cassidy tended bar and Doc Holliday once owned a saloon. Learn all about city history at the **Rough Rider Museum** (☎ 505-454-1401; 725 Grand Ave; open 9am-noon & 1-4pm Mon-Fri, 10am-3pm Sat, noon-4pm Sun). On the historic town square, **Taepetes de Lana Weaving Center** (☎ 505-426-8638; 1814 Plaza; open 8am-5pm Mon-Fri, 10am-5pm Sat) is a community-run cooperative. The 1832 **Plaza Hotel** (☎ 505-425-3591, 800-328-1882; W www.plazahotel-nm.com; 230 Plaza; rooms/suites from $60/110) has Victorian guest rooms, a restaurant and saloon.

Drive back toward Romeroville on I-25, then follow the north frontage road toward **San Jose** and farther west at **Sands**, cross I-25 back to the south side. Continue west into **Rowe**, then head north toward Pecos on NM63. En route, pass **Pecos National Historic Park** (☎ 505-757-6414; admission $3; open 8am-5pm). When the Spanish first arrived, this Indian

ALTERNATE ROUTE TO ALBUQUERQUE

The Santa Fe loop of Route 66 was bypassed during the New Deal. Today this newer alignment offers very little to see, though it cuts about 100 miles off your trip.

To bypass Santa Fe, take I-40 west from Santa Rosa to exit 203, where the dead skeleton of the **Longhorn Ranch**, an Old West–style tourist trap, rattles in the wind. Cross the interstate, turning onto the north frontage road west toward **Moriarty** (exit 197), where you switch again to the south frontage road through town, passing the **El Comedor Restaurant** (☎ 505-832-4442; 1009 Hwy 66) and its 1950s neon rotosphere sign. At the east edge of town, jog left onto NM333.

Follow the highway through **Edgewood**, home of the **Wildlife West Nature Park** (☎ 877-815-9453; 87 N Frontage Rd; admission $5/3; open 10am-6pm, noon-4pm in winter), a haven for rescued unreleasable creatures, **Barton** and **Tijeras**, at the start of the Turquoise Trail scenic byway. A short detour northwest to Sandia Crest reveals the **Tinkertown Museum** (☎ 505-281-5233; admission $3/2.50/1; open 9am-5:30pm Apr-Oct), a wonderland of folk-art carving, mechanized miniatures and eccentric Americana. West of Tijeras, enter Albuquerque on Central Ave.

pueblo was a center of tribal trading; the Franciscan mission was destroyed during the Pueblo Revolt of 1680. For camping in the nearby Santa Fe National Forest, stop by the **Pecos District Ranger Station** (☎ 505-757-6121; open 8am-5pm Mon-Sat in summer) in downtown Pecos. Turn left here onto NM50 to reach **Glorieta**, where a Civil War battle was waged. Rejoin I-25 (exit 299) west to exit 294, then follow the north frontage road past the historical marker and into Santa Fe on NM466 (Old Pecos Trail).

Santa Fe

Santa Fe is an oasis of art and culture lifted 7000ft above sea level, with a backdrop of mountain ranges marching toward Taos. Route 66 follows the Old Pecos Trail into town, turns left onto Water St, then right on Shelby St and left again on Palace Ave, which veers left onto Sandoval and becomes Cerrillos Rd.

The **Santa Fe Convention Center & Visitors Bureau** (☎ 800-777-2489; w www.santafe.org; 201 W Marcy St; open 8am-5pm Mon-Fri) is central. Ask at the **New Mexico Public Lands Information Center** (☎ 505-438-7542; 1474 Rodeo Rd; open 8am-5pm Mon-Fri) about outdoors recreation.

SIGHTS & ACTIVITIES

On the plaza at the end of the historic Santa Fe Trail, Native American artisans sell jewelry and pottery by the historic **Palace of the Governors** (105 W Palace Ave). Its neighbor, the **Museum of Fine Arts** (107 W Palace Ave), focuses on the Southwest. Both museums belong to **The Museum of New Mexico** (w www.museumofnewmexico.org; 4-day all-museum pass $15; museums open 10am-5pm Tue-Sun), which offers history and art walking tours between April and October.

Willa Cather based her novel *Death Comes to the Archbishop* on Jean Baptiste Lamy of **St Francis Cathedral** (131 Cathedral Place), which still shelters an antique Madonna. Nearby, the **Institute of American Indian Arts Museum** (☎ 505-938-8900; w www.iaiancad.org; 108 Cathedral Place; admission $4/2/free; open 9am-5pm Mon-Sat, 10am-5pm Sun) showcases traditional and contemporary arts.

Narrow **Canyon Road** is a gallery district. The walk by the **Cross of the Martyrs** (Paseo de Peralta) memorial has mountain views. The strength of the **Wheelwright Museum of the American Indian** (☎ 505-982-4636; 704 Camino Lejo; admission free; open 10am-5pm Mon-Sat, 1-5pm Sun), at outlying Museum Hill, is its Navajo exhibits.

Summer Santa Fe is festive, with the **Spanish Market** in July, **Indian Market** in late August and grand **Santa Fe Fiesta** around Labor Day.

SLEEPING

Santa Fe is about the most expensive stop between Chicago and LA. In summer, everything books up fast.

The 1950s **Silver Saddle Motel** (☎ 505-471-7663; 2810 Cerrillos Rd) is a friendly, basic option. Others with doubles from the low $40s are **King's Rest Court** (1452 Cerrillos Rd), **Cottonwood Court** (1742 Cerrillos Rd), **Thunderbird Inn** (1821 Cerrillos Rd) and the **Cactus Lodge Motel** (☎ 505-471-7699; 2864 Cerrillos Rd).

The garden-enclosed **El Rey Inn** (☎ 505-982-1931, 800-521-1349; *1862 Cerrillos Rd; rooms & suites $75-175*) and the adobe **Stagecoach Motor Inn** (☎ *505-471-0707; 3360 Cerrillos Rd; rates $79-150*) have high standards.

EATING & ENTERTAINMENT

If you develop a love for New Mexican cuisine, the **Santa Fe School of Cooking** (☎ *505-983-4511;* W *www.santafeschoolofcooking.com; 116 W San Francisco St; 2½-hour classes $45-95*) teaches traditional Southwestern fare, and classes include a meal. As the sun sets over the adobe, head for drinks at the **Hotel St Francis** rooftop lounge.

The free weekly *Santa Fe Reporter* keeps tabs on live entertainment. **The Lensic** (☎ *505-988-1234; 211 W San Francisco St),* a Moorish-style movie palace from 1931, stages anything from ballet to African drumming.

CAFÉ PASQUAL'S

It's deservedly famous for its breakfasts (served until 3pm), using fresh herbs, whole grains and if you wish, home-smoked trout. The communal round table is especially welcoming.

☎ 505-983-9340; 121 Don Gaspar Ave; breakfast & lunch $6-12; open 7am-3pm Mon-Sat, 8am-2pm Sun, dinner 5:30-10:30pm

PAUL'S RESTAURANT

This is a whimsical space, with folk art on the walls, impeccable service and imaginative Southwest-inspired dishes like blue crab cakes with chipotle sauce.

☎ 505-982-8738; 72 W Marcy St; lunch $6-8, dinner $14-20; open 11:30am-2:30pm Mon-Fri, 5:30-9pm daily

EL FAROL

Check out live flamenco, blues, jazz, soul and bluegrass, all inside an 1835 adobe. Grilled cactus is on the Spanish tapas bar menu.

☎ 505-983-9912; 808 Canyon Rd; open 2pm-10pm, bar until 2am, live music usually Wed-Sun

COWGIRL HALL OF FAME

Enjoy down-home barbecue, Tex-Mex and Cajun cooking on the outdoor patio. Live music plays nightly at 9pm (cover $3).

☎ 505-982-2565; 319 S Guadalupe; open 11am-midnight Mon-Fri, 8:30am-midnight Sat-Sun

On the Road

Cerrillos Rd feeds onto I-25 (exit 278) southbound to exit 276. Either detour on NM599A to **El Rancho de los Golondrinas** (☎ *505-471-2261; 334 Los Pinos Rd; admission $5/4/2, free Wed; open 10am-4pm Wed-Sun Jun-Sep),* a living history museum of 18th-century Spanish colonial life, or drive over to the east frontage road, heading south to rejoin I-25 (exit 267).

Take the interstate south. Six miles northwest of exit 259, **Santo Domingo Pueblo** (☎ *505-465-2214)* rebuilt its mission church in 1886 and adorned it with frescoes. Known for beadwork and pottery, this pueblo holds a feast and ceremonial corn dances in early August. Off exit 252, conservative Keresan **San Felipe Pueblo** (☎ *505-867-3381)* holds ceremonial corn dances on May 1.

Leave I-25 (exit 248) and drive south on NM313 through the sleepy hamlet of **Algodones** toward Bernalillo. Turn right on NM550 and drive a mile west to serene **Coronado State Monument** (☎ *505-867-5351; admission $3; open 8:30am-5pm Wed-Mon*). A self-guided walk takes in Kuaua pueblo ruins and its *kiva* murals beside the visitor center. **Coronado Campground** *(tent & RV sites $8-18)* has a few cottonwood trees for shade.

Back on NM313, follow the old El Camino Real into the antiques-filled downtown **Bernalillo**. The bustling **Range Cafe** (☎ *505-867-1700; 925 Camino del Pueblo; lunch/dinner from $5/10; open 7:30am-9pm*) has fresh takes on New Mexican classics such as blue corn enchiladas, plus live music in the Lizard Rodeo Lounge. **Silva's Saloon** (☎ *505-867-9976; 955 El Camino Real*), the quintessential Old West bar, is packed with memorabilia.

Cruise NM313 into Albuquerque, where it becomes 4th St. The **El Camino Motor Hotel** (☎ *505-344-1606; 6800 4th St NW*) is made of pink adobe.

Albuquerque

Albuquerque derives its vitality from its history as a crossroads. It is New Mexico's largest and most populous city. Catholic mysticism mixes with hard-nosed Western attitudes, both leavened by the influence of university life. The **Albuquerque Convention & Visitors Bureau** (☎ *505-842-9918, 800-733-9918;* w *www.abqcvb.org; Convention Center, 401 2nd St NW; open 9am-5pm Mon-Fri*) is downtown.

Route 66 follows two alignments. From Santa Fe, enter on 4th St, making a short detour onto 3rd St at Roma Ave (east> : one-way traffic follows 5th St). From Santa Rosa, follow Central Ave through Nob Hill, the university area, downtown and by Old Town.

SIGHTS & ACTIVITIES

Albuquerque's **balloon fiesta** attracts almost a million spectators in early October. The New Mexico **state fair** features live music and rodeos in September. The **Gathering of Nations Pow Wow** takes place over three days in April.

OLD TOWN

The historic **plaza** has artisan shops, an 18th-century adobe church and the **Rattlesnake Museum** (☎ *505-242-6569; 202 San Felipe NW; admission $2.50/2/1; open 10am-6pm*). Free walking tours are given at 11am Tuesday to Sunday by the **Albuquerque Museum of Art & History** (☎ *505-243-7255; 2000 Mountain Rd NW; admission $3/1, free 1st Wed; open 9am-5pm Tue-Sun*).

visitor center ☎ 505-243-3215; Plaza Don Luis, 303 Romero St NW; open 9am-5pm

PETROGLYPH NATIONAL MONUMENT

Trails of varying difficulty through the high-desert volcanic escarpment lead to 25,000 rock etchings, dating from AD 1300 to the time of early Spanish settlers.

visitor center ☎ 505-899-0205; 6001 Unser Blvd, 3mi north of I-40 exit 154; open 8am-5pm

SANDIA TRAMWAY

One of the world's longest tramways starts its 2.7mi ride in the desert realm of cactus and soars to the pines of Sandia Peak (10,378ft), where there's an observation deck. Mountain bike rentals are available.

☎ 505-856-7325; No 10 Tramway Loop NE, 9mi north of I-40 exit 167; roundtrip ticket $15/12/10; open 9am-9pm in summer

SLEEPING

Midway between downtown and Old Town, the **Route 66 Hostel** (☎ 505-247-1813; 1012 Central Ave SW; dorm beds $16; office hours 7:30-10:30am & 4-11pm) shows its age.

Motels, some of which are quite spruced up, line Central Ave. Built with adobe bricks, the 1930s Pueblo Revival–style **El Vado Motel** (☎ 505-243-4594; 2500 Central Ave SW; singles/doubles from $27/31) has carports. Of similar vintage, the non-smoking **Monterey Motel** (☎ 505-243-3554, 877-666-8379; 2402 Central Ave SW; doubles $38-70) takes pride in its colorful bed sheets and swimming pool.

The downtown Art Deco **Hotel Blue** (☎ 505-924-2400, 877-878-4868; w www.thehotelblue.com; 717 Central Ave NW; rooms & suites $60-110) puts king beds in every room. Historic B&Bs abound, especially around Old Town; ask at the visitor center.

EATING

Near Old Town, stop off at the **Route 66 Malt Shop** (☎ 505-242-7866; 1720 Central Ave SW) for a hot pastrami, Reuben sandwich or to chat with the soda jerk. By the railroad tracks, **66 Diner** (☎ 505-247-1421; 1405 Central Ave NE; open 11am-11pm Mon-Thu, 11am-midnight Fri, 8am-midnight Sat, 8am-10pm Sun) serves comfort food.

ARTICHOKE CAFE
For some refreshing ideas and eclectic fare, check out this award-winning eatery just east of downtown.

☎ 505-243-0200; 424 Central Ave SE; lunch/dinner from $8/14; open 11am-2:30pm Mon-Fri, 5:30-9pm Mon, 5:30-10pm Tue-Sat, 5-9pm Sun

HIGH NOON RESTAURANT & SALOON
Imbibe excellent margaritas and grilled fare in a rough-hewn, 18th-century adobe off the plaza.

☎ 505-765-1455; 425 San Felipe NW; dishes $5-15; lunch from 11am Mon-Sat, from noon Sun, dinner from 5pm daily

---

DETOUR: ACOMA PUEBLO

Known as 'Sky City' for its fantastic mesa-top location – 367ft above the surrounding plateau – Acoma Pueblo, one of North America's oldest continuously inhabited settlements, has been populated since the mid-12th century. Artisans sell traditional pottery here, and the 17th-century **San Esteban del Rey Mission** is New Mexico's largest.

Visitors must join a tour departing from the **visitor center** (☎ 800-747-0181; tours $10/9/7; open 8am-7pm, until 5pm Nov-Mar, tours stop 1hr earlier). Afterward, guests may walk down the trail unescorted. Acoma is about 15 miles south of I-40 exit 108 (east : exit 96) on Indian Route 23.

MAC'S LA SIERRA COFFEE SHOP

On the western outskirts, they've been dishing up unfussy New Mexican standards for over 40 years.

☎ 505-836-1212; 6217 Central Ave NW; open 5:30am-midnight Mon-Sat, 6am-10pm Sun

ENTERTAINMENT

Alibi is Albuquerque's free arts and entertainment weekly. Most nightlife is either downtown or east of the university area in Nob Hill.

KIMO THEATRE

This flamboyant 1927 landmark in 'Pueblo Deco' style has longhorn steer-skull light fixtures with glowing amber eyes.

box office ☎ 505-768-3544; 423 Central Ave NW; self-guided tours 9am-3pm Mon-Fri

CLUB RHYTHM & BLUES

Showcasing blues bands, the club also hosts Latin jazz, funk and open-mic nights. It's not far from **Kelly's Brewpub** *(3200 Central Ave SE)* inside the 1930s Jones Motor Co building.

☎ 505-256-0849; 3523 Central Ave NE; open from 8pm Mon-Sat

CARAVAN EAST

Practice your two-step or line dancing to live country & western bands or graze the complimentary happy-hour buffet.

☎ 505-265-7877; 7605 Central Ave NE; cover $3 Fri-Sat; open from 4:30pm

On the Road

Those with time to spare should cruise the older Route 66 alignment out of Albuquerque, taking 4th St south to Bridge Blvd. Turn right and after crossing the Rio Grande, veer left onto NM314 and follow it south through **Las Padillas**. Keep left onto NM147 to reach **Isleta Pueblo** *(☎ 505-869-3111)*. Pottery shops stand around the 17th-century **San Augustine Mission**.

Turn right onto NM47, then take another right onto NM6 into **Los Lunas**. Beyond the NM314 intersection, a stately 19th-century adobe home, the **Luna Mansion** *(☎ 505-865-7333; meals $8-20; open from 5pm Wed-Sun)* is now a restaurant. Keep on NM6 through peaceful countryside west of town all the way to **Correo**, south of I-40 (exit 126). A 4WD vehicle can follow the old road west over the railroad tracks, to eventually join the north frontage road into **Mesita** (exit 117).

(An alternate rapid route out of Albuquerque follows Central Ave west up Nine Mile Hill, crosses over I-40 [exit 149] and heads west on the north frontage road beside the landmark **Rio Puerco bridge**, a Parker Truss model, joining I-40 [exit 140] westbound to Mesita.)

Keep driving west of Mesita along rust-colored canyons. Turn right onto NM124. Drive west by **Laguna Pueblo** – its 1705 Franciscan mission church, **San Jose de Laguna**, has an ornate interior – and pass through **New Laguna** and **Paraje**.

Heading west on NM124, at **Budville** there's a boarded-up trading post inside a 1930s filling station. Next, Mt Taylor, a boundary of the Navajo world, comes into view approaching **Villa de Cubero**. At the old tourist courts once found here, Hemingway worked on *The Old Man and the Sea*. West of **San Fidel**, cross over I-40 (exit 96) to **McCartys**, with its Spanish Colonial mission church. Except for RVs and other high vehicles, drive west and cross under I-40 via a tunnel, then feed onto NM117.

Santa Fe Ave enters **Grants**, a carrot-growing capital that turned to uranium mining in the 1950s. Tour an underground mine at the **New Mexico Mining Museum** (☎ 505-287-4802, 800-748-2142; 100 N Iron St; $3/2; open 9am-4pm Mon-Sat). Topped by an atomic neon sign, the **Uranium Café** (519 W Santa Fe Ave; open 7am-2pm Mon-Fri, 8am-2pm Sat) serves green chili burgers with heaps of hospitality. Nearby, **The Mission at Riverwalk** (422 W Santa Fe Ave; open 10am-4pm Tue-Sat) has art galleries and a coffee shop. Busy **Monte Carlo Restaurant** (☎ 505-287-9250; 721 W Santa Fe Ave) serves the 'disaster burrito.' Run by friendly folks, the AAA-approved **Sands Motel** (☎ 505-287-2996, 800-424-7679; 112 McArthur St) and **Grants Cafe** (932 E Santa Fe Ave) are neighbors.

For outdoor recreation, camping and trip-planning, visit the **Northwest New Mexico Visitors Center** (☎ 505-876-2783; 1900 E Santa Fe Ave, I-40 exit 85; open 8am-5pm, 9am-6pm in summer), where panoramic windows look onto El Calderon lava flow.

Drive west of Grants on NM122 through a string of small towns – **Milan**, **Bluewater**, **Prewitt** and **Thoreau**, the turn-off to Chaco Canyon – before reaching the **Continental Divide** (7275ft) and rejoining I-40 westbound. **Stauder's Navajo Lodge B&B** (☎ 505-862-7533; w www.rainbirdtrading

---

DETOUR: EL MORRO & EL MALPAIS NATIONAL MONUMENTS

About 40mi south of Grants (see above) on Hwy 53, **El Morro National Monument** (☎ 505-783-4226; entry $3; open 9am-5pm, trails close 4pm) protects pueblo ruins and a 200ft sandstone outcropping called 'Inscription Rock.' It's covered with petroglyphs and also graffiti left by Spanish *conquistadores* and the US Army Camel Corps. En route are the privately owned **Bandera Ice Caves** (☎ 888-423-2283; admission $8/4; open 8am-1hr before sunset), which stay frozen year-round. **El Malpais National Monument & Conservation Area** (☎ 505-783-4774; visitor center open 8:30am-4:30pm) was carved by lava flows millennia old. Its most striking sandstone features – like La Ventana natural arch and The Narrows – are south of Grants along Hwy 117.

.com; *cottage singles/doubles from $75/85),* 3 miles from exit 44, has antique décor and breakfast served in a Spanish hacienda-style house.

From exit 36, drive west on the north frontage road. Outside Gallup is **Red Rock State Park** *(☎ 505-722-3829; tent/RV sites $10/18).* Since the 1920s an **Inter-tribal Indian Ceremonial** gathering has been held here in mid-August. Thousands of Native Americans and tourists throng to not only Gallup, but also the huge amphitheater for markets, a rodeo and ceremonial dancing. Continue into Gallup, via NM118.

Gallup

At a crossroads of cultures – Native American, Mexican and Old West – Gallup, an oft-forsaken yet charming place, makes a jumping-off point for excursions to the Navajo Nation. The **chamber of commerce** *(☎ 800-242-4282; 103 W Hwy 66; open 9am-6pm Mon-Fri)* has Navajo code-talker exhibits.

SIGHTS & ACTIVITIES

Native American culture around the Colorado Plateau is the subject of the fascinating **Gallup Cultural Center** *(☎ 505-863-4131; 201 E Route 66; admission free; open 8am-8pm Mon-Sat)* museum. Ceremonial dances are at 7pm nightly during summer. The circa-1900 Rex Hotel is now the **Gallup Historical Museum** *(☎ 505-863-1363; 300 E Route 66; open 8:30am-3pm Tue-Sat, to 5:30pm summer).*

In a line-up of trading posts, the 1913 **Richardson's Trading Co & Cash Pawn** *(222 W Route 66)* guarantees goods directly purchased from artisans. **Ortega's Indian Arts** *(2107 W Route 66)* displays the world's largest turquoise nugget, worth almost $250,000. Also downtown is the Spanish Colonial–style **El Morro Theater** *(207 W Coal Ave).*

SLEEPING & EATING

The restored 1937 **El Rancho Hotel** *(☎ 505-863-9311, 800-543-6351; 1000 E Route 66;* w *www.elranchohotel.com; motel rooms from $40, hotel singles/doubles from $52/61)* is reason enough to stop overnight. Movie stars John Wayne and Humphrey Bogart slept here, and the neon sign out front still promises the 'Charm of Yesterday, Convenience of Tomorrow.' Its restaurant, shop and lounge are worth visiting.

Many motels are so shady your mother would worry. However, the cheerful **Blue Spruce Lodge** *(☎ 505-863-5211; 1119 E Route 66)* is an exception, and nearby retro-looking **Kristy's Coffee Shop** *(1310 E Hwy 66; open 24hrs)* has good breakfasts. Other vintage establishments are the downtown **Eagle Cafe** *(☎ 505-722-3220; 220 W Hwy 66; open 8am-6pm)* and 1950s **Ranch Kitchen** *(☎ 505-722-25 37; 3001 W Hwy 66; most dishes $8-11; open 7am-10pm),* serving barbecue, New Mexican and Navajo cooking.

On the Road

Take NM118 west of Gallup until the north frontage road dead-ends at **Defiance**. Stay on NM118 by turning left, then right onto the south frontage road. A few miles later, cross I-40 (exit 8) and drive west over the railroad tracks through **Manuelito**, which shares its name with a Navajo chief. Ease over the state line into Arizona.

ARIZONA

Arizona harbors plenty of jaw-dropping nature, from millennia-old volcanic craters to the color-etched sandstone of the Painted Desert to the Grand Canyon itself. Skies are huge here. The state's fierce independence shows itself, not least in its stubborn refusal to observe Daylight Saving Time. Even with at least 400 miles of Route 66 to go, tempting detours may derail the best-intentioned road trip.

In addition to having its longest uninterrupted stretch of old highway, the Mother Road connects the dots between Winslow's windblown streets, Williams' 1940s-vintage downtown, Kingman's mining settlements and gunslinging Oatman, each town a snapshot of a different era. Unpaved dirt segments and notorious bits of old highway, such as Gold Hill Grade up to Sitgreaves Pass, provide a taste of old-school motoring.

The **Historic Route 66 Association of Arizona** (☎ 928-753-5001; **w** www.azrt66.com; PO Box 66, Kingman, AZ 86402) organizes an annual 'Fun Run' motorcade from Seligman to Golden Shores.

On the Road

Enter Arizona by the canyons on the north frontage road, driving past the legendary **Chief Yellowhorse Trading Post**. At Lupton cross I-40 (exit 359) and go west on the south frontage road. Rejoin I-40 (exit 354), traveling westbound through **Allantown** and **Houck** to exit 351. Take the north frontage road west – be prepared for some rough dirt sections – past sleepy rural communities over the 1930s-era **Querino Canyon Bridge** to rejoin I-40 (exit 341) at Ortega Rd. Drive west to **Sanders** (exit 339), then follow the north frontage road again to **Chambers**, turning left onto US91 and getting back on I-40 (exit 333). At Pinta Rd (exit 320), adventurous folks can drive north, then west a few miles along a dirt roadbed to the **Painted Desert Trading Post** ruins.

DETOUR: NAVAJO NATION

Today the Navajo Nation, covering about 27,000 sq miles of high desert and forest, is the largest reservation in the USA. Navajo servicemen (nicknamed 'codetalkers') helped create a secret code during WWII – it was never broken. Despite being over the state line in Arizona, the Navajo Nation observes Daylight Saving Time and is easily approached from Gallup, NM (see page 41). Head north on US491, then west on NM264 to **Window Rock**, home of the tribal council chambers and museum. The annual Navajo Nation Fair, with rodeos and a wild horse race, is held over Labor Day weekend. Thirty miles farther west, the **Lorenzo Hubbell Trading Post** (☎ 928-755-3475; open 8am-5pm, to 6pm May-Sep) is a national historic site.

Petrified Forest & Painted Desert

Since there's not much to see on the interstate, detour instead at exit 311 through the **Petrified Forest National Park** (☎ 928-524-6228; entry per vehicle $10; open 8am-5pm, extended hours in summer). The widely scattered 'forest' is actually broken fossilized logs dating from the Triassic period (over 225 million years ago). The trees have crystallized into quartz. The park's paved, 28 mile-long **scenic drive** passes walking trails, vistas and natural features. Visitors revel in the **Painted Desert's** scenery; there, the land changes colors with the minerals in the earth. Check out petroglyphs at **Newspaper Rock**. Near the north entrance, beyond the **Painted Desert Visitor Center**, is the restored landmark **Painted Desert Inn**, now housing a bookstore. Nearby wilderness **backcountry camping** (free) requires a permit. Ranger-led walks begin near the park's southern entrance at the **Rainbow Museum** and visitor center, which contains the cast of dinosaur fossils found locally in 1984. Outside the south entrance, Hwy 180 travels northwest into Holbrook.

On the Road

Approaching from the national park, enter **Holbrook** by passing over the railroad tracks. At the **Rainbow Rock Shop** (101-103 Navajo Blvd), a giant brontosaurus stands guard over gems, geodes and petrified wood. Drive north of the Navajo-Hopi intersection to the 1898 **courthouse**, where Indian ceremonial dances are performed nightly in summer. Inside is a **historical museum** (☎ 800-524-2459; 100 E Arizona St; open 8am-5pm in summer) that records wild and bloodthirsty 19th-century days.

West of the main intersection on Hopi Dr is the well-kept **WigWam Village Motel** (☎ 520-524-3048; 811 W Hopi Dr; singles/doubles $36/42). Vintage cars slumber outside each concrete tepee, themselves filled with cozy 1950s furniture. The **Plainsman Restaurant** (1001 W Hopi Dr; open 7am-9pm Tue-Sat, 8am-3pm Sun-Mon) coffee shop has a Mother Road mural. Nearer downtown, **Joe & Aggie's Café** (☎ 520-524-6540; 120 W Hopi Dr) has a barbershop out back, but **Romo's Cafe** (☎ 520-524-2153; 121 W Hopi Dr) has flashy margaritas. Both serve Mexican-American fare.

Continue west on Hopi Dr; rejoin I-40 (exit 285) westbound to exit 277. Drive west on the north frontage road through **Joseph City**, founded by Mormon pioneers. Cross over I-40 (exit 274) and follow the south frontage road west, past the **Jackrabbit Trading Post**, dating to 1947 and famous along Route 66 for its 'Here It Is!' billboard campaign. Take I-40 (exit 269) west to exit 257, moving to the south frontage road (Business 40) west into Winslow.

Winslow

It often seems that Winslow, an Old West rail town, could blow away entirely when the wind gusts. Route 66 follows 3rd St (east : one-way traffic uses 2nd St). The **visitor information center** (☎ 928-289-2434; w www.winslowarizona.org; 300 W North Rd, I-40 exit 253; open 8am-5pm) is inconveniently located north of town.

SIGHTS & ACTIVITIES

Every tourist slows down to see the **corner** *(Kinsley Ave & 2nd St)* made famous by The Eagles' 1970s hit single 'Take It Easy.' More worth your time is the **Old Trails Museum** *(☎ 520-289-5861; 212 Kinsley Ave; open 1-5pm Tue-Sat in summer)*, where an eclectic collection includes a Meteor City ashtray, cowboy hash knives and a photo history of the Harvey girls. Outside town, explore petroglyphs and pueblo ruins at **Homolovi Ruins State Park** *(☎ 928-289-4106; north of I-40 exit 257; day-use fee $5, tent/RV sites $12/19)*. Twelve more miles north along Hwy 87, **Little Painted Desert County Park** *(open dawn-dusk)* offers bird watching and vistas.

SLEEPING & EATING

Scruffy **motels** around town charge from $20. Most coffee shops and diners on the east side of town are now Mexican kitchens. Small-plane pilots frequent the **Last Resort Cafe** *(open 11am-8pm Tue-Thu, 11am-9pm Fri-Sat, 11am-4pm Sun)* at the airport.

Exquisite **La Posada Hotel** *(☎ 928-289-4366; w www.laposada.org; 303 E 2nd St; rooms from $80)*, a 1930s Harvey House, achieves a gracious Spanish-Colonial style. Albert Einstein and John Wayne both stayed here. Its **Turquoise Room Restaurant & Martini Bar** *(☎ 928-289-2888; lunch/dinner from $10/15; open 7am-10am, 11:30am-2pm & 5-9pm Tue-Sun)* serves high-caliber Southwest cuisine.

SHOPPING

Inside the historic Lorenzo Hubbell Trading Company building, **Arizona Indian Artists Cooperative (AIAC) Gallery** *(☎ 928-289-3986; 523 W 2nd St; open 8am-5pm Mon-Sat)* sells contemporary artisan crafts and jewelry. Also check out La Posada's antiques-filled **gift shop**.

On the Road

Getting back on I-40 (exit 252) is your only option from Winslow to Flagstaff, but take heart – there are kitschy detours en route. Off exit 233, a 6-mile road leads south past the RV park to **Meteor Crater** *(☎ 928-289-2362, 800-289-5898; admission $12/11/6; open 6am-6pm in summer)*. This 50,000-year-old natural landmark, created in less than 10 seconds, is deeper than the Statue of Liberty is high. Sturdy shoes are a must for a guided hike around the crater rim. Farther west off exit 239, the white geodesic dome of **Meteor City** houses a mish-mash of souvenirs. Outside are concrete tepees and supposedly the world's largest dreamcatcher. Look for the **Twin Arrows** at exit 219 pointing out a long-closed trading post and cafe.

Finally, despite what the song says, forget about **Winona**, a one-horse town off exit 211. Either follow Camp Townsend-Winona Rd toward Flagstaff or drive farther west on I-40 (exit 204). The 13th-century canyon cliff dwelling ruins of **Walnut Canyon National Monument** *(☎ 928-526-3367; admission $5; open 8am-6pm Jun-Aug, 9am-5pm Sep-May)* are south of exit 204. Otherwise, head west on the north frontage road, turn right beyond the railroad tracks, then go left onto US89. Cruise Santa Fe Ave into Flagstaff.

Flagstaff

The heart of the Old West still beats in Flagstaff, but today it's also a cultured college town. The **visitor center** (☎ 800-842-7293; 1 E Route 66; open 7am-7pm in summer) is downtown inside a historic railway depot. Follow US89 through Flagstaff, taking Santa Fe Ave, then turning left onto Sitgreaves St and right onto Old Highway 66 west out of town.

SIGHTS & ACTIVITIES

'Flag,' as locals dub it, is a destination in its own right, with museums, a historical downtown, cultural attractions and northern Arizona's best nightlife.

MUSEUM OF NORTHERN ARIZONA

Focusing on the tribes of the Colorado Plateau, excellent collections explore traditional Indian culture and contemporary fine arts.

☎ 928-774-5213; 3101 N Fort Valley Rd (Hwy 180); admission $5/4/3; open 9am-5pm

LOWELL OBSERVATORY

Famed for its 1930 discovery of Pluto, this working astronomical observatory puts on evening stargazing programs year-round.

☎ 928-774-3358; 1400 W Mars Hill Rd; admission $4/3.50/2; open 9am-5pm with tours at 10am, 1pm & 3pm Apr-Oct

OUTDOOR ACTIVITIES

All around Flagstaff are hiking, mountain-biking and equestrian trails. Adventurers can even ascend Arizona's tallest mountain, Humphreys Peak (12,663ft). Ask at the **Coconino National Forest Supervisor's Office** (☎ 928-527-3600; W www.fs.fed.us/r3/coconino; 2323 E Greenlaw Lane; open 7:30am-4:30pm Mon-Fri) for information.

SLEEPING & EATING

Accommodations fill up quickly in summer. Many **motels** along E Santa Fe Ave cost from $20 in the off-season, $50 in summer. Vintage neon signs may look alluring, but the rooms are decidedly lackluster.

Woody Mountain Campground (☎ 928-774-7727, 800-732-7986; 2727 W Route 66; tent & RV sites $16-22; open Apr-Oct) is forested. Downtown Flagstaff's two **hostels** (☎ 928-774-6731, 800-398-7112; W www.grandcanyonhostel.com; dorm beds $15-17, rooms $30-37) provide complimentary breakfast and off-street parking.

The old-fashioned **Monte Vista Hotel** (☎ 928-779-6971, 800-545-3068; doubles with shared/private bath from $50/60, add $10 Fri-Sat), where Hollywood stars once slept, and quaint **Hotel Weatherford** (☎ 928-779-1919; 23 N Leroux St; rooms without TV or phone $50-60) are welcoming, not luxurious.

Macy's (☎ 928-774-2243; 14 S Beaver St; open from 6am), a European coffeehouse and bakery, roasts its own coffee and cooks light meals. Near the university, **New Frontiers Natural Marketplace & Deli** (☎ 928-774-5747; 1000 S Milton Rd; open 8am-8pm Mon-Sat, 10am-8pm Sun) is a natural-foods nirvana. **Charly's Pub & Grille** (at the Hotel Weatherford; dishes $8-20; open 11am-10pm Mon-Fri, 8am-10pm Sat-Sun) has standout Southwest cuisine.

ENTERTAINMENT

Free *Flagstaff Live!* weekly keeps tabs on the live music and performing arts scene. Charly's **Exchange Pub** *(Hotel Weatherford)* has nightly acts, from New Orleans jazz to ska. The Monte Vista Hotel has a svelte **cocktail lounge** *(open from 6pm)*, starting its music at 9pm Thursday to Sunday (cover $2).

MUSEUM CLUB

At this 1931 roadhouse, nicknamed 'The Zoo' for its taxidermy days, cowboy spirit reigns over a barn-sized wooden dance floor, with free country swing lessons Thursday nights.

☎ 928-526-9434; 3404 E Route 66; open until 3am Fri-Sat

PAY-N-TAKE

Besides the respectable downtown brewpubs, there's also this bright-and-cheery sundries market, which just happens to have a beer, wine and coffee bar. Outside tables are in view of the 1917 Orpheum Theater.

☎ 928-226-8595; 12 W Aspen St

On the Road

Follow Old Highway 66 west of Flagstaff. Rejoin I-40 (exit 191) westbound to Bellemont (exit 185). West along the north frontage road is the so-called **'Deer Farm Loop,'** where Route 66's signature two-lane concrete highway with 'thumpty-thump' expansion cracks alternates with older red-dirt roadbed, which may be impassable during winter or heavy rains. Scattered beside are photo-worthy gas station, cafe and motel **ruins**. After passing through **Brannigan Park** and **Parks**, jog north and turn left onto Deer Farm Rd. Go west back to I-40 (exit 167).

Drive west to exit 165, then cross I-40 and follow south into charming **Williams**, where much of the downtown is on the National Register of Historic Places. One-way traffic follows Railroad Ave west (east⟩ : take Route 66). This railway whistlestop town was the last piece of the Mother Road to be bypassed by the interstate in 1984. The **Williams Chamber of Commerce & USFS Visitor Center** *(☎ 800-863-0456;* w *www .williamschamber.com; 200 W Railroad Ave; open 8am-6:30pm in summer)* has exhibits, books and maps. Rangers help sift through outdoor recreation opportunities, including camping in Kaibab National Forest.

Old-timey steam and diesel locomotives pull the **Grand Canyon Railway** *(☎ 520-773-1976, 800-843-8724;* w *www.thetrain.com; roundtrip adult/child fares from $58/25)* to the canyon rim year-round. Renowned **Turquoise Teepee** *(114 W Route 66)* trading post sells quality artisan goods. East is a vintage 1940s **motel row**; during summer, prices rise sharply and 'No Vacancy' signs appear. **Route 66 Inn** *(☎ 520-635-4791, 888-786-6956; 128 E Route 66)* is basic but tidy. The **Canyon Hotel** *(☎ 928-635-9371, 800-482-3955; 1900 E Rodeo Rd; doubles with breakfast $40-110),* on the eastern outskirts, has a pool. Downtown, the **Red Garter Bed & Bakery** *(☎ 928-635-1484, 800-328-1484;* w *www.redgarter.com; 137 W Railroad Ave; rooms $85-120)* is inside a former Victorian saloon and bordello.

No one will go hungry. For breakfast, stop by **Old Smokey's Pancake House** *(624 W Route 66; open 6:30am-1:30pm).* A slice of pie from **Pine Country Restaurant** *(107 N Canyon Blvd)* shouldn't be skipped. Fresh Mexican fare is dished up at **Pancho McGillicuddy's** *(141 W Railroad Ave;*

DETOUR: GRAND CANYON NATIONAL PARK

The Grand Canyon is arguably the best-known natural attraction in the USA. When President Theodore Roosevelt visited in 1903, he remarked, 'You cannot improve on it.' An incredible spectacle of colored rock strata and the many buttes and peaks within the canyon itself, the meandering South Rim gives access to awesome views. In peak summer season, there is no escaping the crowds.

As a day trip from Flagstaff (see page 45) or Williams (see page 46), allow an hour to reach the **south entrance station** (entry $20 per vehicle). Rangers hand out *The Guide*, with detailed information on everything from interpretive programs to shuttle bus routes. A short drive north by Mather Point is **Canyon View Information Plaza** (☎ 928-638-7888; W www.nps.gov/grca; open 8am-5pm). Nearby Grand Canyon Village has parking lots, modern amenities, accommodations and basic eateries; **Canyon Village Marketplace** (☎ 928-638-2262; open 7am-8:30pm) rents and sells outdoor gear.

Visit early in the day. The foremost attraction is the canyon rim, paralleled by a scenic drive east; and a 9-mile hiking trail west to **Hermit's Rest** (open 9am-5pm, to 7pm summer), which was once a Fred Harvey stagecoach stop. Near the village, **Yavapai Observation Station** (open 8am-5pm, to 8pm summer) has views and a geology museum. **Desert View Watchtower** (open 8am-5:30pm) is 20 miles east, past the 800-year-old **Tusayan Ruin** (open 9am-5pm).

Several trails descend into the canyon. Temperatures are 20°F cooler on the rim than at the bottom, which can exceed 100°F in midsummer. A day hike down to the river and back is foolhardy. Take the well-graded **South Kaibab Trail** only to Skeleton Point for a 6-mile workout. On overnight treks (permits required), return via the less-steep **Bright Angel Trail**. Reservations are needed for **mule rides** (☎ 928-638-2631; half-day trips $120/335).

On the canyon rim, year-round **Mather Campground** (reservations ☎ 800-365-2267; sites $15) books up fast, while remote **Desert View Campground** (sites $10; opens mid-May) is first-come, first-served. Reservations are essential for all other lodging (☎ 303-297-2757, 888-297-2757, same-day availability ☎ 928-638-2631; W www.grandcanyonlodges.com). The 1905 **El Tovar Hotel** (rooms/suites from $130/200) and its elegant **dining room** (dinner reservations ☎ 928-638-2631; breakfast & lunch $8-15, dinner $18-26; open 6:30am-2pm & 5-10pm) are worth every penny. More affordable are the 1930s **Bright Angel Lodge** (rooms/cabins from $55/80), **Trailer Village** (RV sites $25) and **Phantom Ranch** (dorm beds $26) on the canyon floor.

DETOUR: SUNSET CRATER & WUPATKI NATIONAL MONUMENTS

Thirty miles north of Flagstaff (see page 45) via US89, located about midway from the Grand Canyon's east entrance, are the amazing ruins of **Wupatki National Monument** (☎ 928-679-2365). These Ancestral Puebloan sites differ from most others because they are freestanding, rather than built into cliffs or caves. Some of today's Hopi Indians are descended from the 12th-century inhabitants of these pueblos. A 36-mile loop road connects Wupatki's ruins and volcanic **Sunset Crater National Monument** (☎ 928-526-0502), farther back south toward Flagstaff. Combined entry to both monuments costs $5; summer opening hours are 8am to 6pm.

open 11am-10pm Mon-Fri, 10am-10pm Sat-Sun). **Twister's** (417 E Route 66; open 6am-6pm Mon-Sat, 8am-3:30pm Sun) is a 1950s soda fountain, while **Cruisers Café 66** (233 W Route 66; open 4pm-9:30pm) inhabits a 1930s filling station. **Rod's Steak House** (☎ 928-635-2671; 301 E Route 66; open 11:30am-9:30pm) has been cookin' since 1946. Slake a thirst at the **Canyon Club** (132 W Route 66) or 1912 'World Famous' **Sultana Bar** (301 W Route 66), a honky-tonk tavern.

Outside Williams, rejoin I-40 (exit 161) west. A bicycle trail now runs over the 1920s **Ash Fork Hill** loop, a 1920s alignment of Route 66. To reach it, drive north of exit 151 on FR6 and park in the turnout. Back on the interstate, exit 146 leads to Lewis Ave west through tired-looking **Ash Fork**, the 'Flagstone Capital of the World.' Quickly get back on I-40 (exit 144) west to exit 139. Veer right to follow Crookton Rd west toward **Seligman**. Drive slowly; savor the serene landscape and broad horizons on this unchanged stretch of old Mother Road. Turn right, then left about a mile before entering town.

Seligman sure takes its Route 66 heritage seriously! **Angel Delgadillo's Barbershop** (☎ 928-422-3352; W www.route66giftshop.com; 217 E Route 66) is more of a visitor center, run by a man who can reminisce about the Dust Bowl era and has helped spark Route 66 preservation efforts across Arizona. His eccentric brother, Juan, runs the wacky **Route 66 Roadhouse** (☎ 928-422-3291; 301 E Route 66) down the street. Ironically the **Roadkill Café & Steakhouse** (☎ 928-422-3554; 502 W Route 66; open 7am-late) has an all-you-can-eat salad bar. The old-fashioned **Copper Cart Café** (103 W Route 66) sports a tempting sign, but skip the food. Seligman has motels aplenty, with rooms from $30, but nothing special, except for the inviting **Deluxe Inn** (☎ 928-422-3244; 203 E Chino Ave). After dark, shoot some stick or pop quarters in the jukebox at the **Black Cat** lounge.

After Seligman – hold onto your hats – are miles of rolling hills and canyon country, making up the longest uninterrupted stretch of Route 66 yet. Approaching the Hualapai Nation, at the artificially lit **Grand Canyon Caverns** (☎ 928-422-3223; 45min tour $12/8, above-ground motel rooms $45-60; open 8am-6pm in summer), an elevator drops 21 stories underground to caverns as big as a football field. Farther west, **Peach Springs** is a jumping-off point for tribal-led river rafting (May–Oct only) and bus tours of the Grand Canyon West region. Make your reservations through the plain-looking **Hualapai Lodge** (☎ 928-769-2230, 888-255-9550; |w| www.grandcanyonresort.com; singles/doubles from $60/70; restaurant open 6am-9pm). Continue on west through **Truxton** and **Valentine**. At **Hackberry**, the much-loved **general store** and visitor center is chock-full of memorabilia. Pass under I-40 before entering Kingman.

Kingman

Founded in the early 1880s, **Kingman** retains many historic buildings. The wagon-wheel tracks of an old mining route are visible off White Cliffs Rd. Route 66 follows Business 40 (Andy Devine Blvd) through downtown, then veers left onto Beale St.

Pick up self-guided driving tour maps at the **Powerhouse Visitor Center** (☎ 928-753-6106, 866-427-7866; 120 W Andy Devine Ave; open 9am-6pm, to 5pm Dec-Feb), which has a **Route 66 museum** (admission $3) opposite Locomotive Park. Farther west, the **Mojave Museum of History and Arts** (☎ 928-753-3195; 400 W Beale St; admission $3; open 10am-5pm Mon-Fri, 1-5pm Sat-Sun) chronicles Hualapai tribal traditions.

SLEEPING

About 15 miles south of town, **Hualapai Mountain Park** (☎ 928-757-3859, 877-757-0915; Hualapai Mtn Rd; tent/RV sites $10/17, cabins $35-75) offers short trails, camping and 1930s stone-and-wood cabins. Most motels on Kingman's east side have rooms from $25. Try the white pueblo--esque **Arcadia Lodge** (☎ 928-753-1925; 909 E Andy Devine Ave) or the **Hilltop Motel** (☎ 928-753-2198; 1901 E Andy Devine Ave; rooms from $30) for views (it's also where Timothy McVeigh stayed before the Okalahoma City bombing). The **Silver Queen** (☎ 928-757-4315; 3285 E Andy Devine Ave; rooms $30-50) is a definite step up the lodging ladder. The 1909 **Hotel Brunswick** (☎ 928-718-1800; |w| www.hotel-brunswick.com; 315 E Andy Devine Ave; rooms with shared/private bath from $25/50, suites $75-90) has atmospheric downtown digs.

EATING & ENTERTAINMENT

The visitor center has a NY-style deli, **Memory Lane** (open 10:30am-5pm Mon-Sat, 11am-4pm Sun). Down the street is **Mr D'z Route 66 Diner** (☎ 928-718-0066; 105 E Andy Devine Ave). A bit west, **House of Chan** (☎ 928-753-3232; 960 W Beale St) serves steak, seafood and roast duck. In the Hotel Brunswick, **Hubbs Café** (dishes $10-20, multi-course dinner $25; open 11am-2pm & 4:30-9pm) is a genteel Southwest bistro. A martini-glass neon sign hangs outside the **Kingman Club** (312 E Beale St) not far away.

On the Road

Leaving Kingman on Beale St, follow along the railroad tracks, which thread through a claustrophobic canyon. Eventually cross I-40 (exit 44) and drive north to the intersection. Turn left onto Oatman Rd, following it west over a long, dusty stretch of flat highway before it corkscrews into the Black Mountains. Watch for fluorescent-orange tumbleweeds, saguaro cactus (the bloom is Arizona's state flower) and falling rocks as you travel along Gold Hill Grade over **Sitgreaves Pass** (3523ft). Afterward, the road twists and turns, heading past the century-old **Goldroad Mine** (☎ 928-768-1600; 1hr mine tours $12/6; open 10am-6pm, tours depart every 30mins), where you can see actual gold vein. You can drop by the **Prospector Cafe** for chili and apple pie. Trail rides and stagecoach tours are offered October to April only.

Oatman, 2 miles past the mine, is the old Wild West come alive for tourists. Wild donkeys descended from early mine prospectors' pack animals crowd the town's main street of false-front buildings. Gunfight re-enactments are held at 1:30pm and 3:30pm on Saturday and Sunday. Every July 4th there's a sidewalk egg-frying contest. Yes, it's that hot here. Squeezed among antiques shops, the 1902 **Oatman Hotel** (☎ 928-768-4408; 181 N Main St; rooms/suites $35/55) is where Clark Gable and Carole Lombard honeymooned in 1939. Drop by and peruse historical exhibits (donation $1), or order a few tacos and a cold beer at the saloon downstairs. You could also poke around the **Oatman Jail Museum** (140 Oatman Rd; admission $1).

A couple miles west of Oatman, veer left onto the 20-mile **historic byway** that leads through breathtaking high-desert landscape. In spring, the region comes alive with wildflowers, but watch out for flash floods. Keep going through **Golden Shores** – a few cafes, gas stations and watering holes – then curve around through **Havasu National Wildlife Refuge** (☎ 760-326-2853) for migratory and water bird habitats, where desert trails wind along the Colorado River. Contact **Captain Doyle's River Excursions** (☎ 866-284-3262; w www.captdoyle.com; tour $25, 2-person minimum) for petroglyph tours. Farther along, **Topock Gorge Marina** offers boat rentals and pub-style food.

After ducking under the railroad tracks, get back on I-40 (exit 1) to cross into California. The white-piped **Old Trails Arch Bridge** (closed to vehicular traffic), which once carried Dust Bowl–era refugees over the state line, stands to the south.

DETOUR: LAS VEGAS

It would be heresy to drive so far, and to have already seen so much that's in bad taste, without detouring to that tourist trap par excellence, Las Vegas. Casino gambling, hot nightlife and a tissue-thin veneer of glamour can be yours on 'The Strip' (aka Las Vegas Blvd), where hotel rooms start at $25 on weeknights; **Circus Circus Hotel & Casino** (☎ 877-224-7287) has an RV Park. Looking to get hitched? Elvis impersonators await at Vegas' drive-thru wedding chapels. Starting west of Needles (see page 51), Vegas is almost 100 miles north on US95. An alternate return loop via Red Rock Canyon, Death Valley and I-15 to Baker joins Route 66 at Victorville (see page 53).

Ah, California. For down-on-their-luck Okies and optimistic post-WWII travelers along Route 66, this was the promised land. The crashing waves of the Pacific awaited at the end of a long road. After running a brutal gauntlet of Mojave Desert ghost towns, travelers passed a few dusty western railway stops, such as forgotten Barstow and Victorville, before crossing daunting Cajon Summit into San Bernardino, just beyond the reach of Los Angeles.

Keep in mind Route 66 is not always easy to follow through California; sections along the National Old Trails Hwy remain prone to potholes and bumps. The **California Route 66 Preservation Foundation** (☎ 760-868-3320; [w] *www.cart66pf.org; PO Box 290066, Phelan, CA 92329*) website covers news, events and a cyber-tour.

On the Road

After entering California, detour to **Park Moabi** (☎ 760-326-3831; *tent sites $12, RV sites $18-35*) for swimming on the Colorado River. Otherwise, exit at Five Mile Station Rd, following it to its intersection with US95, turning right (northbound) across I-40 into super-hot **Needles**, named for nearby mountain spires. Keep going on Front St past the old mule-train wagon, past the 1920s-era Palm Motel and drive alongside the railroad tracks to **El Garces** (*tours $3; depart 10am, 11am & noon on 2nd Sat Oct-May*), a 1908 Harvey House hotel and train depot, by the helpful **chamber of commerce** (☎ 760-326-2050; *100 G St; open 9:30am-2:30pm Mon-Fri*).

Needles Marina Park (☎ 760-326-2197; *100 Marina Dr; tent & RV campsites $28-30, 4-person cabins $65; office hours 8am-5pm, to 6pm summer*) is down by the river. Vintage motels from $25 abound on the western outskirts. **River Valley Motor Lodge** (☎ 760-326-3839; *1707 W Broadway*) has spacious, well-kept rooms. Nearby **Le Brun** (*2109 W Broadway*) and **Chalet Lodge Inn** (*2306 W Broadway*) also are friendly. By the depot, **Munchies** (*829 Front St; open 24hrs*) sandwich shop serves homemade cheesecake.

Before leaving Needles, stop by the **Desert Information Center** (☎ 760-326-6322; *707 W Broadway; open 8am-4pm Wed-Sun*) to find out

---

MOJAVE MOTORIN'

In the old days, many travelers leaving Needles made the **Mojave Desert** crossing at night, first attaching a tightly woven burlap bag of water to their car's radiator grill as insurance. Even today you should check your car over carefully before braving the desert. Driving out soon after sunrise or in the evening twilight grants cooler temperatures and more subtly shaded landscapes. Always carry a spare gallon or two of water in case of breakdowns. For a major repair (an overheated engine, most likely), it's a long haul to San Bernardino.

about hiking, camping and wildlife watching in the vast Mojave National Preserve. Then head west on Broadway and left onto Needles Hwy. The road crosses the interstate a few times, feeds onto River Rd and finally veers left onto the National Old Trails Hwy west to Park Rd. Rejoin I-40 westbound to exit 133. Take US95 north for 6 miles, then turn west at the railroad tracks for **Goffs**, almost a ghost town. Inside a 1914 schoolhouse, the **Mojave Desert Heritage & Cultural Association** (☎ 760-733-4482; 37198 Lanfair Rd; open 1st weekend Jan-Jun & Oct-Dec) has the best-preserved desert settlement in the Mojave. It's worth a peek, even when closed.

Back on Goffs Rd, drive southwest beyond **Fenner** back to the south side of I-40. Curve right onto the National Old Trails Hwy. West are some largely uninhabited desert towns that died off when the interstate bypassed Route 66. Whiz through **Essex**, **Danby** and **Cadiz** before reaching **Amboy**, a ghost town bought outright by two guys who rent it for movie shoots. Their **Roy's Cafe & Motel** (☎ 760-733-4263; |w| www.rt66roys.com) is famous for its sign. West of 'town' is the turn-off to **Amboy Crater**, a symmetrical 250ft volcanic cinder cone. It's a 1-mile scramble from the parking lot up the volcano's west side (unwise during high winds or summer heat).

Keep driving west by **Bagdad** – one tree is all that's left – past haunting ruins spliced in among the majestic landscape. At **Ludlow** you can get gas. Turn right onto Crucero Rd under I-40, then turn west again. After several bumpy miles, turn left at Lavic Rd. Cross back over I-40, then continue west on National Old Trails Hwy to **Newberry Springs**. Renamed after the 1988 film, the **Bagdad Cafe** (46548 National Trails Hwy; open 7am-6pm Sun-Thu) serves beer and buffalo burgers. The highway passes under I-40 on its way west into **Daggett**, where two geezers smokin' by the railroad tracks is about all the action this town sees. The historic **Stone Hotel**, where desert adventurers like Death Valley Scotty once stayed, is undergoing restorations. In town, take a left onto Daggett-Yermo Rd, then a right to keep heading west. After a couple miles, turn left onto Nebo Rd and rejoin I-40 westbound toward Barstow.

DETOUR: JOSHUA TREE NATIONAL PARK

Fifty miles southwest of Amboy (see above), the dusty town of Twentynine Palms is a gateway to this desert park (information ☎ 760-367-5500; entry $10 per vehicle) known for its spiky Joshua trees. Spend your day rock-climbing, hiking the 8-mile Lost Palms Oasis trail or touring Desert Queen ranch (reservations required; call ☎ 760-367-5555). Children of the '80s, sleep where the band U2 slept at the **Harmony Motel** (☎ 706-367-3351; 71161 Twentynine Palms Hwy; singles/doubles $60/70, cabins $100). Built around the Oasis of Mara, the romantic **29 Palms Inn** (☎ 760-367-3505; 73950 Inn Avenue; doubles $50-145) has a poolside **restaurant** (open lunch & dinner).

Barstow

In sleepy Barstow, a railroad settlement and old Mojave crossroads, murals adorn boarded-up buildings downtown.

East of town, Route 66 exits I-40 at the Marine Corps Logistics Base. Cross south over the interstate by turning left, then take a right onto E Main St, following its twisting path via Business 15 into downtown. On the western outskirts, Main St becomes the National Old Trails Hwy once again.

SIGHTS & ACTIVITIES

Check out the **Mojave River Valley Museum** (☎ 760-256-5452; 270 E Virginia Way; open 11am-4pm) for archaeological and cultural insights and for local books. North over the railroad tracks is **Casa del Desierto**, a circa-1911 Harvey House. Inside is **Route 66 'The Mother Road' Museum** (☎ 760-255-1890; 681 N 1st St; open 11am-4pm Fri-Sun), while outside, the **Western America Railroad Museum** (☎ 760-256-9276; 658 N 1st St; open 11am-4pm Fri-Sun) displays a growing stock collection.

SLEEPING & EATING

Pick from the neon-signed **motels**, most with rooms under $30, strung along Main St. The mom-and-pop-operated **Route 66 Motel** (☎ 760-256-7866; 195 W Main St; doubles $35) has classic cars parked outside.

Good luck finding something to eat, though. The nifty-looking **Palm Cafe** (930 W Main St; open 6am-9pm) cooks up American-Chinese food. At **Barstow Station** (1611 E Main St), a Route 66–themed gift shop, McDonald's operates inside silver-bullet cabooses.

At Rainbow Basin National Natural Landmark, **Owl Canyon Campground** (sites $6) is first-come, first-served. It's about 10 miles north of town, off Irwin Rd.

On the Road

Follow the National Old Trails Hwy west through **Lenwood** and **Helendale**, looking out for abandoned gas stations, broken-down buildings and **Elmer's Place** (24266 National Old Trails Hwy), a folk-art collection of glass bottles, telephone poles and road signs. Adventurous? Call for directions to **Exotic World Burlesque Museum & Striptease Hall of Fame** (☎ 760-243-5261; w www.exoticworldusa.org; 29053 Wild Rd; admission $5; open 10am-4pm Tue-Sun), owned by a former Marilyn Monroe impersonator. In **Oro Grande** the future of the **Iron Hog Saloon** (20848 National Trails Hwy) seemed in doubt, but it may serve BBQ and beer again soon.

Cross the Mojave River on a steel-truss bridge, following the National Old Trails Hwy into the high-desert town of **Victorville**, where Westerns were once filmed. Opposite the transportation center, the mish-mash **California Route 66 Museum** (☎ 760-951-0436; 16825 D St; open 10am-4pm Thu-Mon) sits on the site of the Red Rooster Cafe, featured in the pioneering talkie The Jazz Singer. At the next block, turn right onto 7th

St. Head west past the **country fairgrounds** *(events hotline ☎ 760-261-1854)*, home to the Route 66 Raceway, and the leaping-horse sign outside the **New Corral Motel** *(☎ 760-245-9378; 14643 7th St; doubles $45)*, then veer onto Palmdale Rd by the interstate.

North of town, **Peggy Sue's '50s Diner** *(16885 Frontage Rd, I-15 exit Stoddard Wells Rd; open 7am-8pm, to 9pm Fri)* serves classic diner fare and thick milkshakes. Otherwise take I-15 south, passing the **Summit Inn** *(6000 Mariposa Rd)*, a truck stop with antique gas pumps outside and a lunch counter serving ostrich burgers and date shakes.

Head over the dramatic Cajon Summit (elevation 4190ft). **Silverwood Lake State Recreation Area** *(☎ 760-389-2281, camping reservations ☎ 800-444-7275; tent & RV sites $12-15)* is 11 miles east of exit 138. At Cleghorn (exit 129) abandon the interstate, taking Cajon Blvd south along an ancient section of the Mother Road. Rejoin I-15 at Kenwood Ave (exit 124) southbound onto I-215, exiting at Devore (exit 123). A short dead-end road here leads right to **Peaks Coffee Shop** *(18291 Cajon Blvd)* and **The Screamin' Chicken** *(18169 Cajon Blvd)* saloon, a Harley hangout.

Follow Cajon Blvd south into **San Bernardino**, veering right by the railroad trestle. Turn left onto Mt Vernon Ave, driving south toward downtown. Stop farther east at the **First McDonald's Museum** *(☎ 909-885-6324; 1398 N 'E' St; open 10am-5pm)*, sponsored by the Juan Pollo Chicken company. This volunteer-run museum salutes the McFast Food empire and has historic Route 66 exhibits, mostly photos of the desert towns of yesteryear.

Downtown can be seedy, but vintage motel signs and the 1928 **California Theater** *(☎ 909-885-5152; 562 W 4th St)* of performing arts liven things up. West of the county courthouse on Court St, some landmark buildings have become cafes. Not far away, the **Inland Empire 66ers** *(☎ 909-888-9922; 280 S 'E' St; tickets from $3)* play minor league baseball at Arrowhead Park. San Bernardino's **National Orange Show**

MODEST MUSEUMS

Some mini-museums along Route 66 may not look like much, but be sure not to motor by the following curatorial gems:

Under the Prairie Frontier Archaeological Museum (p11; Elkhart, IL)

Shea's Gas Station Museum (p12; Springfield, IL)

Museum of Transportation (p15; St Louis, MO)

Route 66 Museum (p27; Clinton, OK)

Mesalands Dinosaur Museum (p32; Tucumcari, NM)

Gallup Cultural Center (p41; Gallup, NM)

Old Trails Museum (p44; Winslow, AZ)

Museum of Northern Arizona (p45; Flagstaff, AZ)

Southwest Museum (p56; Pasadena, CA)

comes in May. The **Route 66 Rendezvous** classic car show motors in September.

Take 5th St west of downtown, curving onto Foothill Blvd outside town, passing the run-down **Wigwam Motel** (2728 W Foothill Blvd) and **Holiday Skate** rink (☎ 909-875-4235; 805 E Foothill Blvd) in Rialto. Cruise west through **Fontana**, birthplace of the Hells Angels biker club. The abandoned **Giant Orange** stands forlornly next to boarded-up **Bono's Restaurant & Italian Deli** (15395 Foothill Blvd), a 1930s-era landmark. These fresh juice stands once were a fixture of the bountiful citrus groves along SoCal highways, but no more.

California's first winery was founded in **Rancho Cucamonga**, where the single-A **Quakes** (☎ 909-481-5252; 8408 Rochester Ave; tickets from $6) play minor-league baseball at Epicenter Stadium, south of Foothill Blvd. On the western outskirts, the rustic **Sycamore Inn** (☎ 909-982-1104; 8318 Foothill Blvd; open 5-9pm Mon-Thu, 5-10pm Fri-Sat, 4-8:30pm Sun) restaurant has been hospitable since 1848. Look for the Aladdin-worthy neon sign outside **Magic Lamp Inn** (☎ 909-981-8659; 8189 Foothill Blvd; open 11:30am-2:30pm Tue-Fri, dinner 5-10pm Tue-Thu, 5-10:30pm Fri-Sat, 4:30-9pm Sun), offering steak and seafood dining, cocktails and often dancing. Expect to pay at least $20 for dinner at either place.

Next is **Upland** and the **Madonna of the Trail** (cnr Euclid Ave), a monument to women pioneers at the end of the Old National Trails Hwy. Turn south on Euclid Ave to visit the old-fashioned business district and its antiques shops, bakery and Grove Theater. Back on Foothill Blvd leaving San Bernardino County, the 1929 **Buffalo Inn Restaurant & Tavern** (☎ 909-981-5515; 1814 W Foothill Blvd) serves burgers and beer to rowdy bikers. Farther west, college town **Claremont** claims the world's largest collection of California plants, including wildflowers, palms and cacti, at **Rancho Santa Ana Botanic Garden** (☎ 909-625-8767; 1500 N College Ave; admission $2; open 8am-5pm).

Around **San Dimas**, Foothill Blvd skips north of I-210 and continues west through **Laverne**. In **Glendora**, divert briefly onto Alosta Ave by driving straight ahead. The brick **20th Century Motor Lodge** (☎ 626-335-3348; 1345 E Route 66; doubles $50) has a swimming pool with mountain views. Farther west near Palm Tropics Motel, **The Hat** (☎ 626-857-0017; 611 W Route 66; open 10am-1:30am) has made famous pastrami since 1951.

Back on Foothill Blvd, wind west through **Azusa** past the dead Foothill Drive-In Theatre into **Irwindale**, where Foothill Blvd changes into Huntington Dr. Drive west through **Duarte**, which holds a Route 66 parade every September. The **Route 66 Roadhouse** (☎ 626-357-4210; 1846 E Huntington Dr; open until 2am) has Thursday blues jams. In **Monrovia**, detour north to the 1920s **Aztec Hotel** (☎ 626-358-3231; 310 W Foothill Blvd, cnr Magnolia Ave; singles/doubles from $50/60), which has an ornate Art Deco foyer mural and the **Brass Elephant** restaurant and bar.

On Huntington Dr again, drive west under I-210 into **Arcadia**. The Marx Brothers' A Day at the Races was filmed at **Santa Anita Park** (☎ 626-574-7223; 285 W Huntington Dr; admission $5), where thoroughbreds race the day after Christmas through mid-April and again in the fall. Veer right onto Colorado Place, called Colorado Blvd after Rosemead Ave.

Pasadena

Route 66 follows Pasadena's main street, well-heeled Colorado Blvd. The **Pasadena Convention & Visitors Bureau** (*☎ 626-795-9311; 171 S Los Robles Ave; open 8am-5pm Mon-Fri, 10am-4pm Sat*) has in-depth tour maps. Free *Pasadena Weekly* covers the eating and entertainment scenes.

SIGHTS & ACTIVITIES

Architecture fans should see the **Pasadena Playhouse** (*39 S El Molino Ave)*, where Dustin Hoffman got a career boost, and grand **Pasadena City Hall** (*100 N Garfield Ave)*.

GAMBLE HOUSE
A masterpiece of Arts & Crafts architecture, this bungalow was designed by Greene & Greene in 1908. Tickets sell out quickly, starting at 10am (11:30am Sunday).

☎ 626-793-3334; 4 Westmoreland Pl, off N Orange Grove Blvd; guided 1hr tours $8/5; open noon-3pm Thu-Sun

SOUTHWEST MUSEUM
A formidable array of Native American art and artifacts features tribal basketry, Hopi *kachina* dolls and Navajo textiles.

☎ 323-221-2164; 234 Museum Dr, off Marmion Way, Pasadena Fwy exit Ave 43; admission $6/4/3; open 10am-5pm Tue-Sun

MISSION SAN GABRIEL
Saved from earthquakes, the oldest standing colonial mission church in Southern California is a short drive southeast of Pasadena.

☎ 626-457-3048; 428 S Mission Dr, San Gabriel; admission $5/4/2; open 9am-4:30pm

SLEEPING & EATING

Pasadena's bland motel row stretches along Colorado Blvd. Allegedly, the cheeseburger was invented in 1924 at the **Rite Spot** restaurant.

FAIR OAKS PHARMACY
At a restored turn-of-the-century soda fountain, order up grilled cheese sandwiches and egg creams. Competing **Soda Jerks** (*219 S Fair Oaks Ave)* is hardly as authentic, but sells mountains of retro candy.

☎ 626-799-1414; 1526 Mission St, at S Fair Oaks Ave; open 9am-10pm Mon-Thu, 9am-11pm Fri-Sat, 11am-9pm Sun

MI PIACE
Of all the cookie-cutter Italian joints in Old Pasadena, this standout has a spit-fire wine list, above-decent pasta and Sinatra tunes. An enclave of well-respected eateries – Cuban to nouveau Chinese – hides a block north on N Raymond Ave.

☎ 626-795-3131; 25 E Colorado Blvd; dishes $7-18.50; open 8am-11:15pm

ENTERTAINMENT & SHOPPING

CROWN CITY BREWERY
Not that you would, but customers who sample their 100th world beer at this unpretentious brewpub get a souvenir T-shirt.

☎ 626-577-5548; 300 S Raymond Ave; kitchen open 11am-11pm, bar until after midnight

ALL STAR LANES

On select Saturday nights, Bowl-a-Rama showcases rockabilly bands for the pompadour-and-poodle-skirt crowd, whose classic cars are parked outside.

☎ 323-254-2579; 4459 Eagle Rock Blvd, at York Blvd, Pasadena Fwy exit Verdugo Rd; cover $10-15

ROSE BOWL FLEA MARKET

It's the largest in the land, with thousands of vendors descending upon the stadium monthly.

1000 Rose Bowl Dr; admission $7 after 9am; open 6am-3pm 2nd Sun

Los Angeles: Hollywood & Around

Out of Pasadena, Route 66 once followed Figueroa St. Instead, take the Arroyo Pkwy south onto the Pasadena Fwy, exiting right at Sunset Blvd. Snake along Sunset Blvd into Los Feliz, taking a left at Manzanita, then right onto Santa Monica Blvd. A few blocks north of Sunset Blvd, Hollywood Blvd runs parallel to Santa Monica Blvd.

There is a **visitor center** (☎ 323-467-6412; 6801 Hollywood Blvd, 2nd floor; open 10am-10pm Mon-Sat, 10am-7pm Sun) at Hollywood & Highland mall, a new shopping complex designed to give Hollywood's tattered image a facelift. The Babylon Court frames perfect views of the famed Hollywood sign. The on-street parking nearby is not always secure.

SIGHTS & ACTIVITIES

It's no longer the abode of the stars, but Hollywood is undergoing a revival. Historic movie palaces like the **El Capitan** (☎ 323-467-7674; 6838 Hollywood Blvd) and the **Egyptian Theatre** (☎ 323-466-3456; 6712 Hollywood Blvd) have been lavishly restored.

HOLLYWOOD BLVD

The **Hollywood Walk of Fame** begins at the corner of La Brea Ave. Follow the marble-and-bronze stars east to the **Hollywood Entertainment Museum** (☎ 323-465-7900; 7021 Hollywood Blvd; admission $8.75/5.50/4; open 11am-6pm, closed Wed winter), and the fantastical 1927 **Mann's Chinese Theater** (☎ 323-464-8111; 6925 Hollywood Blvd). Spy Mae West's negligee inside **Frederick's of Hollywood Lingerie Museum** (☎ 323-466-8506; 6608 Hollywood Blvd; open 10am-6pm Mon-Sat, noon-5pm Sun). The **Capitol Records Tower** (1750 Vine St) is designed to look like a stack of records.

GRIFFITH PARK

The **Autry Museum of Western Heritage** (☎ 323-667-2000; admission $7.50/5/3, free Thu after 4pm; open Tue-Sun 10am-5pm, to 8pm Thu), endowed by movie star and singing cowboy Gene Autry, tests myths of the Old West against harsher realities. Railroad buffs like **Travel Town Museum** (☎ 323-662-5874; open 10am-5pm Mon-Fri, 10am-6pm Sat-Sun). On the slopes of Mt Hollywood, **Griffith Observatory & Planetarium** (☎ 323-664-1191) was the scene of James Dean's switchblade fight in Rebel Without a Cause.

TV TAPINGS

Most of 'The Industry' has moved from Hollywood to Burbank and Studio City. The easiest way to get tickets is through **Audiences Unlimited**, which handles the most coveted shows, including Everybody Loves Raymond and Friends. Same-day or next-day tickets (all free!) are usually available from their booth at Universal Studios.

advance tickets ☎ 818-753-3470 ext 812; W www.tvtickets.com

SLEEPING & EATING

Motels with rooms from $50 line Sunset Blvd, but many are questionable. Try instead the **Orbit Hostel** (☎ 323-655-1510, 877-672-4887; 7950 Melrose Ave, West Hollywood; dorm beds $18-20, singles/doubles $55/65).

MAGIC CASTLE HOTEL
Staying here may be the only way into the Magic Castle nightclub, where top-flight magicians perform nightly.

☎ 323-851-0800, 800-741-4915; 7025 Franklin Ave; rooms/suites with kitchens from $70/90

MAISON 140
Inside movie star Lillian Gish's former villa, *French Kiss* meets Far East fantasy with boudoir-style rooms and an intimate lounge.

☎ 310-281-4000, 800-432-5444; W www.maison140.com; 140 S Lasky Dr, Beverly Hills; B&B rooms from $135

MUSSO & FRANK GRILL
A hallowed steakhouse since 1919, stars have reposed inside these high-sided mahogany booths. Martinis will please connoisseurs.

☎ 323-467-7788; 6667 Hollywood Blvd; dishes $10-30; open 11am-11pm Tue-Sat

FARMERS MARKET
Outside CBS Television City, try **Du-par's Pies**, Cajun-style cooking at **Gumbo Pot** or eclectic brunches at **Kokomo Cafe** diner.

6333 W 3rd St, at Fairfax Ave; open 9am-9pm Mon-Fri, 9am-8pm Sat, 10am-7pm Sun

BOB'S BIG BOY
Swing by this 1949 landmark for 1950s classic car shows on Friday night or car-hop service most Saturday and Sunday evenings.

☎ 818-843-9334; 4211 Riverside Dr, Burbank; open 24hrs

ENTERTAINMENT

Free *LA Weekly* covers nightlife. The **Hollywood Bowl** (☎ 323-850-2000; 2301 Highland Ave, Hollywood Hills) has staged symphonies under the stars, Monty Python skits and rock concerts. Drop by the museum before the show or tote your own picnic basket onto the lawn.

At the Cinerama Dome, **ArcLight Hollywood Cinemas** (☎ 323-464-4226; 6360 W Sunset Blvd; 4hr validated parking) multiplex is a romp through the 1960s. Arthouse flicks are screened at the **Egyptian Theatre** (☎ 323-466-3456; 6712 Hollywood Blvd), opened in the same year King Tut's tomb was discovered.

SHOPPING

Vendors of film scripts, original press kits and cinematic memorabilia are **Book City** (Hollywood & Highland, 6801 Hollywood Blvd, 3rd floor; open 10am-10pm Sat, 10am-7pm Sun) and **Larry Edmunds Bookshop** (6644 Hollywood Blvd; open 10am-6pm Mon-Sat).

Standing next to a 15ft-high *Rocky & Bullwinkle* statue, the **Dudley DoRight Emporium** (8200 W Sunset Blvd, West Hollywood; open 11am-5pm Tue, Thu & Sat) salutes Jay Ward's beloved 1960s cartoon characters. In Burbank, **It's a Wrap!** (3315 W Magnolia Blvd, Burbank; open 11am-8pm Mon-Fri, 11am-6pm Sat-Sun) resells TV clothes worn by stars.

End of the Road: Santa Monica

With its restored pier, miles of golden sand and pedestrian promenade, Santa Monica bears little resemblance to the shadowy Bay City depicted by Raymond Chandler. Route 66 follows Santa Monica Blvd in a beeline to the ocean, ending at Palisades Park. Nearby is a **visitor information kiosk** (☎ 310-393-7593; 1400 Ocean Ave; open 10am-5pm, to 4pm winter).

SIGHTS & ACTIVITIES

PALISADES PARK
On a bluff over the Pacific, a **Will Rogers Highway** plaque marks the official terminus of Route 66 – hurrah! **Camera Obscura** (1450 Ocean Ave; open 10am-3pm), an early version of the single-lens reflex camera, was quite the sensation when it opened in 1899; get a key at the Senior Recreation Center.

SANTA MONICA PIER
Ride a 1920s **carousel** featured in The Sting, touch starfish at the **UCLA Ocean Discovery Center** (admission $3; open 11am-5pm Sat-Sun, also afternoons Tue-Fri in summer) or enjoy a sunset atop the world's first solar-powered ferris wheel at **Pacific Park** (open 11am-11pm Sun-Thu, 11am-12:30am Fri-Sat in summer). The summer **Twilight Dance Series** features rock, jazz and soul concerts.

SANTA MONICA STATE & VENICE CITY BEACHES
This is LA's zaniest beachfront. A paved shoreline path has separate lanes for cyclists and rollerbladers. Venice's chief attraction is the bizarre slice of life on mile-long **Ocean Front Walk**. Don't miss bikini-clad bodybuilders at **Muscle Beach**.

WILL ROGERS STATE PARK
A real-life Hollywood cowboy, humorist Will Rogers traded Beverly Hills for this mountain ranch. Spencer Tracy and Walt Disney played polo on the lawn. Hiking trails lead up into the chaparral, including to Inspiration Point.

☎ 310-454-8212; off Sunset Blvd, Pacific Palisades; open 8am-sunset

SLEEPING

Santa Monica has an official HI hostel (☎ 310-393-9913; 1436 2nd St; dorm beds $25-30). Independent hostels charging less are found at Venice Beach. Motels along Ocean Ave, Main St and Lincoln Ave start at $55. **Sea Shore Motel** (☎ 310-392-2787; 2637 Main St; rooms/suites from $75/110) is reliable.

The Art Deco **Georgian Hotel** (☎ 310-395-9945, 800-538-8147; w www.georgianhotel.com; 1415 Ocean Ave; rooms/suites from $170/235) was a favorite hideaway of Clark Gable and Carole Lombard.

EATING & ENTERTAINMENT

Established in 1946, **Hot Dog on a Stick** (1633 Ocean Front Walk) is south of Santa Monica Pier. In Venice, **Jody Maroni's Sausage Kingdom** (2011 Ocean Front Walk) serves plump all-natural 'haut dogs.'

APPLE PAN
Hungry diners crowd around the horseshoe-shaped counter and grandfatherly servers keep things snappy at this 1940s burger shack.

☎ 310-475-3585; 10801 W Pico Blvd, West LA; open 11am-midnight

HARVELLE'S
This 1930s club serves up true blues, R&B and West Coast jazz. Arrive early to dine next door at the Chicago-style rib house.

☎ 310-395-1676; 1432 4th St; open 8pm-2am; cover under $10 (2-drink min)

The Author

A Californian by choice, Sara Benson packed herself off to the Golden State after college graduation with nothing but a suitcase and a few bucks. She has spent the past decade traveling, teaching and writing across Asia, the Pacific Rim and North America, yet always lands right side back up on the West Coast or in her hometown of Chicago. She destroyed her car by driving over 7000 miles to research this book.

From the Author

Thanks to the mom-and-pop motel owners, small-town museum curators and late-night diner staff who made this trip such a blast. Lawrence Charap and Kathleen Munnelly provided key research materials. My parents gave emergency car and computer advice, my grandmother shared her house at the end of the road, Sara Z lent me her laptop and Josh kept on being funny even while shouldering 90% of the editing – thank you.

The Lonely Planet Story

The story begins with a classic travel adventure: Tony and Maureen Wheeler's 1972 journey across Europe and Asia to Australia. There was no useful information about the overland trail then, so Tony and Maureen published the first Lonely Planet guidebook to meet a growing need.

From a kitchen table, Lonely Planet has grown to become the largest independent travel publisher in the world, with offices in Melbourne (Australia), Oakland (USA), London (UK) and Paris (France).

Today Lonely Planet guidebooks cover the globe. There is an ever-growing list of books and information in a variety of media. Some things haven't changed. The main aim is still to make it possible for adventurous travelers to get out there – to explore and better understand the world.

At Lonely Planet we believe travelers can make a positive contribution to the countries they visit – if they respect their host communities and spend their money wisely. Since 1986 a percentage of the income from each book has been donated to aid projects and human rights campaigns, and, more recently, to wildlife conservation.

www.lonelyplanet.com

Lonely Planet's award-winning Web site has information on hundreds of destinations from Amsterdam to Zimbabwe, complete with interactive maps and color photographs. You'll also find the latest travel news, an online shop with all our titles, and a lively bulletin board where you can meet fellow travelers, swap recommendations and seek advice.

About This Book

Commissioned and developed by Kathleen Munnelly • Edited by Rachel Bernstein • Design and layout by Candice Jacobus & Wendy Yanagihara • Maps by Annette Olson & Bart Wright • Cover design by Candice Jacobus • Series Publishing Manager: Maria Donohoe • Thanks to Ruth Askevold, Mariah Bear, Andreas Schueller, Ryan ver Berkmoes and Vivek Waglé

LONELY PLANET

You already know that Lonely Planet produces more than this one guidebook, but you might not be aware of the other products we have on this region. Here is a selection of titles that you may want to check out as well:

USA
ISBN 1-86450-308-4
US$24.99 · UK£14.99

Chicago
ISBN 1-86450-210-X
US$17.99 · UK£9.99

Southwest
ISBN 1-86450-376-9
US$24.99 · UK£14.99

Los Angeles
ISBN 1-74059-021-X
US$15.99 · US£9.99

HIT THE ROAD WITH LONELY PLANET'S OTHER ROAD TRIP TITLES:

Road Trip: California Highway 1
ISBN 1-74059-582-3
US$10.00 · UK£5.99

Road Trip: Napa & Sonoma Wine Country
ISBN 1-74059-581-5
US$10.00 · UK£5.99

INDEX

A

AAA 5
Acomo Pueblo (NM) 38
Adrian (TX) 31
Afton (OK) 21
airports 3, 4
Alanreed (TX) 28
Albatross (MO) 18
Albuquerque (NM) 34, 37–9
Albuquerque Museum of Art & History (NM) 37
Algodones (NM) 36
Allantown (AZ) 42
Allenton (MO) 16
Amarillo (TX) 29–30
Amboy (CA) 52
Amboy Crater (CA) 52
Anheuser-Busch Brewery (MO) 14
Antique Toy Museum (MO) 16
antiques 10, 16, 30, 37
Arcadia (CA) 55
Arcadia (OK) 24
Arizona 42–50
Art Institute (IL) 7
Ash Fork (AZ) 48
Atlanta (IL) 11
Autry Museum of Western Heritage (CA) 57
Avery, Cyrus 3
Avilla (MO) 18
Azusa (CA) 55

B

Bagdad (CA) 52
Bard (NM) 32
Barstow (CA) 53
Barton (NM) 34
baseball 9, 15, 30, 54, 55
Baxter Springs (KS) 20
Bernalillo (NM) 37
Big Texan Steak Ranch (TX) 30
Black Madonna Shrine (MO) 15–6
Bloomington (IL) 10–1
Blue Hole (NM) 33
Bob's Big Boy (CA) 58
books 5, 31
Bourbon (MO) 17
bowling 9, 15, 17, 23, 57
Braceville (IL) 10
Braidwood (IL) 10
Brannigan Park (AZ) 46
Branson (MO) 18–9
Bridgeport (OK) 26
Bristow (OK) 23
Broadwell (IL) 11
Buckhorn (MO) 17
Budville (NM) 40

Bug Ranch (TX) 29
Busch Stadium (MO) 15
Bushland (TX) 31

C

Cadillac Ranch (TX) 29
California 51–9
California Route 66 Museum (CA) 53
Calumet (OK) 26
Canadian County Historical Museum (OK) 26
Canute (OK) 27
Cardinals Hall of Fame (MO) 15
cars
 AAA 4
 museums 17, 22, 33
 races 10
 renting 4
Carthage (MO) 19
Catoosa (OK) 22
caves 16, 19, 40, 48
Chain of Rocks Bridge (IL) 13
Chambers (AZ) 42
Chandler (OK) 23
Chelsea (OK) 21
Chicago (IL) 3, 7–9
children, traveling with 6
Civil War Museum (MO) 19
Claremont (CA) 55
Claremore (OK) 21
climbing 11
Clinton (OK) 27
Coleman Theater (OK) 21
Commerce (OK) 21
Continental Divide (NM) 40
Conway (MO) 17
Conway (TX) 29
Corn Maize (OK) 26
Coronado State Monument (NM) 36
Correo (NM) 39
Cross of the Martyrs (NM) 35
Crystal Cave (MO) 19
Cuba (MO) 17
Cuervo (NM) 33

D

Daggett (CA) 52
Dana-Thomas House (IL) 12
Davenport (OK) 23
Defiance (NM) 41
Depew (OK) 23
Devil's Elbow (MO) 17
Devil's Rope Museum (TX) 28
Discoveryland! (OK) 23
Divernon (IL) 12
diving 33
Dixie Trucker's Home (IL) 11

Dobson Museum (OK) 21
Doolittle (MO) 17
Dorothea B Hoover Historical Museum (MO) 19
Dot's Mini Museum (TX) 31
Duarte (CA) 55
Dwight (IL) 10
Dynamite Museum (TX) 29

E

Eastern Trails Museum (OK) 21
Edgewood (NM) 34
Edmond (OK) 24
Edwardsville (IL) 13
Eisenhower, Dwight 3
El Garces (CA) 51
El Malpais (NM) 40
El Morro (NM) 40
El Rancho de los Golondrinas (NM) 36
El Reno (OK) 26
Elk City (OK) 27
Elkhart (IL) 11
Elmer's Place (CA) 53
Elwood (IL) 10
Endee (NM) 32
English Field Air & Space Museum (TX) 29
Erick (OK) 27
Exotic World Burlesque Museum & Striptease Hall of Fame (CA) 53

F

farmer's markets 15, 58
Farmersville (IL) 12
Fenner (CA) 52
First McDonald's Museum (CA) 54
Flagstaff (AZ) 45–6
folk art 6
Fontana (CA) 55
food 30
Forest Park (MO) 14
Fort Reno (OK) 26
Foyil (OK) 21
Frederick's of Hollywood Lingerie Museum (CA) 57

G

Galena (KS) 20
Gallup (NM) 41
Gamble House (CA) 56
Gardner (IL) 10
Gateway Arch (MO) 14
Geary (OK) 26
Gemini Giant (IL) 10
General Sweeney's Museum (MO) 18
Gilcrease Museum (OK) 22
Glenarm (IL) 12

Glendora (CA) 55
Glenrio (TX) 31
Glorieta (NM) 35
Godley (IL) 10
Goffs (CA) 52
Golden Driller (OK) 22
Golden Shores (AZ) 50
Goldroad Mine (AZ) 50
Grand Canyon (AZ) 47
Grand Canyon Railway
    (AZ) 46
Grant Park (IL) 7
Grants (NM) 40
Griffith Observatory &
    Planetarium (CA) 57
Griffith Park (CA) 57
Groom (TX) 28–9
Guthrie (OK) 24

H
Hackberry (AZ) 49
Halltown (MO) 18
Hamel (IL) 13
Havasu National Wildlife
    Refuge (AZ) 50
Hazelgreen (MO) 17
Heatonville (MO) 18
Helendale (CA) 53
Hell's Half Acre (KS) 20
Heritage Center &
    Historical Museum (KS)
    20
Hext (OK) 27
highlights 5–6
history 3
Holbrook (AZ) 43
Hollywood (CA) 57–8
Homolovi Ruins State
    Park (AZ) 44
Houck (AZ) 42
Hydro (OK) 26

I
Illinois 7–13
Illinois & Michigan Canal 9
Institute of American
    Indian Arts Museum
    (NM) 35
International Bowling
    Museum (MO) 15
Irwindale (CA) 55
Isleta Pueblo (NM) 39

J
Jackrabbit Trading Post
    (AZ) 43
Jericho Gap (TX) 28
Jesse James Wax
    Museum (MO) 16
JM Davis Arms &
    Historical Museum
    (OK) 22
John's Modern Cabins
    (MO) 17
Joliet (IL) 10
Jones, Mary Harris 13

Joplin (MO) 19
Joseph City (AZ) 43
Joshua Tree National Park
    (CA) 52

K–L
Kansas 20
Kellyville (OK) 23
Kingman (AZ) 49
kitsch 6, 33
Laguna Pueblo (NM) 40
Lake Meredith National
    Recreation Area (TX) 29
Landers Theater (MO) 18
Laquey (MO) 17
Las Padillas (NM) 39
Las Vegas (NM) 34
Las Vegas (NV) 50
Laverne (CA) 55
Lebanon (MO) 17
Lela (TX) 28
Lenwood (CA) 53
Lincoln, Abraham 11
Lincoln (IL) 11
Lincoln's New Salem (IL) 12
Litchfield (IL) 13
Los Angeles (CA) 4, 57–8
Los Lunas (NM) 39
Lowell Observatory (AZ)
    45
Ludlow (CA) 52
Luther (OK) 24

M
Mac's Antique Car
    Museum (OK) 22
Mann's Chinese Theater
    (CA) 57
Manuelito (NM) 41
Marsh Rainbow Arch
    Bridge (KS) 20
Marshfield (MO) 17
McCartys (NM) 40
McLain Rogers Park (OK) 27
McLean (IL) 11
McLean (TX) 28
Memoryville USA (MO) 17
Meramec Caverns (MO) 16
Mesalands Dinosaur
    Museum (NM) 32
Mesita (NM) 39
Meteor Crater (AZ) 44
Miami (OK) 21
Midway Airport (IL) 3
missions
San Augustine (NM) 39
San Esteban del Rey (NM)
    38
San Gabriel (CA) 56
Missouri 14–9
Mitchell (IL) 13
Mojave Desert (CA) 51–2
Mojave Museum of
    History & Arts (AZ) 49

Mojave River Valley
    Museum (CA) 53
Monrovia (CA) 55
Montoya (NM) 33
Moriarty (NM) 34
motels 9
motorcycles 4
Mt Olive (IL) 13
Muscle Beach (CA) 59
Museum of Fine Arts
    (NM) 35
Museum of Funeral
    Customs (IL) 12
Museum of New Mexico
    (NM) 35
Museum of Northern
    Arizona (AZ) 45
Museum of Pioneer
    History (OK) 23
Museum of
    Transportation (MO) 15
Museum of Western
    Expansion (MO) 14
museums 54, see also
    individual museums
music 10, 13

N
Narcissa (OK) 21
National Cowboy &
    Western Heritage
    Museum (OK) 25
National Historic Route
    66 Association 3
Navajo Nation (AZ) 42
Needles (CA) 51
New Laguna (NM) 40
New Mexico 32–41
New Mexico Mining
    Museum (NM) 40
Newberry Springs (CA) 52
Newkirk (NM) 33
Normal (IL) 10

O
Oak Ridge Cemetery (IL)
    12
Oatman (AZ) 50
Odell (IL) 10
O'Hare International
    Airport (IL) 3
Oklahoma 21–7
Oklahoma City (OK) 24–5
Old Town Museum (OK)
    27
Old Trails Museum (AZ) 44
Oliver Parks Telephone
    Museum (IL) 12
100th Meridian Museum
    (OK) 27
Oral Roberts University
    (OK) 22
Oro Grande (CA) 53

P
Pacific Park (CA) 59

Painted Desert (AZ) 43
Palace of the Governors (NM) 35
Palisades Park (CA) 59
Paloma (NM) 33
Paraje (NM) 40
Parks (AZ) 46
Pasadena (CA) 56–7
Peach Springs (AZ) 48–9
Pecos National Historic Park (NM) 34–5
Petrified Forest National Park (AZ) 43
Petroglyph National Monument (NM) 37
Phelps (MO) 18
Phillipsburg (MO) 17
Pig-Hip Restaurant (IL) 11
Pioneer West Museum (TX) 28
Pontiac (IL) 10
pueblos 36, 38, 39
Puerto de Luna (NM) 33

Q–R

Quapaw (OK) 21
radio 10
Rainbow Museum (AZ) 43
Rainbow Rock Shop (AZ) 43
Rancho Cucamonga (CA) 55
Rancho Santa Ana Botanic Garden (CA) 55
Rattlesnake Museum (NM) 37
Red Oak II (MO) 18–9
Red Rock State Park (NM) 41
Rescue (MO) 18
restaurants 30
Rialto Square Theatre (IL) 10
Riverside Reptile Ranch (MO) 16
Riverton (KS) 20
rodeos 21, 22, 24, 29
Roger Miller Museum (OK) 27
Rogers, Will 21–2, 59
Rolla (MO) 17
Romeoville (IL) 9
Rosati (MO) 17
Rough Rider Museum (NM) 34
Round Barn (OK) 24
Route 66 Auto Museum (NM) 33
Route 66 Museum (OK) 27
Route 66 Raceway (IL) 10
Route 66 State Park (MO) 15
Route 66 'The Mother Road' Museum (CA) 53

Rowe (NM) 34
Roy Rogers & Dale Evans Museum (MO) 18–9
RS&K Railroad Museum (OK) 27
RVs 4

S

St Clair (MO) 16
St Cloud (MO) 17
St James (MO) 17
St Louis (MO) 14–5
St Robert (MO) 17
San Bernardino (CA) 54
San Dimas (CA) 55
San Felipe Pueblo (NM) 36
San Fidel (NM) 40
San Jon (NM) 32
San Jose (NM) 34
Sanders (AZ) 42
Sandia Tramway (NM) 37
Sands (NM) 34
Santa Anita Park (CA) 55
Santa Fe (NM) 35–6
Santa Monica (CA) 59
Santa Rosa (NM) 33
Santo Domingo Pueblo (NM) 36
Sayre (OK) 27
Sears Tower (IL) 7
Seligman (AZ) 48
Shamrock (TX) 28
Shaw Nature Reserve (MO) 16
Shea's Gas Station Museum (IL) 12
Shirley (IL) 11
Shrine Mosque (MO) 18
Silverwood Lake State Recreation Area (CA) 54
Sitgreaves Pass (AZ) 50
Sky City (NM) 38
Southwest Museum (CA) 56
souvenirs 33
Spencer (MO) 18
Springfield (IL) 11–2
Springfield (MO) 18
Stanton (MO) 16
Staunton (IL) 13
Steinbeck, John 3, 21, 31
stockyards 25, 29
Strafford (MO) 17
Stroud (OK) 23
Sullivan (MO) 16
Sunset Crater (AZ) 48

T

Table Rock State Park (MO) 18–9
Texas 28–31
Texola (OK) 27
theme parks 16, 19, 30
Tijeras (NM) 34

Tinkertown Museum (NM) 34
Totem Pole Park (OK) 21
trains 4, 46, 53, 57
Travel Town Museum (CA) 57
Tri-State Mineral Museum (MO) 19
Tucumcari (NM) 32
Tulsa (OK) 22–3
TV tapings 57

U–V

UCLA Ocean Discovery Center (CA) 59
Under the Prairie Frontier Archaeological Museum (IL) 11
Upland (CA) 55
Vega (TX) 31
Venice Beach (CA) 59
Victorville (CA) 53
views 16
Vinita (OK) 21

W–Y

Waggoner (IL) 13
Walnut Canyon National Monument (AZ) 44
Warwick (OK) 24
Waynesville (MO) 17
Weatherford (OK) 26–7
Wellston (OK) 24
Western America Railroad Museum (CA) 53
Wheelwright Museum of the American Indian (NM) 35
White Oak (OK) 21
WigWam Village Motel (AZ) 43
Wildlife West Nature Park (NM) 34
Wildorado (TX) 31
Will Rogers Memorial Museum (OK) 21–2
Will Rogers State Park (CA) 59
Williams (AZ) 46
Williamson (IL) 13
Williamsville (IL) 11
Wilmington (IL) 10
Wilson's Creek National Battlefield (MO) 18
Window Rock (AZ) 42
Winona (AZ) 44
Winslow (AZ) 43–4
Wright, Frank Lloyd 9, 10, 12
Wrigley Field (IL) 9
Wupatki National Monument (AZ) 48
Yukon (OK) 25

Oxford Handbook of Clinical Medicine 6/e (also available for PDAs and in a Mini Edition)
Oxford Handbook of Clinical Specialties 7/e
Oxford Handbook of Accident and Emergency Medicine 2/e
Oxford Handbook of Acute Medicine 2/e
Oxford Handbook of Anaesthesia 2/e
Oxford Handbook of Applied Dental Sciences
Oxford Handbook of Cardiology
Oxford Handbook of Clinical and Laboratory Investigation 2/e
Oxford Handbook of Clinical Diagnosis
Oxford Handbook of Clinical Haematology 2/e
Oxford Handbook of Clinical Immunology and Allergy 2/e
Oxford Handbook of Clinical Surgery 2/e
Oxford Handbook of Critical Care 2/e
Oxford Handbook of Dental Patient Care 2/e
Oxford Handbook of Dialysis 2/e
Oxford Handbook of Endocrinology and Diabetes
Oxford Handbook of ENT and Head and Neck Surgery
Oxford Handbook for the Foundation Programme
Oxford Handbook of Gastroenterology and Hepatology
Oxford Handbook of General Practice 2/e
Oxford Handbook of Genitourinary Medicine, HIV and AIDS
Oxford Handbook of Geriatric Medicine
Oxford Handbook of Medical Sciences
Oxford Handbook of Obstetrics and Gynaecology
Oxford Handbook of Oncology
Oxford Handbook of Ophthalmology
Oxford Handbook of Palliative Care
Oxford Handbook of Practical Drug Therapy
Oxford Handbook of Psychiatry
Oxford Handbook of Public Health Practice 2/e
Oxford Handbook of Rehabilitation Medicine
Oxford Handbook of Respiratory Medicine
Oxford Handbook of Rheumatology
Oxford Handbook of Tropical Medicine 2/e
Oxford Handbook of Urology

Oxford Handbook of
Geriatric
Medicine

Lesley K. Bowker

Consultant in Medicine for the Elderly,
Norfolk and Norwich University Hospital NHS Trust,
Honorary Senior Lecturer,
University of East Anglia, UK

James D. Price

Consultant in Geriatric Medicine and General
Internal Medicine,
Oxford Radcliffe Hospitals NHS Trust, and
South East and South West Oxfordshire
Primary Care Trusts, UK

Sarah C. Smith

Consultant in Geriatric Medicine and General
Internal Medicine,
Oxford Radcliffe Hospitals NHS Trust,
South East and South West Oxfordshire and
Oxford City Primary Care Trusts, UK

OXFORD
UNIVERSITY PRESS

OXFORD
UNIVERSITY PRESS

Great Clarendon Street, Oxford OX2 6DP

Oxford University Press is a department of the University of Oxford.
It furthers the University's objective of excellence in research, scholarship,
and education by publishing worldwide in

Oxford New York

Auckland Cape Town Dar es Salaam Hong Kong Karachi
Kuala Lumpur Madrid Melbourne Mexico City Nairobi
New Delhi Shanghai Taipei Toronto

With offices in

Argentina Austria Brazil Chile Czech Republic France Greece
Guatemala Hungary Italy Japan Poland Portugal Singapore
South Korea Switzerland Thailand Turkey Ukraine Vietnam

Oxford is a registered trade mark of Oxford University Press
in the UK and in certain other countries

Published in the United States
by Oxford University Press Inc., New York

© Oxford University Press 2006

The moral rights of the authors have been asserted
Database right Oxford University Press (maker)

First published 2006

A catalogue record for this title is available from the British Library
Data available

Library of Congress Cataloging in Publication Data
Data available

Typeset by Newgen Imaging Systems (P) Ltd., Chennai, India
Printed in Italy
on acid-free paper by Legoprint S.p.A.

ISBN 0–19–853029–3 (flexicover: alk. paper)   978–0–19–853029–9 (flexicover: alk. paper)

10 9 8 7 6 5 4 3 2 1

Foreword

Geriatrics is medicine of the gaps—such gaps as we see between surgery and social work, and between psychiatry and orthopaedics. It is the medicine of the gaps between what doctors need to know for their everyday work and what they are taught as medical students. Medical curricula are still structured around diseases and technologies rather than people with diseases and people needing technologies. The majority of such people are old.

Even more importantly geriatrics has to transcend gaps in 'evidence-based medicine'. This is only partly because older people, and especially frail older people, are left out of clinical trials; there is also a philosophical gap. We start life with different levels of health and function and we age at different rates. Older people come to differ from each other more than do younger people; logic requires that they are treated as individuals not as members of the homogenous groups assumed in the rationale of conventional trial evidence.

Some generalizations are possible. It follows from the biology of ageing that the risk of complications, often preventable or curable, from physically challenging treatments will increase with age. But it follows, too, that the benefits of treatments that are not physically challenging will also increase with age. The n-of-1 trial is the relevant but sadly under-used paradigm, its logic (though not its rigour) underlying the better-known 'let's try it but stop if it does not work' trial. With the patient as an active and informed partner even this is better than the unthinking application of the results of a clinical trial of dubious relevance.

Because of the evidence gap, geriatric medicine has to be an art as well as a science—as the authors of this handbook emphasize in their preface. The art of medicine depends, in William Osler's words on 'a sustaining love for ideals' and, at a practical level, on ability to recognize similarities and to distinguish significant differences. Good doctors can draw on structured experience and recognize patterns and warning signals that are unrecorded in the cookbook medicine of trialists and managers. The cookbooks are based on what happens on average and our patients expect us to do better than that.

For some of us its interplay of medicine, biology, and social sciences makes geriatrics a fascinating central interest. But most doctors who meet with ill older people have other responsibilities as well. They will enjoy their work better and be more efficient if they feel able to respond confidently to the commoner problems of their older patients. Not every older person needs a geriatrician any more than every person with heart failure needs a cardiologist. But all doctors need to know what geriatricians and cardiologists have to offer and all doctors must be able to recognize when they are getting out of their depth.

So here is a *vade mecum* written for the caring and conscientious clinician but it is not a cookbook. It outlines how to set about analysing complex clinical situations, and the resources that can or should be called on. The authors are worthy guides; they have gained and given of their experience and wisdom in one of the best and busiest of British hospitals. Their aim is not to supplant but to facilitate thought and good judgement—two qualities that our older patients need, deserve, and expect of us.

John Grimley Evans

Contents

Preface *x*
Acknowledgements *xi*
Abbreviations *xiii*

1	Ageing	1
2	Organizing geriatric services	15
3	Clinical assessment of older people	59
4	Rehabilitation	79
5	Falls and funny turns	115
6	Drugs	135
7	Neurology	163
8	Stroke	191
9	Psychiatry	219
10	Cardiovascular medicine	277
11	Chest medicine	327
12	Gastroenterology	373
13	Renal medicine	409
14	Homeostasis	431
15	Endocrinology	451
16	Haematology	487
17	Musculoskeletal system	509
18	Pressure injuries	545
19	Genitourinary medicine	551
20	Incontinence	573

21	Ears	589
22	Eyes	609
23	Skin	629
24	Infection and immunity	659
25	Malignancy	687
26	Death and dying	699
27	Ethics	715
28	Finances	737

Appendix 745
Index 757

We dedicate this book to our lovely girls: Nina, Jess, Helen, Cassie, and Anna.
We managed to finish despite their arrival!

Preface

This pocket-sized text will function as a friendly, experienced, and knowledgeable geriatrician who is available for advice at all times.

This is a handbook, not a textbook. It is not exhaustive—we have focused on common problems, including practical help with common dilemmas which are not well covered by traditional tomes, whilst excluding the rare and unimportant.

We believe that the practice of geriatric medicine is an art-form and aim to provide guidance to complement the lists and protocols found in many textbooks. The evidence-based literature in geriatric medicine is limited, so advice is often opinion and experience-based.

The satisfaction of good geriatric care is lost to many who become overwhelmed by the breadth and complexity of seemingly insoluble problems. We provide a structured, logical, yet flexible approach to problem solving which we hope will give practical help to improve the care given to older patients in many settings.

Lesley K Bowker
James D Price
Sarah C Smith

Acknowledgements

Sue Burge

Andrew Coull

Adam Darowski

Yaw Duodu

Soroosh Firoozan

Maggie Hammersley

Maxine Hardinge

Helen Herbert

Paula Hickey

Nicola Jones

David Maisey

Rupert McShane

Kneale Metcalf

Jane Parker

Sarah Pendlebury

Lisa Pitkin

Jonathan Price

John Reynolds

Adam Sandell

Lisa Shaw

Sanja Thompson

Victoria Tippett

Adrain Wagg

Bee Wee

Simon Winner

Abbreviations

AAMI	age-associated memory impairment
AAS	admission avoidance scheme
ABG	arterial blood gases
ABPI	ankle brachial pressure index
ACE	angiotensin converting enzyme
ACTH	adrenocorticotrophic hormone
AD	Alzheimer's dementia
ADH	antidiuretic hormone
ADL	activities of daily living
A&E	accident and emergency
AF	atrial fibrillation
AFB	acid-fast bacilli (TB)
ALP	alkaline phosphatases
ALS	advanced life support
AMTS	abbreviated mental test score
ANA	antinuclear antibody
ANCA	anti-neutrophil cytoplasmic antibody
ARDS	adult respiratory distress syndrome
AXR	abdominal X-ray
BPH	benign prostatic hypertrophy
CD	*Clostridium difficile*
CDAD	*Clostridium difficile* associated diarrhoea
CDT	clock drawing test
CF	cardiac failure
CGA	comprehensive geriatric assessment
CH	community hospital
CHD	coronary heart disease
ChEI	cholinesterase inhibitor
CIND	cognitive impairment no dementia
CK	creatine kinase
CLL	chronic lymphocytic leukaemia
CNS	central nervous system
COPD	chronic obstructive pulmonary disease
CPR	cardiopulmonary resuscitation
CRP	C reactive protein
CSF	cerebrospinal fluid

CSS	carotid sinus syndrome
CT	computerized tomography
CTPA	CT pulmonary angiogram
CXR	chest X-ray
DBP	diastolic blood pressure
DH	day hospital
DIC	disseminated intravascular coagulation
DKA	diabetic ketoacidosis
DLB	dementia with Lewy bodies
DNAR	do not attempt resuscitation
DV	domiciliary visit
ECG	electrocardiogram
ED	emergency department
EEG	electroencephalogram
EMG	electromyogram
EMI	elderly mentally infirm
EPOA	enduring power of attorney
ESR	erythrocyte sedimentation rate
ESRF	end stage renal failure
FBC	full blood count
FLD	frontal lobe degeneration
FSH	follicle stimulating hormone
FTD	frontotemporal dementia
GCS	Glasgow coma scale
GDS	Genatric Depression Scale
GI	gastrointestinal
GMC	General Medical Council
GORD	gastro-oesophageal reflux disease
GP	general practitioner
GPSI	GP with special interest
Hb	haemoglobin
HbA_{1c}	glycosylated haemoglobin
HIV	human immunodeficiency virus
HONK	hyperosmolar non-ketotic coma
HRT	hormone replacement therapy
IGT	impaired glucose tolerance
IHD	ischaemic heart disease
im	intramuscular
IP	interphalangeal
ITU	Intensive Therapy Unit
iv	intravenous

JVP	jugular venous pressure
LDH	lactate dehydrogenase
LFT	liver function tests
LH	luteinizing hormone
LHRH	luteinizing hormone releasing hormone
LMN	lower motor neurone
LMWH	low molecular weight heparin
LPA	lasting power of attorney
LTOT	long-term oxygen therapy
LUTS	lower urinary tract symptoms
MAOI	monoamine oxidase inhibitor
MCI	minimal cognitive impairment
MCP	metacarpophalangeal
MCV	mean cell volume
MDI	metered dose inhaler
MDT	multidisciplinary team
MEAMS	Middlesex elderly assessment of mental state
MMSE	mini mental state examination
MRCGP	Membership of the Royal College of General Practitioners
MRCP	Membership of the Royal College of Physicians
MRI	magnetic resonance imaging
MRSA	methicillin resistant *Staphylococcus aureus*
MTP	metatarsophalangeal
NG	nasogastric
NICE	National Institute for Health and Clinical Excellence
NIV	non-invasive ventilation
NPH	normal pressure hydrocephalus
NSAID	non steroidal anti-inflammatory drugs
NSF	national service framework
NVQ	national vocational qualification
OH	orthostatic hypotension
OSA	obstructive sleep apnoea
OT	occupational therapy (or therapist)
PD	Parkinson's disease
PDD	Parkinson's disease with dementia or predicted date of discharge
PE	pulmonary embolism
PEG	percutaneous endoscopic gastrostomy
PLAB	Professional and Linguistic Assessment Board
PMR	polymyalgia rheumatica
POA	power of attorney

PPD	purified protein derivative
pr	*per rectum* (anally)
prn	pro re nata (as-needed)
PSA	prostate specific antigen
PT	physiotherapy (or therapist)
RCT	randomized controlled trial
SALT	speech and language therapy (or therapist)
SAP	single assessment process
SBP	systolic blood pressure
sc	subcutaneously
SLE	systemic lupus erythematosus
SSRI	selective serotonin reuptake inhibitor
STD	sexually transmitted disease
SVT	supraventricular tachycardia
T3	triiodothyronine
T4	levothyroxine
TB	tuberculosis
TCA	tricyclic antidepressant
TFT	thyroid function tests
TIA	transient ischaemic attack
TSH	thyroid stimulating hormone
TTOs	to take out (discharge drugs)
TURP	transurethral resection of the prostate
U, C+E	urea, creatinine and electrolytes
UMN	upper motor neuron
UPDRS	unified Parkinson's disease rating scale
URTI	upper respiratory tract infection
USS	ultrasound scan
VaD	vascular dementia
VBI	vertebrobasilar insufficiency
VF	ventricular fibrillation
WBC	white blood cell

Ageing

The ageing person 2
Theories of ageing 4
Demographics: life expectancy 6
Demographics: population age structure 8
Demographics: ageing and illness 10
Illness in older people 12

The ageing person

There are many differences between old and young people. In only some cases are these changes due to true ageing, i.e. to changes in the characteristic(s) compared to when the person was young.

Changes not due to ageing

- **Selective survival.** Genetic, psychological, lifestyle, and environmental factors influence survival, and certain characteristics will therefore be over-represented in older people.
- **Differential challenge.** Systems and services (health, finance, transport, retail) are often designed and managed in ways that make them more accessible to young people. The greater challenge presented to older people has manifold effects (e.g. impaired access to health services).
- **Cohort effects.** Societies change, and during the twentieth century, change has been rapid in most cases. Young and old have therefore been exposed to very different physical, social, and cultural environments.

Changes due to ageing

- **Primary ageing.** Usually due to interactions between genetic (intrinsic, 'nature') and environmental (extrinsic, 'nurture') factors. Examples include lung cancer in susceptible individuals who smoke, hypertension in susceptible individuals with high salt intake, and diabetes in those with a 'thrifty genotype' who adopt a more profligate lifestyle. Additionally there are genes which influence more general, cellular ageing processes. Only now are specific genetic disease susceptibilities being identified, offering the potential to intervene early and to modify risk.
- **Secondary ageing.** Adaptation to changes of primary ageing. These are commonly behavioural, e.g. reduction or cessation of driving as reaction times increase.

Ageing and senescence

Differences between old and young people are thus heterogeneous, and individual effects may be viewed as:
- Beneficial (e.g. increased experiential learning, increased peak bone mineral density (reflecting the active youth of older people))
- Neutral (e.g. greying of hair, pastime preferences)
- Disadvantageous (e.g. decreased reaction time, development of hypertension).

However, the bulk of changes, especially in late middle and older age, are detrimental, especially in meeting pathological and environmental challenges. This loss of adaptability results from homeostatic mechanisms that are less prompt, less precise, and less potent than they once were. The result is death rates that increase exponentially with age, from a nadir around age 12. In very old age (80–100 years), some tailing off of the rate of increase is seen, perhaps due to selective survival, but the increase continues nonetheless.

Further reading

Evans JG et al. (2003). *Oxford Textbook of Geriatric Medicine*, 2nd edition, Section 2. Oxford: Oxford University Press.

Successful versus unsuccessful ageing

How can success be defined, i.e. towards what aim should public health and clinical medicine be striving? The following definitions are to some extent stereotypical and culture-sensitive. More flexible definitions would acknowledge individual preferences.

- *Successful ageing.* Without overt disease, with good physical and cognitive function, a high level of independence and active engagement with broader society. Usually ended by a peaceful death without a prolonged dying phase.
- *Unsuccessful ageing.* Accelerated by overt disease, leading to frailty, poor functional status, a high level of dependence, social and societal withdrawal, and a more prolonged dying phase where life quality may be judged unacceptable.

Theories of ageing

With few exceptions, all animals age, manifesting as increased mortality and a finite lifespan. Theories of ageing abound, and over 300 diverse theories exist. Few stand up to careful scrutiny, and none has been confirmed as definitely playing a major role. Four examples follow:

Oxidative damage

Reactive oxygen species fail to be mopped up by antioxidative defences and damage key molecules, including DNA. Damage builds up until key metabolic processes are impaired and cells die.

Despite evidence from *in vitro* and epidemiological studies supporting beneficial effects of antioxidants (e.g. vitamins C and E), clinical trial results have been disappointing.

Abnormal control of cell mitosis

For most cell lines, the number of times that cell division can occur is limited (the 'Hayflick limit'). Senescent cells may predominate in tissues without significant replicative potential such as cornea and skin. The number of past divisions may be 'memorized' by a functional 'clock'— DNA repeat sequences (telomeres) shorten until further division ceases.

In other cells, division may continue uncontrolled, resulting in hyperplasia and pathologies as diverse as atherosclerosis and prostatic hyperplasia.

Protein modification

Changes include oxidation, phophorylation, and glycation (non-enzymatic addition of sugars). Complex glycosylated molecules are the final result of multiple sugar-protein interactions, resulting in a structurally and functionally abnormal protein molecule.

Wear and tear

There is no doubt that physical damage plays a part in ageing of some structures, especially skin, bone, and teeth, but this is far from a universal explanation of ageing.

Ageing and evolution

In many cases, theories are consistent with the view that ageing is a by-product of genetic selection: favoured genes are those that enhance reproductive fitness in earlier life but which may have later detrimental effects. For example, a gene that enhances oxidative phosphorylation may increase a mammal's speed or stamina, whilst increasing the cumulative burden of oxidative damage that usually manifests much later.

Many genes appear to influence ageing; in concert with differential environmental exposures, these result in extreme phenotypic heterogeneity i.e. people age at different rates and in different ways.

Demographics: life expectancy

- Life expectancy (average age at death) in the developed world has been rising since accurate records began and continues to rise linearly
- Life span (maximum possible attainable age) is thought to be around 120 years. It is determined by human biology and has not changed.
- Population ageing is not just a minor statistical observation but a dramatic change that is easily observed in only a few generations.
  - In 2002, life expectancy at birth for women born in the UK was 81 years, and 76 years for men.
  - This contrasts with 49 and 45 years respectively at the end of the nineteenth century.
- Although worldwide rises in life expectancy at birth are mainly explained by improvements in perinatal mortality, there is also a clear prolongation of later life in the UK as shown by calculations of life expectancy at 50 or 65 (see Fig.1.1 opposite).
  - Between 1981 and 2002, life expectancy at age 50 increased by four and a half years for men and three years for women.
  - Whilst projections suggest this trend will continue it is possible that the modern epidemic of obesity might slow or reverse this.

Individualized life expectancy estimates

Simple analysis of population statistics reveals that mean male life expectancy is 76 years. However this is not helpful when counselling an 80 year old! The table below demonstrates that as a person gets older their individual life expectancy actually increases. This has relevance in deciding on health care interventions.

Predicted life expectancy at various ages for men, UK		
Age at time of estimate	**Median years left to live**	**i.e. death at age**
40	36.5	76.5
60	17.9	77.9
80	5.6	85.6
90	2.8	92.8

More accurate individualized estimates should take into account sex, previous and current health, longevity of direct relatives, as well as social and ethnic group.

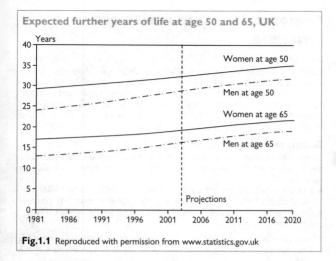

Fig.1.1 Reproduced with permission from www.statistics.gov.uk

Demographics: population age structure

Fertility

Fertility is defined as the number of live births per adult female. It is currently around 1.6–1.7 in the UK. If this rate were maintained, then in the long term population would fall unless 'topped up' by net immigration. In contrast during the 'Baby Boom' years of the 1950s, fertility rates reached almost 3. This bulge in the population pyramid will reach old age in 2010—2030, increasing the burden on health and social services.

Deaths and cause of death

The driver of mortality decline has changed over the twentieth century, from reductions in infant/child mortality to improvements in old age mortality.

- Infant mortality accounted for 25% of deaths in 1901, but had fallen to 4% of deaths by 1950. Currently over 96% of deaths occur >45 years.
- Deaths at age 75 and over comprised 12% of all deaths in 1901, 39% in 1951, and 65% in 2001.

The most common cause of death for people aged 50–64 is cancer (lung in men, breast in women); 39% of male and 53% of female deaths are due to cancer. Over the age of 65, circulatory diseases (heart attacks and stroke) are the most common cause of death. Pneumonia as a cause of death also increases with age to account for one in ten among those aged 85 and over.

All these statistics rely on the accuracy of death certification (p716) which is likely to reduce with increasing age.

Population 'pyramids'

These demonstrate the age/sex structure of different populations. The shape is determined by fertility and death rates. 'Pyramids' from developing nations (and the UK in the past) have a wide base (high fertility but also high death rates, especially in childhood) and triangular tops (very small numbers of older people). In the developed world the shape has become more squared off (see Fig.1.2 opposite) with some countries having an inverted pyramidal shape—people in their middle years outnumber younger people—as fertility declines below replacement values for prolonged periods.

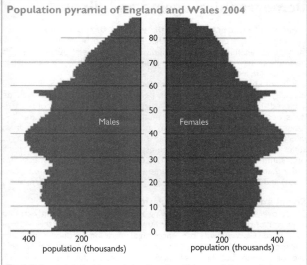

Fig.1.2 Reproduced with permission from http://www.statistics.gov.uk

Demographics: ageing and illness

Healthy life expectancy and prevalence of morbidity

Healthy life expectancy (HLE) is that expected to be spent in good or fairly good health. From both an individual and societal perspective it is desirable to have an equivalent or greater rise in healthy life expectancy as in total life expectancy.

It is not known whether 'compression of morbidity'—where illness and disability is squeezed into shorter periods at the end of life—can be achieved. Trends in data from USA suggests that compression of morbidity is occurring, but challenges to public health are different in the UK. Obesity and lack of exercise may negate diminishing morbidity from infectious diseases; as more people survive vascular deaths they might suffer dementia (and other old age associated diseases). The jury is still out; some data gathered in the UK using self-rated health measurees show that in 1981 the expected time lived in poor health was 6.5 years (men) and 10.1 years (women); by 2001 this was 8.7 and 11.6 years.

Social impact of ageing population

Those over 80 are the fastest growing age group in UK. Currently around a quarter of the population is over 60 years old but by 2030 this will rise to a third. Governments can encourage migration (economic migrants are mostly young) and extend working lives (e.g. increase pensionable age for women) but these will have little effect on the overall shift. The impact of this demographic shift on society's attitudes and economies is huge.

Examples include:
- Financing pensions and health services—in most countries these are financed on a 'pay-as-you-go' system so will have to be paid for by a smaller workforce. This will inevitably mean greater levels of taxation for those in work or a reduction in the state pension. Unless private pension investment (which works on an 'insurance' system of personal savings) improves there is a risk that many pensioners will continue to live in relative poverty.
- Healthcare and Disability services—the prevalence and degree of disability increases with age. American Medicare calculations show that more than a quarter of health care expenditure is on the last year of a person's life, with half of that during the last sixty days.
- Families are more likely to be supporting older members.
- Retired people comprise a growing market and companies/industries that accommodate the needs/wishes of older people will flourish.
- Transport, housing, and infrastructure must be built or adapted.
- Political power of the elderly (the 'grey lobby' in America) will grow.

Further reading

National statistics online www.statistics.gov.uk

Illness in older people

One of the paradoxes of medical care of the older person is that the frequency of some presentations ('off legs', delirium...) and of some diagnoses (infection, dehydration...) encourages the belief that medical management is straightforward, and that investigation and treatment may satisfactorily be inexpensive and low-skill (and thus intellectually unrewarding for the staff involved).

However, the objective reality is the reverse. Diagnosis is frequently more challenging, and the therapeutic pathway less clear and more littered with obstacles. However, choose the right path, and the results (both patient-centred and societal (costs of care etc.)) are substantial.

Features of illness in older people

- Present atypically and non-specifically.
- Cause greater morbidity and mortality.
- May progress much more rapidly—a few hours delay in diagnosis of a septic syndrome is much more likely to be fatal.
- Health, social, and financial sequelae. Failures of treatment may have long-term wide-ranging effects (e.g. nursing home fees >£500/week).
- Co-pathology is common. For example, in the older patient with pneumonia and recent atypical chest pain, make sure you exclude MI (sepsis precipitates a hyperdynamic, hypercoagulable state, increasing the risk of acute coronary syndromes; and a proportion of atypical pain is cardiac in origin).
- Lack of physiological reserve. If physiological function is 'borderline' (in terms of impacting lifestyle, or precipitating symptoms), minor deterioration may lead to significant disability. Therefore, apparently minor improvements may disproportionately reduce disability. Identification and correction of several minor disorders may yield dramatic benefits.

Investigating older people

- *Investigative procedures* may be less well tolerated by older people. Thus the investigative pathway is more complex, with decision-making dependent upon clinical presentation, sensitivity and specificity of test, side effects and discomfort of the test, hazards of 'blind' treatment or 'watchful waiting' and of course the wishes of the patient.
- *Consider the significance of positive results.* Fever of unknown cause is a common presentation, and urinalysis a mandatory investigation. But what proportion of healthy, community-dwelling, older women have asymptomatic bacteriuria and a positive dipstick? (A: around 30%, depending on sample characteristics). Therefore in what proportion of older people presenting with fever and a positive dipstick is UTI the significant pathology? (A: much less than 100%!).

The practical consequence of this is the undertreatment of fever arising from chest, abdominal, or neurological sepsis (attributed to UTI following positive urinalysis).

Treating disease in older people

- *May benefit more than younger people* from 'invasive' treatments— e.g. thrombolysis. On a superficial level, think 'which is more important—saving 10% of the LV of a patient with an ejection fraction (EF) of 60% (perhaps a healthy 50 year old) or of a patient with an EF of 30% (perhaps an 80 year old with heart failure)?'. Note that the significant criterion here is more the LVEF than the age, the principle being that infarcting a poor LV may cause long term distress, morbidity and mortality, whereas infarcting a part of a healthy myocardium may be without sequelae.

- *May benefit less than younger people.* Life expectancy and the balance of risks and benefits must be considered in decision-making. For example, the priority is unlikely to be control of hypertension in a frail 95 year old who is prone to falls.

- *Side effects* of therapies are more likely. In coronary care: beta-blockade, aspirin, ACE inhibitors thrombolysis and heparin may all have a greater life (and quality-of-life)-saving effect in older patients. Studies show these agents are underused in MI patients of all ages, but much more so in the elderly population. The frequency of side effects (bradycardia and block, profound hypotension, renal impairment and bleeding) is greater in older people, although a significant net benefit remains.

- *Response to treatment may be less immediate.* Convalescence is slower, and the doctor may not see the eventual outcome of his/her work (the patient having been transferred to rehabilitation, for example). *The natural history* of many acute illnesses is recovery independent of medical intervention, particularly in the young. Beware false attributions and denials of benefit:
  - The older person frequently benefits from therapy, unwitnessed by medical staff
  - The younger person recovers independent of medical efforts, though his/her recovery is falsely attributed to those interventions (by staff and patient).

Organizing geriatric services

Using geriatric services 16
Acute services for older people 20
The great integration debate 22
Admission avoidance schemes 24
Day hospitals 26
Speciality clinics 28
Intermediate care 30
The national service framework for older people 32
Single assessment process 34
Community hospitals 36
Domiciliary (home) visits 38
   How to... do a domiciliary visit 39
Care homes 40
   How to... advise a patient about residential care 41
Funding of care homes 42
Delayed discharge 44
Home care 46
Informal carers 48
Other services 50
Chronic disease management 52
Primary care 54
Careers in UK geriatric medicine 56
The diploma in geriatric medicine 58

Using geriatric services

Geriatric services have developed rapidly since the inception of the specialty in the 1950s. They have different forms, depending on local resources, experts, and enthusiasts. Every district will offer different services, each with a different spectrum of options. There are some broader national differences within the UK; services in Scotland and Northern Ireland lean more towards rehabilitation and long-term care than in England and Wales. The following is intended as a generic guide to utilising geriatric services in the UK. Diversity will limit applicability.

Services for acute problems

Urgent assessment of the acutely unwell patient, where the disease process is new and severe (e.g. acute myocardial infarction, stroke), or the deterioration is rapid (e.g. delirium).
Examples:
- GP emergency services (p54).
- Emergency departments (p20).
- Acute medical admission service.
- Rapid Access (admission avoidance) services (pp24–5).
- Urgent domiciliary visits (p39).

Choosing which is most appropriate will depend on patient characteristics (e.g. if unstable, then an ambulance to an emergency department is appropriate; if no change is expected over a few days then urgent outpatient assessment may be used) and local service characteristics (availability of urgent clinic slots etc.).

Services for sub-acute problems

Assessment of a patient with a progressive disease process (e.g. increasing falls, worsening Parkinson's in a frail patient), or unexplained potentially serious problems (e.g. iron deficiency anaemia, weight loss), or for diagnosis and management plan (e.g. cardiac failure).
Examples:
- Routine outpatients.
- Speciality clinics (p28).
- Day hospital (p26).
- Intermediate care facilities (p30).
- Elective admission (to acute hospital, rehabilitation wards or community hospital).
- Domiciliary visits (p38).

Again, choice of service will depend on patient factors. Single organ problems can be referred to specialist clinics, less well-defined medical problems to a geriatric outpatients, and problems suggesting the need of multidisciplinary input to the day hospital. Local availability, waiting times and consultant interests will also affect choice—whilst most cardiologists have chest pain clinics, not all will run heart failure services, which may be provided by general physicians or geriatricians.

Services for chronic problems

This includes active, elective management of slowly progressive conditions by GPs, community teams, specialist nurses, and secondary care physicians (see Chronic disease management, pp52–3) and the provision of care for established need.

Care may be provided by a number of means:
- Informal carers (p48).
- Home care and care agencies (pp46–7).
- Day centres (p50).
- Respite care (in care homes or hospitals) (p49).
- Care homes (p40).

Allocation of these usually long-term services is generally after an assessment of need and financial status by a care manager.

Most patients will pass through many aspects of this care spectrum with time, and a flexible, reactive service with good communication between providers is essential. The flow diagram (Fig.2.1 p18) schematically represents possible patient flows through the system.

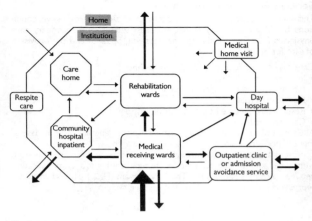

Fig.2.1 An example of a comprehensive geriatric service, including patient flows

Acute services for older people

Since older people present atypically, and are at high risk of serious sequelae of illness, high quality acute services that fully meet their needs are essential. In any setting, older people have special needs. Their needs, and the consequences of not meeting them, are amplified in the setting of acute illness. Specific areas meriting attention include pressure area care, prevention and treatment of delirium, and optimal nutrition and hydration. Accurate early and comprehensive diagnosis is essential.

An acutely unwell older person may present to one of several services. Their distribution between these services will depend on:
- Local service provision.
- The individual's understanding of the system.
- The advice given by others (relatives, health professionals and advice services such as NHS Direct).

Any service aiming to diagnose acute illness amongst older people must have access to immediate plain radiography, ECG and 'basic' blood tests (including prompt results). Specialist clinical assessment (geriatrician, urologist, neurologist, etc.) and more advanced diagnostics (e.g. ultrasound, CT, MRI) must be available on a prompt referral basis, though maybe on another site.

Emergency department (ED, A&E, Casualty)

Older people present commonly to the ED. Presenting complaints include falls, fractures, fits and faints, as well as a broad range of acute surgical and medical problems traditionally referred directly by GPs to surgical or medical teams. Direct referrals of such patients to ED are increasing, as a result of changes in GP out-of-hours services, advice by agencies such as NHS Direct, and changing public behaviour.

The ED is potentially inhospitable and dangerous for older people. The environment may be cold, uncomfortable, disorientating, and lacking dignity and privacy. There is a risk of pressure sores developing due to long waits on hard chairs and trolleys. Provision and administration of food and fluid may be neglected, or inappropriately prohibited on medical grounds. A medical model of care may presume serious illness, prioritizing invasive monitoring, and treatments, at the expense of a more holistic approach that appreciates the downside of these interventions. Staff are experts in emergency medical management, but their expertise in geriatric medicine and nursing is variable.

A strategy to optimize care for older people in ED might include:
- Close liaison with geriatric medical and nursing specialists.
- Medical and nursing rotation between ED and geriatric medical wards.
- Focus on optimizing food and fluid provision and pressure care.
- Provision of alternative modes of admission and assessment, e.g. Rapid Access Clinic, direct admission to geriatric ward.
- Provision of specialist geriatric assessment unit.
- Occupational therapist, physiotherapist, and social worker with expertise in older people based in ED.

The great integration debate

There has been a long-standing debate amongst UK geriatricians about the best model of care for older people in hospital. Historically, age-related care grew out of workhouse facilities and the advent of care provided in mainstream institutions was a major step against ageism. The provision of age-related services on the same site and with equal facilities developed. This defied the label of ageism and professed other advantages. Traditionally, care has been divided into either 'age-related' or 'integrated' but there are many shades of grey in between these two extremes, usually developing locally in response to manpower restraints, ward availability, and the enthusiasm of individuals. The two 'pure' systems may be described as follows:

- **Age-related care.** A separate team of admitting doctors to deal with all patients over a certain age (varies—commonly around 75 years) who then care for these patients on designated geriatric wards.
- **Integrated care.** In truly integrated care, specialists will all maintain additional generalist skills. These generalists will admit all medical patients regardless of age and continue looking after them on general medical wards, in parallel with specialist clinical commitments.

(See table opposite for advantages and disadvantages of each system.)

The debate has never been fuelled by any evidence (there are no studies comparing systems) and it has become less fevered recently as the reduction in junior doctors' working hours has made it impractical in many hospitals to run two entirely separate teams. As a result various hybrid systems have grown up, managing patients pragmatically and sampling the best aspects of both the systems.

A common compromise is that there is integrated acute assessment, with a single admitting team, but rapid dispersal to the most appropriate service—gastroenterology for a patient with acute GI bleed, cardiology for acute MI, and geriatrics for a confused elderly patient etc. This dispersal may be done at a variety of levels and times, again depending on local service strengths and constraints. Models include triage of need ('needs' or 'function' related segregation) by an appropriate person immediately after admission (admitting SpR, experienced nurse, bed-manager etc.), dispersal by a ward allocation system after removal from the admitting ward, or over a period of a few days (by inter-speciality referral) as the special needs become apparent.

As individual systems evolve, the debate recedes and energies are invested into providing the best possible care for all patients through innovation and flexibility within a certain hospital structure, rather than in drawing boundaries and maintaining rigid definitions. Vigilance against ageism in these evolving systems remains essential.

Comparing age-related and integrated care

Age-related care

Advantages	Potential drawbacks
• All old people seen by doctors with a special interest in their care. • All old people looked after on wards where there is a multi-disciplinary team. • Even apparently straightforward problems in older patients are likely to have social ramifications that are proactively managed.	• Possibility of a two-tier standard of medical care developing, with the geriatric patients having lower priority and access to acute investigation and management facilities. • Less specialist knowledge in those doctors providing day-to-day care. • May be stigmatising for all patients of a certain age to be defined as 'geriatric'. • May be less kudos and respect for geriatric practitioners.

Integrated care

Advantages	Potential drawbacks
• As the majority of patients coming to the hospital are elderly, it maintains an appropriate skill base and joint responsibility for their care. • There is equal access to all acute investigative and maintenance facilities, as older patients are not labelled as a separate group. • Trainees from all medical specialties will have exposure to and training in geriatric assessment. • Sharing of specialist knowledge is more collaborative and informal.	• Many generalists will not be skilled in the management of older patients, so those under their care may not fare as well. • Specialist commitments are likely to take priority over the care of older patients. • The multi-disciplinary team input is harder to coordinate effectively where the patients are widely dispersed. • Management of the social consequences of disease tends to be reactive (to crisis) rather than proactive.

Admission avoidance schemes

Admission avoidance schemes (AAS) are very variable in content and name. Schemes may be divided into those that do and do not offer specialist geriatric assessment (provided by a geriatrician, a GP with a special interest, or a geriatric specialist nurse).

Non-medically based schemes

May include emergency provision of carers, district nurse, occupational therapy, and physiotherapy, delivering, for example, prompt functional assessment and increased care after a fall. As medical assessment is not a part of the scheme, treatable illness may be missed. At the least, such schemes should incorporate assessments by healthcare professionals who can recognize the need for specialist geriatric assessment and can access such services promptly.

Schemes with a medical assessment

- Variously titled Early Assessment, Rapid Assessment, Emergency or Rapid Access clinics.
- All aim to provide a prompt response to medical need in older people, with acuity falling somewhere between immediate admission and more elective outpatient services.
- Few schemes aim to provide same-day assessment, most aiming to see patients within one week of referral, and at best the next day.
- There is an assumption that patients are midway between first symptoms and severe disease, and that early intervention may prevent decline, permit less aggressive or invasive treatment, and permit the patient to remain safely at home.
- Services are best accessed via telephoned or faxed referral, with prompt assessment of the content of and response to referrals by an experienced professional.

▶▶ There is a risk that acutely unwell older people who need emergency assessment or treatment are referred to AAS rather than admitted immediately. If in doubt, admit to the emergency medical/geriatric team. Delirium is an example of a presentation where admission to hospital from home is required.

- In practice most AAS do have to admit a modest proportion of patients directly. In some cases this represents optimal care, but in others it is an indication of dangerously delayed response to a clinical situation.
- AAS staffing usually includes senior medical staff (± junior support). Experienced nursing assistance is invaluable, perhaps in the form of a Nurse Practitioner. Nursing roles are variable but may be very extended, to include history taking, and physical and mental state examination.

- Most commonly, AAS are housed in 'general' outpatient facilities. Examples of problems managed here include anaemia or breathlessness.
- A more comprehensive geriatric response is facilitated when AAS is housed in or adjacent to outpatient multidisciplinary services, e.g. Day Hospital.
- AAS should have prompt (ideally same day) access to occupational and physiotherapy services, to support the patient at home whilst the effect of medical interventions become apparent. Patients with complex needs are best managed in this environment, e.g. Parkinson's disease with on/off periods.

Day hospitals

Day hospitals (DH) provide services that lie somewhere between outpatients and inpatients for the elderly. There is multidisciplinary input for patients who usually stay for half or a full day. The case mix and interventions vary widely between units but can include

- Medical—new patient assessments e.g. for falls, weight loss, anaemia, as well as chronic disease management e.g. heart failure, parkinsonism.
- Nursing—e.g. pressure sore and leg ulcer treatment.
- Physiotherapy—e.g. following stroke, fracture, surgery.
- Occupational therapy.
- Diagnostics—facilities for usual blood tests, radiology etc. but also specific therapeutic trials e.g. levodopa challenge tests, Tensilon tests.
- Treatments—e.g. blood transfusions, intravenous furosemide infusions.

There is usually a mixture of new patient assessments, rehabilitation and chronic disease management. Patients may be referred directly from the community, may be booked for a follow-up after an inpatient stay, or be referred from other outpatient settings. Some units have different sessions for specific patient types or services (e.g. movement disorder clinic, admission avoidance clinic).

History and evolution

The first DHs were set up in 1960s. In their heyday many units had collected a huge number of patients who were very frail but had little active intervention and used their visits as social occasions or respite for carers. Unacceptably long waiting lists hindered efficient running in some units. Transport problems often proved to be a weak point, with patients spending lengthy periods of time waiting for, or during, transport.

The monitoring/supporting role has now been largely taken over by day centres and modern DHs tend to have a high ratio of new to existing patients and a rapid turnover. Increasing pressure on acute hospitals has opened up the role of rapid access admission avoidance clinics and early supported discharge schemes. Intermediate services development following the NSF has sometimes augmented services (e.g. falls services) and sometimes denuded them (e.g. where outreach services have taken over).

Pressures to justify the expense of day hospital places led to a flurry of publications looking at effectiveness and cost-effectiveness. While this area remains controversial a systematic review in 1999 found that DH patients did have less functional deterioration, lower rates of institutionalization, and hospital admission than control groups receiving no care. However, DHs did not prove superior to other comprehensive care services (e.g. domiciliary rehabilitation). DH care is costly but this may be offset by decreased inpatient bed usage and institutionalization.

Further reading

Forster A et al. (1999). Systematic review of day hospital care for elderly people. *BMJ* **318**: 837–841.

Speciality clinics

Every region will have different resources, but most will have some speciality clinics run by geriatricians, by other specialists or occasionally combined clinics run by more than one speciality. Examples of clinics are shown in the table opposite.

The advantages of speciality clinics are many:
- Usually simple referral protocol.
- Concentration of expertise.
- Increased training opportunity for juniors.
- Often specialist nursing staff.
- Increased patient education and awareness of the condition—through meeting others with the same diagnosis, through the work of specialist nurses, and through the availability of information leaflets.
- May utilize a rapid access investigation slot on a regular basis (e.g. carotid Doppler ultrasound in TIA clinics).
- Increased use of protocols (may improve quality of care).
- Often rapid turnover.

Where the same clinic is offered by different specialities, or where you are unsure if a referral to a geriatrician or an organ specialist is most appropriate, ask the following:
- **Is this a new or urgent problem?** There are an increasing number of clinics with a protocol-defined maximum waiting time for the urgent assessment of patients. These may prevent admissions and allow rapid outpatient management of many conditions (e.g. TIA, chest pain, possible malignancy) but are prone to being overwhelmed with referrals thereby rendering them less responsive to the needs of the truly urgent cases. Non-urgent cases should be referred to standard outpatient clinics.
- **Is the diagnosis likely to be clear-cut?** A fit patient with cardiac sounding chest pain should go to a cardiology-run clinic, as they will have the fastest access to the appropriate expertise and investigations. If the pain is more nebulous, then waiting for a chest pain clinic appointment only to be given the diagnosis 'non-cardiac chest pain' is unhelpful. Such a patient is better seen in a more general (usually geriatric) clinic.
- **Does this patient have a single problem?** If so, then they are likely to do well in a clinic run by an organ specialist. If, however, they are frail, with multiple pathologies then a geriatric clinic may be better. Here there is time to for example, undress the patient properly, and assess them fully as the allocation time per new patient is likely to be longer. There is also less likely to be a protocol driven response to a single problem without looking at the wider picture (e.g. prescription of multiple medications for angina in a patient prone to falls).
- **Is this patient already attending a geriatric clinic for follow-up?** If so, most new problems can be addressed by that team rather than referring to another speciality.

Examples of speciality clinics

Clinic	Run by
• TIA/stroke	• Geriatrician
	• Neurologist
	• Stroke physician
• Movement disorders (Parkinson's)	• Geriatrician
	• Neurologist
• Chest pain	• Cardiologist
• Cardiac failure	• Geriatrician
	• Cardiologist
	• General Physician
• Abnormal chest X-ray/ haemoptysis	• Chest physician
• Lower GI bleeding/query lower GI malignancy	• GI Surgeon
• Upper GI bleeding/query other GI malignancy	• Gastroenterologist
• Breast lump	• Breast surgeon
• Leg ulcers	• Dermatologist
	• Geriatrician

Intermediate care

There is no universally acknowledged definition of 'intermediate care'. It is used to describe almost any sort of care which lies between an acute inpatient stay and usual primary care. The term first came into general use in 2001 after the NSF described it as a major strategy for improving health care and the UK government promised to invest £900 million over 5 years to implement it. In many instances this led to a re-badging of existing services but there were also an assortment of new and often innovative approaches.

Whilst many geriatricians welcomed the emphasis on non-hospital-based geriatric medicine, others have warned against intermediate care being a covert form of ageism, which allows rationing of acute hospital medicine in favour of less expensive and often less effective care.

Intermediate care is for patients who do not fit into either acute or chronic/stable categories, although these overlap. The emphasis of intermediate care tends to be not primarily medical but multi-disciplinary and holistic. There are two main types of patients:

- Those requiring rehabilitation, re-housing, or both, in a post-acute illness setting—usually recruited from acute wards—'step-down' care.
- Community-dwelling patients who require nursing/therapy input, often following an acute or subacute deterioration, in order to avoid a hospital stay—'step-up' care or admission-avoidance.

The arrangement of intermediate care teams has been developed locally and varies enormously in staffing, facilities, ethos, and access. Some projects concentrate on very specific groups (e.g. post-surgical fractured neck of femur in over 70-year-olds) whilst others are more generic. Most regions have several complementary services.

Some examples of popular models include:

- **Discharge coordinating teams**—nurse, therapy, or social work teams who bridge the interface between hospital and community based services. They often act as gatekeepers for rehabilitation/community beds or supported discharge schemes.
- **Hospital-at-home schemes** where intensive nursing and/or therapy input in the patient's home can allow a patient to receive treatment without the need for admission to hospital, or be discharged earlier.
- **Front door teams** who recruit elderly patients from accident and emergency and assessment wards, to improve assessment (e.g. provide an OT/physio assessment following a fall) and to make referrals to other services such as social workers, clinics etc.

The variety of different models makes it very hard to promote equity of access or research into the effectiveness of the service. Whilst it has been shown possible to provide almost all kinds of geriatric care in a community setting this doesn't necessarily mean that it is more effective, cost-efficient, or even preferable for patient, family, and staff. Research designed to answer these questions is sparse and contradictory.

Intermediate care can occur in different environments, for example
- Nursing outside the acute care setting in traditional community/cottage hospitals, nursing homes, or even residential homes.
- Patient's own home.
- Day hospital or other therapy based sites.

Interventions in intermediate care are often based around a comprehensive geriatric assessment (p78) by a multidisciplinary team. However, more specialized services can be provided by individuals or teams that are missing some vital members (particularly medical or social work) and care is needed that important interventions (such as treatable illnesses or unclaimed benefits) are not overlooked.

Further reading
Steiner A. (2001). Intermediate care—a good thing? *Age and Ageing* **30-S3**: 33–39.

The national service framework for older people

This huge document (over 200 pages) was published by the Department of Health in March 2001. It was one of the first NSFs to be produced and set out the government's agenda to improve health and social services for the elderly with milestones (i.e. deadlines for service changes) stretching over the following four years. There are eight standards.

1. Rooting out age discrimination

'NHS services will be provided, regardless of age, on the basis of clinical need alone. Social care services will not use age in their eligibility criteria or policies that restrict access to available services.' This key standard was widely welcomed and has proved useful in audits with the aim of removing explicit (written policy) ageism in, for example, access to diagnostic services or treatments. Implicit ageism is harder to tackle.

2. Person-centered care

'NHS and social services treat older people as individuals and enable them to make choices about their own care.' This incorporated the introduction of the Single Assessment Process as well as some ideas about shared commissioning of care and equipment between different government agencies. Many of the goal's planned reforms in this standard have had, at best, patchy implementation.

3. Intermediate care

'Older people will have access to a new range of intermediate care services at home or in designated care settings to promote their independence... prevent unnecessary hospital admission and effective rehabilitation services to enable early discharge... and prevent premature or unnecessary admission to long-term residential care.' This standard was accompanied by earmarked funding to develop services and run 5000 new intermediate care beds. It was the most controversial of the standards with many geriatricians arguing that the result of such services would be reduced access to acute hospital care—indeed one target relates to a reduction in the rate of rise of older persons' admissions.

4. General hospital care

'... appropriate specialist care by hospital staff who have the right set of skills to meet their needs.' All hospitals should have a specialist multidisciplinary team for older people with appropriate training.

5. Stroke

'... action to prevent strokes... access to diagnostic services and treated appropriately by a specialist stroke service... programme of secondary prevention and rehabilitation.' This standard has helped drive the development of stroke units (required in all hospitals by 2004 although not fully achieved) and TIA clinics.

6. Falls

'… action to prevent falls and reduce resultant fractures or other injuries. Older people who have fallen receive effective treatment and… advice on prevention through a specialist falls service.' The development of falls services has lagged well behind the suggested timeframe.

7. Mental health in older people

'… access to integrated mental health services To ensure effective diagnosis, treatment and support…' Promotes integrated depression and dementia services.

8. The promotion of health and active life in older age

'… through a co-ordinated programme of action led by the NHS with support from councils.' Targets related to flu vaccination, smoking cessation, and blood pressure treatment etc. are largely implemented in general practice where they are reinforced by the new GP contract (p55).

There was an additional document on:

Medicines and older people

'… gain the maximum benefit from medication… and do not suffer unnecessarily from illness caused by excessive, inappropriate or inadequate consumption of medicines.' Including a pharmacy-led 'medicines review' for at risk elderly people.

As with many other NSFs, translating policy into change has been only partially successful but there is no doubt that the older people's health and social services today have been influenced by this important document.

The new Commission for Health Care Audit and Inspection (CHAI—set up in April 2004) will move away from using rigid targets to assess performance, aiming to use quality indicators instead. This is likely to promote adherence to NICE and NSF standards which may gain renewed importance.

Further reading

The National Service Framework via www.dh.gov.uk

Evans JG Tallis RC, (2001). A new beginning for care for elderly people?—and related correspondence *BMJ* **322:** 807–808.

www.healthcarecommission.org.uk

Single assessment process

This term was introduced in the NSF for older people. The idea is a simple one—'multidisciplinary, interagency assessment of needs ensuring that the elderly receive the relevant services, in an integrated way'. The main aim was to avoid professionals duplicating their assessments e.g. when a patient moves between hospital and community settings. The initial milestone for introducing single assessment process (SAP) was April 2004.

Unfortunately the assessment systems at the heart of health and social security proved much more resistant to change than was anticipated. Geographical variations in systems, distrust between different agencies as well as antiquated technology has meant that the SAP currently exists only as multiple pilot schemes throughout the UK.

Community hospitals

Community hospitals (CH) vary in size, clinical focus, and facilities. In some areas, they represent a substantial inpatient resource, with older patients predominating both as in- and outpatients. Their origins were commonly either as small 'cottage' hospitals or workhouses, providing very limited services from dated buildings. They are now undergoing substantial change and reinvention as a less centralized focus of non-acute, in- and outpatient, medical, and rehabilitation services. Prompts to recent change have included the new GP contract, the NSF (e.g. for falls services), and additional funding for intermediate care.

Often there is substantial community support, both emotional and tangible (volunteers, gifts), for local hospitals. This makes service changes politically sensitive, slow, and difficult. In some cases, CH facilities are in desperate need of reconfiguration to reflect current service priorities.

Facilities may include
- Inpatient beds for between 10 and 60 patients.
- Physiotherapy and OT services (in- and outpatient).
- Day hospital.
- Office/professional base for community-based care, rehabilitation, and social services.
- Outpatient medical facilities—easier access for the frail elderly.
- Psychogeriatric services, outpatient and/or inpatient.
- Local health (e.g. PCT) management base.
- GP out-of-hours service base.
- Minor Injuries Unit—often staffed by nurse specialists.
- Maternity services—midwife office base ± maternity beds.
- Often a GP practice is based on site or close by, with mutual benefits.
- Limited diagnostic testing e.g. blood tests, plain radiography. More complex tests e.g. CT, ultrasound, usually require transport to another hospital.

Medical cover is usually by GPs. In 'cottage hospitals' they admit patients on their own practice list. In other 'community' hospitals a GP may be employed as a clinical assistant. In some hospitals both patterns co-exist. Visits should be both regular—identifying potential problems and planning prospectively—and responsive to acute problems identified by nursing staff.

Specialist medical input may be available, including a visiting community geriatrician and psychogeriatrician. Other specialists e.g. surgeons may hold outpatient clinics on site.

Nurses and therapists are often very experienced in the care of older people, and are able and willing to work more independently from doctors. Nursing staff often lead the discharge planning process including MDT meetings. Staff turnover is often low, with a high proportion of committed, long-term staff.

Groups of patients being admitted include

Rehabilitation and discharge planning

Often transferred from acute hospitals following surgery (elective or emergency) or acute medical problems. Timing of transfer must be appropriate—is the patient medically stable, have relevant investigations been completed?

Palliative care

Where the nature of illness is clear, and cure is not possible, CH can provide high quality nursing care and symptom control when things can no longer be managed in the patient's home. Preferable to admission to acute hospitals. Hospice beds are often very limited, and hospice care focuses on cases where symptom control is especially difficult.

Respite care

Usually now performed out of hospital, in care homes. Some especially complex, or emergency/unplanned respite care may occur.

Acute illness or functional decline

- In general, this should be discouraged because illness in older people is often occult and atypical. Diagnosis is easier and more precise in an acute general hospital with easy access to investigations and specialist opinions. After accurate diagnosis and completion of invasive (e.g. intravenous) treatments, transfer to a CH becomes appropriate.
- Admission to CH may be justified in cases of strong informed patient opinion, where the diagnosis is clear, where invasive treatments and advanced monitoring are highly unlikely to be required, or when logistics dictate (e.g. very long distances).
- Admission may also be appropriate after specialist assessment in a Rapid Access Clinic or at a domiciliary visit.

'Social' admissions

Where staff perceive that the precipitant to admission has been a change in social supports (e.g. death or illness of a carer), not the condition of the patient. Beware occult acute illness on admission, or later—these patients are often very frail. High death rates in such admissions have been reported.

Domiciliary (home) visits

A medical assessment in the home, usually by an experienced geriatrician. This involves visiting the home of the ill person, sometimes alone, but perhaps with a GP or carer. On occasion, a therapist or care manager may also attend. Distinguish this 'medical' home visit from the Home Assessment Visit performed by an OT to determine functional capacity and the needs for aids/adaptations prior to discharge home from hospital.

Historically, domiciliary visits (DVs) were widely used to prioritize patients on the waiting list for admission to hospital, but with the disappearance of such lists for acute medical problems this is now rarely done. There are advantages and disadvantages to medical assessments in the home. The disadvantages, and an appreciation of how much elderly people benefit from selective use of modern, acute hospital facilities have led to a substantial reduction in the number of visits performed. In many areas, they now serve a function predominantly in those who refuse to attend hospital and who appear seriously or terminally ill. They have also been used by some as a method of routine, post-discharge follow-up. Although expensive, the latter may be effective, and overlaps with emerging systems of chronic disease management. They may also be used to assess suitability for admission to non-acute settings e.g. community hospitals.

Disadvantages

- Lack of equipment and other hospital facilities e.g. diagnostic.
- Lack of nursing support (chaperone, lifting/handling during clinical examination).
- An inability to perform other than very basic tests.
- An inefficient use of time—as well as travelling time, patients and family often expect longer discussions and they effectively control the duration of the consultation.

Advantages

- Provision of a second opinion for the primary care team, who may be struggling to diagnose or treat, or need reassurance that they are doing all that is possible.
- Function may be rapidly and effectively assessed, e.g. is there evidence of incontinence, is the larder stocked, is the dwelling acceptably clean, what degree of mobility is achieved (through e.g. 'furniture walking'). Are there appropriate aids and adaptations?
- Assessment of mental state may be more accurate in the patient's home (confusion worsened in hospital setting).
- Assessment of drug compliance (p146).
- Patients appear more frail and vulnerable in a hospital setting.
- No travel for the patient.
- Some patients adamantly refuse assessment in hospital. The experience of the visit itself may persuade a reluctant patient to be admitted.

HOW TO... **do a domiciliary visit**

When?
- Combine with other trips if possible.
- Not too early or late in the day (patient may rise late and settle early).

Will you and your property be safe?
- Danger from patient, relatives/carers, neighbours?
- Tell someone where you are going, and when you should be back.

What do you need to know before you go?
- Name, address, directions (especially in rural areas).
- Do you have a referral letter?
- Review and take any previous medical notes.
- Can the patient's family or carer attend? (One or two is useful— discourage excessive numbers of family members.)
- Will the patient be in? Telephone them in advance and consider ringing again just before you are about to set off.

What to take?
- BP cuff, stethoscope, tendon hammer, auroscope, ophthalmoscope, 'PR tray' (jelly, gloves, wipes), urinalysis sticks.
- Scoring charts (AMTS, MMSE, Barthel, GDS).
- Paper and pen, dictation machine, and cassette.

What will you do?
- History, examination.
- Functional assessment.
- Environmental inspection.
- Medication (check the drug cabinet or top drawer for over-the-counter and prescription drugs).
- Accepting a cup of tea will inform in several areas.
- Discuss your findings and plan with patient and family.

What to do afterwards
- Telephone or fax GP to report findings and discuss plans.
- Dictate letter to be typed, copy to GP, and hospital notes.
- Claim fee if applicable.

Care homes

This area of geriatric care is evolving rapidly with changes driven by:
- Expansion of elderly population.
- Reduced availability of informal carers (e.g. working women, smaller families living further apart).
- Closure of many council-owned homes (previously known as Part III homes).
- Closure of many privately-owned homes (uneconomic at levels of current state funding, especially in view of recent legislation).
- Care home legislation (see below).
- Shortage of staff—both nurses and untrained carers.

Until recently there was a clear division between residential homes (providing hotel-style services and some basic personal care such as help washing/dressing to mobile patients) and nursing homes (providing full nursing to very dependant, often bed-bound patients). This distinction was always arbitrary and as patient's care needs fluctuated or steadily increased with time patients found themselves inappropriately housed. There is now a move towards establishments under the wider term 'care homes' which provide services for the full range of dependencies.

Staffing

Most of the care provided in care homes is by unskilled staff (or those with basic NVQ training) who nonetheless may have extensive experience. The quality of care is a key issue for clients and their relative in selecting a home but it is very variable and difficult to judge from the outside. In homes providing nursing care there has to be a trained nurse available on site at all times.

Care home medicine

Medical care is usually provided by one or more GPs from a local practice (clients are rarely able to keep their own GP). Some community geriatricians routinely visit care homes in their area to provide support and education. Attention should be paid to try to minimize sedative medication, maximize preventative interventions (e.g. flu jabs, calcium and vitamin D) and where possible to involve patients in advance care planning (e.g. decisions about future hospitalization, living wills).

Care homes for patients with dementia

Elderly mentally infirm (EMI) homes are registered to take patients with significant dementia who may have behaviour problems such as aggression, anti-social behavior or wandering. These homes are in particularly short supply. Eligibility for such homes may need to be determined by a psychogeriatrician. They have specially trained staff and often have secure entrances. Some ordinary homes are not registered to take patients with a diagnosis of dementia and decline to do so although many patients in non-EMI homes will have a degree of cognitive impairment.

HOW TO... **advise a patient about residential care**

This task is of grave importance; there are implications for the patient's independence, quality of life and finances, and with rare exceptions it tends to be a one-way step. Ensure that the patient has had a full assessment (ideally involving a specialized, geriatric, multi-disciplinary team) at a point of maximized health and functioning (ie not during an intercurrent illness when an emergency arises). It is unwise to make recommendations based only on your own impression or those of the family—an occupational therapist or social worker can be very helpful. Ensure that the patient has had an adequate trial of rehabilitation. Consider the prognosis of underlying conditions—you would be more likely to recommend residential care where there is rapidly deteriorating disease.

Some patients (often with normal cognition living alone) may choose to go into care and are grateful to others for help with arrangements. Such patients often describe loneliness/isolation or fear. If they are functionally independent ensure that sheltered housing or regular day centre attendance doesn't fit their needs better—care homes have a majority of demented and dependant clients who may not provide the company they seek. Most patients do not want to go into care because of:

- Negative 'workhouse' preconceptions of what care homes are like.
- Emotional attachment to their spouses, homes, pets, neighbours.
- A fear of loss of independence and dignity.
- Anxiety over costs and loss of inheritance for family.
- Stigmatization and perception that they have failed.

Patients with dementia may lack insight into the care they require (p718). Many of the principles of breaking bad news apply e.g. 'warning shots' will prepare the patient. Explain what factors make it advisable to consider residential care and why other options are not feasible— use factual examples (e.g. you need help during the night and we cannot provide this at home). Clarify the contribution that other professionals have made to this assessment. The following positive points can be persuasive:

- By actively choosing a care home they are more likely to get one they like. Leaving it until an emergency may remove any choice.
- All placements arranged by social services are on a trial basis initially with routine review at about a month.
- Emphasize the positive—company, hot meals, less anxiety for family.
- Where placement is from home and is not urgent then a trial stay/respite period of a week or two can sometimes be arranged.
- Reassure there will be help with financial/logistical arrangements.
- Some care homes allow you to take well-behaved pets.
- A privately owned house doesn't always have to be sold e.g. if a family member continues to live there.

Funding of care homes

Funding

- The cost of residential care in 2005 ranges from around £300–£1000 a week depending on client dependency, local costs (e.g. house prices, staff availability) and the quality and variety of facilities provided.
- While in Scotland the state pays for all nursing and personal care, in England and Wales fees are means-tested and calculated on a sliding scale. In 2005 personal care is free where savings/equity are less than £12,250 but those with more than £20,000 have to pay the full cost.
- Regardless of income a small sum for certain kinds of nursing care is provided by the state. Patients needing nursing care have an assessment carried out by specially trained nurses in order to be categorized into one of three bands which entitle then to some state funding (the Registered Nursing Care Contribution—RNCC).
- Funding issues are addressed by a care manager (usually a social worker) using a complex questionnaire.

To complicate this system further a small number of highly dependant patients (who would previously have been provided for in long-stay NHS wards) are eligible for NHS *continuing care*. Examples of such patients include those who require terminal care and those with ongoing complex medical or psychiatric needs who require frequent specialist medical or nursing intervention. Patients eligible for continuing care have 100 per cent of their funding provided by the state regardless of their own financial status. The provision of continuing care has been very inconsistent between health authorities and the health service ombudsman has admitted that tens of thousands of residents have been denied the free care they are entitled to. The assessment systems are still regionally developed and administered.

The national care home standards (www.dh.gov.uk)
These were published following the Care Standards Act in 2000 and define minimum standards. There is guidance about all aspects of care e.g. care planning, documentation and complaints procedures as well as specific requirements about facilities (e.g. all doors 80cm wide, ratio one assisted bath per eight residents) and minimum staffing ratios. Whilst these regulations have improved some facilities they have also forced many smaller homes out of business.

Delayed discharge

Whilst some patients are admitted directly from their home to a care home in a planned move, the majority are admitted following an acute illness. This often occurs via a hospital setting e.g. a patient who has a stroke and doesn't regain sufficient function to return home after rehabilitation. Where patients are held in NHS hospitals after they no longer require hospital treatment while awaiting care home beds they are sometimes called 'bed blockers'. Whilst most geriatricians dislike this stigmatizing term (delayed discharge is better) there is no doubt that such patients cost the NHS millions of pounds a year and reduce the availability of hospital beds for patients that would benefit more.

Delays in placement are due to one or more of the following:

- Shortage in care-home places, especially for EMI homes. Availability varies according to region but stems from financial and staffing shortfall (see p42).
- Overworked social workers may prioritize urgent cases from the community over hospital cases (who are perceived as being in a 'place of safety') which can lead to delays in assessment and processing.
- Social Services who are short of cash may 'ration' the number of new care home places they fund to try to limit costs. From 2004 NHS trusts can charge Social Services £100/day for such delayed discharges—this system (called reimbursement or cross-charging) was designed to improve discharge rates but has created more paperwork and has had a patchy impact.
- Patients/relatives may oppose discharge because they are unwilling to accept that there is no further capacity to recover, and return home.
- Patients/relatives may be reluctant to move from free NHS care to means-tested care because of financial implications.

Role of doctors caring for delayed discharge patients

- Ensure that it is clear to everyone (including the patient and relatives) that the patient no longer requires acute hospital care. Record 'medically fit for discharge' in the notes and document follow-up arrangements for outstanding problems
- Continue medical monitoring—switch to 'care home medicine' priorities (see p40) but remember that these frail patients are prone to new or recurrent illnesses and are at risk from hospital-acquired infections
- Actively drive discharge—communication is key e.g. case conferences and multi-disciplinary meetings
- Consider interim options—the patient may be able to wait in an intermediate care facility such as a community hospital or 'transitional' bed in a private care home arranged by Social Services

Home care

In most countries the majority of people needing personal care remain at home rather than moving into an institution (e.g. care home). Their needs are provided by carer(s) who may be a spouse or other family member, informal carers, or professional carers (self-employed, or employed by a private care agency or public body). In the UK, the care needs of a patient are usually specified by a care manager (Social Services) and then delivered by private and/or state care agencies.

Community care assessment ('needs assessment')

This is the process whereby a care manager determines the needs of a disabled person and how they can be met. Assessing need requires information from the patient and others, often including relatives, OT, physio, and nurse. Meeting those needs requires agreement between care manager and client (patient, or next-of-kin/legal representative if the client is not competent) after considering the options, finances etc.

Delivery of care

- The bulk of care is delivered by care assistants, who should have basic training in delivering personal care, and lifting/handling.
- In specific cases they may be trained further, to deliver care usually the domain of the district nursing team, e.g. bowel care.
- The work is poorly paid (at or close to the minimum wage), but may be very satisfying. Long-term friendships may develop, with a commitment to patient welfare that goes beyond the strict confines of a contract.
- Carers perform important supervision of patients, and are often the first to note the possibility of illness.
- Continuity of care is an important contributor to quality, and is highly desirable, but a lack of continuity is common. There is a risk of physical, emotional, or financial abuse by carers, although such cases are uncommon.

In the UK, there is a national shortage of carers, worse in some geographical areas. This can delay discharge or, at worst, prevent it. It also renders existing care packages vulnerable to unexpected carer absence e.g. due to sickness. Care packages provided by combinations of care agencies may therefore be more stable than those provided by only one.

Tasks performed by carers

- Washing, bathing, dressing.
- Safe moving and handling including hoists.
- Feeding, meal preparation, and housework.
- Supervision of self-medication from Dosett box.
- Emptying of urinary catheter, fitting of penile sheath catheter.
- Bowel care if trained.

Tasks not performed by carers

- Dressings.
- Administration of medications from individual containers.
- Insulin injections.
- PEG feeding.

Home care costs

In the UK, state support for care fees is 'means tested'—a financial assessment is performed by the care manager. Criteria vary locally, but in general only those with no significant savings have the costs of care met by the state.

Purchasing personal care is expensive. In the UK care costs about £20 per hour. A care package consisting of two hours daily would therefore cost around £300 per week—less expensive than a care home, but still a major financial burden for those who meet the fees themselves.

Structuring the care package

- **Tailor to the individual.** A package usually consists of between one and four visits per day, by one or two carers. A common pattern is for two visits daily, one early (wash, dress, toilet, food preparation) and one late (evening meal, ready for bed). Lunch may consist of a pre-prepared meal, frozen and simply reheated by the patient, removing the need for a midday visit. Two carers are needed for 'double-handed care' e.g. turning or transferring a dependent patient.
- **Night-time visits** are rarely needed, and difficult to provide reliably. Roles may include toileting, pressure care (turns) or administering medication, but there may be other solutions (e.g. other continence management, changing medication regimes).
- **Continuous ('24 hour') care** is sometimes requested by patients or family, but close to impossible to provide—sufficient staff are difficult to find, and the care would be extremely expensive; a move into a care home would usually be cheaper. Therefore these packages are usually privately funded. Live-in carers are sometimes employed long-term, but cannot be on hand the whole 24 hours, need holidays, and may go sick unpredictably.
- **Access to the home** by carers can be difficult if the patient is immobile and cannot get to the door. Combination locks or a key safe (conventional key locked within small combination, or key-accessed safe) provide a secure solution.
- **Equipment** may be necessary before a patient can be discharged and a care package initiated, e.g., hoist, bed, chair, cushion. OTs usually assess need and provide.

Commonly reported problems with care packages

- Timing—unpredictable, or too early, or late (e.g. 6pm visit to prepare for bed).
- Carers—variable quality, lack of continuity.
- Cost—often a significant issue. Costs discourage some patients from taking an adequate (or any) care package, and may result in it being stopped after a period.
- Visits—may be brief; carer and patient feels rushed.

The Commission for Social Care Inspection (www.csci.org.uk) inspects and deals with complaints about social care providers. National Minimum Standards must be met if a care agency is to gain and retain a licence.

Informal carers

This term describes anyone who provides regular and substantive care to a person on a non-professional basis, usually without financial reward. This is often a family member, but may also be a friend or neighbour.

- 1 in 10 adults in the UK will provide informal care to another person.
- A total of 6 million people acted as carers in 2003, and this is projected to rise to 9 million by 2037.
- Carers main benefit is worth (in 2004) £44 per week, for an average of 35 hours caring—just £1.26 per hour—saving the economy £57 billion per year.
- 12 per cent of the over 65s act as a carer, a third for > 50 hours a week.
- The health of carers themselves is poor—44 per cent have poor health, compared with 30 per cent of non-carers. The more demanding the care-giver role, the more likely the carer is to suffer ill health.

This vital group of individuals maintain many elderly patients in the community and are the backbone of the care system. For many, having an informal carer is the only way of staying at home. A patient with cognitive problems (especially if mobile) may require constant supervision to ensure safety—a level of care that can only be provided by an informal live-in carer (often a spouse). This level of care will often exceed that which can be provided in a care home leading to dissatisfaction when patients are temporarily or permanently admitted to institutional care.

The importance of this group is recognized in a new government National Strategy for Carers that aims to improve information and support to carers and improve the care they themselves receive—'caring for carers'. This includes the right of a carer to a 'Carer's Assessment', carried out by social services, which addresses the following points:

- Is the carer getting enough sleep?
- Is the carer in good health?
- Does the carer have time for themselves?
- Are relationships adversely affected by the care giving?
- Are there concerns about work?
- Is the carer collecting all available benefits?
- Is all available help being provided? (Services include emotional support, help with household and caring tasks, accessing benefits and local activities, arranging respite care—see box opposite.)

Support for carers is essential—caring can be relentless, unrewarding and often depressing. Elder abuse is a rare but possible consequence of this highly stressful situation. As well as government resources, there are a number of charity and self-help organizations that provide support and practical help:

Carers UK	www.carersuk.org
Princess Royal Trust for Carers	www.carers.org
Crossroads	www.crossroads.org.uk

Respite care

Acting as a carer can be exhausting (both physically and mentally) for the carer and often the patient, who may find accepting so much help from a loved one difficult. Part of any successful care 'package' is sustainability, which includes ensuring that everyone has a break from time to time. Some of the charities listed opposite (e.g. Crossroads) will offer a carer support worker to take over the caring role for a few hours at a time, but a longer break may well be needed.

In such situations, respite care in a residential establishment may provide the solution. Many care homes, particularly those in the independent sector are able to provide extremely flexible respite care packages. These can range from a two-week visit (e.g. to cover a holiday), to day care or even an overnight stay. A regular arrangement can be made, where for example one week on every eight is spent in residential care.

Most local authorities operate a discretionary policy in terms of paying for respite care in care homes, and may fund several weeks a year of respite to help sustain a care arrangement. This is means tested.

NHS respite is rare these days, but does still exist. Patients with psychiatric needs will often have respite on psychogeriatric wards. Long-standing arrangements on community hospital wards and long-stay wards (becoming increasingly rare) may persist. Terminal care patients will often be offered respite care in hospices or community hospital wards. These services are free to the patient.

Other services

Day centres

- Traditionally run by Health and Social Services but now increasingly run by voluntary organizations (e.g. British Red Cross, Age Concern).
- Accessed via Social Services, (who assess need) or by self referral.
- Offer regular visits (e.g. once or twice a week) with transport if needed.
- There is a charge that varies with requirements (e.g. transport, meals).
- Vary enormously, but may include:
  - Catering (e.g. coffee, tea, and lunch).
  - Social support network.
  - Personal care (e.g. bathing facilities, hairdressing etc.).
  - Respite for carers.
  - Skills development (arts and crafts, adult learning classes).
  - Access to services (e.g. podiatry, district nurse).
  - Leisure activities (e.g. quizzes, reminiscence, music, gardening, keep fit, trips out).
  - Enables monitoring of progressive conditions (e.g. dementia) and early referral for extra support to prevent crisis.
  - Rehabilitation and independent living skills (may occasionally have OT, physiotherapy, and SALT input).

Day centres differ from day hospitals in that there is rarely any medical input with clients usually in a stable condition. Attendance is usually long-term and cognitive impairment is more common.

Social clubs

Many different types that vary from county to county. Usually run by voluntary organizations. Information on locally available clubs can be obtained from libraries, the local county council or Age Concern.
Include:

- Lunch clubs (often with transport)—meet up for a hot midday meal.
- Bingo clubs.
- Tea dances.
- Keep fit groups.
- Special interest groups (e.g. all-male, all-female, ethnic groups, hobby groups—gardening, model railways etc.).

Befriending

Scheme run primarily by Age Concern, that provides lonely, isolated older people with a regular volunteer visitor who will sit and chat and help with minor jobs such as fetching library books etc.

Pet schemes

Volunteers bring pets to visit people who can no longer keep them e.g. in care homes.

Holiday support

Voluntary organizations can provide information on suitable holidays for the disabled, and some will offer financial assistance.

Chronic disease management

- Around 60% of the adult population suffer from a chronic condition (commonly asthma, diabetes, hypertension, and cardiac failure), and older people make up the bulk of this group.
- Multiple chronic diseases lead to increasingly complex health care needs and are a particular phenomenon of the elderly population, who become increasingly frail with the accumulation of chronic problems.
- Most of this pathology is managed in primary care, but it impacts frequently on secondary care—10 per cent of the population (who have chronic disease) account for 55 per cent of inpatient days.

There has been a recent shift in UK political emphasis away from acute sector targets, towards the proactive management of these conditions—referred to as 'long term conditions'. Lessons have been learned from so-called 'managed care organizations' (such as Kaiser Permante in California) in the USA, where comprehensive health care is provided to a defined population. There are built in incentives to actively manage chronic disease as this substantially reduces acute expenditure.

There are a number of levels of chronic disease, summarized as follows:

- **Level 1**—accounts for 70–80 per cent of patients, who have a single chronic disease (e.g. hypertension). Management is enhanced by increasing personal responsibility for the condition with education and encouraging active participation in care. Patient experts are developed who take on some of the education of their peers.
- **Level 2**—more complex patients, but still with commonly recognized complications of disease (e.g. Parkinson's disease). Management is at a population level, with broad guidelines for care, protocols, and patient pathways. The approach is multi-disciplinary with innovative ways of delivering a set standard of care (email, telephone, group meetings, nurse clinics etc.).
- **Level 3**—highly complex patients with individual needs (e.g. frail elderly patient with multiple interacting pathologies). Active case management by a key worker (often a nurse) promotes early intervention to prevent crisis and facilitates joined up care.

The emphasis is on proactive management, rather than a 'fire-fighting' approach. Much chronic disease is amenable to preset assessments and has a group of common complications to watch for. This is very successfully implemented by clinical nurse specialists. The frail elderly however are less predictable and so key workers need broader skills and are less able to rely on protocols.

The following are useful ways of managing these patients:
- 'Frailty registers'.
- Specialist geriatric nurses ('community matrons') with close medical back-up.
- District nurses and health visitors.
- Community multi-disciplinary teams.
- Increased liaison between primary and secondary care with free and frequent sharing of information and care goals, and easy access to urgent clinical review (e.g. in urgent assessment clinics).
- Shared patient records.
- GPs with a special interest in geriatrics.
- Utilization of day hospital to monitor those most at risk of acute deterioration.

Further reading
NHS plan for long term conditions www.natpact.nhs.uk, click link to long term conditions.
Lewis R, Dixon J, (2004), Rethinking the management of chronic disease. *BMJ* **328**: 220–222.

Primary care

- 90 per cent of older people see their GP at least once a year.
- Around 20 per cent of general practice consultations are for elderly people.
- Consultations tend to be more complex than in younger patients.
- Of these consultations, about a third will need a home visit, compared to less than 10 per cent of the general population—the trend for home visiting is declining, but older people remain the biggest user group.
- GPs tend to be aware of the health problems of their older patients—those that do not attend tend to be healthy.
- The most common consultations are for respiratory and musculoskeletal problems (whereas secondary care see more complications of vascular disease such as ischaemic heart disease and stroke).
- Half of the over 65s are on a regular medication, and 17 per cent are on three or more—treatment is usually prescribed and monitored by the GP.

Many older people suffer from chronic conditions (such as arthritis, COPD, diabetes etc.) and the day-to-day management is usually carried out by GPs. Input from secondary care may come at a time of crisis (admission to hospital, rapid referral clinics) or may be more structured in the case of more complex chronic diseases, with regular clinic follow-up or day hospital attendance. GPs act as a vital link between hospital and community services—identifying patients at particular risk of crisis so allowing preventative action to be taken (a skill more intuitive than evidence based, which comes with experience).

- Patients with multiple co-morbidities and/or extreme frailty may benefit from identification (so-called 'frailty registers') and elective review—a possible role for day hospitals, GPs with a special interest in geriatrics, district nurses, health visitors, or the new community matrons.
- GPs with a special interest in geriatrics can act as community specialists, working with other MDT members and liaising with hospital departments. They will often take the Diploma in Geriatric medicine.
- GPs play a key role in the long-term management of risk factors for disease—now highlighted by the new GP contract (see box opposite).
- Inpatients in many community hospitals are looked after by GPs.

Primary care has been subject to much reform in the last decade
1. In 2000, the UK government revealed the NHS plan that aimed to modernize the structure, organization, and delivery of health care.
2. In 2002, Primary Care Trusts were created (each with responsibility for a population of 100 000–375 000) and given resources and responsibilities to improve the health of their local population. PCTs are overseen by Strategic Health Authorities, that focus on long-term planning and national priorities (e.g. NSF priorities, see pp32–3).
3. The new GP contract was introduced in 2004.

The 2004 UK GP contract

This contract has altered priorities for many GPs.

Payment points

Delivery of services is reimbursed via a system of payment points.
- Based on achievements in certain clinical areas: coronary heart disease—including heart failure—(121 points), stroke/TIA (31 points), hypertension (105 points), diabetes (99 points), COPD (45 points), epilepsy (16 points), cancer (12 points), mental health (41 points), hypothyroidism (8 points), and asthma (72 points).
- Also points for organizational aspects (184 points), additional services e.g. cervical screening (36 points), the patient experience (100 points), holistic care payments (100 points), and quality practice payments (30 points).

For example, the following refers to cardiac failure:
- Having a register of patients with CHD who have LV dysfunction— 4 points.
- 90% of these patients having the diagnosis confirmed by echocardiography—6 points.
- 70% of these patients being treated with an ACE inhibitor— 10 points.

The standards do not have an upper age limit, all patients needing to have good blood pressure control etc., which is good in theory. However, this may not always be appropriate in the frailer elderly who may, for example, get postural symptoms with ACE inhibition. There is the chance to 'opt out' in an individual because it is 'not clinically appropriate' or the medication is not tolerated, but these standards discourage the individual tailoring of therapy that is essential in geriatric practice.

Documenting evidence consumes large amounts of GP time, which could otherwise be spent seeing patients. In addition, diseases that are NOT covered by the standards may suffer. These include conditions such as Parkinson's disease, depression, and osteoarthritis that are very common in older people.

Out-of-hours

- No longer a requirement to provide out-of-hours services to patients (in fact may be difficult to opt to do so).
- Mostly now provided by centralized PCT services.
- Patients are unlikely to be seen by a doctor who knows them, increasing the rate of referral to hospital.
- Patients are asked to attend a central assessment point, and if they are unable (e.g. immobile), they are likely to be seen by a paramedic or taken to hospital via the 999 system.

Careers in UK geriatric medicine

Consultant career pathway

- After house jobs, a medical SHO rotation is undertaken, which should include some exposure to geriatric medicine.
- Application for a Specialist Registrar post may follow a period of research, but commonly this is done directly after MRCP is obtained.
- Speciality training in geriatrics is almost always paired with another speciality, (resulting in dual accreditation) most commonly General Internal Medicine, but other options include Rehabilitation Medicine or Stroke Medicine.
- Increasing trend to obtain triple accreditation in Geriatric Medicine, General Internal Medicine and Stroke Medicine.

Non-consultant career grade pathway

- Includes staff grades, clinical assistants and associate specialists.
- Responsibilities of the post-holder varies considerable from equivalent to SpR (staff grades) to consultant (associate specialists).
- The main difference from a consultant post is that they do not hold overall clinical responsibility and have variable responsibility for management, administration and training.

Primary care physicians

- GPs may wish to sub-specialize in Geriatric Medicine.
- This often leads to clinical assistant sessions in Geriatric Medicine services (either acute, rehabilitation or community settings).
- These doctors have often had significant experience in Geriatric Medicine during their vocational training scheme, and obtain the Diploma in Geriatric Medicine.

Overseas doctors

- Many overseas doctors wish to work in the UK for a period of time, and it can be difficult and expensive to get a 'foot in the door'.
- Geriatric medicine often provides opportunities for such doctors.
- It is essential to obtain PLAB (www.gmc-uk.org/register/plab.htm).
- Most doctors begin with clinical attachments, which are unpaid observer posts, but enable the doctor to become familiar with the UK healthcare system.
- The next step is to obtain GMC registration and ALS training, before applying for a paid position.
- The least competitive tend to be locum appointments or trust grade posts.
- Obtaining MRCP and the Diploma in Geriatric Medicine help to define an interest and will assist with subsequent appointments.
- A successful period in such a post may lead to success in obtaining a substantive training post (e.g. SHO) after which time the playing field tends to be levelled.

The diploma in geriatric medicine

Qualification awarded by the Royal College of Physicians (UK) to 'give recognition of competence in the provision of care of older people'.

Candidates

Candidates must be two years post-medical qualification, and have held posts in geriatric medicine. Usually taken by GPs with an interest in geriatrics (often trainees) or doctors working in (or applying for) geriatric posts (trust grades, staff grades, associate specialists etc.). Sometimes will count towards other geriatric qualifications (e.g. Masters courses) so may also be done by specialist registrars, although it is not primarily designed for this group. May also be of interest to psychogeriatricians. It is of use to all SHOs doing a geriatric job as it motivates them to study important topics that will recur in MRCGP and MRCP and it gives them something tangible at the end of an attachment.

Examination structure

Written section
- Paper 1 (3 hours)—short notes on 20 topics (e.g. foot care).
- Paper 2 (2½ hours)—longer answers required on 3 wider topics (e.g. osteoporosis). Limited choice available in which questions.

Clinical exam
- One long case (45 min with a patient, then 30 min with examiners).
- Short cases—may include patient assessment, results of investigations, equipment and appliances (20 min).

Syllabus
- Demographic and social factors.
  - UK demography.
  - Social influences on ageing.
- Clinical aspects of ageing.
  - The ageing process.
  - Disease prevention.
  - Features of atypical presentation of disease.
  - Management of common conditions.
  - Domiciliary care for the disabled.
  - Legal and ethical considerations.
  - Terminal care.
- Administrative aspects.
  - Knowledge of social services.
  - Special geriatric services and facilities such as day centres, nursing homes etc.
  - Financial considerations.
  - Audit.

For further information see RCP website
www.rcplondon.ac.uk/professional/exam/exam_dip_geriatric.htm

Clinical assessment of older people

Consultation skills 60
Multiple pathology and aetiology 62
Taking a history 64
Other sources of information 66
Problem lists 68
Physical examination: general 70
Physical examination: systems 72
Investigations 74
Common blood test abnormalities 76
Comprehensive geriatric assessment 78

Consultation skills

There are certain skills that are key to any consultation, but some are more important with an older patient.

Arranging an appointment

- For older patients, attending hospital may be more of a physical and emotional challenge, for which there is a need to feel well. Patients often decide not to attend clinic appointments because they feel ill.
- Hospital transport is often used. Morning appointments usually require a patient to be ready by 8:30 am—daunting for someone who takes time to get going in the morning. Offer late morning or afternoon appointments, using early slots for patients who travel independently.
- When informing the patient about the appointment, make sure that instructions are clear. Demented patients should probably have appointments sent to carers who would ideally attend with them; visually impaired patients may need a large print letter or a telephone call.
- Remind the patient to bring both medication and prescription lists to their appointment. Muddled medications may indicate self-medication problems. Comparison of drugs and list helps to assess concordance.
- Establish who has requested the consultation—e.g. memory clinic appointments are often in response to family concerns, and the patient may not attend as they do not perceive or wish to face the problem.
- Day hospital settings for consultation can be more relaxed, allowing the patient to recover over lunch before facing the trip home again.
- Are hospital attendances really necessary? Discuss with the GP, offering to discharge the patient to his/her care, but supported by open telephone access for advice and a hospital review on request.
- If all else fails, domiciliary visits may be useful.

Rapport

- Good rapport with the patient makes the interview easier, more productive and more enjoyable.
- Smart dress increases patient confidence, especially in older patients.
- Always introduce yourself—shake hands if it seems appropriate, and address formally (Mr/Mrs/Miss) unless invited to do otherwise.
- Be friendly but not patronizing or over familiar. Informal chat can break the ice, and show that you have time for and interest in the person.
- Older patients deserve and expect respect from (inevitably) younger doctors, but often have more respect for the medical profession.
- Patients are likely to have great faith in a trusted GP than in a young junior met for the first time. When asked what is wrong, they may quote the GP diagnosis ('Dr Brown said I had a stroke') rather than offering their experiences. Emphasize that you work as part of a team ('your doctor has asked for our opinion, so we need to go over things again. I will let them know what I think.'). After a hospital admission, explain changes to prescriptions and that you will inform the GP.
- Acknowledge and apologise for waiting times and uncomfortable conditions (e.g. during an emergency admission)—it may not be your fault, but apologising may defuse frustrations that hamper the consultation.

Environment
- Older patients are more likely to feel helpless and vulnerable in hospital if only partially clothed and on a couch. Interviewing a fully dressed patient sitting in a chair gives more dignity and respect.
- Good light, quiet, and no interruptions will minimize problems from visual and hearing impairment.

Giving advice
- Advice is taken more often if rapport has been good during the interview. Appearing knowledgeable and professional increases the chance of agreement to investigations and medication changes. For example, some patients refuse to take aspirin, having been told years ago by a trusted doctor 'never to take aspirin again' because of an ulcer. Take time to explain that risks and benefits change with evolving disease and as new therapies develop. Gain understanding and agreement (see p300).
- Increasingly conditions require multiple investigations and medications. For example, following a TIA the patient may be well, yet tests can include bloods, ECG, CXR, brain scan, and carotid Doppler, and several drugs are often prescribed. Take time to explain the rationale for each, thereby increasing concordance.
- Write a list of planned investigations and medication changes along with their justification. Give the list to the patient. This takes time, but increases the likelihood that advice will be followed.
- Offer to repeat your advice to family members (who may be sitting in the waiting room), to telephone someone who is at home, or to send a dictated letter in the post. A frail spouse may not be able to attend outpatients, or a busy daughter may not have time to attend, yet both may be vital to the delivery of effective ongoing care—e.g. administering medications or organizing appointment diaries.

Multiple pathology and aetiology

Most diseases become more common in an older population. Some conditions such as osteoarthritis are present in the majority (radiographically 70 per cent of over 70s). By the age of 80, it is very likely that an individual will have at least one disease. Many will have more than that (**multiple pathology**). As increasing numbers of medications are advocated by evidence-based medicine, so polypharmacy and adverse effects become more common too.

Many of these diseases will be chronic and stable. The patient may have adapted to the limitations imposed by the disease (e.g. not walking as far or as fast because of OA knees; reading large-print books because of failing vision), or medicated to aid symptom control (e.g. analgesia in arthritis). However, background multiple pathologies should be noted for two main reasons:

- Cumulative chronic disease will cause decline in physiological reserve.
  - The older patient with multiple stable diseases has less resilience to physiological challenge than a fit young person; a smaller insult is needed to cause illness.
  - Non-specific presentations reflect the complexity of the pathology—background problems interacting with new (perhaps seemingly minor) insults to cause acute decline without obvious cause.
- Many patients adapt to impairments, particularly if the functional decline is gradual.
  - Assessment and intervention remains helpful. For example, failing vision is often accepted as a part of ageing, yet is often amenable to treatment.

In an acute presentation, there are several aspects to consider:
- What is the acute precipitant? This may be minor e.g. medication changes, influenza, constipation.
- What are the underlying pathologies making the patient more susceptible to the acute precipitant?
- Note that one acute pathology can lead to another in a vulnerable patient—e.g. a bed-bound patient with pneumonia is at high risk for thromboembolic disease.

So, for any single presentation there are likely to be **multiple aetiologies** which need to be unravelled. This can be difficult, but applying a structured logical approach assists the process:
- Use a **problem list** to help structure the approach.
- Allow **time** for the acute event to settle, physical and psychological adjustments to occur (much slower than in a younger person), stamina and confidence to build up, care arrangements to be put in place etc.
- Involve a **multidisciplinary team** to take a holistic look at the patient and evolve the problem list and action plan.

Taking a history

Histories taken from older people vary as much as the patients themselves, but some common problems make the process more difficult:

- Multiple pathology.
- Multiple aetiology.
- Atypical presentation of disease.
- Cognitive impairment, both acute and chronic.
- Complex social situations.

Failing to recognize the importance of obtaining an accurate and comprehensive history risks misdiagnosis and mismanagement.

The patient interview

The most direct information source, but requires patience and skill.

- An elderly person with multiple problems may give a history that is hard to unravel. Someone with chronic back pain will answer positively to the closed question 'do you have pain?', but it may be no worse than the last ten years and not at all a part of the new presentation. Ask 'is this new?' and 'is it different from usual?'
- Allow time to volunteer symptoms. Avoid interrupting. If a symptom is mentioned in passing, return to it later to enquire about its nature, precipitants etc. Interrupting may cause the main issue to be lost.
- The patient may underplay issues that are emotive (e.g. failing memory, carer abuse, incontinence) or perceived as leading to institutional care. Foster an atmosphere of trust and mutual interest in problem solving.

Cognitive impairment

Patients with dementia or delirium may not answer clearly or succinctly, and symptoms may need to be teased out. Quantities of seemingly irrelevant information may be interspersed with gems of important history. Don't get frustrated and give up—continue with a combination of open questions and careful listening, punctuated by closed questions that may result in a clear 'yes' or 'no'. General inquiries such as 'do you feel well?' and 'does it hurt anywhere?' can be rewarding. A patient who is made to feel silly will often dry up—if you are getting nowhere with specific questions, then broaden the conversation to get dialogue flowing again.

Sensory impairment

Poor vision and hearing make the whole interview harder and more frightening for the patient. Use a well-lit, quiet room. Guide the patient to where you want them to sit. Ensure hearing aids are in, and turned on. Speak clearly into the good ear and do not shout. Use written questions if all else fails. Facilitate communication, however laborious—patients will worry that they appear stupid, and may elect to withdraw completely if obstacles cannot be overcome. (See also sections on hearing, Chapter 21 and vision, Chapter 22)

Terms that should be banned and why

'No history available'	It is almost always possible to get a history: if not from the patient, then from family, carers, GP, community nurse, or ambulance. Nursing homes are staffed 24 hours a day and they all have telephones.
'Poor historian'	The historian is the person recording the history—this term is a self-criticism! If the patient is unable to give a history this is important and the reason should be documented along with evidence e.g. AMTS, GCS.
'Social admission'	A social admission is one caused solely by a change in the social situation e.g. a carer who has died suddenly or a hoist that has broken.
	True social admissions are very rare and should in general not occur: admit to a non-hospital setting (e.g. care home) or increase care at home.
	If the patient's function has changed e.g. new incontinence, falls, confusion, and their unchanged social situation cannot cope then the admission is not social.
	Often there is a combination of altered health and social circumstances.
	It is true that a younger patient might be able to stay at home with a minor change in health (e.g. Colles fracture, flu) whereas an older patient needs hospital care. But by blaming only the social care the doctor is at risk of missing the medicine, stigmatizing the patient, and labelling carers as failures.
'Acopia'	Usually a more accurate description of the clerking doctor than the patient! An unhelpful term—see notes above. Ask yourself why can the patient not cope? What problem has led to this presentation and can it be treated medically?
'Bed-blocker'	Pejorative term that implies that the patient is actively hindering discharge. Delayed discharge is a better term, as it removes any hint of blame from the patient.

▶▶ Patients admitted with the labels 'social admission' or 'acopia' are frail and have a high in-hospital morbidity and mortality. Statistically they are more likely to die in this hospital admission than a patient with myocardial infarction. Just because they are more challenging to diagnose and often require multi-disciplinary assessment does not mean that they should be regarded as time and resource wasters for the system.

Other sources of information

Many patients, especially those with acute illness, are unable to give a full and reliable history. If so, a history must be obtained from other sources.

The family
Often a rewarding source of information, especially at the initial assessment. Older people may underplay their symptoms, fearful of being thought unable to cope, or not wishing to fuss. The family will often have concerns and it is useful to establish these as they may (or may not) be justified; weigh them up as more information is gathered.

Family members often wish to speak away from the patient—this can be useful and is acceptable if the patient gives consent.

▶▶ Your duty is to the patient and you are their advocate. Family members may have louder voices, but take care to listen to those for whom you are responsible. Elderly people are allowed to take risks (e.g. live at home with a high risk of falling) providing that they are competent (see pp718–19).

Neighbours/friends
Elderly patients with no family nearby may be very well-known to their neighbours—perhaps they have been found wandering at night, or unusual behaviour has been noted. The neighbour may not feel obliged to volunteer this information and it may need to be sought. Neighbours may also act as informal carers and can contribute more care than family or formal carers. Common law partners are often heavily involved, yet may not be as prominent in hospital as other family members. Rifts may exist between established family and new partners and these need to be understood when planning care.

Professional carers
They will know the usual functional and cognitive state of the patient, and will often have alerted medical services to a change. They are rarely present at the medical assessment. Contact them and obtain all the information that you can.

General practitioner and community nurse
May well know the patient very well, and have good insight into the dynamics of the care arrangement and family concerns. They can help clarify the medication and past medical history. If a confused patient arrives during GP practice hours, an initial clerking should always include a telephone call to the GP surgery. Patients who are housebound or who have leg ulcers, urinary catheters, or other nursing needs, are usually best known to community nurses.

Ambulance crew
The ambulance crew may be present during the initial hospital assessment of a sick older patient. Ask them what they know. If they have left, examine written ambulance team documentation—this includes timing, symptoms, and clinical signs including vital signs. This is a useful source of information that is under-utilized.

Nursing and residential homes

When patients are admitted from institutional care, a good history can almost always be obtained: information should be sent with the patient, but if not it can be sought by telephone immediately. Information about usual functional state, past medical history, medications, and acute illness should be kept on file at the home.

Old medical notes

Obtain them as quickly as possible, as they will provide essential information. If the patient is not local, arrange for information (letters, discharge summaries etc.) to be faxed or to speak to health professionals who know the patient.

Problem lists

Useful tools to help formulate plans for complex elderly patients in any setting. They act as aides-memoire for multiple pathology and prompt clinicians to consider interacting problems.

Problem lists should include:
- **Acute problems**
  - May be a symptom (e.g. fall) rather than a diagnosis.
  - List possible causes with a plan for investigation.
- **Chronic conditions**
  - How stable is the disease?
  - What management is already in place?
  - What else can be done?

Lists can be generated at any stage in an illness—ideally at presentation—but need to be worked on and evolve as time goes on. Involve members of the multidisciplinary team and make the list part of goal setting and discharge planning.

Example
- An 86-year-old lady who lives at home alone with a carer once a day is admitted to the medical assessment unit with confusion following a fall.
- She has a past medical history of osteoarthritis, myocardial infarction, and polymyalgia rheumatica.
- She has been finding it increasingly difficult to cope at home in the last year or so and is occasionally getting confused.
- Her daughter, who lives abroad, is very concerned.

An initial problem list may read as follows:

Acute problem:	fall and confusion
Possible causes:	sepsis
	constipation
Action plan:	septic screen (MSU, CXR, blood cultures, CRP, ESR, WBC)
	rectal examination
Background problems:	osteoarthritis
	vascular disease
	polymyalgia rheumatica.

- She is found to have an *E. coli* urinary tract infection, which is treated, but remains much less able than prior to admission.
- She is transferred to a rehabilitation ward and the MDT involved.

- The patient makes a slow but steady recovery, and regains mobility with a Zimmer frame, being independent for activities of daily living.
- She is successfully withdrawn from steroids and begins appropriate secondary prevention measures.
- Her home is adapted for downstairs living, and she returns there with a twice-daily care package after five weeks in hospital.

A problem list at this stage may read:

Problem	Status	Action
Coliform urinary tract infection	Recovering.	Complete antibiotic course.
Osteoarthritis	Particularly affects left hip. Pain limits mobility. Takes prn paracetamol.	Regular analgesia. Look into possible joint replacement. Physiotherapy for walking aids and to improve muscle strength. OT to adapt environment to limitations.
Vascular disease	MI in 1980s, no angina for years. Progressive mobility and cognitive decline likely due to diffuse cerebrovascular disease. Takes aspirin, atenolol, nitrates.	Consider stopping nitrates as no angina. Consider statins or ACE inhibitors to limit progression of cerebrovascular disease. MDT input to adapt to chronic changes.
Polymyalgia rheumatica	Diagnosed in 1991. On prednisolone 5mg and calcium and vitamin D. Asymptomatic.	Slow steroid withdrawal. Consider bisphosphonate.
Frailty	Likely multifactorial: osteoarthritis, cerebrovascular disease, steroid myopathy, probable steroid-induced osteoporosis.	Action as above for each disease. Physiotherapy to improve stamina and confidence.
Deafness	Noticed by nurses. Progressive and bilateral. Patient attributes to 'getting older'. Likely presbyacusis.	Referral for hearing aid.
Family concerns	Daughter lives abroad, and is unable to help.	Meet with daughter (with patient's permission) and explain problems and action plan.

Physical examination: general

There are two major ways in which examining an older patient can be more time-consuming and challenging:

- The extent of the examination is **wider:**
  - There are more systems with presenting symptoms.
  - You often need to 'screen' (by examining a wide selection of systems) where presenting symptoms are vague.
  - The chance of detecting incidental pathology (e.g. asymptomatic aortic stenosis, skin cancers) is much higher.
- The procedure itself is **more difficult:**
  - Physical constraints—patients are less agile so undress more slowly and cannot always adopt optimal positions for examination (e.g. lying flat). They can wear many layers of clothing. They are more likely to have pain or to tire during the examination.
  - Cognitive constraints—examinations that require complex instructions to be remembered and followed (e.g. visual field examination) may be too much for a confused elderly person.

Despite these challenges, there are great rewards:

- There is a much higher prevalence of physical signs.
- The examination more often makes the diagnosis e.g. a patient with a non-specific presentation may have an undiscovered abdominal mass or a lobar consolidation.

General advice

- Given the challenges, it is tempting to take short cuts leading to a sub-optimal examination, but this must be resisted
  - There are differing degrees of this—it might be reasonable to auscultate a chest through a thin shirt or nightdress but it is useless to examine an abdomen through a rigid corset or with the patient sat in a wheelchair.
  - Sub-optimal examination is dangerous, especially if inaccurate findings are documented and then acted upon by others. It is better to record that you haven't completed an examination and put a note at the end of your history that you, or another doctor, needs to complete or repeat the procedure.
  - It is sometimes reasonable for a comprehensive examination to take two or three sessions, but start with the most useful elements.
- Make use of nurses, relatives, or other carers to decrease the physical problems of examination. Use electric beds and lifting and handling aids to make examination more comfortable and effective.
- Try to examine all aspects of one portion of the body at the same time. If organized, you should not have to sit a patient up, roll them over or stand them more than once per examination.
- Always inspect the patient fully. For example, look under clothing (especially sacrum and breasts), between toes, and under wound dressings, wigs, and prostheses.

Physical examination: systems

System	Of particular importance	Examples/notes
General examination	Body shape and height, nutritional status, hydration. Mood (e.g. cooperation) insight, anxiety, hygiene, clothing, intellect/presentation, speech.	Comments in this category are powerful in drawing the overall picture e.g. 'a thin (52kg) anxious lady with stuttering but clear speech' is very different from 'an obese, cheerful lady with unkempt clothes and a strong smell of stale urine'.
	Temperature.	Hypothermia is more common. Fever may be absent/minimal on presentation—recheck later.
	Looks ill/well?	If the patient looks ill state this and try to say in what way.
Cognition	Assess and quantify Conscious level (GCS) Orientation (time, place and person) Assessment scale e.g. MMSE or AMTS	Should already be partially assessed during history. If unusual/delusional thoughts record e.g. 'thinks I am her mother' or 'repeated agitated shouts of 'get off'.
Signs of systemic disease	Jaundice, clubbing, lymphadenopathy, cyanosis. Thyroid. Breasts.	Consider breast examination in all women
Skin/nails	Bruising, rashes, purpura.	Carefully record bruising positions if any suggestion of abuse or accident
	Toenail onychogryphosis.	If you don't record it you won't remember to refer to the podiatrist/chiropodist
	Venous disease or ulceration. Cellulitis.	
	Pressure sores.	Always inspect the sacrum if immobile.
	Skin tumours	Basal cell and squamous cell carcinomas and even melanomas are common incidental findings.
Cardiovascular	Check the BP yourself especially if it has been abnormal. Postural BP (see p131).	Consider BP readings in both arms—peripheral arterial disease is common and can cause major discrepancy.

System	Of particular importance	Examples/notes
Respiratory	Respiratory rate is very useful (sensitive marker and part of many early warning scores).	Normal 12–16/min in older people.
	Respiratory pattern.	You may need to watch for >1min to detect Cheyne–Stokes breathing.
	Crepitations only helpful if: • Don't clear with cough. • Mid or upper zone. • Associated with changes in percussion and air entry.	30% of normal elderly chests will have 'basal crepitations'.
	Chest shape and expansion.	Respiratory impairment due to kyphosis common and important.
	Cough.	Listen and examine any sputum.
Abdomen	Bladder.	Silent retention common.
	Rectal examination is almost always relevant.	Constipation as well as bowel and prostate abnormalities.
	Mouth.	Thrush, ulcers, and teeth.
Cranial nerves	Note if vision obviously impaired and why.	Visual fields tricky but important in those with new visual loss or stroke.
		Some loss of up gaze is normal.
	If hearing poor check for wax.	
	Note hearing aids/glasses.	
Peripheral nervous system	Look for patterns e.g.: • Asymmetry of muscle bulk, power, sensation. • Sensory levels. • Peripheral neuropathy. • Global hyperreflexia. If tremor try to qualify (p166–7). Gait and balance.	Some normal elderly will lose ankle jerks and distal (toe) vibration sense. See also Functional assessment.
Musculo-skeletal	Restricted range or deformity.	
	Hot/painful joints.	
	Gouty tophi.	
Functional	Usually through observation during your examination.	Don't help unless they struggle—can they dress (including buttons/socks)? get on/off bed? lie to sit, rollover? 'Get up and go test' = speed and stability while they sit to stand and walk across room.

Investigations

Investigations are often less focused in older patients because:
- Presentation is more frequently non-specific.
- Multiple pathology is more common.
- Screening for many diseases (e.g. thyroid disease) is appropriate.

Simple investigations

Almost all older people who present with new symptoms should have:
- FBC, ESR
- U,C and E
- Glucose
- LFT
- Calcium and phosphate
- CRP
- TFT
- CXR
- ECG
- Urinalysis.

These tests are inexpensive, well tolerated, rapidly available and have a high yield. Coupled with a comprehensive history and examination, they will usually give sufficient information to guide initial management and further investigations. The urgency with which these tests are obtained is often determined more by hospital policy and the need for fast turnaround than by clinical need.

- Don't order repeat tests automatically until you have seen the results of the first set—only abnormal ones need to be repeated the next day.
- If you order a test, record that you have done so in the notes (most doctors write a list of suggested investigations and then tick the ones they have themselves arranged).
- Ensure that results are reviewed and record them in the notes.

Further investigations

Although it is often tempting to order further investigations at presentation it is often not helpful as it may mislead the clinician, lead to unnecessary patient anxiety, and to further time-consuming and expensive assessments. Often the correct course of investigation is very different when an experienced clinician reviews with the benefit of initial results and a short period of observation.

Do not request an investigation if it will not alter management e.g.:
- Carotid Dopplers are unnecessary if endarterectomy would be inappropriate (e.g. poor functional status).
- Urgent CT head scan will not alter management for a deeply unconscious patient dying of stroke.

Sometimes making a diagnosis has value even where definitive treatment is unsuitable. An investigation may alter management even if 'aggressive' treatment options are inappropriate. For example sigmoidoscopy and barium enema may be helpful in a patient with bloody diarrhoea even if colonic resection is not feasible: pathology such as colitis could be treated, and if advanced cancer were found, then the information would help direct:

- Palliative management including 'surgical' procedures such as stenting.
- Non-medical decisions e.g. making a will.
- Discharge arrangements e.g. choosing care home placement over home.
- The diagnosis itself can be reassuring to patients and relatives.

These concepts often have to be explained carefully to patients, family and medical colleagues who may feel that some investigations are unnecessary or that not enough is being done.

Tolerating investigations

In general, non-confused older people accept and tolerate investigations as well as younger patients.

There are a few exceptions, which include:

- Colonoscopy (increased risk of colonic perforation).
- Bowel preparation for colonoscopy or barium enema (more susceptible to dehydration).
- Exercise Tolerance Tests—arthritis, neurological problems etc. often mean that the patient cannot walk briskly. Consider bicycle or chemical provocation testing.

It is often helpful to discuss the procedure with the person performing the test (often a radiologist)—they might have suggestions for modifying the test or substituting a different procedure to make it safer.

You may need to allow more time for gaining consent or the procedure itself especially if the patient is deaf or anxious. Elderly patients are less likely to be aware of what modern medical tests involve than younger patients. Particular problems occur with confused patients, who may benefit from escort by a family member or trusted nurse. The cautious use of sedatives or anxiolytics is sometimes helpful.

In the outpatient setting it is often the trip to hospital rather than the test itself that is traumatic. Minimize visits e.g. by combining a clinic visit with a test or by arranging two tests on the same day. Try asking the GP or district nurse to remove 24-hour tapes. Where a series of tests or complex management needs to be accomplished, admission to hospital may be the best option.

Common blood test abnormalities

A screening series of blood tests in an older person usually yields several that fall outside normal laboratory ranges. The examples that follow are those which are most commonly abnormal in the absence of relevant illness. Unless they are very abnormal or something in the presentation makes them particularly relevant, they can usually be ignored. There are four broad categories:

Different reference range in older patients
- **ESR** may be as high as 30mm/hr for men and 35mm/hr for women in normal 70 year olds (see p488).
- **Haemoglobin.** Some debate, but the reference range should probably be unchanged (see p488).

Abnormal result but common, and rarely imply important new disease
- **TSH**—often low with normal free T4 and T3 during acute illness: sick euthyroid syndrome (p452). Repeat 2–4 weeks after acute illness has resolved.
- **Low blood sodium**—very low levels should always be investigated. (p436) but some patients run with an asymptomatic persistently mild hyponatraemia (≥128mmol/L) due to (overall beneficial) drugs or sometimes without obvious cause.
- **Alkaline phosphatase**—if liver function tests are normal, an isolated raised alkaline phosphatase (ALP) can represent Paget's disease (p524), which is often asymptomatic. ALP remains high for weeks after fractures including osteoporotic collapse.
- **Normochromic normocytic anaemia**—always check B12, folate and ferritin/iron/iron binding. If these haematinics, as well as an ESR and blood film are normal, then it is usually fruitless to look for the cause of mild, non-specific anaemia (p490). Acutely unwell patients are often haemoconcentrated, with a temporarily normal Hb that then falls to a pathological level after a few days, when rehydrated.
- **Asymptomatic bacteriuria** (p678). This is a common finding in older patients and does not always indicate significant urinary infection. Check for the presence of white cells on urine microscopy.

False negative result
- **Creatinine**—low muscle mass can mask poor renal function (p410–11). Consider using a conversion formula to estimate glomerular filtration rate e.g. when judging drug dosage.
- **Urea**—as above. In a frail older person, urea levels in the middle or higher range of normal are consistent with severe dehydration.

False positive rates very high

- **Anti-nuclear antibodies (ANA)**—figures of up to 1:80 are of doubtful significance in older patients
- **D-dimer.** Any form of bruising, infection, or inflammation will increase d-dimer. If it is negative (rarely) it can still a useful test but do not expect it to be useful test to exclude DVT/PE in a frail elderly patient with falls and a UTI.
- **Troponin.** Although this test is very specific to cardiac muscle, low level release can occur with arrhythmias, PE, and heart failure. It is not a useful screening test in older patients with no chest pain and a non-specific presentation.

Comprehensive geriatric assessment

A comprehensive geriatric assessment (CGA) is the evaluation of the patient in his/her environment. It encompasses medical, functional, and psychosocial elements.

The team

CGA usually involves a team including nurses, therapists, and social workers as well as doctors and it should lie at the core of many intermediate care projects. The team should work together with a common form of documentation to avoid duplication of information gathering.

Interventions

CGA usually leads to several recommendations/treatments. There have been many models proposed e.g. based in outpatient settings (to improve independence, admission avoidance) or at the time of discharge from hospital (to improve function and reduce readmission).

The tool of CGA has been adapted to disease-specific management programmes (e.g. heart failure) and to assessing the suitability of older patients for cancer treatments (where age alone is felt too blunt a tool for discriminating who might benefit).

Evidence

Although it is difficult to compare data from such diverse interventions, there is evidence from many studies and one large meta-analysis that CGA can improve outcomes such as survival, function, and quality of life, as well as reducing length of inpatient stay and preventing admissions to hospital and nursing homes. It is not surprising that CGA is more effective when coupled with:

- Systems to improve adherence to advice.
- Long-term follow-up/review.
- Medical management interventions.

Further reading

Stuck AE, Siu AL, Wieland GD *et al.* (1993). Comprehensive Geriatric Assessment; a meta-analysis of controlled trials. *Lancet* **342**: 1032–1036.

Rehabilitation

Rehabilitation *80*
The process of rehabilitation *82*
Aims and objectives of rehabilitation *84*
Measurement tools in rehabilitation *86*
Measurement instruments *88*
Selecting patients for inpatient rehabilitation *90*
Patients unlikely to benefit from rehabilitation *92*
   How to... conduct a multi-disciplinary meeting *93*
   How to... plan a complex discharge *95*
Physiotherapy *96*
Walking aids *98*
Occupational therapy *100*
Occupational therapy assessments and interventions *102*
Doctors in the rehabilitation team *104*
Nurses in the rehabilitation team *106*
Social work and care management *108*
Speech and language therapy and dieticians *110*
Pharmacy *112*
Community nurses and health visitors *114*

Rehabilitation

A process of care aimed at restoring or maximizing physical, mental, and social functioning. Can be used for:

- Acute reversible insults e.g. sepsis.
- Acute non-reversible or partially reversible insults e.g. amputation, MI.
- Chronic or progressive conditions e.g. Parkinson's disease.

Involves both *restoration* of function and *adaptation* to reduced function depending on how much reversibility there is in the pathology. Rehabilitation is an active process done **by** the patient not **to** him/her. It is hard work for the patient (akin to training for a marathon)—it is not 'convalescence' (akin to a holiday in the sun).

Rehabilitation is the 'secret weapon' of the geriatrician, poorly understood, and little respected by other clinicians. Many geriatricians feel it is what defines their speciality and it can certainly be one of the most rewarding parts of the job. The 'black box' of rehabilitation contains a selection of non-evidence-based, common sense interventions comprising:

- Positive attitude. Good rehabilitationalists are optimists—this is partly because they believe all should be given a chance and partly because they have seen very frail and disabled older people do well. A positive attitude from the team and other rehabilitating patients also improves the patient's expectations. Rehabilitation wards should harbour an enabling culture where the whole team encourages independence: patients dressed in their own clothes, with no catheter bags on show and eating meals at a table with other patients.
- Multi-disciplinary coordinated team working. By sharing goals the team can ensure they are consistent in their approach.
- Functionally-based treatment. e.g. the haemoglobin level only matters if it is making the patient breathless while walking to the toilet.
- Individualized holistic outcome goals. These incorporate social aspects which are often neglected. The team concentrates on handicap rather than impairments (see box opposite).

Settings

Specialised rehabilitation wards are not the only place for rehab. If the above considerations are in place then successful rehabilitation can take place in

- Acute wards
- Specialist wards (e.g. stroke units, orthopaedic wards)
- Community hospitals
- Day hospitals
- Nursing and residential homes
- The patient's own home.

These alternative sites often employ a roving rehabilitation team which may be based in a hospital or the community.

WHO classification

- **Impairment**—pathological defect in an organ or tissue.
e.g. homonymous hemianopia due to posterior circulation stroke.
- **Disability**—restriction of function due to impairment.
e.g. inability to drive due to visual defect.
- **Handicap**—the social disadvantage cause by disability.
e.g. unable to visit friends in neighbouring village as unable to drive.

It can be seen that some impairments produce no disability or handicaps and some handicaps are due to multiple interacting impairments. The system allows the social circumstances to be factored in. For example, in the above example the disability produces no handicap if a regular bus route exists. Doctors are generally focused on impairments, poor at assessing disability, and rarely consider handicap.

Despite the attractive logic of such a classification it is actually rarely used in practice. This is probably because geriatricians intuitively consider the wider aspects of illness without requiring the discipline of formal terms.

The process of rehabilitation

1. Selection of patients (pp90–1)

2. Initial assessment—this is not like a medical clerking, you need to get to know your patient on different levels (e.g. their mood, motivation and expectations, complex social factors). Remember it is more meaningful to assess the handicap not just the impairment.

3. Goal setting (p84)

4. Therapy
   - Medical—doctor-led (p104).
   - Physical—mainly physiotherapy (pp96–7) and nurse-led (p106). Mobility, balance, and stamina. Confidence is often a key issue.
   - Self care—mainly occupational therapy (p100) and nurse-led
   - Environmental modification—aids and adaptations.
   - Carer/relative training—it is too late to leave this until just prior to discharge.

5. Reassessment—usually at weekly multidisciplinary team (MDT) meetings (p93). Goals are adjusted and new goals are set. Points 3, 4, and 5 are repeated in a cycle until the patient is ready for discharge.

6. Discharge planning (p95)—should be started as soon as the patient is admitted but the efforts escalate towards the end of the inpatient period. A home visit and family meeting are often held to clarify issues.

7. Follow-up and maintenance—post-discharge home visits, outpatients or day hospital attendance. Ideally done by the same team but in reality this function often taken over by community in which case good communication is vital.

Aims and objectives of rehabilitation

It is essential that the MDT states what it plans to do and to achieve, in clear terms that are shared within the team and can be worked towards. A large part of this is achieved through the agreement and statement of targets at two hierarchical levels: aims and objectives.

Aims

Best set by the team, in discussion with the patient.
One or two, patient-centred targets that encompass the broad thrust of the team's work—a team 'mission statement' for that individual, For example:
- To achieve discharge home, with the support of spouse, at six weeks.
- To transfer easily with the assistance of one, thus allowing return to existing residential home place at four weeks.

Objectives

Best set by individual team members, in discussion with patient.
More focussed targets, usually several, that reflect specific disabilities and help focus the team's specific interventions, e.g.
- To walk 10m independently, with a single stick, at three weeks.
- To achieve night-time urinary continence at four weeks.

Both aims and objectives should have five characteristics, summarized by the acronym 'SMART':
- **Specific** i.e. focused, unambiguous.
- **Manageable** i.e. amenable to the team's influence.
- **Achievable** and
- **Realistic**, acknowledging time and/or resource limitations. It is futile and demoralizing to set targets that cannot be achieved. Conversely, the team (and patient) should be 'stretched', i.e. the target should not be inevitably achievable.
- **Time-bounded**. Specify when the target should be achieved. Many patients are motivated and cheered by the setting of a specific date (especially for discharge). Setting dates for specific functional achievements prompts further actions, e.g. ordering of equipment for the home.

Predicted date of discharge (PDD). Specifying a PDD from the point of admission is useful for patients, carers, and MDT members.
- Emphasizes to the patient that inpatient care is not indefinite, and that a more pleasant home or care home environment is the aim.
- Can be intrinsically motivating for patient and team.
- Prompts carers and MDT to think ahead to pre- and post-discharge phases of care.

Measurement tools in rehabilitation

Principles

The most widely used standardized measurement instruments are structured questionnaires that deliver a quantitative (numerical) output. They vary in precision, simplicity, and applicability (to patient groups or clinical settings). For each domain of assessment several tools of differing size are usually available, reflecting tensions between brief assessments (speed, easy-to-use, well-tolerated) and a more prolonged evaluation (precision improved, give added layers of information).

Measurement tools are helpful at single points (especially entry and exit to a therapy programme), and also in assessing progress.

Advantages

- Quantify.
- Widely understood, and transferable across boundaries.
- Facilitates communication between professionals and settings of care.
- Provide a synopsis.
- May permit a less biased, more objective view of the patient.
- Facilitate a structured approach to assessment and clinical audit.

Disadvantages

- May be time-consuming.
- Scores may conceal considerable complexity—patients scoring the same may be very different.
- Intra-individual, intra-rater and inter-rater variabilities mean that a score may change whilst a patient remains static, e.g. three or four points change in the (20 point) Barthel is needed before a team can be absolutely confident that the patient has changed.
- There are many scales available, and some are not in general use, leading to confusion when staff or patients move between units.

Measurement instruments

Activities of daily living (ADL)

Use a scale appropriate to the patient's level of function:

- Personal ADLs (pADLs) or Basic ADLs (bADLs). Include key personal tasks, typically transfers, mobility, continence, feeding, washing, dressing. A single scale is valid for all. e.g. Barthel (20 point; see Appendix). Score range 0 (dependent) to 20 (independent). The most commonly used scale. Quick, and apparently simple. Not very sensitive to change, as steps within each domain (e.g. transfers) are large. A marked ceiling effect is seen, especially for a range of impaired patients living independently at home, many of whom score 20.
- Extended ADLs (eADLs) or Instrumental ADLs (iADLs). Include key daily household tasks, e.g. housework, shopping. Useful for the more independent person. Scales are selected according to an individual patient's needs. e.g. Frenchay Activities Index, Nottingham ADL Score.

Mobility

e.g. EMS (elderly mobility scale), Tinetti mobility score (TMS), timed get up and go test

Cognition

- Several screening and assessment tools are in common use.
- The 10-point abbreviated mental test score (AMTS, see Appendix) is brief, and useful for screening in both outpatient and inpatient settings.
- The 30-point mini-mental state examination (MMSE) provides sufficient precision to be used for serial assessment—e.g. tracking recovery from delirium, or therapeutic response to cholinesterase inhibitors in dementia—but takes < 10 minutes to administer.
- The Middlesex elderly assessment of mental state (MEAMS) assesses systematically the major cognitive domains, using a range of targeted subtests. Time-consuming (15 minutes), but gives more detailed information. Often used by therapists.

Depression

e.g. Geriatric Depression Scale (GDS). Several versions of this are available, but the most commonly used is the 15 point score (see Appendix), administered in 5–10 minutes. Superficially distressing questions, but well tolerated by most patients. Sensitive (80%) but only moderately specific (60%).

Pressure area risk

Prompt systematic evaluation of patients at risk, and brisk response in those at risk, is essential. Several scores are available, but the most widely used is the Waterlow pressure sore prevention score, a summary score derived from easily available clinical data. High score indicates high risk. Note that the score does not take into account the ability of the patient to lessen risk by changing position, the acuity of the medical condition, etc.

Disease-specific scales

All of the common diseases have dedicated scales, usually developed for use in research, and then introduced variably into clinical practice. They are often more complex than used in general clinical practice, with corresponding disadvantages—time-consuming, less easily transferable. e.g. unified Parkinson's disease rating scale (UPDRS), that quantifies all the motor and behavioural aspects of the disease as a single number.

Selecting patients for inpatient rehabilitation

Most hospitals do not have enough rehabilitation beds to cater for all patients who could benefit, so they are a valuable resource. This is often not understood by the referring service. Patient selection is a time-consuming, important, and complex task. In an environment where there is no cost limit, the approach can be more inclusive.

Who should select patients?

Review of referrals is often done by geriatricians, but can be equally well done by another experienced rehabilitation professional. In some cases, a team assessment is done and discussed in a conference.

Who to choose?

This is difficult. Be aware that some services will refer simply to get the patient out of one of their beds. Two factors need to be considered:
- Which patients will benefit most from what is a limited resource?
- What does the MDT need to keep it positive and functioning well?

In many ways the 'best' rehabilitation patient is one who has had an acute event from which they are recovering (e.g. a fracture), who is motivated and cognitively intact—able to participate in therapy with enthusiasm and who has a clear goal in mind (usually to return home). There are rapid results and fast turnover to keep variety and interest for the team. However, consider whether this type of patient actually needs 'hard core' rehabilitation, or in fact would get better in almost any supported setting with a bit of convalescent time (e.g. intermediate care with nursing, guidance to improve stamina and confidence and perhaps a bit of social support on discharge).

Contrast this with a frail elderly woman with multiple medical problems, moderate cognitive impairment, barely managing at home alone before a prolonged hospital inpatient stay with repeated complications who has gone downhill physically and mentally. If asked, she wishes to go home, but may not appear altogether realistic. Her daughter in Australia thinks she should go into a home for 'her own safety'. It is all too easy to write this patient off, deny them rehabilitation and arrange placement. This is the kind of complex 'heartsink' patient that most needs the expertise of the rehabilitation team. In any other specialty, the most complex cases are dealt with by the specialist—the same should be true of rehabilitation. These types of patients often do remarkably well and should at least be offered a trial of rehabilitation.

Even patients with no recovery potential can benefit from aspects of the teams expertise—be it learning adaptation, teaching skills to carers, or arranging complex discharge packages.

▶▶ In general, the harder a problem seems to be, the less likely it is that it will be sorted out in a non-specialist setting and the more likely it is that the patient will benefit from the rehabilitation team.

In practice it is often a balance between the two, where a broad case-mix is maintained; with some slower stream complex cases and some more rapidly treated simpler cases.

Information required for patient selection

Should be gleaned from all available sources (including primary nurse, hospital notes—medical, nursing and therapy, family, carers, GP, specialists etc.) and may involve telephone calls and/or several visits. Regardless of who does the assessment, the following information should be acquired:

Premorbid features

- Physical problems—list of medical conditions, how active they are and how they impact on life; list of medication.
- Functional limitations—assess by conversation (Did you use a stick? Did you ever go out alone? Could you get up and down stairs? etc.) Formalize by estimating the premorbid Barthel. Ask about physical ability and personal care.
- Social set-up—who do they live with (and how fit and willing to help are they); where do they live (rural or in town); what is the property like (e.g. flat or house, any stairs to access and once inside the property, whether the bedroom and bathroom are up or downstairs); does anyone help out (formally e.g. home carers or informally e.g. neighbours, family, friends); what did they do on a regular basis (e.g. walk to the pub for lunch, attend day centres or lunch clubs, cycle into town for groceries etc.).
- Cognitive state—range from mild memory problems (may predispose to delirium) to significant dementia. Ask about any objective assessments (e.g. MMSE) and the difficulties the problem causes in everyday life.

Acute features

- Nature of acute insult—is it reversible (compare amputation to acute confusional state).
- Interacting co-morbidities.
- What is the expected recovery curve? Varies with the disease: a patient with a large MCA stroke may show very slow progress at outset and then steady but slow progress after several weeks; a patient with a fractured neck of femur by contrast is likely to improve rapidly after the operation and continue to make quick progress; a septic patient is unlikely to improve at all until the acute illness has resolved and is then likely to improve steadily. If the assessor has limited knowledge of the disease then information should be obtained from the specialist currently caring for the patient.

Patient wishes

- Do they understand about the problems they face?
- Do they know what they wish to do when they leave hospital? (E.g. go home as soon as possible, return to their residential home, not go home unless they are able to function as before etc.)

Patients unlikely to benefit from rehabilitation

- Patients in a steady state who are awaiting placement.
- Patients for whom the process of waiting for a rehabilitation bed will delay discharge (e.g. where expected recovery to discharge fitness is under a week).
- Patients with a single requirement for discharge (e.g. provision of commode).
- Patients who are still medically unstable, requiring frequent medical review, investigation or treatment.
- Patients with pure nursing needs (e.g. unconscious patients).
- Probably inappropriate for terminal care patients (palliative care teams likely to be able to support discharge planning when needed).

Dementia and rehabilitation

This can be frustrating and difficult (but also very rewarding). Therapists will often prefer patients with 'carry over'—who are able to recall the last session and build on it. Nurses may find patients with behavioural problems disruptive to the ward. Safety issues are more difficult as awareness of danger and the ability to make an informed decision about risk taking are less. Relatives' anxiety is likely to be high. However, there is still a lot that can be done.

Repeated exercise can build stamina and some learning may occur. Rehabilitation settings allow more time for spontaneous recovery to occur. The more complex the discharge, the less likely it is that this can be managed in a non-specialist setting and the greater the need for the multi-disciplinary team expertise. Demented patients are most at need of an advocate for their rights and wishes, and the expert team assessment of feasibility and risk is the best way to ensure they are respected.

▶▶ In general, dementia alone is not a reason for refusing rehabilitation.

HOW TO... **conduct a multi-disciplinary meeting**

This is a ward or team-based meeting with the primary functions of communication, goal setting, reviewing progress, and discharge planning.

There are also wider aims of
- Team building—there is usually a chance for discussion over tea and biscuits. This is not time wasting—vital for team bonding.
- Education—sharing knowledge and insight into each others jobs.

Usually weekly for inpatient settings but can be less frequent in community or outpatients. Most commonly the team meets in a room away from patients/relatives—sometimes involving the patient by bringing them into the room.

Theoretically any member of the team can 'run'/chair the meeting but in practice where a doctor attends they usually take this role. The chair is responsible for:
- Timing—the last few patients discussed should not be rushed. Some patients take a lot longer than others but this should be a function of need not just where they happen to appear on the list. Don't use the same order each week.
- Involving all team members—ensure each member has an unimpeded opportunity to comment on each patient—some may need prompting. Don't allow assumptions that everyone knows certain information or that it is unimportant. A well-established team may automatically take turns—others may need you to force an order (see opposite page). Ask members to clarify jargon or code that may not be universally understood.
- Ensuring decisions are made/goals are set. Without good leadership a long discussion can occur without a positive action plan. Prompt with 'so what are we going to do about this?', 'who is going to take that on?', 'when will that actually happen?' If discussion is going in circles or there is dispute it can be helpful to summarize what has been said so far to allow things to move on. Where there is agreement on goals make sure they are SMART (p84).
- Maintaining morale—remember case conferences can be stressful. Keep discussions professional and good humoured. Careful use of humour and frequent reminders that individuals and the team have done well are very important.
- Encourage feedback—it is interesting and educational to hear follow-up on discharged patients. Ensure thank you letters etc. are shared as well as news on deaths, readmissions etc.

HOW TO... conduct a multi-disciplinary meeting (continued)

The conventional order of presentation is:
1. Doctor—diagnosis, current management and changes planned, prognosis—particularly if symptoms are limiting therapy.
2. Nurse—nursing requirements, mood and behaviour, continence, sleeping, relatives/visitors comments.
3. Physiotherapist—mobility, equipment, progress and potential.
4. Occupational therapist—functional assessments (e.g. dressing, kitchen), cognition and home visits.
5. Social worker—background, discharge discussions, external liaison (e.g. with council, funding panels etc.).

This order allows discussions to flow naturally from medical background to current function (therapists), to goal planning and discharge plans (social worker). There is no reason why the order should not be different but beware one person dominating and avoid discussing endpoints (e.g. discharge) before going through the logical steps or you will miss something.

Notes of the meeting are vital—ideally they should be written once somewhere that all team members have access to. As a minimum record date, current status, notes about the content of discussion (even if solutions not found), goals, and plans. You have failed if you summarize a 20 minute important discussion as 'continue' or 'aim home next week'!

HOW TO... **plan a complex discharge**

- There is no such thing as a '*safe discharge*', only a safer one. There is widespread misapprehension that hospitals and nursing homes are 'safe' while home is dangerous but this is the wrong way round e.g. rate of falls in institutions is higher (there is just someone there to pick you up) and the increased exposure to infection (e.g. MRSA, flu) can be life-threatening.
- The *timing of discharge* is sometimes obvious (e.g. when the patient returns to pre-morbid functioning) but can be controversial. Some patients want to go before the MDT feels they are ready and others (or their families) wish to stay longer (usually due to unrealistic aspirations or dislike of the chosen discharge destination)—communication is the key to avoiding this. Patients should understand that discharge is not necessarily the end of recovery following an illness.
- Start to *plan discharge* from day one e.g. by obtaining background social history and patient aspirations. Set a target that patient and team are aware of—it is better to revise a projected discharge date or destination than to have none at all because it helps to focus goal-planning.
- *Early relative involvement*—family meetings will ensure effective two-way communication. It will also reduce the chance of 'the daughter from America syndrome' where a relative comes out of the woodwork just before a carefully planned discharge to block or alter the plans.

The multidisciplinary team members should prompt you but the following are common pitfalls which can cause a discharge to fail:
- Care availability (especially night times)—check well in advance with the social worker that the care package you plan is available.
- Modifications and equipment—ideally any environmental modifications should be in place before your patient is ready for discharge otherwise there can be lengthy delays. It is amazing how long it can take for simple measures such as a bed to be moved downstairs. For more complex alterations (e.g. stairlifts, walk-in showers) get an realistic estimate of time—sometimes the patient may need alternative accommodation while these works are completed.
- Appropriate transport available (relative, ambulance)—check not only for patient but also for their equipment.
- Keys—who has got them? Who needs keys/door entry codes?
- Night times—discharge plans often fail because the patient who looks good by day has unanticipated needs at night. Check with the nurses that they are not incontinent, immobile, or confused at night.

Physiotherapy

Training

A BSc Hons physiotherapy degree is 3–4 years full-time. A MSc Physiotherapy can be done as a 2-year accelerated postgraduate course. See UK chartered society of physiotherapists website at *www.csp.org.uk*

The role of the physiotherapist

- Aimed at improving physical functioning by exercise, reducing pain, and providing appropriate aids.
- May be for recovery, adaptation, or preventative e.g. falls.
- Patient needs sufficient motivation, muscle strength, and energy to participate—it is *not* a passive process.
- Duration of therapy may be short initially, but increases as patient tolerates more.
- Cognitive impairment may limit learning and 'carry-over' of skills from session to session, but stamina may be improved with repeated sessions and dementia is not a reason to withhold physiotherapy.
- Rehearsal of skills improves function and patients are given exercises to do alone (often with written instructions). Physiotherapy assistants, nursing staff, and relatives can all assist in this rehearsal process.
- Involved in training others to move dependent patients safely (e.g. carers).

Range of interventions

Increasing range of movement

- Active or passive exercises.
- Use after stroke or prolonged bed rest to increase joint mobility and prevent pain and contractures.

Increasing strength of muscles

- Usually general strengthening to improve stamina.
- Can be targeted at specific areas of weakness and enhanced by the use of resistance and weights.
- Important part of falls prevention.

Improve coordination

- Usually after stroke.
- Repeated movements rehearse skills and improve coordination.
- Improve sitting balance.

Transfers ie the ability to get from one place (bed) to another (chair).
- Strategy depends on patient ability.
- Totally dependent patients are hoisted.
- Once there is sitting balance then transfers with assistance of two people and a sliding board can be attempted.
- Once there is standing ability, then standing transfers with one person, then a frame can be worked on.

Ambulation
- Exercises aimed at improving independence in mobilizing.
- Realistic goals should be set—ideally premorbid state should be achieved, but 10 metres may be adequate for discharge home if this is the distance from chair to kitchen.
- Balance aided by bars then walking aids.

Heat treatment
Using packs, hydrotherapy pools, ultrasound etc. to treat pain and improve joint mobility.

Other treatments
e.g. cold treatments, electrical stimulation for pain relief (e.g. TENS machine).

Provision of aids
Usually ambulatory aids.

Walking aids

These increase stability, leading to improved confidence and function, and decreased number of falls. In general, identifying the need for an aid should prompt consideration of the cause of functional decline (is it reversible?) and provision of a physiotherapy assessment for prescription (correct aid, correct size), education (use of the aid, how to get up after falls), and treatment (strength/balance training).

All walking aids without wheels should be fitted with rubber ferrules to optimise grip, checked for wear regularly.

Stick (or cane (USA)) May be single-ended ('straight'), double-ended ('hemi'- or 'bipod'), three-ended ('tripod') or four-ended (delta-, quadru-pod).The latter offer modest additional stability compared to the straight stick. Held in the hand opposite the most impaired leg, thus unweighting the impaired limb. The level of hand placement should be at the greater trochanter, permitting 20–30 degrees of elbow flexion—the most efficient elbow muscular function.

The choice of handle is important, e.g. *contoured*: improve grip, reduce pressure, in permanent users or those with deformities; *swan neck*: weight is centred over the base of the stick, providing a little more stability; *right-angled*: more comfortable, but not easily secured when not in use; *crook handle*: hooked over the arm when not in use.

Frame A structure of lightweight alloy metal that is self-stabilizing (usually based around four points in contact with the floor), providing unweighting of the lower limbs and greater stability than a stick. Various heights, depths, and widths are available. Bulky, and difficult to transport. Some folding versions (often only three legs) are available. May be used indoors or out. The handgrips should be at wrist level, with the elbows slightly (15 degrees) flexed. Shorter frames are used in patients who fall backwards. To use a non-wheeled frame, lift it and move it 4–12" (10–30cm) in front of the body; then lean forwards a little, taking some weight through the arms before taking two equal steps towards the centre of the frame.

A weighted frame has weights low on the frame structure to provide additional counter-balance against falls. A *wheeled* frame has wheels at the front, permitting faster walking and an improved gait pattern, but it provides a slightly less stable base. Small-wheeled frames are suitable only for smooth surfaces. A *gutter* frame has forearm rests, enabling weightbearing through forearms rather than hands alone, providing additional support in the early stages of mobilization, or when hands/wrists are impaired.

Crutches A full assessment by a therapist is needed before selecting crutches. Crutches may be of the axilla- or elbow- type. Both are available with various features that should be individually prescribed, for example closed elbow cuffs provide added security and enable the user to let go of the handgrip to open a door without the crutch falling to the floor.

Walkers or rollators A frame that has three or four wheels and often hand-operated brakes (for added stability whilst static). Three-wheeled versions usually fold, permitting stowage in a car. Rollators with additional features such as bigger wheels (for uneven ground), a seat or attached basket for shopping or other house/garden tasks are larger than most standard frames and are usually used outdoors.

A trolley walker combines walking support with a means of transporting items from room to room. One or two shelves. The lower shelf is recessed at the back so that it doesn't interfere with walking.

Early walking aids (EWA) e.g. post-amputation mobility aid (PAM-aid). Used early (usually from ~ day 7) following amputation, in patients in whom a permanent prosthesis is planned or being considered.

Occupational therapy

Training
An occupational therapy degree is 3–4 years full-time or it can be done as a 2-year accelerated postgraduate course. The courses are two-thirds academic and one-third field work. See UK society website at www.cot.org.uk

Role of the occupational therapist (OT)
College of Occupational Therapy definition:
'OT enables people to achieve health, well-being and life satisfaction through participation in occupation (i.e. daily activities that reflect cultural values, provide structure to living and meaning to individuals; these activities meet human needs for self care, enjoyment and participation in society)'.

OTs achieve this by assessing both functional status and the environment then advising how to adapt.

Skills vs. habits
- A **skill** is having the ability to start, carry out, and complete a task effectively (e.g. making a cup of tea).
- A **habit** is a task that is actually carried out (e.g. a person may be able to make a meal, but does not do so when alone as they do not feel hungry).

Components of personal ability
Assessed by direct observation during tasks, formal testing, and information taken from carers, relatives and other professionals.
Cognition—to understand the task and why it needs doing. May be limited by dementia, poor concentration span, poor problem-solving skills etc. Assessed with cognitive tests such as MEAMS (p86).
Psychology—wanting to do and complete the task. Limited by depression, apathy, impaired coping skills etc.
Sensorimotor ability—especially in the upper limb.

Occupational therapy assessments and interventions

Assessments

Washing and dressing—aim to be done in the morning, when the patient would normally be carrying out these tasks.

Kitchen—looking at competence and safety for required tasks (depending on circumstances e.g. may need to make a meal on a gas stove, or just pour a drink from a prepared thermos).

Access visits—are done without the patient, to study the layout and potential problems of a patient's own home.

Home assessment visits

- A visit done with the patient, to see them in their own environment.
- Can be done by the OT alone, or with another member of the multi-disciplinary team (e.g. physiotherapist, care manager).
- May be useful to include intended carers (family or professional) as concerns can be addressed during the visit.
- Can be done in the community whilst the patient is still at home, from a hospital ward prior to discharge to ensure that it is feasible and that all possible problems and dangers have been minimized, or after discharge as a follow-up.
- Sometimes surprising—patients may either perform considerably better than expected (as they are in a familiar environment to which they have been adapting for years) or considerably worse (especially when a new physical limitation has occurred, such as stroke, as being at home emphasizes how different life will now be).
- Standard format for assessing all aspects of the property.
- Followed by a report containing observations on client performance and a list of recommendations regarding reorganization of furniture (e.g. bring bed downstairs), equipment provision and care required.
- Often typed and circulated to all MDT members.

Interventions

Teaching new skills (e.g. putting on a jumper with an arthritic shoulder) and habits (e.g. heating up microwave meal every lunchtime). Looking at how much can be done by the patient themselves, and how much help is needed (family or professional carers). Assessing need for equipment and advising about suitability, as well as training carers in its use. Commonly used equipment includes aids to:

- Access—ramps, rails, banisters, stairlifts, perching stools (high stools to enable seated access to a kitchen work surface) etc.
- Transfers—'banana boards' (curved boards that the patient slides across from one horizontal surface to another), swivel mats (two circles that twist to allow easier turning of an immobile patient, usually in a car seat).
- Mobility—wheelchairs, scooters etc.

- Bathing and dressing—bath boards, accessible baths and showers, long shoe horns, grab handles (to allow picking things up without bending) etc.
- Toileting and continence—seat raises, commodes, non-return urine bottles (for use when lying flat) etc.
- Eating and drinking—cutlery and cups with easy grip handles, aids to improve safety with hot water (kettle holders, full cup alarms), tap turners etc.
- Splints—for wrists (prevent pain) and ankles (foot drop).
- Sensory aids—enhanced signals e.g. large dials on a clock or altered signals e.g. flashing light instead of a bell for the deaf.

Doctors in the rehabilitation team

Doctors are commonly part of hospital rehabilitation teams but may be missing from community rehabilitation teams where a nominated doctor (e.g. GP or community geriatrician) can be consulted about specific issues.

When present, doctors tend to chair MDT meetings—this may be partly historical and partly because they are 'professional risk takers' who are more confident at coaxing a shared decision from a team, sometimes in very uncertain circumstances.

Medical ward rounds are less frequent than on acute wards—a weekly round would be usual—and since the patient is usually medically stable, communication with patient and family may predominate over medical management.

In a rehabilitation setting the doctor's main duties to the patient are:
- Selection of patients and maintenance of a waiting list.
- Optimize and stabilize medical treatments (e.g. ensure adequate analgesia).
- Rationalize drug therapy (e.g. stop night sedation).
- Anticipate and treat complications (e.g. pressure sores, Clostridium diarrhoea).
- Diagnose and treat depression.
- Identify and manage co-morbid conditions (e.g. incontinence, skin tumours).
- Initiate secondary prevention (e.g. aspirin for stroke, bisphosphonates following osteoporotic fractures).
- Secondary referral to other specialists (e.g. dermatology, orthopaedics).

Additional duties to the team include:
- Education.
- Team building.
- Context-setting—doctors often cross health-sector boundaries whereas therapists and nurses can be fixed in teams or wards. They should share information about the patients on the waiting list and about those who do not reach the rehabilitation unit and why. This overview can help the team understand pressure on beds etc.

Nurses in the rehabilitation team

The role of rehabilitation nurses in the recovery of a patient is often underestimated. They spend the longest time and often have the most intimate relationship with patients and their relatives.

Their wide role encompasses:

- Rehabilitation helper—particularly rehearsal of new tasks learnt with therapists (e.g. transfers, dressing). It takes longer and more skill to encourage a patient to wash/dress themselves than simply to provide personal care—this is the fundamental difference between rehabilitation and normal ward nursing.
- Overall performance assessors versus snapshot—they can detect any differential performance between what a patient 'can do' with the therapist and what he/she 'does do' when on their own, when tired or when relatives are visiting.
- Communication and liaison—first port of call between members of the team and patient and relatives. Emotive information sometimes more readily revealed in such non-threatening discussions.
- Nocturnal assessment—they are the only professionals able to monitor sleep, nocturnal confusion/wandering, and nocturnal continence/toileting.
- Continence management.
- Pressure and wound care management.
- Medication administering and monitoring self-medication.
- Ward or unit management.

Some senior specialist nurses have roles that overlap with the doctor e.g. in selecting patients for rehabilitation, chairing multi-disciplinary and family meetings, nurse prescribing etc. This is especially true in some community hospitals which can be exclusively run by Nurse Consultants.

Social work and care management

Social workers are trained to degree level (3 or 4 years), or postgraduate diploma. See website www.basw.co.uk. Care managers may have less formal training.

Care managers are based in both community and hospital settings, and may work with patients of all ages. The quality of support that they provide to a geriatric medicine service is a key determinant of patient throughput and quality of care. Any inpatient clinical area managing the needs of older people should have significant input from a social worker with experience in working with older people. 30 per cent of Emergency Departments ('A&E') in UK hospitals now have a dedicated social worker, aiming to avoid admissions by optimising access to social care.

To function effectively, social workers must have a detailed understanding of local services and facilities, how those services are accessed, as well as supporting information such as transport, costs, and waiting lists.

Elements of their role include:
- Assessment of client needs, often informed by the MDT in hospital settings.
- Translation of care needs into a package of care.
- Monitoring delivery of care and modifying its content or providers if necessary.
- Providing patients and families with details of care homes that can meet the patient's needs, in the desired geographical area.
- Providing advice about finances and financial support, care homes and home care.
- Performing financial assessments to determine who will fund their own care, and who will receive assistance.
- Counselling and support, to patients and families.
- Crisis management. For example, if a carer becomes ill or dies, a care package may be increased urgently, or emergency admission to a care home arranged. 'Social admission' to hospital should be a last resort, unless the condition of the patient has also changed, in which case urgent medical assessment, perhaps in a hospital, is essential.
- Arranging short breaks (for the carer) or respite care (for the patient).

Speech and language therapy and dieticians

Speech and language therapy (SALT)
Trained to degree level (3–4 years), or postgraduate diploma. See website www.rcslt.org

Assessment and treatment of swallowing disorders forms the bulk of inpatient work. Careful bedside evaluation of the patient is central to this, complemented if necessary by videofluoroscopy, the assessment 'gold standard'.

Useful interventions include patient positioning, changes in the texture or consistency of food/fluid, and carer supervision or prompting with food boluses. A period of 'nil by mouth' may be necessary until possible recovery of a safer swallow, during which artificial feeding should be considered.

Assessment and treatment of speech disorders forms the remainder of their work, commonly following stroke, or head/neck surgery. Therapists are experts in communication disorders, and their assessments are useful in distinguishing between severe dysarthria and dysphasia, for example. They provide: advice to patient, carers and staff; alternatives to speech, including communication boards, non-verbal strategies and electronic communicators.

Dieticians
Trained to degree level (3 or 4 years), or postgraduate diploma. See website www.bda.uk.com

Malnutrition in older people is common, underdiagnosed and under-treated. Prevalence and severity is especially high with (acute or chronic) comorbidity, and in inpatients. Community-dwelling older people may have an unvaried diet, depleted in fruit and vegetables ('tea and toast'). Dieticians are experts in the assessment and treatment of nutritional problems, but other members of the MDT must be alert to the possibility of malnutrition, and initiate interventions and dietician referral. Screening tools are useful.

Effective interventions include offering attractive food tailored to the individual, asking the family to bring in food, offering food frequently, and providing a dedicated assistant by the bedside to assist with feeding (this could be a staff member, family, or informal carer). Modern packaging (prepacked margarine, snack boxes) can be obstructive.

Where 'normal' feeding is impossible e.g. after acute stroke, the dietician can provide assessment, monitoring and advice to the patient (and family) regarding artificial feeding (p378).

Pharmacy

Pharmacists train for at least 4 years, leading to the M.Pharm degree. See website www.rpsgb.org.uk

Involved in preparation, prescribing, packaging, and dispensing of medicines. A key part of the system delivering quality drug use to out- and in-patients. Gatekeepers of many hospital formularies (limited drug lists optimizing costs and effectiveness). Advise on all aspects of prescribing, especially interactions and dosing.

Issues where pharmacists may help:
- High frequency of adverse drug reactions (up to 17 per cent of hospital admissions).
- Underuse of medications e.g. preventatives in asthma.
- Poor concordance/compliance.
- Poor administration technique e.g. inhalers.
- Frequent and complex changes in medication.
- Poor communication with primary care on discharge.
- Absence of full medication history on admission.

The NSF for Older People states that all patients over 75 should have their medicines reviewed at least annually, and those taking four or more medicines six-monthly. Every area must have schemes for the elderly to get more help from pharmacists in using their medicines.

Community nurses and health visitors

Both are trained nurses with further postgraduate training and experience that enables them to work more independently in community settings. Their precise role and professional relationships varies greatly between districts.

Community nurses

Usually work for one or more GP practices, providing domiciliary nursing services in excess of those provided by non-nurse carers. A district nurse is a community nurse who has undergone further training.

Specialist skills include:
• Wound care—assessment and treatment.
• Insulin injections and diabetes monitoring.
• Continence management.
• Bowel management.
• Chronic disease management.
• Education, of patients and carers (e.g. PEG feed, catheter care).

Although caring for adults of all ages, much of their work involves older people, especially the frail elderly. They are often an excellent source of information about older people admitted to hospital, often having frequent contacts with frail elderly people who are unable to leave the home and are therefore seen only rarely by GPs.

Health visitors (HV)

Again, usually work with one or more GP practice, but the dominant focus is on health promotion. Most work with mothers and babies/children, but they can work with any age group. Some health visitors specialize in working with older people and carers. They may help older people maintain independence by
• Providing information about local activities.
• Advising on benefits.
• Advising on help available from social services to support them in their homes.
• Visiting people at home.
• Arranging respite care.

See www.msfcphva.org (Community Practitioners' and Health Visitors' Association)

Chapter 5

Falls and funny turns

Falls and fallers 116
Assessment following a fall 118
Interventions to prevent falls 120
Syncope and presyncope 122
Balance and dysequlibrium 124
Dizziness 126
    How to... manage multifactorial dizziness—clinical
    example 127
Vertebrobasilar insufficiency 128
Orthostatic (postural) hypotension 130
    How to... measure postural blood pressure 131
Carotid sinus syndrome 132
    How to... perform carotid sinus massage 133
Falls clinics 134

Falls and fallers

A fall is an event that results in a person non-intentionally coming to rest at a lower level (usually the floor). Falls are common and important, affecting one-third of people living in their own homes each year. They result in fear, injury, dependency, insitutionalization, and death. Many can be prevented and their consequences minimised.

Factors influencing fall frequency

Intrinsic factors. Maintaining balance—and avoiding a fall—is a complex, demanding, multi-system skill. It requires muscle strength (power:weight ratio), stable but flexible joints, multiple sensory modalities (e.g. proprioception, vision, eye sight) and a functional peripheral and central nervous system. Higher level cognitive function permits risk assessment, giving insight into the danger that a planned activity may pose.

Extrinsic factors. These include environmental factors e.g. lighting, obstacles, the presence of grab rails and the height of steps and furniture, as well as the softness and grip of the floor.

Magnitude of 'stressor'. All people have the susceptibility to fall, and the likelihood of a fall depends on how close to a 'fall threshold' a person sits. Older people, especially with disease, sit closer to the threshold, and are more easily and more often pushed over it by stressors. These can be internal (e.g. transient dizziness due to orthostatic hypotension) or external (e.g. a gust of wind, or a nudge in a crowded shop); they may be minor or major (no-one can avoid 'falling' in hurricane force winds or during complete syncope).

If insight is preserved, the older person can to some extent reduce risk, by limiting hazardous behaviours and minimizing stressors (e.g. walking only inside, avoiding stairs or uneven surfaces, using walking aids, or asking for supervision).

Factors influencing fall severity

In older people, the adverse consequences of falling are greater, due to:
- **Multiple system-impairments** which lead to **less effective saving mechanisms.** Falls are more frightening and injury rates per fall are higher.
- **Osteoporosis** and increased fracture rates.
- **Secondary injury** due to post-fall immobility, including pressure sores, burns, dehydration, and hypostatic pneumonia. Half of older people cannot get up again after a fall.
- **Psychological adverse effects** including loss of confidence.

Falls are almost always multifactorial. Think:
- **'Why today?'** Often because the fall is a manifestation of acute or sub-acute illness e.g. sepsis, dehydration or drug adverse effect.
- **'Why this person?'** Usually because of a combination of intrinsic and extrinsic factors that increase vulnerability to stressors.
- ▶▶ A fall is often a symptom of an underlying serious problem.

Banned terms

The terms **'simple fall'** and **'mechanical fall'** are used commonly, but they are facile, imprecise, and unhelpful. 'Simple' usually refers to the approach adopted by the assessing doctor.

- For every fall, identify the intrinsic factors, extrinsic factors, and acute stressors that have led to it.
- Within each of these categories, think how their influence on the likelihood of future falls can be reduced.

Assessment following a fall

Think of fall(s) if a patient presents:
- Having 'tripped'.
- With a fracture or non-fracture injury.
- Having been found on the floor.
- With secondary consequences of falling (e.g. hypothermia, pneumonia).

Patients who present having fallen are often mis-labelled as having 'collapsed', discouraging the necessary search for multiple causal factors. Practice opportunistic screening—ask all older people who attend primary or secondary care whether they have fallen recently.

History

Obtain a corroborative history if possible. In many cases, a careful history differentiates between falls due to:
- Frailty and unsteadiness.
- Syncope or near syncope.
- Acute neurological problems (e.g. seizures, vertebrobasilar insufficiency).

Gather information about:
- Fall circumstances (e.g. timing, physical environment).
- Symptoms before and after the fall.
- Drugs, including alcohol.
- Previous falls, fractures and syncope ('faints'), even as a young adult.
- Previous 'near-misses'.
- Comorbidity (cardiac, neurological (stroke, Parkinson's disease, seizures), cognitive impairment, diabetes).
- Functional performance (difficulties bathing, dressing, toileting).

Drugs associated with falls

Falls may be caused by any drug that is either directly psychoactive or may lead to systemic hypotension and cerebral hypoperfusion. Polypharmacy (>4 drugs, any type) is an independent risk factor.

The most common drug causes are:
- Benzodiazepines and other hypnotics
- Tricyclic antidepressants
- Antipsychotics
- Skeletal muscle relaxants e.g. baclofen, tizanidine
- Opiates
- Diuretics
- Antihypertensives, especially ACE-inhibitors and alpha-blockers
- Hypoglycaemics, especially:
  - Long-acting oral drugs (e.g. glibenclamide)
  - Insulin.

Examination

This can sometimes be focused if the history is highly suggestive of a particular pathology. But perform at least a brief screening examination of each system.

- **Functional.** Ask the patient to stand from a chair, walk, turn around, walk back and sit back down. Assess gait, use of walking aids and hazard appreciation (e.g. leave an obstacle in the way and see how they negotiate it).
- **Cardiovascular.** Always check lying and standing BP. Check pulse rate and rhythm. Listen for murmurs (especially of aortic stenosis).
- **Musculoskeletal.** Assess footwear (stability and grip). Remove footwear and examine the feet. Examine the major joints for deformity, instability or stiffness.
- **Neurological.** To identify stroke, peripheral neuropathy, Parkinson's disease, vestibular disease, myelopathy, cerebellar degeneration, visual impairment, and cognitive impairment.

Tests

Many tests are of limited value, but the following are considered routine:

- FBC
- B12, folate
- U,C+E
- ECG
- Glucose
- Calcium, phosphate
- TFT.

If a specific cause is suspected, then test for it, e.g.:
- 24 hour ECG if there are frequent episodes suggestive of arrhythmia.
- Tilt table testing if unexplained syncope.

Interventions to prevent falls

The complexity of treatment reflects the complexity of aetiology.
- Older people who fall more often have remediable medical causes.
- Do not expect to make only one diagnosis or intervention—making minor changes to multiple factors is more powerful.
- Tailor the intervention to the patient. Assess for relevant risk factors and work to modify each one.

Reducing fall frequency

Priorities are likely to include:
- **Drug review.**
  - For each drug, weigh the benefits of continuing with the benefits of reduction or stopping. Stop if risk ≥ benefit. Reduce if benefit is likely from the drug class, but the dose is excessive for that patient.
  - Taper to a stop if withdrawal effect likely e.g. benzodiazepine.
- **Treatment of orthostatic hypotension.**
- **Strength and balance training.** In the frail older person (often by Physiotherapist, p96). May be delivered via exercise classes, or disciplines such as Tai Chi.
- **Walking aids.** Provide an appropriate aid and teach the patient how to use it (pp98–9).
- **Environmental assessment and modification** (often by Occupational Therapist; p100).
- **Reducing stressors.** This involves decision-making by the patient or carers. The cognitively able patient can judge risk/benefit and usually modifies risk appropriately—e.g. limiting walking to indoors, using a walking aid properly and reliably, and asking for help if a task (e.g. getting dressed) is particularly demanding. However:
  - Risk can never be abolished.
  - Enforced relative immobility has a cost to health.
  - Patient choice is paramount. Most will have clear views about risk and how much lifestyle should change.
  - Institutionalization does not usually reduce risk (see below).

Preventing adverse consequences of falls

Despite risk reduction, falls may remain likely. In this case, consider:
- **Osteoporosis detection and treatment.**
- **Teaching patients how to get up.** Usually by a physiotherapist.
- **Alarms** e.g. pullcords in each room or a pendant alarm (worn around the neck). Often these alert a distant call centre who summon more local help (home warden, relative, or ambulance).
- **Supervision.** Continual visits to the home (by carers, neighbours, family, and/or voluntary agencies) reduce the duration of a 'lie' post-fall.
- **Change of accommodation.** This sometimes reduces risk, but is not a panacea. A move from home to a care home rarely reduces risk—care homes are unfamiliar, often have hard flooring surfaces, and staff cannot provide continuous supervision.

Preventing falls in hospital

Falls in hospital are common, a product of admitting acutely unwell older people with chronic comorbidity into an unfamiliar environment. Multifactorial interventions have the best chance of reducing falls:

- Treat infection, dehydration and delirium actively.
- Stop incriminated drugs and avoid starting them.
- Provide good quality footwear, and an accessible walking aid.
- Provide good lighting and a bedside commode for those with urinary or faecal urgency or frequency.
- Keep a call bell close to hand.
- Care for the highest risk patients in a bay under continuous staff supervision.

Interventions that are rarely effective and may be harmful

- **Bedrails (cotsides).** Injury risk is substantial: limbs snag on unprotected metal bars and patients clamber over the rails, falling even greater distances onto the floor below.
- **Restraints.** These increase the risk of physical injury, including fractures, pressure sores, and death. Also increase agitation.
- **Hip protectors.** Impact absorptive pads stitched into undergarments. Increasing evidence suggests that they are not effective, largely due to practical issues and resulting poor compliance—they are difficult to put on, can be uncomfortable, and multiple pairs (£40 each) are needed if incontinence is a problem.

Further reading

Parker MJ, Gillespie WJ, Gillespie LD. Hip protectors for preventing hip fractures in older people. The Cochrane Database of Systematic Reviews 2005, Issue 3.

Syncope and presyncope

Syncope is a sudden, transient loss of consciousness due to reduced cerebral perfusion. The patient is unresponsive with a loss of postural control (i.e. slumps or falls).

Presyncope is a feeling of light-headedness that would lead to syncope if corrective measures were not taken (usually sitting or lying down).

These conditions:

- Are a major cause of morbidity in the elderly population (occurring in a quarter of institutionalized older people), and are recurrent in a third. Risk of syncope increases with advancing age and in the presence of cardiovascular disease.
- Account for 5% of hospital admissions, and many serious injuries (e.g. hip fracture).
- Cause considerable anxiety and can cause social isolation as sufferers limit activities, in fear of further episodes.

Causes

These are many. Older people with decreased physiological reserve are more susceptible to most. They can be sub-divided as follows:

- **Peripheral factors**—hypotension may be caused by the upright posture, eating, straining, or coughing; and may be exacerbated by low circulating volume (dehydration), hypotensive drugs or intercurrent sepsis. Orthostatic hypotension is the most common cause of syncope.
- **Vasovagal syncope ('simple faint')**—common in young and old people. Vagal stimulation (pain, fright, emotion etc.) leads to hypotension and syncope. Usually, an autonomic prodrome (pale, clammy, light-headed) is followed by nausea or abdominal pain, then syncope. Benign, with no implications for driving. Diagnose with caution in older people with vascular disease, where other causes are more common.
- **Carotid sinus syndrome.**
- **Pump problem**—myocardial infarction or ischaemia, arrhythmia (tachy- or brady-cardia e.g. VT, SVT, fast AF, complete heart block).
- **Outflow obstruction**—e.g. aortic stenosis.

The main differential is seizure disorder, where the loss of consciousness is due to altered electrical activity in the brain (p176).

▶▶ Stroke and TIA very rarely cause syncope, as they cause a focal not a global deficit. Brainstem ischaemia is the rare exception.

History

The history often yields the diagnosis, but accuracy can be difficult to achieve—the patient often remembers little. Witness accounts are valuable and should be sought.

Ensure that the following points are covered:

- **Situation**—was the patient standing (orthostatic hypotension), exercising (ischaemia or arrhythmia), sitting or lying down (likely seizure), eating (post-prandial hypotension), on the toilet (defaecation or micturition syncope), coughing (cough syncope), in pain or frightened (vasovagal syncope)?

- **Prodrome**—was there any warning? Palpitations suggest arrhythmia; sweating with palpitations suggests vasovagal syndrome; chest pain suggests ischaemia; light-headedness suggests any cause of hypotension. Gustatory or olfactory aura suggests seizures. However, associations are not absolute; e.g. arrhythmias often do not cause palpitations.
- **Was there loss of consciousness?**—There is much terminology (fall, blackout, 'funny turn', collapse etc.), and different terms mean different things by each term. Syncope has occurred if there is loss of consciousness with loss of awareness due to cerebral hypoperfusion; however, many (~30%) patients will have amnesia for the loss of consciousness and simply describe a fall.
- **Description of attack**—ideally from an eyewitness. Was the patient deathly pale and clammy (likely systemic and cerebral hypoperfusion)? Were there ictal features (tongue biting, incontinence, twitching)? Prolonged loss of consciousness makes syncope unlikely. A brain deprived of oxygen from any cause is susceptible to seizure; a fit does not necessarily indicate that a seizure disorder is the primary problem. Assess carefully before initiating anticonvulsant therapy.
- **Recovery period**—ideally reported by an eyewitness. Rapid recovery often indicates a cardiac cause. Prolonged drowsiness and confusion often follow a seizure.

Examination

Full general examination is required. Ensure that the pulse is examined, murmurs sought and a postural blood pressure is obtained.

Investigation

- **Bloods**—check for anaemia, sepsis, renal disease, myocardial ischaemia
- **ECG**—for all older patients with loss of consciousness or pre-syncope. Look specifically at PR interval, QT interval, trifascicular block (prolonged PR, RBBB, and LAD), ischaemic changes, and LVH (occurs in aortic stenosis).
- **Other tests** depend on clinical suspicion e.g. tilt test if symptoms sound orthostatic but diagnosis is proving difficult (lying and standing blood pressures will usually suffice; tilt testing is a very labour intensive test, and should not be requested routinely); brain scan and EEG if seizures suspected; Holter monitor if looking for arrhythmias.

Treatment

- Treat the cause.
- Often not found, or multifactorial, so treat all reversible factors.
- Review medication (e.g. diuretics, vasodilators, cholinesterase inhibitors, tricyclic antidepressants).
- Education about prevention and measures to abort an attack if there is a prodrome. Advise against swimming or bathing alone, and inform about driving restrictions. (Varies from no restriction to a 6-month ban, depending on the type of syncope. See details at www.dvla.gov.uk/at_a_glance)

Balance and dysequilibrium

Balancing is a complex activity, involving many systems.

Input

There must be awareness of the position of the body in space, which comes from:

- **Peripheral input**—information about body position comes from peripheral nerves (proprioception) and mechanoreceptors in the joints. This information is relayed via the posterior column of the spinal cord to the central nervous system.
- **Eyes**—provide visual cues as to position.
- **Ears**—provide input at several levels. The otolithic organs (utricle and saccule) provide information about static head position. The semicircular canals inform about head movement. Auditory cues localize a person with reference to the environment.

Assimilation

Information is gathered and assessed in the brain stem and cerebellum.

Output

Messages are then relayed to the eyes, to allow a steady gaze during head movements (the vestibulo-ocular reflex) and to the cortex and the cord to control postural (antigravity) muscles.

When all this functions well, balance is effortless. A defect(s) in any one contributing system can cause balance problems or dysequilibrium:

- **Peripheral nerves**—neuropathy is more common (see p184). Specifically, it is believed that there is a significant age-related loss of proprioceptive function.
- **Eyes**—age related changes decrease visual acuity. Disease (cataracts, glaucoma etc.) is more common (see Chapter 22).
- **Ears**—age related changes decrease hearing and lead to reduced vestibular function. The older vestibular system is more vulnerable to damage from drugs, trauma, infection and ischaemia (see Chapter 21).
- **Joint receptors**—degenerative joint disease (arthritis) is more common in older people.
- **Central nervous system**—age related changes can slow processing. Disease processes (ischaemia, hypertensive damage, dementia etc.) are more common with age.
- **Postural muscles**—more likely to be weak, because of inactivity, disease, medication (e.g. steroids) or the reduced muscle mass of ageing.

In the older person, one or more of these defects will occur commonly. In addition, skeletal changes may alter the centre of gravity, and cardio-vascular changes may lead to arrhythmias or postural change in blood pressure, exacerbated further by medications.

An approach to dysequilibrium

- Aetiology is usually multifactorial.
- Consider each system separately, and optimize its function.
- Look at provoking factors (medication, cardiovascular conditions, environmental hazards etc.) and minimize them.
- Work on prevention:
  - Alter the environment (e.g. improve lighting).
  - With the physiotherapist, develop safer ways to mobilize and increase strength, stamina, and balance.
- Small adjustments to multiple problems can make a big difference, e.g. when appropriate, combine cataract extraction, a walking aid, vascular secondary prevention, a second stair rail, brighter lighting, and a course of physiotherapy.

▶▶ If falls persist despite simple (but multiple) interventions, refer to a Falls Clinic.

Dizziness

A brain that has insufficient information to be confident of where it is in space generates a sensation of dizziness. This can be due to reduced sensory inputs, or impairment of their integration. Dizziness is common, occurring in up to 30% of older people.

However, the term dizziness can be used by patients and doctors to mean many different things, including:
- Movement (spinning) of the patient or the room—vertigo (see pp600–1).
- Dysequilibrium or unsteadiness—(see p125).
- Light-headedness—presyncope (see pp122–3).
- Mixed—a combination of these sensations.
- Other—e.g. malaise, general weakness, headache.

Distinguishing these is the first step in management, as it will indicate possible causal conditions. This relies largely on the history. Discriminatory questions include:
- 'Please try to describe exactly what you feel when you are dizzy?'
- 'Does the room spin, as if you are on a roundabout?' (Vertigo.)
- 'Do you feel light-headed, as if you are about to faint?' (Presyncope.)
- 'Does it occur when you are lying down?' (If so, presyncope is unlikely.)
- 'Does it come on when you move your head?' (Vertigo more likely.)
- 'Does it come and go?' (Chronic, constant symptoms are more likely to be mixed or psychiatric in origin.)

Causes

The individual conditions most commonly diagnosed when a patient complains of dizziness are:
- Benign paroxysmal positional vertigo (p601)
- Labyrinthitis (p601).
- Posterior circulation stroke (p601)
- Orthostatic hypotension
- Carotid sinus hypersensitivity
- Vertebrobasilar insufficiency
- Cervical spondylosis (p530)
- Anxiety and depression.

In reality, much dizziness is multifactorial, with dysfunction in several systems. This means that precise diagnosis is more difficult (and often not done) and treatment is more complex.

▶▶ Making small improvements to each contributing problem can add up to a big overall improvement (perhaps making the difference between independent living or institutional care).

HOW TO... manage multifactorial dizziness—clinical example

History

Mrs A is 85, and has fallen several times. She complains of dizziness, specifically she feels 'muzzy in the head', usually when standing. When this occurs, if she sits down promptly it will pass, but often she doesn't make it and her legs 'just give way'. She also feels 'muzzy' in bed sometimes when turning over. Past medical history includes hypertension (she takes atenolol 100mg) and osteoarthritis. She lives alone in unmodernized accommodation.

Examination

She is thin and has a kyphotic spine. Pulse is 50 per minute; supine blood pressure is 130/80, falling to 100/70 on standing. There is limited movement at the hips and cervical spine. Neck movement causes unsteadiness.

Investigations

Blood tests are normal. ECG shows sinus bradycardia; X-rays show severe degenerative change of the hip joints and cervical spine, with some vertebral wedge fractures.

Diagnosis and treatment plan

This is a multifactorial problem. Some of the relevant factors include:

- Postural instability: caused by arthritis, kyphosis and low muscle mass.
- Presyncope: caused by bradycardia and mild postural drop.
- Possibly vertebrobasilar insufficiency due to cervical spine degeneration.
- Extrinsic factors (e.g. poor lighting) are almost certainly contributing.

Approach this problem by listing each contributing factor, and identifying what can be done to improve it. For example:

Contributing factor	Management
Osteoarthritis	Optimize analgesia
	Consider referral for joint replacement
	Physiotherapy (provision of walking aids; strength and balance training)
Kyphosis	Consider bisphosphonate, calcium and vitamin D to prevent progression
	Walking aids will improve balance
Low muscle mass	Take a dietary history
	Consider nutritional supplements
	Physiotherapy; encourage exercise
Bradycardia and postural drop	Consider stopping (or reducing) atenolol
	Monitor blood pressure
Environment	Occupational therapy review to:
	—Provide grab rails and perching stool
	—Improve lighting and flooring
	—'De-clutter' the home

Vertebrobasilar insufficiency

Vertebrobasilar insufficiency (VBI) is a collection of symptoms attributed to transient compromise of the vertebrobasilar circulation. There is often associated compromise of the anterior cerebral circulation.

Symptoms

These arise from functional impairment of the midbrain, cerebellum or occipital cortex, and can include:

- Abrupt onset, recurrent dizziness or vertigo
- Nausea and/or vomiting
- Ataxia
- Visual disruption (diplopia, nystagmus)
- Dysarthria
- Limb paraesthesia.

Causes

Impairment of the posterior cerebral circulation leads to VBI:

- Atherosclerosis of the vertebral or basilar arteries.
- Vertebral artery compression by cervical spine osteophytes (due to degenerative joint disease), at times triggered by neck movement.
- Obstructing tumour.

Diagnosis

This is based mainly on the history, supported if necessary by investigations. Invasive tests such as angiography are very rarely indicated.

- Check for vascular risk factors (see p194).
- Cervical spine X-ray may show osteophytes, although these are common and very non-specific.
- CT brain may demonstrate tumour or ischaemic change. MRI is more sensitive for posterior circulation ischaemic change.
- MR angiography may reveal occlusive vertebral artery disease.
- Doppler ultrasound (rarely) to examine vertebral artery flow.

Treatment

- Vascular secondary prevention measures (see p324).
- Limiting neck movements, if these are a precipitant for symptoms, can be useful. Soft collars can be worn, and act mainly as a reminder to the patient to avoid rapid head turns.
- There is no evidence that anticoagulants are effective.

'Drop attack'

This term refers to unexplained falls with no prodrome, no (or very brief) loss of consciousness, and rapid recovery.

- The proportion of falls due to 'drop attack' increases with age
- There are several causes, including:
  - Cardiac arrhythmia
  - Carotid sinus syndrome
  - Orthostatic hypotension
  - Vasovagal syndrome
  - Vertebrobasilar insufficiency.

The first four causes listed usually lead to syncope or pre-syncope, with identifiable prior symptoms (e.g. dizziness, pallor); those episodes would not be termed 'drop attacks'. However, such prior symptoms are not universal, and may not be recollected, leading to a 'drop attack' presentation.

In most cases, following appropriate assessment, cause(s) can be identified, and effective treatment(s) begun.

▶▶ Making a diagnosis of 'drop attack' alone is not satisfactory; assess more completely, and where possible determine the likely underlying cause(s).

Orthostatic (postural) hypotension

Orthostatic hypotension (OH) is common. About 20% of community-dwelling and 50% of institutionalized older people are affected.
- An important, treatable cause of dizziness, syncope, near-syncope, immobility, falls, and fracture. Less frequently leads to visual disruption, lethargy, neck- or backache.
- Often most marked after meals, exercise, at night, and in a warm environment, and abruptly precipitated by increased intrathoracic pressure (cough, defaecation, or micturition).
- Often episodic (coincidence of precipitants) and covert (ask direct questions; walk or stand the patient and look for it). May occur several minutes after standing.

Diagnosis
Thresholds for diagnosis are arbitrary. A fall in BP of ≥ 20mmHg systolic or 10mmHg diastolic on standing from supine is said to be significant.

Causes
- **Drugs** (including vasodilators, diuretics, negative inotropes or chronotropes (e.g. β-blockers, calcium channel blockers), antidepressants, antipsychotics, opiates, levodopa, alcohol)
- **Chronic hypertension** (↓ baroreflex sensitivity and LV compliance)
- **Volume depletion** (dehydration, acute haemorrhage)
- **Sepsis** (vasodilation)
- **Autonomic failure** (pure, diabetic, Parkinson's disease, etc.)
- **Prolonged bed rest**
- **Adrenal insufficiency**
- **Raised intrathoracic pressure** (bowel or bladder evacuation, cough).

Treatment
- Treat the cause. Stop, reduce or substitute drugs incrementally.
- Reduce consequences of falls (e.g. pendant alarms).
- Modify behaviour: stand slowly and step-wise; lie down at prodrome.
- If salt or water deplete (e.g. diuretics, diarrhoea), supplement with:
  - Na (liberal salting at table or NaCl tabs e.g. Slow Sodium 5–10g/day).
  - Water (oral or iv (iv fluid as isotonic dextrose or saline)).
- Consider starting drugs if non-drug measures fail:
  - Fludrocortisone (0.1–0.2mg/day).
  - α-agonists e.g. midodrine (2.5mg tds, titrated to maximum 40mg/day); unlicensed in UK; contraindicated in IHD.
  - Desmopressin 5–20mcg nocte.
  - In all cases, monitor electrolytes and for heart failure and supine hypertension. Caution if supine BP rises > 180mmHg systolic. Dependent oedema alone is not a reason to stop treatment.
- The following may help:
  - Full-length compression stockings.
  - Head-up tilt to bed (decreases nocturnal natriuresis).
  - Caffeine (strong coffee with meals) or NSAIDs (→ fluid retention).
  - Erythropoietin or octreotide.

Postprandial hypotension

Significant when associated with symptoms and fall in BP ≥20mmHg within 75 minutes of meals. A modest fall is normal (and usually asymptomatic) in older people. Often more severe and symptomatic in hypertensive people with OH or autonomic failure.

Diagnosis

Measure BP before meals and at 30 and 60 minutes after meal. Symptoms and causes overlap with OH.

Treatment

- Avoid hypotensive drugs and alcohol with meals.
- Lie down or sit after meals.
- Reduce osmotic load of meals (small frequent meals, low simple CHO, high fibre/water content).
- Caffeine, fludrocortisone, NSAIDS and octreotide are used rarely.

HOW TO... **measure postural blood pressure**

1. Lay the patient flat for ≥5 minutes.
2. Measure lying blood pressure with a manual sphygmomanometer.
3. Stand the patient upright rapidly, if necessary with assistance.
4. Check BP promptly (within 30 seconds of standing).
5. Whilst standing, repeat BP measurement continually—at least every 30 seconds for > 2 minutes.
6. Record:
   - Supine BP
   - Nadir of systolic and diastolic BP
   - Symptoms.

Note that:

- **Lying-to-standing measurements** are more sensitive than sitting-to-standing or lying-to-sitting. The latter are sometimes all that is possible for less mobile patients, even with assistance.
- **Consider repeat assessment** at different times of day—OH is more common after a meal and when relatively fluid depleted (early morning).
- **Automatic (oscillometric) BP devices** (e.g. 'Dinamap') should not be used—they cannot repeat measurements rapidly, nor track a rapidly changing BP.
- **Consider referral to a Falls Clinic** for prolonged upright head-up tilt table testing if symptoms suggest syncope or near-syncope after more prolonged standing.

Carotid sinus syndrome

Carotid sinus syndrome (CSS) is episodic, symptomatic bradycardia and/or hypotension due to a hypersensitive carotid baroreceptor reflex, resulting in syncope or near-syncope. It is an important and potentially treatable cause of falls.

CSS is common in older patients, and rarely occurs under 50 years. Series report a prevalence of 2% in healthy older people, and up to 35% of fallers over 80 years. It is a condition that has been identified recently, and not all physicians are convinced that we fully understand the normal responses of older people to carotid sinus massage or the significance of the spectrum of abnormal results.

Normally, in response to increased arterial blood pressure, barorecep-tors in the carotid sinus act via the sympathetic nervous system to slow and weaken the pulse, lowering blood pressure. This reflex typically blunts with age, but in carotid sinus syndrome it is exaggerated, probably centrally. This hypersensitivity is associated with increasing age, atheroma and the use of drugs that affect the sinoatrial node (e.g. β-blockers, digoxin, and calcium channel blockers).

Typical triggers include:
- Neck turning (looking up or around)
- Tight collars
- Straining (including cough, micturition and defaecation)
- Meals, ie post-prandial
- Prolonged standing.

Often however no trigger is identified.

There are three subtypes:
- **Cardioinhibitory** (sinus pause of >3seconds)
- **Vasodepressor** (BP fall >50mmHg)
- **Mixed** (both sinus pause and BP fall).

The diagnosis is made when all three of the following factors are present:
- Unexplained attributable symptoms
- A sinus pause of >3 seconds and/or systolic BP fall of >50mmHg in response to 5 seconds of carotid sinus massage (see box opposite)
- Symptoms are reproduced by carotid sinus massage.

CSS is often associated with other disorders (vasovagal syndrome and orthostatic hypotension), probably due to shared pathogenesis (auto-nomic dysfunction). This makes management more challenging.

Treatment
- Stop aggravating drugs where possible.
- Pure cardioinhibitory carotid sinus hypersensitivity responds well to AV sequential pacing, resolving symptoms in up to 80%.
- Vasodepressor related symptoms are harder to treat (pathogenesis is less well understood), but may respond to increasing circulating volume with fludrocortisone or midodrine (not licensed), as for orthostatic hypotension.

HOW TO... **perform carotid sinus massage**

1. As this is a potentially hazardous procedure:
   - Perform it in conditions that optimize test sensitivity—e.g. on a tilt table, at a 70–80 degree tilt, massaging on the right hand side.
   - Ensure that resuscitation facilities are available (full cardiac arrest trolley, another health professional close by, telephone).
2. Check for contraindications—do not perform after recent MI (increased sensitivity), in cerebrovascular disease or if there is a bruit present unless carotid Doppler is normal.
3. Advise the patient about possible side effects—arrhythmias (most common if taking digoxin) and neurological symptoms (usually transient, occurring in about 0.14% of tests).
4. The patient should be relaxed, with the head turned to the left, lying on a couch with the body resting at 45 degrees (or on a tilt table at 70–80 degrees).
5. Attach the patient to a cardiac monitor with printing facility (to provide documentary evidence of asystole). The fall in BP is usually too brief to be detected by conventional (sphygmomanometric) methods, but continuous ('beat-to-beat') blood pressure monitoring (using e.g. Portapres or Finapres devices) enables the detection of pure vasodepressor CSS.
6. Identify the carotid sinus—the point of maximal carotid pulsation in the neck.
7. Massage with steady pressure in a circular motion for 5–10 seconds.
8. Look for asystole and/or hypotension during massage or shortly (seconds) afterwards.
9. If clinical suspicion is high, and the result of right-sided massage is negative, repeat on the left side (do not do this routinely).

Falls clinics

The assessment and secondary prevention of falls are complex processes best performed by an experienced multi-disciplinary team with expert knowledge, functioning within a 'falls clinic'.

Falls clinics have become much more common, initially a result of trials showing the power of multidisciplinary interventions to reduce falls in community-dwelling older people. More recently the NSF required universal UK provision.

The team structure, diagnostic approach and delivery of care varies enormously, but there are broadly two complementary approaches taken by falls clinics:

- Focus on identifying and reducing syncope and near-syncope, with a low threshold to further investigation including tilt table testing and arrhythmia detection.
- More global approach in which cardiovascular evaluation is an important but minor part of the assessment.

Reflecting the differing approaches, some clinics (often those practising a more medical model) take place in outpatient clinics, whilst others occur in day hospitals and are more routinely multi-disciplinary.

Falls clinics are often led and delivered by non-physician health professionals such as experienced nurses, occupational therapists, and physiotherapists. Screening for modifiable medical factors should be a routine part of all assessments, with referral to a medical specialist (e.g. GPSI or geriatrician) if such factors are identified.

Referral criteria

Falls are so common that health services would be swamped if all who had fallen were referred. Instead, refer those with more sinister features suggesting a likelihood of recurrent falls, injury, or an underlying remediable medical cause. Referral criteria might include:

- **Recurrent** (≥ 2) falls.
- **Loss of consciousness**, syncope or near-syncope.
- **Injury**, especially fracture or facial injury (the latter suggesting poor saving mechanisms or loss of consciousness).
- **Polypharmacy** (≥ 4 drugs).

Sources of patients include:

- **A&E** (assess most people with non-operatively managed fractures).
- **Acute orthopaedic units** (hip and other operatively managed fractures).
- **GP or Community Nurse.**
- **Medical wards.**
- **Self-presenting.** Some services advertise directly, via posters and other media.

Further information

National Service Framework for Older People. www.dh.gov.uk

Drugs

Drugs and older patients 136
Rules of prescribing 138
Pharmacology in older patients 140
Drug sensitivity 142
Taking a drug history 144
   How to... improve concordance 146
Adverse drug reactions 148
   How to... manage drug-induced skin rashes 149
ACE inhibitors 150
   How to... start ACE inhibitors 151
Amiodarone 152
   How to... manage amiodarone-induced thyroid
   dysfunction 153
Analgesia in older patients 154
   How to... manage pain in older patients 155
Steroids 156
Warfarin 158
   How to... initiate warfarin 160
Breaking the rules 162

Drugs and older patients

The commonest intervention performed by physicians is to write a prescription. Older patients will have more conditions requiring medication, and polypharmacy is common.

In the developed world:

- The over 65s typically make up around 14% of the population yet consume 40% of the drug budget.
- 66% of the over 65s, and 87% of the over 75s are on regular medication.
- 34% over the over 75s are on three or more drugs.
- Care home patients are on an average of eight medications.

Good prescribing habits are essential for any medical practitioner, but especially for the geriatrician.

Rules of prescribing

1. Is it indicated?

Treatment of new symptom

Some symptoms trigger a reflex prescription (e.g. constipation—laxatives; dizziness—prochlorperazine). Before starting a medication, consider:

- What is the diagnosis? (e.g. dizziness due to postural drop.)
- Can something be stopped? (e.g. opioid analgesia causing constipation.)
- Are there any non-drug measures? (e.g. increase fibre for constipation.)

Optimizing disease management

E.g. a diagnosis of cardiac failure should trigger consideration of loop diuretics, spironolactone, ACE inhibitors, and β-blockers.

- Ensure the diagnosis is secure before committing the patient to multiple drugs (may be difficult where there is no clear diagnostic gold standard, e.g. with TIAs).
- Do not deny older patients disease modifying treatments simply to avoid polypharmacy.
- Do not deny treatment because of potential side effects—whilst these may impact on functional ability, or cause significant morbidity (e.g. low blood pressure with β-blockade in cardiac failure) and need to be discontinued, this should usually be after a trial of treatment with careful monitoring.
- Conversely, do not start treatment to improve mortality from a disease if the patient has limited life span for other reasons (e.g. extreme frailty).

Preventative medication

E.g. blood pressure and cholesterol lowering.

- Limited evidence base in older patients—be guided by biological fitness (see p324).
- Ensure the patient understands the rationale for treatment.

2. Are there any contraindications?

- Review past medical history (drug-disease interactions common).
- Contraindications often relative, so a trial of treatment may be indicated, but warn patient, document risk and review impact e.g. ACE inhibitors when there is renal impairment.

3. Are there any likely interactions?

- Review the medication list.
- Computer prescribing assists with drug-drug interactions, automatically flagging up potential problems.

4. What is the best drug?

Choose the broad category of drug (e.g. which antihypertensive) by considering which will work best in this patient (e.g. ACE inhibitors work less well in Afro-Carribeans), which is least likely to cause side effects (e.g. calcium channel blockers may worsen cardiac failure) and is there any potential for dual action? (e.g. a patient with angina could have a β-blocker for both angina and blood pressure control).

Within each category of medication, there are many choices:
- Develop a personal portfolio of drugs with which you are very familiar.
- Hospital formularies will often dictate choices within hospital.
- Cost should be a consideration—e.g. simvastatin is now off patent and likely to be cheaper than a newer statin.
- Pharmaceutical companies will try to convince you of the benefits of a new brand. Unless this is a novel class of drug, it is likely that existing brands have a greater proven safety record with similar benefit. Older patients have greater potential to suffer harm from new drugs, and are unlikely to have been included in clinical trials. Time will tell if there are real advantages—in general stick to what you know.
▶▶ Never be the first, or last of your peers to use a new drug.

5. What dose should be started?
- 'Start low and go slow.'
- Drugs are usually better tolerated at lower doses, and can be optimised if there are no adverse reactions.
- In most cases, benefit is seen with drug initiation, further increments of benefit occurring with dose optimization (e.g. ACE inhibitors for cardiac failure, where 1.25mg ramipril is better than 10mg with a postural drop).
- However, do not under treat—use enough to achieve the therapeutic goal (e.g. for angina prophylaxis, a β-blocker dose should be adequate to induce bradycardia).

6. How will the impact be assessed?
Schedule follow-up looking for:
- Efficacy of the drug e.g. has the bradykinesia improved with a dopamine agonist? Medication for less objective conditions (e.g. pain, cognition) requires careful questioning of patient and family/carers.
- Any adverse events—reported by the patient spontaneously, elicited by direct questioning (e.g. headache with dipyridamole) or by checking blood tests where necessary (e.g. thyroid function on amiodarone).
- Any capacity to increase the dose to improve the effect (e.g. ACE inhibitors in cardiac failure).

7. What is the time frame?
- Many older patients remain on medication for a long time. 88% of all prescriptions in the over 65s are repeats. 60% of prescriptions are active for over 2 years, 30% over 5 years, and 6% over 10 years.
- This may be appropriate (e.g. with antihypertensives) and if so, the patient should be aware of this and seek an ongoing supply from the GP.
- Some drugs should never be prescribed long term e.g. prochlorperazine, night sedation.
- Medication should be regularly reviewed and discontinued if ineffective or no longer indicated e.g. some psychotropic medications (e.g. lithium, depot antipsychotics) were intended for long-term use at initiation, but the patient may have had no psychiatric symptoms for years (or even decades). They can contribute to falls, and cautious withdrawal may be indicated.

Pharmacology in older patients

Administration challenges include:
- Packaging may make tablets hard to access—childproof bottles and tablets in blister packets can be impossible to open with arthritic hands or poor vision.
- Labels may be too small to read with failing vision.
- Tablets may be large and difficult to swallow (e.g. co-amoxiclav) or have an unpleasant taste (e.g. potassium supplements).
- Liquid formulations can be useful, but accurate dosage becomes harder (especially where manual dexterity is compromised).
- Any tablet needs around 60ml of water to wash it down and prevent adherence to the oesophageal mucosa—a large volume for a frail older person. Some tablets (e.g. bisphosphonates) require even larger volumes.
- Multiple tablets, with different instructions (e.g. before/after food) are easily muddled up, or taken in a sub-optimal way.
- Some routes (e.g. topical to back) may be impossible without assistance.

Absorption
- Many factors are different in older patients (increased gastric pH, delayed gastric emptying, reduced intestinal motility and blood flow etc.).
- Despite this, absorption of drugs is largely unchanged with age—exceptions include iron and calcium, which are absorbed more slowly.

Distribution
- Some older people have a very low lean body mass, so if the therapeutic index for a drug is narrow (e.g. digoxin) the dose should be adjusted.
- There is often an increased proportion of fat compared with water. This reduces the volume of distribution for water-soluble drugs giving a higher initial concentration (e.g. digoxin). It also leads to accumulation of fat-soluble drugs, prolonging elimination and effect (e.g. lidocaine, diazepam).
- There is reduced plasma protein binding of drugs with age, which increases the free fraction of protein-bound drugs such as warfarin and furosemide.

Hepatic metabolism
- Specific hepatic metabolic pathways (e.g. conjugation) are unaffected by age.
- Reducing hepatic mass and blood flow can impact on overall function which slows metabolism of drugs e.g. theophylline, paracetamol, diazepam, nifedipine.
- Drugs that undergo extensive first pass metabolism (e.g. propranolol, nitrates) are most affected by the reduced hepatic function.
- Many factors interact with liver metabolism (e.g. nutritional state, acute illness, smoking, other medications etc.).

Renal excretion
- Renal function declines with age (GFR, tubular excretion—see p552), which has a profound impact on the handling of drugs that are predominantly handled renally.
- Drugs, or drugs with active metabolites, that are mainly excreted in the urine include digoxin, gentamicin, lithium, furosemide and tetracyclines.
- Where there is a narrow theraputic index (e.g. digoxin, aminoglycosides) then dose adjustment for renal impairment is required (see UK *BNF* Appendix 3).
- Impaired renal function is exacerbated by dehydration and urinary sepsis—both common in older patients.

Drug sensitivity

Many older patients will have altered sensitivity to some drugs, for example:

- Receptor responses may vary with age. Alterations in the function of the cellular sodium/potassium pumps may account for the increased sensitivity to digoxin seen in older people. Decreased beta adrenoceptor sensitivity means that older patients mount less of a tachycardia when given agonists (e.g. salbutamol) and may become less bradycardic with beta-blockers.
- Altered coagulation factor synthesis with age leads to an increased sensitivity to the effects of warfarin.
- The ageing central nervous system shows increased susceptibility to the effects of many centrally acting drugs (e.g. hypnotics, sedatives, antidepressants, opioid analgesia, antiparkinsonian drugs, and antipsychotics).

Certain adverse reactions are more likely in older people, because of this altered sensitivity:

- Baroreceptor responses are less sensitive, making symptomatic hypotension more likely with antihypertensives.
- Thirst responses are blunted, making hypovolaemia due to diuretics more common.
- Thermoregulation is blunted, making hypothermia more likely with prolonged sedation.
- Allergic responses to drugs are more common because of altered immune responses.

Drugs that may require an adjustment of dose in older patients

Despite the variations in drug handling, most drugs have a wide therapeutic index, and there is no clinical impact.

Only drugs with a narrow therapeutic index or where older patients may show very marked increased sensitivity may require dose alteration:

- ACE inhibitors (pp150–1).
- Aminoglycosides (dose determined by weight, and reduced if impaired renal function).
- Diazepam (start with 2mg dose).
- Digoxin (low body weight older patients rarely require more than 62.5 micrograms maintenance dose (see p299).
- Non-steroidal anti-inflammatory drugs (see p154).
- Opiates (start with 1.25–2.5mg morphine to assess impact on CNS)
- Oral hypoglycaemics (increased sensitivity to hypoglycaemia with decreased awareness—avoid long-acting preparations such as glibenclamide, and start with lower doses of shorter acting drugs e.g. gliclazide 40mg).
- Warfarin (load more cautiously—see pp158–9).

Taking a drug history

An accurate drug history includes the name, dose, timing, duration, and reason for all medication. Studies have suggested that patients will report their drug history accurately around half of the time, and this figure falls with increasing age.

Problems arise because of

- Inadequate information to the patient at the time of prescribing.
- Multiple medications.
- Multiple changes if side effects develop.
- Use of both generic and brand names.
- Variable doses over time (e.g. dopa agonists, ACE inhibitors).
- Cognitive and visual impairment.
- Over the counter drugs.

Useful sources of information

- The patients actual drugs—they will often bring them along in a bag to outpatients or when admitted.
- Many seasoned patients will carry a list of their current medication—written either by them or a healthcare professional.
- Computer-generated print outs of current medication from the GP.
- Dosett and Nomad systems will incorporate information about the medication they contain.
- A telephone call to the GP surgery will yield a list of active prescriptions (but not over the counter medication).
- Family members will often know about medication, especially if they help administer them.
- Medical notes will often contain a list of medication at the last hospital attendance.

These can be extremely useful, but have limitations. A prescription issued does not mean that it was necessarily dispensed, or that the medication is being taken correctly and consistently. Previously prescribed medications may still be being taken and patients may occasionally use other patient's medication (e.g. a spouse).

Good habits

- Every time a patient is seen (in clinic, day hospital, admission etc.) take time to review the medication and make an up-to-date list.
- Begin correspondence with a list of current medication.
- If changes are made, or a new medication tried and not tolerated, document the reason for this, and communicate this to all people involved in care (especially the GP).
- Always include allergies and intolerances in the drug history.

Solutions

1. Take the drug history with meticulous care—ask directly about:
   - Inhalers.
   - Topical medication (creams, eye drops, patches etc.).
   - Occasional use medication.
   - Intermittent use medication (e.g. 3 monthly B12 injections, depot antipsychotics, weekly bisphosphonates etc.).
   - Over the counter medication (a growing number of drugs are available to buy this way, including proton pump inhibitors and statins).
   - Herbal and traditional remedies.
2. Clarify how often occasional use medication is taken—analgesia may be used very regularly, or not at all.
3. Be non-judgmental. If you suspect poor concordance (e.g. blood pressure failing to settle despite multiple prescriptions) then the following questions can be useful to elicit an accurate response:
   - 'Have you managed to take all those tablets I suggested?'
   - 'Which tablets do you find useful?'
   - 'Do any of the tablets disagree with you?'—if yes, then 'how often do you manage to take it?'
   - 'What triggers you to remember?' (e.g. take with each meal, leave by toothbrush etc.).
4. Scrutinize computer-generated lists carefully. Remember to look at when the prescription was last issued and estimate when they would be due to run out (e.g. 28 tablets to be taken once a day, last issued 3 months ago means that the drug has either run out, or not been taken regularly).
5. The gold standard is to ask the patient to bring in all of the medication that they have at home—both old and new. Go through each medication and ask them to explain which they take, and how often. This allows:
   - Comparison with a list of medication that they are supposed to be taking.
   - Old drugs to be discarded (if necessary retain them and return to pharmacy).
   - Concordance to be estimated (by looking at date of dispensing and number of tablets left).
   - Clarification of doses, timings, and rationale for treatment. In a less pressured setting (e.g. day hospital) it is useful to generate a list for the patient to carry with them (see p147 for example).
   - Education of patient and family where needed (e.g. reason for taking).

HOW TO... improve concordance

Simplify prescription regimes

- Convert to once a day dosing where possible (e.g. change captopril tds to ramipril od).
- Try to prescribe medications to be taken at the same time of day—this may challenge firmly held views (e.g. warfarin must be taken at night).
- Try to use medications that have dual indications for the patient (e.g. beta blockade for both hypertension and angina).
- Consider a daily dose reminder system (e.g. Dosett box) or a monitored dosage system (e.g. Nomad).

Educate the patient and family

- Do they understand the reason for taking the medication, and how to take it correctly? Are there any problems the patient is attributing to the medication (perhaps incorrectly)?
- Medication summaries (see example opposite) can assist with this.
- Warn of predictable side effects that are likely to pass (e.g. nausea with citalopram, headache with dipyridamole).
- Promote personal responsibility for medication—this should not be something that the patient feels has been imposed.
- Enlist support of family and carers in monitoring.

Monitor

- Check tablet boxes and see if they are gone.
- Look at how often a repeat prescription has been requested.
- Some medications can have serum levels checked (e.g. digoxin, phenytoin, lithium).

Some medications will produce changes detectable at physical examination (e.g. bradycardia with beta blockade, black stool with iron therapy).

Example of a patient drug summary sheet

Medication	Brand name	Reason	Dose	Morning	Lunch	Evening	Duration
Aspirin		Thin blood, prevent heart attack	75mg	√			Lifelong
Simvastatin	Zocor	Lower cholesterol Prevent heart attack	40mg			√	Lifelong
Ramipril	Tritace	Lower blood pressure Prevent heart attack	5mg			√	Lifelong
Atenolol	Tenormin	Lower blood pressure, Prevent angina attacks	50mg	√			Lifelong
Isosorbide mononitrate	Ismo	Prevent angina attacks	20mg	√	√		Lifelong
GTN spray		Treat angina	1 puff				As needed
Amoxicillin	Amoxil	Antibiotic for chest infection	500mg	√	√	√	7 days

Adverse drug reactions

More common and complex with increasing age—up to 3 times more frequent in the over 80s. Drug reactions account for considerable morbidity, mortality, and hospital admissions (one study estimated a quarter of US hospital admissions relate to medication complications).

Older people are not a homogeneous group, and many will tolerate medications as well as younger ones, but a number of factors contribute to the increased frequency:

- Altered drug handling and sensitivity occur with age, made worse by poor appetite, nutrition and fluid intake.
- Frailty and multiple diseases make drug-disease interactions more common, for example:
  - Anticholinergics may precipitate retention in a patient with prostatic hypertrophy.
  - Benzodiazepines may precipitate delirium in a patient with dementia.
- These relationships become even more complex when the large numbers of drugs that are prescribed for multiple conditions interact with the diseases as well as each other e.g. an osteoporotic patient is prescribed a bisphosphonate, then sustains a vertebral crush fracture and is given a non-steroidal which exacerbates gastric irritation and causes a gastrointestinal bleed.
- Errors in drug taking make adverse reactions more likely. Mistakes increase with:
  - Increasing age.
  - Increasing numbers of prescribed drugs (20% of patients taking 3 drugs will make errors, rising to 95% when 10 or more drugs are taken).
  - Cognitive impairment.
  - Living alone.

Strategies to minimize adverse drug reactions

- Prescribe sensibly—see pp138–9.
- Consider possible drug-drug and drug-disease interactions whenever a new drug is started.
- For every new problem, consider if an existing medication could be the cause. Try to avoid the so-called **prescribing cascade**, where side effects are treated with a new prescription, rather than discontinuing the offending drug. If multiple medications are possible culprits then stop one at a time and watch for improvement.
- Optimize concordance (see p146).

HOW TO... manage drug-induced skin rashes

Common side effect in older patients—thought to be due to altered immune function. Rarely life threatening, but cause considerable distress.

Make the diagnosis

- Variable in appearance, but most commonly toxic erythema—symmetrical, erythematous, itchy rash, trunk > extremities, lesions may be measles-like, urticarial, or resemble erythema multiforme.
- Certain drugs may produce predictable eruptions:
  - Acneiform rash with lithium.
  - Bullous lesions with furosemide.
  - Target lesions with penicillins and phenytoin.
  - Psoriasis-like rash with beta-blockers.
  - Urticaria with penicillin, opiates and aspirin.
  - Fixed drug eruption (round purple plaques recurring in the same spot) with paracetamol, laxatives, sulphonamides and tetracyclines.
- Toxic epidermal necrolysis is a rare, serious reaction to drugs such as non-steroidals, allopurinol and phenytoin. The skin appears scalded, and large areas of epidermis may shear off causing problems with fluid and electrolyte balance, thermoregulation and infection.
- Take a careful drug history to elicit a temporal relationship to medication administration—e.g. within 3 days of starting a new drug (may be as long as 3 weeks), or becoming worse every morning after a regular drug is given.

Stop the drug

- Stop multiple medications one at a time (stop drugs started closest to the onset of the rash first), and watch for clinical improvement.
- May get slightly worse before improving.
- Usually clears within 2 weeks.
- Advise the patient to avoid the drug in the future.

Soothe the skin

- Emollients, cooling agents like calamine and topical steroids may help.
- Oral antihistamines are often given with variable success. Sedating antihistamines (e.g. hydroxyzine 25mg) may help sleep.

Treat the complications

More likely if extensive and prolonged.
Risks include:
- Hypothermia
- Hypovolaemia
- Secondary infection.

▶▶ Consider dermatology referral if not improving after 2 weeks off the suspected drug.

ACE inhibitors

Common indications include blood pressure control, vascular risk reduction, heart failure, and diabetic nephropathy.

Cautions

Renal disease

- Use ACE inhibitors with extreme caution if there is a known history of renal artery stenosis, as renal failure can be precipitated. If the clinical suspicion of this is high (renal bruit, uncontrolled hypertension that is unexplained) then consider investigating for renal asymmetry with an ultrasound before starting treatment.
- Renal impairment per se is not a reason to withhold ACE inhibitors (indeed they are effective treatment for some types) although the dose may need to be reduced.
- Monitor renal function before and after treatment (see opposite). Sudden deterioration may indicate renal artery stenosis, and the ACE should be stopped pending investigation.
- If a patient becomes unwell (dehydrated, septic etc.) they may need temporary withdrawal of the ACE inhibitor (see box opposite).

Hypotension

- Early ACE inhibitors (e.g. Captopril) were associated with a risk of first dose hypotension, and so many patients were given an in-hospital test dose.
- This is rare with newer ACE inhibitors, and cautious outpatient initiation is acceptable (see box opposite).
- Older patients are more prone to postural hypotension. Check blood pressure lying and standing, and ask about postural symptoms (e.g. light-headedness).
- The risk of hypotension is greater with volume-depleted patients— e.g. those on high dose diuretics, on renal dialysis, dehydrated from intercurrent illness or in severe cardiac failure. Correct dehydration before initiation where possible.
- ACE induced Hypotension is common in patients with severe aortic stenosis, and should probably be avoided (unless under cardiological supervision).
- 'Start low, and go slow'. Monitor carefully. This may take multiple clinic visits, but avoids complications.

Cough

- Many ACE inhibitors cause a persistent dry cough. Always warn the patient about this, as it can cause considerable distress. Forewarned is forearmed, and many patients will be prepared to accept this side effect if the ACE inhibitor is the best choice for them.
- Changing to an angiotensin receptor blocker (ARB) removes the cough in most cases, but there is increasing evidence that these are not equivalent drugs in terms of risk reduction.

Hyperkalaemia
- There is a risk of hyperkalaemia when ACE inhibitors are used with potassium-sparing diuretics e.g. spironolactone (in heart failure) or with non-steroidals.
- Be aware, and monitor electrolytes. Most tolerate a potassium of up to 5.5mmol/L.
- The tendency to hyperkalaemia can be useful in patients who are also on potassium-losing diuretics (e.g. furosemide) as the two may balance each other out—overall hypokalaemia is more common in patients with cardiac failure.

HOW TO... start ACE inhibitors

Screen for contraindications (see opposite).
Check baseline renal function and electrolytes.
Warn patient about possible cough and postural symptoms.

An example of initiation/titration is as follows:

Week 1
Start ramipril 1.25mg at night.

Week 2
Check renal function, blood pressure (lying and standing) and check for postural symptoms.

Week 4
Increase ramipril to 2.5mg at night.

Week 6
Check renal function, blood pressure (lying and standing) and check for postural symptoms.

Week 8
Increase ramipril to 5mg at night.

Continue titrating the dose upwards as tolerated, but most older patients will develop postural symptoms at higher doses, increasing the risk of falls. The goal should be for safe optimization.

Once established on an ACE inhibitor, periodic renal monitoring is sensible (perhaps annually).

If a patient becomes acutely unwell
- Dehydration increases susceptibility to ACE induced renal failure and hypotension.
- Correct the dehydration first—treat cause, give fluid supplementation, and stop diuretics.
- Temporary cessation of ACE may be needed if dehydration prolonged (>24 hours).
- Monitor renal function daily.
- Remember to restart the ACE after recovery.

Amiodarone

Indications include rate control and prevention of supraventricular cardiac arrhythmias (commonly atrial fibrillation) and prevention of paroxysmal ventricular arrhythmias.

Intravenous amiodarone is now included on the Advanced Life Support protocols for cardiac arrest (www.resus.org.uk).

Cautions

- Interacts with many drugs, including warfarin, which is often co-prescribed for AF stroke prophylaxis. A steady state will be reached if both drugs are taken regularly, but careful INR monitoring is needed with initiation.
- Can cause deranged thyroid function tests in either direction. Baseline thyroid function should be taken before initiation and then at six monthly intervals. Measure TSH, free T4 and free T3—see box. opposite.
- Photosensitivity can occur, so amiodarone is unlikely to be suitable for avid gardeners or outdoor workers.
- Corneal microdeposits often occur, that can cause a glare with night driving—if this is likely to be a problem then avoid the medication. These are reversible.
- Liver function can become deranged—check at baseline and every six months.
- Pulmonary problems may occur (fibrosis, alveolitis, pneumonitis) and any new respiratory symptoms on treatment should trigger a chest X-ray.
- Peripheral neuropathy may occur—be alert for early signs of this and stop the drug promptly to avoid progression.

Starting oral amiodarone

1. Check thyroid and liver function tests.
2. Load with:
   - Week one—200mg tds.
   - Week two—200mg bd.
3. From week three onwards use the maintenance dose of 200mg od.
4. See the patient at six–eight weeks to check for adverse effects and efficacy.
5. In the longer term, the dose may be reduced further in frail older patients to 100mg od (or even alternate days) without losing efficacy.

Despite this long list of side effects, amiodarone is often well-tolerated and effective in older patients, and is less negatively inotropic than many of the alternatives—do not be put off.

HOW TO... **manage amiodarone-induced thyroid dysfunction**

Amiodarone contains 37% iodide, which impacts on thyroid homeostasis, causing alterations in thyroid function tests in up to 50% of patients.

Early amiodarone changes:

- Alterations in thyroid function tests in a euthyroid patient most common.
- Usually high thyroid stimulating hormone (TSH) or decreased thyroxine (T4) concentrations.
- This is typically transient, resolves after about three months and does not indicate that hypothyroidism has occured.
- Monitor at three monthly intervals.

Changes with longer-term amiodarone therapy include:

Euthyroid changes

- Minor increase in T4.
- Suppression of triiodothyronine (T3).
- Suppression of TSH.
- Manage by monitoring thyroid function every 6 months.

Hyperthyroidism

- More common when there is occult underlying thyroid disease and in areas with low oral iodine intake (up to 12% incidence).
- Diagnose with increased free T3 and free T4 with suppressed TSH concentrations.
- Patients on amiodarone may be apparently euthyroid with a low TSH and high T4. ▶▶ Always check T3 as well.
- Withdraw amiodarone where possible.
- No immediate improvement as amiodarone has a long half-life.
- Where amiodarone needs to be continued, this can be treated with carbimazole as for standard hyperthyroidism. May be resistant. Adding steroids may help.
- Amiodarone can also cause a destructive thyroiditis, releasing thyroid hormone into the circulation and causing hyperthyroidism. Treatment is with high dose steroids.

Hypothyroidism

- More common in areas with low iodine intake (up to 13% incidence).
- Diagnose with decreased free T3 and free T4 concentrations with elevated TSH concentrations.
- An elevated TSH alone is not diagnostic—may be transient, especially in the first three months of treatment. If the patient is well, recheck in 3 months.
- Amiodarone withdrawal is rarely necessary. Adding levothyroxine sodium will correct the problem.

Analgesia in older patients

Older patients are more likely to suffer chronic pain than younger ones, owing to the increased frequency of conditions such as osteoarthritis, osteoporosis etc.

Pain management is more challenging and a standard 'pain ladder' approach not always useful because of the altered sensitivity of the older patient to certain classes of analgesic medication.

Non-steroidal anti-inflammatory drugs (NSAIDs)

Includes aspirin (especially at analgesic doses).

Potential problems

- Fluid retention causing worsening hypertension, cardiac failure and ankle swelling.
- Renal toxicity—risk of acute tubular necrosis, exacerbated by intercurrent infection or dehydration.
- Peptic ulceration and gastrointestinal bleeding—there is an increased risk with increased age, and the bleeds tend to be more significant.
▶▶ The number of older patients requiring hospitalization because of NSAID-induced deterioration in renal or cardiac function actually exceeds the number with GI bleeds.
- Age itself is probably not an independent risk factor for most complications of NSAID treatment, but factors such as co morbidities, co medications, hydration, nutritional status and frailty are linked to an increased risk, all of which are more common with advancing age.

Guidance for use in older patients

- NSAIDs should be used with extreme caution in older patients, and avoided altogether in the very frail.
- Should be given for a short period only.
- Use low-dose, moderate potency NSAIDs (e.g. Ibuprofen 1.2g daily).
- Never use two NSAIDs together (this includes aspirin 75mg).
- Consider co-prescription of a gastric protective agent (e.g. Omeprazole) for the duration of the therapy.
- Avoid using ACE inhibitors and NSAIDs together—they have opposing effects on fluid handling, and are likely to cause renal toxicity in combination.

Opioid analgesia

Wide range of drugs sharing many common features, but with qualitative and quantitative differences.

Potential problems include constipation, nausea and vomiting, confusion, drowsiness and respiratory depression.

Guidance for use in older patients

- Most of these are dose dependant, and careful up-titration will obtain the right balance of analgesic effect and adverse effects.
- Constipation is common (worse in older people) but can be managed with good bowel care (p397).
- Most adverse effects are reversible once the medication is reduced or discontinued.

HOW TO... manage pain in older patients

Diagnose the cause

Chronic abdominal pain may be due to constipation that will respond to bowel care rather than analgesia.

Consider non-drug measures

- Weight loss and physical activity helps with many pains (e.g. arthritis).
- Temperature treatments (e.g. hot/cold packs applied to painful joint).
- TENS machines.
- Alternative therapies (e.g. acupuncture, aromatherapy) can help.
- Avoidance of (non essential) activity that provokes pain if possible.

Consider targeted therapy

E.g. Topical capsaicin for post-herpetic neuralgia, local nerve blocks for regional pain, massage for musculoskeletal pain, joint replacement for arthritic pain or radiotherapy for pain from bony metastases.

Regular paracetamol

- Well-tolerated and with few side effects.
- Before moving from this, ensure that the maximum dose is being taken regularly (i.e. 1g taken four times a day) for optimal analgesic effect. Many patients will find taking an occasional paracetamol ineffective—explain that regular dosing increases analgesic effect.

Opioid analgesia

- Second line therapy in most older patients.
- Options to deal with mild (e.g. codeine, dihydrocodeine), moderate (e.g. tramadol) and severe pain (e.g. morphine, diamorphine, fentanyl).
- Compound preparations are useful when adding an opioid to regular paracetamol, as it limits the number of tablets taken. Co-codamol (codeine and paracetamol) has variable doses of codeine (8mg, 15mg, or 30mg per tablet) allowing up titration of the opioid component.
- All affect same receptors, so use as a continuum—if regular maximum dose codeine is not working, then step up to the next level of opioid strength (e.g. if 60mg codeine qds is not sufficient then change to tramadol 50mg qds or MST 5mg bd).
- Various formulations for the delivery of strong opiates. Liquids are useful if there are swallowing problems (e.g. oramorph). Slow release tablets (e.g. MST) and transdermal patches (e.g. fentanyl) provide constant analgesic effect for continuous pain. Parenteral opiates are used in terminal care (subcutaneous injections of morphine and diamorphine for intermittent pain; 24-hour infusion pumps for constant pain.
- Monitor for side effects—active bowel care with initiation.

Other drug options

- Very fit older patients can be given short courses of NSAIDs.
- COX-II inhibitors have a limited role.

Psychological factors

- Depression is often coexistent (consequent or causal). Treatment can help with overall pain management.
- Positive mental attitude and learning to live with a degree of discomfort may be preferable to side effects of analgesic medication.

Steroids

Oral steroids (usually prednisolone) are given for many conditions in older patients, commonly COPD exacerbations, polymyalgia rheumatica, rheumatoid arthritis and colitis. Treatment may be long-term, and although the benefits of treatment usually outweigh the risks, awareness of these can often minimize harm.

Cautions

- **Osteoporosis**—this is most marked in the early stages of treatment. Older people will have diminishing bone reserves anyhow, and there is a strong argument for putting all steroid-treated older patients on bone protection at outset, unless the course is certain to be very short (less than 2 weeks, say). This should consist of daily calcium and vitamin D, along with a bisphosphonate (weekly preparations e.g. alendronate 70mg, improve concordance).
- Steroids can precipitate **impaired glucose tolerance or frank diabetes**. Monitor sugar levels periodically (perhaps weekly finger-prick tests, or urine dipstick) in all steroid users. They will also worsen the sugar control in known diabetics, necessitating more frequent monitoring.
- **Hypertension** may develop because of the mineralocorticoid effect of prednisolone, and this should be checked for regularly.
- **Skin changes** occur, and are particularly noticeable in older patients with less resilient skin. Purpura, bruising, thinning, and increased fragility are common.
- **Muscle weakness** occurs with prolonged use, dominantly proximal in distribution. This leads to problems rising from chairs, climbing stairs etc. and may be the final straw for a frail older person with limited physical reserve.
- There is an **increased susceptibility to infections** on steroids, and the presentation may be less acute, making diagnosis harder. Candidiasis (oral and genital) is particularly common and should be treated promptly (see p640).
- High doses (as used in treatment of giant cell arteritis) can cause **acute confusional states**, and older people are particularly prone. As treatment is often initiated as an outpatient, be sure to warn the patient and carers of this.
- **Cataracts** may develop with long-term steroid use. If vision declines, look for cataracts with an ophthalmoscope and consider referral to an ophthalmologist.
- **Peritonitis may be masked** by steroid use—the signs being less evident clinically. Remember to have a higher index of suspicion of occult perforation in a steroid-treated older patient with abdominal pain. There is also a weak association between steroid use and peptic ulceration.
- Adrenocortical suppression means that the **stress response will be diminished** in chronic steroid users. If such a patient becomes acutely unwell (e.g. septic), the exogenous steroid dose will need to be temporarily increased (e.g. double the usual oral dose, replace with intramuscular hydrocortisone if unable to take by mouth).

Stopping treatment

Many patients are on fairly low doses of steroids for a long period. It can be difficult to completely tail the dose, as steroid withdrawal effects (fevers, myalgia etc.) can often be mistaken for disease recurrence, and this often needs to be done very slowly (perhaps reducing by as little as 1mg a month). There is no such thing as a 'safe' dose of steroid, so for every patient you see on steroids, ask the following:

- Can the dose be reduced?
- Could a steroid sparing agent (e.g. azathioprine) be used instead?
- Is the patient taking adequate bone protection?
- What is the blood pressure and blood glucose?

Warfarin

Common indications range from absolute (pulmonary embolus, deep vein thrombosis, artificial heart valve replacement) to relative (stroke prophylaxis in atrial fibrillation).

Cautions

- Risk is higher if the patient is unable to take medication accurately—not suitable without supervision for cognitively impaired patients, or those who self-neglect. If there is an absolute indication, then consider supervised therapy (by spouse, family, or carers via a dispensing system) or (rarely) a course of low molecular weight heparin instead.
- Risk is also higher if there is a high probability of trauma e.g. recurrent falls. Warfarin may be inappropriate.
- GPs will often be good judges of risk—consider discussing borderline cases.
- Bleeding is the major adverse event, ranging from an increased tendency to bruise to major life-threatening bleeds. The most significant include intracerebral haemorrhage and GI blood loss. Warfarin does not cause gastric irritation, but may accelerate blood loss from pre-existing bleeding sources. Ask carefully about history of non-steroidal use (including aspirin) and GI symptoms (indigestion, heartburn, weight loss, abdominal pain, altered bowel habit, rectal bleeding etc.). If any are present then quantify risk with further testing—full blood count and iron studies might indicate occult blood loss. If the warfarin is not essential, then a full GI work-up may be appropriate before starting in the fitter patients. In frailer patients, consider warfarin with empirical proton pump inhibitor.
- Nosebleeds are common in older patients, and may become more significant on warfarin. Often due to friable nasal vessels that are amenable to treatment by ENT surgeons, so reducing the risk of epistaxis on warfarin.
- Co-morbidity may increase sensitivity to warfarin (e.g. abnormal liver function) and should be screened for if there is suspicion.

Usual targets

Indication	Target	Duration
Atrial fibrillation	2.5	Lifelong
Venous thromboembolism	2.5	Varies. Usually 6 months. Lifelong if recurrent or with ongoing precipitant (e.g. malignancy)
Recurrent venous thrombo-embolism whilst on warfarin	3.5	Lifelong
Mechanical prosthetic heart valves	3.5	Lifelong

What to do when the INR is too high

- If there is no sign of bleeding, then simply stop the warfarin and monitor the INR as it falls. Do not give vitamin K at this point, as anticoagulation will be difficult for weeks afterwards.
- Always look for the reason why the INR became elevated and correct this factor.
- If there is bleeding, then the warfarin needs reversing with vitamin K (5mg slow iv injection) and fresh frozen plasma.

Further reading

British National Formulary. Oral anticoagulants section, www.bnf.org.

HOW TO... initiate warfarin

Discuss risks and benefits of treatment with the patient—the indication is rarely absolute. See p301 for an example.

Ensure the patient is told:

- There will be frequent blood tests and monitoring.
- Many medications interact with warfarin, so before taking any new medication (including over the counter) always check compatibility with the doctor, dentist or pharmacist.
- Use paracetamol or codeine-based analgesia (never NSAIDs).
- Alcohol interacts with warfarin metabolism, and should be taken in moderation and on a regular basis (avoid binge drinking).
- If trauma occurs, bleeding may last longer. Apply pressure to wounds and seek medical help if it does not stop.
- Give the patient an anticoagulant treatment book (see *BNF* for stockists) that will hold details of their treatment schedule and reinforce information that you give them.

Induction

- Check baseline clotting.
- Prescribe warfarin to be taken at 6pm.
- Medical notes should state indication, target INR and duration of therapy.
- The normal adult induction dose (10mg day one, 10mg day two then an INR) is rarely appropriate in older patients who are more sensitive to its effects.
- Reduce the dose if the patient is frail, has a low body weight, has multiple co-morbidities, or a deranged baseline clotting.
- For most older patients 5mg /5mg /INR is a safer approach.
- If there are multiple factors causing concern, then 5mg /INR is better.
  ▶▶ There is no rush. If the indication is absolute, then the patient should also be on therapeutic heparin until the INR is in range. It is much easier to increase the dose of warfarin, than to deal with bleeding from an overdose.
- The INR will then need checking daily, then alternate days until a pattern becomes clear. (See *Oxford Handbook of Clinical Medicine*, 6th edn, Oxford University Press, 2004 for example of dosing).
- Many haematology departments will offer automatic dosing with a schedule for retesting.
- The INR testing can gradually be done less frequently, stretching to 12 weekly in long term users.

Breaking the rules

Much prescribing in geriatric practice relies on individually tailored assessment and pragmatic decision-making. Whilst much of what is described in the preceding pages is appropriate for many, there are always times when the rules must be broken in the best interests of the individual patient. This requires experience, and the patient should always be followed-up to assess the impact of the decision.

Polypharmacy causes problems, but is not always universally regarded as bad—depriving patients of beneficial treatments because they are old, or already on multiple other medications is also wrong. In a recent study of medication changes during a geriatric admission, the total number of drugs was the same at admission and discharge, but they had often been changed. In other words, there was active evaluation of medication going on—the goal being not just to limit the number of drugs, but also to optimize and individually tailor treatment.

Where side effects are very likely, but the drug is definitely indicated, then it may be appropriate to co-prescribe something to treat the expected adverse effect, for example:
- Steroids and bisphosphonates.
- Opiates and laxatives.
- Furosemide and a potassium sparing diuretic (or an ACE inhibitor).
- Non-steroidals and a gastric protection agent.

Whilst certain disease drug interactions are very likely, and should be avoided, others may be an acceptable risk. For example:
- Beta-blockers are to be used with caution with asthma, yet they have such a good impact with on cardiovascular risk reduction that these cautions should not be absolute. Often the 'asthma' is in fact COPD with little beta-receptor reactivity, so cautious beta-blockade initiated in hospital whilst monitoring the lung function may be appropriate.
- Diabetics often have cardiovascular disease and the risk of beta-blockade is usually outweighed by the benefits.
- The risk of beta-blockers in peripheral vascular disease is a modest reduction in walking distance, reversible on stopping the drug. This is often outweighed by the reduction in risk of cardiac death.
- Fludrocortisone (for postural drop) will worsen hypertension and cause ankle swelling, yet if the postural drop is so profound that the patient cannot mobilize then it may be appropriate to accept the hypertension and associated risk.
- Amlodipine may worsen ankle swelling in a patient with chronic venous insufficiency, but if this is the best way of controlling hypertension, it may be appropriate to accept a cosmetic problem.

Neurology

The ageing brain and nervous system 164
Tremor 166
Neuralgia 168
Parkinson's disease (PD) 170
   How to... treat challenging symptoms in
   Parkinson's disease 172
Diseases masquerading as Parkinson's disease 174
Epilepsy 176
Epilepsy: drug treatment 178
Neuroleptic malignant syndrome (NMS) 180
Motor neuron disease 182
Peripheral neuropathies 184
Subdural haematoma 186
Sleep and insomnia 188
   How to... use benzodiazepines (BZ) for insomnia 189
Other sleep disorders 190

The ageing brain and nervous system

As in other systems, intrinsic ageing (occurs in all) is often hard to distinguish from extrinsic ageing mechanisms (caused by disease processes). See p220 for discussion of cognitive ageing.

Histological changes in the brain include:

- Each neuron has fewer connecting arms (dendrites).
- Around 30% of brain cells are lost by the age of 80.
- There is deposition of pigment (lipofuscin) in the cells and amyloid in the vessels.
- The presence of senile plaques and neurofibrillary tangles does increase with age but they are not diagnostic of dementia.

Age-related change	Consequences
Loss of neurons (cannot be regenerated) Decrease in brain weight (by around 10% at age 80)	Cerebral atrophy common on brain scans (although this doesn't correlate well with cognitive function)
Some neurons become demyelinated and have slowed nerve conduction speed and increased latency (time taken to recover before transmitting next impulse)	Reflexes which have long nerve tracts (e.g. ankle jerks) can be diminished or lost Minor sensory loss e.g. fine touch/vibration sense may be lost distally
Neurotransmitter systems alter (e.g. cholinergic receptors decrease)	Increased susceptibility to some neuromodulating drugs
Increasing frequency of periventricular white matter changes seen on cerebral imaging	Probably not a normal finding Significance unclear—assumed to be representative of small vessel vascular disease but poor post-mortem correlation

Tremor

Tremor is commoner with increasing age. It can be disabling and/or socially embarrassing.

▶▶ It is important to try to make a diagnosis as treatment is available in some cases.

Examine the patient first at rest (relaxed with arms supported on lap) then with outstretched hands and finally during movement (pointing or picking up a small object). Tremors fall roughly into three categories:

1. **Rest tremor**—disappears on movement and is exaggerated by movement of the contralateral side of the body. Commonest cause is Parkinson's disease.
2. **Postural tremor**—present in outstretched limbs, may continue during action but disappears at rest. Commonest cause is benign essential tremor.
3. **Action tremor**—exaggerated with movement. When tremor is maximal at extreme point of movement called an intention tremor. Commonest cause is cerebellar dysfunction.

Benign essential tremor

- The classic postural tremor of old age, worse on action (e.g. static at rest but spills tea from teacup) may have head nodding (titubation) or jaw/vocal tremor, legs rarely affected. May be asymmetrical.
- About half of cases have a family history (autosomal dominant).
- Presents in middle age, occasionally earlier and worsens gradually.
- Often more socially embarrassing than physically impairing.
- Improved by alcohol, primidone, and beta-blockers but these are often unacceptable treatments in the long-term. It is worth considering beta-blockers as a first choice in treatment of other conditions such as hypertension where benign essential tremor is a symptom.

Parkinson's disease (see p170)

Cerebellar dysfunction

The typical intention tremor is associated with ataxia.

- **Acute** onset is usually vascular in the elderly.
- **Sub-acute** presentations occur with tumours (including paraneoplastic syndrome), abscesses, hydrocephalus, drugs (e.g. anticonvulsants), hypothyroidism, or toxins.
- **Chronic** progressive course is seen with:
  - Alcoholism (due to thiamine deficiency—always give thiamine 100mg od orally or iv preparation if in doubt, it might be reversible).
  - Anticonvulsant (e.g. phenytoin—may be irreversible if severe, commoner with high plasma levels but can occur with longterm use at therapeutic levels).
  - Paraneoplastic syndromes (e.g. ovary anti-Yo, bronchus anti-Hu) anti-cerebellar antibodies can be found.
  - Multiple sclerosis.
  - Idiopathic cerebellar atrophy.
  - Many cases defy specific diagnosis. Consider multisystem atrophy (p174).

Other causes of tremor

Diagnosis	Recognition and characteristics	Management
Thyrotoxicosis	Fine resting tremor This is actually commoner in younger patients	See p472
Rigors	Sudden onset coarse tremor with associated malaise and fever	Diagnose and treat underlying cause
Asterixis (tremor and incoordination) with hepatic, renal or respiratory failure	Coarse postural tremor in a sick patient with physiological disturbance A less dramatic, often fine, tremor can occur with metabolic disturbance such as hypoglycaemia or hypocalcaemia	Diagnose and treat underlying condition
Withdrawal of drugs e.g. alcohol, benzodiazepines, SSRIs, barbiturates	Always consider when patient develops tremor ± confusion soon after admission	For alcohol consider sedation with e.g. chlordiazepoxide 5mg tds and thiamine 100mg od or iv forms For therapeutic drugs recommence and consider gradual controlled withdrawal at later date
Drug side effects e.g. lithium, anticonvulsants		Check serum levels are in therapeutic range. Consider a different agent
Anxiety/stress—increased sympathomimetic activity	Fine tremor	Rarely necessary to consider beta-blockers
Orthostatic tremor—rare, benign postural tremor of legs	Fine tremor of legs on standing diminished by walking/sitting. Can palpate muscle tremor in legs. Patient feels unsteady but rarely falls	Provide perching stools etc. to avoid standing for long

Neuralgia

This describes pain originating from nerve damage/inflammation. It is often very severe and debilitating and seems to be commoner in the elderly. The pain is usually sharp/stabbing and is often intermittent being precipitated by things like movement and cold. Traditional analgesics (paracetamol, NSAIDS, opiates) are not very effective and there is a long list of 'neuromodulating' drugs which may give superior pain control but often have important side effects (mainly sedation). Non-pharmacological treatments such as TENS (transcutaneous nerve stimulation) can be helpful.

Post-herpetic neuralgia

Severe burning and stabbing pain in a division of nerve previously affected by shingles (p687). Pain may be triggered by touch or temperature change. Shingles and subsequent persisting neuralgia is much commoner in the elderly, it can go on for years, be difficult to treat and have major impact on quality of life.

Prevention: start antiviral therapy within 72 hours of rash (e.g. famciclovir 250mg tds)

Treatment: low dose (5–10mg nocte) amitriptyline should be introduced early on if pain persists after rash has healed. Topical lignocaine or capsaicin ointments. Other drugs worth trying include gabapentin, carbamazepine, and valproate but side effects may be unacceptable; start with low doses and increase slowly. Referral to pain clinic is warranted if pain control is difficult, they may try nerve blocks or thermocoagulation.

Trigeminal neuralgia

Causes unilateral severe stabbing facial pain, usually V2, V3 rather then V1. Triggers include movement, temperature change etc. Time course—years with relapse/remission. Depression and weight loss can result. Differential diagnoses include temporal arteritis, toothache, parotitis, and temporomandibular joint arthritis. Consider neuroimaging esp. if there are physical signs i.e. sensory loss or other cranial nerve abnormality suggestive of secondary trigeminal neuralgia. Bilateral trigeminal neuralgia suggests multiple sclerosis.

Treatment: as for post herpetic neuralgia.

Neuralgia can also occur with
- Malignancy
- Cord compression
- Neuropathy.

Parkinson's disease (PD)

A common idiopathic disease, (prevalence 150/100,000) associated with inadequate dopamine neurotransmitter in brainstem. There is loss of neurons and Lewy body formation in the substantia nigra. The clinical syndrome is distinct from Lewy Body dementia (p230) but there is overlap in some pathological and clinical findings leading to suggestions they might turn out to be related conditions.

The clinical diagnosis of PD is based on:
- **Bradykinesia** (slow to initiate and carry out movements, expressionless face, fatigability of repetitive movement)
- **Rigidity** (cogwheeling = tremor superimposed on rigidity)
- **Tremor** ('pin rolling' of hands—worse at rest)
- **Postural instability**.

Other clinical features:
- Usually an asymmetrical disease.
- Autonomic features (e.g. postural hypotension, dribbling, and constipation) are late but common in the elderly.
- No pyramidal or cerebellar signs but reflexes are sometimes brisk.
- Dementia and hallucinations can occur in late stages but drug side-effects can case similar problems.
- Dysphagia can lead to nutrition and swallowing problems.

Investigations

Diagnosis is clinical, but a trial of dopamine supplementation with quantified parameters (e.g. 2 min walking distance, sit-to-stand time, tapping or bead transferring test) before and after treatment period can aid diagnosis and help titrate dopamine treatment.

Brain imaging (e.g. CT) can be used to exclude other conditions that may mimic PD (e.g. vascular disease). Functional imaging scans are becoming more widely used to assist diagnosis.

Treatment

Drugs

There is controversy about ideal drug treatment strategy—a large trial (PD MED) will finish recruiting in 2005 and, when results are in, will hopefully clarify cost-effectiveness of different treatment regimens. In the meantime start treatment with one of:
- **Levodopa plus decarboxylase inhibitor** (prevents peripheral breakdown of drug) (Madopar®/Sinemet®). Start low (e.g. 62.5mg tds) and titrate to symptoms.
- **Dopamine agonists** (ropinirole, pergolide, cabergoline). Psychiatric side effects (confusion, hallucinations), postural hypotension and nausea often limit therapy.
- **Monoamine oxidase inhibitor**—selegiline. Early trials seemed to show increased mortality in mild PD when in combination with levodopa (cf levodopa alone) so use alone or late in disease. New buccally absorbed preparation is better tolerated and useful in swallowing difficulties.

With time you may need to increase dose or add a second agent from above list or try:

- **COMT inhibitor** (entacapone). Will smooth fluctuations in plasma levodopa concentrations. Give with each levodopa dose—sometimes will need levodopa dose decrease. Stains urine orange.
- **Amantidine**—weak dopamine agonist which can reduce dyskinetic problems.
- **Apomorphine**—s/c injections. Specialist treatment—rarely useful in the elderly except to cover periods of nil by mouth.

NB **Anticholinergics** (benzhexol, orphenadrine) are mild anti-Parkinsonian drugs rarely useful in elderly due to severe psychiatric side effects. They do have a beneficial effect on tremor and are possibly the drug of choice where tremor is more of a problem than bradykinesia.

Psychiatric features (e.g. hallucinations) can often be decreased by reducing dopaminergic therapy. Where this fails, or is intolerable, some patients may respond to antipsychotics such as quetiapine or olanzapine. If features suggest Lewy Body dementia a trial of anticholinesterases (Aricept®) may be warranted.

Surgery

Ablation (e.g. pallidotomy) and stimulation (electrode implants) used in highly selected populations. Older patients often excluded due to high operative risk.

Other therapeutic options

- Patients and carers benefit from regular review by a specialist doctor or nurse. Many services now have specialist Parkinson's disease nurses.
- A course of physiotherapy can be helpful to boost mobility.
- Occupational therapy plays a vital role in aids and adaptations for disability.
- Speech and language therapists, along with dieticians can help when swallowing becomes a problem.
- Occasionally inpatient assessment is helpful but be aware that hospital routines can rarely match home treatment and some patients deteriorate in hospital.
- Depression is common—be vigilant and treat actively but beware antidepressants can exacerbate movement disorder and postural hypotension.
- Parkinson' Disease Society (www.parkinsons.org.uk) has plenty of information and advice.

HOW TO... treat challenging symptoms in Parkinson's disease

Wearing off—progression of disease—patients require higher doses or more frequent dosing to produce same effect

Possible that levodopa itself is toxic to neurons and enhances progression. In younger patients/milder disease start with selegiline or dopamine agonists

Dyskinesias

Reduce levodopa dose if possible (either alone or with addition of an agonist). Add amantadine

Motor fluctuations with choreodystonic 'on' phases and freezing 'off' phases develop and worsen with duration of treatment

Reduced levodopa dose more frequently (dose fractionation) or controlled release preparations or add entacapone or add dopamine agonist

Other drug **side effects** (confusion and hallucinations, constipation, urinary retention, nausea and vomiting) are a particular problem in elderly and often limit treatment to sub-ideal levels

Domperidone (30mg tds PO) is the best antiemetic

In general, **patients prefer dyskinetic side effects** than 'off spells'—relatives/carers may find the opposite easier to cope with especially if patient confused or falling when 'on'

Ensure you talk to the patient as well even if it is easier to talk to the carer. Compromise may be necessary

Quantifying response to treatment is very difficult

Get patients/carers to fill in a 24 hour chart. A formal quantified drug trial by therapists can be very helpful

Morning stiffness

Use a rapid acting drug (e.g. Madopar® dispersible or apomorphine) in bed on waking or try a long acting drug last thing at night

End-stage disease

Ultimately drug responsiveness so poor and side effects so marked that decreasing and withdrawing therapy may be appropriate. Palliative treatment and social support important

Diseases masquerading as Parkinson's disease

The majority of slow, stiff or shaky elderly on geriatric wards do not have true PD. As many as 1 in 4 diagnoses of PD made by general practitioners are incorrect. It is important to get the diagnosis right or you will subject patients needlessly to the harmful side effects of medications. Coexistence of more than one syndrome can further complicate diagnosis.

- **Atherosclerotic pseudoparkinsonism/multi-infarct dementia**
Due to neurovascular damage—consider in those with stroke/TIA or with atherosclerotic risk factors e.g. hypertension. Short stepping, wide-based unstable gait with relative preservation of arm and facial movements (lower body Parkinsonism). Head scan may show lacunae or white matter change.

- **Benign essential tremor**
Often inherited (autosomal dominant), worse on action (spills tea from teacup), improved by alcohol and beta-blockers, may have head nodding or vocal tremor.

- **Lewy body dementia**
Lewy bodies are widely present throughout cortex not predominantly in substantia nigra as with true PD. Psychiatric symptoms e.g. visual hallucinations tend to precede physical ones.

- **Drug-induced Parkinsonism**
Neuroleptics are the commonest cause but remember that Stemetil® (prochlorperazine) for dizziness and metaclopramide for nausea are also causes. Some irritable bowel treatments (Motival® Motipress®) contain neuroleptics.

- **Other causes**
Alzheimer's disease, hydrocephalus, and even severe polyarthritis can sometimes cause diagnostic confusion. Rare differential diagnoses include Wilson's disease, Pick's disease, carbon monoxide poisoning, multiple head injuries (ex boxers), and post encephalitis or anoxic brain injury.

Parkinson's-Plus syndromes

This is a confusing array of rare disorders including:
- **Multi-system atrophy** (aka Shy-Drager syndrome, olivopontocerebellar atrophy)—early autonomic failure (incontinence and postural instability), cerebellar signs, aphonia and dysphagia. Not dementia.
- **Progressive supranuclear palsy** (aka Steele-Richardson-Olszewski Disease)—down-gaze palsy, axial rigidity and falls, dysarthria and dysphagia, frontal lobe dementia.

Further reading
Quinn N. (1995). Parkinsonism- recognition and differential diagnosis. *BMJ* **310**: 447–452.

Clues to distinguish Parkinson's disease

	True PD	Pseudo-PD (esp. atherosclerotic)
Response to L-dopa	Good	Poor or transient
	Develop dopa dyskinesias	Dopa dyskinesias unusual
Age of onset	40–70	70+
Tremor	Unilateral or asymmetrical	Absent or mild
	Resting tremor prominent	
Progression	Slow progression/long history	Rapid progression
Dementia	Only at late stage	Prominent or early
Instability/falls	Late	Early and prominent
Dysphonia, dysarthria or dysphagia	Late	Early and prominent
Other neurology (pyramidal signs, downgaze palsy, cerebellar signs)	Rare	Common

Epilepsy

Primary epilepsy most commonly presents around the time of puberty but the incidence of new fits is actually higher in the over 70s (>100 per 100,000) because of the increasing amount of secondary epilepsy (caused by e.g. cerebrovascular ischaemia, subdural haematomas, brain tumours).

In addition fits can be precipitated by:
- Metabolic disturbance (e.g. hyponatraemia)
- Drugs (e.g. ciprofloxacin)
- Infection (at any site but particularly meningitis/encephalitis)
- Withdrawal from alcohol or drugs such as benzodiazepines
- Wernicke's encephalopay (due to thiamine deficiency in malnourished e.g. alcoholics).

Many of these conditions are commoner in older patients who also have a lower fit threshold for any given level of stimulus.

Diagnosis
- See also 'funny turns' (p122).
- An eye witness account is the most useful diagnostic tool.
- Look particularly for post-event confusion/drowsiness which is rare in cardiac syncope.
- The classic features of prodrome, tongue-biting, and incontinence are not so useful in distinguishing cardiac from neurological syncope in the elderly.
- Remember that cerebral hypoperfusion from any cause (e.g. bradycardia) can cause fits so epilepsy can co-exist with other causes of syncope. In these cases treatment of the primary syncope/hypoperfusion is more effective than anti-epileptics.

Investigations
- Routine blood screening, CXR, and ECG to look for precipitants and differential diagnoses.
- CT scan is vital to exclude a structural lesion.
- EEGs can be helpful when positive but very commonly have non-specific changes and low sensitivity ie normal EEG does not rule out epilepsy.

General management
- Ensure the patient is not taking medication that lowers the fit threshold (check the *BNF*—common examples include tricyclics, ciprofloxacin and phenothiazines. Think about over the counter drugs (e.g. Ginkgo biloba) and stimulants such as cocaine.
- Correct any metabolic derangement (especially glucose, sodium, sepsis).
- Advise about driving restrictions—don't assume they don't drive.
- Detect and treat complications e.g. aspiration, trauma, pressure injuries.

Driving regulations and epilepsy

You have a duty to ensure that the patient informs DVLA. Patients have at least a one year ban on driving for a first fit (unless a 'provoked fit' e.g. following brain surgery or stroke, when this may be shorter period—individual decision). They can then reapply for a licence as long as they remain fit-free. Patients must also refrain from driving for six months after withdrawing epilepsy medication.

Further information available at www.dvla.gov.uk

Epilepsy and stroke

Onset seizures (within a week, most commonly within 24 hours) occur in 2–5% of strokes. Commoner with haemorrhages, large cortical strokes and venous infarction. Consider also alcohol/drug (especially benziodiazepine) withdrawal for early fits. Long-term anticonvulsants not usually prescribed unless fits recur.

After the first week stroke remains a risk factor for new epilepsy—first year 5% fit, subsequently 1.5% annual incidence. Many such patients develop transient neurological worsening (Todd's paresis) or permanent worsening without CT evidence of new stroke—in these patients it is usually worth considering long-term anticonvulsants.

Epilepsy may occur secondary to clinically 'silent' cerebral ischaemia and 3% of patients with stroke have a past history of fits, most occurring in the preceeding year. Some epilepsy experts suggest that aspirin is prescribed for new onset seizures in an elderly patient once structural lesions have been excluded.

Epilepsy: drug treatment

Acute treatment

- Start with benzodiazepines (5–10mg rectal diazepam or 2–10mg iv Diazemuls® or 0.5–2mg, lorazepam iv or im).
- If fits continue, consider setting up loading dose infusion of phenytoin (use a cardiac monitor) until oral medication can be taken.
- Rarely the patient may need intubating and paralysing to stabilize them or to allow an urgent CT scan.

Chronic treatment

- Because of side effects and long duration of treatment most doctors will resist starting anticonvulsants until after a second fit, especially if the diagnosis is unclear or if there is a reversible precipitant. Presence of underlying structural abnormality or wishing to return to driving may tip the balance in favour of treatment.
- Phenytoin (200–400mg nocte) and carbamazepine (100mg od gradually increasing to 200mg tds) are effective but particularly sedative, Valproate (300mg CR bd) is better tolerated and often used first line in older patients but plasma levels are unhelpful in monitoring compliance or side effects.
- All anticonvulsants have significant side effects e.g. sedation, confusion, rash, tremor, and ataxia. Serious liver, blood and pulmonary side effects can also occur—ongoing monitoring to optimize dose and minimize side effects is necessary.
- Many anticonvulsants interact with each other as well as other drugs and can increase toxicity or reduce effectiveness—if in doubt consult a pharmacist.
- Avoid abrupt withdrawal of antiepileptics—fits may be provoked.
- Partial seizures (e.g. face/arm twitching) are rarely dangerous and often distress bystanders more than the patient, but they can progress to secondary generalized seizures. The same drugs can be employed. Partial seizures often indicate structural lesions and an early CT scan is advisable.
- Sometimes a trial of anticonvulsants in patients with recurrent unexplained collapse can be revealing

Refer to an epilepsy specialist if control is proving difficult and multiple drugs are required.

Neuroleptic malignant syndrome (NMS)

Rare but important syndrome in patients taking neuroleptics (e.g. haloperidol, chlorpromazine, risperidone) with triad of:
- Fever
- Rigidity and tremor
- Rhabdomyolysis with secondary renal failure (p550).
▶▶ Can be fatal (up to 30%) and early recognition important.

Diagnosis

May arise at any time during treatment ie patient may have recently:
- Started (most common) or stopped neuroleptics.
- Increased the dose or been stable on them for a long time.
- Added a second drug e.g. tricylic antidepressant, lithium.

Reintroduction of the offending drug at a later date may not reproduce symptoms. Contributing factors such as intercurrent illness, metabolic derangement may be important in the aetiology.

Clinical features:

- The patient looks unwell with fever, severe lead-pipe rigidity, bradykinesia, occasionally tremor, and decreased conscious level.
- Time course—onset usually over 1–3 days, starts with rigidity/altered mental state.
- Seizures and abnormal neurological signs can occur.
- Autonomic dysfunction causes sweating, tachycardia, and hypertension.
- Multiorgan failure can occur and there is a leucocytosis and creatinine kinase levels may be over 1000IU/L.
- Lumbar puncture, CT scan and EEG are often required to exclude other diagnoses such as CNS infection.
▶▶ The most common cause of a similar presentation is sepsis in a patient with pre-existing cerebrovascular disease.

Management

Paracetamol and cooling—fans and damp sponging. Intravenous fluids with careful monitoring of electrolytes and renal function. Dantrolene (direct muscle relaxant) can speed recovery. Short term dialysis is sometimes required. Early transfer to intensive care unit may be wise—death most commonly occurs by hypoventilation/pneumonia or renal failure. There are sometimes persisting neurological sequelae.

Serotonin syndrome

A similar syndrome to NMS in patients taking serotonin reuptake inhibitors especially if combined with tricyclic or monoamine oxidase inhibitor. Patients tend to be agitated and delirious rather than unconscious. Gastrointestinal symptoms (diarrhoea/vomiting) occur. Onset may be within 2 hours, resolution usually quicker than NMS.

Motor neuron disease

A progressive idiopathic disease with selective degeneration of motor neurons causing weakness and wasting. There is a variety of manifestations depending on the site of damage; the commonest site for lesions is in the anterior horn cells of spinal cord (LMN), but descending motor pathway (UMN) may be affected in the corticospinal tracts, brainstem and motor cranial nuclei.

- Onset rises steeply with age with peak incidence late 50s/early 60s. Very rare before age 40. Overall prevalence 7 per 100,000 but incidence 1 per 10,000 age 65–85.
- Under-diagnosed in the elderly (confused with cerebrovascular disease, myasthenia—especially bulbar onset forms, cervical myelopathy, motor neuropathy, syringomyelia, and paraneoplastic syndromes).
- Slightly commoner in males.
- 5% will have a family history (autosomal dominant is most common but can be recessive or X-linked).

History

- Weakness, cramps and fatigue in limbs. Weakness usually begins in a focal area and spreads to contiguous muscles, onset in upper limbs is most common.
- Palatal and vocal cord paralysis can cause stridor, dysarthria, dysphagia, and aspiration pneumonia.
- Paresis of respiratory muscles can cause respiratory failure (may present to chest physicians/ITU).
- Intellect, sensation and continence are usually retained. Some forms associated with frontotemporal dementia (<5%). Depression common.

Examination

- Look for wasting with fasciculation (LMN) especially in tongue, shoulders, and legs. NB fasciculations may be a normal finding in hands and calves of older people.
- Head drop/droop can occur.
- Brisk reflexes, clonus, and upgoing plantars (UMN). This is one condition that can cause absent ankle jerks with upgoing plantars.
- Atrophy and weakness are less specific signs.
- 'Donald Duck' speech.
- Sensory changes should make you question the diagnosis.

Investigations

- Creatine kinase (CK) may be elevated.
- CT, MRI, and muscle biopsy are usually normal.
- EMG shows denervation of muscles caused by anterior horn cell degeneration and is diagnostic.

Clinical pictures

Diverse presentations and rate of progression including;
Amyotrophic lateral sclerosis is the commonest form: classical picture of mixed UMN and LMN. Term used commonly in USA.
- Progressive pseudobulbar or bulbar palsy: speech and swallow predominantly affected.
- Primary lateral sclerosis: upper motor neurons predominantly affected.
- Progressive muscular atrophy: lower motor neurons predominantly affected.

Treatment

Riluzole (sodium channel blocker) 50mg bd. Prolongs survival by a few months but not function. Licensed and endorsed by NICE for ALS only. Expensive and should be supervised by specialist. Monitor liver function and check for neutopaenia if febrile illness.

Supportive
- Chest: antibiotics and physiotherapy, tracheostomy, non-invasive nocturnal ventilation (for diaphragmatic palsy, sleep apnoea).
- Speech: early referral to speech therapy for communication aids.
- Nutrition: initially pureed food and thickened fluids. Malnutrition and aspiration are indications to consider artificial feeding.
- Muscle spasm: baclofen, physiotherapy.
- Mobility/independence: OT for wheelchairs and adaptations.
- Pain/distress: opiates or benzodiazepines (but beware respiratory suppression).

Other
- This is a devastating diagnosis to give to a patient—mean life expectancy is 2–5 years. Matters are often worse because there is often a considerable delay between symptoms and a concrete diagnosis being made (sometimes initial diagnosis may have been incorrect). Emphasize the retention of cognition and aspects of supportive care available. Offer regular follow-up appointments.
- Specialist Neurology/MND nurses are available in some areas.
- Refer to Motor Neurone Disease Association for support.
- Consider enduring power of attorney and advance directives.

Further reading
www.mndassociation.org

Peripheral neuropathies

Some minor degree of sensory loss in the feet and reduced or absent ankle jerks is so common in older people (up to 50% of over 85 year olds) that some class this as a normal ageing change, but remember:
- Even mild, asymptomatic neuropathies can contribute to postural instability and falls.
- The diagnosis is often missed because of non-specific symptoms and insidious onset with slow progression.

Clinical features
- Signs of lower motor neuron weakness with wasting and loss of reflexes.
- Sensory loss often with joint position and vibration loss before touch and pain.
- Neuralgia-type pain may be present (esp. diabetes and alcohol).
- Autonomic failure and cranial nerve involvement can also occur.
- Severe cases may affect respiration.

Classification

Try to determine if the signs are focal or generalized and whether they are predominantly sensory or motor because this can help identify the likely underlying pathology. Further classification by pathology (axonal or demyelinating) requires nerve conduction studies or biopsy.

The commonest pattern produces widespread symmetrical sensory loss (typically glove and stocking). This may be combined with distal muscle weakness (mixed motor and sensory neuropathy) or sometimes there is a pure motor neuropathy. Where signs are focal consider mononeuritis multiplex.

Causes

The causes are legion and often multiple in elderly patients. Idiopathic neuropathies are very common (25% defy diagnosis in most studies). The following list is not exhaustive:
- Idiopathic
- Diabetes
- Carpel tunnel syndrome
- Paraneoplastic syndromes (e.g. small cell lung cancer)
- Alcoholism (often combined with vitamin deficiency)
- Renal failure
- B12 or folate deficiency
- Guillain–Barré syndrome (commonest acute onset)
- Hypothyrodism
- Vasculitides (e.g. Wegener's granulomatosis)—actually multiple mononeuropathy
- Drugs (e.g. isoniazid, nitrofurantoin, vincristine, amiodarone)
- Paraproteinaemias and amyloid
- Chronic inflammatory demyelinating polyradiculoneuropathy (rare autoimmune motor neuropathy).

Investigations

- Always check B12, glucose, TFT, serum and urine immunoglobulins, ESR, and CRP before labelling a neuropathy idiopathic.
- Look carefully for an occult tumour (e.g. breast examination and CXR).
- Nerve conduction studies will confirm nerve damage and distinguish demyelination from axonal damage (which sometimes helps with differential diagnosis) but they are not always required in straightforward cases.
- Further specialist tests include immunology, tumour markers, lumbar puncture, molecular genetics tests, and nerve biopsy.

Treatment

The important thing is to identify reversible causes quickly but even treatable causes rarely respond dramatically—the aim is usually prevention of further deterioration. Chronic inflammatory polyradiculoneuropathy is treated by steroids, plasma exchange, and intravenous immunoglobulin but most other chronic neuropathies have no specific treatment. Supportive and symptomatic treatment (e.g. appropriate footwear, analgesia, environmental adaptation) is important.

Acute neuropathy due to Guillain–Barré syndrome is a medical emergency which responds to intravenous immunoglobulins or plasmapheresis. These patients can deteriorate rapidly and should be managed in conjunction with specialist neurology units. Even patients that look well should have their vital capacity measured daily to warn of impending respiratory failure.

Subdural haematoma

A condition which is much commoner in old age because as the brain shrinks the veins which lie between it and the skull are much more likely to get torn following trauma (even minor injury). Older people are also more likely to have falls/head injuries and are more commonly on predisposing drugs (e.g. aspirin, warfarin). Other risk factors include alcoholism, epilepsy, and haemodialysis.

Features

▶▶ Subdurals frequently present with very non-specific symptoms in a frail confused patient. A high index of suspicion is required.

- Subdurals can occur acutely (and present within hours of an accident) or more slowly as the classical 'chronic subdural haematoma' although this distinction doesn't help guide management.
- A history of head injury occurs in only about half of patients.
- Common features include drowsiness and confusion (rarely fluctuant), postural instability, progressive focal neurology (e.g. hemiparesis, unequal pupils), headache, blurred vision.
- Rarely transient neurology (mimicking TIA) or Parkinsonism can occur.
- Some patients are asymptomatic and large collections can be incidental findings.
- Examine for papilloedema, focal neurology, and long tract signs.

Diagnosis

CT head scan: look for crescent-shaped haematoma compressing sulci (hypodense/black is old blood, hyperdense/white indicates recent bleeding) and midline shift. All patients who have new upper motor neuron signs with confusion and/or drowsiness should be scanned. It is harder to decide when to scan a confused patient without such signs—most agree it is reasonable to look for other causes of acute confusion before asking for a head scan as long as the patient is being observed for any change in neurological signs or conscious level.

▶▶ Have a lower threshold for scanning patients on aspirin or warfarin and for those who have evidence of falls, particularly facial bruising.

MRI is slightly superior and useful when CT changes are subtle (an isodense phase occurs on CT in transition between hyperdense and hypotense changes) or very small haematomas are suspected.

Management

Decisions are usually made in conjunction with the local neurosurgical team (although in practice only about one third of patients will end up having surgery). Stop aspirin and reverse warfarin therapy if possible. Observation (with or without dexamethasone to reduce intracerebral pressure) is frequently used in:

- Asymptomatic patients
- Those with small bleeds who are stable/improving
- Those not fit for transfer/surgery.

When conservative management is adopted, record conscious level (Glasgow coma scale—see Appendix) and any focal neurology at least daily or if there is any change. Any deterioration should prompt repeat CT scan and reconsideration of surgery.

Burrhole surgery is not complex and is done under local anaesthetic. Recovery after surgery can be dramatic. Complications include rebleeding and seizures. Use symptoms (especially conscious level) not CT appearance to decide on surgery. Mortality is around 10%—highest with depressed conscious level and bilateral haematoma. Those left with residual neurology should receive rehabilitation as in stroke.

Sleep and insomnia

With increasing age less sleep is needed (approx one hour less than young adults), circadian rhythm is less marked, and sleep becomes more fragmented with greater difficulty getting to sleep. Deep (stage 3 and 4) sleep is reduced but dreaming sleep/REM (rapid eye movement) is preserved.

Insomnia is a symptom which correlates poorly with observed actual sleep time (i.e. patients who complain of poor sleep may be observed by nurses/family to sleep well whilst those who sleep very little do not necessarily complain). It can be very distressing and is associated with increased morbidity and mortality. Around 25% of elderly people suffer chronic insomnia—even higher rates are found with psychiatric and medical conditions. Insomnia is a particular problem in an unfamiliar, noisy ward environment and doctors are often under considerable pressure to prescribe sedatives.

Treatment of insomnia

First ensure that underlying causes are looked for and treated. For example:
- Pain at night—consider using analgesics with sedative side effects e.g. opiates.
- Co-morbidities e.g. orthopnoea, nocturia, oesophageal reflux, Parkinson's disease.
- Depression/anxiety—very common—use of an antidepressant will improve sleep much better than a hypnotic.
- Alcohol dependence.
- Drugs—corticosteroids, omeprazole, phenytoin, amiodarone, sulphasalazine, atorvastatin, ramipril, as well as psychiatric drugs e.g. paroxetine, haloperidol and chlorpromazine can cause insomnia. Beta-blockers and levodopa cause nightmares.

The following **non-pharmacological interventions** (sleep hygiene) can be tried:
- Reduce or stop daytime 'catnapping'.
- Avoid caffeine, heavy meals and alcohol in the evening (alcohol helps you fall asleep but reduces sleep quality).
- Use a bedtime routine.
- Ensure environment is dark, quiet, comfortable.
- Relaxation and cognitive behavioural techniques can be useful.
- Try warm milky drinks.

Drugs

- Benzodiazepines (e.g. temazepam 10mg) are licensed for short term (less than 4 weeks) management of insomnia and anxiety. They do work well when used correctly—see box opposite.
- The newer Z-drugs (e.g. zopiclone, zolpidem and zeleplon) are only for insomnia. They have shorter half-lives and fewer side effects (although zopiclone is still a cause of daytime drowsiness). Overall they are probably slightly superior to benzodiazepines but the same cautions about dependence apply.
- Other hypnotics (e.g. chloral hydrate, chlormethiazole, antihistamines) can be toxic esp. in overdose and provide no major advantages over the above two examples.

HOW TO... use benzodiazepines (BZ) for insomnia

Tolerance develops after only 4 weeks and BZ fail to produce a useful sedative effect, however it only takes this long for dependence to occur. Dependence may be physical (with rebound insomnia, anxiety, or even delerium) and/or psychological (the patient believes they will not be able to sleep without tablets). The shorter the half-life the greater the withdrawal effects. BZ use has been associated with increased falls, reduced functional status, road traffic accidents, depression and memory impairment.

Although awareness of these problems has reduced the number of long-term BZ users there is still over-prescribing.

Prevention of dependence

- Do not use BZ for mild or non-distressing insomnia—try non-pharmacological measures first.
- Never prescribe BZ for more than 4 weeks.
- Never prescribe BZ medication at discharge from hospital.
- All patients/carers should receive warnings about BZ side effects (esp. dependence) and the reason for limiting course length at the outset.
- GPs should limit repeat prescriptions and audit their practice.

Treatment of dependence

- Explain and motivate patient/carers.
- Gradual reduction regimen e.g. diazepam by 2–2.5mg every 2 weeks.
- In difficult cases switch to equivalent dose of diazepam first—long half life produces milder withdrawal symptoms.
- Continuing support.
- Occasionally acute withdrawal is undertaken by mistake (e.g. drug accidentally not prescribed for a couple of weeks during acute admission with fractured neck of femur). In these cases no not automatically re-start the BZ but do explain to the patient or they will just re-start it when they return home.

Other sleep disorders

Hypersomnolence

This is excessive daytime sleepiness despite a normal night of sleep. Causes include brain disease (e.g. dementia, stroke), cardiopulmonary disease (e.g. cardiac failure, COPD), obstructive sleep apnoea, hypothyroidism, narcolepsy, and sedative drugs.

Restless legs syndrome

A common (10% of older people), unpleasant sensation in limbs which increases with drowsiness and is eradicated by movement. Can be associated with limb jerking during sleep with sleep disturbance. Both symptoms respond to benzodiazepines. Dopamine agonists are also used with some success.

Circadian rhythm disorders

Jet-lag is the best known but advanced sleep phase syndrome (sleepiness occurs too early in evening, but there is early morning wakening) and delayed sleep phase (sleepiness comes too late at night) can occur without such a precipitant. Treat by gradually altering bedtime and bright light therapy when wakefulness desired.

Sleep apnoea in the elderly

Obstructive sleep apnoea (OSA) and central sleep apnoea are very common in elderly people and can cause daytime sleepiness, accidents, and heart failure. Unfortunately periods of apnoea are less likely to be symptomatic than in the young, and where symptoms do exist they are often multifactorial so diagnosis and compliance with therapy (non-invasive positive pressure ventilation) can be problematic.

Further reading
Harbison J. (2002). Sleep disorder in older people. *Age and Ageing* **31**: 6–9.

Stroke

Definition and classification 192
Predisposing factors 194
Acute assessment 196
   How to... assess for inattention 197
Investigations 198
Acute management 200
   How to... perform a bedside swallowing assessment 202
Stroke units 204
   How to... estimate prognosis after stroke 205
Thrombolysis 206
Ongoing management 208
   How to... protect your patient from another stroke 210
Complications 212
   How to... manage urinary incontinence after stroke 213
Longer term issues 214
TIA clinics 216

Definition and classification

Definition

Stroke is the sudden onset of a focal neurological deficit, lasting more than 24 hours or leading to (earlier) death, due to either infarction or haemorrhage.

- Infarction: emboli, in situ thrombosis or low flow.
- Haemorrhage: spontaneous (not associated with trauma). Excludes sub-dural and extra-dural haematomas, but includes spontaneous sub-arachnoid haemorrhage.

Use of the term cerebrovascular accident is now discouraged.

Transient ischaemic attacks (TIAs) are focal neurological deficits (including monocular visual loss) due to inadequate blood supply that last less than 24 hours (in reality, most TIAs last just minutes).

Infarction and TIAs have the same pathogenesis, and the distinction is likely to become less helpful with time. Acute stroke treatments are being developed and will need to be started as soon as possible (pp200–1) so waiting 24 hours before the diagnosis of stroke is made will be nonsensical. The term 'brain attack' is being used to describe the full spectrum of disease severity from TIA to fatal stroke, where early intervention to save brain tissue has parallels with approaches to myocardial salvage in coronary syndromes.

Stroke burden

- Incidence of first ever stroke is about 200 per 100,000 per year.
- Prevalence is around 5–12 per 1000 population, depending on the age of the sample.
- It is a disease of older people (over two-thirds of cases occur in the over 65s, less than 15% occur in under 45s) and is the subject of Standard 5 in the National Service Framework for Older People (p32).
- Globally it is the third most common cause of death (after coronary heart disease and all cancers).
- In England and Wales it accounts for 12% of all deaths and is the most important cause of severe disability amongst community dwellers.

Classification

Various methods:

- *Infarct or haemorrhage* (also haemorrhagic infarcts).
- *Pathogenesis*: large vessel, small vessel, cardioembolic (AF or LV mural thrombus), valve disease, infective endocarditis, non-atheromatous arterial disease (vasculitis, dissection), blood disorders etc.
- *Vessel affected*: anterior circulation (mainly middle cerebral artery), lacunar (deep small subcortical vessels), posterior circulation (vertebral and basilar arteries).
- *Bamford classification*: clinical features to define likely stroke territory; used in major trials giving prognostic information about each group (see table opposite).

Bamford Classification

Total anterior circulation stroke (TACS)

Features	1. Hemiparesis and hemisensory loss
	2. Homonymous hemianopia
	3. Cortical dysfunction (dysphasia, visio-spatial or perceptual problems)
Infarction (TACI)	85%
Haemorrhage (TACH)	15%
Causes	Occlusion ICA, MCA, or ACA
	Emboli from heart, aortic arch or carotids, in situ thrombosis.
Prognosis at one year	Dead	60%
	Dependent	35%
	Independent	5%

Partial anterior circulation stroke (PACS)

Features	Two of the three listed above	
	OR cortical dysfunction alone	
Infarction (PACI)	85%	
Haemorrhage (PACH)	15%	
Causes	As for TACS	
Prognosis at one year	Dead	15%
	Dependent	30%
	Independent	55%

Lacunar stroke (LACS)

Features	Hemiparesis	
	OR Hemisensory loss	
	OR Hemisensorymotor loss	
	OR Ataxic hemiparesis	
	(with NO cortical dysfunction)	
Infarction (LACI)	95%	
Haemorrhage (LACH)	5%	
Causes	Small perforating arteries microatheroma	
	Hypertensive small vessel disease	
Prognosis at one year	Dead	10%
	Dependent	30%
	Independent	60%

Posterior circulation stroke (POCS)

Features	Brainstem symptoms and signs (diplopia, vertigo, ataxia, bilateral limb problems, hemianopia, cortical blindness etc.)	
Infarction (POCI)	85%	
Haemorrhage (POCH)	15%	
Causes	Occlusion of vertebral, basilar or posterior cerebral artery	
	Emboli from heart, aortic arch or vertebrobasilar artery	
Prognosis at one year	Dead	20%
	Dependent	20%
	Independent	60%

Predisposing factors

Fixed

- *Age*: stroke risk increases with increasing age (this is the strongest risk factor).
- *Sex*: males > females.
- *Ethnicity*: Probably higher in Blacks and Asians than Whites living in the West—likely due to increased obesity, hypertension and diabetes.
- *Family history*: positive family history increases risk. Not simple inheritance—complex genetic/environmental interaction.
- *Previous stroke/TIA*: risk of recurrence is about 10–16% in the first year, being highest in the acute phase.
- *Other vascular disease*: presence of any atheromatous disease (peripheral vascular disease, ischaemic heart disease, renovascular disease) increases risk of stroke, as atheroma is rarely organ specific.

Modifiable by lifestyle change

- *Smoking*: causal, dose-related risk factor. Risk diminishes 5 years after quitting.
- *Alcohol intake*: J-shaped relationship, where heavy drinking is a risk factor, but moderate intake is protective.
- *Obesity*: increased risk of all vascular events in obesity—confounded by increase in other risk factors (hypertension, diabetes) but probably weak independent factor, especially central obesity.
- *Physical inactivity*: increased stroke in less active—again confounded by presence of other risk factors in the inert; to date limited evidence that increased activity lowers risk.
- *Diet*: healthy eaters have lower risk, but such individuals often have healthier lifestyles in general. Low salt, high fruit and vegetable, high fish and anti-oxidant diets are likely to be protective, but trials have failed to show an effect.
- *Oestrogens*: oral contraceptive pill confers a slightly increased risk of stroke and should be avoided in the presence of other risk factors. Post-menopausal hormone replacement therapy has recently been shown to increase risk of ischaemic stroke, but not of TIA or haemorrhagic stroke.

Medically modifiable

- *Hypertension*: clear association between increasing blood pressure and increased stroke risk across all population groups. Risk doubles with each 5–7 mmHg increase in diastolic blood pressure. Also increases with systolic rises and even isolated systolic hypertension.
- *Diabetes*: risk factor for stroke independent of increased hypertension.
- *High cholesterol*: weaker risk factor than in heart disease—likely due to diversity of stroke aetiologies.
- *Atrial fibrillation*: risk of stroke increased in AF (p296).
- *Carotid stenosis*: risk increases with increasing stenosis and with the occurrence of symptoms attributable to the stenosis.
- *Other co-morbidity*: increased stroke risk in some conditions, such as sickle-cell anaemia, blood diseases causing hyperviscosity and vasculitides.

Acute assessment

History

- Is it a focal neurological deficit?
- Did it come on 'at a stroke' or is there a hint of progression? (Simple stroke may worsen over several days, but think of alternative diagnoses, e.g. tumour.)
- Is there headache or drowsiness? (Haemorrhage more likely.)
- Was there a fall or other head trauma? ▶▶ Think subdural and request urgent scan.
- What are the vascular risk factors?
- What was the pre-morbid state?
- What are the co-morbidities? (Increases chance of poor outcome.)
- What are the medications? (Call GP surgery if unknown.)
- Where do they live, and with whom? Who are the significant family members?

Examination

Glasgow Coma Scale (see Appendix). Designed for use in head injury, it is used as a standardized measure to assess neurological deterioration. Unconsciousness or deteriorating GCS suggests haemorrhage, large infarct with oedema or brainstem event.

NIH stroke scale. Clinical evaluation instrument with documented reliability and validity. Used increasingly to assess neurological outcome and degree of recovery in stroke. Grades the following areas: consciousness, orientation, obeying commands, gaze, visual fields, facial weakness, motor function in the arm and leg, limb ataxia, sensory, language, dysarthria, and inattention.

General examination

- General inspection (head trauma, signs of fitting—incontinence or tongue biting, evidence of self neglect, frailty and general condition e.g. skin).
- Temperature (especially after a long period on the floor).
- Cardiovascular examination (pulse rate and rhythm, blood pressure, cardiac examination for source of cardiac emboli, cardiomegaly, carotid bruits).
- Respiratory examination (aspiration pneumonia or pre-existing respiratory conditions).
- Abdominal examination (palpable bladder, organomegaly).

Neurological examination (may need to be adapted if patient drowsy)

- Cranial nerves: especially visual fields and visual inattention (if difficulty with compliance, test blink response to threat, and look for a gaze preference which may occur with hemianopia or neglect), test swallow (not gag).
- Limbs: tone (may be diminished acutely), any weakness (grade power for later comparison. Is the distribution pyramidal—arm flexors stronger than extensors, leg extensors stronger than flexors. If weakness subtle, assess for pyramidal drift and fine movements of both

hands—dominant should be better), coordination (limited if power is diminished), sensation (easy bedside tests for fine touch and proprioception. If sensation intact, also test for sensory inattention.), reflexes (initially may be absent, then become brisker with time. Plantars extensor on affected side.).

- Gait: assess in less severe stroke—is it safe?
- Speech: dysarthria (trouble enunciating because of e.g. facial weakness or posterior circulation stroke) or dysphasia (cortical disruption of speech—may be receptive and/or expressive).
  - Receptive dysphasia is an inability to understand language. Test with one-stage commands—'close your eyes' and progress to more complex tasks 'put your left hand on your right ear'. If comprehension intact, reassure the patient that you know they can understand, but are having difficulty finding the right words.
  - Expressive dysphasia—problems producing speech—may be fluent (lots of words that make no sense), or non-fluent. Nominal dysphasia is part of an expressive dysphasia and is tested by asking the patient to name increasingly rare objects (e.g. watch, hand, second hand.).

HOW TO... assess for inattention

Occurs with parietal cortex damage, where there are errors in awareness of self—the patient's 'automatic pilot' has gone wrong.

In extreme cases, the patient will not recognize their own arm, and only wash half of their body. Lesser degrees are more common, and complicate the rehabilitation process, as the patient must constantly be reminded of the existence of the affected side.

To test:

1. Establish that sensory input is present bilaterally—i.e. check that the patient can feel a touch to each hand individually and does not have a hemianopia (may be hard to establish where extreme gaze preference exists).
2. Provide two stimuli at once (touch both hands together, or move fingers in both sides of the visual field) and see if the patient preferentially notices the sensory input on the good side. If so, there is inattention of the bad side.

Even if formal testing does not reveal inattention, sometimes it will become apparent during rehabilitation, often noted by therapists.

Investigations

Test	Rationale
Full blood count	• Anaemic or polycythaemic • Elevated white count suggestive of sepsis • High or low platelet count
Urea and electrolytes	Look for evidence of dehydration, and assess fluid replacement Aim for electrolyte normalization
Liver function tests	• Baseline assessment • Evidence of co-morbidity
Creatine kinase	Evidence of muscle breakdown (if prolonged lie on floor)
Glucose	Diabetic—old or new diagnosis (Elevated sugars initially may represent hyperglycaemic stress response) Hypoglycaemia ▶▶ may mimic stroke
Cholesterol	Vascular risk factor
ESR	Elevation in vasculitis or sepsis (including endocarditis)
CRP	Any evidence of sepsis (e.g. aspiration pneumonia etc.)
Blood cultures	Consider if sepsis possible or new heart murmur heard (endocarditis)
Urinalysis	• Diabetic • Vasculitis • Urinary infection
ECG	• Assess rhythm • Evidence of ischaemic heart disease/myocardial infarction or previous hypertension
Chest X-ray	Not routinely advised in guidelines, but often useful in elderly—look for any sign of aspiration, what is the heart size etc.
CT brain	• Guidelines advise scan within 24 hours, or sooner if there is doubt about diagnosis e.g. possible subarachnoid or sub-dural, likely bleed where the patient is on warfarin, or has a sudden drop in GCS suggesting possible hydrocephalus. • CT will distinguish stroke from non-stroke diagnoses such as tumour, identify whether this is a bleed or an infarct—facilitating antiplatelet therapy, and identify the likely cause of the event—carotid territory infarcts from stenosis, multiple infarcts from cardiac emboli etc. • Blood appears white in early CT; infarcts may not show acutely (first few hours), developing low-density areas ± surrounding oedema after a few days. • Small infarcts may never be seen, and the diagnosis is made clinically. ▶▶ A normal CT does not exclude a stroke
Carotid Doppler	Request in carotid territory events with good recovery where the patient is a candidate for endarterectomy
Echocardiogram	Consider where multiple (? cardio embolic) infarcts, in AF, after recent MI (looking for thrombus) or where there is a murmur.

Acute management

Guidelines for acute care have been published by the Royal College of Physicians, (www.rcplondon.ac.uk/pubs/books/stroke/), echoed in the NSF (p32).

Diagnosis

- Care should occur on an acute stroke unit.
- Diagnosis should be made clinically (including assessment of likely cerebral area affected) and reviewed by a clinician with expertise in stroke.
- CT scan should be performed within 24 hours unless there is a good clinical reason for not doing so (e.g. dying patient for terminal care).

Medical interventions

- Aspirin (300mg) should be given as soon as possible after the onset of stroke symptoms if the diagnosis of haemorrhage is considered unlikely (usually after a scan—can be given NG or PR if no swallow).
- Neurosurgical opinion should be sought for all cases of hydrocephalus (due to bleeds).
- Centrally-acting drugs should be avoided (e.g. sedatives).
- Debate about the optimal blood pressure in the acute phase—high blood pressure is harmful long term, but may be required to provide perfusion pressure with altered cerebral auto regulation acutely—trials ongoing. Guidelines advise that blood pressure should not be lowered acutely in general, but existing antihypertensives continued.
- Oxygen supplementation should be given to hypoxic patients.
- Hydration should be maintained to ensure euvolaemia and biochemical normality, and monitored appropriately. This usually means giving 2 litres of normal saline intravenously in the first 24 hours, (unless the patient is alert and swallowing normally). This would be altered if admission electrolytes were deranged (e.g. hypokalaemia) and reviewed after a repeat electrolyte measurement on day two.
- Glucose should be measured and euglycaemia maintained—likely to improve recovery of ischaemic penumbral tissue.
- Pyrexia should be lowered with treatment of the underlying cause, fan, paracetamol, and sponging. High temperatures are associated with poorer outcomes, but the causal nature of this association is unknown.
- stockings.
- Seizures may occur (pp177–8).
- There should be a nominated physician to keep up-to-date with new developments in stroke care, and new drugs should only be used as part of randomized controlled trial.
- Thrombolysis with tissue plasminogen activator should only be given in a specialist centre with appropriate experience and expertise (p206).

Multi-disciplinary acute input

Protocols should be developed for early management, including monitoring consciousness level, assessing swallow (not gag), risk assessment for pressure sores (including nutritional status), cognitive impairment, bowel and bladder care (avoiding catheterization if possible) and moving and handling requirements.

Early speech and language therapy assessment should be done for all with swallow or language difficulties.

Early mobilization with the physiotherapist is advised, the therapist having expertise in stroke rehabilitation.

HOW TO... perform a bedside swallowing assessment

General examination
- Is the patient conscious and cooperative? If not, reassess later.
- If there is facial weakness, dysarthria, dysphasia, drooling, or respiratory symptoms then the likelihood of swallow impairment is higher.

Preparation
- Sit the patient upright.
- Listen to the chest to establish baseline.
- Ask the patient to cough, and note the strength and effectiveness.
- Find a cup of tepid water, and a teaspoon.

Why water?
Use water for convenience—this is a screening test to establish whether the patient should have further assessments. A small volume is used to minimize the consequences of aspiration.

Assessment
1. Give the patient a teaspoon of water, and ask them not to swallow.
2. Look for leakage of water from the closed mouth.
3. Ask the patient to swallow the water.
4. Check for prompt, coordinated swallow with elevation of the tracheal cartilage.
5. Watch for signs of aspiration—coughing and spluttering. These may not occur for several minutes. Do not leave the bedside immediately.

What next?
If the patient swallows without difficulty:
- Try a half-glass of water (drunk slowly).
- If they manage this safely, then allow them to eat and drink.
- Reassess if concerns arise later.

If there are problems:
- Ask the patient to remain 'nil by mouth' and inform the nursing staff.
- Alternative means of hydration will be required at once— an iv drip, or NG tube are common (the latter also allows medication to be given).
- Further assessment will be needed by SALT, who can stratify the swallow impairment and make a plan for safe oral intake, reviewing at regular intervals.
- Nutrition will need to be considered if the swallow is not safe— consider NG feeding, and involvement of a dietician.

Stroke units

Definition

Geographically-defined unit staffed by a coordinated multi-disciplinary team with expertise in stroke.

The gold standard is probably to admit strokes directly and continue care through to discharge—known as a comprehensive stroke unit. Resource limitations may mean that not all stroke patients pass through the unit, or that the length of stay is cut short. Some units deal with acute admissions only, others with the post-acute rehabilitation phase only. Coordinated stroke care can also be provided on a general rehabilitation ward or by roving stroke teams who visit all stroke patients on general wards.

Benefits

Stroke units, when compared with general ward care, result in lower rates of death, dependency, and institutional care, without lengthening hospital stay. The number needed to treat in a stroke unit to prevent one death or dependency is 18.

Rationale

The majority of improvement seems to occur in the first four weeks, and the mechanism is unclear.

Key components of stroke units include:
- Meticulous attention to physiological homeostasis
- Attention to prevention of complications (such as thromboembolic disease and pressure sores)
- Early mobilization
- Coordinated multi-disciplinary team care
- Interest, expertise, and motivation of staff.

The individual impact of each of these is unknown, but combined they confer significant benefits to the stroke patient.

Further reading

Stroke Unit trialist's collaboration (2001). Organised inpatient (stroke unit) care for stroke. *The Cochrane Database of Systematic Reviews*. Issue 3. www.cochrane.org

HOW TO... estimate prognosis after stroke

After first ever stroke, death occurs in 12% by a week, 31% at a year, and 60% at 5 years.

Indicators of a poor prognosis include:
- Impaired consciousness
- Gaze preference
- Dense weakness
- Cardiac co-morbidity
- Urinary incontinence
- Pupillary abnormalities
- Urinary incontinence.

The risk of recurrent stroke amongst survivors is 10–16% at one year, thereafter falling to about 4–5% per anum. The risk is higher with increasing number of risk factors.

Recovery is usually slow, and a clear time-frame established early on in the disease with the patient and the relatives is helpful. Recovery is most rapid in the first 3 months, and this tends to be 'front loaded' so the most dramatic improvements occur in the early weeks. Recovery then tends to slow, but may continue for up to 2 years.

▶▶ Each patient is different—recovery may be delayed by infections, depression etc., and this time frame should be a guide only.

The risk of not returning to independence varies with stroke type. Overall, about 20–30% of survivors are completely dependent at a year, and 40–50% are independent.

Thrombolysis

Rationale

In acute ischaemic stroke, an artery becomes occluded by thrombus in situ or embolus, and blood supply is compromised. Death of surrounding brain tissue results in deficits in function associated with that part of the brain. Early recanalisation of the vessel by lysing thrombus may limit the extent of brain injury.

Agents

The most frequently used agent is intravenous recombinant tissue plasminogen activator (r-tPA).

Risks

Treatment with thrombolysis leads to an excess in death due to intracranial haemorrhage (a five-fold increase compared with placebo).

Benefits

Despite early excess of deaths due to haemorrhage, treatment with thrombolysis leads to 44 fewer dead or dependent patients per 1000 treated with r-tPA within 6 hours, and 126 fewer dead or dependent patients per 1000 treated with r-tPA within 3 hours.

Imaging

This should be done prior to giving thrombolysis to exclude haemorrhage. Perfusion and diffusion weighted MRI scans may give more information than CT. Both need to be interpreted by someone with the appropriate experience prior to thrombolysis.

Use

Overall, use is recommended in specialist centres with sufficient expertise in stroke, and with facilities to deal with complications. In these centres, intravenous r-tPA is considered in all patients with definite ischaemic stroke who present within 3 hours of the onset of symptoms.

Careful discussion with the patient and family of risks and benefits is required.

Exclusion criteria

- Previous haemorrhage or active bleeding site
- Seizure at onset
- Mild or rapidly improving deficit
- Impaired coagulation
- Caution with very severe stroke.

Ongoing management

Should involve all of the multi-disciplinary team:

Dietician Calculate food and fluid requirements for each individual patient; adapt diet for specific needs (e.g. diabetic, weight loss); develop regimens for NG or PEG feeds; advise on provision of modified diets for stages of swallow recovery (thickened, pureed etc.); review nutrition as recovery alters needs.

Doctors Confirm diagnosis; manage medical complications; establish therapies.

Nurses Monitor patient continuously; assist with basic care (physiological and physical); ongoing bowel and bladder management; ongoing skin care; facilitate practise of skills acquired in therapy; promote functional independence; first point of call for relatives.

Occupational therapist Optimize functional ability (usually begin with upper limb work, coordinating with the physiotherapist); specific assessments of certain tasks (washing and dressing, kitchen safety, occupational tasks etc.) as recovery continues; adaptation to home environment by a series of home visits, with and without the patient, and the supply of aids (rails, bed levers, toilet raises, bath boards etc.), provision of wheelchairs where needed.

Pharmacist Review charts; promote safe prescribing.

Physiotherapist Assess muscle tone, movement and mobility; maximize functional independence by education and exercise; monitor respiratory function; initial bed mobility, then work on sitting balance, then transfers and finally standing and stepping; help prevent complications such as shoulder pain, contractures and immobility associated problems (pressure sores, DVT/PE).

Psychologist Assess psychological impact of stroke on patient and family; allow the patient to talk about the impact of the illness; monitor for depression and other mood disorder, highlighting the need for medication; document cognitive impairment; assist in retraining where neglect is prominent.

Social worker Psychosocial assessment of patient and family; support with financial matters (accessing pension, arranging power of attorney, financing placement etc.); advice and support for patient and family on accommodation needs, especially finding a care home placement; link to community services (care package, community rehabilitation, day centres etc.)

Speech and language therapist Assess swallow (bedside ± video swallow testing) and establish plan for safe oral intake; reassess, and plan nutritional route during recovery; language screening (dysarthria, dysphasia and dyspraxia) with intervention to improve deficits.

Feeding and stroke

Many patients will have impairment of swallow acutely, and early identification is necessary to prevent aspiration. Hydration is essential at
this time, but if the problem persists beyond 24 hours or so (research
has not showed significant advantages in feeding in the very acute
phase), then nutritional support should be given unless the patient is
terminal. Passing a NG tube allows medication to be given as usual as
well as feeding, but it is uncomfortable and may become dislodged. If
the patient continues to have swallowing problems, then a PEG feeding
tube may be inserted. The need for this should be regularly reviewed,
and it can fairly easily be removed, making it appropriate for both
medium and long term feeding. See p384 for discussion of the ethics of
feeding.

HOW TO... protect your patient from another stroke

Ensure that the following are addressed:

- Smoking, diet and exercise.
- Antiplatelet therapy:
  - Aspirin reduces relative risk of further event by about 25%. Dose probably not important—generally use 75–300mg.
  - Events that occur on aspirin ('aspirin failures') do not necessarily imply that aspirin is inadequate, but there may be an argument for increasing the dose (may be dose-dependent aspirin resistance), adding another antiplatelet agent (e.g. dipyridamole) or rarely changing the agent (e.g. to clopidogrel).
  - Adding clopidogrel to aspirin increases antiplatelet activity, but has been shown to increase the risk of cerebral haemorrhage and is no longer recommended for secondary prevention of stroke.
- Lower blood pressure: choice of agent debated. The important thing is probably just to lower the blood pressure, but there is growing evidence for the use of ACE inhibitors and thiazide diuretics as first line. If there are no contraindications, lowering blood pressure per se is likely to be beneficial, but aim for <130/85.
- Lower cholesterol: known for some time that lowering cholesterol is useful secondary prevention in coronary disease, but it has only been recently with the Heart Protection Study that benefit has also been shown in stroke, and also specifically in older patients. The cut off for treatment in this trial was 3.5, and so, as with blood pressure, it may be the lower the better.
- Anticoagulation for AF: see p300. In infarction, likely to be safe to start warfarin after 2 weeks. With haemorrhage, judge each case individually (probably wait several months for haemorrhagic transformation; may never be appropriate in primary bleed).
- Carotid endarterectomy: >70% symptomatic stenosis carries a stroke risk of about 15% per year, and is an indication for endarterectomy where there is good recovery and the patient is fit for surgery (which can be done with local anaesthesia). Perform early for greater benefit.

Complications

During a prolonged admission for a large stroke, a number of problems occur frequently:

Contractures Longer term complication.

Faecal incontinence May be due to immobility, cognitive problems or neurological impairment. Regulate bowel habit where possible with high fibre diet and good fluid intake and toilet regularly. If all else fails then deliberately constipating the patient with codeine and using regular enemas can work. See p586.

Infection Commonly chest or urine. Think of it early if a patient becomes drowsy, confused, or appears to deteriorate neurologically. Prompt septic screening and treatment with antibiotics, oxygen, and hydration are indicated in the majority of patient in the acute phase (stroke outcome very unclear initially) but may be withheld in a more established stroke where the prognosis can more confidently be assessed as dismal (decision made with the family).

Muscle spasm Very common on affected side. Arthritic joints are exacerbated by spasm, and antispasmodics may need to be used alongside analgesia for effective pain relief. Try baclofen 5mg (initially twice a day), or tizanidine 2mg daily (increased slowly after a few days if needed, up to a maximum of 24mg daily)—watch out for drowsiness and loss of tone in the affected side that can hinder therapy.

Pain Commonly shoulder pain in a paralysed arm. Usually multifactorial—e.g. joint subluxation (treat with physiotherapy to strengthen muscles and arm support) interacting with muscle spasm and shoulder arthritis as above. Central post-stroke pain tends to afflict all of the affected side and can be treated with amitriptyline (start low e.g. 10mg at night).

Pressure sores Should be avoidable in the majority of patients, see p546.

Psychological problems Low mood is extremely common post-stroke (at 4 months, a quarter will be depressed, and over half of these remain depressed at a year). This is unrelated to the stroke type, but is associated with a worse outcome (perhaps because of less motivation to participate in therapy). It should be actively sought (the screening question 'do you think you are depressed?' is quick and effective; it may also be noticed by nurses, therapists, or family; tools such as the Geriatric Depression Scale can also be used, but may be confounded by dysphasia). Treatment is with psychosocial support and antidepressants (e.g. citalopram 20mg). Anxiety is also very common, and often responds to explanation and empowerment.

Thromboembolism Very common post-stroke especially if very immobile. Mobilize early and use full-length compression stockings as well as aspirin to prevent occurrence. Low dose heparin (5000 IU bd sc) may have a role in bed-bound patients, but there is some evidence against it (increased risk of haemorrhage when all doses are considered). Have a low threshold for investigating a leg that becomes swollen or painful.

HOW TO... manage urinary incontinence after stroke

This is very common, more so after severe stroke. It does however improve over time, and a flexible approach is required to ensure that a patient does not get catheterized and remain so.

- Initially, try to manage with pads and regular toileting.
- If the skin starts to break down, or if the burden on carers is heavy, then a catheter can be inserted *for a limited time span*.
- Once mobility improves, try removing the catheter—ensure this is seen by all as a positive and exciting step back towards independence, as it can cause considerable anxiety.
- If this fails, check for and treat urinary tract infection then try again.
- If this fails, then replace the catheter and use bladder stabilizing agents for about 2 weeks (e.g. tolterodine 2mg bd) before removing it again.
- If all this fails, consider sheath catheter devices or bottles (with non-return valves for use in bed) in men; commodes next to the bed for women.

▶▶ The need for a permanent catheter post stroke should be reviewed regularly as the condition is likely to improve. See also p578–81.

Longer term issues

Return to the community

Best coordinated by the stroke multi-disciplinary team. Early discharge may be useful if the patient can transfer, and there is a specialist community stroke team available. Later discharges are planned by the team, usually after careful assessment of needs (home alterations, care packages etc.). The general practitioner should be alerted to continue medical monitoring, in particular optimizing secondary prevention. Community teams (district nurses, community rehabilitation teams, home carers etc.) should be aware of the patient's needs (continence, diabetic monitoring, ongoing therapy needs etc.) and ideally be involved in the discharge planning. The patient and family should have adequate information and training, as well as a contact point in case of problems (stroke coordinators often take this role). Voluntary agencies (e.g. the Stroke Association—www.stroke.org.uk) are often helpful, and the patient should be alerted to them.

Ensure that the patient is aware of driving restrictions before they are discharged.

Driving regulations with cerebrovascular disease

- TIA/stroke with full neurological recovery—one month off driving.
- Recurrent TIAs—3 months off driving following last TIA.
- Stroke with residual neurological deficit after 1 month—the patient must notify the DVLA, and the decision is made on a case by case basis, with evidence from medical reports. Hemianopia, inattention, and impaired cognition are definite markers of lack of fitness to drive (this can be decided by a GP, or hospital physician). Dysphasia is harder—cognitive state is difficult to assess and associated impairments (such as problems reading street signs or misinterpreting the environment) are not readily identified out of context. Pure limb weakness can often be safely managed with car adaptation. If there are any doubts and the patient wishes to drive then they should be seen in a driving assessment centre (usually the patient will have to pay).
- Stroke with seizure—this is treated as a provoked seizure. May be less than 1-year ban depending on circumstances.

See www.dvla.gov.uk/at_a_glance/content.htm

Follow-up

Some follow-up should be offered to all stroke survivors. The intensity and duration of inpatient care can contrast sharply with home. The realities of living with disability begin to sink in, and many questions and anxieties arise. Even minor strokes or TIAs require a further point of contact, as they will have been committed to lifelong medication and will need monitoring of risk factors. In addition, stroke recovery continues (albeit at a slower pace) for up to 2 years (or even longer) and management plans made at discharge may need to be adapted.

Checklist for follow-up
(Usually 2–4 months after discharge)
Secondary prevention
Check drugs, blood pressure, diabetic control and cardiac rhythm.
Continence
- Are there continence problems?
- If a catheter is in situ, has mobility improved to a point at which trial removal can be done?
- If the patient was discharged on bladder stabilizing drugs, and has remained continent, can these be tailed off?
Nutrition
- Is nutrition adequate? If not, refer to dietician.
- If a PEG tube is in place, is it still required?
- Does the patient warrant another assessment of swallowing (by SALT) to allow oral nutrition to begin?
Communication and speech
- Are there still problems?
- Is there a need for a speech and language therapy review?
Mood
- Is the patient depressed?
- Do they need referral to a psychologist or (rarely) psychiatrist?
- If discharged on an antidepressant, can it be discontinued?
Physical progress
- Is there ongoing physical therapy?
- If not, is there continued improvement? If there has been deterioration then refer back for assessment for further therapy (RCP guidelines).
Contractures
- Are there any contractures developing? If so, refer to physiotherapy.
Muscle spasms
- Have these developed, or lessened since discharge?
- Review need for anti-spasmodic medication—titrate down if no longer required.
Pain
- Commonly in shoulder, or post-stroke pain.
- Has this developed, or lessened?
- Review need for medications.
Daily living
- Are there any issues in managing day-to-day?
- Is all the necessary equipment in place? (And is it still needed e.g. a commode can be returned when the patient is able to mobilize to the toilet alone.)
- Is there anything that they would like to be able to do that they cannot? (E.g. read a book, take a bath.)
- Would a further review by a therapist be helpful?
- Do they wish to drive? (See opposite.)
Support
Are they in contact with a community stroke coordinator (if available)?
Are they aware of voluntary organizations?

TIA clinics

Rapid outpatient assessment of TIA and minor stroke, to establish diagnosis, commence secondary prevention and lower risk of subsequent event.

How fast?

Guidelines suggest as soon as possible and certainly less than 7 days. New data suggests that the risk of second event after TIA or minor stroke is 8–12% at one week, making earlier assessment seem sensible. Daily clinics or specialist services based in Emergency Departments may not be easily achieved, but may prove to be optimal as stroke medicine evolves. Currently, early antiplatelet agents and early endarterectomy are known to be beneficial. The timing of blood pressure lowering and statin use has yet to be quantified. New therapies are being developed aimed at limiting the ischaemic penumbra, where timing is likely to be crucial. The concept of 'brain attack' where 'time is brain' (analogous to 'heart attack') is evolving fast.

Function

Confirm diagnosis: very variable, but up to a third of referrals to a TIA clinic are non-cerebrovascular. Main alternatives are cardiac dysrhythmias, orthostatic hypotension, other systemic disease (infection, endocrine) or, rarely, brain tumour or demyelination.

Arrange investigations: to aid diagnosis (e.g. CT brain) or investigate risk factors (e.g. full blood count, ESR, glucose, cholesterol, ECG, carotid dopplers, possibly chest X-ray and echocardiogram).

Modify risk factors: set targets for blood pressure and glucose control, advise about antiplatelet agents and anticoagulation in AF, advise about statin use, refer for carotid endarterectomy, advise about smoking cessation.

Rehabilitation: point of referral for physiotherapy, occupational therapy, speech and language therapy as outpatient or inpatient as required.

Education: of patients, relatives, primary care doctors. Discuss stroke disease and its modification, time frame for recovery, psychological aspects of stroke, driving restrictions.

Structure

Varies enormously. Ideally would have:

Rapid referral protocol—perhaps a standard referral sheet and fax number for GPs, possibly via a single phone call to an answering machine.

Stroke specialist nurse—can take history including standardized risk factor analysis, measure BP, provide education (leaflets, individual action plans), coordinate investigations and follow-up. Role can be extended into community—point of access for patients.

Time for explanation: many patients will feel overwhelmed by the amount of information they are being given. The specialist nurse can be very helpful in clarifying things, and leaflets allow the information to be revisited at home. Remember, we are often prescribing several new tablets, or even suggesting surgery for a patient who feels well. Comprehension is vital for concordance.

Rapid access to investigations: particularly carotid dopplers, CT scanning and echocardiography. Many clinics run a 'one-stop' service, where all assessments, investigations, and conclusions are completed at a single visit. Other clinics have dedicated slots into which they have to prioritize the patients attending that day.

Prompt communication to general practitioner: advice about risk reduction must be relayed promptly to the GP for maximum benefit. Ideally same day by fax or delivered by the patient.

Psychiatry

Cognitive ageing 220
Impairments in cognitive function without dementia 222
Dementia: overview 224
    How to... investigate a patient with dementia 226
Dementia: common diseases 228
Dementia and Parkinsonism 230
Dementia: less common diseases 232
Normal pressure hydrocephalus 234
Dementia: non-drug management 236
    How to... manage the driver who has dementia 237
Dementia: risk management and abuse 238
Dementia: cholinesterase inhibitors 240
    How to... treat with cholinesterase inhibitors 241
Dementia: other drug treatments 242
Dementia: managing behavioural problems 244
Dementia: prevention 246
Compulsory detention and treatment 248
    How to... manage the older person refusing treatment 249
Psychosis 250
Delirium: diagnosis 252
Delirium: causes 254
Delirium: clinical assessment 256
    How to... distinguish delirium from dementia 258
Delirium: treatment issues 260
Delirium: non-drug management 262
Delirium: drug treatments 264
    How to... prescribe sedating drugs in delirium 265
Squalor syndrome 266
Depression: presentation 268
    How to... distinguish dementia from a depressive
    pseudodementia 269
Depression: clinical features 270
    How to... assess depression 271
Depression: non-drug management 272
Depression: drug treatments 274
Suicide and attempted suicide 276

Cognitive ageing

Cognitive, or thinking, ability is the product of:
- 'Fixed intelligence', the result of previous thinking, which often increases with age, i.e. 'wisdom'.
- 'Fluid intelligence', i.e. real-time information processing, which declines modestly in older age.

Broadly, intellectual function is maintained until at least 80 years, but processing is slower. Non-critical impairments include forgetfulness, modestly reduced vocabulary and slower learning of, e.g., languages. These changes are to be expected, their consequences can be managed, and they do not cause significant reduction in functional level.

Three factors support a diagnosis of normal ageing rather than disease:
- The ability to maintain function in normal life through aids (e.g. aides-memoire: lists or calendars) or adaptations (of one's environment or of one's expectations).
- Very long time-scale of decline: 10–30 years, compared to months or a few years in disease.
- Relative decline e.g. the academic who holds her own at the graduates' reunion.

Impairments in cognitive function without dementia

Age-associated memory impairment (AAMI) or benign senescent forgetfulness

Older people learn new information and recall information more slowly, but given time their performance is unchanged. This is distinct from the impairment in dementia, in that in AAMI overall function is unimpaired, and usually only less important facts are forgotten. It is often more bothersome to the patient than a concern to relatives (compare dementia, when often the family are much more concerned than the patient).

AAMI can present early (age 40s–50s) when high achievers become frustrated by modest deterioration in speed of new learning. It may be exacerbated by performance anxiety, creating a vicious cycle, and is often helped by psychological strategies to assist memory.

Minimal cognitive impairment (MCI) or cognitive impairment no dementia (CIND)

Impairments are more broad than memory alone, and are felt to be pathological (e.g. secondary to cerebrovascular disease), but the full criteria for a diagnosis of dementia are not met—for example because there is not yet significant impact on day-to-day functioning.

Progression to dementia occurs in between 5% (community studies) and 10% (memory clinic studies) annually. Thus with time, many patients do develop dementia, but many do not, and in some there is no deterioration.

Diagnosis is important in order to:
- Reassure the patient (by distinguishing from dementia).
- Modify risk factors for progression.
- Monitor deterioration such that intervention can begin promptly if progression occurs.

Dementia: overview

Dementia is an acquired decline in memory and other cognitive function(s) in an alert (i.e. non-delirious) person that is sufficiently severe to affect daily life (home, work, or social function). Each of the elements within the definition must be present in order to make the diagnosis.

Prevalence increases dramatically with age: 1% of 60–65 year olds, >30% of over 85 year olds. Over 50% of nursing home residents have dementia.

Major dementia syndromes (and proportion of cases in older people) include:
- Dementia of Alzheimer type (60–70%)
- Vascular dementia (10–20%)
- Other neurodegenerative dementias (5–10%) e.g. dementia with Lewy bodies, Parkinson's disease with dementia, frontotemporal dementia
- Reversible dementias (<5%) e.g. drugs, metabolic, subdural, normal pressure hydrocephalus.

Mixed pathology (especially Alzheimer's and vascular) is common.

Diagnostically, there are many false-positive and false-negative cases. Mild to moderate dementia is easy to miss on a cursory, unstructured assessment. Patients labeled incorrectly as having dementia may be deaf, dysphasic, delirious, depressed, or under the influence of drugs.

History

The most important component of assessment. Take from both patient and informant. Note onset, speed of progression, symptoms. Take a careful drug history, including over-the-counter drugs and recreational drugs (especially alcohol).

Usually there is a progressive decline in cognitive function over several years, ending with complete dependency and death (usually due to dehydration, malnutrition, and/or sepsis). Deterioration may be stepwise (suggesting stroke/vascular aetiology), abrupt (after a single critical stroke) or rapid (weeks/months, suggesting a drug, metabolic, or structural cause e.g. tumour, subdural).

Deterioration occurs in:
- Retention of new information (e.g. appointments, events, working a new household appliance); short-term memory loss is often severe, with repetitive questioning.
- Managing complex tasks (e.g. paying bills, cooking a meal for family).
- Language (word-finding difficulty with circumlocution, inability to hold a conversation).
- Behaviour (e.g. irritability, aggression, poor motivation, wandering).
- Orientation (e.g. getting lost in familiar places).
- Recognition (failure to recognize first acquaintances, then friends or distant family, then close family e.g. spouse).
- Ability to self-care (grooming, bathing, dressing, continence/toileting).
- Reasoning: poor judgment, irrational or unaccustomed behaviours.

Also ask about a family history of early dementia and a personal psychiatric history of e.g. depression.

Physical examination

- To determine possible causes of a dementia syndrome, including reversible factors.
- Look for vascular disease (cardiovascular, peripheral vascular and cerebrovascular), neuropathy, Parkinsonism, thyroid disease, malignancy, dehydration, (alcoholic) liver disease.

Mental state

- Exclude delirium. Features include agitation, restlessness, poor attention and fluctuating conscious level.
- Exclude depression. Features include low affect, poor motivation, and a negative perspective. Perform a Geriatric Depression Scale.
- Measure cognitive function. Serial testing may be helpful in borderline cases—is there evidence of progression? Many measurement tools are available, e.g. MMSE, Mini-Cog, number of animals named in one minute, clock-drawing test (see p88).
- Neuropsychological assessment (detailed, prolonged assessment by a specialist psychologist) may be helpful in distinguishing between dementia and depression, between age-associated memory impairment and early dementia, and between focal impairments (e.g. aphasic or amnesic syndromes) and dementia.

HOW TO... investigate a patient with dementia

Cases of reversible dementia are uncommon, but their identification is important, as effective treatment may reverse the impairment and prevent progression. Therefore screen for them.

Blood tests

The following are generally considered useful:

- FBC
- B12
- Calcium
- TSH
- Random glucose
- ESR
- U, C and E
- LFT
- CRP

Request syphilis serology if there are atypical features or special risks.

Resting ECG

Plain radiology

Chest radiograph (evidence of heart disease, occult malignancy).

Neuroimaging

It is arguable whether every person with dementia should undergo brain imaging. Imaging is indicated where there is:

- Early onset (<60 years old)
- Sudden onset or brisk decline
- High risk of structural pathology (e.g. known cancer, falls with head injury)
- Focal CNS signs or symptoms.

In more typical cases suggestive of either Alzheimer's, vascular, or mixed (Alzheimer's–vascular) dementia, the diagnostic yield is very low. Thus, in most cases, imaging does not alter the clinical management based on history, examination, and lab tests alone. If a patient or carer is particularly anxious (e.g. fear of brain tumour), imaging may help allay fears, although of course dementia is a far from benign diagnosis.

- **CT** is the usual imaging modality.
- **MRI** identifies posterior circulation vascular pathology with much greater sensitivity.
- **SPECT (single photon emission CT)** is used rarely, usually in specialist centres, to more reliably differentiate between Alzheimer's and vascular dementia.

Dementia: common diseases

Alzheimer's disease (AD; Dementia of Alzheimer type (DAT))

- The most common cause of a dementia syndrome.
- Insidious onset, with slow progression over years.
- Early, profound short-term memory loss progresses to include broad, often global cognitive dysfunction, behavioural change, and functional impairment.
- Behavioural problems are common, usually occurring in moderate to severe dementia, but sometimes preceding cognitive impairments.
- Diagnosis is made clinically, based on the typical history, mental status examination, and unremarkable physical examination.
- Early-onset AD (<65 years old) is uncommon, has a stronger genetic component, and is more rapidly progressive.

Vascular dementia (VaD)

- The next most common cause.
- Suggested by vascular risk factors e.g. diabetes mellitus, hypertension, smoking or other vascular pathology, with other supporting evidence on history, examination, or tests.
- Cognitive impairment may be patchy, compared to the more uniform impairments seen in AD.
- Frontal lobe, extrapyramidal, pseudobulbar features, and emotional lability are common.
- Urinary incontinence and falls without other explanation are often early features.
- Other features may be mostly cortical (mimicking AD) or subcortical (e.g. apathy, depression).
- Onset is often associated with stroke, or the deterioration is abrupt or stepwise.
- Physical examination often shows:
  - Focal neurology suggesting stroke or diffuse cerebrovascular disease (hyperreflexia, extensor plantars, abnormal gait, etc.).
  - Other evidence of vascular pathology e.g. atrial fibrillation, peripheral vascular disease.
- Neuroimaging shows either:
  - Multiple large vessel infarcts.
  - A single critical infarct (e.g. thalamus).
  - White matter infarcts or periventricular white matter changes.
  - Microvascular disease, too fine to be seen on neuroimaging, may cause a significant proportion of VaD, apparent only post-mortem.

Thus using 'multi-infarct dementia' as a synonym for VaD is imprecise and its use should be discouraged.

Differentiating between Alzheimer's and vascular dementia

The importance of differentiating between Alzheimer's and VaD can be overemphasized. Their presentations overlap, and pathologies commonly coexist. Pragmatically:

- In cases where vascular risk factors and/or signs exist, treat vascular risk factors aggressively, whether or not there is significant cerebrovascular pathology on brain imaging.
- A trial of cholinesterase inhibitors (effective in Alzheimer's but much weaker evidence in vascular dementia), is probably worthwhile where vascular risk factors and/or pathology exists, but Alzheimer's may be contributing to the presentation.

Dementia and Parkinsonism

Dementia with Lewy bodies (DLB) and Parkinson's disease with dementia (PDD) may be considered as extremes of a continuum. In PDD, motor impairments precede cognitive impairments and are more severe. In DLB, cognitive and behavioural impairments precede motor phenomena and are more severe.

The distinction may be even more complex if combined with contributions from Alzheimer's or vascular pathology.

Dementia with Lewy bodies (DLB)

- A gradually progressive dementia, with insidious onset.
- Fluctuations in cognitive function and alertness.
- Prominent auditory or visual hallucinations, often with paranoia and delusions.
- Parkinsonism is commonly present, but often not severe.
- Typical antipsychotics (e.g. haloperidol) are very poorly tolerated, leading to worsening confusion or deterioration of parkinsonism. Atypical antipsychotics (e.g. risperidone, and especially quetiapine) may be better tolerated, but great caution is advised in their use.
- Levodopa or dopamine agonists may worsen confusion.

Note that several features are common to both DLB and delirium, e.g. fluctuations, effect of drugs, perceptual and psychotic phenomena. When comparing the two, the following is true of DLB:

- Onset is insidious and progression gradual.
- No precipitating illness (e.g. infection) is found.
- Hallucinations are complex and not the result of misperception of stimuli.
- Delusions are well-formed and may be persistent.

Parkinson's disease with dementia (PDD)

- People with Parkinson's disease (PD) are much more likely to develop dementia, especially older people, those in the later stages of the disease, and those who become confused on PD medication.
- Typical motor features of PD are present, and may be severe.
- The presentation and neuropathology is variable, and may resemble Alzheimer's disease, vascular dementia, or DLB.
- By definition, if features of PD precede dementia by more than a year, then the diagnosis is of PDD, not DLB. This applies even if the dementia syndrome is otherwise typical of DLB.

Minimal cognitive impairment in Parkinson's disease

Many patients with PD have subtle impairments of cognition, too mild to justify a diagnosis of dementia. Slowed thinking and deficits in visuospatial attention and executive function are commonly seen.

Other conditions

Multiple system atrophy, progressive supranuclear palsy, and corticobasal degeneration may also present with both Parkinsonism and dementia.

Dementia: less common diseases

Frontotemporal dementia (FTD)

- Neurodegenerative disease, with insidious onset and slow (several years) progression.
- Onset is often early (age 35–75), and either behavioural or language difficulties dominate the clinical picture. Forgetfulness is mild. Insight is lost early. Difficulties at work may be the first sign.
- Commonly used assessment tools (e.g. MMSE) do not test frontal lobe function, so do not be put off the diagnosis by 'normal' cognitive screening tests.
- Behavioural problems are most common and include disinhibition, mental rigidity, inflexibility, impairment of executive function, decreased personal care, and repetitive behaviours.
- Language dysfunction may include word-finding difficulty, problems naming or understanding words, lack of spontaneous conversation, or circumlocution.
- Later, impairments become more broad, similar to severe Alzheimer's.
- Neuroimaging usually demonstrates frontal and/or temporal atrophy.
- FTD presents as a clinical spectrum. More specific conditions within that spectrum include:
  - Frontal lobe degeneration (FLD). Frontal greater than temporal degeneration.
  - Pick's disease. Similar to FLD, but uncommon. Classical 'Pick bodies' seen post-mortem.
  - MND with dementia. Usually late in the progression of MND.
  - Progressive nonfluent aphasia and semantic dementia. Temporal degeneration.
- Family history is positive in 50% of cases.

Dementia and drugs/toxins

- Alcohol-associated dementia may occur after many years of heavy drinking, presenting with disproportionate short-term memory impairment.
- Psychoactive drugs may cause a dementia-like syndrome that is substantially reversible.

Dementia and infection

- Neurosyphilis is becoming more common. Serological tests for syphilis should be performed if a dementia syndrome has atypical features (e.g. seizures) or risk factors for sexually transmitted disease (including mental illness, history of other STD, drug/alcohol abuse). Beware false positive serological tests in Afrocaribbeans with a history of yaws. If neurosyphilis seems possible, sample cerebrospinal fluid and seek microbiology advice with a view to penicillin treatment.
- HIV-associated dementia generally affects younger people, reflecting the epidemiology of HIV infection. It occurs late in HIV, rarely if at all at presentation.

Vasculitis

- Suggested by elevated CRP or ESR without other cause.
- Heterogeneous presentation, including as delirium or dementia.
- Examine the patient for evidence of systemic vasculitis.
- Perform lumbar puncture and CSF examination, to exclude infection or neoplasm.
- Potentially treatable, so pursue this diagnosis vigorously if necessary.

Normal pressure hydrocephalus

Normal pressure hydrocephalus (NPH) classically presents with the triad:
- Gait disturbance (wide-based)
- Incontinence of urine
- Cognitive impairment (psychomotor slowing, apathy, appear depressed).

Most with this triad have other (unrelated) causes, or have diffuse cerebrovascular disease.

Assessment

Neuroimaging
- Shows ventricles that are enlarged disproportionately compared to the degree of cerebral atrophy.
- Neuroimaging for unrelated reasons (e.g. TIA) may reveal ventricular enlargement that appears disproportionate to the degree of cerebral atrophy, suggesting possible NPH. In the absence of clinical features of NPH, the diagnosis cannot be supported, and the patient may be reassured

Lumbar puncture
- Diagnostic and therapeutic procedure.
- Usually performed if clinical and radiological findings suggestive of NPH.
- Before the procedure, assess baseline gait (e.g. timed walk) and cognition (e.g. MMSE, clock-drawing test).
- Opening pressure is normal in NPH.
- Remove 20–30ml of cerebrospinal fluid.
- Check for improvement in gait and cognition after 1–2 hours.

Treatment

Ventriculoperitoneal shunting is effective for some, but many do not benefit. Gait is more likely to improve than is cognition. It is a major procedure, and complications are common, e.g. infection and subdural haematoma. Decision to proceed requires:
- A confident diagnosis (may require specialist neurological review).
- Support of patient and carer for the procedure.
- An assessment that the likelihood of benefit is high.

Benefit is more likely in those who:
- Have a short history (days or weeks).
- Have a known cause—usually trauma or subarachnoid haemorrhage.
- Have normal brain substance on neuroimaging.
- Have no significant comorbidities. Cerebrovascular disease is especially relevant.
- Benefit from lumbar puncture and large volume cerebrospinal fluid removal.

Dementia: non-drug management

- Modify reversible factors, commonly multiple but minor (e.g. constipation, low grade sepsis, mild anaemia or drug side effects).
- Encourage physical and mental activity, including social activities (e.g. social clubs, day centers, p50).
- Suggest simple interventions to improve coping (e.g. lists, calendars, alarms).
- Treat depression. SSRIs are much preferred to tricyclics. Repeat cognitive assessment 2–4 months after treatment to determine if cognitive impairment remains.
- Create a safe, caring environment, usually in the patient's own home. A predictable routine is helpful. OT home assessment identifies hazards, provides visual safety cues, etc.
- Organise carers to assist with ADLs, prompt medication etc.
- Support caregivers:
  - Enquire about caregiver burden, and psychiatric symptoms.
  - Caregiver support groups.
  - Respite care—usually in care homes, for a few days to two weeks.
  - Sitting services—usually for 2–3 hours once or twice weekly.
  - Family Support Visitor—provides emotional and practical support.
- Educate patients and families about the disease and how to cope with its manifestations. This includes appropriate modifications to the home environment and learning to communicate and interact with the patient with dementia. Counselling and support delays admission to care homes.
- Simplify medication, and provide Dosett boxes or similar, to aid concordance. In the later stages, drugs such as antihypertensives may become pointless if not harmful (ie risk > benefit).
- Inform patient and carers of legal and ethical issues including:
  - Driving (see box opposite)
  - Enduring power of attorney (p720)
  - Wills (p740)
  - Discussion of end-of-life issues (artificial feeding, comfort versus life prolongation) may be appropriate.
- Disclosure of diagnosis. Each case should be considered individually, but in general the diagnosis should be revealed. Disclosure:
  - Is consistent with the patient's right to know (autonomy). Most older people say that they would want to know the diagnosis.
  - Facilitates medical, financial, and care planning, e.g. advance directives, power of attorney, living arrangements.
  - Allows for consent to treatment and facilitates participation in research.
  - Facilitates discussion between patient and carer.

Arguments against disclosure include a possible depressive reaction, accentuated by a perceived lack of effective treatments. Such a reaction is minimized by sensitive multidisciplinary support that emphasizes the positive therapeutic solutions available.

HOW TO... **manage the driver who has dementia**

Road traffic accident and injury risk increase with the severity of dementia. In most countries it is mandatory for the driver to report important health factors to the licensing authority, who will then request further information from the patient's medical team. Patients and carers should be reminded of this responsibility at diagnosis.

Assessment of driving ability during a hospital outpatient or general practice consultation is often difficult. In some cases, whether a patient is safe to drive will be obvious—either in the very earliest stages of cognitive impairment, or in more severe dementia. In other cases, usually of mild (to moderate) cognitive impairment, the following evidence is useful:

- Reports of driving problems, incidents (e.g. near-misses) or accidents. Are relatives/friends concerned to get into the passenger seat? Have they tried but failed to limit or prohibit driving? Some evidence is of less value e.g. getting lost is a poor indicator of safety.
- Reports of how driving patterns have changed, and why. Are journeys now brief, infrequent, and confined to quiet local roads?
- Clinical evidence of major impairment in visuospatial function, attention or judgment. However, a combination of modest impairments may be as important.
- Presence of non-cognitive impairments (e.g. visual, joint function) or other conditions that affect driving safety (e.g. seizures, syncope).

Each case should be reassessed intermittently, either at regular intervals or at points prompted by critical incidents.

The best assessment of driving ability is by a professional driving assessor, in the patient's own vehicle on the public roads. Such professionals, often occupational therapists, can deliver the confident, robust opinion that is often required, as well as offering useful practical advice to the cognitively or physically impaired driver.

In general:

- It is preferable that the patient, family, and doctor should agree that stopping voluntarily is advisable. Compulsory licence withdrawal by the authority generates great anger and distress.
- The issue is best discussed early in the course of the disease, when the patient has best insight.
- If driving is safe for the moment, encourage patient and family to think ahead, to a time when driving cannot be continued—is local public transport sufficient, or will a spouse have to hone long-lost driving skills?

Rarely, a patient continues to drive when clearly unsafe and having been informed that they must stop. In most cases, further clear statements of this, backed up by the threat of medical reporting to the authorities, are sufficient to prompt cessation. If driving continues, the clinician is ethically justified in reporting this to the authorities, and will usually have the strong support of the family.

Dementia: risk management and abuse

Risk management is an essential part of care.

- Is there a risk of harm to the patient or to others?
- How great is the risk, over how long is the patient (or other person) exposed to it, and how severe are the consequences of the risk?

Common risks include:

- *Falls.* Moving from own home to institutional care is rarely the answer. Supervision is far from continuous in any institution, the environment is less familiar, and the floors are often uncarpeted and unforgiving.
- *Wandering.* Usually more distressing to carers than risk-presenting to the patient.
- *Aggression by a patient towards carers or family.* Usually verbal, but sometimes physical or sexual. May lead to carers refusing to work with a patient.
- *Aggression towards a patient by carers or family.* Less easy to identify, as the patient may not complain, through fear or due to cognitive problems. Be concerned if there are unexplained 'falls' or unusual patterns of bruising.
- *Self-neglect.* Often with denial. May manifest as poor diet, poor hygiene, etc.
- *Fire risk.* May be easily modifiable, through removal or modification of kitchen appliances, gas fires, etc. Cigarette smoking is more problematic.
- *Driving.*
- *Financial abuse.* For example:
  - Theft or fraud
  - Modification of wills
  - Misuse or transfer of a patient's money.

Having determined the nature and magnitude of a risk, consider 'can the risk be reduced?' and 'should it be reduced?'

If risk reduction can be done without impacting on the patient's independence or enjoyment of life, then go ahead.

If reducing risk involves curtailing liberty or restricting enjoyable activity (walking, wandering, living alone), then consider:

- What is the patient's attitude to risk?
- If unable to express this, what was his/her pre-morbid attitude, and what would he/she now want?
- What is the view of carers?

Commonly, discussions around risk occur when a patient is perceived by some (carers, relatives, nursing or therapy staff) to have become unsafe to remain at home. This should prompt multidisciplinary assessment and discussion, including whether a move to institutional care would involve a change of risk patterns rather than a reduction in overall risk.

Dementia: cholinesterase inhibitors

Cholinesterase inhibitors (ChEIs) are the first drug class proven to improve cognition in some patients with dementia.

Effectiveness

They are far from miracle drugs, with very variable response. In general:

- ChEIs offer symptomatic benefit through a one-off increment in cognition. The underlying disease continues to progress at the same rate.
- Of the dementias, AD, DLB, and PDD have the greatest cholinergic deficit, and these are the dementia types known to benefit most from ChEI treatment.
- About half of patients show no benefit, a significant minority show moderate improvements ('clock turned back a few months') and for a small minority there is substantial improvement.
- In some, there is a worsening in cognition, or onset of agitation that may be temporary or respond to a change in drug.
- Early studies focused on effects on cognitive function, and these are overall modest. However, small improvements in cognition can translate into significantly improved day-to-day function, reducing carer burden (by ~30 minutes daily in moderate dementia).
- There is some evidence that ChEIs can reduce the requirements for home care, and can delay placement in nursing home.
- Benefit has been demonstrated for mild to moderate dementia, not in severe dementia.

Choosing a drug

The three ChEIs currently available are:

- **Donepezil** (Aricept®) 5mg od increased to 10mg od after 4 weeks
- **Galantamine** (Reminyl®) 4mg bd increased to 8mg bd after 4 weeks, 12mg bd after 8 weeks
- **Rivastigmine** (Exelon®) 1.5mg bd increased to maximum 6mg bd within 3 months.

Selecting an agent is difficult, as there are no head-to-head comparisons. Effectiveness seems broadly similar, and choice can be made based on costs, and the team's experience. There is most evidence for donepezil in Alzheimers disease and for rivastigmine in Lewy body dementia. Overall, the evidence for ChEIs is strongest in Alzheimer's and Lewy body dementia, and weakest in vascular dementia.

HOW TO... treat with cholinesterase inhibitors

Introducing and monitoring ChEIs is a specialist area, usually undertaken by psychogeriatric teams, or by geriatricians or neurologists working in the setting of a memory clinic.

In general, ChEIs should not be initiated in inpatient medical or rehabilitation settings, as the effects of environmental changes, physical illness, or drugs may dominate those of the ChEI, rendering assessment of effect impossible. It is preferable to initiate treatment when the patient is physically well and living in their own home.

Where given for behavioural disturbance or non-cognitive symptoms (e.g. hallucinations), ChEIs may be initiated more urgently in an institutional setting.

Before treatment
- Consider the relative risks and benefits and discuss them with patient and carer.
- Explain that the drugs do not provide a cure, and may reasonably be deferred until symptoms worsen.
- Consider how concordance can be assured.

Treatment trial
- There are significant side effects, commonly gastrointestinal (nausea, dyspepsia, diarrhoea, anorexia). These occur especially during the dose titration phase at higher doses, and are often short-lived.
- A ChEI should be given for an initial treatment period of 2–3 months. If there is no effect at maximum tolerated dose, the drug should be discontinued. There is probably little benefit from trying other ChEIs if one has failed.

Assess impact using:
- Clinician's subjective global assessment, based on the views of relative(s) or carer(s) and serial clinical observations.
- The results of cognitive tests e.g. MMSE, clock-drawing test.

Continuing therapy
- If benefit appears to have occurred, the drug should be continued at that dose. Benefit may be absolute, or relative: a small decline would be expected during the 2–3 month evaluation period, so an absence of deterioration may be attributed to drug benefit.
- ChEIs can be given indefinitely, but should be withdrawn periodically (18 months) to determine whether benefit continues. If the patient deteriorates promptly after drug withdrawal (within weeks, thus probably secondary to drug withdrawal rather than disease progression), then ChEI is restarted. The evidence for ChEIs in advanced dementia is weak, and they are generally withdrawn at this point.

Dementia: other drug treatments

Memantine (Ebixa®)

- There is limited evidence for this drug, a blocker of NMDA receptors that may reduce glutamate-mediated destruction of cholinergic neurones.
- It appears to have a small beneficial effect in severe dementia of Alzheimer's or vascular aetiology.
- It is unclear whether there are important effects on quality of life, caregiver time or insitutionalization.
- It is well tolerated. Uncommon side effects include hallucinations and worsening confusion.
- Avoid in severe renal failure.
- Memantine enhances the effect of levodopa and dopamine agonists.

Preventing progression

No drugs have been proven to slow or halt progression, although dementia is seen as so catastrophic, the following are often used:

- **Vascular secondary prevention.** e.g. aspirin, lipid-lowering drugs, ACE-inhibitors, and other antihypertensives. For patients with vascular dementia and mixed (Alzheimers–vascular) dementia, aggressive risk factor modification and tailored drug treatment akin to that following stroke is logical and may slow progression, although is not well evidenced.
- **Vitamin E.** High doses (e.g. 400–800 IU bd) are widely used by patients, and have been supported by some doctors, but recent evidence is much less convincing than earlier studies of an effect in either primary prevention or on slowing of progression. In conjunction with recent evidence suggesting no benefit in cardiovascular disease, high dose vitamin E supplementation cannot be recommended.
- **Ginkgo biloba.** A supplement widely used by people with memory impairment or dementia to enhance memory and other cognitive functions, but not convincingly supported by trial evidence. Preparations are expensive, vary in strength, and have antiplatelet activity—caution with anticoagulants.

Dementia: managing behavioural problems

Problems arise because of agitation, anxiety, phobias, irritability, wandering, hoarding, aggression, socially inappropriate behaviour (e.g. sexual disinhibition, inappropriate urination, attention-seeking), hallucinations, and delusions.

These are common in dementia, including Alzheimer's, and may occur early in the disease. Often it is behavioural problems rather than cognitive impairment that leads to insitutionalization; managing them successfully may enable a patient to remain in their own home.

General

- Consider whether acute illness (e.g. sepsis), pain (e.g. urinary retention), or changes in drug treatment (e.g. anticholinergics) have contributed, especially if behaviour has deteriorated rapidly.
- Consider whether agitation or aggression is a manifestation of depression (consider an SSRI) or of fear (which may respond if care is given in a non-challenging way by a familiar team).
- Symptomatic treatment may not be needed if symptoms are transient, do not cause the patient significant distress, and are not threatening care of the patient in the current environment.

Non-drug management

These are preferred, and may alone be sufficient.
- Avoid precipitants.
- Effective therapies include music, bathing, exercise, pets, art therapy, aromatherapy, etc.
- The environment should be home-like, familiar and interesting.
- Activities may reduce boredom, wandering and aggression.
- Delusions and hallucinations may be helped by distraction and reassurance.
- Anxiety may respond to relaxation, or a discussion of worries.
- The psychogeriatric team will be able to offer helpful advice.

Drug treatment

The best drug is that which, for that patient with that problem, has worked well previously.

For *agitation, anxiety, and irritability:*
- Consider trazodone (a sedating antidepressant), initially 50mg nocte, increased as needed, maximum 300mg daily.
- If this fails, or side effects (usually oversedation) occur, introduce an atypical antipsychotic (risperidone 0.5mg bd—2mg bd, olanzapine 2.5mg od—10mg od, quetiapine 25mg od—200mg od; NB risk of stroke may be increased).
- Anxiolytics such as benzodiazepines may be used for brief, anxiety-inducing situations.
- If depression is prominent, try an SSRI such as citalopram.

For ***problematic psychotic symptoms*** (delusions, hallucinations, paranoia):
- Atypical antipsychotics should be used at the lowest dose that is effective.
- Given the possible increased stroke risk, consider alternatives such as trazodone, especially where sleep disturbance is a problem and aggression is only verbal.
- In DLB, use antipsychotics with great caution, in low dose, under close supervision, and only when other non-pharmacological and pharmacological measures have been exhausted. Atypical antipsychotics are preferred.

Cholinesterase inhibitors may improve behaviours as well as cognition. They have few side effects, and may be given 'first-line', especially if symptoms are moderate and not acute in onset.

Review drug use regularly, being aware of potential side effects such as falls, immobility or confusion. Behavioural problems are often periodic, so consider trials off treatment, especially in those whose behavioural disturbance was not severe and has responded to treatment.

▶▶ Beware iatrogenic deterioration. Modest behavioural deterioration in a patient with moderate dementia at home may lead to hospital admission, with a loss of all familiar routine, physical environment, and caregivers. Thus further behavioural decline, administration of sedatives and further worsened confusion. Where appropriate, manage the patient at home, with a brief but thorough outpatient attendance if there is concern about physical precipitants.

Dementia: prevention

Lifestyle interventions

- **Physical activity.** Conflicting data. Physical activity may well not protect against dementia, but should be encouraged for other reasons.
- **Cognitive activity.** Observational studies suggest that games, reading, etc. are protective, but these associations may not be causal, and there are no good randomized studies.
- **Diet.** Again, observational studies suggest benefits from a high fish oil diet, but there is no high quality prospective evidence.

Drugs

- *Hormone replacement therapy (HRT).* Conflicting data from epidemiological and prospective studies. In one large prospective study, HRT doubled dementia risk. Cannot be recommended for prevention.
- *NSAIDs.* Large prospective cohort studies suggest that long-term NSAID use is protective, especially when used several years before dementia onset. RCTs are ongoing. NSAIDs may function by reducing amyloid formation, and this may be specific to only some NSAIDs (e.g. ibuprofen). Side effects are considerable for long-term users.
- *Antioxidants.* High dietary intake of antioxidants (e.g. vitamins C and E) is associated with lower risk of dementia, but methodological concerns exist (e.g. does subclinical cognitive impairment reduce recall during questionnaire surveys of diet?). Extrapolating from in vitro studies, and some early positive studies in CHD (now largely refuted), some recommend high dose (>400 IU/day) vitamin E supplements.
- *Antihypertensives.* Conflicting data. Dementia prevention is not in itself a reason to lower blood pressure.
- *Statins.* Associated with a lower frequency of dementia, but this may be spurious, due to prescribing bias (e.g. physicians less likely to prescribe to those with sub-clinical cognitive impairment).

Overall, there are few high quality randomized controlled trials of primary prevention in dementia, but many epidemiological studies. Usual practice is to encourage physical and mental activity ('use it or lose it'), to optimize blood pressure and to encourage low dose aspirin in those with, or at high risk of, cerebrovascular disease. Some physicians are treating patients at high risk of AD with NSAIDS and antioxidants, but this is not generally advised because there are several examples where promising epidemiological evidence was followed by evidence of harm when RCTs finally reported (beta-carotene, HRT). In vascular dementia, there is little evidence for atheroma reduction, but it is usual practice to modify general vascular risk factors (p324), and those with clear clinical or radiological evidence of TIA or stroke should have the usual measures.

Further reading

1. Shumaker S, Legault C, Rapp SR, et al. (2003). Estrogen plus progestin and the incidence of dementia and mild cognitive impairment in postmenopausal women. *JAMA* **289**: 2651–62.
2. Etminan M, Gill S and Samii A. (2003). Effect of non-steroidal anti-inflammatory drugs on risk of Alzheimer's disease. *BMJ* **327**: 128.

Compulsory detention and treatment

Older people in need of medical assessment, treatment, or continuing care commonly lack the capacity to judge the risk and benefit of interventions. They may therefore refuse care when its benefit is clear, and where it may be judged confidently that, had they mental capacity, they would agree.

In the United Kingdom, there are several legal procedures, which may support a doctor in the compulsory treatment, admission or detention of patients.

Common law

The most commonly used legal support for actions when the patient lacks capacity. Actions may include:

- Admission to hospital.
- Treatment and detention on a ward or within a hospital.
- Treatment in the home (e.g. in delirium secondary to infection, but refusing antibiotics).
- Detention in the home (e.g. wandering presents danger to the patient).

Actions should be:

- Justifiable and reasonable. Based on a consideration of the risks/benefits for that patient, and their likely wishes were they competent. Consider alternatives.
- Proportionate to the situation.
- Carefully documented.

Section 5 (2) of the Mental Health Act, England and Wales

- This permits the detention of an inpatient in a general or psychiatric hospital for up to 72 hours after submission of a report, whilst their mental health needs are assessed. Outpatients or day hospital patients do not fall within this section.
- It should be considered if a patient is highly resistive to treatment or restraint, formalizing actions taken under Common law.
- It is sensible to seek the advice of a psychogeriatrician to confirm that it is appropriate, and during the 72 hour period to perform assessment and help guide further management.
- Detention is authorized when the registered medical practitioner in charge of treatment or a fully registered deputy (ie consultant or fully registered junior doctor; not pre-registration house staff) completes a report ('form 12') and submits it to the duty hospital manager.

Section 2 of the Mental Health Act, England and Wales

- This permits the admission to hospital and detention of a patient for assessment and treatment.
- The patient must be suffering a mental disorder that warrants detention in the interests of the patient or for the protection of others.
- Application is made by a relative or approved social worker, and supported by two registered medical practitioners.
- The assessment period is up to 28 days and is not renewable.

Section 47 of the National Assistance Act 1948

- This permits compulsory transfer from home to a place of safety (e.g. a hospital or care home).
- Necessary criteria would include that the patient is 'aged or infirm', and that they require care but have not received it, usually due to refusal. Often conditions are very squalid.
- It is now rarely used, as if there is mental illness, then common law or a Section may be most appropriate, and if the patient is competent, then compulsion is usually inappropriate, however squalid others judge conditions.
- Most commonly used if there is care refusal in a competent patient, and where conditions are sufficiently squalid that they present a health hazard to others.

HOW TO... manage the older person refusing treatment

In practice, compulsion is possible only in hospital environments. Brief interventions against a patient's will are sometimes possible in the home (e.g. restraint to prevent dangerous wandering; forced administration of antibiotics in a septic patient with delirium), but can rarely be sustained—the necessary resources are not available, and staff feel legally and physically vulnerable.

Use **common law** to admit in cases of:
- Dementia with acute physical illness (to acute medical or geriatric ward).
- Delirium with moderate behavioural disturbance (to acute medical or geriatric ward).

Use the **Mental Health Act** to admit in cases of:
- Dementia, with risk to self e.g. dangerous wandering (to psychiatric ward). But alternatives must be explored and considered.
- Delirium with severe behavioural disturbance (to psychiatric, medical or geriatric ward).
- Psychotic state, severe with risk to self or others (to psychiatric ward).
- Depression, severe with psychosis or risk of self-harm (to psychiatric ward).

Use Section 47 of the **National Assistance Act** in cases of people living in squalor, without psychiatric illness, but with risk to the health of others (to care home or other place of safety).

Compulsory admission is not justified and/or not legal in cases of:
- Physical illness, refusing treatment but no psychiatric illness.
- Psychotic state or other psychiatric illness of moderate severity, without significant risk to self or others.

These are guidelines. If in any doubt, seek emergency advice from the local psychogeriatric team.

Psychosis

Psychotic symptoms e.g. delusions and hallucinations, are common in older people, particularly in those who are acutely unwell, hospitalized or in care homes. These symptoms are distressing to the patient, cause anxiety amongst caregivers, and often indicate important, treatable disease.

What is psychosis?

A state of severe impairment of assessment of reality. The results include:

- Distortions of perception e.g. illusions (misperceptions: distortions of actual perceptions) and hallucinations (perceptions not the result of external stimulus).
- Distortions of thought content, i.e. delusions—beliefs held with great conviction despite contrary evidence. These are usually secondary, i.e. a response to abnormal occurrences such as hallucinations or low mood.

Causes of psychotic symptoms in older people

The most common causes are 'organic'. In order of frequency:

- Dementia
- Delirium
- Drugs e.g. levodopa
- Other neurological causes e.g. cerebrovascular disease, brain tumour.

Less common causes are 'functional' or 'non-organic', e.g.:

- Persistence into late life of chronic schizophrenia
- Delusional disorder of later life ('late paraphrenia')
- Psychotic presentation of affective disorder (mania or depression).

Treatment of patients with psychotic symptoms

- Can usually be managed on the general medical wards, or at home, but early specialist psychogeriatric team support is advised.
- Avoid reinforcing a patient's paranoid beliefs: don't avoid contact, don't seek rapid transfer from the ward, etc.
- Make a diagnosis and treat the underlying cause e.g. stop drugs leading to delirium.
- Attend to hearing and visual impairments.
- Treat underlying mood disorder.
- In dementia, especially Alzheimer's and DLB, consider ChEIs.
- If symptoms are distressing and persistent, consider the use of antipsychotics e.g. haloperidol, risperidone, olanzapine; usually after specialist advice. Be cautious in patients who may have DLB.
- On discharge, offer opportunities for social interaction and practical home support.

Delirium: diagnosis

Beware sloppy language.

- The term 'confusion' means only that: muddled thinking, or an inability to think clearly. It is an important symptom of acute 'organic' brain disorders such as delirium but is not confined to them, i.e. low specificity. It may also be seen in depression, dementia, and less commonly in some primary psychotic disorders.
- The term delirium (acute confusional state) refers to an acute brain syndrome, effectively acute brain failure, characterised by impairment of consciousness (however slight).

▶▶ Use the term confusion when describing a presentation, but never as a diagnosis.

In summary, delirium is a syndrome of disturbance of consciousness accompanied by change in cognition not accounted for by preexisting dementia.

Key features include

- **A disturbance of consciousness** (decreased clarity of awareness of the environment). Decreased ability to focus, shift, or sustain attention. Distractability. Loses thread of conversation. Leads to uncertainty about time of day. Impairment is often not obvious, especially if onset gradual; but, after recovery, memory for the period will be poor. This feature is not seen in early dementia, or in primary psychotic disorders.
- **Change in cognition.** Often widespread, e.g. memory impairment (often recent memory), disorientation (time, place; person less common), language disturbance (e.g. dysgraphia, dysnomia), perceptual impairment (misinterpretations e.g. slamming door = gunshot), illusions (usually visual, e.g. bedclothes animated), hallucinations. Thinking may be slow and muddled, but is often rich in content.
- **Acute onset, and fluctuates.** Usual onset over hours or a few days. Sometimes changes are subacute (weeks to a few months) and may be misdiagnosed as dementia. Severity varies during the day.

Other features (not essential to make the diagnosis) include

- Disturbance of the sleep-wake cycle. May be complete reversal.
- Disturbed psychomotor behaviour. May be 'up' (restless, picking, wandering) or 'down' (slow, immobile).
- Emotional disturbance. e.g. fear, depression, anger, euphoria, lability. Fear and aggression may be a consequence of threatening hallucinations or delusions. The patient may call out, scream, or moan continually. In an institutional setting this may be problematic, especially at night. At a lesser level, the patient may appear simply perplexed and bewildered.
- Delusions (often persecutory) are common, but usually transient and poorly elaborated.
- Poor insight is typical.

Delirium is a varied syndrome. As well as fluctuating day-to-day or hour-to-hour, it is variable in nature, manifesting distinctly in different patients, or in the same patient at different times. For example, two patterns (ends of a spectrum) have been described:

- 'Up': oversensitive to stimuli, psychomotor agitation, repeatedly getting out of bed, noisy, psychotic symptoms, aggression.
- 'Down': psychomotor retardation, lethargy, quiet, paucity of speech, few psychotic symptoms.

Making the diagnosis can be difficult. Delirium may be misdiagnosed when it is not present (for example in deaf, or blind, or dysphasic patients). More commonly, the diagnosis is not made when it is present. Therefore screening tests (typically the AMTS) are valuable, and should be performed in all cases when delirium is possible—certainly at the time of admission, and during admission if changes in clinical condition occur.

Usually there is evidence of the medical condition that has led to delirium. Although this is not necessary to make the diagnosis, it is necessary to treat it effectively.

Delirium: causes

A particular case is often multifactorial, i.e. several factors (individually modest and alone insufficient) combine to push a patient across a threshold to frank delirium. Chronic factors (e.g. overt or incipient dementia) may maintain a person closer to that threshold, and impaired homeostasis of older age increases the systemic—and cerebral—effects of illness.

Delirium is therefore especially likely to occur in the very elderly, in the physically frail, or if there is preexisting dementia, defective hearing or vision, or brain damage of any kind e.g. idiopathic Parkinson's disease. In these cases more minor acute illnesses may cause delirium.

Factors that may contribute to delirium

▶▶ Usually, there is evidence from either the history, or examination, or simple tests, of the factor(s) that have contributed to delirium.
These factors include:

- **Infection**. Viral or bacterial. Not necessarily severe, especially in those with minimal cognitive impairment, dementia, or other contributory factors. Common sources are chest, urine, skin (cellulitis). Remember other infections e.g. CNS, endocarditis, biliary infection, diverticulitis, pancreatitis, abdominal perforation, and abdominal or pelvic collection.
- **Drug intoxication**. Especially anticholinergics, anxiolytics/hypnotics, anticonvulsants, opiates (see box opposite).
- **Disorders of electrolyte/fluid balance** e.g. dehydration, uraemia, hypo-/hypernatraemia, hypercalcaemia. Modest degrees of hyponatraemia (>130mM) are unlikely to be the sole cause of delirium.
- **Alcohol or drug withdrawal**.
- **Organ failure** e.g. cardiac, respiratory, liver.
- **Endocrine**. High or low blood sugar, hypo- or hyperthyroid.
- **Epileptic**. Post-ictal state following unrecognized seizures. Consider if there has been an unwitnessed 'collapse', with amnesia, and any ictal features (incontinence, tongue biting).
- **Intracranial pathology** e.g. head injury, space-occupying lesion, increased intracranial pressure of whatever cause, infection, pre-existing cognitive impairment or acute/chronic cerebrovascular disease. However, acute stroke is rarely the sole cause of delirium.
- **Pain**.

These factors may be accentuated on admission to hospital by environmental disorientation, a lack of information, sensory over- or under-stimulation, impersonal setting, changes in staff or wards, poorly understood investigations and treatments, and being away from a familiar home and family/carers.

Drugs causing delirium

Drug-induced delirium is common. Incidence of delirium is closely associated with anticholinergic activity. Therefore tricyclic antidepressants and neuroleptics constitute high-risk groups. Many more are less frequently associated with delirious reactions.

- **Anticholinergics** (used for either cardiac or GI effects, e.g. atropine, hyoscine, propantheline)
- **Antipsychotic drugs ('neuroleptics')** e.g. chlorpromazine, trifluoperazine, thioridazine
- **Antihistamines** e.g. chlorphenamine, diphenhydramine
- **Hypnotics/anxiolytics** e.g. barbiturates, benzodiazepines, 'Z-drugs' (zolpidem etc.)
- **Antidepressant drugs** especially tricyclics
- **Anticonvulsant drugs** e.g. phenytoin, carbamazepine
- **Opiates and opiate-like drugs** including codeine, dihydrocodeine and tramadol
- **Corticosteroids** including prednisolone
- **Lithium**
- **H2 receptor blockers** e.g. cimetidine (rarely)
- **L-dopa (Sinemet®, Madopar®), dopamine agonists.** Caution in treating Parkinsonism in patients with Lewy body dementia
- **Digoxin.**

'Recreational' drugs that may cause delirium include alcohol, marijuana, LSD, amphetamines, cocaine, opiates, and inhalants.

A drug may be the 'final straw' that leads to overt delirium. For example a dry, septic patient who has tolerated co-codamol when well, may become delirious when it is again administered in hospital.

Delirium: clinical assessment

History and examination

- Most factors leading to a presentation with delirium can be identified by taking a history and examining the patient. Even confused, forgetful patients report ongoing symptoms (e.g. pain, dysuria) if asked.
- Always obtain a collateral history, paying careful regard to recent minor/major symptoms e.g. cough, as well as drug history, and an exploration of the nature and duration of memory or cognitive symptoms.
- Always assess cognition objectively—e.g. using the AMTS, MMSE, or Clock-drawing test. This may yield surprising results (better or worse than expected), and permits tracking of progress.
- If a patient is non-compliant with examination, use distraction (e.g. chatting whilst examining) or complete the examination in sections. Sedation will only rarely be necessary.
- Focus the examination on important areas—is there evidence of infection (examine all lung areas, abdomen), or of new focal neurology? Is the patient dehydrated or overloaded?
- Repeat vital signs regularly, especially temperature.
- Check arterial oxygen saturation off oxygen—even modest hypoxaemia (sats ≤95%) may indicate important cardiopulmonary pathology.

Investigation

- One contributing factor may be obvious (e.g. urinary tract infection), but do not assume that this is the sole—or even the most important—factor, until others have been excluded.
- All should have some baseline tests (see box opposite). These will vary according to the clinical picture, the availability of tests, and whether a clear cause is already apparent.
- If the cause remains unclear despite a careful history, examination, and 'simple' tests, then repeat clinical assessment, consider less common causes, and consider more advanced tests such as CT/MRI brain or CSF examination.

Baseline investigations in delirium

- **FBC, ESR.** Evidence of infection, anaemia (unlikely on its own to cause delirium).
- **U, C and E.** Hypo-/hypernatraemia, dehydration, renal impairment.
- **Glucose.** Hypo-/hyperglycaemia. The sugar may now be normal—but what was it an hour/day ago?
- **LFTs and amylase.**
- **TFTs.** Hypo- or hyperthyroidism are common and treatable. Both may contribute to a presentation of delirium
- **CRP.** A very useful test, but may be normal early in the course of infection.
- **Calcium and phosphate.**
- **CXR.** Clinical examination is relatively insensitive to early/localized pathology e.g. infection.
- **ECG.** Silent ischaemia/infarction common in older people. Consider troponin.
- **Urinalysis ± urine microscopy and culture.** Asymptomatic bacteriuria is common; a positive dipstick may not therefore explain a patient's delirium. Look for additional causes.
- **Blood culture.** Always send before starting antibiotics. Occult bacteraemia is common.
- **Blood gases.** Hypoxaemia or hypercapnia may contribute to delirium.

HOW TO... distinguish delirium from dementia

The most common issue in diagnosing the older patient with confusion ('brain failure') is whether the patient has delirium alone, dementia alone, or a delirium superimposed on a preexisting dementia.

Achieve this by combining information from the history with a physical examination and mental state examination.

The history is key. The duration of symptoms is most important. Information from medical records, carers, and family will help determine whether dementia was present before onset of delirium. 'When was his memory last as good as yours?'.

Feature	Delirium	Dementia
Mode of onset	Acute or subacute	Chronic or subacute
Reversibility	Often reversible	Rarely reversible
Fluctuation	Diurnal or hour-to-hour fluctuation common	Generally little diurnal variation, although some deteriorate during the evening; 'sundowning'. Day-to-day fluctuation more common in Lewy body dementia
Poor attention	Yes (but variable hour-to-hour)	In severe dementia
Conscious level	Usually affected but may be subtle and variable	Normal
Hallucinations and misinterpretations	Common	Usually occurs late in the disease. Visual hallucinations earlier in the disease, especially when symptoms fluctuate, suggests Lewy body dementia
Fear, agitation, aggression	Common	Uncommon in early stages
Disorganized thought, unreal ideas	Common	Late. Often poverty of thought
Motor signs	Tremor, myoclonus, asterixis common	Late only
Speech	May be dysarthric, dysnomic	Normal
Dysgraphia	Often present	Usually late
Short and long term memory	Poor	Long-term memory often normal until late

Delirium: treatment issues

▶▶ Initiate treatment early: delirium is a medical emergency.

Where to treat?

In many cases the patient should be admitted to an acute general hospital where there are advanced diagnostic facilities (including CT) and staff trained to manage acute illness. Outside an acute hospital—in a domestic setting, care home, community or psychiatric hospital—the medical team must in each case balance the benefits of advanced diagnostics, treatment and monitoring with the possible detrimental effect of transfer e.g. of ambulance transport, a change of environment, less familiar care staff, etc. There is little place for a 'treat at home and hope' approach, unless:

- The dominant cause is clear.
- Effective treatment can be given.
- Appropriate care and supervision can be assured.
- The risks of transfer to an acute environment are considered to outweigh the benefits.

Keep the admission brief. With appropriate support and monitoring, discharge home or transfer to a less acute environment can often be achieved early.

The underlying cause

▶▶ Making the diagnosis of delirium is half the job. The second part is eliciting and treating cause(s).

- However, don't treat totally blindly, e.g. there is little place for blind, broad-spectrum antibiotics, unless the patient is very ill and sepsis appears likely.
- Always check the drug chart. Consider each drug in turn: at this time, does risk equal or exceed benefit? If so, stop the drug, at least temporarily.
- Ensure adequate fluid and nutrition. The patient may not be dry or malnourished on admission (though they commonly are), but may soon become so.
- If alcohol dependency or severe malnutrition is known or suspected, high dose parenteral vitamin B supplements may be needed.
- Occasionally, the cause of delirium is not apparent. In such cases:
  - Initiate general supportive measures (fluid, pressure care, nutrition etc.).
  - Continually re-examine and consider more advanced tests.

Competency

Patients with delirium are not usually competent to direct treatment. Common law allows assessment and treatment in their best interests. This may include:

- Holding within a ward or hospital if a patient attempts to leave.
- Temporary physical restraint (e.g. whilst drugs are administered).
- Covert administration of essential drugs.

Clear explanations should be given to staff and family of the need for such interventions, and their ethical and legal justification. Document clearly in the medical notes why the team considers that such measures are necessary.

Delirium: non-drug management

Delirious patients feel ill, frightened, bemused, and disorientated. There are problems with attention, memory, and perception. Therefore do what you can to make life easier for the patient:

- Provide a quiet environment free from worrying sounds; appropriate clothes; quality lighting, at an appropriate level for the time of day; a clock or outside view to aid orientation.
- Optimize visual and auditory acuity by providing spectacles and hearing aids that work.
- Reassure the patient repeatedly and calmly.
- Explain who you are and what you wish to do. Check for understanding.
- Patients will sense a doctor's manner, particularly aggression or frustration. At all times appear relaxed, unhurried, and pleasant.
- Use non-verbal communication: sit down, smile, and appear friendly rather than professional.
- Don't argue, or correct delusions—the product will be aggravation and lesser compliance.
- Visitors who are heightening emotion should be asked to leave.
- Explain to relatives, and enlist their help, in supervising, feeding, and bringing in items familiar to the patient.

Physical restraint

Restraint is terrifying and has adverse mental and physical sequelae. It is only rarely needed, but is sometimes (inappropriately) used as a substitute for supervision and guidance by an experienced carer/nurse.

In cases of severe aggression, where parenteral drugs are required, brief immobilization of the patient using the minimum force necessary may on balance be in the patient's interests.

Thinking about discharge

Once a patient is admitted, multiple barriers to discharge often appear:
- Carers and family will fear that recent deterioration will persist, and may resist discharge.
- Care packages may be cancelled, taking weeks to restart.
- Therapists may assess function as suboptimal in the unfamiliar hospital environment, judging that discharge is unsafe.

Therefore once the acute event has been diagnosed and treatment begun, encourage the team to begin promptly to plan for home.

Delay in discharge leads to:
- Increased prescription of psychotropic drugs
- Institutionalization
- Increased likelihood of care home placement.

▶▶ In those whose functional status declines significantly, remember that full recovery may take weeks if not months—beware making irreversible decisions (e.g. home vs. residential care)—before the final functional level is known.

Delirium: drug treatments

Drugs are needed only when the agitation that accompanies delirium is:
- Causing significant patient distress.
- Threatening the safety of the patient or others.
- Interfering with medical treatment (e.g. pulling out of iv lines, aggression preventing clinical examination).

Having decided that drug treatment is in the patient's interests, remember that:
- Drugs should complement, not replace, non-drug approaches.
- The correct dose is the minimum effective dose.
- The response (adverse and beneficial) and prescription must be reviewed regularly.
- It is preferable to use only one drug, starting at low dose, and increasing the dose incrementally at intervals of 30–60 minutes.

The relative merits of differing drug classes and drugs are debated, but a reasonable consensus is presented opposite.

In cases where behaviour remains problematic, seek urgent advice from the local psychogeriatric team.

HOW TO... prescribe sedating drugs in delirium

Typical antipsychotics (e.g. haloperidol)

- Usually the first-line. Compared to low-potency antipsychotics, there are fewer side effects (e.g. sedation, hypotension, anticholinergic).
- Begin with a small dose, e.g. 0.5mg orally, as tablet or liquid, as required. Repeat doses after 1–2 hrs, and increase the dose size as needed and tolerated. Total daily oral dose is usually 0.5–4mg.
- Response is idiosyncratic: some patients are very sensitive to low dose, others only to very large doses.
- In older people the half-life of haloperidol may be as long as 60 hrs. Dosing can be cumulative. Failure to titrate the dose correctly may render the patient semi-conscious for days.
- The oral liquid formulation of haloperidol is colourless and odourless, aiding covert administration (e.g. in a drink) if required.
- In the very agitated consider haloperidol 1–2mg im repeated after one hour (approximately 2:1 oral to intramuscular dose equivalence).
- The incidence of extrapyramidal side effects is high. Avoid haloperidol in DLB and in all causes of severe Parkinsonism.

Short acting benzodiazepine (e.g. lorazepam)

- Useful if sleep disturbance is prominent, or as a second line treatment for severe distress or agitation.
- Short acting benzodiazepines are preferred, e.g. lorazepam 0.5mg po/im repeated as necessary/tolerated, to maximum 3mg/day.
- Dependence and tolerance is possible, so review regularly and discontinue as soon as possible. Avoid inclusion on TTOs if possible.
- Long-acting benzodiazepines are especially useful for the treatment of delirium caused by alcohol or benzodiazepine withdrawal. Use chlordiazepoxide, in reducing dose.
- In extreme cases only (e.g. severe distress/agitation, with imminent danger to self/others), consider giving a small intravenous dose of a short-acting benzodiazepine (e.g. midazolam 1–2.5mg), carefully titrated to response. Monitor closely both clinically and with oximetry—the major risk is respiratory depression.

Atypical antipsychotics (e.g. risperidone, olanzapine)

- The place of the newer atypical antipsychotic medications (e.g., risperidone, olanzapine) remains unclear, following concerns of increased risk of stroke.
- Should be considered when response to other strategies is poor.
- Risperidone liquid can be diluted in water, black coffee, or juice.
- Risperidone 0.5mg has similar potency to haloperidol 1mg.

Combination treatment

Benzodiazepines and antipsychotic medications are sometimes combined in the management of delirium symptoms, generally under specialist advice.

Stopping treatment

Once behaviour has improved, consider step-wise dose reduction, aiming to stop the drug as soon as possible without prompting relapse.

Squalor syndrome

Also referred to as senile self-neglect (inappropriately derogatory) or Diogenes syndrome.

Clinical features

- Affected people, usually elderly, live in conditions of severe self-neglect, are socially withdrawn, and lack insight into the unusual nature of their behaviours and effects on others.
- Financial problems are rare.
- Homes are typically dirty, their upkeep neglected, and are often the repository for hoarded rubbish. This often causes distress and anxiety to neighbours, social and health professionals, much more so than to the patients themselves. Thus they come to the attention of many agencies, health, social, and public (e.g. environmental health).

The syndrome is not uncommon. Diagnosis is made when the above features exist, without major psychiatric illness (dementia, depression) to explain it. The best guess is that the syndrome is an unusual manifestation of longstanding personality disorder, and that isolated frontal lobe dysfunction commonly plays a part.

Risk factors

- Borderline personality ('eccentricity')
- Early dementia or depression
- Recent bereavement (commonly spouse)
- Lack of close family
- Social isolation
- Sensory impairment (often visual).

Management

- This should include identification and treatment of contributing psychiatric illness and secondary physical illness e.g. malnutrition.
- Patients often decline ongoing social support. Psychiatric day care may maintain more mainstream behaviour for a time, but relapse is common. Institutional care is a long-term solution, if accepted.
- Usually such people are competent to decide to maintain their unusual lifestyle, and to decline offers of support.
- Caring for them can be frustrating, but adverse consequences for the patient are often surprisingly few, and a watching brief is usually sufficient, with prompt intervention when decompensation occurs.

Depression: presentation

The most common psychiatric illness in older people. Probably 10–15% prevalence over 65 years, severe in 3%.

Risk factors for depression include:
- Disability and illness (especially if serious).
- Care home residents.
- Bereavement. Reactive depression is more common in older people, who suffer more bereavement, illness and other life events. The reaction may be understandable, but there is benefit from treatment (see pp704–5).
- Social isolation.
- Chronic pain.
- Sensory impairment (e.g. hearing or sight).

Comorbidity may mask or precipitate depression, which may be:
- Physical (Parkinson's, stroke, cancer, or post-acute illness).
- Psychiatric (dementia).

Depression is **underdiagnosed** in older people, for the following reasons:
- Perception that depression carries a social stigma, so not volunteering symptoms.
- Presentation with symptoms suggesting physical rather than psychiatric disease (e.g. weight loss rather than sadness).

▶▶ Have a low threshold for opportunistic screening.

HOW TO... distinguish dementia from a depressive pseudodementia

Pseudodementia is a severe depression that presents with poor memory and concentration and impaired functional capacity, e.g. for Activities of Daily Living.

It is usually distinguishable from dementia, because:

- The history is often short and the onset relatively abrupt.
- Patients often complain about poor memory and are despairing.
- Assessment of cognition often results in 'don't know' responses.
- Memories are often accessible with 'hints' or cues from the assessor—they remain 'stored'.
- There is often a past history of depression, or an identifiable precipitant.

The prognosis is variable. In some, mood and cognition respond to antidepressants. However, many go on to develop dementia, usually of Alzheimer type.

Coexistence of depression and dementia

- Both depression and dementia are relatively common, and may coexist coincidentally.
- Over 20% of people with an early dementia may be depressed, suggesting a depressive reaction to the onset of dementia— especially common and understandable if insight is preserved.
- This is quite different from pseudodementia (where there is no actual dementia).

General guidance

- Treat depression whatever the cause—whether a 'true' pseudodementia, or a combination of dementia and depression.
- Avoid mislabelling a depressed patient as also demented— the management and prognoses are very different.
- Always screen for depression when assessing patients with cognitive disorders, including short-term memory loss alone.

Depression: clinical features

Sadness

Commonly denied, and not necessary in order to make a diagnosis of depression. Tearfulness is uncommon, especially in men. Also ask about biological symptoms, anhedonia (inability to enjoy—ask 'what do you enjoy or look forward to?') and depressive thoughts (guilt, worthlessness, low self-esteem, self-blame, suicidal thoughts, hopelessness and help-lessness)

Anorexia and weight loss

Common to both depression and to serious physical illness. In the patient who presents in this way, without evidence of a physical cause after clinical examination and basic tests, it is a matter of judgement whether and when an antidepressant trial should begin, and whether more invasive tests should be delayed pending the results of that thera-peutic trial.

Sleep disturbance

Typically early morning wakening, but a full sleep history is useful, as early wakening may be appropriate, e.g. if sleeping during the day. Some older people do sleep much less than when younger—the key is whether they wake refreshed, or wake anxious and fearful, keen to return to sleep but unable to do so.

Disturbance of behaviour

May include attention-seeking, aggression, irritability, cries for help (e.g. intentional falls), self-neglect, malnutrition, social withdrawal.

Cognitive impairment

Poor attention and concentration may result in impairments in several cognitive domains, typically memory. If severe, this may manifest as a 'depressive pseudodementia'.

Suicidal ideation and self-harm

Should always be taken seriously, as completed suicide is relatively com-mon in older people, especially those with physical illness. Self-harm (e.g. drug overdose) may be medically trivial, but psychiatrically very serious, and should mandate psychiatric referral. Parasuicide—a 'cry for help' or 'manipulative' self harm event—is very rare; most older people who self-harm are at least moderately depressed.

Physical slowness

Exclude physical causes, including Parkinsonism, cerebrovascular disease, and hypothyroidism. May manifest as increased dependence or 'failure to cope'. May be severe, with very reduced mobility or total immobility—the depressed, bedbound, motionless, anorexic patient must be treated as an emergency.

Somatization

This expression of psychological problems as physical symptoms is common, as is hypochondriasis (disproportionate concern over health). In the patient presenting with somatization or hypochondriasis, the risks are of failing to investigate and treat when a true physical illness is present, or conversely, of failing to appreciate that antidepressant treatment is actually what is needed.

HOW TO... assess depression

Depression rating scales
E.g. Geriatric Depression Scale (see Appendix), which is known to be valid in community and hospital settings, and maintains specificity in mild to moderate dementia.

Two or three simple questions can be effective screening tools. Simply asking 'do you feel low?' has reasonable sensitivity and specificity for depression.

Psychiatric history and examination

Physical history and examination
Targeting evidence of physical illness contributing to or mimicking depression, and contraindications to drug treatments.

Cognitive assessment screen
E.g. Mini-Mental State Examination, clock-drawing test. Is there coexisting cognitive impairment? If so, does it improve with treatment for depression? i.e. pseudodementia (see p269).

Blood tests
- FBC (anaemia leading to lethargy; high MCV in alcohol excess)
- ESR (malignancy, vasculitis)
- B12 and folate (low levels may contribute to depression, or result from anorexia)
- U,C and E (uraemia, dehydration)
- Calcium (hypercalcaemia leading to depression, fatigue)
- Thyroid function (hypo- and occasionally hyperthyroidism may present as depression)
- Liver function (malignancy, alcohol excess).

Depression: non-drug management

Depression is undertreated as well as underdiagnosed. Treatment should be started promptly, its intensity (e.g. drug dose) increased as needed, and continued until the likelihood of relapse off treatment is low.

Supportive treatment

- Includes counselling and relief of loneliness.
- Treat physical symptoms and pain.
- Address rational anxieties, e.g. financial, housing, physical dependency.
- Consider stopping contributory drugs (beta-blockers, benzodiazepines, levodopa, opiates, steroids).

Psychotherapy

As effective as antidepressants for mild to moderate depression, and may be preferred by some. May complement drug treatment in resistant cases. Cognitive behavioural therapy has the most evidence. Often limited availability.

Electroconvulsive therapy (ECT)

ECT offers a safe, rapid and reasonably certain response in cases where:
- Rapid response is necessary.
- Patients with depression have been intolerant to or have not responded to drug treatment.
- Depression is very severe and manifests as psychosis, severe physical retardation, depressive stupor or food/fluid refusal.

Relative contraindications include coronary, cerebrovascular, and pulmonary disease.

Specialist referral

Consider psychogeriatric assessment if:
- Treatment is unsuccessful after 6–8 weeks.
- Depression is severe, e.g. with delusions.
- The diagnosis is unclear e.g. when depression and significant cognitive impairment co-exist.
- A patient is refusing treatment or otherwise threatening self-harm.
- There are questions of competency.

Depression: drug treatments

Drug treatment is generally effective, well-tolerated and non-addictive, although patients often believe otherwise. There is significant stigma associated with taking antidepressants, and this may need to be explored and addressed. In reactive depression, consider saying 'this won't stop you feeling sad, that's understandable, but it will help you to cope better with those feelings'. Inform the patient that response takes time but is usual.

Treatment should be continued for up to a year. If depression has been severe and/or recurrent, consider continuing indefinitely.

Stopping drugs

Withdrawal reactions (anxiety, mania, delirium, insomnia, GI side effects, headache, giddiness) may occur if drugs are stopped abruptly after 8 weeks or more. Therefore reduce dose gradually, over 4 weeks. In those on long-term treatment, reduce over several months.

Switching drugs

'Gradual cross-tapering' is generally advised, i.e. the incremental reduction of the 'old' drug, and incremental increase of the 'new' drug. Rarely, a wash-out period between drugs is required (e.g. before MAOIs).

Selective serotonin reuptake inhibitors (SSRIs)

E.g. citalopram (10–30mg od) or sertraline (50–100mg od).

- Generally now the first class of antidepressant prescribed.
- Compared to tricyclic antidepressants such as amitriptyline, they are less sedating, have fewer anticholinergic and cardiotoxic side effects, fewer drug interactions, and are much safer in overdose.
- Response may take up to 8 weeks.
- Common side effects include gastrointestinal symptoms (nausea and diarrhoea), postural hypotension, anxiety and restlessness, and hyponatraemia. Hyponatraemia is usually moderate (Na >125mM) and asymptomatic, and especially common in combination with diuretics.
- Start at low doses to minimize side effects, and build up as needed to give a useful response.
- If there is no response to an adequate dose of one SSRI, there is little point trying another. Instead, switch class.

Tricyclic antidepressants

E.g. amitriptyline, nortriptyline.

- Much less prescribed than previously.
- They still have a role, for example:
  - If anticholinergic effects are desirable (urge incontinence).
  - When there is neuropathic or other pain that may respond to its coanalgesic effect.
  - In depression resistant to other drugs.
- The secondary amines (e.g. nortriptyline) are preferred, causing less orthostatic hypotension than tertiary amines (e.g. amitriptyline, imipramine). Anticholinergic side effects are less troublesome if doses start low and are increased weekly.

Serotonin and noradrenaline reuptake inhibitors (SNRIs)

E.g. venlafaxine.
- For severe depression, or when poor response to SSRIs after 6 weeks.
- Starting dose 37.5mg bd, increased after several weeks if needed to 75mg bd (75mg–150mg od as modified release formulation).
- May cause less orthostatic hypotension than the SSRIs, but other side effects similar.

Mirtazapine

- An atypical antidepressant.
- It has fewer anticholinergic side effects, but is more sedating than tricyclics.
- Use when a degree of sedation is desirable.

Mononamine oxidase inhibitors (MAOIs)

E.g. meclobemide.
Occasionally used, under expert guidance, but dietary and drug interactions are problematic.

Suicide and attempted suicide

Older people, especially men, have a higher risk of completed (rather than attempted) suicide. Following an attempted suicide, further attempts—and successful suicide—are common.

Risk factors include being male, single (i.e. unmarried, divorced/separated or widowed), socially isolated, having financial problems, having made previous attempts, and suffering recent bereavement. Unlike younger people, the substantial majority of older people who attempt suicide are psychiatrically unwell at the time of the attempt; most are depressed. Many seek contact with medical services prior to the attempt, although they may not express depressive or suicidal thoughts at that visit.

Suicidal behaviours may be overt or covert.

Overt behaviours include:
- Intentional drug overdoses (opiates, antidepressants, paracetamol, benzodiazepines; more common in women).
- Self-injury (hanging, shooting, jumping, drowning; more common in men).

Covert suicide is relatively more common in older people, and includes:
- Social withdrawal.
- Severe self neglect.
- Refusal of food, fluid, or medication.

This may manifest in subtle ways that encourage extensive investigation to exclude physical illness, whilst the psychiatric problem goes unrecognized and untreated.

Suicidal ideation is more common in institutional settings (acute and rehabilitation hospital wards, and care homes) and in people with acute or chronic physical illness. Risk factors here include depression, chronic pain, sleep disturbance, functional impairment, drug abuse, and psychotropic drug prescription. At their mildest, suicidal ideas manifest as common and relatively benign doubts about whether life is worth living. At their most worrying, they are carefully considered, well formulated, and strongly-held beliefs that death is preferable to life, and how that could be achieved.

Assessment of the 'severity' of an attempt requires an effort to determine perceived risk from the patient's perspective at the time of the attempt. This may not parallel the medical seriousness. Consider:
- Degree of planning vs. impulsivity.
- Likelihood of interruption during attempt.
- Reaction to interruption to attempt (disappointment or relief?).
- Suicide note and its contents.
- Planning for future (e.g. making of will, contents of suicide note).
- Personal view of suicide as a reasonable 'life choice'.

Specialist referral. Always in cases of attempted suicide, suicidal ideation or 'covert suicide'. Probably not in cases of non-persistent, or poorly formulated views that life is not worth living.

Cardiovascular medicine

The ageing cardiovascular system *278*
Chest pain *280*
Angina *282*
Coronary syndromes *284*
Myocardial infarction *286*
Hypertension *288*
Hypertension: treatment *290*
  How to... use antihypertensives in a patient with
  co-morbid conditions *291*
Arrhythmias: presentation *292*
Arrhythmias: management *294*
Atrial fibrillation *296*
Atrial fibrillation: treatment *298*
  How to... use digoxin *299*
Atrial fibrillation: anticoagulation *300*
  How to... discuss warfarin for atrial fibrillation *301*
Bradycardia and conduction disorders *302*
Common arrhythmias and conduction abnormalities *304*
Cardiac failure: assessment *306*
  How to... investigate a patient with suspected
  cardiac failure *307*
Acute cardiac failure *308*
Chronic cardiac failure *310*
Dilemmas in cardiac failure *312*
Diastolic heart failure *314*
Valvular heart disease *316*
Peripheral oedema *318*
Peripheral vascular disease *320*
  How to... measure an ankle brachial pressure index
  (ABPI) *321*
Gangrene in peripheral vascular disease *322*
Vascular secondary prevention *324*

The ageing cardiovascular system

The cardiovascular system changes with age. As with all systems, the relative contribution of cumulative exposure to risk factors (extrinsic ageing), disease acquisition (often occult) and intrinsic ageing is unknown. It is known that the changes described opposite do not occur in all older people, and that a fit older person can have a 'healthier' cardiovascular system than an unfit younger person.

The table opposite addresses the three important questions:
- What are the common changes with age?
- How does that impact on function?
- What are the clinical implications?

Age related change	Impact on function	Clinical implications
Proximal arteries become thicker, dilated, elongated, and less elastic	Systolic pressure peak increases, causing hypertension	Intimal thickening probably predisposes to atheroma
	Increased peripheral vascular resistance (variable)	Systolic hypertension common in older patients
		Chest X ray may show enlarged aortic knuckle—'unfolding' of the aorta
Fibrosis and fat infiltration of SA node and conducting system	Slower conduction from SA node and through the conducting system	First degree heart block and bundle branch block common
		Left axis deviation more frequent
		More vulnerable to clinically significant bradyarrhthmias
Maximum heart rate falls by 10% at rest and 25% during stress	Decreases capacity for cardiac output—largely compensated for at rest, but limits response to stress	Less able to mount a tachycardia, so less reliable sign of acute illness
Left ventricular wall thickens as myocyte size increases	Increases cardiac filling pressures and allows compensation for drop in heart rate	A degree of cardiac enlargement seen on chest x-ray is normal. Worse with hypertension, so always check BP and treat as needed
Left atrial size increases due to alterations in cardiac filling		Predisposes to atrial fibrillation
Myocardial contractility impaired at high demand	Contractility preserved at low stimulation, but with stress cannot increase, meaning (along with heart rate factors) that cardiac output cannot be increased	Decreased cardiac reserve to stress—may become haemodynamically compromised in response to acute illness earlier than younger patients
Increased circulating catecholamines with down-regulated receptors (especially beta adrenergic)	Impairs ability to mount a stress response	As above—decreased cardiac reserve to stress
		More prone to cardiac failure
Impaired oxygen consumption on exercise	Varies considerably between individual older patients—unchanged in those used to exercise, up to 60% reduction in unfit	Contributes to reduced cardiovascular reserve to stress

Chest pain

A common complaint in all settings. May be primary symptom (presenting to GPs and general medical take) or mentioned only in response to direct questioning. Also occurs commonly during inpatient stays for other pathologies.

There are very many causes, the majority of which become more common with age. Many are benign, but some are serious and even life-threatening, so a thorough and sensible approach is needed.

Common conditions not to be missed include: cardiac pain; pleuritic pain due to pulmonary infarction or infection; peptic pain (including bleeding ulcers); pain from dissecting aortic aneurysm, and pneumothorax (especially in COPD).

Other possibilities include: muscular pain (e.g. after unaccustomed exertion); chostochondritis (local tenderness at sternal joint); pain from injury (e.g. after a fall); referred pain from the back and neck (e.g. osteoarthritis) and referred pain from the abdomen.

Differentiating these depends on accurate history taking and careful examination, both of which can be more of a challenge in older patients. Presentation may be atypical, and the patient may have many other problems so teasing out which are the important symptoms can be difficult (experience improves the ability to 'feel' your way around the history). It may be the last symptom mentioned in a long list, however, mention of chest pain should always trigger a careful assessment.

History

- Is this a new symptom? (E.g. may suffer from chronic angina.)
- If not, is it any different from the usual pain?
- What is the nature of the pain? (E.g. pleuritic, heavy, tight etc. This is often hard to do, and hand gestures can help—a clenched fist for a heavy pain, a stabbing action for a sharp pleuritic pain etc.)
- How acute is the onset?
- Are there any associated symptoms?

Patients with cognitive impairment can be particularly difficult to assess, but allowing free conversation may reveal symptoms, followed by closed questions that may prompt appropriate answers. Family members may have noted signs or symptoms e.g. clutching the chest after walking and are an invaluable aid to assessment.

Examination

- How does the patient look? A sweaty, clammy patient needs urgent and exhaustive assessment, whereas a patient drinking tea and chatting is less likely to have a devastating condition.
- What are the basic observations?
- Signs of shock alert to a serious condition (ischaemic heart disease, pulmonary infarction, dissection, sepsis, blood loss) but remember these may be late signs and are less useful in older patients. The patient may usually be hypertensive, so a BP of 120/80 may be very low for them; they may be on a beta-blocker, so unable to mount a tachycardia etc.

Temperature may be raised in sepsis.

Oxygen saturation may be low with pulmonary problems.

Different blood pressures in the arms may indicate dissection (but may also occur with atheroma).

Listen to the heart—are there any new murmurs (dissection or infarction) or a rub (pericarditis)?

Listen to the lungs—is there consolidation (sepsis) or a rub (consolidation or infarction)?

Look at the legs—is there any clinical deep vein thrombosis?

Investigations

Some tests can be less useful in older patients, and should be individually tailored to the patient. Sending off every single test on all patients with chest pain will only lead to confusion.

ECG: should be done on the majority of patients with chest pain. Remember the baseline ECG may well be abnormal in an elderly person, and comparison with old traces is extremely useful. If your patient has a very abnormal ECG (e.g. left bundle branch block) it is useful to give them a copy to carry with them.

Chest X-ray: looking for lung abnormalities and widening of the mediastinum. Remember that the aorta often 'unfolds' so a careful look at the contours of the aortic arch and/or comparison with old films is needed to assess possible dissection. Remember that a patient can look fairly well in the early stages of aortic dissection.

Blood tests: basic haematology, biochemistry and inflammatory markers are often useful. Remember that in acute blood loss, the haemoglobin may not drop immediately, and that an elderly septic patient may take a day or two to develop an elevated white cell count and CRP.

Troponin: useful in a patient with suspected cardiac chest pain (for risk stratification). It is NOT a useful test if you do not think this is cardiac pain—there are many false positives that will only cause confusion.

D-dimer: only useful if negative in cases of suspected thromboembolism. There are a huge number of causes of a positive d-dimer (including old age itself) and a positive result does not imply the diagnosis of PE.

Further tests: (e.g. CT thorax for suspected dissection, exercise testing for angina, lung perfusion scans for thromboembolism etc.) depend on clinical factors.

▶ Always attempt to explain a chest pain—both for the patient and future clinicians. A 'diagnosis' of non-cardiac chest pain is rarely helpful.

Angina

Coronary artery disease is clinically evident in 20% of those >80 years. Management is often sub-optimal. It is unacceptable to leave a patient with symptoms, however frail, until all available options have been looked at, and it has been proven (by trying it) that a certain treatment cannot be tolerated. A step-wise, slow introduction of tablets allows insight into adverse effects and may require multiple clinic visits. Symptom diaries can assist with this process.

Stable angina

Risk factor reduction

- Cholesterol and blood pressure less likely to be lowered in older patients, but the risk reduction is equal if not greater than for younger subjects.
- Diabetic control is less likely to be tight, in part due to justifiable concerns about the dangers of hypoglycaemia.
- Life style advice (exercise, smoking, and diet) should be given.

Medication

- Under utilized, particularly aspirin (concerns about bleeding) and beta-blockade but there is evidence that they are both equally useful in reducing risk.
- A trial and error approach to treatment is needed—add one or two treatments at a time to minimize the risk of side effects (most commonly orthostatic hypotension) and stop if there are problems, trying something else instead.
- Start on low doses, and titrate upwards (e.g. atenolol 25mg).
- Long acting agents (e.g. diltiazem MR) reduce compliance problems.
- Nicorandil (10–20 mg bd) is often better tolerated than other anti-anginals in this age group.
- Choice of medication should be pragmatic—if a patient has a bradycardia for example, a non-negatively chronotropic drug is most appropriate (e.g. amlodipine 5–10mg). If the patient also has COPD, it may be wise to avoid beta-blockade. If a patient has cardiac failure, a cardioselective beta-blocker (e.g. carvedilol, metoprolol, bisoprolol) is a better choice than a fluid retaining calcium-channel-blocker.
- GTN can cause considerable problems with hypotension, and instruction on correct use is essential. Tablets can be spat out once the pain starts to settle, so (in theory) the dose can be titrated to symptoms. In practice, the spray is often easier to use. It should be used sitting down if possible and prophylactically before significant exertion.

Aggravating conditions

Such as cardiac failure, anaemia, thyroid disease, arrhythmias, valvular heart disease. More common in older people and should be corrected.

Revascularization

Should be considered (ideally after risk stratification by stress testing), as for younger patients, if symptoms persist despite maximal medical therapy (see p285).

Palliation

Consider if diffuse disease, not amenable to revascularization with ongoing symptoms (e.g. home oxygen therapy, opiates to allow sleep).

Coronary syndromes

Coronary heart disease (CHD) incidence rises with increasing age. Management in general is as for younger patients, but there are some points relating to older patients in particular:

- **Atypical presentation:** more likely to present with atypical or vague symptoms (e.g. intense dyspnoea, syncope or weakness); ECG changes may not be present in up to a quarter of acute MI, with the full diagnostic triad (chest pain, ECG changes and biochemical changes) present in under a third of those >85 years.
- **Different pathology:** more pre-existing coronary artery disease with more multivessel disease; more likely to have a non-ST elevation MI (NSTEMI); more likely to develop heart failure, AV block, atrial fibrillation and cardiogenic shock after a coronary event.
- **Later presentation:** increased prevalence of angina so less alarmed by chest pains; may modify lifestyle to avoid symptoms (if climbing a hill gives them chest pain, they may just stop doing it); increased occurrence of 'silent ischaemia' (especially in diabetics); increased social and attitudinal factors ('I didn't want to bother the doctor'). A third of patients over 65 with MI will present later than six hours after symptom onset.
- **Increased co-morbidity:** making diagnosis difficult (e.g. a patient with COPD who has exertional breathlessness) and therapy less well-tolerated (e.g. beta-blockers with peripheral vascular disease). Also as co-morbidities add up, so frailty increases and medications are generally less well-tolerated (e.g. symptomatic hypotension from antianginals).
- Higher in-patient **mortality** from acute coronary syndromes, so prioritize for specialist monitoring where there are limited resources.
- Less likely to receive **aggressive acute therapy** (e.g. less thrombolysis, angiography and angioplasty, coronary artery bypass grafting, and maximal medical treatment).
- Less likely to have **full secondary prevention** measures implemented.

Management of the older cardiac patient is therefore more difficult and more likely to result in death than in younger patients. Older people therefore need the highest quality clinical care—yet too often they are denied access to coronary care facilities and aggressive therapy. Lack of evidence does not mean that there is no benefit—rather that it has not been proven, as is the case with many commonly used therapies (for example loop diuretics in pulmonary oedema).

Common sense dictates when to use an aggressive approach, considering the patient as a whole including:

- Patient preference where possible
- Co-morbidities (alter risk profile)
- Current medication
- Frailty and likely life expectancy
- Apparent biological age rather than chronological age.

There are many well-defined treatment algorithms, and older patients should be included at every step unless there are good reasons not to. If you plan to exclude a patient from treatment, you should clearly document your rationale.

Revascularization procedures

Includes percutaneous coronary angiography and intervention (PCI) and coronary artery bypass grafting (CABG).

When?

- Used when stable symptoms persist despite maximal medical therapy, or when unstable symptoms fail to settle.
- Risk stratify with exercise testing and troponin measurements. Older patients may be unable to exercise, but consider bicycle exercise, stress echocardiography, or an isotope myocardial perfusion scan to look for evidence of reversible ischaemia.

What are the risks?

- PCI: higher risk of death, renal failure, and infarction in elderly. Age is an independent predictor of increased complication, but so too are diabetes, cardiac failure, and chronic renal impairment, all of which are more common in older patients.
- CABG: increased early mortality and stroke in older patients.

What are the benefits?

- PCI: may be only way to control intrusive symptoms in stable angina, and the only way to settle an acute coronary syndrome. Variable evidence from studies—all agree increased early complications, but longer-term benefits in older patients are reported as equivalent or even better.
- CABG: probably better with triple vessel disease, poor exercise tolerance, poor left ventricular function and diabetes. Generally well tolerated in elderly, with similar long-term improvements in symptoms and quality of life to younger patients. New minimally invasive techniques, that do not require bypass, are likely to reduce the early complications without impairing outcome.

Overall recommendations

Consider all patients that fail medical treatment for revascularization procedures, regardless of age. The early complication rate is higher in older patients, but the eventual benefit is equal if not better than for younger patients.

Approach a cardiologist with a record of treating older patients.

Crucial to include the patient in the decision, with a frank and indi- vidualised discussion about risks and benefits.

urther reading

ongmore M, Wilkinson I, Rajagopalan S (2004). Acute coronary syndromes. In *Oxford Handbook of Clinical Medicine*, 6th edn. Oxford: Oxford University Press.

Myocardial infarction

Around two thirds of all myocardial infarctions occur in patients over 65 years old and a third in patients over 75. Overall, the incidence of MI has decreased, but this is not the case for older patients. Despite this, evidence regarding optimal management is lacking, as older patients tend to be underrepresented in clinical trials. The table below summarizes what is known.

Therapy	Evidence
Aspirin	Equivalent risk reduction in elderly population.
Thrombolysis	Less ST elevation, so fewer eligible in the first place.
	Increased risk of complications e.g. cerebral bleeding (but can predict those at higher risk if hypertensive, low body weight, previous stroke, or on warfarin).
	Contradictory evidence regarding mortality—large RCTs suggest increased absolute risk reduction of mortality in elderly (e.g. ISIS-2) but these are selected, probably fitter patients, and do not include the very old. Observational trials of actual practice suggest equivalent benefit in older patients, or possibly even a survival disadvantage. Probable equivalent proportional mortality reduction, so absolute reduction greatest in elderly who have the highest mortality.
	Overall, consensus is that thrombolysis should be used in older patients as routine, with rare exceptions for the very frail or where individual risk seems to outweigh benefit.
Primary PTCA	Trials suggest same overall mortality in elderly and young, and the risk of haemorrhagic stroke occurring with thrombolysis avoided. However, procedural risk increases with age, and it is probably less likely to succeed with increasing age. No direct comparisons of thrombolysis and PTCA in elderly. Pragmatically speaking, in the UK, this is unlikely to be available, and thrombolysis remains the treatment of choice.
Low molecular weight heparin	Effective in NSTEMI, and possibly more effective in older patients.
GP IIb/IIIa inhibitors	Trials using this therapy in unstable angina and NSTEMI show benefit that is equal in the older patients.

As a general rule, all appropriate therapies should be considered in all patients post MI, regardless of age. Whilst evidence is lacking in older patients, it is more reasonable to extrapolate from a younger population than to deny treatment. This approach must of course be tempered with common sense and individually tailored decision-making.

Cardiac rehabilitation

- Used after MI and multiple presentations of CHD and congestive cardiac failure.
- Involves structured exercise programme.
- Proven to improve exercise tolerance and decrease readmission.
- Under used for older cardiac patients—less referral, and sometimes there are upper age limits in place.
- Benefit seen in older patients is equivalent to that in younger patients, although they start from a less fit baseline.
- Older people adhere well to programmes and seem to suffer no complications.
- Some adaptations are needed (more time to warm up and cool down, longer breaks, avoidance of high impact activity, lower intensity for a longer time).
- Benefits include improved fitness, increased bone mineral density, improved mood, and fewer falls as well as improved cardiovascular fitness.

Hypertension

Hypertension is an important risk factor for vascular disease. Under diagnosed and treated, especially in older patients.

Incidence of hypertension overall rises with age, reaching a prevalence of 60–80% beyond 65. After this age, systolic blood pressure (SBP) rises linearly while diastolic blood pressure (DBP) falls leading to widening of the pulse pressure and relative frequency of isolated systolic hypertension (ISH) (reflects reduced arterial compliance, likely disease related and not a part of 'normal' ageing per se).

Hypertension is an independent risk factor for stroke, ischaemic heart disease, peripheral vascular disease, congestive cardiac failure, renal failure and dementia in all age groups, but in older patients it is systolic blood pressure and widened pulse pressure that are the strongest predictors of adverse cardiovascular outcome.

Definitions

	Grade	Systolic BP (mmHg)	Diastolic BP (mmHg)
Mild	1	>140	>90
Moderate	2	>160	>100
Severe	3	>180	>110
ISH	1	>140	<90
ISH	2	>160	<90

Assessment

- **Ask about** symptoms (including hypotensive), co-morbidity, and smoking.
- **Measure** with a well-maintained, calibrated device, with an appropriate sized cuff.
  - Check supine and standing blood pressure (orthostatic hypotension can cause symptoms when treatment initiated).
  - Take at least two measurements in a single consultation.
  - Never initiate treatment based on a single reading.
  - Consider ambulatory measurements if drug resistance, variable BP, white coat hypertension, or postural symptoms.
- **Examine** for causes (drugs and renal disease are most common) and evidence of target organ damage (stroke, dementia, carotid bruits, cardiac enlargement, ischaemic heart disease, peripheral vascular disease, renal disease, retinal changes).
- **Investigations** to look at target organs (urinalysis, blood urea and electrolytes, ECG) and for risk factor analysis (glucose, lipids).

Treatment thresholds and goals
- Depends on individual.
- In active elderly population with reasonable life expectancy treat as for younger patients i.e. >160/100mmHg and with lower threshold (>140mmHg) in high-risk patients (e.g. smokers, diabetics, evidence of target organ damage, high estimated 10 year risk).
- No clear evidence for optimal target. Probably the lower the better as long as tolerated.
- Caution in ISH—try not to lower DBP<65mmHg.
- There is even less data for very elderly (>85 years) people and a pragmatic approach based on apparent biological age is appropriate.

Hypertension: treatment

Similar approach to that used in younger patients, but it is important to bear the following in mind:

- Side effects are more common and more debilitating in older patients (due e.g. to more sluggish baroreceptors and reduced cerebral autoregulation).
- There is a greater risk of drug interactions as older patients are more often victims of polypharmacy.
- Co-morbidity is common and should direct the choice of antihypertensive agents (see box opposite).
- Hypertension should be seen as a risk factor and the decision to treat should be weighed along with other risk factors. In a very frail elderly person with a limited life expectancy, the side effects suffered may far outweigh any future benefits from risk factor modification. This however should be an active decision reached if possible with the patient, and not a simple omission.
- Begin with lower doses and titrate up slowly ('start low and go slow') to minimize adverse reactions. It is better to be on something at a low dose than nothing at all.

Non-pharmacological measures

Lifestyle modifications are as important and effective in reducing blood pressure in older patients as in the young. Salt restriction, weight reduction, and regular exercise are particularly effective. Moderate alcohol intake is advised. Smoking cessation and decreasing saturated fat intake helps with overall risk reduction.

Choice of medication

There have been many large trials comparing the different classes of antihypertensive with little consistency in results. Overall, it seems that it is lowering the blood pressure per se that is the important factor, and this benefit continues up until at least 84 years (possibly beyond—evidence pending). In older patients, with much co-morbidity, there may be compelling reasons for using, or not using certain agents (see box opposite). Try to use a drug that will treat both blood pressure and a co-existing disease to limit polypharmacy. If not, then the British Hypertension Society recommends using the AB/CD approach:

A ACE inhibitors and angiotensin receptor blockers
B Beta-blockers
C Calcium channel blockers
D Diuretics

In younger, white patients, begin with A or B. In older patients and all black patients begin with C or D.

If inadequate control:

1. Try another drug within the initial group
2. Then (A or B) plus (C or D)
3. Then (A or B) plus C plus D
4. Then A plus B plus C plus D
5. Finally, consider adding alpha-blocker or spironolactone.

Try to avoid B and D together (increased risk of diabetes).

HOW TO... use antihypertensives in a patient with co-morbid conditions

Calcium channel blockers

E.g. diltiazem SR 90mg (rate limiting).
- Use when there is angina or atrial fibrillation.
- May make cardiac failure worse.
- Dihydropyridine calcium channel blockers (e.g. amlodipine, felodipine) are excellent in ISH.

Thiazide diuretics

E.g. bendrofluazide 2.5mg.
- Useful first line therapy in most older patients—may help with ankle swelling and cardiac failure symptoms.
- Avoid if severe gout, urinary incontinence or profound dyslipidaemia.

Beta-blockers

E.g. atenolol 25mg.
- Useful with angina, atrial fibrillation and stable cardiac failure.
- Avoid with peripheral vascular disease, COPD, asthma, heart block.

ACE inhibitors

E.g ramipril 2.5–10mg.
- Use for secondary prevention after vascular event (stroke, TIA, heart attack), in diabetes, heart failure and chronic renal impairment.
- Avoid in renal artery stenosis and aortic stenosis.

Angiotension receptor blockers

E.g. losartan 50mg
- Use when ACE intolerant (usually cough) where an ACE is indicated.
- May cause less orthostatic symptoms than ACE inhibitors.

Alpha blockers

E.g. doxazosin 1mg.
- Excellent for resistant hypertension in older patients.
- Use if prostatic hypertrophy.

Further reading

Dahlof B, et al. Sept 2000. STOP Hypertension 1 and 2 (1st and 2nd Swedish Trial in Old People with hypertension). Heart (84) supplement I : i2–i4.

SHEP (Systolic Hypertension in the Elderly Program) Cooperative Research Group JAMA **284** (4): 465–471 Jul 2000.

British Hypertension Society Guidelines, 2004 (www.hyp.ac.uk).

NICE guidelines on management of hypertension in adults in primary care (www.nice.org.uk).

Arrhythmias: presentation

Arrhythmias are very common in older people, but are not so common as a presenting complaint. A patient with recurrent presyncope preceded by palpitations presents very little diagnostic challenge. What is much more common is for an arrhythmia to be the explanation for a rather more vague presentation such as:

- Recurrent falls
- Patient covered in bruises who has been explaining them away as clumsiness
- General fatigue
- Dizzy spells
- Light-headedness
- 'Collapse query cause'
- Blackouts
- Worsening/new angina or cardiac failure.

History

It is important to ask about palpitations with any of these problems, (indeed it should form part of the systems review in all older people) but be aware of the following points:

- Clarify carefully what you mean—many people do not understand what we mean by 'palpitations' and may be describing an ectopic heart beat followed by a compensatory pause, or even just an awareness of the normal heart beat e.g. when lying in bed at night.
- Do not exclude the possibility of an arrhythmia just because the patient does not complain of palpitations—especially with confused patients.
- Where there are palpitations and light-headedness, establish an order wherever possible. Postural drop is also very common in older patients, and can produce a similar set of symptoms (falling BP causing light-headedness, then a compensatory tachycardia)—in theory the palpitations should come first in an arrhythmia.
- Are there any constant features of the symptoms? For example, dizziness occurring on standing is more likely to be postural drop; dizziness on exertion may have an ischaemic component; dizziness on turning the head may be due to vestibular problems, or carotid sinus hypersensitivity (see p132); dizziness that can occur anywhere or at any time is much more likely to be due to an arrhythmia.
- A history of injury with a blackout increases the chances of finding particularly a bradycardia requiring pacing.
- Always take a full drug history—antiarrhythmics can be pro-arrhythmogenic, many drugs cause bradyarrhythmias (commonly beta-blockers, digoxin or rate-limiting calcium-channel-blockers such as diltiazem), and antidepressants (especially the tricyclics) can predispose to arrhythmias.

Examination
- Should always include lying and standing blood pressures, assessment of the baseline pulse character, rate and rhythm and full cardiovascular examination to look for evidence of structural cardiac disease (e.g. cardiomyopathy, heart failure, valvular lesions) all of which may predispose to arrhythmias.
- General problems require a full general examination—it is rarely appropriate to examine a single system only in an elderly patient. A rectal examination, for example, may reveal a rectal tumour causing anaemia and hence palpitations.
- It may also be appropriate to examine the vestibular system (p603) and central nervous system.

Investigations
- *Blood tests*: including FBC (anaemia), urea, creatinine, and electrolytes (low K predisposes to arrhythmias), thyroid function, digoxin levels.
- *ECG*: look for baseline rhythm and any evidence of conducting system disease (e.g. a bundle branch block, or any heart block). Check the Q-T interval. Also look for LV hypertrophy (arrhythmias more likely) or ischaemia.
- *CXR*: look at cardiac size.
- *Holter monitoring*: a prolonged ECG recording. Usually a 24 hour period initially. Remember this is a very small snapshot, and of limited value especially if symptoms are infrequent. Can be useful if the symptoms are experienced whilst the monitor is on, and the ECG trace shows normal sinus rhythm. If the suspicion of arrhythmias is high, then repeat the test, or arrange for transtelephonic event recording or even an implantable loop recorder where the symptoms are severe enough (e.g. sudden syncope).

Arrhythmias: management

Management of arrhythmias in older patients does not differ significantly from management in other age groups, but remember the following:

- Presentation may be atypical with confusion or falls rather than palpitations.
- There is more likely to be underlying cardiac pathology—always check for ischaemia and structural heart disease even for apparently benign arrhythmias (e.g. SVT).
- Always check for common precipitants in older patients:
  - Electrolyte abnormalities (especially hypo or hyperkalaemia, hypocalcaemia)
  - Anaemia
  - Myocardial ischaemia
  - Antiarrhythmic toxicity (especially digoxin)
  - Sepsis
  - Hypothermia
  - Any other acute illness.
- If the precipitant cannot be remedied immediately (commonly sepsis) then the arrhythmia is likely to be recurrent—consider cardiac monitoring during this period.
- Tachycardia may be less well tolerated than in a younger patient causing significant hypotension, angina or cardiac failure.
- Hypotension itself may be less well tolerated than in younger patients (risk of cerebral injury) and so prompt action is required.
- Where there is cardiac failure because of an arrhythmia, fluids cannot be used for resuscitation and so definitive action is required sooner rather than later. Begin by using standard treatment for acute heart failure (oxygen, intravenous diuretics, and opiates etc.) whilst organizing cardioversion (usually electrical for speed) or rate limitation (appropriate for atrial fibrillation—use intravenous digoxin).
- Bundle branch block is common, and so there may be confusion between supraventricular and ventricular arrhythmias. There are numerous subtle ways of distinguishing between these but in an emergency:
  - If the patient is compromised, then electrical cardioversion will treat both effectively.
  - If the patient is unwell, but stable, then an amiodarone infusion will treat both effectively, and has the advantage of causing little myocardial depression.
- Elderly patients are much more likely to be on an antiarrhythmic drug already.
- ▶▶ Check the medication carefully before administering any therapy. See opposite for common pitfalls.
- Electrical cardioversion is well tolerated by most older patients, usually effective and less likely to cause side effects than many medications. It should be considered early where there is significant compromise. Anaesthetic support is required, which can take some time to arrange, so prompt referral is recommended. It is less useful in acute sepsis where the arrhythmia is likely to recur, and it is hard to establish whether compromise is caused by the sepsis or the arrhythmia.

Common pitfalls with antiarrhythmic medication

Adenosine
- Its action is prolonged by dipyridamole (now commonly prescribed with aspirin in stroke), so avoid using together.
- Exacerbates asthma and is antagonized by theophylline, so avoid in asthmatics.

Amiodarone
- Risk of ventricular arrhythmias when used with disopyramide, procainamide and quinidine, so avoid concomitant use.
- Increases plasma half-life of flecainide, so reduce dose.

Atropine
- Can precipitate glaucoma, so avoid in patients with this condition.

Flecainide
- Contraindicated when there is ischaemic heart disease, cardiac failure, and haemodynamic compromise.
- Probably best avoided in most older patients, who may well have occult cardiac disease.

Verapamil
- Do not use intravenously in a patient already on a beta-blocker (high risk of asystole and hypotension).

General guidance

Most antiarrhythmic medication used concomitantly increases the risk of myocardial depression and arrhythmias. This effect is more pronounced in older patients. Caution when using more than one, and consider using sequentially rather than additively if one alone is ineffective.

Atrial fibrillation

Common arrhythmia, becoming more common with age (risk doubles with each additional decade of age, rising to 7% of over 85 year olds). Often associated with other disease (e.g. hypertension, coronary artery disease, mitral valve disease, thyrotoxicosis) but also occurs in 1–2% of otherwise healthy elderly. Unlike other arrhythmias, it is often chronic.

Disorganized atrial activity with variable conduction to the ventricles leads to an irregularly irregular pulse rate and volume. Up to a third of older patients with atrial fibrillation (AF) will have AV nodal disease that limits the rate to less than 100bpm, often making it asymptomatic. It is therefore often noted incidentally during routine examination—but should never be ignored.

Assessment

Should include examination for hypertension and valve disease, blood tests for thyroid disease, and an ECG to confirm the diagnosis (may be sinus rhythm with ectopics). Paroxysmal AF may cause intermittent symptoms and should be looked for with Holter monitoring.

Complications

AF causes an increase in morbidity and mortality, even if there is no underlying cardiac disease.
- Pulse >120 often causes palpitations, light-headedness, or syncope.
- Rapid rate may also cause angina or cardiac failure.
- General malaise may also result from a chronically sub-optimal cardiac output.
- AF is often associated with periods of AV conduction delay ('pauses') and if >3 seconds these may cause syncope.
- The main complication is stroke from cardiac emboli.

Atrial flutter

- Rapid, regular atrial activity (usually 300 per minute).
- Characteristic saw tooth appearance on ECG (revealed by carotid sinus massage if rate high).
- Rate depends on degree of AV block (150bpm if 2:1 block, 75bpm if 4:1 block etc.). ▶▶ Always think of atrial flutter when the pulse rate is 150.
- Commonly associated with COPD or ischaemic heart disease.
- Lower embolic risk than atrial fibrillation, but only if pure flutter—often the patient will flip in and out of flutter and fibrillation.
- Treat with rate control and stroke prophylaxis. This rhythm is usually amenable to cardioversion, but if there is significant co-morbidity or structural heart disease, sinus rhythm is unlikely to be sustained.

Atrial fibrillation: treatment

Acute AF
- Treat underlying condition e.g. sepsis, ischaemia, cardiac failure.
- If compromised, consider electrical cardioversion.
- Otherwise, control rate (usually with digoxin; alternatives include a beta-blocker or verapamil if no contraindication e.g. heart failure).
- May resolve once precipitant has been dealt with.

Chronic AF
- Rate control if necessary, using digoxin which slows AV conduction (see box opposite).
- Alternatives include beta-blockade (e.g. atenolol 25–50mg) or calcium-channel-blockers (e.g. diltiazem) which should be considered if needed to treat co-morbidities e.g. hypertension, angina.
- Where chemical cardioversion is considered on symptomatic grounds give amiodarone (initially 200mg tds for a week, then 200mg bd for a week, then 200mg od thereafter. May be able to drop dose further to 100mg a day, or even every other day). ▶▶ Remember that amiodarone interacts with warfarin and regular monitoring of INR will be needed if the two are used together—as is often the case. Also can cause thyroid abnormalities, and this should be monitored with TFTs (see p152).
- Consider stroke prophylaxis with aspirin or warfarin.
- Electrical cardioversion for chronic AF should only be attempted after a period of anticoagulation (minimum 3 weeks). It is more likely to succeed (and less likely to recur) where there are fewer of the following present:
  - Structural heart disease (hypertrophy, atrial enlargement, valvular heart disease etc.)
  - Co-morbidity (especially hypertension, cardiac failure)
  - Increasing age.

Recent evidence suggests that an older patient with several of the above is better off being treated with rate control and anticoagulation only, without attempting cardioversion.

Paroxysmal AF
- Equal embolic risk, so consider anticoagulation as for chronic AF.
- Remember that digoxin does not prevent AF.
- Amiodarone (as above) or beta-blockers (e.g. atenolol 25mg) are useful to prevent paroxysms of AF.

HOW TO... use digoxin

Indications
- Rate control of atrial fibrillation.
- Mild positive inotrope sometimes used in cardiac failure.

Not useful for
- Paroxysmal AF prevention.
- Exercise induced fast AF.

Loading with digoxin
1mg in divided doses over 24 hours.
This dose is always required, regardless of renal function—modify maintenance doses only in renal impairment.
Example: Day one: 8am digoxin 500mcg po, 8pm digoxin 500mcg po.
          Day two: 8am digoxin at maintenance dose

Deciding a maintenance dose
- Main determinant is renal function—digoxin is excreted this way, so use low dose with renal impairment.
- Consider also body mass e.g. start with 62.5mcg for a small elderly lady—the dose can always be increased if there is inadequate rate control.
- Dosage is determined clinically, but serum levels can be used to assess toxicity or concordance.

Digoxin toxicity
- Hypokalaemia predisposes to this, so always monitor potassium and supplement if needed. Target [K] > 4.0mmol/L.
- Symptoms include confusion, nausea, vomiting, arrhythmias (especially nodal bradycardia and ventricular ectopics), and yellow or green visual haloes.
- ECG may show ST depression and inverted T wave in V5 and V6 (reversed tick).
- Treat by stopping medication, rehydrating and correcting hypokalaemia.
- Life-threatening poisoning can be treated with digoxin-specific antibody fragments.

Atrial fibrillation: anticoagulation

This is a complex and often emotive issue. Many older people will have very strong views about stroke ('I'd rather die than ever have a stroke') or warfarin (many know it as rat poison, or have known someone who had a bleed whilst on warfarin). As we are dealing with population risks and benefits, it is impossible to accurately predict for a single individual what will happen to them if they do, or do not take preventative therapy. Conveying this concept is difficult, but because the decision is complex, involvement of the patient becomes key. This takes time and patience.

It is important to have a simple way of explaining the facts as they are known, perhaps writing them down for clarity, then allowing time for them to sink in before coming to a final decision. There is no enormous urgency—the stroke risks quoted are per annum, and it is worth giving the patient time to think things over if required.

Address each of the following questions:

What is the risk of stroke in this patient with AF?

Overall, the risk is about 5 times greater than a person with similar health and age who does not have AF. Paroxysmal AF carries the same embolic risk.

This risk may be more accurately quantified by the following:

High risk (6–12% chance of stroke per year)
- Older than 65 with cardiovascular risk factors (hypertension, diabetes)
- Previous stroke or TIA
- Cardiac disease (MI, cardiac failure)
- Echo abnormalities (poor LV function on echo, atrial clot)
- Thyroid disease.

Medium risk (3–5% chance of stroke per year)
- Older than 65 but with none of the high risk characteristics
- Younger than 65 with cardiovascular risk factors (hypertension, diabetes).

Low risk (less than 1% chance of stroke per year)
Younger than 65 with no additional risk factors detailed above.

What is the risk of therapy?

Warfarin when taken correctly and monitored carefully has around 1% per year risk of major bleeding in primary prevention of stroke, and 2.5% risk in secondary prevention.

How effective is therapy at reducing risk?
- Warfarin reduces stroke risk in atrial fibrillation by around two-thirds.
- Aspirin (300mg) reduces risk by around 20–25%.

What are the recommendations?

Where there are no contraindications, any patient with a stroke risk estimated at greater than 4% per year should have warfarin (i.e. the high and most of the moderate risk groups above), those with a risk of 1–4% should have aspirin and those with a risk <1% should have no treatment.

HOW TO... discuss warfarin for atrial fibrillation

Your patient is an 86-year-old woman with hypertension, ischaemic heart disease, and mild cardiac failure. She currently takes aspirin, atenolol, bendrofluazide, frusemide, and ramipril. She has newly diagnosed AF, which is rate-controlled because of the atenolol.

You wish to discuss starting warfarin with her. The conversation may go as follows:

Doctor: 'You have a condition called atrial fibrillation—where the heart beat is irregular. It is not causing you any problems at the moment, it is common and it is not a dangerous heart condition. However, there is a risk that this irregular beat could send a clot to the brain and cause a stroke and I would like to consider a treatment to reduce the risk of this happening.'

Patient: 'A stroke? I'm going to have a stroke?'

Doctor: 'If we took 100 people in your situation, then in a year about 10 of them would have a stroke—but 90 would not.'

Patient: 'I would hate to have a stroke. What can you do?'

Doctor: 'We can thin your blood with a drug called warfarin.'

Patient: 'I've heard of that—isn't it very dangerous?'

Doctor: 'You would need to have regular blood tests to make sure the dosage was right. If those 100 people all took warfarin, then one of them would have a serious problem with bleeding.'

Patient: 'But it will stop me from having a stroke?'

Doctor: 'Going back to those 100 people—if they all take the warfarin, then only 3 or 4 will have a stroke instead of the original 10. The risk is reduced by about 2/3.'

Patient: 'Which 3 or 4 people?'

Doctor: 'There is no way of predicting who will benefit from treatment and who will have a problem. What we do know is that overall, the risk is lower with warfarin, and so we do recommend treatment for someone like you.'

Patient: 'Do I have to?'

Doctor: 'No, of course not. It is your decision. I will give you an information leaflet. Why don't you go away and think it over? We will talk again.'

See also p160 (initiating warfarin checklist).

Bradycardia and conduction disorders

As the heart ages the function of the cardiac pacemaker (the sinoatrial node) and the conducting system (bundle of His and Purkinje fibres) tends to decline, due to:

- Declining numbers of cells in the SA node
- Increasing prevalence of disease (atheroma, amyloid and hypertension)
- Degeneration with fibrosis and fat infiltration.

This is not inevitable, but around 50% of older patients will have some ECG evidence of conduction delay (prolonged PR and QT interval, left axis deviation etc.) and be prone to symptomatic bradycardia and conduction disorders.

Causes

- **Medication**: digoxin, amiodarone, beta-blockers, calcium-channel blockers.
- **Sick sinus syndrome**: isolated sinus node dysfunction, very common in older patients, with uncertain cause (theories include vascular insufficiency or amyloid infiltration, but often no cause is found).
- **Ischaemic heart disease**
- **Systemic disease**: hypothyroidism, liver failure, hypothermia, hypoxia, hypercapnia, cerebral disease (e.g. stroke, raised intracranial pressure, haemorrhage).

Presentation

- Often picked up incidentally on an ECG.
- When symptomatic, bradycardia causes low output syndromes ranging from fatigue, dizziness, dyspnoea and presyncope, syncope and falls, to angina, cardiac failure, and shock.
- May be intermittent (with paroxysmal brady arrhythmias), chronic (with stable arrhythmias), or occur acutely (usually post MI).

Management

Not every bradycardic patient needs an urgent pacemaker—the local cardiology service will help if in doubt. For every problem, consider the following:

Is the patient acutely compromised? If so then urgent treatment is required in order to minimize cerebral injury. For shock, lie the patient down, and elevate the legs. Use intravenous fluids. Try to increase the heart rate using atropine (0.6mg iv, repeated up to total dose of 3mg), an isoprenaline infusion or temporary pacing (external pads are quick and often well tolerated; if the situation persists, insert a temporary pacing wire). Tailor your treatment to each individual—if the cause of the bradycardia is a catastrophic intracerebral event, then putting the patient through a temporary wire is not sensible—try external paddles to increase the heart rate and see if this has a positive impact on consciousness level whilst a CT scan is organized. Conversely, an acute inferior MI may cause significant short-term problems with bradycardia yet little longer-term cardiac damage.

Are there any symptoms? If so, are they attributable to the bradycardia?
Is the condition likely to resolve? Occurs after acute MI, in which case
support the patient during the acute episode as needed (non-invasively if
feasible).

How frequent are the symptoms?
- Continuous: temporary wire may be needed before permanent pacing.
- Exertional: consider bed rest pending permanent pacing instead of a
  temporary wire (reduces risk of infection and makes insertion of
  permanent wire easier).
- Infrequent: elective permanent pacemaker can be organized.
- No symptoms: no action is required unless there is a high risk of future
  asystole. This is the case with second-degree heart block type II where
  there is also bundle branch block. It is also true of complete heart
  block. Pacemaker is required for these conditions.

Are there any reversible factors?
- Check medication. Digoxin (especially with toxicity), amiodarone,
  beta-blockers and calcium channel blockers can all cause or exacerbate
  bradycardia.
- Check thyroid function.
- Acutely, hypothermia can also cause bradycardia.

Permanent pacemakers

Indications
- Over 85% are used for patients over 64 years old.
- 50% are for sick sinus syndrome and AV block.
- Increasingly used for vasodepressor carotid sinus hypersensitivity
  (p132).
- Occasionally used for recurrent syncope where no cause is found.

Pacemakers
- Dual chamber pacemakers are more expensive but tend to produce
  a better cardiac output and less AF than single chamber ones.
- Permanent pacing should be programmed to minimize paced beats
  allowing the intrinsic rhythm to get through as much as possible.
- With LV dysfunction pacing may need to include multisite pacing as
  RV pacing can worsen dysynchrony and exacerbate LV failure.

Insertion
- Relatively simple procedure, done whilst awake that is usually well
  tolerated by even very frail patients, with often dramatic improvements in quality of life—consider in most where indicated.
- Technical problems can occur with insertion if the patient cannot lie flat.
- Usually straightforward, but rare complications during insertion
  include arrhythmias (commonly AF) and rarely perforation of the
  right ventricle.
- Later problems include sepsis and failure of pacemaker output.
Regular follow-up is required to check the pacemaker function and
battery reserve.

Common arrhythmias and conduction abnormalities

Condition	Clinical features	Treatment
Sinus bradycardia	• Intrinsic SA nodal disease • Pulse rate <60 • Common incidental finding • Drugs are common cause • Acute onset associated with inferior MI and raised intracranial pressure • Consider hypothyroidism	• Treat only if symptomatic (rarely causes problem) • Check thyroid function
Supraventricular ectopics	• Narrow complex QRS without a p wave, followed by a compensatory pause • Patient may be aware of this, and describe an 'early beat' with a gap afterwards	• Benign • Reassure the patient • No action required
Sinoatrial block	• Intermittent inability of SA node to depolarise atrium • ECG shows pauses that are multiples of the PR interval	• Usually asymptomatic • Treat only if symptoms
Slow AF	• Combination of AF and SA nodal disease very common. • Symptomatic pauses frequent	• Anticoagulation for stroke prevention • High index of suspicion for pauses if suggestive symptoms—check with Holter monitor and treat with pacemaker
Sick sinus syndrome	• Sinoatrial node dysfunction (degenerative or due to ischaemic heart disease) causing a bradycardia—includes sinus bradycardia and slow AF. Often associated with other conduction problems	• Treat symptoms
Tachybrady syndrome	• Combination of slow underlying rate (sinus bradycardia of slow AF) with tendency for runs of SVT that often terminate with a long pause. • Symptoms due to both slow and fast pulse	• Usually requires pacemaker for bradycardia and rate limiting drugs to control tachyarrhythmias.

Table (*Contd.*)

Condition	Clinical features	Treatment
First degree heart block	• PR > 0.22 seconds	• Benign if isolated, but always check for co-existing 2nd or 3rd degree block. No action required
Second degree heart block, Mobitz type I (Wenckebach)	• PR interval increases progressively until a QRS is dropped	• Often occurs transiently post MI • Usually appropriate to monitor until resolves
Second degree heart block, Mobitz type II	• Fixed PR interval, but conduction to the ventricles does not occur on every beat. Usually in a fixed pattern (conducting every second, third or fourth beat) • Often associated with bundle branch block	• Often symptomatic • High risk of progression to complete heart block • Usually requires elective pacing.
Complete heart block (third degree)	• Complete dissociation of atrial and ventricular activity. P waves visible, but not conducted. QRS originates at ventricular pacemaker (escape rhythm). If this is in the AV node then the rate is around 60 and the QRS morphology narrow. If it is more distal then the rate tends to be around 40 with wide QRS complexes.	• Usually symptomatic although if rate >50 may only be on exertion • If chronic, limit activity until permanent pacing arranged • If acute (e.g. post MI) likely to resolve • When associated with hypotension, angina or cardiac failure at rest, may need temporary pacing wire
Bundle branch block	• Widened QRS due to delayed conduction. • Not related to rate, so asymptomatic • Right bundle branch block is a common finding in healthy elderly and is usually benign, but if acute consider acute pulmonary embolism • Left bundle branch block is associated with hypertension and ischaemic heart disease	• Acutely, LBBB may indicate acute infarct • If found incidentally tell the patient (aids future emergency treatment) and consider giving a copy of the ECG to the patient.

Cardiac failure: assessment

Cardiac failure (CF) is very common, occurring in 1 in 10 of the over 65s and accounting for 5% of admissions to medical wards and 1–2% of all healthcare costs. Overall prevalence is 3–20 cases per 1000 population, but this doubles with each decade over 45 years. Becoming more common as population ages and survival from coronary events improves.

Pathology

- Poor left ventricular (LV) function (systolic or diastolic) decreases cardiac output.
- Sympathetic nervous system activated (increased pulse, myocardial contractility, peripheral vasoconstriction and catecholamines).
- Renin–angiotensin system activated (increases salt and water retention).
- Vasopressin and natriuretic peptides increase.

Causes

Usually due to coronary heart disease (especially in Caucasians—CHD risk factors are markers for CF) and hypertension (especially Afro-Carribeans). Other causes include valve disease, arrhythmias, pericardial disease, pulmonary hypertension (e.g. with COPD or multiple pulmonary embolisms), high output states (look especially for anaemia, thyroid disease and Paget's disease), and cardiomyopathy (check alcohol history).

Diagnosis

Cardiac failure is a complex clinical diagnosis, with no universally agreed diagnostic criteria. Often difficult to diagnose accurately, particularly in older patients with increased co-morbidity and symptoms. Many older people are put on a diuretic for presumed heart failure, but diuretic use as a marker of CF is 73% sensitive but only 41% specific. This predisposes to postural symptoms, and adds to polypharmacy.

Symptoms

Ask are these symptoms cardiac and what is the underlying disease causing them? Exertional dyspnoea is 100% sensitive for CF (i.e. every CF case has it), but only 17% specific (i.e. many other causes of exertional dyspnoea exist—the main one being respiratory). Fatigue and ankle swelling are also very common in CF but occur in many other diseases too. Orthopnoea and paroxysmal nocturnal dyspnoea are much more specific, but occurring late in the disease are not sensitive.

Signs

Again, early signs are sensitive, but not specific (e.g. tachycardia, pulmonary crepitations, peripheral oedema). Later signs are more specific, but not sensitive (e.g. elevated JVP—98% specific, 17% sensitive; gallop rhythm—99% specific and 24% sensitive).

▶▶ Overall, clinical features tend to be sensitive OR specific, but not both. The multiple pathology of older patients poses a particular challenge in diagnosis. Clinical suspicion should then be supported by investigation before embarking on a trial of treatment.

HOW TO... investigate a patient with suspected cardiac failure

Use investigations to support a clinical diagnosis and establish cause.

- **ECG**: abnormal in over 90% of cases (Q waves, T wave /ST segment changes, LVH, bundle branch block, AF). Consider Holter monitor if paroxysmal symptoms.
- **Chest X-ray**: look for cardiac enlargement (although this is absent with acute onset e.g. post MI or PE), upper lobe blood diversion, fluid in the horizontal fissure, Kerley B lines, bat wing pulmonary oedema, pleural effusions (usually bilateral; R >L if unilateral), any other cause for breathlessness.

▶▶ Combination of a normal CXR and ECG makes CF very unlikely indeed.

- **Blood tests**: FBC (?anaemic), biochemistry (?renal function, sodium low in severe CF), glucose and lipids (CHD risk factors), liver function (?congestion), thyroid function. BNP if available see box, p315.
- **Echocardiography**: 2D doppler echo should be done for all with suspected cardiac failure (NICE guidelines) to help confirm diagnosis, establish cause and grade disease severity. Looks for LV function (systolic and diastolic, see p314), estimates ejection fraction, looks for evidence of valve disease, cardiomyopathy, regional wall abnormalities from ischaemic heart disease, pericardial disease, intracardiac shunts, LV aneurysms or cardiac thrombus. Open access echo (i.e. direct GP referral) has improved the number of patients who have an echo, but the results are only as good as the echo technician and there can be problems with interpreting results (e.g. diastolic problems). Overall, only 25% of those referred for echo have LV systolic dysfunction.
- **Pulmonary function tests**: may help distinguish cardiac from respiratory breathlessness (PEFR and FEV1 reduced in CF, but less than in COPD). Remember many patients have both.

Acute cardiac failure

Treatment

- Immediate treatment with oxygen, intravenous loop diuretic and nitrates (if adequate blood pressure), opiate, and antiemetic.
- Address cause (e.g. acute myocardial infarction, arrhythmia).
- Consider ventilatory support (begin with non-invasive positive pressure ventilation which can be done in a non-ITU setting and does not present problems of weaning).
- After improvement is seen begin to plan ongoing treatment—write up regular loop diuretic and usually ACE on the drug chart and make plans for further assessment.

Prognosis

Patients with acute heart failure look extremely unwell yet can often make apparently 'miraculous' recoveries as the precipitant is dealt with. Remember that it is the pre-morbid state and the nature of the acute injury, never age alone, that should determine how aggressively to manage the acute condition.

Rapid atrial fibrillation and cardiac failure

- A common combination in older patients.
- It is rarely clear which came first.
- Treat both simultaneously.
- Digoxin is the drug of choice to slow AF in this situation (load 1mg of digoxin over 24 hours in divided doses—e.g. 500mcg iv or orally repeated at 12 hours, followed by the maintenance dose) as it is does not depress the myocardium, unlike amiodarone.
- Always look for a precipitant—sepsis, MI, PE, etc.

Further reading

Longmore M, Wilkinson I, Rajagopalan S (2004). Severe pulmonary oedema and management of heart failure, in *Oxford Handbook of Clinical Medicine*, 6th edn. Oxford: Oxford University Press.

Chronic cardiac failure

▶▶ Begin by reviewing basis for diagnosis as it means a poor prognosis and a commitment to a large number of medications.

A multi-disciplinary approach is preferable, involving the patient in monitoring where possible (e.g. daily weighing). Best done by those with an interest, and with facilities for ongoing follow-up e.g. day hospitals (particularly suited to the frailer elderly), cardiac failure clinics, by cardiac failure specialist nurses or GPs with a special interest.

Lifestyle

Address cardiovascular risk actors, reduce alcohol intake, increase aerobic exercise (ideally as part of a rehabilitation programme).

Medication

Large evidence base for a large number of drugs (see box opposite). It may be tempting to limit the number of drugs in older patients, justified by concerns about side effects, but if the diagnosis is secure then all classes should be at least attempted. It is probably better to prescribe a low dose of an ACE with a beta-blocker, rather than a maximum dose of ACE when the blood pressure may be insufficient to introduce the beta-blocker.

Treating cause

- Atrial fibrillation should be slowed and anticoagulation started (cardioversion unlikely to succeed once LV dysfunction).
- Hypertension should be treated until disease progression drops cardiac output and hence blood pressure.
- Valvular disease should be assessed for surgical correction where appropriate (especially aortic valve disease—discuss with patient early after onset of CF).
- Treat anaemia and thyroid disease.

Vaccination

Offer influenza vaccination annually and pneumococcal vaccination (once only).

Monitoring

Should include:

- Clinical assessment of symptoms and functional capacity (how far can they walk without stopping etc.).
- Blood pressure, including postural measurements.
- Fluid status (weigh regularly. Estimate dry weight, record it, and use this to titrate future management. Examine for JVP, oedema, and lung crepitations).
- Cardiac rhythm (clinical and by ECG).
- Cognitive state (common problem with CF due to vascular disease and low blood pressure. Pre-emptive questioning allows planning, so ask about problems encountered and consider a 30-point rating scale—see Appendix).

- Nutritional state (malnutrition common in CF. Ask about appetite, assess muscle bulk, check albumin—consider build-up drinks or dietician input).
- Medication review (are they on all appropriate drugs at maximum tolerated doses?).
- Side effects (especially ask about postural symptoms, check urea, creatinine and electrolytes).
- Psychological and social review, done by a multidisciplinary team (how are they and carers coping with problems of chronic disease? Do they need any social support?).

Medication for chronic cardiac failure

Loop diuretics: (e.g. furosemide) Use to control symptoms. Begin with 40mg (20mg in very elderly) and titrate upwards (guided by symptoms and examination findings). Monitor renal function and electrolytes.

ACE inhibitors: should be started early in all with a diagnosis of systolic heart failure unless valvular cause, or renal artery stenosis suspected. Again begin low (e.g. ramipril 2.5mg) and titrate upwards monitoring renal function and postural symptoms.

Beta-blockers: should be started in all stable patients with LV systolic dysfunction after diuretics and ACE inhibitors regardless of whether there are continuing symptoms (improves prognosis). Use beta-blocker licensed for cardiac failure e.g. carvedilol 3.125mg, bisoprolol 2.5mg and titrate upwards.

Spironolactone: use for continuing symptoms despite loop and ACE. Dose 25mg. Watch potassium levels as ACE and spironolactone will raise this.

Digoxin: use in AF, and where there are continuing symptoms despite maximal other therapy in sinus rhythm.

Thiazide diuretics: can be added to loop diuretics in end-stage CF, eg bendroflumethazide 2.5mg, or metolazone 5mg (monitor electrolytes closely; may be used on alternate days if causes excess diuresis).

Warfarin: use in AF, or where echo has shown intracardiac thrombus.

Angiotensin receptor blockers (ARBs): (e.g. losartan) useful where ACE intolerant, this class is rapidly gaining evidence of its efficacy in cardiac failure. *May* be role for ARBs in addition to ACE inhibitors.

Aspirin/statins: use for risk factor modification where cause is ischaemic heart disease.

Further reading

NICE guidelines for the management of chronic heart failure in adults in primary and secondary care (www.nice.org.uk)

Dilemmas in cardiac failure

The cardiac failure seesaw

One of the commonest dilemmas is balancing drugs in a patient with both cardiac failure and chronic renal failure.

Aggressive diuretic use will improve the cardiac failure but lead to thirst, malaise, hyponatraemia, uraemia, postural hypotension and ultimately anuria. Hydrating to improve renal function will lead to worsening pulmonary oedema.

Each patient will need a carefully planned balance, accepting moderate elevations in urea and/or a bit of oedema, which enables the patient to exist in the greatest comfort. This balance will take time and skill to achieve.

The following will help:
- Make all changes slowly and wait for impact—large dose changes increase oscillation between wet and dry states.
- If a patient is still losing weight on a therapy regime, they are likely to continue to do so—do not discharge after an acute event until steady state is reached, otherwise they will come back into hospital with dehydration and renal failure.
- Get to know the ideal weight, and use this to guide therapy.
- Involve patients and carers wherever possible.
- Admit and stabilize in hospital (may take weeks).
- Get to know the patient—continuity of care is very helpful, and cardiac failure nurses may play a key role in this.

Terminal care

- Chronic heart failure is a grim diagnosis with a poor outlook (only 25% will survive 3 years—worse than many cancers).
- Consider broaching this with all patients in clinic (ideally in a stable phase of the illness) to allow future plans to be made and resuscitation issues discussed.
- As the disease progresses ensure appropriate palliative care measures are taken with careful review of symptoms and patient/family anxieties.
- Opiates (e.g. oramorph 2.5–10mg) can be given to help relieve the distress of dyspnoea and allow sleep.
- Continuous oxygen therapy may ease discomfort.
- Intermittent iv boluses of furosemide in day hospital can keep people out of hospital.

Further reading

Stewart S and McMurray J J V (2002). Palliative care for heart failure. *BMJ*; **325**: 915–16.

Diastolic heart failure

- Clinical syndrome of cardiac failure with preserved left ventricular ejection fraction seen on echocardiography (>50%), where there is no major valvular disease.
- Accounts for around a third of clinically diagnosed heart failure, and is more common in older patients, especially females, hypertensives and those with left ventricular hypertrophy.
- Not a benign condition—ambulatory patients do better than those with systolic heart failure, but the mortality is equivalent in older patients or hospitalised. Fourfold increase in mortality when compared with controls without heart failure.

▶▶ Important to recognise and treat, and not to discontinue heart failure treatment on basis of normal LV function.

Pathology

Thick walled left ventricle with a small cavity. Slow to relax and allow filling in diastole, causing increased diastolic pressures (hence pulmonary pressures and so dyspnoea) and a low cardiac output (hence fatigue).

Diagnosis

- **Clinical suspicion** (history as for all systolic heart failure [SHF]) and **examination** findings (elevated JVP, pulmonary oedema, hypertension, murmur in the aortic area, 4th heart sound) are key.
- **Chest X-ray** will show pulmonary congestion, and the **ECG** evidence of hypertension.
- **Echocardiography** shows preserved LV function and in skilled hands may show evidence of abnormal diastolic relaxation (Doppler studies show a reduced ratio of early (E) to late or atrial (A) ventricular filling velocities—E:A < 0.5 is suggestive of diastolic dysfunction). However, these changes are very common in older patients (E:A often < 1) and it is unclear as yet whether asymptomatic diastolic dysfunction warrants treatment. Thus treatment is based on symptoms, not echo results.
- **BNP** (see box opposite) may be useful in cases where there are multiple possible aetiologies of dyspnoea as a negative result makes heart failure unlikely, helping to limit polypharmacy.

Management

- **Prevention:** by blood pressure control at population level.
- **Relieve precipitants:** treat arrhythmias, anaemia, thyroid disease, ischaemia, malnutrition.
- **Acute symptoms:** control blood pressure with oral agents as priority. Use diuretics cautiously as can drop cardiac output still further.
- **Chronic disease management:** less evidence than for SHF. Control of blood pressure key. Diastolic relaxation agents (e.g. beta-blockade) not proven. Use where dual indication e.g. AF or ischaemic heart disease. ACE and ARB likely to help (some trial evidence that ARBs reduce readmission rates modestly). Improve exercise tolerance with physical activity.

B-type natriuretic peptide (BNP)

Three types of natriuretic peptide known, with effects on heart, kidneys, and the nervous system. B-type is found mainly in the heart in humans and increases with pressure overload of the heart, acting as a biochemical marker for cardiac failure. BNP concentration correlates with the severity of heart disease and is 97% sensitive and 84% specific for the diagnosis in symptomatic primary care patients.

Problems

- What is a high level? Different assays produce different numbers, and there is a continuum of results making a diagnostic cut-off necessary.
- What is the gold standard for diagnosis in order to evaluate the test? (Echo has limitations.)
- Cost effectiveness unknown.
- Limited clinical trial evidence.
- Significance of a high level in an asymptomatic patient is unclear.
- Currently not widely available in the UK.

►► Overall, a 'negative' (i.e. very low) result in a breathless patient makes cardiac failure very unlikely, and other causes should be sought. May be useful to help preselect patients for echocardiography.

Valvular heart disease

The majority of valvular heart lesions in the UK are degenerative (e.g. senile calcification is the main cause of aortic stenosis) so valve defects are very common in older patients. The following must be remembered:

- Listen to the heart of all elderly people—many valve lesions are detected incidentally.
- Think of valvular disease when a patient presents with dyspnoea, cardiac failure, angina, palpitations, syncope, or dizziness. Examine them carefully (see table opposite).
- When a murmur is heard, echocardiography should be requested in order to document the valve lesion and formulate a management plan. ►► Remember endocarditis if a murmur is heard in the context of an unexplained fever.
- Once the valve lesion is known, decide whether valve replacement is indicated yet (see table opposite). In many lesions (e.g. mitral valve disease and aortic regurgitation) the progression of symptoms alerts to the need for pre-emptive surgery. In aortic stenosis however, a prompt response to the development of early symptoms is required, and so the approach is different.
- After deciding whether intervention is required, consider whether or not the patient is a surgical 'candidate'. Remember that many lesions are amenable to percutaneous interventions (feasible in much frailer patients). Always ask the patient what they think—often there will be strong views that come as a surprise to the physician. Make it clear that obtaining a surgical opinion is not committing the patient to surgery—indeed the surgeon may feel that the risks outweigh the benefits—but that it is an important first step.
- If surgery is not yet indicated, then ensure there is some sort of call-back/surveillance system in place—whether repeat echo-cardiography, or clinic review, or simply ensuring that the patient knows what symptoms should trigger medical review.
- If it is decided that surgery is not an option, ensure that full palliative care measures are in place.
- Remember antibiotic prophylaxis for invasive procedures (indicated in all acquired valve disease).

Talking to patients about potential surgery

Many older people are terrified at the prospect, and the gut reaction may be to avoid it at all costs. Others will not want to take responsibility for the decision—'whatever you think, doctor' is a common response. Having a frank and useful discussion about risks and benefits is often difficult, but should always be attempted before referral is made. Pig valves can be used in older patients, which have a shorter life span than metal valves, but obviate the need for warfarin. Ensure you have enough time and take it slowly giving plenty of opportunity for questions. They may wish to go away and think about it, perhaps returning with a spouse or child—encourage this and do not force a decision.

Common valve lesions

Valve lesion	Symptoms	Complications	Treatment	Who to consider for surgery?
Mitral stenosis	• Dyspnoea • Fatigue • Palpitations • Chest pain • Haemoptysis	• Atrial fibrillation • Systemic emboli • Pulmonary hypertension • Pulmonary oedema • Pressure effects from large LA • Endocarditis	• Rate control of AF (digoxin and/or beta-blocker) • Anticoagulation if AF • Diuretics if CF • Antibiotic prophylaxis for invasive procedures	• Symptoms despite medical management. • If pliable valve, may be candidate for balloon valvuloplasty
Mitral regurgitation	• Dyspnoea • Fatigue • Palpitations	• Pulmonary oedema • Atrial fibrillation • Endocarditis	• Rate control of AF • Anticoagulation if AF • Diuretics if CF • Antibiotic prophylaxis for invasive procedures	• Deteriorating symptoms—aim to replace valve before extensive LV damage • Condition progresses slowly, so not if asymptommatic
Aortic stenosis	• Angina • Dyspnoea • Cardiac failure • Dizziness • Syncope • Sudden death	• Angina • Pulmonary oedema • Syncope • Sudden death • Endocarditis	• Consider surgical referral • If not suitable, then treat angina and heart failure symptomatically • Avoid ACE inhibitors. • Antibiotic prophylaxis for invasive procedures	• Once symptomatic prognosis poor (2–3yrs), so refer for valve replacement early after symptom onset. • Asymptommatic patient with deteriorating ECG should also be referred • Valvuloplasty may be an option for frail patients
Aortic sclerosis	• None	• None	• None	• Not applicable
Aortic regurgitation	• Dyspnoea • Palpitations • Cardiac failure	• Pulmonary oedema • Endocarditis	• Diuretics if CF • Antibiotic prophylaxis for invasive procedures	• Worsening symptoms, worsening cardiomegaly, ECG deterioration • Aim to replace valve before extensive LV damage

Peripheral oedema

Swollen ankles are extremely common in older patients. Starting a diuretic must not be an immediate reaction as this treats only one of several causes and may cause harm. As with all geriatric medicine, a careful assessment, diagnosis and appropriate treatment should be carried out.
▶▶ Swollen ankles does not always indicate cardiac failure.

Causes
- Often, mild ankle swelling occurs in an otherwise fit person: this tends to be worse on prolonged standing and in the heat (sometimes referred to as 'dependant oedema'). It is likely that there is some minor venous disease causing the oedema, but it is essentially benign.
- Peripheral venous disease: chronic oedema due to damage to deep veins causing venous hypertension, increased capillary pressure and fibrinogen leakage. Usually bilateral, but one side is often worse than the other (see p646).
- Cardiac failure: usually bilateral, look for associated signs e.g. raised JVP, cardiac enlargement, pulmonary crepitations etc.
- Acute oedema may be due to superficial thrombophlebitis (red, hot, very tender venous cord with surrounding oedema) or a new deep vein thrombosis (painful swollen calf with pitting oedema of ankle. Review thrombotic risk factors).
▶▶ Always consider DVT with new onset unilateral swelling.
- Drug side effect: commonly calcium channel blockers (especially amlodipine) and non-steroidal anti-inflammatory drugs.
- Low serum albumin: nephrotic syndrome, gastrointestinal loss, malnutrition, chronic disease, acute sepsis etc.
- Lymphatic obstruction: consider obstructing pelvic tumours. If oedema is severe, perform rectal and groin examination.
- Traumatic: after forcefully dorsiflexing the foot (usually when walking), leading to rupture of the plantar tendon or injury to gastrocnemius. This oedema tends to be unilateral, tender, above the ankle and with associated bruising to the calf. Treat with rest and non-steroidals.
- Other e.g. hypothyroidism, osteoarthritis of the knee, ruptured Baker's cyst, post stroke paralysis.

Assessment
- History: how acute was the onset? Is it unilateral or bilateral? Is it painful, red and hot? What are the associated physical symptoms—importantly dyspnoea (may indicate PE or cardiac failure)?
- Examination: look for physical signs as above. Always listen to the heart and lungs and look for sacral oedema when ankle swelling is found. Consider rectal/groin examination.
- Investigations: be guided by your clinical suspicion. Consider ECG (unlikely to be normal in cardiac failure), urea and electrolytes, albumin, full blood count, thyroid function tests.

▶▶ D-dimer in elderly patients with swollen ankles is rarely helpful. Whilst a negative result effectively rules out deep vein thrombosis, many elderly patients will have an elevated d-dimer—only use the test if you would proceed to ultrasound scanning in the event of a positive result.

Treatment

All patients with ankle swelling should have a careful assessment for disease as above, with treatment dependant on cause:

- Stop drugs if they are responsible (replace with alternatives).
- If cardiac failure, then full assessment and treatment is required.
- For chronic venous disease use leg elevation and compression bandaging (p646).
- With severe lymphoedema, massage and pneumatic boots can be useful.
- If low albumin, treat cause and increase dietary intake.

If no disease is found then management is pragmatic. Patients may find the ankle swelling unsightly, have difficulty fitting on their shoes or even complain of an aching pain. Support hosiery may help. It may then be appropriate to start a low dose of thiazide diuretic (e.g. bendroflumethiazide 2.5mg) but this will necessitate occasional monitoring of electrolytes and clinical review to ensure the benefits of treatment still outweigh the risks. Many patients may be happy to tolerate the minor inconvenience once they have been assured that there is no serious pathology.

Ankle swelling and nocturnal polyuria

During the day, a large amount of fluid can collect in the interstitial space in the ankles. At night, when the legs are elevated, this fluid is partly returned to the circulating volume and can cause a diuresis—hence nocturnal polyuria.

Paradoxically, treating such a patient with diuretics to limit the swelling will ultimately help with the polyuria.

Peripheral vascular disease

Peripheral vascular disease (PVD) is common in older patients, causing symptoms in 10% of those over 70 years. Only a third of older patients will have the classic symptoms of intermittent claudication and often decreasing activity levels will mask developing disease.

Claudication pain may progress to ischaemic rest pain (night-time pain, often relieved by hanging foot over bed), then to ulceration—due to trauma with poor healing (small, punctate, painful ulcers at pressure points e.g. toes, lateral malleolus, metatarsal heads) and possibly gangrene.

Around 80% of patients with claudication remain stable or improve; only 20% deteriorate, and 6% require amputation (ongoing smokers and diabetics are most at risk).

Examination reveals a loss of pulses (best discriminator is an abnormality of the posterior tibial pulse), possibly bruits, coolness to touch, slow capillary refill (over 2 seconds), shiny hairless skin with atrophic nails and poor wound healing.

PVD as a marker of other vascular disease

- 5-year mortality in PVD is 30%, mostly due to cardiovascular disease.
- It is easy to detect PVD non-invasively by measuring ABPI (see box opposite).
- The impact of broad vascular risk management on subsequent vascular disease burden has yet to be quantified, but is likely to be substantial.
- ▶▶ If a patient complains of leg pains, screen for PVD and if detected initiate full vascular secondary prevention.

PVD as a cause of significant morbidity

Although very common, many elderly people will modify their lifestyle to reduce symptoms. It is important to actively seek out symptoms.
Adopt the following treatment approach:
- Modify risk factors.
- Advise increasing exercise (NOT decreasing).
- Commence antiplatelet agent—commonly aspirin.
- Consider other drugs—phosphodiesterase inhibitors (e.g. cilostazol) have antiplatelet activity and act as vasodilators. The herbal remedy Ginkgo biloba may have a modest impact also.
- Do not necessarily stop beta-blockers (traditionally thought to worsen claudication). The evidence for this is weak and beta-blockers have a major role in modifying cardiac risk.
- Refer for revascularization when appropriate. Percutaneous revascularization is relatively low risk and should be considered for lifestyle-limiting claudication that does not respond to medical therapy, where there is a focal stenosis or when there is limb-threatening ischaemia in a patient who is not fit for surgery. Elective surgery is usually reserved for low risk patients (under 70 years with no diabetes and no distal disease) who are fit enough to tolerate the procedure. Age has a significant impact on surgical risk—relative risk of mortality increases by 1.62 with each decade.

HOW TO... measure an ankle brachial pressure index (ABPI)

When?

- To confirm PVD as a cause of claudication.
- To diagnose vascular disease before implementing secondary prevention.
- To diagnose the aetiology of (venous) ulcers.
- To ensure compression bandaging is safe.

Equipment

- Blood pressure cuff with sphygmomanometer.
- Hand-held Doppler probe.

Method

- Inflate the cuff around the upper arm as usual and use the doppler probe over the brachial artery to measure the systolic blood pressure.
- Repeat in the other arm.
- Next inflate the cuff around the ankle and use the probe to measure the systolic pressure in the dorsalis pedis and posterior tibial arteries.
- Take the highest of the four ankle readings and divide by the higher of the two arm readings to give the ABPI.

Interpretation

- >1.3   Non-compressible calcified vessels—reading has limited value
- 1.0–1.3 Normal range
- <0.9   Angiographic peripheral vascular disease very likely
- 0.4–0.9 Likely to be associated with claudication
- <0.4   Advanced ischaemia.

Gangrene in peripheral vascular disease

The onset of gangrene is relatively common in people with severe PVD and causes considerable distress. It often poses management difficulties, as many frail elderly are judged inappropriate for surgery.

Slowly progressive disease with dry gangrene

- Cyanotic anaesthetic tissue with necrosis.
- Distal, with clear demarcation.
- Often a low-grade inflammatory response (elevated WBC and CRP). The patient may feel unwell and anorexic.
- Non-urgent surgical review is appropriate, but the approach is often to allow auto-amputation—a lengthy and sometimes distressing process, for patient and family.
- Surgical amputation may be considered but as there is often inadequate local circulation to allow healing, this may need to be extensive, or combined with bypass (the latter carrying a significant operative risk). Sometimes amputation vastly improves the quality of life for a bed-bound patient with gangrene. Discussion about possible amputation should be approached with tact and sensitivity—patients are often very against loss of a limb, even when they have not walked for years. Ensure that the patient and family are aware of the rationale for treatment, and that there is regular review of analgesia requirements.

Wet gangrene

▶▶ This is a life threatening condition and urgent surgical review is required, in all but the most terminal of patients.

- Moist, swollen, and blistered skin—usually in diabetics.
- The usual approach to management is for debridement and amputation.

Acute ischaemia

▶▶ This is a limb threatening condition and demands urgent action.

- Usually due to embolization.
- **Distal emboli** cause so-called 'blue toe syndrome'. The main object of treatment is to prevent recurrence as little can be done to salvage occluded small vessels. This may include angiography to establish the source, and/or anticoagulation depending on the fitness of the patient.
- **Proximal emboli** cause diffuse acute ischaemia. Revascularization of the limb is nearly always attempted (unless there is already irreversible ischaemic changes) and the approach can be tailored to the frailty of the patient—ranging from thrombolysis, percutaneous thromboembolectomy (possible under local anaesthetic) to emergency bypass procedures.

Vascular secondary prevention

Atheromatous vascular disease (cardiac, peripheral vascular, and cerebral) accounts for a huge amount of morbidity, mortality and expenditure. Secondary prevention measures evolve continually as individual clinical trials reach completion. Although some interventions are primarily applied to a specific pathology (e.g. statins in cardiovascular disease), most impact on all vascular systems. The cumulative effect of therapies is not yet known, but the consensus is that they will substantially reduce the burden of future vascular events.

Traditionally, older patients have been under-provided with secondary prevention measures, for a number of reasons:

- There is often polypharmacy, and reluctance amongst patients and healthcare professionals to add to this.
- It was thought that secondary prevention benefits were seen only with long term (perhaps 5 to 10 years) treatment. Unless life expectancy was greater than this, therapy was not begun.
- It may be 'shutting the door after the horse has bolted'—the damage has already been done.

But consider several contrary points:

- Recent evidence suggests that some therapies (statins and ACE inhibitors) act quickly, possibly due to endovascular stabilization.
- Although older patients are under-represented in clinical trials, where older patients have been included (e.g. the Heart Protection Study) the benefits have been equal, if not greater than in younger patients.
- Do not assume that a disabled person will not benefit from prevention of further events. In a bed-bound stroke patient who has to be spoon fed a further stroke that removes swallowing ability altogether may deprive that person of their only pleasure in life.
- As with much of geriatric medicine, frank discussion with the patient is advised. Many patients will have strong views and fall into one of two groups—the fatalists, who prefer not to take medication 'just in case', and the 'belt-and-braces' patients who welcome all possible measures.
- Drug doses are determined by clinical trial evidence—often a high dose in generally robust patients. Adopt a pragmatic approach in frail patients, with lower doses as these may be effective.

We do not advocate the blind prescription of all secondary prevention to all of older patients—such an approach would be clinically inappropriate for some and unlikely to be cost effective. What we do suggest is that each case is considered on a case-to-case basis, and where possible discussed with the patient to reach an individually tailored action plan.

Further reading

The Heart Protection Study Collaborative Group (HPS) (2002). *Lancet.* July 6; **360** (9326):7–22.
Heart Outcome Prevention Evaluation (HOPE) Study (2000). *N Engl J Med;* **342**:145–53.
Clopidogrel versus aspirin in patients at risk of ischaemic events (CAPRIE) (1996). *Lancet;* **348**: 1329–8.

Table to show main secondary prevention agents:

Agent	Dose	Action	Outcome	Special points for older patients
Aspirin	75–300mg od	Antiplatelet activity	Prevention of all vascular events	Use lower doses Beware gastric irritation Consider co-prescription of proton pump inhibitor Enteric coated formulations unlikely to be very useful
Clopidogrel	75mg od	Antiplatelet activity	Mainly as an alternative to aspirin where not tolerated, or as an addition in cardiac disease.	Reportedly, lower gastric side effects than aspirin Slightly higher efficacy than aspirin as monotherapy
Dipyridamole MR	200mg bd	Antiplatelet activity	Addition to aspirin in cerebrovascular disease NOT for cardiac disease (can exacerbate angina)	Start slowly as commonly causes headache Low bleeding risk
Antihypertensives	Various agents	Blood pressure reduction	Prevention of all vascular events	The lower the blood pressure, the greater the benefit, but take care to avoid hypotensive side effects
ACE inhibitors	e.g. Ramipril 10mg od	Blood pressure reduction and possible endovascular effect	Prevention of all vascular events	Dose stated is often not tolerated in older patients—aim as high as tolerated, but start with 1.25mg
Statins	e.g. Simvastatin 40mg od	Cholesterol lowering and possible endovascular effect	Prevention of all vascular events	Should be prescribed for vast majority Lower doses (eg. 10mg) may be better tolerated

Note: consider also smoking cessation, increasing physical activity, and for stroke–endarterectomy and AF prophylaxis.

Chest medicine

The ageing lung 328
Respiratory infections 330
Influenza 332
　How to... treat influenza-like illness in older
　people 333
Lower respiratory tract infection 334
Pneumonia: treatment 336
　How to... manage the patient with pneumonia who fails to
　respond to treatment 338
Vaccinating against pneumonia and influenza 340
Pulmonary fibrosis 342
Rib fractures 344
Pleural effusions 346
　How to... aspirate a sample of pleural fluid 347
Pulmonary embolism 348
Pulmonary aspiration 350
Chronic cough 352
Asbestos-related disease 354
Lung cancers 356
Tuberculosis: presentation 358
Tuberculosis: investigation 360
　How to... perform and interpret a tuberculin skin test 361
Tuberculosis: treatment 362
Asthma and COPD: assessment 364
Asthma and COPD: drug treatment 366
　How to... improve drug delivery in asthma or COPD 367
Asthma and COPD: non-drug treatment 368
Oxygen therapy 370

The ageing lung

Most of the functional impairment of the lungs that is seen in older people is due to disease, often smoking-related. Intrinsic ageing leads only to mild functional deterioration. The respiratory system has a capacity well in excess of that required for normal activity. Therefore, intrinsic ageing:

• Does not lead to symptoms in the non-smoker without respiratory disease.
• In those with respiratory disease (e.g. emphysema) will cause progressively worsening symptoms with age even if the disease itself remains stable.
• In acute disease, e.g. pneumonia, may cause earlier decompensation or a more severe presentation.

The specific changes seen in healthy older people are similar to those seen in mild chronic obstructive pulmonary disease, and include:

• Decreased elastic recoil, therefore small airways collapse at low lung volumes.
• Increased chest wall stiffness, due to:
  • Degenerative change in intercostal, intervertebral and costovertebral joints.
  • Osteoporosis and kyphoscoliosis.
• Weaker respiratory muscles that may have lower endurance.
• Reduced gas exchange and increased ventilation-perfusion mismatch, due to collapse of peripheral airways whilst perfusion remains intact.
• Impaired chemoreceptor function, leading to lessened ventilatory response to decreased P_aO_2 or increased P_aCO_2.
• Impairment of microbial defence mechanisms. Less effective mucociliary clearance and less sensitive cough reflex.

Generally observed consequences of these changes include:

• Increased susceptibility to infection (underventilation of and inability to clear sputum from dependent lung zones).
• Lower maximum minute ventilation (weaker musculature acting against a stiffer chest).
• An approximately linear fall in P_aO_2 with age (~0.3%/year). Since alveolar oxygen tension remains stable, the alveolar-arterial (A-a) oxygen gradient rises.
• Reduced exercise capacity. However, oxygen consumption and cardiac output decline in proportion to lung function, so the lungs are rarely the limiting factor in exercise performance.

Breathlessness in older people is often multifactorial:

• Chronic breathlessness in an individual may be the result of e.g., decreased fitness, obesity, an inefficient gait (osteoarthritis or stroke), kyphosis, previous lung damage (e.g. apical fibrosis due to TB) and intrinsic ageing. In this example, note that only one of the factors is specific to the lung.
• In the acutely breathless patient, pathologies commonly coexist, e.g. infection, fast atrial fibrillation and heart failure. The classically administered combination of digoxin, frusemide and amoxicillin is therefore often appropriate.

Respiratory infections

Cough with or without sputum, shortness of breath, fever or chest pain is a very common presentation in elderly patients. It is very important to try to distinguish which part of the airway is primarily affected because this implies completely different pathogens, prognoses and treatment strategies. Try to avoid aggregating all such patients together using the imprecise term 'chest infection'.

Upper respiratory tract infection (URTI)

These are caused by viruses, e.g. rhinovirus, respiratory syncitial virus, influenza and parainfluenza. Symptoms include nasal discharge and congestion, fever and sore throat. These may extend to the lower tract and then include cough, wheeze, sputum production or worsening of existing cardiopulmonary disease.

With increasing age:

- URTI becomes less frequent, but more severe.
- The risk of complications increases. These include:
  - Lower tract infection such as bronchitis or pneumonia, which may be bacterial or viral.
  - Bronchospasm.
  - Extra-pulmonary manifestations such as falls, immobility and delirium.
- Post-infection weakness, fatigue, and anorexia is more severe and prolonged, maybe lasting several weeks.
- Frequency of hospital admission and death increases substantially.

Influenza

This is the most serious viral respiratory tract infection, and is often a severe, systemic illness with pulmonary bacterial superinfection (*Staphylococcus aureus, Haemophilus influenzae, Streptococcus pneumoniae*). It occurs most commonly in December–February. Antigenic shifts result in periodic pandemics (large scale epidemics).

Presentation is similar in young and old ie rapid onset of fever (rigors, chills), myalgia, headache and fatigue with variable degrees of prostration. Compared to less threatening viruses such as rhinovirus:
- Nausea, vomiting, diarrhoea, high fever, rigors and ocular symptoms (e.g. photophobia) are more common.
- Rhinorrhoea is less common.

Less common serious complications include myocarditis and meningoencephalitis. Mild meningism is common, and if combined with other sinister features (e.g. altered conscious level) is an indication for CSF sampling.

Diagnosis is usually based on combining clinical assessment with epidemiological data, particularly current influenza incidence. Some other viruses can cause an identical clinical syndrome, and serological test results are not immediately available. Thus an initial assessment cannot produce an absolutely confident microbiological diagnosis. The syndrome may therefore most precisely be labeled 'influenza-like illness'.

Positive virological diagnosis in the context of increased community incidence or a care home outbreak is helpful by prompting vigorous attempts to reduce transmission of infection (see below and p340).

Reducing viral transmission

Mass outbreaks of respiratory viral infection are common in care homes and hospitals. They can occur at any time of year but are commonest from autumn to spring. Viruses are spread by aerosol or hand-to-hand contact (sometimes indirect, via fomites such as cutlery or drinking vessels). During an outbreak:
- Reduce transfers of healthy patients into, or symptomatic patients out of, the affected area.
- Reduce staff movement across work areas (especially applicable to short-term staff who may work in many clinical areas in a short time).
- Care for symptomatic patients in single rooms, or in ward bays with similarly infected patients.
- Exclude visitors who have respiratory or other symptoms of viral illness from the ward.
- Ensure that staff caring for patients have been immunized against influenza.
- Ensure that scrupulous hand-washing procedures are followed.
- Consider using face masks for staff caring for symptomatic patients.

HOW TO... treat influenza-like illness in older people

The following guidance is generic, and should be tailored to the patient, their illness and their care environment. If the highest quality care cannot be provided, then a prompt step-up of care should be arranged. This may include hospital admission.

- Do not underestimate the disease. Mortality and morbidity increases exponentially with age and frailty.
- Give excellent supportive and symptomatic care. Its effectiveness should not be underestimated.
  - **Fluids**. Reduced intake and increased losses (fever) lead to volume depletion and end-organ dysfunction. Encourage frequent oral fluid. Consider early initiation of subcutaneous or intravenous fluids if a vicious spiral of dehydration and poor intake seems likely to ensue.
  - **Nutrition**. Encourage high calorie, high protein drinks or solids. If the illness is especially severe, prolonged, or complicated, or if the patient is especially frail or malnourished, consider a period of nasogastric feeding. Involve a dietician early.
  - **Paracetamol**. If fever, discomfort or pain occur.
  - **Maintain mobility**. Bed-rest may sentence the patient to death or dependency. Carers may need clear, firm advice about this.
- Identify and treat complications promptly.
  - Carers may need information about important warning signs and the need to seek prompt medical advice.
  - Perform regular observations of blood pressure, pulse, and temperature where possible.
  - Common serious complications include delirium, secondary bacterial infection, bronchospasm, pressure sores, and circulatory collapse.
- Antiviral agents (the neuraminidase inhibitors zanamivir and oseltamivir) can reduce both the severity and duration of influenza.
  - Recently introduced, they are not yet widely used.
  - They are indicated in patients over 65 years who have a influenza like illness during a period of high community incidence providing they present early (<48 hours).
  - They are well tolerated, reduce symptom severity and duration and they may reduce mortality.
  - Zanamivir is inhaled (10mg bd for five days; two blisters of 5mg each via Diskhaler). Oseltamivir is taken orally (available as capsules or suspension; 75mg bd for five days).

Lower respiratory tract infection

This includes bronchitis and (lobar or bronchial) pneumonia.

Acute bronchitis

This has fewer systemic features and a better prognosis. It can be managed less aggressively, with more reliance on bronchodilators than antibiotics. Often viral in origin, if an antibacterial is thought appropriate then give amoxicillin to cover *Streptococcus pneumoniae* (erythromycin or clarithromycin if penicillin-sensitive).

Pneumonia

- This is a syndrome of acute respiratory infection with shadowing on CXR. Symptoms may be mild and are often non-organ specific.
- Common presenting scenarios include cough (often unproductive), delirium, reduced conscious level, lethargy, anorexia, falls, immobility, and dizziness. Rarely patients can present with shock, coma, and adult respiratory distress syndrome (ARDS).
- Chest pain, dyspnoea, and high fever are less common than in younger people. Signs may be minimal:
  - The patient may be well or unwell. Assess severity using the CURB criteria (p336).
  - Fever is often absent, but vasodilatation is common.
  - Tachypnoea is a sensitive sign, as is at least moderate hypoxaemia (≤ 95% on air) on oximetry.
- Tests often guide management
  - Chest radiograph often reveals minimal infective infiltrate. Associated problems can include malignancy, effusion or heart failure.
  - Blood cultures should be sent, but sputum culture is not useful unless TB is suspected.
  - White cell count may be normal.
  - CRP is often normal early in the illness. A very high CRP suggests pneumococcal disease or severe sepsis of any cause.
  - Urea, creatinine, and electrolytes guide fluid management. Renal impairment is a sign of poor prognosis.
  - Arterial blood gas (ABG) sampling is not usually necessary, unless oxygen saturations are < 90%; oximetry is much better tolerated and usually sufficient to guide oxygen therapy.
- Organisms (see table opposite):
  - Often no causative organism is identified.
  - Pneumococcus is a common pathogen in all settings, including hospital.
  - Viral pneumonia, especially influenza, is underrecognised, and is the second most common cause of community-acquired pneumonia.
  - Legionella and Mycoplasma pneumonias are uncommon. Mycoplasma is much more frequent during epidemics, occurring every three years or so.
  - Unusual organisms are more common in frail patients, in higher dependency environments and in those who have recently received courses of antibiotics. These organisms include Gram negatives (which colonize the oropharynx) and anaerobes (a result of aspiration of gut contents).

Pneumonia pathogens in various care settings; in approximate order of frequency

Community-acquired	Care home	Hospital
Streptoccus pneumoniae (>30% of cases)	*Streptoccus pneumoniae* (>30% of cases)	Gram negative aerobic bacilli e.g. Klebsiella, *Pseudomonas aeruginosa*
Viral e.g. influenza, parainfluenza, respiratory syncitial virus	Viral e.g. influenza, parainfluenza, respiratory syncitial virus	Anaerobes e.g. Bacteroides, Clostridium. Especially in those at risk of aspiration e.g. immobility, swallowing difficulty, prolonged recumbency or impaired conscious level
Haemophilus influenzae	Gram negative aerobic bacilli e.g. Klebsiella, *Pseudomonas aeruginosa*	*Staphylococcus aureus*
Gram negative bacilli e.g. Klebsiella, *Pseudomonas aeruginosa*	*Haemophilus influenzae*	*Streptoccus pneumoniae* and *Haemophilus influenzae*. NB These may be the most common pathogens • In non-acute settings e.g. rehabilitation wards • In the well, less frail patient
Legionella pneumophila. Mycoplasma pneumoniae if epidemic	Anaerobes e.g. Bacteroides, Clostridium. Especially in those at risk of aspiration e.g. immobility, swallowing difficulty, prolonged recumbency or impaired conscious level	Viral e.g. influenza, parainfluenza, respiratory syncitial virus
Other, e.g. TB	Other, e.g. TB	
Following influenza, think of secondary bacterial infection, especially with *Streptococcus pneumoniae* (most common), *Haemophilus influenzae* or *Staphylococcus aureus*	Following influenza, think of secondary bacterial infection, especially with *Streptococcus pneumoniae* (most common), *Haemophilus influenzae* or *Staphylococcus aureus*	

Pneumonia: treatment

Treatment is much more than antimicrobials alone:
- Assess and optimize fluid volume status; give oral, subcutaneous or intravenous fluid as appropriate. Concurrent heart failure is common, but volume depletion more so.
- If there is subjective dyspnoea or moderate/severe hypoxaemia, then supplement oxygen, titrating the inspired oxygen concentration upwards to achieve arterial oxygen saturations > 90%. For lesser degrees of hypoxaemia, it is not necessary to subject patients to claustrophobic, uncomfortable oxygen masks: consider not supplementing oxygen, simply monitoring saturations.
  - Exercise caution in COPD: observe the patient closely, both clinically and with serial ABG sampling.
  - Avoid the use of nasal specs acutely: if ventilatory drive is poor, inspired oxygen concentrations are very uncontrolled.
- Encourage mobility. If immobile, sit upright in bed, and sit out in a chair.
- If dyspnoea, anxiety or pain is very distressing, consider opiates. Side effects include respiratory depression, sedation and delirium, so begin with small doses and assess effect.
- Request physiotherapy if there is a poor cough, or lobar/lung collapse.
- Use saline nebulizers to loosen secretions which are difficult to expectorate and bronchodilator nebulizers when wheeze suggests associated bronchoconstriction.
- Minimize risk of thromboembolism through early mobilization, compression stockings and in high risk cases prophylactic heparin.
- Assess pressure sore risk and act accordingly.
- Anticipate possible deterioration, and judge in advance the appropriate levels of intervention. Would renal dialysis, ventilation and/or cardiopulmonary resuscitation be effective and kind?
- Keep the family informed. Where possible, enlist their help, e.g. in encouraging eating and drinking.

Characteristics of severe pneumonia: the CURB-65 score

Five key criteria (acronym 'CURB-65') determine prognosis:
1. Confusion (AMTS ≤8)
2. Urea (serum urea >7mmol/L)
3. Respiratory rate (≥30/min)
4. Blood pressure (<90 systolic and/or ≤ 60mmHg diastolic)
5. 65 years of age or more

The score has a six point scale (0–5 adverse prognostic features):
- Score 0 or 1. Low risk of death (0–3%). Possibility of home treatment (but consider other factors e.g. functional status, hypoxaemia.
- Score 2. Intermediate risk of death (13%). Hospital treatment is indicated.
- Score 3, 4 or 5. Severe pneumonia, with high risk of death (score 3: mortality 17%, 4: 41%, 5: 57%). Consider intensive care admission.

A five point scale (CRB-65; urea excluded) can be applied outside hospital and also discriminates effectively between good and poor prognoses (e.g. mortality with score 1: 5%, score 3: 33%).

Antimicrobials

Refer to local guidelines, reflecting pathogen sensitivities and drug costs.

Community or care home settings

- Amoxicillin 500mg tds po is usually effective (vs. *Streptococcus pneumoniae* and *Haemophilus influenzae*). Erythromycin or clarithromycin if penicillin-allergic.
- Add clarithromycin 500mg bd (or erythromycin which has more gastric side effects) if there are features of atypical pneumonia, there is a *Mycoplasma* epidemic, or the patient may have had influenza.
- Co-amoxiclav 375mg tds po has added activity against some Gram negatives and *Staphyloccus aureus*, and may be more effective in the frail patient or where aspiration is likely.
- Ciprofloxacin alone should be used rarely—it has Gram negative activity, but is less effective against *Streptococcus pneumoniae*, an important pathogen in most settings. If an antimicrobial is sought that will cover both chest and urinary sepsis, a better choice may be co-amoxiclav or trimethoprim.
- Intravenous antibiotics are necessary if the patient is very unwell or unable to swallow. Cefuroxime and erythromycin is a good choice in the unwell patient, treating all likely pathogens effectively. Convert to oral therapy and change broad to narrower spectrum drugs when the patient's condition improves and/or culture results are known. Often, only 48 hours or less of broad spectrum, intravenous therapy is needed.

Hospital-acquired infection

This presents a difficult dilemma. Hospitalized patients, especially those who are more frail and have spent longer in hospital, are prone to Gram negative and anaerobic pulmonary infections. However, they are also susceptible to the adverse effects (especially diarrhoea) of broad spectrum antimicrobials.

A hierarchical approach is sensible, considering likely pathogens and illness severity:

- In the less frail patient who remains well, begin amoxicillin alone, co-amoxiclav or a combination of amoxicillin and ciprofloxacin (all po). Broaden the spectrum only if the patient deteriorates or culture results suggest that the likely pathogen is insensitive:
- If a patient is at high risk of Gram negative infection (frail, dependency, prolonged stay, invasive procedures, aspiration risk), begin with intravenous cefuroxime (or equivalent). Narrow the antimicrobial spectrum when the patient's condition improves and/or a pathogen is identified.
- If the patient has received multiple courses of treatment, seek microbiology advice.
- In all cases take blood cultures, and monitor the patient carefully.

HOW TO... manage the patient with pneumonia who fails to respond to treatment

Is the diagnosis correct?
- Consider other chest pathology such as heart failure, pulmonary embolism, pleural effusion, empyema, cancer, or cryptogenic organizing pneumonia. Extrathoracic pathology mimicking pneumonia includes acidosis (tachypnoea), and biliary or pancreatic pathology.
- Review the history, examination, and investigations.
- Consider admission to hospital and further tests.

Is there a complication?
For example effusion, empyema, heart failure, silent myocardial infarction, or pulmonary embolism.

Is the antibiotic being taken regularly and in adequate dose?
- Is concordance a problem? Could a friend or relative help prompt tablet-taking, or would a Dosett box help?
- Syrups may be swallowed more easily than tablets. An experienced nurse can help where there are swallowing difficulties.
- If swallowing remains ineffective, or drug absorption in doubt (e.g. vomiting) then consider intravenous therapy.

Is the organism resistant?
- Take more blood cultures.
- Consider a change in antimicrobial, taking into account likely pathogens and their known sensitivities.
- Consider atypical infection: send urine for Legionella antigen test, especially if the patient is immunocompromised or if a patient with a community-acquired pneumonia appears disproportionately unwell.

Could other elements of care be more effective?
For example fluid balance, oxygenation, nutrition, posture, and chest physiotherapy.

Is this an end-of-life situation?
- Is treatment to extend life now inappropriate, the failure to respond a sign that the diagnosis is of 'dying' (see p732)?
- If the patient cannot tell you their wishes, determine their likely views by discussing with family and friends, a decision informed by your judgment of where in their life-cycle your patient sits.
- In determining prognosis consider comorbidity—is this an abrupt, potentially reversible illness in an otherwise fit person, or a further lurch downhill for a patient with multi-organ failure.
- Not for nothing is pneumonia referred to as 'the old man's friend', sometimes bringing to a brisk and welcome end a period of irrevocable decline and suffering.

Vaccinating against pneumonia and influenza

Vaccine delivery

- Both vaccines should be offered in October or early November to all aged over 65 years, especially:
  - The frail
  - Care home residents
  - The immunosuppressed
  - Those with comorbidity e.g. heart failure.
- Reliable delivery of these vaccinations depends upon effective information management systems in general practice, and substantial efforts by patients, carers, district nurses and GP practice nurses.
- A common reason to have missed immunization is to have been a long-term inpatient (e.g. undergoing rehabilitation) during the autumn immunization period. Hospitals should ensure that these inpatients are immunized.
- Vaccinating healthcare workers, especially those working in long-term care settings, reduces the spread of infection and therefore death due to influenza amongst patients.

Pneumococcal vaccine

- Pneumovax II, a multivalent pneumococcal polysaccharide vaccine, is effective against 65% of serotypes.
- Immunity remains for at least five years, perhaps for life.
- Bacteraemia is reduced by at least 50%. The effect on incidence of pneumonia itself is less clear.

Influenza vaccine

- The trivalent vaccine is prepared from currently prevalent serotypes.
- Immunity develops in less than two weeks, and it is therefore useful during epidemics.
- Immunity remains for up to eight months.
- The risk of pneumonia, hospitalization or death due to influenza is reduced by over half.

Post-exposure antiviral prophylaxis

There are two patient groups for whom pharmacological prophylaxis of influenza is recommended (NICE 2003).

- Unimmunized adults who have had close contact with a person with influenza-like illness
- Immunized or unimmunized residents of care homes where there are new cases of influenza-like illness. In this case, prophylaxis should be offered regardless of immunization status.

The neuraminidase inhibitors oseltamivir (see p333) is recommended (available as capsules or suspension; 75mg od for at least seven days; consider for up to six weeks during epidemic).

Consider why immunization was not performed. Is it too late to administer this year (this contact may not have flu, but the next one might)? If not, then optimize the chances of immunization next year.

Pulmonary fibrosis

This common problem is much underdiagnosed due to a combination of under-investigation and overlap of clinical signs with common pathologies such as heart failure.

Consider when breathlessness coexists with profuse fine chest creps, with or without clubbing. On CXR, there may be bilateral pulmonary shadowing consistent with pulmonary oedema, but with little supporting evidence (e.g. normal heart size, absent Kerley B lines).

Causes

- Idiopathic. The most common type in older people, known as usual interstitial pneumonia (UIP).
- Connective tissue disease e.g. rheumatoid arthritis (most common), systemic lupus erythematosus, sarcoidosis. Lung involvement is sometimes the first manifestation of the multisystem disease.
- Drugs (e.g. amiodarone, nitrofurantoin rarely).
- Occupational exposure e.g. asbestos, silica.
- If localized, consider TB, bronchiectasis and radiotherapy.

Tests

- The diagnosis is usually confirmed by high-resolution CT scanning, which can also help distinguish subgroups likely to respond to immunosuppressive treatment.
- Respiratory function tests may be useful (a restrictive picture with decreased transfer factor is usual) but typically adds little in the frail older person.
- Refer to a respiratory physician to confirm diagnosis and guidance on management.

Prognosis

This is very variable—about a third are clinically stable, a third improve, and a third deteriorate at rates that vary greatly between individuals. Some can live with pulmonary fibrosis for years without significant functional impairment.

Treatment

- Treat or remove any underlying cause e.g. drugs.
- A minority respond slowly (over weeks) to immunosuppression, usually with steroids (e.g. 30–60mg od prednisolone and azathioprine). Monitor closely for side effects (see p156). In non-responders, tail off and stop. In responders, reduce dose cautiously. Ensure bone protection with calcium, vitamin D and bisphosphonates.
- Home oxygen therapy is often useful.
- Give opiates for distressing dyspnoea.
- In those in whom dyspnoea progresses, consider end-of-life issues including treatment limitation, and a change of focus from life-extending measures to a purely palliative approach.

Rib fractures

Common in older people.
- Often a result of falls or even minimal bony stress such as coughing in a person with osteoporosis.
- Consider the possible contribution of alcohol, which causes both falls and osteoporosis.

Fractures should be diagnosed clinically—point tenderness and crepitus are found. CXR, even with multiple projections, is insensitive to fracture, but is useful in excluding early complications such as pneumo- or haemothorax.

Rib fractures heal without specific treatment. The major problem is pain, which commonly leads to voluntary splinting of the injured area. There is hypoventilation and a failure to clear secretions, and secondary pulmonary infection can occur. The patient should be encouraged to breathe deeply and to cough.
- Supporting the injured area when coughing, using a small pillow, minimizes pain.
- Regular analgesia should include paracetamol, plus a weak opiate in most cases. A short course of NSAIDs may be helpful.
- Admit to hospital if pain is severe and the patient unable to cough, or if complications (usually infection) have occurred.
- In cases of severe pain (e.g. multiple fractures), consider strong opiates or intercostal/paravertebral blocks. Involve the local Pain team.

Strapping of the affected area is no longer done, as it increases complication rates. Reassure the patient that the injury itself is not severe, will heal without immobilization and that coughing will prevent complications, not cause further damage.

Pleural effusions

A frequent (clinical or radiological) finding, sometimes incidental. Common causes are heart failure, post-pneumonia, pulmonary embolism and malignancy especially lung primary, mesothelioma, leukaemia, lymphoma, and metastatic adenocarcinoma (ovary, stomach).

The differential is wide, but narrowed when the results of CXR and pleural fluid aspiration are known.

Differentiating cause, by protein level

Transudate (protein <25g/L)	Exudate (protein >35g/L)
Heart failure	Malignancy
Hepatic cirrhosis	Infection, including TB
Hypoproteinaemia e.g. malabsorption, sepsis	GI causes e.g. pancreatitis
Nephrotic syndrome	Multisystem disorders e.g. rheumatoid
(Exudative causes if low serum protein)	(Heart failure after diuresis)

- Empyemas, malignancy and TB produce exudates with low pH (<7.2), low glucose (<3.3mmol/L) but high LDH.
- Transudates are usually not due to focal lung pathology, and so usually affect both lungs. Unilateral effusions due to transudates occasionally do occur, more commonly on the right side.
- Effusions due to heart failure are typically small and bilateral, with cardiomegaly; they can be unilateral, but usually a tiny contralateral effusion is seen, manifesting as blunting of the costophrenic angle; if the angle remains sharp, other causes are more likely.
- A massive unilateral effusion is usually due to malignancy.
- A uniformly bloodstained effusion is usually due to infection, embolism, malignancy or trauma.

Chronic effusions

- If bilateral transudates, should be treated as for heart failure.
- If the diagnosis is not clear after CXR and aspiration consider chest physician referral and tests including CT, pleural biopsy (CT-guided rather than blind), thoracoscopy and echocardiogram.
- For large, recurrent effusions, consider chest physician referral for continuous outpatient external fluid drainage via a semipermanent intrapleural ('Pleuryx') catheter.
- Frail patients may not tolerate, or desire, the more invasive tests. In this case, consider:
  - Repeated aspiration, combining diagnostic with therapeutic taps and sending larger volumes of fluid for cytology and AFB culture.
  - 'Watching and waiting', with regular clinical review.
  - A trial of diuretics, especially if the effusion is a transudate.

HOW TO... aspirate a sample of pleural fluid

Aspiration is safe without ultrasound guidance in the compliant patient with anything larger than a tiny effusion. This can be done in five minutes on the ward or in outpatients.

1. Sit the patient leaning forwards and resting comfortably. Make yourself comfortable.
2. Clinically identify the effusion (review the CXR; percuss to find maximum dullness).
3. Using permanent ink, mark this point.
4. Clean and disinfect the skin. Attach a green hub (21 gauge) needle to a 10ml syringe.
5. Using aseptic technique, insert the needle close to the marked point, but above a rib in order to avoid the neurovascular bundle.
6. Advance slowly, applying moderate suction to the syringe, until the pleural space is entered and fluid flows.

If a larger volume of aspirate is needed, swap to a larger syringe, holding the needle quite still.

Ultrasound detects small effusions (50–100ml) and aids diagnostic aspiration in patients with a small effusion.

Tests on the aspirate should usually include microscopy/culture, cytology, protein, LDH, glucose and pH. If tuberculosis or cancer is suspected, then send larger volumes (e.g. 50ml) to microbiology and cytology respectively.

Pulmonary embolism

Pulmonary embolism (PE) is common, yet as 'the great pretender' (of other pathology), is underdiagnosed and underreported on death certificates. It commonly coexists with and is confused with other lung disease e.g. pneumonia, heart failure, and COPD—and is a common cause of deterioration in such patients.

Presentation

The classic symptom triad of pain, dyspnoea, and haemoptysis is seen less commonly in older people.

Common presentations include:
- Brief paroxysm(s) of breathlessness or tachypnoea.
- Collapse, cardiac arrest, syncope, pre-syncope, or hypotension.
- Pulmonary hypertension and right heart failure, presenting as chronic unexplained breathlessness.
- Puzzling signs e.g. fever, wheeze, resistant heart failure, arrhythmia, confusion, or functional decline.

Investigations

Determining the likelihood of PE rests on combining clinical judgment (the product of history, examination and immediately available tests such as CXR) with appropriate imaging such as ventilation–perfusion (V/Q) lung scan. The common clinical features of PE—tachypnoea, tachycardia and modest degrees of hypoxaemia—are common in ill older people, so clinical judgment alone is rarely enough.

Moreover, a confident diagnosis is essential because:
- The risk of anticoagulation is higher in older people.
- The risk of a missed diagnosis is higher in older people (less physiological reserve).

Possible PE in older people should be investigated in the usual way, with the choice of tests guided by local facilities and expertise. The following issues are especially relevant:
- In a patient without known lung disease, the combination of breathlessness and a CXR showing clear lung fields strongly suggests PE. Further test(s) (usually lung perfusion scan) are indicated.
- CXR abnormalities may be minor (atelectasis or small effusions), or major (usually reflecting comorbid conditions rather than PE itself). Classical wedge shadows or unilateral oligaemia are rare.
- PE in the absence of lower limb deep vein thrombosis is common (10–20% of cases), so do not be put off by an absence of clinical signs of the leg, or a negative venogram or ultrasound.
- Arterial blood gases have some value in diagnosis, but the common abnormalities (low P_aO_2, low P_aCO_2, and increased alveolar–arterial (A–a) oxygen gradient) are neither sensitive nor specific.
  - In healthy older people, an increased A–a gradient is common.
  - In older people following PE, a normal A–a gradient is seen in >10%.

- Echocardiogram may be normal following PE. However, in a patient with a high clinical probability, typical features of PE on echocardiogram usually provide sufficient diagnostic confidence to permit anticoagulation without further imaging.
- In the patient with unexplained right heart failure, consider PE: obtain an ECG and echocardiogram (ask for PA pressures) and request imaging that details the lung parenchyma (high resolution CT: pulmonary fibrosis?) and the vasculature (CTPA: pulmonary embolism?).
- In the patient who does not respond to treatment for chest infection, heart failure or acute exacerbation of COPD, consider whether PE may be responsible.

Treatment

Anticoagulation

Standard treatment is low molecular weight heparin (LMWH e.g. dalteparin 200U/Kg/24hrs, enoxaparin) followed by warfarin. Once the possibility of PE is raised, it is essential to treat with LMWH pending investigation results, unless there are particular treatment risks.

To minimize bleeding risk:
- Anticoagulate with caution. Check baseline clotting. Give 5mg (not 10mg) warfarin dose on day 1 (p158).
- Beware the older patient with mild anaemia or a low MCV—do they have occult blood loss?
- In the very frail, sick, unstable patient in whom anticoagulation with warfarin would present significant risk, consider a period of anticoagulation with LMWH. Start warfarin when clinical stability returns.

Thrombolysis

Consider thrombolysing, balancing risks and benefits, where there is life-threatening PE, manifesting as acute right heart strain and systemic hypotension. Both risk and benefit increase with age, so age itself is not a contraindication.

Inferior vena cava (IVC) Filter

Consider an IVC filter ('Greenfield filter'). These are inserted by interventional radiology, and cannot be removed once *in situ*.
Indications include:
- Strong contraindication to anticoagulation e.g.
  - Active bleeding
  - A high risk of bleeding, e.g. newly diagnosed peptic ulcer or very recent haemorrhagic stroke.
- Massive thromboembolism with contraindication to thrombolyis.
- Ongoing thromboembolism despite anticoagulation.
- Embolism from a septic focus.

Pulmonary aspiration

The involuntary entry of extrinsic material into the pulmonary airways. This is a common problem, ranging from subclinical micro-aspiration of oropharyngeal mucus to major inhalation of gastric contents.

Causes

- Swallowing problems
- Gastro-oesophageal disorders leading to reflux
- Impaired conscious level including seizures
- Sedative drugs
- Previous aspiration or non-aspiration pneumonia
- Artificial feeding—either nasogastric or gastrostomy.

Diagnosis

- Commonly, the occurrence of pneumonia in a patient with risk factor(s) suggests the diagnosis.
- CXR may show consolidation in dependent lung zones e.g. R lower lobe, although any zone may be affected.

Treatment

- The role of antibiotics is debated. Much of the radiographic response may be a chemical pneumonitis ie inflammatory reaction to caustic gastric contents, rather than infective pneumonia.
- The choice of antibiotics is also contentious. Many cases respond well to amoxicillin or co-amoxiclav, but consider broad spectrum intravenous antibiotics to cover Gram negatives and anaerobes in:
  - The unwell
  - The especially frail
  - High dependency settings
  - Where aspiration has been major.
- If possible, treat the underlying cause. If risk factors persist (e.g. impaired swallow or continual seizures), consider a 'nil by mouth' order until they are addressed.
- Where the swallow may be impaired, perform a formal swallowing assessment (see p202) and manage according to the results.
- In palliative care:
  - Consider anticholinergics to dry secretions
  - In advanced dementia, it is often appropriate to accept the risk of aspiration. Insertion of a gastrostomy (commonly a PEG, percutaneous endoscopic gastrostomy) risks medicalizing the final months whilst achieving nothing—aspiration is common in patients with a PEG
  - It is often cruel and futile to deny a dying patient food that he/she may enjoy, even if the risk of aspiration and a life-shortening pneumonia exists. 'Nil by mouth' orders are usually inappropriate in end-of-life situations.

Chronic cough

A common problem, with causes ranging from the trivial to the sinister. Even where the underlying cause is benign, chronic cough can be both distressing and disabling.

Causes

- Asthma. Cough is a common presenting symptom in older people.
- Silent pulmonary aspiration.
- Gastro-oesophageal reflux disease (GORD).
- Postnasal drip. Due to:
  - Sinusitis.
  - Chronic rhinitis. Frequently allergic in origin, but in older people, symptoms are often not seasonal.
- Drugs e.g. ACE-inhibitors (may take weeks or months to develop), beta-blockers (leading to bronchospasm).
- Persistent benign cough following URTI. May persist for 2–3 months.
- Chronic pulmonary pathology e.g. COPD, TB, bronchiectasis.
- Heart failure, with high pulmonary pressures.
- Thoracic malignancy, either primary or secondary.

Investigation

Consider both tests and trials of treatment. Their pace and extent depends on the differential diagnosis following careful history and examination. Consider the following tests:
- CXR (mandatory).
- Sinus X-ray.
- Spirometry, with assessment of response to bronchodilators.
- Regular monitoring of peak expiratory flow rate, looking for morning drops suggesting asthma.
- Sputum microscopy and culture is unlikely to be helpful.

Next, consider a trial of treatment for the most likely cause, e.g.:
- Bronchodilators (and inhaled steroids) for possible asthma.
- A proton pump inhibitor for possible GORD.
- Assess the effect of treatment of possible chronic rhinitis with:
  - Nasal corticosteroids. Probably the treatment of choice e.g. beclometasone, budesonide.
  - Decongestants. Should be used in short courses only (since rebound phenomenon).
  - Antihistamines. Most useful for obviously allergic rhinitis. Should be used with caution; select those with fewer anticholinergics properties e.g. cetirizine or loratidine.

In all cases, trials of treatment need to be prolonged ($\geq$ 8 weeks).

Treatment

This is of the underlying cause. Where this cannot be treated effectively (e.g. advanced malignancy), specific treatments aimed at reducing cough may be of benefit. These include opiates such as codeine (15–60mg 4-hourly) or morphine (starting dose 5mg 4-hourly). Simple cough linctus may be useful for irritating dry cough following URTI.

Asbestos-related disease

The period between asbestos exposure and overt (or covert) disease is usually long, often over 20 years, and may not be clearly recollected by the patient. However, confirming the diagnosis is important. Compensation may be due if disease can confidently be shown to have arisen as a consequence of asbestos exposure. If the diagnosis could not be confirmed during life, then post-mortem confirmation may lead to compensation payments to relatives.

Pleural plaques

Discrete areas of thickening of the pleura that often calcify. Benign. A marker of asbestos exposure, but of no further clinical significance. However, compensation is payable for this alone, if the claim is made promptly following diagnosis.

Asbestosis

Progressive fibrosis, clinically and radiographically similar to idiopathic pulmonary fibrosis. Usually due to prolonged and substantial occupational exposure.

Mesothelioma

A malignant, incurable tumour of the pleura, presenting as cough, chest pain, effusion or dyspnoea. Very poor prognosis; few survive over two years. Treatment is palliative; the tumour is not respectable, and is insensitive to chemotherapy or radiotherapy. Asbestos exposure may have been only transient.

Bronchial carcinoma

There appears to be a synergistic effect between asbestos and tobacco.

Lung cancers

The commonest cause of cancer deaths, and largely a disease of older people.

- Symptoms may be non-specific (e.g fatigue, weight loss), or else pulmonary in origin but attributed to existing non-malignant pathology (e.g. dyspnoea in a patient with COPD).
- Have a high index of suspicion and a low threshold for further investigation. Have an even higher degree of suspicion in older smokers presenting with pneumonia.
- In those presenting with pneumonia, sinister features include:
  - Haemoptysis, especially if significant, e.g. with persistent blood clots.
  - Regional or generalized symptoms of cancer (e.g. hoarse voice, weight loss).
  - Cough and consolidation without obvious infective symptoms (e.g. fever).
  - Symptoms that continue to be troublesome despite antibiotics.

If sinister features are present, it is unacceptable to wait (up to six weeks) before repeating a CXR to confirm resolution. Refer promptly for urgent specialist assessment and consider CT scanning.

- Treatment has improved and is now more effective, both in extending life and in palliating symptoms. Therefore, 'benign neglect', i.e. simply observing an older person with probable lung cancer, is now only rarely acceptable. It may be appropriate, for example, in cases of extreme frailty or severe cognitive impairment.
- Older people with probable lung cancer remain under-investigated and under-treated:
  - Tests such as bronchoscopy and a histopathological diagnosis are less commonly obtained. This makes palliative treatment and prognostication difficult.
  - Treatment such as surgery or chemotherapy are less commonly considered or administered. To an extent this reflects appropriate decisionmaking based on functional status.
- Treatment decisions should be made by expert teams who consider the patient's functional status, comorbidities and cancer characteristics.

▶▶ Refer all patients with suspected or confirmed lung cancer for a specialist opinion.

Non-small cell carcinoma (squamous cell, adeno- and large cell carcinoma)

- Surgery may lead to cure if:
  - There is adequate pulmonary function (arbitrarily, $FEV_1 \geq 1.5$ litre).
  - There is no distant spread (but >50% of cancers have spread at presentation).
  - The patient is relatively well with good functional status and no serious comorbidity.
- Surgical procedures are high risk (e.g. at 70 years, lobectomy has 10% perioperative fatality, and pneumonectomy 20%). However, the condition is always fatal without treatment, so the patient's view is critical.
- Radiotherapy. When surgery is not feasible, either because of the nature of disease, or the fitness of the patient, then radiotherapy may be used either:
  - Palliatively, to control symptoms (see below).
  - Curatively, in high dose (CHART). Success rates are lower than for surgery.

Small cell carcinoma

- Relatively more common in older people: >20% of cases.
- Most cases are advanced at presentation, and treatment is palliative.
- Most tumours are chemoresponsive. Frail patients are unlikely to tolerate aggressive treatment and it risks reducing the quality of the brief life that remains. Therefore, chemotherapy regimes are tailored to the patient, determined by structured assessment of performance status. In general, frail patients undergo fewer but similar chemotherapy cycles compared to the more robust.
- Surgery is the treatment of choice, but is seldom useful because tumours are rarely localised at presentation.

Palliative interventions

- Radiotherapy for superior mediastinal obstruction, bronchial obstruction, chest pain, haemoptysis, or painful bony metastases. This is generally well tolerated, although ~10% develop radiation pneumonitis weeks after treatment, and it is on average more severe in older people.
- Opiates for cough.
- Aspiration of pleural effusion for breathlessness.
- Endobronchial therapy (e.g. stenting, diathermy).

Tuberculosis: presentation

In older people, tuberculosis (TB):
- Incidence is much higher, especially in the very old.
- Outcomes, including mortality, are much less good.
- Is most commonly due to reactivation of previous disease, the primary infection having been asymptomatic or unrecognized. In the early twentieth century, primary infection of young adults was common. By the mid-late twentieth century, primary infection of younger people had diminished. When this cohort reaches old age, TB reactivation will be much less common.
- Reactivation (postprimary disease) occurs due to decreased immunity (see p662), itself due to intrinsic ageing, disease (e.g. diabetes mellitus, renal failure), malnutrition (e.g. chronic alcohol excess) or drugs (e.g. steroids).
- A few patients develop new infection from open cases. Care home residents are most vulnerable, infection passing from fellow residents or from care home staff.

Presentation

Pulmonary disease

- Sometimes similar to that in younger people, ie cough, sputum, fatigue, weight loss, and anorexia.
- Night sweats, fevers and pulmonary symptoms may be less common.
- May present as pneumonia that fails to resolve, or as an incidental finding, suggested on CXR.

Extrapulmonary disease

Most (>75%) presentations are pulmonary, but extrapulmonary cases are relatively more common in older people, e.g.:
- **Miliary**. Diffuse, overwhelming infection with fever, weight loss and hepatosplenomegaly
- **Urogenital and renal**. May affect any part of the renal tract. Sterile pyuria, haematuria, abdominal or back pain, genital sinuses or pelvic masses may occur, or disease may be asymptomatic.
- **Meningeal**. Consider this in the very frail, malnourished, or immuno-suppressed patient with non-specific cerebral signs (e.g. confusion, dementia-like syndrome, headache, or reduced conscious level). Meningism may be absent, and the CSF virtually acellular.
- **Skeletal**. Bone infection most commonly affects the spine (usually thoracic or lumbar), presenting as pain and tenderness. TB arthritis usually affects large weight-bearing joints (see pp534–5).
- **Other** e.g. lymph nodes, intestine.

Sequelae of previous treatment

Lung collapse therapy was used widely in the treatment of pulmonary TB in the 1930s to 1950s. Procedures included therapeutic pneumothorax, thoracoplasty and plombage (expanding the extrapleural space with artificial materials). Sequelae include empyema, sinus formation, bronchopleural fistulae, and ventilatory failure. TB, pyogenic or fungal organisms may be isolated. Early specialist input is essential.

Tuberculosis: investigation

CXR

Changes are more variable than in younger people, and may mimic other benign or malignant disease (e.g. bacterial pneumonia, cancer).

- Usually upper zone infiltrates with cavities, but more common features in older people include mid/lower zone infiltrates, miliary (diffuse nodular) and bilateral change.
- Healed old disease is usually seen i.e. calcified hilar nodes, a peripheral primary complex, pleural thickening and diffuse apical fibrosis and calcification.
- Pleural effusions are common.
- Rare changes include mass lesions or isolated lymphadenopathy.
- Very rarely the CXR may be normal, e.g. occasionally in miliary or endobronchial disease.

Sputum for microscopy and culture

The standard method of confirming TB.

- Conventionally, three early morning sputum specimens are obtained and stained by acid fast staining (e.g. Ziehl–Neelsen). The quality and persistence of the microscopist is important, as the scanty organisms can be easily missed on cursory examination.
- If a patient cannot expectorate, obtain 'induced sputum', through physiotherapy, or nebulized normal saline (rarely nebulized hypertonic saline). If this fails, or clinical suspicion is high despite negative smear and culture, consider bronchoscopy with washings.

Other tests

- Raised **ESR** and **CRP** are usual.
- **FBC**. Mild (normocytic) anaemia and reduced WCC are more common in older people.
- Obtain three **early morning urine** specimens in case of possible genitourinary infection.
- **Tissue sampling**. Where possible, sample tissue e.g. lymph node, pleura, bone marrow. Send samples to both microbiology (microscopy and culture) and to histology. Typical histological features, of caseous necrosis with granuloma formation (with or without acid fast bacilli) support strongly the diagnosis of TB.
- **Tuberculin skin testing** is complex. See box opposite.

HOW TO... **perform and interpret a tuberculin skin test**

In these diagnostic tests, tuberculin purified protein derivative (PPD) is injected in a standardized manner, and the reaction assessed quantitatively.

The Heaf test has been used in screening larger numbers of younger patients, often as pre-vaccination screening programmes. Tiny droplets of high concentration PPD are administered using a multiple tine (Heaf) apparatus. High concentration PPD is no longer manufactured, and the test is not further described here.

The Mantoux test is most commonly performed where TB is suspected in an individual patient. Fixed volumes of less concentrated PPD are injected intradermally.

- The standard dose is 5 tuberculin units (0.5ml of 1 in 10,000 dilution).
- Examine the skin after 48 to 72 hours and measure the diameter of induration, reflecting the extent of the cell-mediated immune response.
- A positive test indicates immunity, not necessarily infection. This may be a result of previous (probably asymptomatic) TB infection, or immunization (although reactivity to the BCG vaccine often disappears after 10 years).
- The degree of induration correlates approximately with the likelihood of infection. However, the post-test probability of infection is a product of both the pre-test probability and the test result.
    - ≥ 15mm indicates a significant reaction and the probability of active infection.
    - 5–15mm may be significant if pre-test probability is high e.g. close contacts, suggestive CXR. Consider causes of a false negative reaction (see below).
    - < 5mm is negative, usually indicating a low probability of active infection. However, if the pre-test probability is very high, consider treatment.
- The test may be falsely negative (or equivocal) with steroid use, lymphoma, malnutrition, sarcoid, overwhelming TB infection, or when there is concurrent other infection.
- Ageing itself impairs the immunological reaction to tuberculin, and may produce a false negative or equivocal test in patients previously infected with TB. Giving a second (booster) tuberculin dose within two weeks of the first often produces a positive test, defined as when induration > 10mm and augmentation of induration (test 1 – test 2) exceeds 6mm.

Tuberculosis: treatment

Given the complexities of treatment, specialist referral is mandatory
Pulmonary disease is treated for a total of six months:

- Usually six months of rifampicin and isoniazid, with pyrazinamide (and ethambutol) for the first two months only.
- Ethambutol may be omitted if the risk of resistance to isoniazid is low.

Longer treatment periods may be needed for extra-pulmonary disease.

In older people:

- Drug resistance is rare, as most infections are recurrences of primary disease, contracted decades ago.
- Failures of treatment are usually due to poor concordance. Combination drug preparations may improve this (e.g. rifater = rifampicin + isoniazid + pyrazinamide).
- Side effects are more common, including ocular toxicity from ethambutol (reduce dose in renal impairment) and hepatitis from isoniazid. Close monitoring is important.

Asthma and COPD: assessment

Presentation

Asthma and chronic obstructive pulmonary disease (COPD) in older people:
- Are both diseases characterized by airflow obstruction.
- Commonly coexist, e.g. in the childhood asthmatic who has smoked.
- May both be mimicked by other common diseases e.g. cancer, pulmonary embolism, heart failure.
- May present late: older people are less aware of hypoxaemia, breathlessness or bronchoconstriction.
- Are underdiagnosed and undertreated, especially in older people.

Asthma
- May present in old age as true 'late onset asthma'. There are also increasing numbers of people who have grown old with the disease.
- In older people, cough may dominate, symptoms fluctuate less, triggers (e.g. cold, smoke, allergens) are less frequent and the association with hay fever or eczema is less strong.
- Nocturnal cough or dyspnoea, including paroxysmal nocturnal dyspnoea, may be caused by asthma.
- NSAIDs and beta-blockers (oral or ocular) may worsen bronchoconstriction.

COPD
- Is much more common in older age, the consequence of intrinsic ageing and progressive disease.
- Is caused by environmental exposure, usually to tobacco smoke, in genetically susceptible people. Significant disease can develop in those who have not smoked for years, as acquired lung damage depends more on 'total pack years' smoked rather than duration alone.
- Symptoms are usually more chronic and slowly progressive, without significant variability.
- If bronchitis is significant, there is a productive cough (most days of at least three months of two consecutive years). Fatigue and sleep disturbance are common. Daytime somnolence suggests ventilatory failure.

Investigations

- *Oximetry* will determine the presence and degree of hypoxaemia. In moderately or severely hypoxaemic patients (O_2 saturation <92%), consider **arterial blood gases** to determine whether long-term oxygen therapy may be of benefit and, in the acutely unwell, to guide oxygen administration.
- *CXR, ECG, and FBC* will help to exclude other pathology e.g. anaemia, dysrhythmia.

- *Peak expiratory flow rate* (PEFR), measured regularly (bd–qds) for up to two weeks, helps determine whether variable airways obstruction (asthma) exists. Variability ≥ 20% is significant. Older people may find using PEFR meters and charting the results difficult. Ask them to demonstrate technique, reading the device and charting in clinic.
- *Spirometry*. Obtain at least FEV_1 and FVC. An FEV_1 : FVC ratio of <70% suggests obstruction.
  - Older people often have difficulty performing pulmonary function tests; an experienced technician in a respiratory laboratory will help provide accurate results.
  - Assessments for **bronchodilator responsiveness** using inhaled bronchodilators are now considered less helpful, as they are poorly predictive of the response to treatment, and do not distinguish reliably between asthma and COPD. However, airflow obstruction that completely and repeatedly resolves after bronchodilator administration does exclude COPD.
  - Assessments for **steroid responsiveness** can be helpful in distinguishing between asthma and COPD (response is greater in asthma than COPD, although there is overlap). Perform spirometry before and after steroids (either two weeks of prednisolone 30mg od, or six weeks of inhaled beclometasone 400mcg bd).
  - Some patients show improvement in FVC or functional status (walking distance or speed) despite no significant change in FEV_1.

Asthma is suggested by:
- A modest degree of fixed airways obstruction (this is uncommon in younger people).
- Significant or full reversibility.
- ≥20% variability in PEFR.

COPD is suggested by:
- A greater degree of airways obstruction.
- No, or only minimal, reversibility.
- <<20% variability in PEFR.
- Greater age and significant smoking history.

Asthma and COPD: drug treatment

In general, treatment principles are similar to those in younger people, and are described in detail in British Thoracic Society guidelines. However, some differences and some similarities benefit from emphasis:

Bronchodilators

- Older people perceive symptoms less reliably, so where there is evidence of variable airways obstruction, give bronchodilators regularly rather than as required.
- In older age, response to anticholinergics e.g. ipratropium, tiotropium, may be better than to beta-agonists e.g. salbutamol.
- High dose beta-agonists, e.g. from nebulizers, may cause tachycardia and rate-related angina. Nebulizers are rarely required. Try higher inhaled doses via a spacer (e.g. salbutamol 400–800mcg (four to eight puffs of a standard MDI)), or long-acting beta-agonists e.g. salmeterol.
- Anticholinergic bronchodilators uncommonly cause side effects such as dry mouth or blurred vision, more often with higher (nebulized) doses and with long-acting preparations. Acute glaucoma is a rare but important complication—reduce ocular exposure by nebulizing via a mouthpiece rather than a facemask.

Corticosteroids

- Long-term oral steroids are rarely beneficial.
- In those receiving regular courses of oral steroids for acute exacerbations, give osteoporosis prophylactic treatment. Inhaled steroids alone probably do not cause osteoporosis.

Theophylline

- Toxicity is common in older people. Plasma levels are increased by febrile illness, heart failure, and drugs e.g. erythromycin and ciprofloxacin. Serious side effects e.g. convulsions may be the first sign of toxicity.
- Check levels when titrating dose. Most of the therapeutic effect is seen by the lower end of the therapeutic range, so target this first.
- Before introducing oral theophylline, optimize inhaled bronchodilator and steroid therapy, including the use of long-acting and higher dose preparations if necessary.

Other

- Influenza and pneumococcal vaccine should be given.
- Exercise extreme caution in the use of **respiratory depressants** e.g. benzodiazepines or opiates. In general:
  - In acutely unwell patients with CO_2 retention, stop them, reintroducing only if withdrawal effects occur.
  - In stable patients with or without CO_2 retention, withdraw or reduce them where possible.
  - In severe, end-stage COPD, if dyspnoea or cough are distressing and cannot be otherwise relieved, consider giving opiates. Give small doses initially, but increase as needed to relieve distress, even if respiratory function deteriorates. Explain the rationale to staff, as well as to relatives and the patient if appropriate.

HOW TO... improve drug delivery in asthma or COPD

- The traditional metered dose inhaler (MDI) alone is rarely adequate, due to difficulties in coordinating device activation and the onset of inhalation.
- Adding a large volume spacer device abolishes the need to coordinate activation and inhalation, improving drug delivery and reducing side effects (e.g. oral thrush).
- Breath-activated devices provide an alternative to the MDI, although lung volumes may not be adequate to activate the device. They vary widely in design, and patients vary greatly in ability to use them.
- Assess and advise on technique regularly, involving both hospital and community teams (doctor, nurse, and pharmacist) as well as the family and other carers.
- Nebulizers are rarely required. An MDI via a large volume spacer device is usually just as effective. Patients in whom nebulized drugs are being considered should be referred for specialist assessment.
- Where concordance is an issue, e.g. in a person with dementia living alone:
    - Give long-acting preparations where possible e.g. salmeterol in place of salbutamol, tiotropium in place of ipratropium.
    - Give combined preparations e.g. Combivent® in place of salbutamol and ipratropium.
    - Once daily inhaled steroid is better than none.
    - Supervise taking of medication as often as possible, but accept that for pulmonary drugs, taking medications irregularly is probably better than taking them not at all.
- Rarely, inhaled drugs are administered too frequently by cognitively impaired people. This very rarely causes side effects, but relatives may need reassurance that this is the case.
- Occasionally, oral beta-agonists are useful, in patients in whom all inhaled preparations have been unsuccessful.

Asthma and COPD: non-drug treatment

- *Pulmonary rehabilitation* is as effective as inhaler therapy, and should be a key part of treatment. It is a complex intervention tailored to the individual, with exercise, behavioural, and educational components. Individual action plans can be followed by older people, facilitating self-management and early intervention.
- *Smoking cessation* should be advised, except in the very advanced or terminal phase, where it may lack benefit and be unkind.
- *Weight reduction* is beneficial in the obese. However weight commonly falls in advanced disease as the work of breathing exceeds calorific intake, and *nutritional supplements* may be needed.
- *Comorbidities* including depression are common and should be treated aggressively.
- *Exercise* is beneficial, sometimes available as part of a pulmonary rehabilitation scheme. Elements should include aerobic and strength-based exercises as well as specific breathing exercises.

Assisted ventilation

- Consider this in cases of respiratory arrest, respiratory acidosis, delirium, exhaustion, or deteriorating respiratory function despite full treatment. Hypercapnia rather than hypoxaemia is usually the key contributor to delirium; sedation is likely to worsen ventilation and precipitate coma.
- For some patients with acute-on-chronic deterioration, ventilation will be futile and inappropriate. Make such a decision after considering:
  - The nature of the chronic illness and recent deterioration.
  - The presence of reversible factors.
  - The patient's current physiological status.
  - The views of the patient or others who represent him/her.
  - If in doubt, request guidance from the ITU team.
- Non-invasive ventilation (NIV) e.g. nasal intermittent positive pressure ventilation provides an acceptable alternative to invasive ventilation (usually endotracheal intubation). NIV is often well-tolerated, can be delivered on specialist wards or high dependency areas, and provides a modest level of ventilatory support that can be weaned promptly as the patient recovers.

Social and practical interventions

- Provide appropriate mobility aids including electric wheelchairs, stairlifts.
- Treat social isolation.
- Provide alarm systems e.g. pendant alarm.

Palliative interventions

- Reassure—many patients are terrified. Assure them that their symptoms of suffocation can and will be treated.
- Positioning—sit up, day and night.
- Involve the palliative care team. Their advice and support is often valuable and can continue into the community if discharge occurs.

Oxygen therapy

- Oxygen is a drug—it has clear indications, and common and important side effects.
- Precision and care in prescribing maximizes benefit and reduces harm.
- In older people, dyspnoea may be accepted, leading to underprescribing.
- However, indiscriminate prescribing, particularly the use of high concentration oxygen, risks respiratory depression and CO_2 narcosis. This is common in older people with COPD.

Long-term oxygen therapy (LTOT)

This improves prognosis in severe COPD and in moderate COPD with features of cor pulmonale. To reduce pulmonary hypertension, arterial pO_2 should be raised above 8kPa for at least 15 hours each day. Concentrations of inspired oxygen (FiO_2) of 24–28% usually achieve this. Respiratory depression is very rarely a problem in patients with stable respiratory failure who receive low oxygen concentrations.

Specific criteria must be met before prescribing LTOT. Measure arterial blood gases twice, on air, at least three weeks apart, and at least four weeks after an acute exacerbation.

Criteria include:
- P_aO_2 7.3–8.0kPa in COPD with complications such as peripheral oedema, evidence of pulmonary hypertension, or polycythaemia.
- P_aO_2 <7.3kPa in COPD without the above complications.

Intermittent oxygen therapy (IOT)

This is useful for a variety of cardiorespiratory conditions, e.g. COPD, advanced heart failure, lung cancer. It relieves distress and improves exercise tolerance and mobility. Low concentrations (24–28%) can achieve significant symptomatic benefit. Prognosis is unaltered.

High concentration oxygen therapy

Oxygen at 40–60% is useful for short-term use in respiratory failure without hypoventilation and CO_2 retention, commonly seen in acute heart failure, pulmonary embolism, and pneumonia. Even in these cases, high flow oxygen may reduce respiratory drive, leading to CO_2 narcosis. This is especially common in older people, those with a smoking history, the acutely unwell and where respiratory depressants (e.g. opiates, benzodiazepines) are co-administered.

Avoid this by:
- Keeping saturations just below normal (90–94%) rather than normal or above normal (98–100%).
- Avoiding respiratory depressants.
- Monitoring closely for signs of CO_2 retention.

Oxygen delivery systems

Supply patients with an administration device applicable to their circumstances.

Constant performance oxygen delivery systems (e.g. Ventimask® 28%) provide a stable FiO_2 (24%, 28%, 32% etc.) for a range of ventilation rates. 28% is suitable for most patients receiving LTOT. These must always be used for hypoventilating patients with elevated P_aCO_2.

Variable performance oxygen delivery systems. FiO_2 varies. The system delivers oxygen at a given rate which mixes with room air at rates dependent on ventilation. Systems include:
- Nasal cannulae. Often better tolerated by patients, and allow them to eat and talk. With oxygen flows of 1–2 litres/minute, FiO_2 is usually low (less than 28%), but can approach 30% if the patient hypoventilates.
- Simple face mask e.g. Hudson. Provides variable FiO_2 up to 40%.
- Non-rebreathing mask with reservoir bag. Provides variable FiO_2 up to 60%.

Oxygen gas supply

Oxygen concentrators are costly to purchase but running costs are low. They are cost-effective when needing low flow oxygen for prolonged periods ($\geq$ 8 hours per day). Oxygen is piped to convenient position(s) in the home, and usually administered via nasal cannulae. Urgent installations can usually be arranged within 24 hours.

Oxygen bottles are useful for:
- Patients on LTOT via an oxygen concentrator who wish to leave their home for short periods.
- Patients needing oxygen as required, who do not meet the LTOT criteria.
- Patients who are likely to have a short-term need for continuous oxygen, e.g. for end-of-life palliation, for whom installation of an oxygen concentrator may not be worthwhile.

A small oxygen cylinder ('PD oxygen cylinder'; 300 litres, lasting 2 hours) is available which is convenient for wheelchair excursions, or travel in a car.

▶▶ Smokers should stop smoking before beginning oxygen therapy. The risk of fire is substantially increased.

Gastroenterology

The ageing gastrointestinal system *374*
The elderly mouth *376*
Nutrition *378*
Enteral feeding *380*
Parenteral feeding *381*
   How to... insert a fine bore nasogastric feeding tube *382*
The ethics of artificial feeding *384*
   How to... manage weight loss in older patients *386*
Oesophageal disease *388*
Dysphagia *390*
Peptic ulcer disease *392*
   How to... investigate and manage persistant unexplained
   nausea and vomiting (N+V) *393*
The liver and gallbladder *394*
Constipation *396*
Diverticular disease *398*
Inflammatory bowel disease *400*
Diarrhoea in the elderly patient *402*
   How to... investigate and manage chronic diarrhoea *403*
Other colonic conditions *404*
The 'acute surgical abdomen' *406*
Obstructed bowel in older patients *408*

The ageing gastrointestinal system

Teeth

- Change colour—yellow and less translucent.
- Become worn (enamel does not regenerate).
- Decreased vascularity and sensitivity of dentine and pulp.
- Caries, peridontitis and tooth loss are common but not inevitable in older patients. Being 'long in the tooth' refers to gum retraction seen with periodontal disease which increases with poor oral hygiene and xerostomia, both common in older people.

Mouth

- Mucosa—thinner and more friable, rarely a functional problem.
- Salivary glands do not produce less saliva but causes of xerostomia (p377) are more frequent with increasing age.
- Bone resorption occurs in the mandible alongside osteoporosis. This is accelerated with periodontitis and progresses fast once teeth are lost leading to a change in facial appearance.
- Orofacial muscle tone can also diminish with consequent dribbling.

Taste

Olfactory function, and hence taste discrimination, decreases gradually with normal ageing but an acute change or complete absence of taste should prompt investigations for a cranial tumour.

Oesophagus

- Slight changes in innervation produce clinically insignificant changes in swallow and peristalsis.
- The misnamed presbyoesophagus is a distinct disease, not a universal age change.
- Hiatus hernias and reflux are very common—probably related to anatomical and postural changes.

Stomach

- Increased incidence of atrophic gastritis (with reduced acid production) but in the absence of disease most older patients maintain normal pH levels.
- Reduction in gastric emptying is common.
- Increased mucosal susceptibility to damage.
- Increased *Helicobacter pylori* carriage but this is less likely to cause ulceration.

Small intestine

- Function well preserved except for calcium absorption which is decreased.
- Increased incidence of bacterial overgrowth with malnutrition and diarrhoea.

Large intestine
Decreased rectal sensation contributes to high incidence of constipation.

Pancreas
Structural changes including atrophy but function is well-preserved.

Liver
- Hepatic weight and volume decrease by around 25% and there is brown (lipofuscin) pigment build-up, but liver function (and therefore liver function tests) are not affected.
- Some older patients have a slightly low bilirubin and albumin level but results still remain within the normal range.

Gallbladder
- Incidence of gallstones increases (40% females over age 80), probably related to reduced rate of synthesis and excretion of bile.
- Most gallstones are asymptomatic.

The elderly mouth

Mouth examination

Use gloves. Be systematic. Check:
- *Parotid glands* (enlarged in parotitis, alcoholism, CLL).
- *Temporomandibular joint* (arthritis causes crepitus, subluxation, pain). Dislocation can cause pain and inability to close mouth.
- *Soft tissues*: tongue and floor of mouth commonest site for oral cancer in smokers/alcoholics. Angular stomatitis.
- *Salivation*: (for xerostomia see opposite).
- *Teeth*: how many missing, how many restorations, pain/sensitivities. Caries are increased by poor brushing and low fluoride exposure, diet of soft sweet foods, xerostomia, poor fitting dentures, and infrequent dentist visits.
- *Dentures*: cleanliness, integrity, and fit.

Interventions

- Nursing help with dental/mouthcare is vital for anyone unable to help themselves.
- Referral to a dentist. Dental checkups should continue every six months regardless of age/disability. This is very difficult to arrange for inpatients but maxillofacial surgeons (who are also trained as dentists) will sometimes help out in severe/urgent cases.
- Consider chlorhexidine mouthwash for patients with poor oral self-care e.g. stroke, dementia.
- Severe periodontal disease may require antibiotics (topical or systemic) and surgical debridement to arrest progress.
- Poor oral and dental health contributes to poor appetite and malnutrition—consider nutritional support (p378).

Facial pain

Consider trigeminal neuralgia, temporal arteritis, parotitis, temporomandibular joint arthritis, dental caries/abscess, aphthous mouth ulcers, or the idiopathic benign 'burning mouth syndrome'.

Sore tongue

Can be a side effect of drugs, glossitis (B12, iron, or folate deficiency), candida/thrush especially after antibiotics or in diabetes (see opposite). A black tongue may be due to Aspergillus colonization and is treated with nystatin lozenges/mouth rinse.

Parotitis

Acute bacterial parotitis is not uncommon in frail older patients who are not eating. Low salivary flow (dehydration and not eating) and poor oral hygiene predispose to parotid gland infection with mouth flora (staphylococci and anaerobes). Treat with aggressive rehydration, intravenous flucloxacillin and chlorhexidine mouth rinses. Response to treatment is usually dramatic—if not consider abscess formation or MRSA.

Xerostomia

Perception of dry mouth is closely related to salivary flow. Saliva is needed for:

* *Taste*: dissolves food to present to taste buds
* *Swallow*: helps form food bolus
* *Protection* of teeth and mucosa: contains antibacterials, buffers and mucin. Rapid tooth decay is a risk of xerostomia.

Xerostomia is not a normal ageing change and should always be investigated. Causes include:

* Drugs with anticholinergic side effects (e.g. tricyclic antidepressants, Madopar®).
* Sjogrens syndrome (an autoimmune destruction of salivary glands) can be primary or associated with other autoimmune conditions.
* Irradiation, salivary stones, tumors, siladenitis (viral or bacterial infections).

Treatment depends on cause—stop or decrease causative drugs, stimulate saliva with grapefruit juice/sugarfree sweets or mints and promote frequent careful mouth care. Artificial saliva (e.g. Glandosane® spray) can provide symptomatic relief for some patients.

Oral candidiasis

May manifest as oral thrush (with removable white plaques on erythematous base), angular stomatitis (sore cracks in corner of mouth), or, rarely, hyperplastic or atrophic forms. Always consider and reverse where possible risk factors such as antibiotics, steroids, hyperglycaemia and immunosuppression. Use nystatin 1ml qds rinsed around mouth for several minutes. In cases with painful swallowing/dysphagia (ie might have oesophageal involvement) and those that cannot comply with rinses use oral fluconazole 50–100mg od for 7–14 days. Dentures should be kept out where possible and soaked in chlorhexidine during treatment.

Mouth ulcers

Simple apthous ulcers and ulcers due to poorly fitting dentures should be treated with topical anti-inflamatories (salicylate gel or triamcinolone). Ulcers can occur as part of a systemic disease such as inflammatory bowel disease. Any oral lesion persisting more than 3 weeks merits referral and or biopsy to exclude cancer but most mouth cancers are painless.

Oral manifestation of systemic diseases/drugs

There is a very long list including common and general (e.g. oral candidiasis in immunosuppression) as well as rare and specific (e.g. oral lichen planus). Remember that many drugs also affect the mouth e.g. xerostomia (see above), tardive dyskinesia with antipsychotics, gum hypertrophy with phenytoin.

Systemic manifestation of dental diseases

Poor oral hygiene with dental or periodontal disease can cause septicaemia or infective endocarditis. Poor teeth can contribute to poor nutrition.

Nutrition

With normal ageing…
- Calorie requirement falls due to reduced activity and lower resting metabolic rate (decreased muscle mass).
- Appetite diminishes (anorexia of ageing).
- There are lower reserves of both of macro and micronutrients (vitamins and minerals).

In the presence of disease older patients quickly become malnourished, and malnutrition is a powerful predictor of outcome (increased functional dependency, morbidity, mortality, and use of health-care resources).

Malnutrition is extremely common in the elderly frail or institutionalized population, and studies have shown that once in hospital most patients' nutritional status actually declines further. Protein energy undernutrition affects:
- 15% of community-dwelling older patients.
- 5–12% of housebound patients with multiple chronic problems.
- 35–65% of patients acutely admitted to hospital.
- 25–60% of institutionalized elderly persons.

Nutritional assessment
- Body mass index (weight in kg/(height in m)^2) is often impractical as height cannot be accurately measured in immobile patients or those with abnormal posture.
- Simple weight is still useful especially if the patient knows their usual weight—rapid weight loss (> 4kg in 6 months) is always worrying even in obese patients.
- Nutrition screening tools are often employed by nursing staff to target interventions but many have not been well validated.
- More complex tools (e.g. Mini Nutritional Assessment) are helpful but time-consuming and rarely used outside research.
- Biochemical measures including hypoalbuminaemia, anaemia, and hypocholesterolaemia develop at a late stage and are confounded by acute illness.

Nutritional support
- Involve a dietician if possible.
- Record food intake carefully.
- Make mealtimes a priority and provide assistance with feeding.
- Offer tempting, high calorie foods.
- Prescribe sip feeds (e.g. Complan or Fortisip), but be aware that compliance is often poor.
- Consider the role of enteral feeding.

Enteral feeding

Consider enteral feeding early if there is dysphagia (e.g. stroke, motor neurone disease, dementia) or failure of oral feeding (e.g. severe anorexia, intensive care unit) with an intact gastrointestinal tract.

There are three common methods:
1. **Fine bore nasogastric (NG) tubes**: simple, quick and inexpensive. The preferred method for short-term feeding. Some patients (usually confused/drowsy) repeatedly pull out NG tubes. Interference with the tube increases the risk of aspiration. Persistence, supervision and careful taping can sometimes help but often a PEG or RIG is required. There are promising early studies using NG tubes which are held in place via a nasal loop. Trained practitioners can insert these by the bedside and removal by the patient is very rare.
2. **Percutaneous endoscopic gastrostomy (PEG)**: the risks of insertion include perforation, bleeding, and infection for a patient who is usually already frail. The patient has to be fit to undergo sedation. Problems obtaining consent from a competent patient and 'agreement' from next of kin for an incompetent one are not uncommon. Once established, this method is discreet and better tolerated than NG tubes and is the method of choice for medium/long-term enteral feeding.
3. **Radiographically inserted gastrostomy (RIG)**: useful if gastroscopy technically difficult (e.g. pharangeal pouch) and sometimes if small bowel feeding preferred over gastric feeding. Similar complication rate to PEG.

Complications for all methods include

- **Aspiration pneumonia:** there is a common misconception that enteral feeding eliminates aspiration in dysphagic patients. This is not true—reflux of food into oesophagus is common and this along with salivary secretions and covert oral intake may still be aspirated. Always check the position of the tube if patient becomes unwell, feverish, or breathless. If aspiration is ongoing despite correct tube position slow the feed, feed with patient sitting upright (ie not at night) and add promotility drugs e.g. metoclopramide 10mg tds or erythromycin 250mg tds (pre meals). A nasojejunal tube or jejunal extention to a PEG tube can also reduce aspiration rates.
- **Re-feeding syndrome:** occurs when patient has been malnourished for a long time. When feeding commences, insulin levels cause minerals (especially phosphorus) to move rapidly into intracellular space and fluid retention occurs causing hypophosphataemia, hypomagnesmia, and hypokalaemia. This in turn can cause life-threatening heart failure, respiratory failure, arrhythmias, seizures, and coma. Avoid by 'starting low and going slow' when introducing feed. It is important to check and correct any abnormal biochemistry before feeding starts and then monitor frequently (check U+E, Ca, Mg, Phos and glucose daily for a few days, then weekly). Supplementation of minerals may be done intravenously or by adding extra to NG feed.

- **Fluid overload and heart failure**: decrease volume infused and add diuretics.
- **Diarrhoea**: exclude infection (especially *Clostridium difficile*). Try slowing the feed rate or changing the feed to one containing more or less fibre.

Parenteral feeding

Should be considered when the gut is not functioning. It requires central venous access and should only be undertaken when supervised by an experienced nutrition team. It is usually a temporary measure e.g. post-gastrointestinal surgery. Complications such as fluid overload, electrolyte disturbance, and intravenous catheter sepsis are common in older patients.

Further reading
Potter J, Langhorne P, Roberts R. (1998). Routine protein energy supplementation in adults: systemic review. *BMJ* **317**: 495–501.

HOW TO... **insert a fine bore nasogastric feeding tube**

This task is often performed by nursing staff who may be very experienced. Doctors are often asked to help when insertion is proving difficult.

1. Get the patients consent—if they refuse come back later. They may well have just had several uncomfortable failed attempts.
2. Have the patient sitting upright with chin tucked forward (patients often hyperextend their neck which makes it harder). Draw the curtains (this can be an unpleasant procedure to have done or to watch).
3. Leave the guide wire in the tube and lubricate with lots of jelly.
4. Feed the tube down one nostril about 20cm (until it hits the back of the throat).
5. If there is a proximal obstruction try the other nostril.
6. If possible ask the patient to swallow and advance the wire.
7. Check the back of the throat carefully—you should be able to see a single wire going vertically down. Start again if there is a loop.
8. Secure the tube yourself immediately with tape to both nose and cheek.

Once you believe the tube is in place you need to check it is in the stomach by one or both of the following methods BEFORE you use the tube.

- A chest X-ray. If you leave the guide wire in, the tube shows more easily. The tip of the tube should be clearly below the diaphragm.
- Aspiration of gastric contents that are clearly acidic with pH indicator paper (not just blue litmus paper).

The method of blowing air down the tube and listening for bubbles has now been discredited as a bubbling sound can be generated due to saliva and pulmonary secretions.

The ethics of artificial feeding

Feeding is a highly emotive issue. It is seen by many (especially relatives) as a basic need and hence failing to provide adequate nutrition is seen as a form of neglect or even euthanasia. In contrast, others (often nurses) feel that artificial enteral feeding is a cruel and futile treatment performed on incompetent patients which only postpones a 'natural' death that involves anorexia or dysphagia.

There are numerous high-profile legal cases regarding feeding (usually withdrawal of) and controversial cases should always be referred to the courts.

▶▶ The key to steering a course through this minefield is communication.

Initiating treatment

- Establish if the patient is competent—even dysphasic patients may understand a little with non-verbal cues etc.
- If the patient is competent ensure they understand the chosen method (and its risks) and projected duration of feeding. Patients with dysphagia must realize that they will be expected to dramatically decrease, or stop, oral feeding.
- For incompetent patients ensure you have communicated with all interested carers and family. There is sometimes disagreement between interested parties and these are best detected and 'thrashed out' early. A case conference is often helpful.
- Establish that everyone accepts the indications for feeding and the aims of treatment and set a date for review e.g.
  - 2 weeks of NG feeding in a patient with dysphagia following a stroke, which is hoped will resolve.
  - PEG insertion in a patient with motor neurone disease and malnutrition with recurrent aspiration pneumonia, to be reviewed if patient requests or if enters terminal phase of disease.
- Don't be afraid of a therapeutic trial (e.g. if you don't know whether the patient's lethargy/drowsiness/depression is related to malnutrition). Always ensure everyone understands and agrees on review dates and criteria for reassessment. Patients/relatives can be reassured that PEG tubes can be removed if improvement occurs.
- Record discussions and plan carefully in medical record.
- If there is still dispute get a second opinion. As a last resort legal advice may be needed.

Withdrawing treatment

▶▶ Withholding treatment is not morally different to withdrawing it.
There are however, technical and emotional differences, which is why many
more ethical problems arise when withdrawing and why some doctors are
resistant to trials of treatment.

Artificial feeding can be withdrawn because:

- It is no longer required (rarely controversial).
- A therapeutic trial has failed (see opposite—sometimes controversial).
- Although feeding is successful the patient's quality of life is felt to be
  unacceptable (nearly always controversial).

BMA advice is that all cases of withdrawal of long-term feeding be
referred to the courts. This is certainly true if there are any parties who
object but there are non-controversial cases in elderly patients where
this is not necessary.

HOW TO... manage weight loss in older patients

Peak body mass is reached at age 40–50 and weight loss can occur after this due to decreased lean mass, although the proportion of fat is relatively increased so overall weight is often remarkably stable.

As a rule of thumb unintentional weight loss of more than 5lb (2.3kg)/5% of body weight in a month or 10lb (4.5kg)/10% body weight in 6 months is worrying.

Always try and get recorded weight (rather than relying on patient/carer memory)—a search of old outpatient clinic and primary care records can help. Record weight regularly while you investigate to look for ongoing trends.

Dramatic weight loss should always prompt a search for remediable pathology. It is important to consider:
- Dementia (pp224–5)
- Depression (p268)
- Malignancy (p694)
- Chronic infection/ disease e.g. COPD, heart failure, TB
- Inflammatory conditions e.g. giant cell arteritis (p520)
- Malabsorbtion (pp402–3)
- Drug causes e.g. digoxin, theophyllines
- Metabolic disorders e.g. hyperthyroidism, uraemia
- Swallowing problems
- Persistent nausea or abdominal pain/reflux (p393)
- Social causes e.g. inability to cook, poverty, social isolation, alcoholism.

A careful history (including dietary history and mental state), examination and routine screening tests (p695) will usually give clues of significant underlying pathology. If preliminary investigations are negative a 'watch and re-weigh and wait' plan is reasonable—be reassured if weight is actually stable or rising, re-examine and re-screen if further loss occurs.

Obviously if a remediable cause is found and treated then weight loss may be halted or reversed. Where no such cause is found, or where it is not reversible, interventions are still possible.
- Prioritize and help with feeding (sounds obvious but often neglected in hospital). Involving relatives at mealtimes can be beneficial.
- Offer high fat/high calorie food (e.g. substitute full fat milk and yogurt if they are on the lower fat variety).
- Refer to a dietician especially if anorexia is prominent.
- Keep a diet diary—this highlights deficiencies in intake and helps identify where interventions might help.
- Prescribe dietary supplements between meals.
- Appetite stimulants e.g. prednisolone can increase weight but side effects usually outweigh benefits.

Oesophageal disease

Gastro-oesophageal reflux disease (GORD)

- The symptoms (retrosternal burning, acid regurgitation, flatulence, atypical chest pain) correlate poorly with the pathology (normal mucosa to severe oesophagitis).
- Sinister features which might suggest malignancy include sudden or recent onset, dysphagia, vomiting, weight loss and anaemia. They should guide management.
  - In the absence of sinister features a 'blind' trial of treatment is given.
  - If there are sinister features then a gastroscopy should be arranged.
- Oesophageal pH monitoring is rarely necessary.
- **Barrett's/columnar-lined oesophagus**—where gastric mucosa replaces the oesophageal squamous cell mucosa—is associated with an increased risk of malignancy and should have regular endoscopic surveillance regardless of symptoms.

Treatment Check if the patient is taking prescribed or over-the-counter NSAIDs, steroids, or bisphosphonates and stop or minimize the dose. Proton-pump inhibitors (PPIs) have revolutionized treatment making antacids and H2 blockers such as ranitidine almost redundant. They are very effective (for symptoms and healing) and safe. They are used for prophylaxis—often at a lower dose (e.g. lansoprazole 15mg with aspirin) as well as treatment and some are licenced for intermittent symptomatic use (e.g. Esomeprazole®). Rarely elderly patients can have side effects of diarrhoea or confusion.

Hiatus hernia

- Very common in older patients, occurring to a degree in almost all.
- Laxity of structures at the gastro-oesophageal junction allows oesophago-gastric junction or portions of stomach to move up (permanently or intermittently) into the thorax.
- May be asymptomatic but often presents with GORD symptoms and occasionally with dysphagia.
- Very large intrathoracic hernias can impair respiratory function and strangulate/perforate.

Diagnosis on CXR (stomach or fluid level behind heart), at endoscopy, or on contrast radiology.

Treatment to reduce reflux suggest: loose weight, avoid alcohol and caffeine, eat small meals often, avoid eating before bed, and sleep propped up on pillows or elevate head of bed on blocks. PPIs will nearly always relieve symptoms, consider investigations if they don't. Prokinetic agents e.g. metoclopramide 10mg tds sometimes help. Younger patients with intractable problems can be assessed for surgery—laparoscopic surgery now available.

Achalasia

- An idiopathic neurological degeneration causing impaired peristalsis and a lack of lower oesophageal sphincter relaxation.
- A dilated oesophagus and aspiration can develop but gastroscopy is usually normal.
- Barium swallow may show abnormalities but 24 hour manometry is the gold standard.
- Despite the lack of anatomical abnormality endoscopic balloon dilation can relieve dysphagia.

Oesophageal candidiasis

- Can present with dysphagia or pain.
- Consider in frail or immunosuppressed patients especially if oral candidiasis is present.
- Characteristic appearance on endoscopy (biopsy confirms) or barium swallow.
- Treat with fluconazole 50–100mg od for 2 weeks.

Dysphagia

Dysphagia (difficulty in swallowing) is a common symptom in older patients.

History

- Ask what type of food is difficult (solids or liquids) and the level at which food sticks (mouth/throat, retrosternal, or epigastric).
- Distinguish dysphagia from early satiety and regurgitation (when successfully swallowed food returns after seconds/minutes), which usually occurs with gastric outlet obstruction.
- If the swallow 'tires' through a meal consider myasthenia.
- Cough, wheeze, or recurrent aspiration pneumonia can be a presentation of swallowing problems which cause aspiration.

Signs

Look for weight loss, oral thrush (may be associated with oesophageal candida), supraclavicular lymphadenopathy, and a gastric splash (implies gastric outlet obstruction). Watch the patient swallow some water and food—the diagnosis might be clear.

Causes

These can be divided into two.

1. **Structural lesions (worse with solids)**
   - Oesophageal or gastric cancer
   - Benign strictures—scarring following e.g. oesophagitis, scleroderma, polymyositis, radiotherapy
   - Pharyngeal pouch
   - Oesophageal candida or severe oesophagitis
   - Hiatus hernia can produce obstruction symptoms
   - External obstruction e.g. bronchial tumor, aortic aneurysm or cervical osteophyte
   - Foreign bodies (e.g. hair balls) are commoner in demented patients.

2. **Functional problems (often worse with fluids)**
   - Pharynx/throat—commonest neurological cause is stroke but can occur in advanced dementia and motor neurone disease. Rarer neurological conditions include myasthenia gravis, inclusion body myositis, multiple sclerosis, and Parkinson's Plus syndromes.
   - Oesophagus—dysmotility problems are relatively common in older patients and include achalasia and diffuse oesophageal spasm.

Investigations

Gastroscopy is now the primary investigation and is well-tolerated even in frail elderly patients. Sometimes a barium swallow is performed first if there is felt to be a high risk of perforation with an endoscope, but gastroscopy allows biopsy and therapy e.g. dilation. Videofluoroscopy provides functional imaging and is useful diagnostically, but the correlation between observed aspiration and clinically significant problems is poor.

Treatment of dysphagia

- An empirical trial of PPI can be used in the very frail and who are deemed unfit for investigation.
- If oral thrush is present try fluconazole 50–100mg od for a week.
- Oesophageal dilation ± stenting can be very successful for benign or malignant strictures.
- For functional problems always involve a speech therapist. Changing the consistency of food and fluids, and positioning patient correctly can minimize problems.
- Oesophageal dysmotility—try PPI and calcium-channel blocker (e.g. nifedipine) or a nitrate (e.g. isosorbide mononitrate M/R).
- Gastroparesis causes early satiety and vomiting. It can be very hard to treat—try metoclopramide 10mg tds, or erythromycin 250mg tds, or domperidone 30mg pr tds if oral route not viable. Electrical gastric 'pacing' or surgery may provide relief.
- Nutritional support—elderly patients with dysphagia are usually malnourished to start with and are then put nil by mouth for investigations. Refer to the dietician and consider dietary supplements and early enteral feeding (p380).

Aspiration pneumonia is largely a chemical rather than infective insult treated by:

- Preventing/minimising aspiration (nil by mouth, NG feeding)
- Oxygen therapy
- Chest physiotherapy
- Intravenous antibiotics (Augmentin® or cefuroxime and metronidazole) are given to prevent superinfection.

There is a group of patients who have dysphagia, weight loss, and recurrent aspiration due to progressive neurological conditions such as dementia who merit palliative treatment. It is not always appropriate to aggressively manage such patients who are frequently incompetent and derive pleasure from eating normally (see p378). Adopting a palliative policy is impossible unless everyone, including the whole multidisciplinary team and relatives, understand and sympathise with the aims of management.

Peptic ulcer disease

This disease is becoming much rarer with the advent of effective medical treatment. It remains predominantly a disease of the elderly population. NSAID use (see p154) is the commonest cause, followed by *Helicobacter pylori*.

H. pylori is a spiral Gram negative bacterium which colonizes the gastric mucosa causing gastritis. Carriage rates increase with age—40% at age 50, 75% at age 70. Infection is usually asymptomatic but is the commonest cause of dyspepsia in older patients. *H. pylori* is strongly associated with duodenal ulcers and their recurrence and may have a link with NSAID associated ulceration.

Presentation

Acute bleeding, pain (epigastric, retrosternal, or back), indigestion, 'heartburn', dysphagia, perforation (peritonitis), iron deficiency anaemia, or an incidental finding (e.g. on endoscopy).

Investigation

- Upper GI endoscopy is very safe and well-tolerated in older patients. It can often be performed without sedation using local anaesthesia in throat only. *H. pylori* can be detected with gastric biopsy and histology or with a test for urease activity (Clo test).
- Serological tests remain positive but titres gradually decline after eradication.
- Breath tests can detect *H. pylori* colonization but obviously don't demonstrate pathology.

Treatment

Dietary restriction is unnecessary (worth specifically mentioning because older patients can remember harsh or bizarre anti-ulcer diets). Stop any NSAIDs. Where there is *H. pylori* and ulceration/gastritis treat with one of the many 'triple therapy' antibiotic PPI regimens (e.g. Amoxil®, clarithromycin or metronidazole, and omeprazole 20mg for 6 weeks). In the absence of *H. pylori* just a PPI will suffice. Arrange a repeat scope at 6 weeks to check healing of all gastric ulcers and malignant-looking duodenal ulcers.

For bleeding

- Resuscitation with blood product is life-saving.
- Early interventional endoscopy with adrenaline injection (or other modalities e.g. heater probes or clips) into bleeding point is suitable for almost all patients—don't delay because of age/comorbidity.
- Post-endoscopic intervention omeprazole 80mg iv stat followed by infusion of 8mg/hr for 72 hours reduces re-bleeding.
- Continued bleeding/re-bleeding despite endoscopic treatment is an indication for surgical intervention. These patients have a high mortality but overall do benefit from operative intervention.

For perforation (p406)

Remember 'silent' perforation (without signs of peritonitis) is commoner in the elderly population. Mortality is high due to delayed diagnosis, reluctance to perform surgery and post operative complications.

HOW TO... **investigate and manage persistent unexplained nausea and vomiting (N+V)**

This group of patients can be very challenging but you should actively manage them from an early stage because they are often very uncomfortable and bedbound. There is often reversible disease and they are at high risk of dehydration/malnutrition and complications of immobility.

N+V can be the major presenting feature of illnesses as diverse as pneumonia, myocardial infarction, intracerebral haemorrhage, and constipation.

- Start with a careful history (especially drug history).
- Thorough examination (including rectal examination and neuro assessment).
- Regular observations of vital signs (looking for intermittent pyrexia, arrhythmia etc.).
- Screening blood tests (including calcium, thyroid function, CRP), urinalysis, CXR, and ECG.

Drugs

Look very carefully at drug history—almost any drug can cause N+V but digoxin (even with therapeutic serum levels), opiates, tramadol, entacapone, antidepressants, NSAIDs and PPIs are some of the common candidates. New drugs are the most likely but remember poor compliance with drugs at home which are prescribed in hospital e.g. cocodamol used occasionally at home may be written as 2 qds in hosp. If there is polypharmacy try stopping the drugs one at a time. Some drugs can take days to 'wash out'.

Central causes

Raised intracerebral pressure can occasionally present this way. A CT scan is needed if there is drowsiness, focal neurology, or a past history of intraventricular blood (exclude hydrocephalus). If there is vertigo or tinnitus consider labyrinthitis or posterior circulation stroke (pp598–9).

Gut causes

Constipation is a very common cause of nausea even without obstruction. An AXR should be done early on to exclude obstruction. Consider repeating this if symptoms persist and you remain suspicious. Plain radiology will remain normal in high obstruction and an OGD or small bowel follow through may help. Severe gastritis/peptic ulceration can present with N+V without pain/bleeding. Gastroparesis is commonest in diabetics and is very hard to treat—try metoclopromide, domperidone, or erythromycin.

The liver and gallbladder

Abnormal liver function tests

Can be transiently elevated e.g. with sepsis, drugs (e.g. statins, coproxamol, penicillins—can occur up to six months after exposure to drug) and viruses (parvovirus, Epstein–Barr and adenovirus). If persistently elevated should always prompt investigations (ultrasound/ CT scan). An isolated elevated ALP is often from a bone source (commonly Paget's disease) but don't assume this—liver metastases can present this way.

Cirrhosis

Chronic liver disease can present for the first time in elderly people. The presentation is often non-specific. The prognosis is worse than for a younger person with the same degree of liver damage. Common cause include alcohol, hepatitis C, autoimmune hepatitis, and non-alcoholic fatty liver. A proportion are cryptogenic (thought to be 'burnt out' auto immune hepatitis or non-alcoholic fatty liver disease).

- **Hepatitis C** may have been transmitted from blood products received before 1991 when screening was introduced. Alcohol consumption is known to increase the percentage of those infected with Hepatis C who develop cirrhosis.
- **Alcohol excess** can present with falls, confusion and heart failure at any age but older patients are less likely to volunteer (or be asked!) their alcohol history.

▶▶ Always enquire about alcohol no matter what your social predjudice!

- **Non-alcoholic fatty liver disease** is not always a benign condition (half will be progressive and 15% develop cirrhosis). Obesity, hyperlipidaemia, and type II diabetes are risk factors so this condition is more common in older patients.

If you suspect cirrhosis your initial investigations should include

Alpha-1-antitrypsin, autoimmune profile (ANA, SMA, LKM, antimitochondrial antibody, and immunoglobulins), ferritin and iron studies hepititis B and C serology, and ultrasound including dopplers of porta and hepatic vein.

Gallstones

- Very common (1:3 elderly females) and mostly asymptomatic although troublesome symptoms often misdiagnosed as gastro-oesophagel reflux or diverticulitis in older age groups.
- Management largely as for younger patients but the risks of surgical intervention are higher so conservative/less invasive approaches often adopted.
- Acute cholecystitis in older patients may present atypically (e.g. without pain) and is not always associated with gallstones. It has a 10% mortality and should be aggressively treated with iv antibiotics and supportive care. Failure to improve should prompt early surgical review.

Constipation

The term constipation is used in different ways, indicating one or more of the following:

- The time between bowel evacuations is longer than normal.
- The stool is harder than normal.
- The total faecal mass present is increased.

The most precise definition may be delayed alimentary tract transit time: this is delayed in age, in the institutionalized and in those eating a Western diet.

There are said to be three types of constipation:

1. Hard faeces present in the rectum (often in massive amounts).
2. The whole distal large bowel loaded with soft, putty-like faeces that cannot be evacuated.
3. High (proximal) impaction which may be due to obstructing pathology (e.g. diverticular disease, carcinoma).

Diagnosis

The diagnosis is largely clinical (based on history and examination alone). ►► Ask specifically as some patients are embarrassed to trouble doctors with bowel symptoms. Constipation may, rarely, be the primary cause of delirium but commonly contributes to the presentation of the frail elderly with other pathology such as sepsis or renal failure.

Rectal examination may be diagnostic, and sometimes the rectum will barely admit the examining finger. If the rectum is empty, consider high impaction. In a thin patient, high impaction is unlikely if the loaded colon cannot be felt during abdominal examination. In more obese subjects a plain abdominal X-ray will be necessary to confirm high impaction, but is insensitive in the very obese.

►► Do not exclude constipation as the cause of faecal incontinence until there has been an adequate therapeutic trial for high faecal impaction.

Causes

- *Reduced motility of the bowel*: chronic laxative abuse, drugs (e.g. opiates, iron, anti-cholinergics, anti-depressants), immobility, constitutional illness, electrolyte disturbances, dehydration, hypothyroidism, lack of dietary fibre, hypercalcaemia.
- *Failure to evacuate the bowels fully*: any painful condition of the rectum or anus, difficulty in access to the toilet, lack of privacy, altered daily routine.
- *Neuromuscular*: Parkinson's disease, diabetic neuropathy, pseudo-obstruction.
- *Mechanical obstruction of the bowel:* carcinoma of the colon, diverticular disease.

Prevention and treatment

Precipitating causes such as dehydration, hypothyroidism, hypercalcaemia, and drugs should be identifed and reversed.

Non-pharmacological measures including regular exercise, improving access to the toilet, adequate dietary fibre and adequate hydration are effective.

Laxatives should be used in combination with non-pharmacological measures.
- Unless there are reversible factors, always prescribe regular laxatives. Waiting for constipation to occur, then using 'prn' doses is far less effective.
- You will need to titrate the laxative dose with time and changing patient circumstances.
- Stimulant laxatives such as senna (1–4 tabs/day) or bisacodyl (5–20mg/day), or stimulant suppositories, may be appropriate for those with bulky, soft faecal overloading.
- Avoid stimulant laxatives in patients with hard rocks of faeces as this may produce abdominal pain. Use a stool softening laxative instead such as lactulose (10–40ml/day) or Movicol® (½ –2 sachets/day).
- Long-term use of stimulant laxatives has been said to cause 'bowel tolerance'/neuronal damage leading to a dilated, atonic colon that required even more laxatives. There is very little evidence to support this, and stimulant laxatives are now considered safe, in moderate doses, for long-term use[1].
- Sometimes stimulant and osmotic laxatives are used in combination, typically in severe constipation (e.g. opiate-induced) that has been unresponsive to a single drug.
- Stool bulking agents such as methylcellulose (Celevac®) or ispaghula (Fybogel®) are useful in prophylaxis, but are less effective in treating established constipation; both fibre and other bulking agents will increase stool volume and may increase problems.
- Costs of laxatives vary enormously, and there is no correlation between cost and patient acceptability. Try cheaper preparations first (fibre, senna).

Faecal retention severe enough to cause incontinence nearly always needs a determined effort to clear the colon (see p587).

---

1 Muller-Lissuer SA, Kamm MA, Scarpignato C et al. (2005). Myths and misconceptions about chronic constipation. *Am J Gastroenterol* **100**: 232–242.

Diverticular disease

Narrow-necked pockets of colonic mucosa which occur adjacent to blood vessel penetrations of the muscle bands, like 'blow outs' on a tyre. Occur anywhere in large bowel but most commonly in the sigmoid.

* *Rare* below age 40, increasing frequency with age and almost universal over age 85.
* *Cause*: thought to be raised intraluminal pressure due to low fibre Western diet.
* *Investigation*: colonoscopy/flexible sigmoidoscopy or barium enema are usually diagnostic and rule out other pathology. CT cologram (abdominal CT with oral contrast) is increasingly used as a better tolerated test in the frail elderly.

Treatment

▶▶ The majority of cases are asymptomatic the majority of the time. On other occasions innocent diverticulae are blamed for symptoms that arise from other pathology e.g. constipation, irritable bowel disease, or gastro-enteritis. The previous diagnosis of diverticular disease should not stop the careful evaluation of new bowel symptoms to exclude important diagnoses such as colitis or cancer.

The treatment depends on presentation:

Pain: especially if associated with constipation, can be improved by a high fibre diet with or without extra stool bulking drugs (e.g. Fybogel® 1 sachet/day).

Diverticulitis: should be thought of as 'left-sided appendicitis'. Infection occurs within a pocket and may be due to a faecolith blocking the neck so avoiding constipation is key to prevention. Abdominal pain and tenderness, diarrhoea, and vomiting occur with fever and raised inflammatory markers. Treat with antibiotics (include anaerobic cover e.g. ciprofloxacin 500mg bd with metronidazole 400mg tds)—mild cases oral antibiotics at home, severe cases may need admission for intravenous rehydration, antibiotics and liaison with surgical services.

Haemorrhage: selective angiography can be used to demonstrate bleeding point.

Diverticular abscess: ultrasound or CT for diagnosis and radiographically guided drainage under local anaesthetic.

Perforation/peritonitis—see p406.

Fistula: most commonly to bladder causing urinary infection and bubbles in urine (pneumaturia). Cystoscopy or CT scan for diagnosis. Surgery is required but simple defunctioning colostomy is often sufficient.

Inflammatory bowel disease

Ulcerative colitis (UC) and Crohns disease (CD) are chronic, relapsing conditions caused by inflammation of the bowel wall. Inflammatory bowel disease is idiopathic and has an increasing incidence in the population as a whole. Initial presentation is usually in adolescence but there is a second peak of incidence in older patients. Diarrhoea and urgency in this age group can be particularly disabling and may result in incontinence and social isolation.

Features

- Diarrhoea (often with blood), malaise, weight loss, and abdominal pain. Delayed presentation may result from embarrassment or fear of cancer. Delayed diagnosis more common in elderly because symptoms are ascribed to one of the common differential diagnoses such as diverticular disease, colonic carcinoma, and ischaemic colitis.
- Associated conditions include arthritis, iritis, sclerosing cholangitis, ankylosing spondylitis, and skin disorders (pyoderma gangrenousum, erythema nodosum).
- Complications include thromboembolism, malabsorbtion and malnutrition, perforation, stenosis with obstruction, fistula formation, colonic and biliary malignancy.

Investigations

- Exclude infection with stool culture and examination for ova, cysts, and parasites and *Clostridium* toxin (if in hospital or recent antibiotics).
- ESR and CRP are usually elevated but may be normal in localized disease.
- A normochromic normocytic anaemia is common but if there is excessive bleeding, iron deficiency can develop.
- Plain X-rays are usually normal but contrast studies are often diagnostic.
- Sigmoidoscopy/colonoscopy and biopsy have high diagnostic yield.

Treatment

Confirmed cases are best managed by gastroenterologists who have specialist nurses and dieticians working with them. Treatment in older patients is not greatly different and is aimed at obtaining and then maintaining remission. There are many new treatments (e.g. cyclosporin, infliximab) which are beyond the scope of this text. Some principles for treating elderly include:

- Exacerbations of distal colitis are usually treated with topical mesalazine and steroids given as enemas—this may be impractical in older patients unless a carer can help and oral steroids can be a better option.
- Budesonide is a new steroid with high topical potency (poor absorption and rapid first pass metabolism) so equivalent doses cause fewer side effects.
- Side effects, drug interactions, and polypharmacy may be more problematic in older patients e.g. always consider bisphosphonates with oral steroids therapy.

- Look for and treat proximal constipation which can impair the efficacy of treatment of a distal colitis.
- Oral 5-aminosalicylic acid preparations (e.g. slow release mesalazine such as Pentasa®) are often successful (for exacerbations and maintainence) and well-tolerated.
- The risk of malignancy is higher the longer the patient has active disease so theoretically many older patients should be under surveillance by a gastroenterologist. Unfortunately the risk of colonic perforation during colonoscopic screening is higher in the elderly population so many screening programmes stop at age 75.
- For failure of medical management elective colectomy is well-tolerated and may give the best quality of life. In contrast emergency surgery in older patients has high mortality.

Diarrhoea in the elderly patient

Acute

Short-lived bouts of diarrhoea are most commonly due to viral gastroenteritis. Supportive management (rehydration, light diet) is usually sufficient for this self-limiting condition. However, if diarrhoea persists, always send samples for culture, OCS (ova, cyst, and parasites) and *Clostridium difficile* toxin (pp672–3).

Chronic

There is a group of elderly who suffer chronic or recurring episodes of diarrhoea that merit active investigation—untreated they suffer high morbidity (especially if diarrhoea induces faecal incontinence) and many causes are treatable. The box opposite gives a suggested plan of investigation.

Malabsorbtion

Patients do not always have diarrhoea. Look for low BMI and falling weight despite reasonable oral calorie intake. Biochemical markers of malnutrition e.g. hypoalbuminaemia may be present. Anaemia is caused by malabsorbtion of iron, B12 or folate and is therefore microcytic, macrocytic, or normocytic.

The common causes of malabsorbtion in older patients often co-exist and include:
- **Coeliac disease/gluten sensitive enteropathy**
  - Peak incidence age 50 but can manifest for the first time in old age with weight loss, bone pain (osteoporosis), fatigue (anaemia), and mouth ulcers.
  - Duodenal biopsy should be performed in all who present with iron deficiency.
  - Anti-endomysial antibodies have very high specificity (100%) and reasonable sensitivity (around 85%). False negatives can occur with low IgA so always check serum immunoglobulins at the same time.
- **Pancreatic insufficiency** Can occur without history of pancreatitis, alcoholism, or gallstones.
- **Bile salt malabsorbtion** Ileal resection or disease allows bile salts to reach colon which causes diarrhoea.
- **Bacterial overgrowth** Particularly common in any person with anatomical abnormality of gut (e.g. post-gastrectomy, small bowel diverticula) but can also occur with normal gut architecture.

HOW TO... investigate and manage chronic diarrhoea

Diagnoses to consider in the elderly population include:
• Inflammatory bowel disease
• Malabsorbtion
• Colonic tumour
• Diverticular disease
• Chronic infections
• Constipation with overflow diarrhoea.

History

Ask about foreign travel, antibiotic exposure, full drug history, previous gut surgery/pancreatitis, family history of inflammatory bowel disease. Ask patient or carer to make a record of stool frequency/texture.

Examination

Abdominal and digital rectal examination. If rectum is loaded be highly suspicious of overflow diarrhoea.

Investigations

1. Stool: culture, *Clostridium difficile* toxin, ova, cysts, and parasites.
2. Blood tests: FBC (anaemia) haematinics (iron, B12, folate deficiency) endomysial antibody (and IgA levels), CRP, and ESR.
3. Radiology: plain abdominal X-ray is rarely diagnostic (except unexpected, left sided faecal loading).
4. Sigmoidoscopy: biopsy in several places even if mucosa looks normal to exclude microscopic colitis (p404).

More complex investigations:

5. Colonoscopy or barium enema.

Treatment

Obviously depends on cause but in patients in whom diagnosis is not clear and they are not fit for, or refuse, more complex investigations there is a place for a trial of empirical treatment. One such strategy is at least 2 week trials of:
• Metronidazole (for overgrowth/diverticular disease)
• Creon® (pancreatic disease)
• Questran® (bile salt malabsorption)
• Steroids (inflammatory bowel disease).

Pick the most likely or try each in turn for a few weeks.

Other colonic conditions

Irritable bowel syndrome (IBS)

A chronic, non-inflammatory condition characterized by abdominal pain, altered bowel habit (diarrhoea or constipation), and abdominal bloating, but with no identifiable structural or biochemical disorder.

- This diagnosis should not made 'de novo' in older patients without very careful exclusion of structural disease (particularly colonic tumors and diverticulitis).
- Lifelong sufferers may continue with symptoms in later life but if the symptoms change the patient should also undergo investigations.
- Pain or diarrhoea that wakes a patient at night, blood in stool, weight loss, or fever are NEVER features of IBS.
- Some drugs used to treat IBS (e.g. tricyclic antidepressants) are less well tolerated in older patients. Mebeverine might be better tolerated for spasm.
- Dietry advice should be given (low fibre for bloating or wind, high fibre or Fybogel® for diarrhoea or constipation).

Angiodysplasia

Tiny capillary malformations (like spider naevi) that can occur anywhere in the gut are important only because they bleed.

- Slow blood loss leads to unexplained recurrent iron deficiency anaemia, brisk loss may produce life-threatening haemorrhage.
- Unless they are inherited in a syndrome (e.g. hereditary haemorrhagic telangiectasia) they are acquired and therefore have increased prevalence with age (most cases aged over 70).
- Asymptomatic angiodysplasia in older patients is common. Diagnosis is often by exclusion of other causes of iron deficiency anaemia.
- Sometimes colonoscopy can visualize lesions (which can then be treated by diathermy).
- Selective mesenteric angiography can demonstrate lesions that are actively and rapidly bleeding.
- Tranexamic acid and oestrogens are sometimes successful in controlling chronic blood loss.

Microscopic colitis (also known as collagenous colitis or lymphocytic colitis)

An idiopathic condition causing chronic or episodic watery, non-bloody diarrhoea but with no gross structural changes seen at colonoscopy.

- Biopsy changes are diagnostic with collagenous thickening of the subepithelial layer and infiltration with lymphocytes.
- Peak incidence in 50s.
- There is no increased risk of cancer.
- Keep treatment as simple as possible—start with diet and anti-diarrhoeal drugs, mesalazine then steroids.

Ischaemic colitis

Underdiagnosed cause of acute diarrhoea ± blood in dehydrated, hypotensive elderly patient with vascular disease. Often self-limiting if volume depletion corrected.

The 'acute surgical abdomen'

▶▶ Peritonitis/perforation often presents in a non-specific or non-dramatic way. Patients often present to medicine rather than directly to surgeons. The diagnosis is easily missed so always have a high index of suspicion and examine the abdomen carefully and repeatedly in sick elderly patients without a diagnosis

Common causes in older patients include:
• Complications of diverticular disease
• First presentation of tumour (gut, pancreatic)
• Ischaemic bowel (emboli in patients with atrial fibrillation)
• Strangulated hernias (always remember groin examination)
• Ruptured abdominal aortic aneurysm
• Duodenal ulcer perforation (becoming less common)
• Biliary stones/sepsis (stones) and pancreatitis.

Signs
Peritonitis/perforation may not have guarding or rigidity, particularly in the very old, those on steroids or diabetics. Lack of bowel sounds can be helpful. Signs may develop with time, so repeated assessments are helpful.

Investigations
Erect CXR can reveal air under the diaphragm (this is sometimes the only indication of a 'silent' perforation). Ultrasound or CT imaging will often reveal the cause.

Management
Always involve the surgical team even where patient is unsuitable for operation as they can advise on conservative management and occasionally an 'interval' procedure is appropriate (e.g. gallstone surgery once cholecystitis has settled). Ensure that surgical decisions are made on the basis of frailty, co-morbidity, or occasionally on an informed, competent patient decision and not just age alone.

Medical management involves:
• Broad spectrum intravenous antibiotics (e.g. cefuroxime 750mg tds or ciprofloxacin 500mg bd with metronidazole 500mg tds).
• Resting the bowel (nil by mouth, NG tube if vomiting).
• Careful monitoring of fluid balance—heart failure from fluid overload or renal failure from dehydration are often the mechanisms of death. A urinary catheter and central venous pressure monitoring are sometimes necessary.
• Consider prophylactic low molecular weight heparin.

It is surprising how often patients survive with conservative measures so continue to monitor the patient and adjust treatment carefully. Once the signs/symptoms recede try to get the patient eating, on oral antibiotics, and mobilizing as soon as possible to avoid the complications of malnutrition, pressure sores, venous thrombo-embolism and *Clostridium difficile* colitis which may be more lethal than the initial peritonitis!

Obstructed bowel in older patients

As with peritonitis this often presents in a non-specific or non-dramatic way.

Common causes in older patients include:
- Constipation
- Colonic tumors
- Sigmoid volvulus
- Strangulated hernias (remember to examine groins)
- Adhesions (look for old abdominal scars)
- Complications of diverticular disease (abscess, localized perforation, stricture).

Signs
Consider excluding obstruction (with plain X-ray) in any patient with persistent vomiting and/or abdominal bloating (ask the patient if their tummy is a normal size for them). Pain/colic, absence of defaecation, tinkling bowel sounds, and gastric splash are helpful when present but are often not. Always examine the groins in both sexes for obstructed herniae.

Investigations
Plain AXR shows dilated bowel—standing AXRs have fluid levels but are often impractical in older patients and rarely add diagnostic information to a supine film. Ultrasound or CT imaging may localize a cause. Contrast radiology and gastroscopy are sometimes useful.

Management
Always involve the surgical team who can advise on diagnosis and conservative management e.g. insertion of a flatus tube for sigmoid volvulus. General management usually involves:
- Resting the bowel (nil by mouth and wide bore NG tube).
- Careful monitoring of fluid balance—heart failure from fluid overload or renal failure from dehydration are often the mechanisms of death.
- Consider wide spectrum antibiotics if there is fever or features of coexistent perforation.
- Consider prophylactic low molecular weight heparin.

Where conservative management fails and an operation is necessary, less invasive/palliative procedures are often more appropriate (e.g. defunctioning colostomy rather than anterior resection).

Pseudo-obstruction presents with vomiting and dilated bowel on X-ray but is due to an atonic bowel so bowel sounds are absent or decreased rather than increased. Can occur with electrolyte abnormality (especially low potassium) or any severe illness (e.g. septicaemia) and reverses with correction of the underlying abnormality.

Renal medicine

The ageing kidney *410*
Acute renal failure *412*
Acute renal failure: management *414*
Acute renal failure: investigations *416*
Chronic renal failure *418*
   How to… estimate the glomerular filtration rate *419*
Chronic renal failure: complications *420*
Renal replacement therapy: dialysis *422*
Renal replacement therapy: transplantation *424*
Nephrotic syndrome *426*
Glomerulonephritis *428*
Renal artery stenosis *430*

The ageing kidney

Renal function tends to decline with age, but unless there is additional renal disease, function is usually sufficient to remove waste and to regulate volume and electrolyte balance, and it is only when stressed that the lack of renal reserve becomes apparent. The relative contribution of cumulative exposure to risk factors (extrinsic ageing), disease acquisition (often occult), and intrinsic ageing is unknown, but not all the changes described are universal in an older population.

Falling renal reserve

Glomerular filtration rate (GFR) falls steadily after the age of 40 in most healthy older people, maybe due to the following age related changes:
- Rise in blood pressure within the 'normal' range.
- Numbers of glomeruli fall (~50% fewer age 70 than age 30).
- Increase in sclerotic glomeruli.

Renal blood flow decreases by around 10% per decade (cortex more than medulla, leading to patchy cortical defects on renal scans).

Lower GFR and renal blood flow are the major causes of reduced renal reserve, with the following clinical implications:
- Renally excreted substances are likely to be retained longer in the body (especially drugs) making prescription amendments necessary (see p140).
- Reduced threshold for damage with ischaemia or nephrotoxins.

The normal range for plasma urea and creatinine levels does not change with age. However, as production of urea and creatinine decreases with falling body muscle mass, renal function may be substantially diminished in an older person, even with apparently normal blood chemistry.

▶▶ GFR is a better estimate of renal function than plasma urea and creatinine.

Blunted fluid and electrolyte homeostasis

The following changes occur with age:
- A blunted response to sodium loading and depletion, so equilibrium is achieved more slowly.
- Less ability to dilute and concentrate urine (falls by 5% every decade).
- Lower renin and aldosterone levels (30–50% less than younger people).
- Loss of the sensation of thirst, even when plasma tonicity is high, for reasons that are unclear (may relate to altered baroreceptor function, dry mouths, or altered mental capacity).
- Lesser response to vasopressin.
- In addition, many commonly prescribed drugs interfere with renal function (diuretics, NSAIDs, ACE inhibitors, lithium, sedatives etc.).

Hyponatraemia is therefore common (low sodium intake combined with renal sodium wasting), but in times of acute illness (increased fluid demand and decreased intake) the slower adaptive mechanisms make hypernatraemic dehydration more common.

Hypokalaemia is common because of poor intake and frequent diuretic use, but lower GFR and hypoaldosteronism lead to a vulnerability to hyperkalaemia especially when exacerbating drugs (NSAIDS, spironolactone, ACE inhibitors) are used.

There is a loss of the circadian rhythm, owing to altered sodium handling and patterns of aldosterone secretion, so that over that age of 60 the proportion of water, sodium and potassium excretion occurring at night increases, causing nocturia.

Structural changes

- Renal mass falls by 20–30% between 30 and 90 years, making kidneys appear smaller on ultrasound scanning, without necessarily implying disease.
- Distal nephrons develop diverticulae (3 per tubule by age 90) that may become retention cysts (benign finding in older people).

Other changes

Renal 1-hydroxylase activity decreases with age leading to decreased vitamin D production. Combined with low phosphate intake, this can mildly elevate parathyroid hormone levels.

Acute renal failure

More common in older people, but with a similar prognosis if occurring de novo and then treated correctly.

▶▶ Do not deny treatment based on age alone—even anuric patients can make a full recovery.

Causes

80% of cases of acute renal failure (ARF) are caused by pre-renal failure and acute tubular necrosis (ATN).

Pre-renal causes

Due to poor renal perfusion. May be caused by:
- Dehydration (commonly associated with sepsis)
- Volume loss (e.g. bleeding, over-diuresis)
- Volume redistribution (e.g. with low serum albumin)
- Poor cardiac output (e.g. post MI)
- Aggravated by many drugs (e.g. diuretics, ACE inhibitors, NSAIDs).

Older patients are prone to sepsis, have less capacity to maintain circulating volume in the face of stress and are more likely to be on aggravating medications, making this a very common problem (e.g. urinary sepsis in a patient taking diuretics and NSAIDs can often cause pre-renal renal impairment, and responds well to antibiotics, fluids and drug cessation).

▶▶All unwell elderly patients should have renal function checked routinely and repeatedly. Consider stopping diuretics and ACE inhibitors during an acute illness.

Renal causes

Due to direct damage to the kidney. Commonly ATN, which may be:
- Ischaemic (occurs when pre-renal failure is not corrected quickly e.g. with sepsis, surgical procedures, prolonged hypotension etc.)
- Nephrotoxic (usually medication such as aminoglycoside antibiotics e.g. gentamicin)
- Due to pigment deposition (e.g. myoglobin in rhabdomyolysis).

Older people are more susceptible. Other (rarer) causes include glomerulonephritis (diffuse inflammatory change to glomeruli with resulting haematuria and red cell casts) and acute interstitial nephritis. These less common causes are important because they are often responsive to specific treatment (usually steroids). The patient should be assessed by a renal physician promptly to make this decision (often after biopsy).

Post-renal causes

- Obstruction of the renal tract at some point e.g. prostatic enlargement, renal stones, urethral strictures, pelvic tumours.
- Ultrasound scan shows a dilated collecting system.
- These conditions are all more common in older people, and are very responsive to treatment if found early, often with full recovery of renal function.

Acute renal failure: management

Is this acute renal failure?

Older people are more likely to have underlying chronic renal impairment, and this confers a worse prognosis. Check old notes, ask the patient, family, and GP about known history, and look back at computer blood test results.

Generally, management does not differ significantly from younger patients:

Investigations

See table pp416–17.

Treat cause

Older people respond as well to most treatments.

Monitor meticulously

- Pulse and blood pressure, cardiac monitor, input (iv and oral) and output (urine, faecal matter, vomit, drains, sweat).
- May be best done on HDU.
- Aim for euvolaemia (assessed clinically—may need to correct deficit) then maintain by matching input to output on an hourly basis initially.
- Fluid balance is likely to be harder in older people because of co-morbidity (especially heart failure).
- ▶▶ The presence of peripheral oedema does not necessarily indicate fluid overload. Circulating volume is best assessed by blood pressure, pulse, JVP, and skin turgor.
- May need CVP and urinary catheter initially, but remove as soon as possible because of infection risk.
- Document daily weight and total fluid balance summary.
- Be prepared for polyuria in the recovery phase, and ensure that the patient does not become fluid depleted.

Treat complications

Importantly hyperkalaemia, acidosis, and pulmonary oedema.

Refer early for further renal support (filtration or dialysis)—a patient can remain oliguric for some time whilst renal recovery is occurring, but it is sensible to make the relevant teams aware of a potential patient. The indications for renal replacement therapy are as follows:

- Refractory pulmonary oedema (older people are particularly prone to this after over enthusiastic initial fluid replacement)
- Persistent hyperkalaemia (K > 7 mmol/L) that cannot be controlled by insulin/dextrose infusions and intravenous calcium
- Worsening acidosis (pH < 7.2)
- Uraemic pericarditis
- Uraemic encephalopathy.

Further reading

Longmore M, Wilkinson I, Rajagopalan S (2004). *Oxford Handbook of Clinical Medicine* 6th edn, pp272–5. Oxford: Oxford University Press.

Acute renal failure: investigations

Investigation	Rationale	Special points in older people
Urea and creatinine	Elevated in renal failure	Elderly people with very little muscle mass will have lower baseline levels, so a urea of 10 in a small elderly lady will represent significant renal impairment Urea:creatinine ratio can be useful—elevated in pre-renal failure, acting as a marker of dehydration
Electrolytes	Potassium rises dangerously in ARF	More prone to cardiac complications of electrolyte disturbance—monitor carefully
Arterial blood gases	Monitor pH which falls in ARF	pH can also be checked on a venous sample
Inflammatory markers (ESR, CRP, WCC)	Check for infection	Common precipitant of ARF in older people (may be occult)
Urine dipstick	Check for leucocytes and nitrites (infection), blood and protein (active renal lesion likely)	High rate of positive urine dipstick in older people—does not always imply infection
Urine microscopy	Looking for casts (red cell casts in glomerulonephritis, white cell casts in infection etc.) and blood cells	Always send for culture, even when the dipstick is negative
Blood and urine cultures	Identify microbes	Ensure these are sent on all patients (who may have occult infection) prior to starting antibiotics

Creatinine kinase	Elevated in rhabdomyolysis	Always check after falls (especially after a long period on the floor before being found). Even if there is not full blown rhabdomyolysis, an elevated CK level indicates the need for hydration and monitoring of renal function
Urinary sodium	Helps distinguish between pre-renal failure (urinary Na < 20mmol/L as kidney still functioning to preserve sodium) and ATN (urinary Na > 40mmol/L as kidney not functioning, so losing Na)	Particularly useful in older people where clinical assessment of fluid balance may be harder because of peripheral oedema etc. Not helpful if the patient has taken diuretics (increase sodium excretion)
CXR	Looking for evidence of cardiac disease, source of infection, pulmonary oedema or pulmonary infiltrates (vasculitis)	More prone to pulmonary oedema—extra caution with fluid replacement if there is cardiomegaly, even where there is no history of cardiac failure
ECG	Looking for evidence of cardiac disease and monitoring for hyperkalaemia	Again alerts to occult cardiac disease if ECG is abnormal
Renal ultrasound	Assess renal size and look for evidence of hydronephrosis	Very useful in older people to help establish if renal failure is truly acute (small kidneys with chronic failure). Also checks for treatable obstructive causes—common in this age group
Other tests	All should have FBC and LFTs. Usually also send autoantibodies (ANA, ANCA), immunoglobulins, complement and electrophoresis of blood and urine	

Chronic renal failure

Chronic renal failure (CRF) is a substantial, irreversible, long-standing, and usually progressive loss in renal function.

More common in older people—incidence in the over 75s is ten times higher than in the under 40s. Half of all renal replacement therapy is now started for patients over 65 years, and this of course does not truly represent the burden of renal impairment, as the majority will die with and not of renal failure, many never encountering a renal physician.

Much renal impairment is discovered incidentally by finding elevated urea and creatinine levels—there are adaptive mechanisms that maintain reasonable health with failing renal function until severe damage has occurred. (Glomerular filtration rate (GFR) of 10–15ml/min.).

Common causes include hypertension, diabetes, obstruction (usually due to prostatic enlargement), glomerulonephritis, and renovascular disease. A significant proportion presenting late remains idiopathic.

When abnormal renal function is discovered, firstly consider the circumstances—is the patient acutely unwell? Are they being overdiuresed? Correct all of these factors, and recheck renal function in a stable clinical state.

If it remains deranged, then do the following:

- Estimate the GFR (see box opposite) Consider checking GFR when creatinine is within the 'normal range' for an older patient with a low body weight.
- Identify and treat any modifiable factors (e.g. diabetes, hypertension and obstructive uropathy).
- Delay disease progression by controlling diabetes and hypertension and by using an ACE inhibitor (or an ARB). Low protein diets, lipid lowering, and correcting anaemia may also help.
- Avoid exacerbating factors such as volume depletion, intravenous contrast, urinary obstruction, and nephrotoxic drugs.
- Identify and treat complications as they arise (see p420).
- Prepare for the end-stage. Try to establish the rate of decline, using previous creatinine measurements. Deterioration tends to be steady and so it is often possible to estimate when interventions are likely to be needed. A frail old person with limited life expectancy and moderate impairment is likely to die of other causes before complex renal issues become a problem. Most other patients benefit from early renal review (ie when impairment is moderate to severe) to clarify diagnosis, optimize management and discuss renal replacement therapy (see p424). Late referral for dialysis is associated with a poor outcome.

Further information
UK National Service Framework for Renal Services www.dh.gov.uk

HOW TO... **estimate the glomerular filtration rate**

Although elevated urea and creatinine levels often alert the clinician to renal impairment, they give a poor estimate of extent, as the levels are determined by many factors as well as GFR. Creatinine, for example is directly related to muscle mass, which tends to fall with age.

This means that:

- A small rise in urea and creatinine in an elderly person is significant, and should be taken seriously.
- A creatinine within the 'normal range' may represent renal failure in a small old patient (see below).

GFR is a better measure of renal function, but is hard to measure. Creatinine clearance approximates GFR and can be measured with a 24-hour urine collection, or estimated using the Cockcroft–Gault formula:

$$\text{Creatinine clearance} = \frac{[(140 - \text{age in years}) \times \text{weight in kilograms}]}{\text{Plasma creatinine } (\mu\text{mol/L}) \times 0.82}$$

This figure needs to be reduced slightly for women.

It can be seen that patient of 80, weighing 50kg with a creatinine of 140 will have an estimated GFR of 26 (i.e. severe failure). Another patient of 30, weighing 70kg with a creatinine of 140 however will have an estimated GFR of 67 (i.e. mild failure)

Using this derived figure, renal impairment has been classified by the Kidney Disease Outcomes Quality Initiative (KDOQI) as follows:

GFR (ml/min)	Average creatinine for patient of 30 yrs weighing 70kg	Average creatinine for patient of 80 yrs weighing 50kg	Degree of renal failure
60–89	125	50	Mild failure
30–59	220	85	Moderate failure
15–29	420	165	Severe failure
<15	>1500	>700	End-stage renal failure

Chronic renal failure: complications

Hypertension
- Can occur at any point in the disease.
- Cause and consequence of CRF.
- Monitor blood pressure regularly in all patients.
- Treat with an ACE inhibitor (saves renal function).

Hyperlipidaemia
- May contribute to renal damage.
- Treat with a statin.

Atherosclerosis
- Accelerated atheroma occurs with renal impairment.
- Ensure that all vascular risk factors are addressed.

Salt and water retention
- Onset with moderate impairment.
- Consider loop diuretics for oedema (e.g. furosemide—high doses (250mg) may be required, but start low and increase as needed).
- Restrict dietary salt intake.
- Fluid restriction may be necessary with more severe renal impairment.

Secondary hyperparathyroidism
- Onset usually with moderate impairment.
- Low calcium, high phosphate and appropriately high parathyroid hormone (PTH).
- Ensure calcium, phosphate, and PTH are checked.
- Consider dietary phosphate restriction (milk, cheese, eggs etc.), phosphate binders (e.g. Calcichew®), calcium supplements, and vitamin D analogues (e.g. alfacalcidol) if there is a problem.
- Risk of renal bone disease (renal osteodystrophy).

Anaemia
- Onset usually with moderate impairment.
- Check for alternative causes of anaemia (iron deficiency, chronic disease, etc.).
- If none found, consider erythropoietin injections to keep Hb > 11g/dL (usually initiated by renal physician).

Neuropathy
- Onset with severe impairment.
- Includes peripheral neuropathy, autonomic neuropathy and encephalopathy.

Acidosis and hyperkalaemia
- Onset with severe impairment.
- Indicate need for renal replacement therapy, or plans for terminal care.

Further reading
www.kidney.org/professionals/kdoqi

Renal replacement therapy: dialysis

This includes haemodialysis (HD—usually done at a dialysis centre and accounting for around 80% of dialysis in the older age group) and peritoneal dialysis (PD—mainly managed at home).

Survival

Older patients have a shorter survival on dialysis than younger patients, probably because of an increase in complications (see below) yet can still expect a 20–40% five year survival (mean life expectancy 3–5 years).

Those over 80 years on dialysis have a median survival of 26 months, irrespective of the age at onset of treatment.

Effectiveness

Some older patients may mistakenly be under dialysed (low muscle mass leads to lower urea and creatinine levels that do not reflect the need for dialysis). In addition, dialysis sessions are more commonly stopped early because of hypotension. This adversely affects outcome. Using other means to calculate dialysis frequency and optimizing health with nutritional support, erythropoietin, and appropriate buffer selection can vastly improve effectiveness in older people.

Complications

In older people:
- Nausea, vomiting, and hypotension during dialysis are more common (due to autonomic dysfunction and decreased cardiac reserve).
- Malnutrition occurs in up to 20%.
- There is increased risk of infection (ageing immune system and malnutrition), depression, and GI bleeds (from uraemic gastritis, diverticulosis and angiodysplasia).

Quality of life

Many older patients on dialysis enjoy a high quality of life. They resent the intrusion of visits to a dialysis centre less than younger patients and can find it offers positive social interaction. Many of this highly selected cohort (frailer elderly with renal impairment do not reach this service) retain their independence, with over 90% maintaining good community social contacts, and over 80% regularly going outdoors. Around 40% rate their health positively. However, for some it becomes tiring and burdensome, especially if relying on hospital transport for attendance.

Who should be offered dialysis?

Dialysis is expensive, and the number of elderly people with end-stage renal failure (ESRF) is large. Many elderly patients with ESRF elect to have dialysis if offered, but offering it to all is not sensible or feasible.

It should not be offered to simply delay dying—rather used if the renal failure is the main threat to continued survival. Severe dementia, advanced malignancy (except possibly multiple myeloma) or advanced liver disease generally makes dialysis inadvisable. Caution should be exercised before offering dialysis to patients with severe heart or lung disease, or frail patients with multiple co morbidities.

What next?

Many patients need to swap dialysis modalities for some reason. The rate of voluntary withdrawal (overall about 5%) increases with age and is usually because of general dissatisfaction with life or the development of significant co morbidity (often cancer). 40% would like to proceed to transplant.

Renal replacement therapy: transplantation

This is the 'gold standard' of renal replacement therapy for ESRF, as it improves survival and quality of life when compared with dialysis, as well as releasing the patient from the burden of regular dialysis sessions.

Transplant recipients are getting older—10% of transplants in 2002 were performed for patients over 65, compared with only 5% a decade ago. However, as the majority of ESRF occurs in the elderly population this still represents an imbalance.

Donated kidneys are in short supply, and tend to be given to those who will get the most use out of them—namely younger patients with a longer natural life expectancy.

The most common cause of graft failure in older people is death of the host with a functioning graft. This is due to a number of factors:
- One of the most common causes of death after transplantation is cardiovascular disease.
- Older people have altered immune responses—this makes it less likely that they will reject a donated kidney, and allows for modified immunosuppressive medication. However, it also increases the risk of serious infection.
- Older people have increased side effects to immunosuppressive medication, particularly steroids.
- Other common conditions make the transplant procedure more complicated, e.g. peripheral vascular disease (technical surgical problems), diverticular disease (predisposes to post transplant perforation), and cholelithiasis (predisposes to biliary sepsis).

There are limited outcome data for older patients, but the following is known:
- Patients over 60 have a 70% 5-year survival post transplant.
- Transplant carries a greater chance of survival than dialysis, in older as in younger patients (around 10 years compared with 6 on dialysis for those aged 60–74).
- Dialysis is often well-tolerated by older people, and may be less intrusive as there are fewer work and domestic commitments.

Each individual must be considered separately, taking into account biological and not chronological age. Careful screening for co-morbidity will reveal those most likely to benefit, regardless of age. The use of older donors for older recipients could partially redress the imbalance, as the grafts themselves will have a limited life-span and so be most appropriate for an age-matched recipient.

Nephrotic syndrome

Increased glomerular permeability to protein causes proteinuria (>3g/day), hypoalbuminaemia, generalized oedema, and hyperlipidaemia. There is an increased susceptibility to infection, thrombosis, and renal failure.

▶▶ More common in older people, but often missed as oedema may be attributed to cardiac failure, and a low serum albumin to poor nutrition—always dipstick urine for protein in an oedematous patient.

Causes

Membranous and minimal change nephropathy, glomerulonephritis and amyloid are common pathologies. Look for associated conditions, including malignancy (e.g. carcinoma, lymphoma), infection (e.g. hepatitis B), systemic disease (e.g. SLE, rheumatoid arthritis, chronic infection), and diabetes. NSAID use may be the only cause.

Presentation

Frothy urine, anorexia, malaise, muscle wasting, oedema (mobile depending on gravity—moves from sacrum and eyelids at night to legs during day), and effusions (pleural, pericardial, ascites). Blood pressure varies. Patients are prone to intravascular depletion with increased total body water, especially when over-diuresed due to assumed cardiac failure.

Investigations

- Routine blood screen (FBC, U,C and E, glucose, LFT)
- Urinalysis
- 24 hour urinary protein
- ANA, ANCA, complement
- Urine and serum electrophoresis, immunoglobulins
- Hepatitis serology
- Renal ultrasound
- Refer to renal team for possible biopsy.

Treatment

Usually requires admission.
- Monitor U&E, fluid balance, blood pressure
- Fluid and salt restriction
- Diuretics (e.g. furosemide 80–250mg)
- Prophylactic heparin s/c
- Monitor closely for infection
- Specific treatment with steroids/immunosuppressants after histology known (specialist advice)
- Control of hypertension in diabetics.

Glomerulonephritis

- A diffuse inflammatory process involving the glomeruli.
- Presents with renal failure, hypertension, oedema, haematuria, red cell casts, and proteinuria.
- Older people often present non-specifically (e.g. with nausea, malaise, arthralgia, and pulmonary infiltrates due to vasculitis).

▶▶ Often misdiagnosed initially, causing delay in treatment. In unwell older people, always dipstick the urine. Think of glomerulonephritis if there is haematuria (see p676).

Causes

- Post infectious (usually streptococcal).
- Systemic disease (vasculitis, lupus, Wegener's granulomatosis etc.).
- Primary renal cause of unknown aetiology.

Treatment

- Supportive.
- 20% require dialysis.
- Steroids can be used for all but post-infectious, so refer early to a renal team to confirm diagnosis (usually by renal biopsy).

Outcome

Worse in older people. More die, and more progress to chronic renal failure.

Renal artery stenosis

More common with increasing age. Usually due to atheroma, so occurs in patients with known vascular disease in other areas. Think of it in the following circumstances:

- When renal function deteriorates after starting an ACE inhibitor. Stopping the drug promptly should reverse the changes.
- When blood pressure is hard to control.
- When there is unexplained hypokalaemia (due to low aldosterone levels).
- When a renal bruit is heard on clinical examination.
- When there is a unilateral small kidney seen on imaging.

As there are often no symptoms, conservative management with blood pressure control, optimizing vascular secondary prevention but avoiding ACE inhibitors is often appropriate. If, however, renal function declines or blood pressure cannot be controlled, then percutaneous angioplasty or stent insertion is well-tolerated even in very old people.

Homeostasis

Volume depletion and dehydration 432
   How to… administer subcutaneous fluid 434
Hyponatraemia: assessment 436
Hyponatraemia: treatment 438
Syndrome of inappropriate ADH 440
   How to… do a short ACTH stimulation test (short
   Synacthen® test) 441
Hypernatraemia 442
Hypothermia: diagnosis 444
Hypothermia: management 446
Heat-related illness 448
   How to… monitor temperature 449

Volume depletion and dehydration

Losses of water and sodium that may be isotonic or hypotonic.

An important, common, easily missed clinical condition, especially in older people. Highly prevalent amongst acutely unwell older people admitted to hospital due to a combination of increased fluid loss (fever, GI loss) and decreased intake (nausea, anorexia, weakness).

Causes
- Blood loss
- Diuretics
- GI losses (e.g. diarrhoea, nasogastric drainage)
- Sequestration of fluid (e.g. ileus, burns, peritonitis)
- Poor oral intake
- Fever.

Symptoms and signs
- Thirst is uncommon in older people.
- Malaise, apathy, weakness.
- Orthostatic symptoms (lightheadedness or syncope) and/or hypotension.
- Nausea, anorexia, vomiting in severe uraemia. Oliguria.
- Tachycardia, hypotension (late signs, and seen also in fluid **overload**).
- Decreased skin turgor, sunken facies, absence of dependent oedema.

The symptoms and signs of clinically important dehydration may be subtle and confusing. It is therefore under-recognized. Continual clinical assessment, assisted by basic tests (urinalysis; urea, creatinine and electrolytes) is essential. Invasive monitoring or other tests are rarely needed.

Older patients commonly become dehydrated because:
- They are 'run dry' on the wards, as medical (and nursing) staff fear precipitating acute pulmonary oedema through excessive intravenous fluid administration.
- Intavenous infusions often run more slowly than prescribed, or cannot run for periods if iv access is lost.
- Moderate leg oedema is very poorly specific for heart failure—don't treat this sign alone, in the absence of supporting evidence, with diuretic.
- Poor urine output on the surgical (or medical) wards is more often a sign of dehydration than of heart failure. Diuretics are the wrong treatment.

▶▶ There is no sensitive biochemical marker of dehydration—urea and creatinine are commonly in the normal range.

Management

- Treat the underlying cause(s).
- Continually reassess clinically, assisted by urinalysis/U, C and E. Measure and document intake, output, and weight.
- If mild: oral rehydration may suffice. Old frail people need time, encouragement and physical assistance with drinking. Encourage relatives and friends to help.
- More severe dehydration, or mild dehydration not responding to conservative measures, will require other measures—usually parenteral treatment, either subcutaneous or intravenous.
- The speed of parenteral fluid administration should be tailored to the individual patient, based on volume of fluid deficit, degree of physiological compromise and perceived risks of fluid overload. For example, a hypotensive patient who is clinically volume depleted with evidence of end-organ failure should be fluid resuscitated briskly, even if there is a history of heart failure. In the absence of end-organ dysfunction, rehydration may proceed more cautiously, but continual reassessment is essential, to confirm that the clinical situation remains benign, and that progress (input > output) is being made.

HOW TO... **administer subcutaneous fluid**

This method (hypodermoclysis) was widely used in the 1950s, but fell into disrepute following reports of adverse effects associated with very hypo/hypertonic fluid. Fluids that are close to isotonic delivered by competent staff are a safe and effective substitute for iv therapy.

- A simple, widely accessible method for parenteral fluid and electrolytes.
- Fluid is administered via a standard giving set and fine (21–23 G) butterfly needle into subcutaneous (sc) tissue, then draining centrally via lymphatics and veins.
- Sc fluid administration should be considered when insertion or maintenance of iv access presents problems, e.g. difficult venous access, persistent extravasation, or lack of staff skills.
- Iv access is preferred if rapid fluid administration is needed (e.g. GI bleed), or if precise control of fluid volume is essential.

Sites of administration Preferred sites include abdomen, chest (avoid breast), thigh, and scapula. In agitated patients who tear out iv (or sc) lines, sites close to the scapulae may foil their attempts.

Fluid type Any crystalloid solution that is approximately isotonic can be used, including normal (0.9%) saline, 5% dextrose and any isotonic combination of dextrose–saline. Potassium chloride can be added to the infusion, in concentrations of 20–40mM/L. If local irritation occurs, change site and/or reduce the concentration of added potassium.

Infusion rate Typical flow (and absorption) rate is 1ml/min or 1.5L/day. Infusion pumps may be used. If flow or absorption is slow (leading to lumpy, oedematous areas):

- Change site.
- Use hyaluronidase (a 'digester' of connective tissue). Add 150 to 300 units to each litre fluid and/or pre-treat site with 150 units.
- Use two separate infusion sites at the same time.
- Using these techniques, up to 3L of fluid daily may be given. For smaller volumes, consider an overnight 'top-up' of 500–1000ml, or two daily boluses of 500ml each (run in over 2–3 hours) leaving the patient free of infusion lines during the daily rehabilitation/activity. Some patients need only 1L/alternative nights to maintain hydration.

Monitoring Patients should be monitored clinically (hydration state, input/output, weight) and biochemically as they would if they were receiving intravenous fluid. Be responsive and creative in your prescriptions of fluid and electrolytes. One size does not fit all.

Potential complications Rare and usually mild. They include local infection, and local adverse reactions to hypertonic fluid (e.g. with added potassium) or to hyaluronidase.

Contraindications

- Exercise caution in thrombocytopaenia or coagulopathy.
- Sc infusion is not appropriate in patients who need rapid volume repletion.

Hyponatraemia: assessment

A common problem. May safely be monitored rather than treated if modest in severity ([Na]>125mM), stable and without side effects, and if there is an identifiable (often drug) cause.

Clinical features

- Subtle or absent in mild cases.
- Typically between [Na]=115–125mM: lethargy, confusion and altered personality.
- At <115mM: delirium, coma, fits, and death.

Causes

Iatrogenic causes are most common. Acute onset, certain drugs, or recent intravenous fluids make iatrogenesis especially likely.

Important causes include:

- Drugs. Many are implicated (see below).
- Excess water administration—either nasogastric (rarely oral) or intravenous (5% dextrose).
- Failure of heart, liver, thyroid, kidneys.
- Stress response, e.g. after trauma or surgery, exacerbated by i.v. colloid or 5% dextrose.
- Hypoadrenalism: steroid withdrawal or Addison's disease.
- Syndrome of inappropriate ADH secretion (SIADH).

In older people, multiple causes are common e.g. heart failure, diuretics, and acute diarrhoea.

Approach

Take a careful drug history. Examine to determine evidence of cause and volume status (JVP, postural BP, pulmonary oedema, ankle/sacral oedema, peripheral perfusion).

Investigations

Clinical history and examination, urine and blood biochemistry are usually all that are needed. Ensure that the sample wasn't delayed in transit or taken from a drip arm. If genuine hyponatraemia, take:

- Blood for creatinine, osmolarity, TFT, LFT, glucose.
- Spot urine sample for sodium and osmolarity.

Consider a short ACTH test to exclude hypoadrenalism, particularly if the patient is volume-depleted and hyperkalaemic.

Hyponatraemia: treatment

Treatment (see flow chart opposite)
- Combine normalization of [Na] with correction of fluid volume and treating underlying cause(s).
- The rate of correction of hyponatraemia should not be too rapid. Usually, correction to the lower limit of the normal range (~130mM) should be achieved in a few days. Maximum correction in any 24 hour period should be < 10mM. Full correction can reasonably take weeks.
- Rapid correction risks central pontine myelinolysis (leading to quadriparesis and cranial nerve abnormalities) and is indicated only when hyponatraemia is severe and the patient critically unwell.

▶▶ By definition, hyponatraemia is a low blood sodium concentration. Therefore a low level may be a result of low sodium, high water, or both. Dehydration and hyponatraemia may coexist if sodium depletion exceeds water depletion. This is common—don't worsen the dehydration by fluid restricting these patients!

Drugs and hyponatraemia
- Most commonly diuretics (especially in high dose or combination), SSRIs, carbamazepine, NSAIDs.
- Other drugs include opiates, other antidepressants (MAOIs, TCAs), other anticonvulsants e.g. valproate, oral hypoglycaemics (sulphonylureas e.g., chlorpropamide, glipizide) and barbiturates.
- Combinations of drugs (e.g. diuretic and SSRI) are especially likely to cause hyponatraemia.

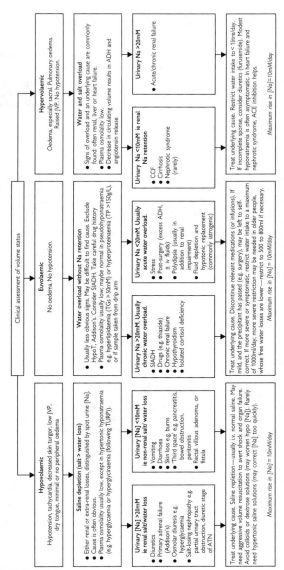

Fig 14.1 Hyponatraemia: aetiology and treatment

Syndrome of inappropriate ADH

Definition
Less than maximally dilute (ie inappropriately concentrated) urine in the presence of subclinical excess body water.

▶▶ Syndrome of inappropriate antidiuretic hormone secretion (SIADH) is massively over-diagnosed, especially in older people, leading to inappropriate fluid restriction. Consider it a diagnosis of exclusion—drugs or organ impairment cause a similar clinical syndrome.

Diagnosis
Essential features include:
- Hypotonic hyponatraemia ([Na]<125mM and plasma osmolarity <260mOsm/L).
- Normal volume status ie euvolaemia—there is slight water overload, but not clinically identifiable.
- Normal renal, thyroid, hepatic, cardiac, and adrenal function.
- Inappropriately concentrated, salty urine: osmolarity >200mOsm/L and [Na]>20mM.
- No diuretics, or ADH-modulating drugs (opiates, anticonvulsants, antidepressants, NSAIDs, barbiturates, and oral hypoglycaemics). Drug effects may take days or weeks to diminish.

Causes
Common causes include:
- Surgical stress
- Neoplasms (especially bronchogenic, pancreatic)
- CNS disease (especially trauma, subdural haematoma, stroke, meningo-encephalitis)
- Lung disease (TB, pneumonia, bronchiectasis).

Treatment
- Treat underlying cause.
- If mild, and the precipitant has passed (e.g. surgery), may be left to self-correct.
- If more severe and/or symptomatic, restrict water intake to a maximum of 1000ml/day; more severe restriction may restriction may be needed in older people, whose free water losses are lower—restrict to 500 to 800ml if necessary.

HOW TO... do a short ACTH stimulation test (short Synacthen® test)

The diagnosis of adrenocortical insufficiency is made when the adrenal cortex is found not to synthesize cortisol despite adequate stimulation. Within 30 minutes of ACTH stimulation, the normal adrenal releases several times its basal cortisol output.

Performing the test
- The test can be done at any time of day.
- Take blood for baseline cortisol. Label tube with patient identifiers and time taken.
- Give 250 mcg Synacthen® (synthetic ACTH, 1–24 amino acid sequence). Give intravenously if intravenous access is present; otherwise im.
- 30 minutes after injection, take more blood for cortisol. Label tube with patient identifiers and time taken.

Interpreting the test

A normal response meets three criteria:
- Baseline cortisol level > 150nmol/L
- 30 minute cortisol > 500nmol/L
- 30 minute cortisol greater than baseline cortisol by 200nmol/L or more.

The absolute 30 minute cortisol carries more significance than the baseline −30 minute increment, especially in patients who are stressed (ill) and at maximal adrenal output.

A normal Synacthen® test excludes Addison's disease. If the test is not normal:
- Consider further tests such as the prolonged ACTH stimulation test, usually after specialist advice, e.g.:
  - ACTH level (elevated in primary, and low in secondary hypoadrenalism).
  - The prolonged ACTH stimulation test.
- If the patient is very unwell, give hydrocortisone 100mg iv pending confirmation of hypoadrenalism.

Hypernatraemia

Causes

- Usually due to true 'dehydration' i.e. water loss > sodium loss.
- Not enough water in, or too much water out, or a combination e.g. poor oral intake, diarrhoea, vomiting, diuretics, uncontrolled diabetes mellitus.
- Rarely due to salt excess—iatrogenic (iv or po), psychogenic or malicious (poisoning).
- Very rarely due to diabetes insipidus (urine osmolarity low) or mineralocorticoid excess (Conn's).

Commonly seen in septic older people: increased losses (sweating) + reduced oral intake + reduced renal concentrating (water conserving) mechanism.

Clinical features

- Hypotension (supine and/or orthostatic)
- Sunken features
- Urine scanty and concentrated
- Lethargy, confusion, coma, and fits.

Tests

Urea and creatinine are often high, but may be in the high normal range; the patient is still water-depleted. Haemoglobin and albumin often high (haemoconcentration), correcting with treatment.

Treatment

- Encourage oral fluid.
- Usually intravenous fluid is required; rarely subcutaneous fluid will be sufficient.
- Fluid infusion rates should not be too cautious: e.g. 3–4 litres/24 hours is reasonable, guided by clinical and biochemical response. Too rapid infusions risk cerebral oedema, especially in the more chronically hypernatraemic patient.
- Ensure the patient becomes clinically euvolaemic as well as normo-natraemic: most dehydrated patients have a normal [Na], and [Na] will correct into the normal range before the patient is fully hydrated.
- Many patients are Na-deplete as well as water-deplete; therefore consider alternating normal saline with 5% dextrose infusions.

Hypothermia: diagnosis

A common medical emergency in older people, occurring both in and out of hospital.

Definition
- Core temperature <35°C, but <35.5°C is probably abnormal.
- Mild: 32–35°C, moderate: 30–32°C, severe: <30°C.
- Fatality is high and correlates with severity of associated illness.

Causes
- Cold exposure (clothing, defective temperature discrimination, climate, poverty).
- Defective homeostasis (failure of autonomic nervous system-induced shivering and vasoconstriction; decreased muscle mass).
- Illness (drugs, fall, pneumonia).

In established hypothermia, thermoregulation is further impaired and is effectively poikilothermic (temperature varies with environment).

▶▶ Hypothermia is a common presentation of sepsis in hospital in older people, and probably an indicator of poor prognosis. Don't ignore the temperature chart.

Diagnosis
Rectal temperature is the gold standard but well-taken oral or tympanic temperature will suffice.

Ensure the thermometer range includes low temperatures (mercury-in-glass thermometer range usually 34–42°C, thereby underestimating severity in all but the mildest cases).

Presentation
Often insidious and non-specific. Multiple systems affected.
- *Skin* May be cold to touch (paradoxically warm if defective vasoconstriction). Shivering is unusual (this occurs early in the cooling process). There may be increased muscle tone, skin oedema, erythema or bullae.
- *Nervous system* Signs can mimic stroke with falls, unsteadiness, weakness, slow speech and ataxia. Reflexes may be depressed or exaggerated with abnormal plantar response and dilated sluggish pupils. Conscious level ranges from confused/sleepy to coma. Seizures and focal signs can occur.
- *Cardiovascular system*:
  - Initially vasoconstriction, hypertension and tachycardia.
  - Then myocardial suppression, hypotension, sinus bradycardia.
  - Eventually extreme bradycardia, bradypnoea and hypotension. May lead to false diagnosis of death, however, the protective effect of cold on vital organs means survival may be possible.
  - Dysrhythmias include atrial fibrillation (early), ventricular fibrillation, and asystole (late).

- *Renal* There is early diuresis with later oliguria and acute tubular necrosis.
- *Respiratory* Respiratory depression and cough suppression occur with secondary atelectasis and pneumonia. Pulmonary oedema and ARDS occur late.
- *Gastrointestinal* Hypomotility may lead to ileus, gastric dilation and vomiting. Hepatic metabolism is reduced (including of drugs). There is a risk of pancreatitis with hypo- or hyper-glycaemia.
- *Other* DIC and rhabdomyolysis.

Investigations

- FBC, ESR
- U, C+E
- Glucose
- Amylase
- CRP

- LFT
- TFT
- Blood culture
- Drug/toxin screen
- CXR.

CK, urinalysis This may show rhabdomyolysis.

ABG Looking for metabolic and respiratory acidosis, lactate acidosis. Do not correct for temperature.

ECG Abnormalities include prolonged PR interval, J waves (peak between QRS and T in leads V4-6) at <30°C and dysrhythmia.

Serum cortisol Consider if there are features of hypoadrenalism or hypothermia is unexplained or recurrent.

▶▶ It is important to repeat key investigations during rewarming e.g. U, C+E, ECG, and ABG.

Hypothermia: management

Monitoring

Regular blood pressure, pulse, temperature, respiratory rate, oxygen saturation, glucose; continuous ECG; consider urinary catheter. Consider ITU.

Treatment principles

- The features of severe hypothermia may mimic those of death. In these cases, begin resuscitation whilst gathering information that permits a decision as to whether further intervention is likely to be futile or else not in the patient's interests. Stop resuscitation according to clinical judgment; generally don't declare dead until re-warmed, or re-warming fails.
- System support: maintain airway, ventilate as necessary. Good iv access. Warm iv fluid: may need large volumes as warming causes vasodilatation. Treat organ dysfunction as appropriate. Cardiac pacing is indicated only if the bradycardia is disproportionate to the reduced metabolic rate.
- If severe, or multiple organ failure, consider ITU. Handle carefully—rough handling and procedures (including intubation) may precipitate VF.
- Rewarming: rate should approximate that of onset (0.5–1°C per hour if not critically unwell). Caution, as rewarming may lead to hypotension. A combination of the following modalities is usually sufficient:
  - Passive external: surround with dry clothes, blankets/space blankets.
  - Active external: hot air blanket ('Bair Hugger™'), hot water bottle, bath.
  - Active internal: heated oxygen, fluid and food.

Sudden, severe hypothermia ± cardiac arrest (e.g. due to water immersion) is uncommon in older people. If it occurs, manage in the usual way with rapid, invasive rewarming, supported by ITU.

Drug treatment

Consider:
- Empirical antibiotics (most have evidence of infection on careful serial assessment)
- Adrenal insufficiency (Rx hydrocortisone 100mg qds)
- Hypothyroidism (Rx liothyronine 50mcg then 25mcg tds IV, always with hydrocortisone)
- Thiamine deficiency (malnourished or alcoholic) (B vitamins oral or iv) (as Pabrinex®).

Drug metabolism is reduced, and accumulation can occur. Efficacy at the site of action is also reduced. Exercise caution with sc/im drugs (including insulin) that may accumulate and be mobilized rapidly as perfusion improves.

Prevention

Before discharge, establish why this episode occurred—is recurrence likely? (consider housing, cognition, hypoglycaemia, sepsis, etc.). Consider how further episodes may be prevented, or terminated early.

Heat-related illness

An important cause of morbidity and mortality in older people, but the risk is much less appreciated than that of hypothermia. The contribution of heat stress to death is rarely mentioned on death certificates, but epidemiological studies indicate significant excess morbidity and mortality during extended periods of unaccustomed hot weather (e.g. France 2003: 15,000 excess deaths). There is an increased incidence of acute cerebrovascular, respiratory and, especially, cardiovascular disease.

Risk factors
- Consider older people as being relatively poikilothermic ie, lacking close control of body temperature in some circumstances. Homeostasis is weakened due to raised sweating threshold, reduced sweat volume, altered vasomotor control and behavioural factors (e.g. lessened sensation of temperature extremes).
- Climate: high temperature, high radiant heat (sitting in sunshine, indoors or out), high humidity.
- Drugs: e.g. diuretics, anticholinergics, psychotropics.
- Comorbidity: frailty, cerebrovascular, and cardiovascular diease.

A spectrum of illness
The presentation is usually different in older people, typically occurring not after extreme exertion, but during heatwaves in temperate zones.
- *Prickly heat ('miliaria')*: itchy, erythematous, papular rash. Rx: cool, wash, antihistamines.
- *Heat oedema*: peripheral oedema, usually self-limiting.
- *Heat syncope*: increased syncope risk due to fluid depletion and vasodilation.
- *Heat exhaustion* is a potentially catastrophic illness. Dehydration and heat stress leads to non-specific presentation with collapse, immobility, weakness, vomiting, dizziness, headache, fever, and tachycardia. However, treatment should result in rapid improvement.
- *Heat Stroke* occurs when untreated heat exhaustion progresses to its end-stage (hyperthermic thermoregulatory failure). Core temperature is generally >40°C, mental state is altered (confusion → coma), circulatory and other organ failure is common, and sweating is often absent. CNS changes may be persistent and severe. Prognosis reflects pre-existing comorbidity, severity and complications, and is often poor.

Management
- *Individual response*. Emergency inpatient treatment required. Identify and reverse precipitants. Cool rapidly until temperature 38–39°C—fan, tepid sponging, remove clothing. Close monitoring (temperature, BP, P, saturation, urine output); consider CVP. Cool iv fluids according to assessment of fluid/electrolyte status.
- *Community response*. Local environment modification—fans, air conditioning, shade windows, open windows at night, seek cooler areas, avoid exercise, maintain or increase cool fluid intake, light/loose clothing. Education of patient and carers. Governments should have public health measures in place to reduce the impact of heatwaves.

HOW TO... monitor temperature

No method is absolutely precise.
- Traditional mercury-in-glass thermometers are now rarely used in hospital, replaced due to risks to patients, staff and public.
- Digital electronic and infrared thermometers can provide reliable results when used correctly and in accordance with manufacturer's instructions.
- Thermochromic (forehead) thermometers are imprecise, although they may be useful for screening or with uncooperative patients.

Digital electronic thermometers

These may permit oral, axillary, or rectal measurement. They typically require a small (1 to 2 seconds) period of equilibration, and a degree of patient compliance.

Infrared ('tympanic') thermometers

These measure the temperature of tissue within and close to the eardrum, returning a value rapidly. Ensure that the earlobe is gently pulled posteriorly and superiorly, straightening the external ear canal, before inserting the probe fairly firmly.

Ear wax has only a slight effect, reducing measured temperature by <0.5°C.

Note that tympanic thermometers may offer a choice of displaying temperature as either 'true tympanic' or the derived value 'oral equivalent'. Ensure that you are familiar with the thermomometers in use in your hospital and what output they give: tympanic or 'oral equivalent'.

Measurement in practice

- Precise temperature measurement is fundamental in detecting and monitoring disease.
- Fever may be due to to infection, malignancy, inflammation, connective tissue disease, or drugs.
- A reduced or absent fever response to sepsis is seen in some elderly patients. Do not dismiss modest fever (<37.5°C) as insignificant, or rule out infection because the patient is afebrile.
- Hypothermia occurs inside and outside hospital, and may be missed unless thermometers with an appropriate range (30–40°C) are used.
- Temperature varies continuously: lowest in peripheral skin, highest in the central vessels and brain. No site is truly representative of 'core' temperature. Typically, when compared to oral temperature, axillary temperatures are 1.0°C lower, and rectal and tympanic temperatures 0.5–1.0°C higher (but see notes on tympanic thermometry, above).
- Where clinical suspicion is high, make measurements yourself, complementing monitoring by nursing staff. Body temperature changes continuously, and a fever may manifest only after the patient has rewarmed following a cooling ambulance journey.
- The hand on the forehead to assess core temperature (and on the palm of the hand, to determine peripheral vasodilation) is of value in screening for sepsis, and can be incorporated into daily rounds without time penalty.

Endocrinology

The ageing endocrine system 452
Diabetes mellitus 454
  How to… diagnose diabetes in older people 455
Diabetes: treatment 456
Diabetes: oral drug treatment 458
  How to… manage older diabetic people in care homes 459
Diabetes: insulin treatment 460
Diabetes: complications 462
Diabetic emergencies 464
  How to… manage diabetes in the terminally ill patient 466
Hypothyroidism: diagnosis 468
Hypothyroidism: treatment 470
Hyperthyroidism: diagnosis 472
Hyperthyroidism: investigation 474
Hyperthyroidism: drug treatment 476
Hyperthyroidism: non-drug treatment 478
Primary adrenal insufficiency 480
Adrenal 'incidentalomas' 482
Hormone replacement therapy (HRT) and the menopause 484

The ageing endocrine system

Ageing and thyroid function

Normal thyroid function is preserved in healthy older people. Median thyroid stimulating hormone (TSH) levels drift upwards very slowly with age, but remain within normal limits in the absence of disease. Lower triiodothyronine (T3) and TSH levels seen in institutionalized older people and in very advanced old age (>95 years) are probably due to illness.

Sick euthyroid syndrome

- TFTs are often abnormal in euthyroid patients who are ill with non–thyroid systemic disease.
- Changes depend on illness severity, and when TFTs are checked (during acute illness or recovery).
- TSH secretion decreases early in the illness. Falls in levothyroxine (T4) and (especially) T3 may follow, the result of reduced TSH, lower thyroid hormone binding and reduced peripheral T4 → T3 conversion.
- Changes are more likely due to true hypothyroidism if
  - Free T4 levels are low.
  - Changes are severe.
- Secondary hypothyroidism (due to hypothalamo-pituitary failure) causes a similar pattern of TFTs, but is very much less common, and other features of pituitary failure are present (e.g. hypogonadism)
- In the convalescent phase following illness, TSH may be elevated as low thyroid hormone levels drive TSH production. For a time, TSH may be high and T4/T3 low, mimicking primary hypothyroidism. TFTs repeated a few weeks later are usually normal.

Ageing and glucose metabolism

In older people:
- Glucose-induced insulin release is delayed and reduced in size.
- Insulin-induced suppression of hepatic glucose production is delayed.
- Insulin-mediated peripheral (muscle and fat) glucose uptake is reduced.

In addition to reductions in physical activity and lean muscle mass, the above factors lead to higher frequency of impaired glucose tolerance (IGT) with age. IGT is associated with macrovascular disease but not with specific diabetic complications. A minority of people with IGT progress to diabetes.

Diabetes mellitus

Diabetes is much more common with age: about 40% of new diagnoses are in people over 65. Prevalence in people over 65 is 20% in the UK, up to 50% in some ethnic groups and the obese.

Comparing type 1 and type 2 diabetes

- Both type 1 (insulin-dependent; IDDM) and type 2 (non-insulin-dependent; NIDDM) diabetes can occur in older people. The onset of type 2 is much more common.
- In overweight older people, diabetes is mostly due to peripheral tissue insulin resistance (type 2). Glucose-induced insulin release is normal.
- Lean older people with diabetes often have impaired insulin release and may have islet cell antibodies more typical of type 1 diabetes. They respond poorly to oral hypoglycaemics.
- There are increasing numbers of older people with type 1 diabetes who developed diabetes in early or mid-life and have survived decades on insulin, sometimes with no or few complications.
- Many people with type 2 diabetes progress to require insulin to achieve acceptable glycaemic control. This group is insulin-requiring (hence IRDM) and are unlikely to develop ketoacidosis if insulin is withdrawn.
- When assessing a patient on insulin, determine whether they are insulin-dependent (type 1; must always have background insulin infused) or insulin-requiring (type 2; in which insulin may safely be withheld for a time, without risk of ketosis).

Secondary diabetes

More common in older people. Causes include:
- Drugs. Often steroids, sometimes high dose thiazides, rarely other drugs.
- Pancreatic disease e.g. chronic pancreatitis.
- Other endocrine disease e.g. Cushing's, hyperthyroidism.

Presentation

- Diabetes often presents atypically or late in older people.
- Up to 50% of older people with diabetes are undiagnosed. This is at least partly due to physiological age-related changes, e.g. the renal threshold for glucose increases (glucosuria and polyuria occur later) and the thirst mechanism is impaired (polydipsia occurs later).
- The diagnosis is often made by screening blood or urine tests, or during intercurrent illness.
- Think of diabetes in many clinical circumstances e.g. coma, delirium, systemic stress (e.g. pneumonia), oral or vaginal thrush (candida), vulval itch (subclinical candida), cellulitis (and necrotizing fasciitis), weight loss, urinary incontinence, polyuria, malaise, vascular disease, or peripheral neuropathy.
- Steroid administration may reveal a diabetic tendency—always monitor, especially when high doses are used.

HOW TO... diagnose diabetes in older people

- Confirm the diagnosis with a random blood sugar or fasting blood sugar. Criteria are the same as for younger patients (see below).
- In general, the diagnosis is confirmed with a second measurement, unless the diagnosis is clear (e.g. severe hyperglycaemia with metabolic decompensation).
- In some older diabetic people, fasting sugars may be normal. This is more common in lean older people, who have only postprandial hyperglycaemia. If in doubt, do an oral glucose tolerance test
- Elevated glycosylated haemoglobin (HbA_{1c}) levels are only moderately specific and sensitive to diabetes and are not sufficient either to confirm or to exclude the diagnosis. HbA_{1c} is helpful in monitoring established disease.
- Screen annually in those with risk factors (e.g. family history, obesity), at least every three years in those without.

Diagnostic criteria
At least one of the following criteria must apply:
- Symptoms + **random plasma glucose** >11.1mmol.
- **Fasting plasma glucose** >7.0mmol.
- 2-hour plasma glucose >11.1 mmol during **oral glucose tolerance test** (75g anhydrous glucose or the equivalent volume of a proprietary glucose drink such as Lucozade®).

Obtaining a fasting blood sugar
- Give the completed request card to the patient.
- The patient should make an early morning appointment with a phlebotomist or GP practice nurse.
- There must be no caloric intake for at least eight hours before the blood test.
  - Tell the patient to go for the blood test before breakfast.
  - Clear fluids (water; tea or coffee without milk or sugar) may be taken.
  - Other beverages or food must be avoided.

Diabetes: treatment

- In all patients, aim to avoid symptoms of hyperglycaemia.
- In the more robust older patient, good glycaemic control probably reduces complication rates:
  - Aim for HbA_{1c} levels close to normal (6.5–7.5%) and fasting sugar of 5–7mmol.
- The frail, and the very old (>80 years) have not been included in most prospective treatment studies. There is therefore doubt whether tight glycaemic control improves long-term outcome. Shorter-term benefits may include improved cognition, functional status, mood, and vitality.
  - Balance the potential benefits of tight control with the risk of drug-induced symptomatic hypoglycaemia, falls, and fractures.
  - Symptoms of hypoglycaemia may go unrecognised or be considered an ageing change by carers.
  - Reasonable targets for the frail are HbA_{1c} 7.5–8.5% and fasting sugar 7–10mM.
  - Vulnerable older patients are probably at higher risk of hypoglycaemia (e.g. causing confusion and falls) than hyperglycaemia. In some circumstances (e.g. where glucose levels appear very variable) it may be safest to accept very high ceiling levels (e.g. up to 20mM).

▶▶ In general, in frail older people, the approach is to reduce symptoms, not to normalize sugars.

Diet

- Dietary change is often the only treatment needed in obese people with type 2 diabetes.
- Wholesale changes to diet may not be accepted, but even small changes are worthwhile and on their own can result in much increased insulin sensitivity within weeks.
- Full compliance may not be possible for the functionally or cognitively impaired, but an experienced dietician or nurse working with the patient and family is usually effective.
- Severe dietary restrictions are often not appropriate, especially for the very old or very frail.
- Beware the strict diet that takes enjoyment from (the last months of) life whilst giving little back.

Education

- Educate family, carers, and nursing home staff continually.
- Provide simple written information and instructions.
- The approach must be tailored to the individual, taking note of cognitive and sensory impairments.

Other interventions

- Exercise, especially endurance exercise (e.g. walking, cycling) improves insulin sensitivity.
- Weight loss. Even modest reductions are beneficial.
- Reduction of other vascular risk factors, including smoking.
- Home or pendant alarm systems.

Disease surveillance

Patients should be reviewed at least annually. In the very frail or dependent, regular reviews remain vital, e.g. to ensure that treatments remain appropriate and that adverse effects have not occurred.

- Assess diet/drug concordance.
- Check weight.
- Optimize cardiovascular risk factors including blood pressure and lipids.
- Assess glycaemic control.
- Blood glucose testing, supplemented by 6-monthly HbA$_{1c}$ estimation is the preferred method.
- Urine glucose testing is less reliable, due to increased renal glucose threshold.
- Examine for evidence of complications, including microalbuminuria, an early sign of nephropathy.
- Check feet and advise on their care (see pp536–8).

▶▶ Utilize the advice and support of nursing staff with specialist knowledge of diabetes—either Community Nurses with a special interest, or dedicated Diabetes Specialist Nurses.

Diabetes: oral drug treatment

Sulphonylureas e.g. gliclazide (start at 40mg od)
- Commonly used as first-line drug therapy in lean elderly patients (where impairment in insulin release predominates).
- Can cause hypoglycaemia. This is uncommon if short-acting agents (gliclazide, glipizide, tolbutamide) are used. Avoid long-acting drugs (chlorpropamide, glibenclamide) which can cause prolonged and damaging hypoglycaemia. In patients taking these (often for years without problems), consider a switch to shorter-acting drugs.
- Commonly cause weight gain.

Biguanides e.g. metformin (start at 500mg od)
- Commonly used as first-line drug therapy in obese (BMI > 25) elderly patients (where insulin resistance predominates).
- Do not cause hypoglycaemia.
- Common side effects are nausea, diarrhoea, anorexia, and weight loss. These are less common if the drug is introduced slowly (500mg od, increased incrementally each week to max. 850mg tds).
- Can cause lactic acidosis in patients with hepatic or renal impairment, or where tissue hypoxia increases lactate production.
  - Do not use in patients with renal impairment (creatinine > 130 µmol/L; have a lower threshold in women and those with low muscle mass), hepatic impairment, or heart failure (even if treated). Age itself is not a contraindication.
  - Stop in acutely unwell patients (especially with sepsis, respiratory failure, heart failure, or myocardial infarction).
  - Discontinue before anaesthesia or the administration of radiographic contrast media, restarting if/when renal function normalizes.

Alpha-glucosidase inhibitors e.g. acarbose (start with 25mg bd twice daily, taken with the first mouthful of food)
- Only moderately effective (HbA_{1c} reduction 0.5–1%), either as first-line or add-on therapy. Despite modest potency and side effects, they have a place, and may e.g. help delay or avoid the need for insulin.
- GI side effects (flatulence, bloating, diarrhoea) usually settle with time and are less severe if the dose begins low and is increased slowly.
- There are no severe side effects. Hypoglycaemia is never a problem.

Thiazolidinediones e.g. rosiglitazone (start with 4mg od)
- Recently developed, they appear effective in older people, and do not cause hypoglycaemia. May be used:
  - As monotherapy, if intolerant of sulphonylureas and biguanides.
  - In combination with either a sulphonylurea or biguanide if control with that combination has been unsatisfactory.
  - Rarely, as part of triple therapy (combination of sulphonylurea, biguanide, and thiazolidinedione) to avoid introducing insulin.
- Liver function tests must be monitored. Stop if dysfunction occurs.
- Can be used in mild/moderate renal failure. Avoid in heart failure.

HOW TO... **manage older diabetic people in care homes**

In care homes

- The prevalence of diabetes is very high.
- Individual diabetic patients are at great risk of complications.
- Hypoglycaemia and other medication side effects are frequent.

To enhance quality of care

- Every resident should be screened for diabetes on admission to the home and each year thereafter. Blood sampling is far more sensitive than urinalysis.
- Every resident with diabetes should have an individual care plan including at least: diet, medications, glycaemic targets and monitoring schedule. Monitoring should be varied in time (pre-/post-prandial; breakfast, lunch, evening meal, late evening), to provide a more complete picture of glycaemic control.
- An annual diabetes review should be performed by either a nurse with specialist training in diabetes, a general practitioner or a specialist (geriatrician or diabetologist).
- An annual ophthalmic screening assessment should be performed. Rarely, domiciliary screening is available. Usually, the resident will need to leave the home, to attend a specialist screening centre, but this is usually worthwhile, as vision contributes significantly to quality of life.
- There should be easy access to specialist services including podiatry, optometry, diabetic foot clinic, dietetics, and diabetes specialist nursing.
- Each home with diabetic residents should have a diabetes care policy. Staff should have received training in the identification and treatment of diabetic emergencies and the prevention of complications.

Diabetes: insulin treatment

- Insulin is essential for the treatment of type 1 diabetes.
- Insulin is started in type 2 diabetes when oral agents fail to achieve adequate control, if hyperglycaemia is severe (especially if the patient is lean, and insulin deficiency likely), if a patient is unwell and if oral drugs are contraindicated (e.g. hepatorenal impairment).
- Side effects include:
  - **Weight gain.** Common. Lessened if an oral drug (especially metformin) is co-prescribed.
  - **Hypoglycaemia.** Much more common with insulin than with any oral agent.

Insulin regimes

- In general, use twice-daily insulin injections. Use either pre-mixed insulins (e.g. Mixtard® 30 or Humulin® M3; 30% fast-acting and 70% long-acting) or an intermediate-/long-acting insulin alone (e.g. Monotard®, Ultratard®).
- Consider long-acting insulin once daily (a.m.), perhaps supplemented by oral hypoglycaemics during the day.
- Very long-acting insulins (insulin glargine and insulin detemir) are effective if given just once daily, and are helpful in those who:
  - Require assistance (relative, nurse) with injections.
  - Are frequently hypoglycaemic on other regimes, especially at night.
  - Would otherwise need twice-daily insulin injections plus oral drugs.
- If eating is very erratic, consider giving short-acting insulin after each meal based on what has been eaten—a simple sliding scale.
- Regimes based on rapid-acting insulin alone or a basal-bolus structure (the mainstay of management in younger type 1 diabetics; provide an insulin profile as close to health as possible), are rarely appropriate in older people unless lifestyle (meals and activity) are especially chaotic and the patient has the cognitive and physical ability to manage dosing.

Initiating insulin

- Involve the multi-disciplinary team. Insulin administration is very time-consuming for community nurses. Explore other options first.
- Patients may be very reluctant to begin, because of fears about injections, hypos, or learning new skills.
- Remember insulin administration issues: cognition, dexterity and vision.
- Pre-mixed insulins avoid having to draw up multiple types of insulin.
- Insulin pens make the measuring of doses much easier for patients, but syringes are more suitable when insulin is drawn up by a third party (relative or nurse).
- In disposable pens, the vial is pre-loaded. This is helpful for patients who are not so dexterous.
- Some patients are able to self-inject, but cannot safely draw up insulin into syringes or use an insulin pen. In this case, doses may be drawn up in syringes by relatives or community nurse, and stored in a refrigerator until needed.
- If insulin is given by a relative, what happens during family holidays?

Changing insulin requirements

Always consider whether your patient is on the correct insulin regime (type and dose).

- Earlier in the course of the disease, insulin requirements often rise as disease severity increases.
- In advanced old age, insulin requirements often fall as appetite declines, body weight drops and renal function deteriorates. Type 2 diabetics on insulin may get off insulin altogether. Stop insulin, maximize oral drug treatment and monitor regularly.

Further reading

Clinical Guidelines for Type 2 Diabetes Mellitus. European Diabetes Working Party for Older People. www.eugms.org/academic/guidelines.jsp

Diabetes: complications

In general, these are more common in older people, especially vascular complications. Evidence for risk reduction in the very old diabetic is weak. In practice, evidence from younger age groups is extrapolated to apply to older groups, except in the very frail and/or those with very poor life expectancy where a more conservative approach may be appropriate. Make an individual decision.

Vascular

A very common cause of morbidity and mortality. The risk of myocardial infarction is as high in diabetics without known coronary disease as it is in non-diabetics who have had an infarct.

- Improve glycaemic control to the extent that it is possible without inducing hypoglycaemia
- Treat hypertension if it is persistent despite lifestyle management.
  - Target blood pressure <140/<80mm Hg.
  - In the frail, target blood pressure <150/<90mm Hg.
  - The drug class used is less important than the reduction in blood pressure achieved. Beta-blockers are not contraindicated. ACE-inhibitors may have an important additional effect in preventing nephropathy.
- Treat hyperlipidaemia except in the very elderly and frail. Statins are well tolerated. The Heart Protection Study demonstrated benefit in diabetics with cholesterol >3.5mmol.
- Stop smoking. Health benefits begin in 3–6 months.
- Low dose aspirin should be offered to all older patients with diabetes (since 10-year coronary risk is >15%) unless there is a contraindication. Control hypertension beforehand.

▶▶ In older people, blood pressure control is as important as glycaemic control in reducing cardiovascular risk.

Neuropathy

This is more common in older diabetic people and is often asymptomatic although may contribute to falls (see pp124–5). Annual screening is necessary: check pinprick, vibration sense, light touch (nylon monofilament), and reflexes.

- Classically and most commonly a distal symmetrical polyneuropathy is seen. Consider other causes.
- Mononeuropathy is usually of sudden onset, asymmetrical and resolves over weeks or months. Often painful. May coexist with polyneuropathy. For example:
  - Third nerve palsy. Most common. Causes ophthalmoplegia.
  - Diabetic amyotrophy. Pelvic girdle and thigh muscle weakness and wasting. Difficulty rising from chair.
- Diabetic neuropathic cachexia. Painful peripheral neuropathy, depression, anorexia and weight loss.

Treatment of all the above is to exclude other causes, to optimise glycaemic control, to control pain and to support the patient through the illness, treating complications (e.g. depression) as they arise.

Nephropathy

A major problem in older diabetic people.

- Microalbuminuria indicates a group at high risk of progression. Treat hypertension aggressively (preferentially with ACE-inhibitors or angiotension-2 receptor antagonists), target BP 125/75 and optimise glycaemic control
- If renal function deteriorates rapidly, exclude papillary necrosis by obtaining emergency renal tract ultrasound

Eyes

Retinopathy, glaucoma, and cataract are common (see p624). All diabetic people should have annual screening ophthalmic assessment that includes retinal examination (fundoscopy via a dilated pupil) and visual acuity testing. This is usually provided by ophthalmic specialist clinics or by diabetologists (or other physicians) with particular expertise. Indications for urgent referral for specialist assessment include:

- Inadequacy of fundoscopic examination e.g. due to cataract.
- Diabetic maculopathy. Either exudates close (< 1 optic disc diameter) to the macula, or suspicion of macular oedema (nothing may be observed that is abnormal, but visual acuity is impaired).
- Preproliferative changes (many cotton wool spots, flame or blot haemorrhages, venous change (beading, loops)).
- Proliferative changes (pre-retinal or vitreous haemorrhage new vessels, retinal detachment).

▶▶ Preventing blindness depends on early diagnosis of diabetes, good glycaemic control, effective retinal screening and early treatment of maculopathy and retinopathy.

Ears

Malignant otitis externa, manifesting as severe ear pain, is more common in diabetes (see p665).

Teeth

Gum disease and caries are more common. Good oral hygiene and regular dental assessment are essential.

Feet

Neuropathy and vascular disease lead to infection, injury and ischaemia. Outcomes include pain, ulceration, immobility and amputation. Impeccable foot care is essential (see pp536–8).

Diabetic emergencies

Two presentations are especially common—hyperosmolar non-ketotic coma (HONK) and hypoglycaemia. However, older patients can present with any diabetic problem, including diabetic ketoacidosis (DKA).

Hyperosmolar non-ketotic coma

- A complication of type 2 diabetes, and may be the first presentation. Most common in older people.
- Often severe. Mortality is very high (10–20%).
- There is often underlying sepsis, particularly pneumonia. Leucocytosis is common, with or without infection. Have a low clinical threshold to beginning antibiotics, after blood and urine cultures.
- There is usually enough endogenous insulin to suppress ketogenesis but not hepatic glucose output. Therefore there is usually only a mild metabolic acidosis (pH > 7.3), and ketonaemia is absent or mild. Blood glucose is often very high (>30mmol).
- Subacute deterioration occurs. Impaired thirst and an impaired 'osmostat' contributing to severe dehydration with high serum osmolarity, hypernatraemia, and uraemia. The fluid deficit is often around 10 litres.
- Neurological problems are common and include delirium, coma, seizures, or focal signs e.g. hemiparesis. Only a small proportion are in coma.
- Treatment elements include:
  - *Fluid volume resuscitation.* Frequent and careful clinical assessment and fluid prescription is usually sufficient to determine rate and volume, but consider insertion of a central line in those with cardiac or renal disease or who are shocked. In general, fluid administration should be slower than in the younger patient with diabetic ketoacidosis. For the patient who is sick but not moribund, two litres in the first three hours and a total of three or four litres in the first 12 hours is often optimal. The exception is the shocked patient, where filling should be more aggressive, with the advice and support of Intensive Care colleagues if appropriate.
  - *Correction of electrolyte abnormalities.* Initially give normal saline. If plasma sodium is very high (>155mmol) consider giving half-normal saline if available, or 5% dextrose when sugars are under control (e.g. <12mmol). Maintain serum potassium in the range 4–5mmol. Give potassium with fluid even if the patient is normokalaemic, as patients are usually total body potassium-depleted, and insulin will drive potassium into cells. Hypokalaemia is a major cause of dysrhythmias and sudden cardiac death.
  - *Hyperglycaemia* often responds well to rehydration and treatment of an underlying cause (e.g. sepsis). Intravenous insulin is often needed, but modest doses (e.g. 1–3 units per hour) are usually enough. Patients with HONK are more insulin-sensitive than those with diabetic ketoacidosis.
  - *Thromboprophylaxis.* Full anticoagulation with low molecular weight heparin can be justified because the thromboembolic complication rate is very high.
  - *Pressure care.*

- Although mortality rates are high, many patients recover promptly. The severity of presentation does not correlate closely with the severity of underlying disease, and in some, the diabetes may subsequently be controlled with diet alone.

Hypoglycaemia

Risk of severe hypoglycaemia increases massively with age. In older people:
- The physiological response to hypoglycaemia is weaker (e.g. reduced glucagon secretion).
- Autonomic warning symptoms (e.g. sweating, tremor) are less marked.
- Psychomotor response may be slow, even if symptoms are recognized.

Other risk factors include frailty, comorbidity, renal impairment, care home residency, social isolation and previous hypoglycaemia.

Clinical features are often not recognized or are atypical:
- Check a sugar in any unwell known diabetic.
- Focal neurological signs or symptoms may be misdiagnosed as stroke. Signs may persist for some time after correction of blood sugar.
- Acute severe or chronic hypoglycaemia can cause a dementia-like syndrome.

Prevention
- Assess each patient's risk of hypoglycaemia, and individualize therapy.
- Balance the lifetime risk of hypoglycaemic attacks with reduction in long term complications.
- If altering medications, monitor sugars closely afterwards.
- Educate patient and carers about signs and symptoms, and the therapeutic response.
- Put in place alarm systems—pendant alarms, 'check' telephone calls, neighbour visits etc.
- Accept higher target glucose levels for those at high risk.

Treatment
- 'Hypos' can persist for hours or days and can recur late, especially if a long-acting insulin or oral drug is responsible. If severe, monitor closely (if necessary by admission) for two to three days.
- Post-event, explore why the 'hypo' occurred. How might the next be prevented, or better treated? Many patients have lost weight or appetite and require a substantially reduced hypoglycaemic prescription.

HOW TO... **manage diabetes in the terminally ill patient**

- This includes end-of-life situations in all disease, not just cancer.
- The sole aim of therapy is to minimize symptoms of hypo- and hyper-glycaemia.
- Ensure that family and carers understand the changed aims of treatment and the rationale for medication changes.
- Involve community nursing teams and diabetes specialist nursing teams early, particularly if you are planning a discharge from hospital to home.

Drug treatment

- As weight declines and oral intake falls, lower doses of insulin and oral drugs are usually needed.
- Dose reductions will also be needed as renal function declines.
- Make stepwise reductions in drug(s) and assess response.
- In some cases, drugs may be phased out completely. For example, type 2 patients on insulin may now manage on oral drugs alone; those on oral drugs may be asymptomatic off them.
- Type 1 patients require insulin until the very latest stages of dying (e.g. coma). Simplification of an insulin regime (e.g. a move to once daily insulin) is often helpful, and may allow a patient to be cared for at home.

Diet

Encourage food and fluid of whatever type is acceptable and attractive to the patient. Rigidly imposed diabetic diets are futile and unkind—it is usually better to encourage food of whatever type can be taken, and to accept the (usually modest) consequences for glycaemic control.

Blood glucose monitoring

- Monitoring should be tailored to the individual patient. In general, testing can be relaxed.
- In all cases, test if symptoms suggest hypo- or hyperglycaemia.
- In patients who are clinically stable (ie their condition is steady) or slowly deteriorating, testing can be infrequent (perhaps once on alternate days).
- In patients whose condition is deteriorating, or in those who have begun steroids, or where diabetes treatment has recently been changed, then testing should be more frequent.
- In the patient who is moribund or comatose due to terminal illness, testing is pointless.

Hypothyroidism: diagnosis

Common: up to 5% prevalence in older men, 15% in older women. Incidence increases with age.

Causes

Primary autoimmune disease (Hashimoto's disease, usually without goitre) is by far the most likely cause, unless iatrogenic causes are present (e.g. drugs (amiodarone, antithyroid drugs), previous hyperthyroidism treatment (radioiodine or surgery), head/neck radiotherapy).

Presentation

- Onset is usually insidious: over months, years or decades.
- Very variable presentation, often unmasked by intercurrent illness. In older people, symptoms and signs are more often mild and non-specific. None or all of the following may occur:
  - Hypothermia, cold intolerance
  - Dry skin, thinning hair
  - Weight gain or loss, constipation
  - Malaise
  - Falls, immobility, weakness, myalgia, arthralgia, elevated creatine kinase
  - Bradycardia, heart failure, pleural or pericardial effusion, non-pitting oedema (feet and hands)
  - Depression or cognitive slowing. Frank dementia is very rare
  - Hyporeflexia with delayed relaxation phase; ataxia or non-specific gait disturbance
  - Anaemia. Often normocytic; less commonly macrocytic or microcytic (reduced Fe absorption)
  - Hyponatraemia, hypercholesterolaemia, hypertriglyceridaemia.
- Symptoms of hypothyroidism are very common in the euthyroid older population. Often, only treatment reveals which symptoms were due to hypothyroidism.

Investigation

- *Have a low threshold* for thyroid function testing, in view of high disease incidence, poor sensitivity of clinical assessment alone, and the ease and effectiveness of treatment.
- *Opportunistic screening* of older people in primary care (e.g. at yearly health assessment) and secondary care (e.g. on presentation to acute medical take) is probably justified. But beware of abnormal TFTs due to sick euthyroid syndrome.
- *Overt primary (thyroid gland failure) hypothyroidism* is confirmed when TSH is high and free T4 low. TSH elevations may be less marked in older people.

- *Subclinical or 'compensated' hypothyroidism* is suggested when TSH is high, but free T4 is normal (although often towards the lower end of the normal range). T3 production from T4 is stimulated by TSH, so may be well maintained. The patient is often asymptomatic, but may have higher risks of atherosclerosis and myocardial infarction. Careful screening often reveals symptoms consistent with hypothyroidism.
- Thyroid masses are sometimes found on examination. USS will help characterize them.
- Anti-thyroid antibodies have reasonable sensitivity and specificity in confirming autoimmune hypothyroidism, and may help management in subclinical disease (see next page).

▶▶ Patients may be persistently lethargic despite successful treatment. Consider the presence of other autoimmune disease, e.g. coeliac disease, Addison's disease or pernicious anaemia.

Hypothyroidism: treatment

- *Overt (or 'clinical') hypothyroidism* should always be treated. The patient might believe themselves to be asymptomatic, but could feel much improved with treatment
- *Subclinical hypothyroidism* should be treated if there are symptoms. Consider treatment if:
  - TSH is particularly high, or free T3/T4 only just within normal limits.
  - Thyroid autoantibodies are positive (rate of transformation to overt hypothyroidism is much higher: ~25% compared with 5% per annum) or there is another autoimmune condition.

In other cases, monitor clinically and biochemically every 6–12 months, but have a low threshold for starting what is a very safe treatment.

Starting treatment

- Begin levothyroxine (T4) at low dose—usually 25mcg daily. More rapid initiation risks precipitating angina, insomnia, anxiety, diarrhoea, and tremor.
- Dosing is optimized biochemically—symptoms and signs alone are very misleading.
- Repeat TFTs monthly or six-weekly, increasing the dose of T4 in 25mcg increments.
- TSH levels guide dosage; T3 and T4 levels are not needed.
- Aim for a TSH in the mid-range of normal, say 1–3 mU/L.
  - Overtreatment (TSH too low) risks AF and osteoporosis.
  - Undertreatment risks physical and cognitive slowing, weakness and depression.
- Older people usually require slightly less T4—usually 50–125mcg daily is sufficient.
- Heavier people require proportionately more T4 than lighter people.
- T4 half life is around one week. Therefore, if fine-tuning of dosing is needed, simply alternate higher and lower doses, e.g. 100/125mcg on alternate days

Long-term management

- Tell the patient that treatment is for life.
- Check thyroid function every year and if clinically indicated.
- In the very long-term, thyroxine requirements may rise, fall or remain unchanged.

Administration

- Foods reduce absorption—take on an empty stomach, usually first thing in the morning.
- If a dose is missed, take it as soon as remembered, and the next dose as normal.
- If compliance is a problem, twice weekly or weekly administration (of proportionately higher doses) gives acceptable control.

Drug interactions
- *Antiepileptics* (phenytoin, primidone and carbamazepine), *barbiturates* and **rifampicin** increase thyroid hormone metabolism, so a higher T4 dose may be needed.
- *Colestyramine, iron, calcium, and antacids (e.g. aluminium hydroxide)* reduce T4 absorption. Give T4 at least two hours beforehand.
- *Amiodarone* has complex effects. Monitor TFTs regularly. See p153.
- *Beta-blockers* may reduce conversion of T4 to T3.
- As thyroid disease is controlled, dose changes of the following may be needed: *diabetic drugs (insulin and oral hypoglycaemics), digoxin, warfarin, theophylline, corticosteroids.*

Hyperthyroidism: diagnosis

Subclinical hyperthyroidism is more common in older people (prevalence 3%), but severe disease is less common (incidence 0.1% per year in older women, 0.01% per year in older men).

Causes

- **Toxic nodular goitre.** The most common cause in older people. There is often slow (years) progression from smooth goitre (euthyroid) to multinodular goitre (euthyroid). Then nodule(s) begin autonomous function, with subclinical and then clinical hyperthyroidism. It does not remit, but may be relatively mild and indolent.
- **Grave's disease.** The thyroid is stimulated by autoantibodies. Exophthalmos and diffuse goitre are less common than in younger people; no goitre is palpable in 40%. Many remit within a year, perhaps more so than in younger patients.
- **Exogenous levothyroxine**, i.e. overtreatment of hypothyroidism. This usually occurs insidiously when age-related slowing in T4 metabolism is not paralleled by reductions in the dose of T4.
- Less common causes include:
  - **Amiodarone** (see p152), and other sources of excess iodine.
  - **Subacute thyroiditis and Hashimoto's thyroiditis.** There is transient thyroid hormone excess due to gland destruction. Suspect if acute hyperthyroidism occurs with sore throat or tender neck. There may be an associated viral syndrome or upper respiratory tract infection.
  - **Single autonomous nodules** (Plummer's disease).
  - Malignant T4-secreting thyroid tumours and pituitary/non-pituitary TSH-secreting tumours.

▶▶ Distinguishing between the two very common causes (toxic nodular goitre and Grave's disease) is relatively unimportant, as treatment is similar. However, always consider the possibility of drugs (thyroxine or amiodarone) or acute thyroiditis, where treatment is clearly different.

Presentation

In older people with overt hyperthyroidism:
- Presentation may be more subtle, with fewer symptoms and signs.
- Diagnosis is often delayed. Features are attributed to comorbidity or suppressed by beta-blockers.
- 'Negative' symptoms may dominate ('apathetic hyperthyroidism') e.g. anorexia, weight loss, fatigue, weakness, and depression. Non-specific symptoms are more common e.g. nausea, weakness, functional decline.
- More classical symptoms of sympathetic overactivation may be absent e.g. tremor, restlessness, sweating, tachycardia, and hypertension.
- Cardiovascular complications are more common e.g. angina, heart failure, atrial fibrillation (although ventricular response may be slow).
- Constipation is more common than diarrhoea.
- Increased bone turnover leads to hypercalcaemia and osteoporosis.

Life-threatening thyroid emergencies

Thyroid storm

A rare but life-threatening manifestation of hyperthyroidism.

- Most commonly seen in patients with undiagnosed hyperthyroidism, often precipitated by non-thyroidal illness (including surgery, sepsis or trauma), or administration of iodine-containing drugs.
- Very rarely seen after radioiodine treatment.
- Features include delirium, restlessness, coma, fever, vomiting, heart failure, tachycardia, and myocardial ischaemia.
- The diagnosis is clinical—TFTs are no worse than in typical hyperthyroidism.
- Support failing organs, treat the underlying cause(s), and seek urgent specialist advice.
- Antithyroid drugs and iodide may be given intravenously to reduce thyroid hormone synthesis.
- Beta-blockers and corticosteroids reduce the peripheral activity of thyroid hormones.

Myxoedema coma

A rare but life-threatening manifestation of hypothyroidism.

- More common in older people, presenting as circulatory and respiratory failure, and progressive drowsiness leading to coma, often with fits.
- There is usually an acute precipitant (e.g. infection) in a patient with chronic hypothyroidism.
- Think of this also in patients who have stopped taking or absorbing levothyroxine.

Hyperthyroidism: investigation

Thyroid function tests

- Have a low threshold for testing in older people, especially if there is a personal or family history of thyroid disease.
- Screening is recommended by some—at least every five years in women over 60.
- Low TSH is sensitive but not specific to hyperthyroidism.
  - Drugs or non-thyroidal illness can suppress TSH below normal, but it usually remains detectable (0.1–0.5mU/L).
  - Very low TSH levels (<0.1mU/L), indicating total suppression of TSH secretion, are more specific to hyperthyroidism.
- *Overt hyperthyroidism.*
  - In most cases, TSH is undetectable and both T4 and T3 are high.
  - Elevated T3 without T4 ('T3 toxicosis') suggests toxic nodules or relapsing Grave's, and is treated as hyperthyroidism.
  - Elevated T4 but normal T3 (due to reduced peripheral conversion) suggests intercurrent illness.
  - In severe hyperthyroidism, T4 may be normal (reduced binding globulin). Free T4 remains high.
  - Acute systemic illness in euthyroid people may cause transient (days) elevation of T4. TSH will be normal or moderately low.
- *Subclinical hyperthyroidism.*
  - This is common: up to 5% point prevalence of decreased TSH in healthy older people. TSH levels are low, with normal (often high normal) free T3 and T4.
  - In most cases, TSH levels revert to normal within a year.
  - Progression to overt hyperthyroidism occurs in up to 10% per year.
  - Symptoms are few, but there is an increased risk of osteoporosis, atrial fibrillation, left ventricular hypertrophy, and possibly dementia.
  - Consider the possibility that non-thyroidal illness (rather than thyroid hormone excess) may be suppressing TSH production.

Anti-thyroid antibodies

- Their presence supports a diagnosis of Grave's disease, especially if a smooth goitre is also palpable, but they are not wholly specific.
- Antibody tests are usually negative in toxic nodular goitre.
- Grave's and toxic nodular goitre are both common and can coexist. In that case a nodular goitre may be palpable, with positive antibodies.
- If Grave's disease is likely, screen for pernicious anaemia and coeliac disease (using relevant autoantibody tests and vitamin B12 levels).

Thyroid radioisotope scanning

This can help confirm the cause of hyperthyroidism and to determine glandular size prior to radioiodine treatment.

- In thyroiditis, uptake is low or very low. Inflammatory markers are up.
- In Grave's, there is a diffuse pattern of increased uptake.
- In toxic nodular goitre, there are multiple 'hot' nodules with surrounding 'cold' tissue.
- A single autonomous 'hot' nodule is surrounded by 'cold' tissue.

Hyperthyroidism: drug treatment

Overt hyperthyroidism should always be treated, even if mild. Several options are available for immediate and long-term treatment. Select on an individual basis, depending on the likely diagnosis, severity of illness and patient characteristics and preferences.

Drug treatment: thioamides (carbimazole or propylthiouracil)

- Suitable for initial management of Grave's disease or toxic nodular goitre.
- In *Grave's disease* this is an option for long-term therapy, as there is a greater probability of long-term remission than in younger people. Duration of treatment is usually 18 months, after which treatment is stopped and regular monitoring continues. Relapse risk is ~50% and is more likely if disease is severe, there is a large goitre, or antibody levels are high. If relapse occurs, begin thioamides again, and refer for definitive treatment (usually radioiodine).
- In *toxic nodular goitre*, long-term remission is less commonly achieved using thioamides. They are therefore used either:
  - Short-term, to achieve euthyroidism prior to definitive treatment (usually radioiodine).
  - Long-term, in the frail patient in whom life expectancy is short.
- Initial daily dose: carbimazole 20–40mg, propylthiouracil 200–400mg (once daily or divided dose).
- Full thyroid suppression takes several weeks. Continue the initial dose for 4–8 weeks, until euthyroid. Base assessment on free T4 measurements each two weeks. TSH may be suppressed for months despite adequate treatment.
- Once control is achieved, there are two options, with similar outcomes:
  - *Titration regimen*. Thioamide dose is reduced gradually, guided by TFTs, to a maintenance dose of carbimazole 5–15 mg or propylthiouracil 50–150mg daily.
  - *Block and replace regimen*. Thioamide dose is maintained high, entirely switching off thyroid synthetic function. Introduce levothyroxine once free T4 is suppressed.
- Side effects include:
  - Skin rash or pruritus. Continue treatment. Try antihistamines. Try switching thioamides.
  - Fever, arthralgia, headache, and gastrointestinal symptoms are usually mild.
  - Agranulocytosis. This is uncommon, but more frequent in older people. Usually occurs early in treatment. Check FBC regularly. It is vital to advise patient and/or relative that the drug must be stopped and urgent advice sought if fever, sore throat, mouth ulcers, or other symptoms of infection develop.

Drug treatment: beta-blockers

Used for rapid symptomatic treatment (tremor, anxiety, angina) and to reduce the risk of dysrhythmia. There is no effect on the hypermetabolic state itself.

May be especially useful in those with known structural or ischaemic heart disease or who are tachycardic, but should be introduced cautiously, with regular monitoring. Digoxin is ineffective in controlling atrial fibrillation in hyperthyroidism.

Check carefully for contraindications (e.g. asthma).

All beta-blockers are effective. Atenolol is a good choice, as it may be given od. Metoprolol and propranolol must be given tds or qds (increased hepatic metabolism in hyperthyroidism).

They have a role:

- In Grave's or toxic nodular goitre as an adjunct to thioamides. Where hyperthyroidism is only mild, beta-blockers may be the only drugs needed prior to definitive treatment with radioiodine.
- In thyroiditis. The hyperthyroid state is transient, and beta-blockers alone may be sufficient treatment until the disease moves onto euthyroidism or hypothyroidism.

Subclinical hyperthyroidism

If due to excess T4 in a patient with treated hypothyroidism, reduce dose by 25mcg and recheck TFT in six weeks.

In other cases, in order to protect bone, heart and brain, consider treatment as for overt hyperthyroidism. This is especially indicated if:

- There is osteopaenia or heart disease, or significant risk factors.
- Suppressed TSH is persistent, or severe, or T3/4 levels are at the higher limits of normality.

If treatment is not begun, reassess every 3–6 months.

Atrial fibrillation and hyperthyroidism

Occurs in 10–15%. Most revert to sinus rhythm within weeks of becoming euthyroid, unless AF has been present for many months. Digoxin is usually ineffective in controlling ventricular rate. Beta-blockade is more effective.

Consider cardioversion if AF persists for 4 months in new-onset AF. Anticoagulate with warfarin to target INR 2–3. Whilst hyperthyroid, patients are relatively hypersensitive to warfarin.

See p296.

Amiodarone and thyroid disease

Incidence of amiodarone-induced thyroid disease is high in older people because of this cumulative exposure and the drug's very long half-life.

Clinical assessment alone is insensitive. Check TFTs before amiodarone treatment, and then every 3–6 months. If amiodarone is stopped, continue TFT monitoring for several years.

For the clinical features and management of amiodarone-induced hypo- and hyper-thyroidism, see p153.

Hyperthyroidism: non-drug treatment

Radioiodine (I^{131})

- Radioiodine is effective, well tolerated, safe and simply administered. The sole contraindications are:
  - When safe disposal of radioactive body fluids after treatment cannot be guaranteed (e.g. home drainage is not into the main sewer). This can usually be overcome.
  - In early treatment of hyperthyroidism, when administration of the iodine load can precipitate thyrotoxic crisis.
- Radioiodine is especially useful if there are drug intolerances, polypharmacy or comorbidities.
- Give once initial symptomatic control has been achieved with drugs.
- Thioamides must be stopped several days before administration of radioiodine (to permit uptake) and is usually restarted several days after (to prevent thyroid storm). Permanently discontinue thioamides after 3–4 months if TFTs are satisfactory.
- Estimating the dose of I^{131} required to render a patient euthyroid is difficult.
  - On average, larger doses are needed for patients with toxic nodular goitre (cf Grave's), larger goitres, in severe disease and in men.
  - Most centres give a single larger dose (400–600MBq) that controls hyperthyroidism in most cases, but leads to early hypothyroidism in up to 50%. A second dose is needed for a minority who remain hyperthyroid.
- Post-treatment, TFTs should be checked each 4–6 weeks for the first year, and then lifelong at reduced frequency but at least every year for life.
- Secondary hypothyroidism may occur early (weeks, often transient)) or late (years). Eventually up to 90% become hypothyroid. There may be an early (weeks) rise in TSH that is transient and does not need treatment if there are no symptoms.
- If the patient remains hyperthyroid at six months, then repeat I^{131} dosing is usually needed.

Surgery

This is rarely performed in older people, considered only if both drug and radioiodine treatment are problematic, or if a large goitre is especially troublesome. The patient must be euthyroid before surgery; beta-blockade alone is not sufficient. Lifelong post-operative thyroid function monitoring is essential.

Primary adrenal insufficiency

Presentation
Usually insidious and often non-specific onset:
- Symptoms include fatigue (helped by rest), weight loss, anorexia, abdominal pain, nausea, constipation, hypotension (orthostatic and supine), depression, delirium, and decreased functional status.
- Skin and mucous membrane hyperpigmentation is common, but is a late sign and may be absent. Pigmentation affects sun-exposed and unexposed areas, especially scars and pressure points.
- Electrolyte disturbance (hyponatraemia and hyperkalaemia) and a mild acidosis (bicarbonate 15–20mmol) are usual. Hypoglycaemia and mild anaemia may be present.

▶▶ In some people with impaired adrenocortical function, there may be no symptoms when well, but acute stress (trauma, illness, psychological) leads to adrenal crisis with shock.

Causes
- Mostly autoimmune. Often evidence of other autoimmune disease.
- TB is relatively more common in older people.
- Uncommonly due to: metastases, lymphoma, haemorrhage or infarction. Very rarely due to: drugs e.g. ketoconazole.

Diagnosis
If the possibility of adrenal insufficiency crosses your mind, then test for it, with a Synacthen® test.
- *Serum cortisol.* Cortisol is secreted episodically, so do not make or exclude a diagnosis on the basis of a single measurement.
  - A very low cortisol level (<100nmol) makes adrenal insufficiency likely, especially if the patient is stressed/unwell at the time.
  - A moderately high (>300nmol) cortisol level makes adrenal insufficiency unlikely.
  - In Addison's, a random cortisol may be low or normal ie normal level does not exclude Addison's.
  - Early morning (6–8am) cortisol levels should be higher—a low level is more likely to be significant.
- *Short ACTH stimulation test ('Synacthen® test').* The only test that has good sensitivity and specificity. See box on p441.
- *Adrenal autoantibodies* are positive in many autoimmune cases.
- *AXR and CXR* may show signs of TB (e.g. calcification).
- *Adrenal CT or MRI* reveals a small gland in autoimmune disease, large if infection or tumour.

If adrenal insufficiency is diagnosed, exclude secondary adrenal insufficiency (pituitary failure).
- Check *gonadotrophins* (FSH, LH) and *TSH.*
- *ACTH* is elevated in primary adrenal insufficiency, low in secondary.

Treatment
- If the patient is unwell, do not delay treatment pending the results of tests: fluid resuscitate with iv normal saline, normalize electrolytes and give high dose intravenous hydrocortisone (100mg iv tds). Improvement should occur quickly.
- Long-term treatment includes glucocorticoid (usually hydrocortisone 20mg am, 10mg pm) and mineralocorticoid (usually fludrocortisone 0.1mg)
- On treatment, older people are much more likely to develop hypertension that may require mineralocorticoid dose reduction and non-diuretic antihypertensive drugs.
- Older people have a worse prognosis, due to more sinister causation (TB, malignancy) and possibly later presentation.

Adrenal 'incidentalomas'

- An 'incidentaloma' is a tumour detected by scanning (ultrasound, CT, or MRI) that is unrelated to the indication for the scan.
- Adrenal incidentalomas are relatively common (0.5–1% of scans). They are more common in older people and the hypertensive. Key questions are 'is it malignant?' and 'is it functional?'.
- Adrenal insufficiency does not occur unless both glands are almost totally destroyed.
- Signs of a functional nodule include hypertension and hypokalaemia.

Adrenal adenomas are very common and usually small (< 2cm), benign and non-functional. Fine-needle biopsy helps exclude malignancy if scan appearances are worrying, but usually only observation (periodic scanning) is needed. The larger the tumour, the higher the chance of malignancy. Large tumours should generally be excised, as biopsy may not identify foci of malignancy.

Metastases are common (primary: breast, bronchus, bowel). Scan appearances are usually diagnostic.

Cysts and lipomas make up most of the remainder.

Benign adrenal cysts are common in older people and may be due to cystic degeneration or local infarction.

Tuberculosis may seed haematogenously, causing adrenal masses, often calcified.

Non-functional **adrenal carcinoma** usually presents late, with retroperitoneal spread and distant metastases.

Hormone replacement therapy (HRT) and the menopause

The menopause (cessation of menstruation due to ovarian failure) occurs typically between ages 45 and 55. The diagnosis can usually be made clinically. If the presentation is atypical, consider alternative diagnoses, e.g. hyperthyroidism. Following menopause, the risk of osteoporosis and vascular disease increases substantially. Symptoms can occur for several years before and after menopause and can be disabling. They include:

● Hot flushes
● Genitourinary atrophy
● Insomnia, depressed mood and cognitive symptoms.

HRT with oestrogen (plus progestogen in those with an intact uterus):

● Is an effective treatment for peri-menopausal symptoms.
● Does not improve well-being in those with no symptoms.
● Does not improve cognitive function or prevent dementia.
● Increases the risk of stroke, coronary events, pulmonary embolism and breast cancer. Increased risk (cumulative serious events) is 1 in 1000 if treated for one year, one in 100 if treated for five years.
● Reduces colon cancer and hip fracture by small amounts.

In those with menopausal symptoms:

● Consider non-systemic treatments, e.g. topical oestrogens for atrophic vaginitis (vaginal cream or tablets, given daily for 2 weeks, then once or twice weekly for 6–8 weeks; sometimes needed long-term). There is some systemic absorption; the risk of endometrial cancer is unknown. In those with reduced manual dexterity, consider a slow-release vaginal ring (replaced after 90 days).
● Other drugs that can help, but are less effective than systemic oestrogens include:
  • Progestogens e.g. medroxyprogesterone, megestrol.
  • Herbal remedies, some of which may have oestrogen-like activity
  • Clonidine (an alpha-adrenoceptor stimulant; usual dose 50–75mg bd) may reduce hot flushes. Side effects are often problematic. Watch blood pressure.
● If symptoms continue, discuss HRT, explaining the risks and benefits. Start treatment at low dose, increasing gradually until symptoms are controlled.
● Every few months, taper the dose of HRT, assessing whether ongoing treatment is needed. Hot flushes usually cease after a few months to a few (<5) years.

Increasing numbers of women have taken HRT for very prolonged periods and are being seen more frequently in geriatric practice. In each case, the risks and benefits of continuing HRT must be assessed. In most cases, the advice will be to stop HRT:

- Risk is probably cumulative (dose and duration).
- Risk is probably multiplicative (non-HRT risk × HRT-related risk). As background risk of cancer and vascular disease rises exponentially in older people, so the net added risk of HRT is higher in older people.
- In most cases, HRT may be withdrawn without recurrence of menopause symptoms.
- In most cases, HRT will have been started (and the patient last advised) when the risks were not appreciated.

▶▶ HRT is an effective treatment for symptoms, but has potentially serious side effects.

Further reading

Crawford F and Langhorne P, (2005). Time to review all the evidence for hormone replacement therapy. *BMJ* **330**: 345.

Haematology

The ageing haematopoietic system 488
Investigating anaemia in older people 490
Iron deficiency anaemia: diagnosis 492
    How to... investigate iron deficiency anaemia 493
Iron deficient anaemia: treatment 494
Macrocytic anaemia 496
Anaemia of chronic disease 498
Myelodysplasia and myelodysplastic syndrome 500
    How to... transfuse an older person 501
Chronic lymphocytic leukaemia 502
Paraproteinaemias 504
Multiple myeloma 506

The ageing haematopoietic system

There are very few changes as the bone marrow ages.

▶▶Be very reluctant to ascribe changes seen on testing to age alone—pathology is much more likely.

Haemoglobin

- Epidemiological studies show that population haemoglobin (Hb) concentration gradually declines from age 60.
- There is debate as to whether the reference range should be adjusted since lower Hb levels are associated with increased morbidity and mortality compared with older patients who maintain normal levels.
- Thus anaemia is common in old age (between 10–20% will have Hb less than 12g/dL in females or 13g/dL in males), but this is due to disease(s) not ageing per se.
- The decision about whether to investigate anaemia should be made not on the absolute value but the clinical scenario. Consider symptoms, past medical history, severity of anaemia, and rate of fall of Hb, the mean cell volume (MCV) and finally patient's wish/tolerance of investigation.
- A fit elderly man with no significant past history merits investigation with an Hb of 11.5g/dL (especially if his Hb g/dL was 13 last year or if the MCV is abnormal) while a patient with known rheumatoid arthritis, renal failure and heart failure who has a normocytic anaemia 10.5g/dL for years usually does not.

Erythrocyte sedimentation rate (ESR)

- The height of the red cells in a standard bottle of blood, after being allowed to sediment for 60min.
- This is a simple, old fashioned and non-specific test. However it is inexpensive and remains useful for screening and monitoring disease in older people.
- Red cells fall gradually because they are more dense, but the rate of fall increases where the cells clump together.
- This occurs in disorders associated with elevated plasma proteins (fibrinogen and globulins).
- ESR rises with age and is slightly higher in women so values up to 30mm/hr for men and 35mm/hr for women can be normal at age 70.
- Anaemia and numerous acute and chronic disorders can elevate ESR.
- Very high levels (>90) are commonly found with paraproteinaemias (p504), giant cell arteritis (p520) and chronic infections such as tuberculosis (p358).

Investigating anaemia in older people

A low hemoglobin is a frequently encountered abnormality in geriatric practice. It is worth remembering the following:

- Other parameters, usually documented in the full blood count report (e.g. MCV) will greatly assist in characterizing the anaemia, and should be scrutinised.
- Looking up old FBC results will often reveal a pattern e.g. a frail older person may run a chronically low Hb because of chronic disease or marrow failure. If there is a recent change, this should prompt more urgent investigation.
- Unwell older patients may have low Hb as a result of fluid overload or marrow suppression. Repeat FBC as they recover, and see if it persists.
- Dual pathology is common, so check a full range of blood tests in all anaemic older patients.
- It is very important to check that the laboratory have received the correct blood specimens for these tests before arranging blind replacement therapy or a transfusion—subsequent samples will be invalid for haematinics.

Most anaemic patients will require:
- Blood film
- Ferritin, serum iron and total iron binding capacity (or transferrin)
- B12, folate.

It is also usually worth doing:
- Renal, liver, and thyroid function tests
- If the ESR is raised check blood and urine electrophoresis and look for Bence–Jones proteins in urine.

Once the anaemia has been characterized (e.g. iron deficient, macrocytic etc.), then decisions can be made about the nature and extent of further testing. See following pages for details.

Iron deficiency anaemia: diagnosis

This is the commonest cause of microcytosis (but beware the occasional patient with lifelong microcytosis who has an inherited thalassamia or sideroblastic anaemia).

Causes
- Commonest is occult blood loss in the gut, especially in patients taking non-steroidal anti-inflammatory drugs (even 75mg aspirin).
- Malabsorbtion (e.g. coeliac disease, gastrectomy).
- Malnutrition is very unusual.

Diagnosis
History is vital (ask specifically about weight loss and gut, kidney, or ENT blood loss). Pallor (conjunctivae and nail beds) may be found. The emphasis of examination should be to find rectal or abdominal masses, hepatomegaly and lymphadenopathy, which could indicate a source of blood loss.

Investigations
- Microcytosis is usually found but can be absent in combined deficiency or with acute blood loss.
- Low serum ferritin levels (<12mgm/L) are diagnostic. Moderately low levels (12–45mgm/L) may also point to the diagnosis as ferritin levels rise with age. Ferritin is an acute phase reactant so normal/high levels don't rule out deficiency.
- Serum iron levels will be low with high iron binding capacity ie the ratio of iron/iron binding will be low (<15%). This is a useful way of distinguishing the anaemia of chronic disorder where both iron and iron binding are low (and the ratio will be normal).
- Low iron stores on a bone marrow trephine are diagnostic but this investigation is painful and rarely required.
- Faecal occult blood are of limited value in cases of established iron deficiency—they are usually positive and you may feel that further GI tests are needed anyhow.
- Haematuria sufficient to cause anaemia is rare, and usually severe. Urinalysis may be indicated in patients with poor vision or cognition to look for renal tract blood loss.
- Iron deficiency without anaemia should still be investigated but the lower the Hb the higher the likelihood of finding attributable pathology.

Characteristic findings in iron deficiency and chronic disease

Test	Iron deficiency	Chronic disease
MCV	Microcytic	Normocytic
Iron	Low	Often low
Transferrin or TIBC	Normal or high	Low
Iron: TIBC ratio	Low (<15%)	Normal
Ferritin	Low is diagnostic	Normal or high

HOW TO... investigate iron deficiency anaemia

The main dilemma is deciding how far to take investigations.

A **fit patient**, who would be a candidate for surgery, should have a minimum of OGD and barium enema or colonoscopy (this has higher rate of perforation in older people, and may be refused in some units). These should proceed regardless of the degree of anaemia and whether there are symptoms. The finding of oesophagitis or an upper GI ulcer should not stop a screening test for the colon to rule out a coexisting neoplasm. If these tests are negative, screen for coeliac disease (e.g. endomysial antibody) and haematuria. Small bowel barium studies are sometimes helpful. If there is intermittent overt GI blood loss mesenteric angiograms can demonstrate small angiodysplastic lesions.

At the other extreme a **frail, bed-bound, nursing home patient** with dementia will probably merit empirical iron and proton pump inhibitor therapy without further investigations.

In **between these extremes** physicians often adopt a 'half way house'. Some examples of this compromise include:

- Not proceeding to lower GI tests if upper GI pathology is found.
- Where NSAIDs are the likely problem, stop the drug, start iron and a proton pump inhibitor, and only investigate if the anaemia or evidence of bleeding continues after a suitable therapeutic trial.
- Not performing lower GI tests if not a candidate for surgery.
- Performing a flexible sigmoidoscopy rather than a full colonoscopy (80% of tumours can be excluded this way without complete bowel preparation and with less risk and discomfort).
- Using oral contrast-enhanced CT cologram to image the colon (better tolerated with lower perforation rates than colonoscopy. Will miss small lesions but good for excluding large tumours).
- Assuming very longstanding and stable iron deficiency (several years) are low risk for a malignant source.

There are **no hard rules** about making these decisions but it is advisable that any risk-taking is shared with the patient and/or relative and that you record your discussions in the notes. Remember that:

- Investigations are often better tolerated than you would expect e.g. OGD remains a very safe test even in the very old.
- Sometimes it is worth doing tests even if definitive treatment is not available e.g. for a frail patient with bloody diarrhoea, a sigmoidoscopy may yield a treatable diagnosis or guide future palliative therapy if a tumour is found.
- A second medical opinion may help.

Most patients are highly persuadable—if you really want them to take an active part in decisions you will need to give an unbiased view of their options—'you don't want one of those unpleasant dangerous barium enemas do you?' is not a fair choice.

Iron deficiency anaemia: treatment

Treatment is often simple. Treat the underlying cause, and replenish iron stores. The underlying marrow is usually healthy. Hb should rise by about 0.5mg/week.

Blood transfusion is expensive, unnecessary, and can be dangerous. It should be used only for severe symptoms (e.g. unstable angina) or where ongoing acute bleeding is present.

Enteral iron
- Oral supplements (ferrous sulphate 200mg od to tds) are very effective but compliance is often poor due to GI side effects (constipation, nausea, diarrhoea).
- Sometimes a different preparation (ie ferrous gluconate or fumarate) is better tolerated.
- Start with low dose and increase to full dose as tolerated. It is better to take a lower dose for longer than abandon treatment after a few days due to side effects.
- If stool is not greeny-black, concordance is poor.
- Avoid slow-release preparations, as they are often poorly absorbed.

Parenteral iron therapy
- This is rarely required. A few patients cannot tolerate any form of oral therapy and occasionally there is iron malabsorption.
- Single intravenous infusions of iron sucrose (Venofer®) or an intramuscular preparation iron dextran (Cosmofer®) can be given weekly.
- Parenteral iron can cause anaphylaxis so a test dose must be given with resuscitation facilities available.

Duration of iron therapy
Always continue iron for three months after the Hb concentration has normalized (to replenish the iron stores) but don't leave them on life-long treatment unless you are unable to trace or treat the cause of ongoing blood loss. Monitoring Hb off iron can guide management by telling you whether blood loss continues and iron overload is not without risk.

Macrocytic anaemia

Causes

- B12 deficiency—usually malabsorption
- Folate deficiency—often dietary in elderly but also consider coeliac disease
- Myelodysplasia
- Aplastic anaemia
- Hypothyroidism
- Myeloma
- Liver failure and alcohol excess
- Drugs e.g. methotrexate, phenytoin, azathiaprine, hydroxycarbamide
- Reticulocytosis.

Megaloblastic anaemia

- Caused by vitamin B12 and folate deficiency.
- Bone marrow shows big erythroblasts with immature nuclei due to defective DNA synthesis while blood film may show hypersegmented neutrophils.
- Can also cause suppression of white cell and platelet production (pancytopaenia) and a mild jaundice with raised LDH due to low-grade haemolysis.
- Lack of B12 and/or folate also affects brain (rare cause of reversible dementia) and nerve function (peripheral neuropathy and spinal cord degeneration—sub acute combined degeneration of the cord—SACDC). There is a poor correlation between the degree of anaemia and the presence of neurological sequelae.

Pernicious anaemia

80% of B12 deficiency cases have an autoimmune gastritis resulting in an absence of gastric intrinsic factor and therefore B12 malabsorbtion. It is more common in elderly females with a history of autoimmune disease. Proving the diagnosis (gastric biopsy, Schilling's test to look for malabsorbtion and autoantibodies for intrinsic factor and parietal cells) is fiddly and rarely undertaken. Treatment is empirical and pragmatic.

Treatment

- In combined deficiency or blind treatment always correct both deficiencies simultaneously as treating one can precipitate acute deficiency of the other and worsen neurology (especially SACDC).
- Folic acid 5mg od is very well-tolerated.
- Hydroxycobalamin loading is 1mg by intramuscular injection three times a week for 6 doses then 1mg every 3 months indefinitely.
- Those with low B12 levels without anaemia can go straight to the 3 monthly regimen.

Anaemia of chronic disease

This is the commonest cause of anaemia in older people. Illness such as infection, malignant disease, renal disease, or connective tissue disorder may be accompanied by a moderate anaemia (9–10g/dL).

Diagnosis

Often a diagnosis of exclusion. Normocytic and normochromic. There is a low serum iron and iron binding capacity with a normal or raised serum ferritin concentration. Bone marrow aspiration is rarely indicated but will usually demonstrate increased iron stores.

The underlying condition may not always be apparent even after a careful history and examination and screening tests should include:
- Blood film, ESR, and immunoglobulins
- Liver and renal function
- CXR
- Autoantibody screen
- Urine analysis
- Thyroid function tests
- PSA.

If no diagnosis is made at this stage symptomatic treatment should be given and the patient should be kept under regular review.

Treatment

- Hb will improve only after treatment of the underlying condition.
- Patients are often placed on both long-term iron and folate supplements for no reason.
- Iron overload can occur and has theoretical risks.
- Symptomatic blood transfusion may be warranted.
- Consider a trial of erythropoietin therapy in patients with poor renal function.

Myelodysplasia and myelodysplastic syndrome

A group of neoplastic disorders of the haemopoetic stem cell characterized by increasing bone marrow failure with qualitative and quantitative abnormalities of all three cell lines resulting in varying degrees of:

- Anaemia (macrocytic or normocytic)
- Neutropaenia (sometimes with a monocytosis)
- Thrombocytopaenia.

A single cell line may be affected, especially at presentation. The qualitative abnormalities mean that function may be poor even with normal counts (e.g. susceptibility to infection without neutropaenia).

Common and underdiagnosed with peak incidence age 80. Cause unknown (except a tiny proportion who have myelodysplasia secondary to previous cytotoxic therapy).

Usually a hypercellular bone marrow (some normocellular/hypocellular) with dysplastic changes and up to 20% blast cells. Some patients have ring sideroblasts (iron deposits in ring shape around nucleus). Transformation to acute myeloid leukaemia (AML) where blasts >20% occurs in a significant proportion (up to 30% eventually)—especially those with a high blast count at diagnosis.

Diagnosis

Around half of patients are asymptomatic at diagnosis (incidental finding on blood test). The rest present with anaemia, infections, or bleeding. Splenomegaly (10%) and/or hepatomegaly in the minority. Skin purpura common.

First exclude B12 and folate deficiency, alcohol excess, cytotoxics and thyroid/liver/renal failure. If characteristic features on blood film and mild disease, bone marrow examination may be unnecessary but confident diagnosis/staging will usually require trephine and aspirate. Subclassification based on bone marrow morphology and karyotyping can be done by haematologists and aids prognostic precision.

Management

- Asymptomatic patients require nothing more than monitoring with regular blood counts—often stable for many years.
- Mainstay of symptomatic treatment is blood transfusions.
- Recurrent infections and bleeding complications should be treated with antibiotics and platelet transfusions respectively.
- Younger patients (age <70) with poor-risk disease are sometimes suitable for bone marrow transplantation or cytotoxic treatment but these have a very high morbidity and mortality in older patients.
- Growth factors such as erythropoetin or granulocyte colony stimulating factor are occasionally used.
- Average survival ranges from 6 months (high risk) to 4 years (low risk) and around one third die of unrelated causes.
- Transformation to AML has a very poor prognosis—palliative treatment only.

HOW TO... transfuse an older person

Acute transfusions
E.g. haematemesis, post operative blood loss.
- Speed of transfusion should be determined by the haemodynamic status (postural BP useful, remember elderly patients, especially those on beta-blockers and with pacemakers, may not be able to mount an appropriate tachycardia).
- Furosemide not required in a volume-depleted patient.
- Reassess fluid balance and repeat Hb frequently—it is very easy to under or overestimate blood requirements and older patients do not tolerate this as well.

When not to transfuse
- Older people admitted acutely may have an alarmingly low Hb (often an unexpected finding on a screening blood test) but this should not automatically trigger urgent, fast, or large transfusion.
- Most of these patients have a newly diagnosed chronic anaemia and can come to harm if transfused overenthusiastically—indeed many of these patients are better managed as an outpatient.
- First assess patient's haemodynamic status and symptoms (fainting, very breathless, new confusion, unstable angina or severe peripheral ischaemia are indications to transfuse; simple tiredness/malaise is not).
- B12 injections or oral iron therapy can cause Hb to rise by 0.5–1g/dL per week and may avoid inpatient care and the risks of transfusion.
- If you do elect to transfuse, 2 units may be sufficient (even for an Hb of 6) to tide the patient over until other treatments work.

Routine/planned symptomatic transfusions
E.g. myelodysplasia
- In general, transfuse only when Hb drops to below 8 (unless symptoms e.g. angina occur at higher levels).
- Outpatient transfusion is now frequently done in day hospitals, with the patient sitting in a chair rather than bed-bound.
- Some units now give up to 4 units/day (2 hourly) unless patient has heart failure or previous reactions.
- Usually with oral furosemide cover (20–40mg/bag of blood).
- A careful system for cross matching in primary care (e.g. some units send out a pack containing pre-labelled bottles, request cards and patient bands to district nurses to collect at home or in GP surgery) can minimize traumatic journeys to hospital.

Chronic lymphocytic leukaemia

Chronic lymphocytic leukaemia (CLL) is the commonest of the lymphoid leukaemias. Malignant proliferation of mature B lymphocytes causes persistent lymphocytosis. Peak incidence age 60–80. Female:male 1:2.

Clinical features

- Often picked up incidentally on blood film when asymptomatic.
- Symmetrical non-tender lymphadenopathy (also tonsillar enlargement).
- Splenomegaly and/or hepatomegaly (in later stages).
- Increased susceptibility to infections (e.g. thrush, herpes zoster, bacterial) due to low immunoglobulins and/or neutropaenia.
- Bruising/purpura due to thrombocytopaenia.

Investigations

Abnormal findings include:

- Lymphocytosis (>5 x 10/9 per litre)—may be >100 x 10/9 per litre.
- Normocytic, normochromic anaemia, and thrombocytopaenia can occur.
- Marrow trephine/aspiration replaced by lymphocytes (20–95% of cells).
- Reduced immunoglobulins develop with advanced disease.
- LDH raised in some (indicating poor prognosis).

Staging systems use blood and marrow counts, degree of lymphadeno-pathy and organ involvement to predict survival and therefore guide management.

Treatment

- Asymptomatic patients with non-progressive early-stage disease are just observed/reviewed in haematology clinics.
- In later stages and progressive disease aim for symptom control (not correction of the lymphocytosis) with:
  - Short courses of oral chemotherapy using chlorambucil or fludarabine.
  - Prednisolone can help with anaemia, neutropaenia or thrombocytopaenia and reduces hepatosplenomegaly.
  - Radiotherapy useful for bulky lymph nodes.

Most patients respond to treatment initially but relapse after time.

Prognosis

- Varies according to stage and prognostic factors but in most patients is a chronic, non-aggressive disease.
- Like myelodysplasia and prostate cancer many elderly patients are likely to die with, rather than of, the disease.
- However patients with aggressive disease have a life expectancy of 2–3 years.

Paraproteinaemias

Abnormal expansion of a single line of plasma cells, which produce a monoclonal immunoglobulin. This is a malignant, or potentially malignant condition that increases in prevalence with advancing age.

▶▶ A polyclonal hyperglobulinaemia is a common benign reaction to many illnesses and infection and is not related to the paraproteinaemias.

It is important to exclude this group of conditions in any older patient with an unexplained anaemia or raised ESR. This is easily done with:

- Serum immunoglobulin levels.
- Serum and urine electrophoresis to look for a monoclonal immunoglobulin.
- Bone marrow aspirate/trephine if one is found.

Monoclonal gammopathy of undetermined significance (MGUS)

- This is the commonest paraproteinaemia, occurring in 3% of over 70-year-olds.
- It is benign and has no clinical manifestations.
- There is a small/moderate monoclonal band (<20g/L), a low level of plasma cell expansion in the marrow (<10%), and a raised ESR but no other clinical or laboratory features of multiple myeloma (MM).
- The paraprotein level should remain stable over time.
- 'Smouldering myeloma' is sometimes diagnosed where the monoclonal band or plasma cell levels are higher than the above thresholds but there are no other features of MM—this is treated in the same way as MGUS.
- The importance of MGUS is that up to a quarter of the patients will eventually develop another haematological disease (usually MM). The median transformation time is 10 years and many patients die of unrelated illness during follow up. There is no test which can predict which remain stable and which transform so all should receive an annual clinical and laboratory review.

Multiple myeloma

Incidence in people over 80 is 30/100,000/yr. The marrow plasma cell expansion is malignant and causes bone erosion and marrow failure. Bence Jones protein (light chains excreted in urine) may contribute to renal failure. Plasma hyperviscosity syndrome can occur.

▶▶ Exclude multiple myeloma (MM) in anyone with an unexplained high ESR or anaemia.

Clinical features

- Malaise/fatigue (anaemia)
- Bone pain, pathological fracture, and cord compression (bone erosion)
- Thirst, confusion, and renal impairment (hypercalcaemia)
- Infections/fever (immuneparesis and neutropaenia)
- Bleeding (thrombocytopaenia)
- Hepatomegaly (20%) and splenomegaly (5%)
- Rarely neuropathy or amyloidosis can occur.

Investigation

- Serum immunoglobulins and electrophoresis—monoclonal
  band (sometimes two)—usually over 30g/L with suppression
  'immuneparesis' of other immunoglobulins. IgG paraprotein
  commonest, then IgA and light chains.
- Other blood tests:
  - High ESR—usually above 100
  - Normochromic normocytic anaemia
  - Neutropaenia and thrombocytopaenia occur late
  - Hypercalcaemia
  - Renal impairment
  - Note that alkaline phosphatase may be normal despite bone lesions
    and hypercalcaemia
  - Hypoalbuminaemia
  - High beta$_2$ microglobulin levels.
- Urine immunoglobulins—light chains occur as Bence–Jones protein in 75%.
- Plain X-rays show lytic lesions or generalized osteopaenia.
- Isotope bone scans may be negative and are not recommended.
- MRI may show non-specific patchy high signal marrow replacement.
- Bone marrow aspirate and trephine— >30% plasma cells.

A confident diagnosis can be made with at least two of:

- >30% plasma cells in marrow
- Evidence of bone involvement
- A myeloma protein present in serum or urine or both.

Unfortunately many cases are not this straightforward and cases are found with a normal ESR, no serum protein band (just Bence–Jones) or less than 30% plasma cells (where marrow expansion is patchy or occurring in a single plasmacytoma deposit).

Management

Should usually be shared care with a haematologist.

Most patients will receive **symptomatic treatment:**

- Blood product transfusion.
- Analgesia for bone pain.
- Radiotherapy for localized bone pain/pathological fracture and for spinal cord compression.
- Treatment of hypercalcaemia—see p697.
- Social and psychological support.

Disease-modifying options include:

- Melphalan ± prednisolone chemotherapy. This is given orally for 4 days on a 4–6 week cycle, is relatively simple and can effect a remission in about half of suitable patients. One or more further courses can be successful but resistance eventually develops.
- Thalidomide. Recently introduced with promising results.
- More complex and aggressive treatments with vincristine, adriamycin, dexamethasone and cyclophosphamide can produce slightly higher remission rates but are less well-tolerated.
- In younger (usually under 65), fitter patients a bone marrow transplant is sometimes recommended.

Prognosis

- Median survival even with treatment is 4 years and palliative care should not be neglected at the end.
- Severe anaemia (Hb < 9g/dL), renal impairment and hypercalcaemia are all associated with a poor prognosis.

Musculoskeletal system

Osteoarthritis 510
Osteoarthritis: management 512
Osteoporosis 514
Osteoporosis: management 516
   How to... manage non-operative fractures 517
Polymyalgia rheumatica 518
Temporal arteritis 520
   How to... manage steroid therapy in temporal arteritis 522
Paget's disease 524
Gout 526
Pseudogout 528
Cervical spondylosis and myelopathy 530
Contractures 532
Osteomyelitis 534
The elderly foot 536
The elderly foot: management 538
The painful hip 540
The painful back 542
The painful shoulder 544

Osteoarthritis

Osteoarthritis (OA) is the most common joint disorder in older patients causing massive burden of morbidity and dependency. It is not inevitable with ageing.

A disorder of the dynamic repair process of synovial joints causing:

- Loss of articular cartilage (joint space narrowing)
- Vascular congestion
- New growth of cartilage and bone (osteophytes)
- Capsular fibrosis.

Inherited factors determine susceptibility but individual genes not identified. Increasing age is the strongest risk factor. Females and those with high bone density are at higher risk. Obesity, trauma, and repetitive adverse loading (e.g. miners or footballers) are potentially avoidable factors. Congenital factors (e.g. hip dysplasia) can result in secondary OA.

Clinical features

- Pain—assess severity, disability and impact on life (handicap). Usually insidious in onset and variable over time, worse with activity and relieved by rest. Chronic pain may cause poor sleep and low mood.
- Only one or a few joints are affected with minimal morning stiffness and often worsening of symptoms during the day.
- Restricted movement—e.g. walking, dressing, rising from a chair.
- Severe OA can contribute to postural instability and falls.

Examination

- Heberden's nodes (asymptomatic bony swellings on distal fingers) associated with inherited knee OA
- Limp with jerky 'antalgic' gait
- Deformity including:
  - Muscle wasting
  - Knees may have valgus (knees apart, feet together), varus (knees together, foot outwards) or flexion deformity
  - Hip shortening/flexion (check on couch by flexing opposite hip to see if affected hip lifts off bed—Trendelenberg test)
- Restricted range of movement
- Crepitus
- Effusions.

Investigations

▶▶ OA is a clinical diagnosis. Symptoms correlate poorly with radiological findings. The main role of X-ray is in assessing severity of structural change prior to surgery. Features include joint space narrowing, osteophytes, sclerosis, cysts, and deformity. Blood tests are normal even when an osteoarthritic joint feels warm—reconsider your diagnosis if inflammatory markers are elevated.

Osteoarthritis: management

OA is the most common, chronic painful condition. Drug dependence and side effects are a big problem.

▶▶ Always consider non-pharmacological treatments first.

Non-drug treatments

- Exercise: stretching and strengthening. Swimming, yoga, and Tai Chi are particularly good. Encourage the patient to exercise despite the pain—no harm will be done.
- Heat packs: but be very careful to avoid burns in patients who may have decreased temperature awareness.
- Weight loss: not a quick fix but influences other health outcomes.
- Sensible footwear: soft soles with no heels. Trainers are ideal.
- Walking aids: e.g. stick (in contralateral hand).
- Education and support: can improve pain and function.
- Osteopaths or chiropractors help some patients but are expensive.

Drug treatments

▶▶ No patient should be offered more dangerous medication unless they have tried and failed regular paracetamol in maximum dose (1g qds) (p154). Patients may need persuading to try a regular prophylactic dose, perceiving it as a 'weak' drug.

- The next step is to add a low potency opiate—often combined with paracetamol e.g. codydramol (dihydrocodeine 10mg/paracetamol 500mg ii qds). Beware constipation and sedation.
- A short course of oral NSAIDs can be useful in acute exacerbations but try to avoid long-term use.
  - If NSAIDs are used for more than 2 weeks or in the presence of known dyspepsia or ulceration, reduce the GI risk by co-prescribing e.g. misoprostol 200mcg tds or lansoprazole 15mg od
  - The COX-2 selective inhibitors have better GI tolerability but have fallen from favour due to vascular adverse events.
- Intra-articular steroids (e.g. triamcinolone hexacetonide 20mg) can be rapidly effective particularly if the joint is hot/very painful. There is a substantial placebo effect, but symptoms tend to recur after 4–6 weeks. Side effects limit use to 4 injections/joint/year. The cumulative systemic effect risks osteoporosis.
- Topical NSAIDs can be helpful and are lower risk than oral medications.
- Counter-irritants e.g. capsaicin cream are safe and have some analgesic effect.
- Oral chondroitin and glucosamine are available unlicensed over-the-counter and are very widely used. They may have a slow-onset mild analgesic action and may slow the progression of disease. There are no significant side effects.

Osteoporosis

Osteoporosis (OP) is the reduction in bone mass and disruption of bone architecture, resulting in increased bone fragility and fracture risk. Results from prolonged imbalance in bone remodeling where resorption (osteoclastic activity) exceeds deposition (osteoblastic activity).

OP is very common and very much under-recognised and under-treated. In combination with falls (see p134) OP contributes to the high incidence of fractures in older people. In the UK 30% of women aged 70 have at least one vertebral fracture and 32% aged 90 will have had a hip fracture.

▶▶ If you make the diagnosis do not delay initiating secondary prevention. Always think of OP when assessing post-operative orthopaedic patients.

Pathology

- Total bone mass increases throughout childhood and adolescence, peaks in the third decade, and then declines at about 0.5% per year.
- Bone loss is accelerated after the menopause (up to 5% per year) and by smoking, alcohol, low body weight, hyperthyroidism, hyperparathyroidism, hypoandrogenism (in men) renal failure, and immobility.
- Steroids, phenytoin, long-term heparin, and cyclosporin cause secondary osteoporosis.
- High peak bone mass reduces later risk. Determined by genetics, nutrition (plenty of calcium/vitamin D especially in childhood and the heavier the better) and weight-bearing exercise.
- There are changes in bone structure as well as bone mass. Both contribute to fragility.
- Diagnosis is complicated by the common coexistence of asymptomatic osteomalacia (defective mineralization) in older people with low sunlight exposure.

Clinical features

- OP itself is asymptomatic—it is the fractures that cause problems.
- Often presents with an acute fragility (ie low energy) fracture—wrist, femoral neck, or crush fracture of vertebral body.
- Wedging of vertebrae is caused because there is higher load-bearing by the anterior part of the vertebral body. This can present as:
  - An incidental, asymptomatic finding (in around a third).
  - Acute painful fracture.
  - A progressive kyphosis ('Dowager's hump'). The bent-over posture is not just unattractive, it causes loss of height, protuberant belly, abdominal compression, oesophageal reflux, and impaired balance with further predisposition to falls and fracture. Restricted rib movements lead to restrictive lung disease.

Diagnosis

▶▶ Blood tests are normal (except after a fracture). If calcium or alkaline phosphate is elevated consider alternative diagnosis e.g. metastases or Paget's disease.

- X-rays may show fractures and give an idea of bone density.
- The gold standard is dual X-ray absorptiometry (DEXA) scanning (rarely employed in the elderly population but useful in younger women). Usually 2 scores are quoted at hip and spine. The T-score compares bone density to peak bone mass while Z score compares it to age/sex/weight-matched sample. A T-score less than −2.5 indicates OP with scores −1 to −2.5 indicating osteopaenia.
- Think of secondary causes:
  - TSH in all
  - Testosterone levels in men.

In a woman aged over 65 years, a pragmatic approach is to assume that OP exists where there is a:

- Low energy fracture of wrist, femoral neck, or vertebra.
- Progressive kyphosis without features of malignancy.

Osteoporosis: management

Primary prevention

- Sensible public health measures (e.g. diet, exercise, stop smoking, reduce alcohol) should be advised but generally affect peak bone mass i.e. too late for older people.
- Prophylaxis for those taking steroid therapy (see below)
- Hormone replacement therapy (HRT) is not particularly effective—postmenopausal bone loss returns after it is stopped. Increase thromboembolic, cancer and vascular risk argue strongly against its use.

Treatment

- **Oral calcium and vitamin D** is cheap and effective, especially in frail institutionalized people (possibly due to treatment of osteomalacia and associated myopathy as much as OP). Tablets are large and chalky and can be unpalatable. Effervescent tablets or granules may be better tolerated. Take two combination tablets daily (e.g. CalciChew® D3 Forte or Adcal® D3). Probably not helpful as monotherapy in fit older people.
- **Bisphosphonates** are very effective. NICE recommends initiation in any woman aged over 75 following a fragility fracture without the need for DEXA scanning.
  - The weekly dose regimens (risedronate 35mg or alendronate 70mg once weekly) are easier to remember and to tolerate than daily dosing, but patients should still take daily calcium and vitamin D.
  - Upper gut ulceration occurs rarely. Use bisphosphonates cautiously when there is dysphagia or a history of dyspepsia. Must be taken on an empty stomach 30 minutes before breakfast or other medicines. Swallow the tablet whole with a full glass of water whilst sitting or standing. Remain sitting or standing for 30 minutes after swallowing.
  - Currently also recommended prophylactically at onset of 'significant' steroid therapy (>7.5mg prednisolone for >1 month).
  - Up to 15% of patients are 'non-responders' and continue to lose bone mass (measured by chemical bone turnover markers). Such patients are unlikely to be detected in geriatric medicine because bone turnover is not monitored but consider change in treatment if fragility fractures continue.
  - Contraindicated in hypocalcaemia. Manufacturers advise avoiding in renal impairment, but it is often given if the indication is strong.
- **Raloxifene** is an oestrogen-like drug which decreases bone loss without measurable effects on the uterus. It is used if bisphosphonates are not tolerated or in non-responders.
- **Strontium ranelate** is still being evaluated but is probably beneficial and is useful if bisphosphonates are not tolerated.

Less common drugs, usually advised only by specialist teams include:
- **Calcitonin** available in nasal spray and improves pain after acute vertebral fracture
- **Teriparitide** a recombinant fraction of parathyroid hormone, given by sc injection. Expensive. Maximum course 18 months.

HOW TO... **manage non-operative fractures**

- Fractures that very rarely require operative intervention include pelvis, humerus, wrist, and vertebra.
- Other fractures, often immobilized surgically in younger people, may be treated more conservatively in older patients to avoid periopera-tive risks (e.g. fractured tibial plateaux may simply be immobilized by plaster of Paris (POP) or splinting).
- Patients with these 'non-operative' fractures are often cared for by geriatricians having been transferred either:
  - From A&E, to medical, ortho-medical or ortho-geriatric units.
  - From orthopaedic wards for ongoing rehabilitation.
- Minor fractures can result in significant functional impairment e.g. a Colles fracture and POP may prevent an older person washing, dressing and toileting. Even walking may not be possible (if a frame can no longer be used).

General principles of management include

- **Control pain**. This allows earlier mobilization and reduces the risks of immobility (pressure sores, pneumonia, thromboembolism).
  - Consider novel treatments such as heat, TENS, calcitonin, or bisphosphonates for vertebral fracture.
  - A short course of NSAIDs is sometimes appropriate in low risk patients but remember to reduce analgesia as soon as possible.
- **Encourage mobility and independence as early as possible**. Best achieved in a rehabilitation unit. Patient and family often expect 'bedrest' after a fracture and may need to be educated.
- **Maintain contact with orthopaedic colleagues**. They can advise on when to replace/remove plasters and how much exercise/weight bearing is appropriate. Ask for re-assessment if progress is poor e.g. ongoing severe pain, or apparent malunion—sometimes a diagnosis has been missed or an interval operation is needed.
- Consider **prophylactic heparin** if there are multiple risk factors for thromboembolic disease.
- Consider **osteoporosis treatment** (there is no evidence that bisphosphonates reduce callus formation or delay bone union)
- Start to plan discharge early.
  - Many patients can be managed at home with a care package and outpatient rehabilitation.
  - Others may need transitional care beds (e.g. while they wait to be weight-bearing or for plasters to be removed) after which return to an active rehabilitation programme prior to going home.
- **Consider the mechanism of the fall** and injury (p118)—are there medical risks that could be reduced? E.g. sedating medication, excessive antihypertensive use, undiagnosed illnesses (e.g. urinary infection or uncontrolled AF), need for aids/adaptations.

Further reading
NICE guidelines www.nice.org.uk/pdf/TA087guidance.pdf

Polymyalgia rheumatica

Polymyalgia rheumatica (PMR) is a common inflammatory syndrome causing symmetrical proximal muscle aches and stiffness. It affects only older people (do not diagnose it under age 45). There is rapid (days) onset of shoulder and then thigh pain that is worse in mornings. Sometimes associated malaise, weight loss, depression, and fever. Often quite disabling with little to find on examination.

Pathology

Identical to that seen in giant cell arteritis (temporal arteritis).

Diagnosis

- Suggestive symptoms with raised inflammatory markers (ESR/CRP) and no other apparent cause.
- Often have normochromic normocytic anaemia and mild abnormalities of liver (especially ALP) or renal function.
- Clinical examination, muscle enzymes, and EMG are normal.
- Temporal artery biopsy is positive in less than 25% and is rarely done.

Exclude other causes (e.g. connective tissue disease, tumour, chronic infection, neurological diseases) particularly if a patient does not respond quickly to steroids. A difficult diagnosis to make reliably—a significant number of patients are misdiagnosed.

Treatment

- Prednisolone (doses more than 15mg are rarely required) usually produces a complete resolution of symptoms in a day or two.
- Treat until symptom-free and ESR/CRP normalize then reduce dose slowly (1mg/month) checking for relapse of symptoms or blood tests.
- Some patients can be taken off steroids after 6–8 months but most need long-term steroids (mean duration 2–3 years).
- Always give bone protection (e.g. alendronate 70mg once weekly with calcium and vitamin D).
- Azathioprine or methotrexate may be used as steroid-sparing agents.
- Educate and involve the patient in monitoring disease.

Diagnostic dilemma and steroid 'dependency'

Some patients were diagnosed with PMR years ago, no longer exhibit nor remember their symptoms and are suffering steroid side effects. They may resist steroid withdrawal or suffer symptoms as steroids are decreased or withdrawn, even if the characteristic syndrome and inflammatory responses are not displayed.

Many other diseases (even simple osteoarthritis) respond to steroids (although usually less dramatically). Steroid withdrawal itself can cause general aches which some have called 'pseudorheumatism'.

Avoid this difficult situation by:

- Comprehensive assessment at onset with good record-keeping, so that others can reappraise the diagnosis if response to treatment is poor.
- Considering the differential diagnosis carefully.
- Discussing diagnosis and treatment with the patient.
- Agreeing with the patient a clear plan, for reviewing steroid therapy.

Temporal arteritis

Temporal arteritis (TA), or giant cell arteritis is a relatively common (18 per 100,000 over age 50) systemic vasculitis of medium to large vessels. Mean age of presentation 70 (does not occur age <50). More common in women and Scandinavia/Northern Europe.

Pathogenesis
- Giant cell arteritis identical to PMR but different distribution.
- Possibly an autoimmune mechanism but no antibodies/antigen isolated.

Clinical picture
- **Systemic:** fever, malaise, anorexia and weight loss
- **Muscles:** symmetrical proximal muscle pain and stiffness as in PMR.
- **Arteritis:** tenderness over temporal arteries—not so much a headache as scalp tenderness. Classically unable to wear a hat or brush hair. If an artery occludes, distal ischaemia or infarction occurs
  - **Headache** is present in 90% (due to ischaemia or local tenderness of facial or scalp arteries).
  - **Jaw claudication** (occlusion of maxillary artery).
  - **Amaurosis fugax** or **blindness** are due to occlusion of the ciliary artery, which supplies the optic nerve—this causes a pale swollen optic nerve but not retinal damage (which is a feature of central retinal artery occlusion with carotid disease).
  - **Stroke** (carotid artery).
  - Any large artery including the aorta can be affected.

▶▶ Always suspect TA if amaurosis fugax involves both eyes (atheroma is more commonly unilateral).

Investigations
- ESR usually >100.
- CRP also very high and falls faster with treatment than ESR.
- May have normochromic normocytic anaemia and renal impairment.
- Temporal artery biopsy (TAB) is highly specific, and therefore the gold standard test. Because the vasculitis may be patchy, TAB is not always positive, ie the sensitivity is moderate. TAB becomes negative quickly (one to two weeks) with treatment.

Treatment
- Amaurosis fugax due to TA is an ophthalmological emergency. Give 80–100mg oral prednisolone or high dose methyl prednisolone IV.
- Never delay treatment while waiting for a biopsy.
- Even without visual symptoms, higher doses and slower dose reduction are required than for PMR (start at 30–40mg).
- Between a third and a half of patients are able to come off steroids by two years.
- After stopping steroids, continue to monitor as relapse is common.
- Osteoporosis prophylaxis should be started at initiation of steroids (usually a bisphosphonate with calcium and vitamin D).

Azathioprine and methotrexate are sometimes used as steroid-sparing agents once therapy is established. Consider them if:
- Steroid side effects are prominent
- High steroid doses are required
- There is slow tailing off
- There is recurrent relapse off treatment.

HOW TO... **manage steroid therapy in temporal arteritis**

Suggested protocol for steroid treatment in temporal arteritis

Diagnosis

↓

Prednisolone 80mg od with
Biphosphonate
Calcium and Vitamin D tablet
Monitor for glycosuria/BM's in known diabetics
See p156

↓

Initial review (2 weeks)

↓

Clinical improvement—usually rapid—if not reassess diagnosis
Repeat inflammatory markers—ESR/CRP

If ESR/CRP still elevated
continue at 80mg and recheck
in 2 weeks

If ESR/CRP normal/near normal
decrease to 70mg and review 2 weeks
continue to reduce by 10mg/fortnight while
markers remain satisfactory

↓

If still no improvement
reconsider diagnosis

When reach 20mg then slow reduction by
2.5mg/fortnight

↓

When reach 10mg then slow reduction by
1mg/fortnight

- If rebound of symptoms or inflammatory markers occurs, then take
  2 steps back on the reduction schedule. Wait 4 weeks before reducing again.
- Beware a steroid-withdrawal syndrome, which can occur without
  arteritis recurrence. ESR and CRP are normal.
- Other blood parameters (anaemia, impaired liver function) may help
  guide treatment.

Paget's disease

This is a very common bone disease of old age (up to 10% prevalence more common in men). It is usually clinically silent—only about 5% are symptomatic.

It is thought to be due to a slow viral infection of osteoclasts, which causes abnormal bone remodelling. Most commonly affects pelvis, femur spine, skull, and tibia. The resultant bone is expanded and disordered and can cause pain, pathological fracture, and predisposes to osteosarcoma.

Presentation
- Most commonly as asymptomatic elevated alkaline phosphatase (ALP).
- Often an incidental finding on a pelvis or skull X-ray.
- Less commonly as:
  - **Pathological fracture** (especially hip and pelvis).
  - **Bone pain:** constant pain commonly in legs, especially at night. The diseased bone itself can be painful or deformity can lead to accelerated joint disease at e.g. hip, knee or spine. Fracture or osteosarcoma can cause suddenly increased pain.
  - **Deformity:** bowing of legs or upper arm is often asymmetrical. The skull can take on a characteristic 'bossed' shape due to overgrowth of frontal bones.
  - **Deafness:** bone expansion in the skull compresses the 8th cranial nerve causing conduction deafness, which can be severe.
  - **Other neurological compression syndromes** e.g. spinal cord (paraplegia), optic nerve (blindness), brainstem compression (dysphagia and hydrocephalus).

Investigations
- ALP is constantly elevated.
  - The bone isoenzyme is more specific and useful when liver function is abnormal.
  - Rarely (e.g. if only one bone is involved), total ALP can be normal but the bone isoenzyme is always raised.
- Other markers of bone turnover e.g. urinary hydroxyproline are raised.
- X-rays show mixed lysis and sclerosis, disordered bone texture, and expansion (a diagnostic feature).
- Radioisotope bone scans show hot spots.
- Immobile patients with very active disease can become hypercalcaemic although this is rare. If calcium and ALP are raised, there is more likely to be another diagnosis (e.g. carcinomatosis, hyperparathyroidism).

Management

As most cases are asymptomatic, often no treatment is required. Symptomatic cases may warrant referral to a rheumatologist.

- Analgesia and joint replacement may be needed.
- Fractures often require internal fixation to correct deformity and because they heal poorly.
- Bisphosphonates (e.g. risedronate 30mg od for 2 months or intermittent iv infusions of pamidronate) are very useful. They have several effects:
  - Reduce pain
  - Reduce vascularity before elective surgery
  - Improve healing after fracture
  - Improve neurological compression syndromes
  - Reduce serium calcium in hypercalcaemia.
- Calcitonin and mithramycin are now rarely used.
- Alkaline phosphatase, other bone turnover biochemical markers and occasionally nuclear bone scans can be used to monitor the effectiveness of treatment.

Gout

Uric acid crystals deposit in and around joints and intermittently produce inflammation. Serum urate levels equate poorly with the disease manifestations.

Increased incidence with age due to:
- Worsening renal function and impaired uric acid excretion.
- Increased hyperuricaemic drug use e.g. thiazides, aspirin, cytotoxics.
- Common acute precipitants e.g. sepsis, surgery.

Presentation
- **Acute monoarthritis** in feet or hands is most common, but can also occur in large joints such as knee or shoulder. The joint is very painful, hot and red. Patients often refuse to bear weight or move the joint. The patient can look unwell and sometimes has a fever.
- **Chronic tophi** (usually painless) over finger joints and in ears can occur, associated with a chronic arthritis. Sometimes mistaken for other more common arthritides.
- **Olecranon bursitis.**
- **Uric acid kidney stones.**

Investigations
- During an acute attack **serum uric acid** may be normal or high.
- **WBC, ESR, and CRP** are usually high or very high.
- **Joint fluid:**
  - May be cloudy or frankly purulent on visual inspection.
  - Microscopy shows many inflammatory cells.
  - Under polarized light, negatively birefringent uric acid crystals are seen in joint fluid or in phagocytes.
- **X-rays** are usually normal (rarely see small punched-out erosions in fingers in chronic tophaceous cases).

The main aim is to exclude an infective arthritis.
▶▶ If in doubt, consider using iv antibiotics until cultures are negative.

Treatment
- **For acute gout:**
  - Use **paracetamol** with a course of **NSAIDs** (consider gastric protection).
  - If you have ruled out infection, local steroid injections are often effective (e.g. methylprednisolone 40mg intraarticular).
  - If NSAIDs are contraindicated (e.g. renal impairment) use a short course of oral **steroids** (e.g. prednisolone 40mg od for 7 days) or **colchicine** 0.5mg stat then 0.5mg every 6–8 hours until pain is controlled or diarrhoea/vomiting side effects prohibit further use. Colchicine is an effective drug but difficult to use correctly—you will need to explain this protocol carefully to patient/carers.
- **For chronic arthritis** with or without tophi: should be treated with allopurinol or uricosuric drugs (probenecid and sulphinpyrazone). Uricosuric drugs are contraindicated in renal stones.

Prevention

One or two attacks of gout probably do not warrant prophylaxis especially as such drugs can precipitate further attacks). Instead, try:
- Changing drugs (stop thiazides and aspirin).
- Lifestyle advice:
    - Reduce alcohol (beer is preferable to lager or wine)
    - Reduce dietary purines (meat)
    - Lose weight.
- Do not leave patients on long-term NSAIDS. Very early use of NSAIDs or colchicine can abort a severe attack of gout.

Several attacks of gout merit slow introduction of allopurinol (start at 100mg od and build up to 300mg od) or uricosuric agents. This may cause a flare of acute gout—cover the introduction of therapy with NSAIDs or low dose colchicine.

Pseudogout

Features

This is an acute, episodic synovitis closely resembling gout except that:
- Calcium pyrophosphate rather than uric acid crystals (with positive rather than negative birefringence) are found.
- Large joints are more commonly affected (especially knees but also shoulder, hips, wrists and elbows).
- It is not associated with tophi, bursitis, or stones.
- X-rays often show calcification of articular cartilage 'chondrocalcinosis' in the affected joint.
- It doesn't respond to allopurinol or uricosuric agents—so consider this diagnosis where recurrent attacks persist despite allopurinol.

As with gout the patient has an acutely inflamed joint which is very painful to move. They may be systemically unwell with a fever and highly elevated inflammatory markers. Serum calcium is normal.

Management

Make a confident diagnosis. This usually involves immediate synovial fluid sampling and urgent microscopy to exclude infection and gout.
Effective treatments for acute pseudogout include:
- Intra-articular steroid injections
- Oral NSAIDs
- Oral corticosteroids
- Colchicine.

Long-term preventative treatment is very rarely needed.

Cervical spondylosis and myelopathy

Degeneration in the cervical spine causes neurological dysfunction with both radiculopathy (compression of nerve roots leaving spinal foramina) and myelopathy (cord compression). The resulting mixture of lower (nerve root) and upper (cord) nerve damage causes pain, weakness and numbness. Progress is usually gradual but can be sudden (especially following trauma). The disease is unusual before the age of 50. Mild forms are very common in the elderly population.

History

- Neck pain and restricted movement may be present but are neither specific nor sensitive markers of nerve damage. Pain may radiate to shoulder, chest or arm in a dermatomal distribution.
- Arms and hands become clumsy especially for fine movements (e.g. doing up buttons). Weakness, numbness and paraesthesia can occur.
- Leg symptoms usually occur later, with an upper motor neurone spastic weakness and a wide-based and/or ataxic gait, often with falls.
- Urinary dysfunction is unusual and late.
- Rarely can cause vertebrobasilar insufficiency symptoms (see p128).

Signs

- Arms have predominantly lower motor signs with weakness, muscle wasting, and segmental reflex loss. The classical 'inverted supinator' sign is due to a C5/6 lesion where the supinator jerk is lost but the finger jerk (C7) is augmented: when the wrist is tapped, the fingers flex.
- Legs may have brisk reflexes, increased tone, clonus and upgoing plantars. In severe cases a spastic paraparesis with a sensory level can develop.

Differential diagnosis

This is wide and includes:
- Syringomyelia
- Motor neurone disease (look for signs above the neck and an absence of sensory symptoms/signs)
- Peripheral neuropathy (no upper motor neurone signs)
- Vitamin B12 deficiency
- Other causes of spastic gait disorders.

Investigations

- **Plain X-rays** in older people almost always show degenerative changes, which correlate poorly with symptoms. They are only useful in excluding other pathology or in demonstrating spinal instability.
- **MRI scanning** is the investigation of choice. Bone and soft tissue structures and the extent of cord compression are all well demonstrated.
- **CT scanning** may also be useful in diagnosis and planning treatment.
- **Nerve conduction studies** can help confirm the clinical impression and exclude other pathology.

Management

Cervical collars do not influence progression but can sometimes help with radicular pain and may provide partial protection from acute decline following trauma.

The only definitive treatment is **surgical:** laminectomy with fusion for stabilization. Surgery is indicated for:

- Progressive neurology (especially if rapidly progressive)
- Severe pain unresponsive to conservative measures
- Myelopathy more than radiculopathy.

Discuss the risks and benefits with the patient—function is rarely restored once lost but pain improves and further damage is usually avoided.

Contractures

Contractures are joint deformities caused by damaged connective tissue. Where a joint is immobilized (through depressed conscious level, loss of neural input, or local tissue damage) the muscle, ligaments, tendons, and skin can become inelastic and shortened causing joints to be flexed.

Common causes worldwide include polio, cerebral palsy, and leprosy; in geriatric medicine common causes include stroke, dementia, and musculoskeletal conditions e.g. fracture. Contractures are an under-recognized cause of disability—they occur to some degree in about a third of nursing home residents and it is still not uncommon to find patients who are bedbound and permanently curled into the foetal position.

Problems

- **Pain:** especially on moving joint but can occur at rest.
- **Hygiene:** skin surfaces may oppose (e.g. the hand after stroke or groins in abduction/flexion contractures) making it difficult for carer and painful for the patient to keep clean and odourless.
- **Pressure areas:** abnormal posture can put pressure areas at increased risk.
- **Aesthetics:** although the lack of movement causes most disability the abnormal posture/appearance can be more noticeable and distressing.
- **Function:** chronic bedbound patients may become so flexed that they are unable to sit out in a chair.

Prevention

- Where immobilization is short-term e.g. after a fracture, passive stretching followed by exercise regimens should be initiated promptly.
- All health care staff should understand the importance of maintaining mobility (including sitting out of bed for short periods) and positioning of immobile patients.
- Preventative measures are rarely successful at preventing contractures in joints with long-term immobility e.g. in residual hemiparesis after stroke. Splinting might help mould the position.

Treatment

- Periodic injection of **botulinum toxin** is often successful where muscle spasticity is the major problem. There are no real adverse effects but some patients develop an antibody response after repeated treatment, which renders therapy less effective. Newer Botox® preparations are less immunogenic.
- There is little point using **muscle relaxants** except to help with pain. Even then drugs such as baclofen, dantrolene and diazepam usually cause side effects of drowsiness before they reach therapeutic levels.
- **Surgery** e.g. tendon division has a place in severe cases.
- **Physiotherapy** can to some extent reverse established changes, especially if not severe and of relatively recent onset.
- Repositioning with serial plaster casts takes a long time and is really only used in younger patients.

Osteomyelitis

Infection of the bone that is commonest in the very young and the very old. It is important in geriatric practice because it complicates conditions that are common in older patients yet presentation is often non-specific and indolent, so the diagnosis may be missed.

Vertebral osteomyelitis

- Most common in older patients.
- Usually affects the thoracolumbar spine.
- Patients complain of mild back ache and malaise and will often have local tenderness. When examining a patient with PUO, always 'walk' the examining fingers down the spine, applying pressure to find local bony pain.
- Vertebral osteomyelitis (commonly T10–11) may lead to:
  - Perivertebral abscess with a risk of cord compression.
  - Vertebral body collapse with angular kyphosis.
- Discitis occurs when the infection involves the intervertebral disc. The patient is relatively less septic, and X-rays appear normal until disease is very advanced (at which point end-plate erosion can occur).
- Haematogenous spread is most common, often after urinary tract infection, catheterization, intravenous cannula insertion, or other instrumentation.
- Commonly due to *Staphylococcus aureus*, less commonly Gram negative bacilli, rarely tuberculosis.

Osteomyelitis of other bones

- Generally more common in children, but arise in older patients in some circumstances:
  - As a complication of orthopaedic surgery.
  - As a complication of ulceration (venous or pressure ulcers).
  - In susceptible individuals (e.g. diabetics with vascular disease and neuropathy are prone to osteomyelitis of the small bones of the feet).
- Organisms include *Staphylococcus aureus, Staphylococcus epidermidis* (especially with prostheses), Gram negative bacilli, and anaerobes.

Clinical features of osteomyelitis

- Pain is usual but may be missed if there is a pre-existing pressure sore, or the patient has peripheral neuropathy and foot osteomyelitis (e.g. diabetics).
- Malaise is common.
- Fever may be absent.

Investigations
- Blood cultures should be taken in all, and are positive in around half.
- Leucocytosis is variable.
- ESR and CRP are usually raised (although very non-specific).
- X-ray changes lag behind clinical changes by about 10 days. Initially normal, or showing soft tissue swelling. Later develop classic changes: periosteal reaction, sequestra (islands of necrosis), bone abscesses, and sclerosis of neighbouring bone.
- Radioisotope bone scanning will show a 'hot spot' with osteomyelitis, but will not distinguish this from many other conditions (e.g. fracture, arthritis, non-infectious inflammation, metastases etc.). MRI is the most sensitive and specific test. Changes may be diagnostic, even in early disease.
- Biopsy or FNA of bone is required to guide antibiotic therapy—this may be done through the base of an ulcer, or using radiological guidance (ultrasound is useful here).
- Wound swabs reveal colonizing organisms, and are often misleading.

Treatment
- General measures such as analgesia and fluids if needed.
- The joint/bone should be immobilized where possible.
- Obtaining tissue specimens permits bacterial culture and determination of antimicrobial sensitivity. After specimens are obtained but prior to results, 'best guess' therapy may be started after microbiological advice (e.g. clindamycin and fusidic acid for haematogenous spread, and a broader spectrum antibiotic when a complication of pressure sores).
- Surgical drainage should be considered after 36 hours if systemic upset continues, or if there is deep pus on imaging (required in ~30%).
- Treatment is initially intravenous, often later converted to oral therapy. Total treatment duration is usually many weeks or months (depending on sensitivity of organism and extent and location of infection).

Complications
- **Metastatic infection**
- **Suppurative arthritis**
- **Chronic osteomyelitis** infection becomes walled off in cavities within the bone, discharging to the surface by a sinus. Symptoms relapse and remit as sinuses close and reopen. Bone is at risk of pathological fracture. Management is long and difficult—this is a miserable complication of joint replacement. Culture organisms and use appropriate antibiotics to limit spread. Surgical removal of infected bone and/or prosthesis is required for cure. Involve specialist bone infection teams if possible.
- **Malignant otitis externa** occurs when otitis externa spreads to cause osteomyelitis of the skull base. Occurs particularly in frail, older diabetics. Caused by pseudomonas and anaerobes. Facial nerve palsy develops in half, with possible involvement of nerves IX–XII. Requires prolonged antibiotics, specialist ENT input, and possible surgical debridement.

The elderly foot

Foot problems are very common (>80% over 65) and can cause major disability including increased susceptibility to falls. A particular problem in older people because:

- Multiple degenerative and disease pathologies occur and interact.
- Many older people cannot reach their feet: monitoring and basic hygiene (especially nail cutting) may be limited.
- Patients think foot problems are a part of ageing or are embarrassed by them and do not seek treatment.
- Health professionals often neglect to examine feet and are too slow to refer for specialist foot care. It is common to find a patient naked under a hospital gown but still with thick socks on.
- Inappropriate footwear may be worn—most older people cannot afford or refuse to wear 'sensible' shoes such as trainers.
- Simple chiropody services are not available on the NHS (rationed to diabetics and those with peripheral vascular disease in most areas).

Nails

- **Very long nails** can curl back and cut into toes.
- Nails thicken and become more brittle with age. This is worsened by repeated trauma (e.g. bad footwear), poor circulation, or diabetes. Ultimately the nail looks like a rams horn (**onychogryphosis**) and cannot be cut with ordinary nail clippers.
- Fungal nail infection (**onychomycosis**) produces a similar thickened discoloured nail.
- **Ingrowing toenails** can cause pain and recurring infection.

Skin

- Calluses (hard skin)
- Corns (painful calluses over pressure points with a nucleus/core)
- Cracks and ulceration (p644)
- Cellulitis.

Between the toes

Fungal infection ('athlete's foot') is very common. The skin maceration that results is a common cause of cellulitis.

Bone/joint disease

- A **bunion** (hallux valgus) is an outpointing deformity of the big toe, which can overlap the second toe.
- **Hammer toes** are flexion deformities of proximal IP joints.
- **Claw toes** have deformities at both IP joints.
- **Osteoarthritis or gout** of the MTP joint causes pain and rigidity.
- **Neuropathic foot:** longstanding severe sensory loss in a foot (e.g. diabetics, tabes dorsalis) with multiple stress fractures and osteoporosis disrupting the biomechanics of the joints (**Charcot's joint**). The foot/ankle is swollen and red but painless with loss of arches (**rockerbottom foot**).

Circulation impairment

Common. Assess vasculature if there is pain, ulceration, infection or skin changes.

Sensory impairment

Touch, pain, and joint position sense are all important to maintaining normal feet.

Other foot problems

- Obesity
- Oedema
- Skin disorders.

The elderly foot: management

Prevention

- Inspect both feet frequently (at least every other day). A hand mirror assists inspection of the sole.
- ▶▶ If a patient cannot see, reach or feel their feet, someone else should be helping them regularly.
- Examine for swelling, discolouration, ulceration, cuts, calluses, or corns.
- If these are identified, consult a health professional (podiatrist, nurse or doctor) promptly.
- Wash feet twice daily in warm water with mild simple soap. If feet are numb, check that the water temperature is not too hot with a hand or with a thermometer (35–40°C is best).
- After washing, dry feet thoroughly, particularly between the toes.
- Changes socks or stockings daily.
- Dry, hard or thick skin should be softened with emollients such as aqueous cream or liquid and white soft paraffin ointment ('50:50').
- Footwear should be supportive but soft. Take particular care with new footwear, inspecting feet frequently after short periods of wear to ensure that no sores have developed.
- Avoid barefoot walking.
- Cut nails regularly, cutting them straight across and not too short.

Treatment

- Qualified podiatrists or chiropodists will debride calluses/corns and use dressings and pressure relieving pads to prevent them recurring. Unfortunately availability on the NHS has been severely restricted recently (only diabetics qualify in most regions) so cost may deter patients.
- Treat athlete's foot (e.g. with co-trimazole cream twice daily for one week).
- Distinguish between thick discoloured nails due to onychomycosis from simple onychogryphosis by sending nail scrapings for microscopy for fungal hyphae. Topical antifungal treatment is often not practical and tablet treatment (e.g. terbinafine) can take 12 months to be effective so the vast majority of elderly remain untreated. If you do decide to use terbinafine, monitor liver function and be wary of drug interactions.
- Surgery may be used to remove nails or correct severe bone deformity.

The painful hip

▶▶ The important diagnosis not to miss in the frail elderly is **fracture**. Having a low threshold of suspicion and investigation is key.

Hip fracture

- The absence of a recent fall and ability to weight bear should not put you off obtaining an X-ray if recent onset, or severe pain.
- In any bed-bound patient after a fall look for inability to lift the leg off the bed and pain on movement (especially rotation) even if they are not fit to stand. A shortened externally rotated leg is a useful sign but will occur in many who have replacement hips and is not seen in all.
- Some patients can walk on a fractured hip.
- Always:
  - Get two views (AP and lateral) of the pelvis and proximal femur.
  - Have the X-ray films reported by a radiologist—some fractures can be subtle.
  - Check for pubic ramus fractures as well as fractures of the femoral head and shaft.
- If initial films are normal but clinical suspicion is high, consider repeating X-ray in a few days (bone fragments can move apart) or proceed to an MRI or bone scan. It is important to make the diagnosis early—do not be afraid to argue your case with radiology.

Almost all hip fractures require surgical repair no matter how frail the patient (conservative management with or without traction is painful and has a massive morbidity and mortality). By contrast, low energy pelvic fractures in older people rarely require surgery (p517). Even with surgery the 30-day mortality for a fractured neck of femur is high (over 15%). Remember to initiate osteoporosis treatment.

Osteoarthritis

- Pain is 'boreing' and stiffness occurs after rest.
- Restriction of movement occurs in all planes.
- OA can significantly increase chance of falls.
- Total hip replacement is now widely available and very effective.
  - Consider referral for radiographic moderate/severe disease with ongoing pain or disability despite trial of conservative treatment.
  - There is a 1% mortality but older people often have a good long-term result. Revision surgery is rarely needed because activity levels are lower than in younger people (and life expectancy less).

Other causes of hip pain

- **Paget's disease:** also causes secondary osteoarthritis.
- **Radicular pain** referred from spine.
- **Metastases**.
- **Septic arthritis:** rare and difficult diagnosis to make but consider joint aspiration, under ultrasound if your patient appears septic with a very painful hip especially after recent hip surgery.
- **Referred pain** from the knee.
- **Psoas abscess**.

The painful back

Assessment

- History should include position, quality, duration, and radiation of pain as well as associated sensory symptoms, bladder, or bowel problems and a systems review.
- Undress the patient and look for bruising and deformity.
- Apply pressure to each vertebra in turn looking for local tenderness.
- Look for restriction of movement and gait abnormality.
- Always check neurology and consider bowel/bladder function.

Causes

Osteoarthritis of the facet joints becomes more common than disc pathology with advancing age (discs are less pliable and less likely to herniate)(pp510–12).

Osteoporosis and vertebral crush fractures can cause acute well-localised pain, chronic pain or no pain at all (pp514–16).

Metastatic cancer should always be considered especially if pain is new or severe, there are constitutional symptoms such as weight loss, or pain from an apparent fracture fails to improve.

Vertebral osteomyelitis and infective discitis (p534–5) should be considered in those with fever and raised inflammatory markers especially if they are immunosuppressed (e.g. rheumatoid arthritis on steroids).

▶▶ Not all back pain comes from the spine. Differential diagnoses to not miss include pancreatitis or pancreatic cancer, biliary colic, duodenal ulcer, aortic aneurysm, renal pain, retroperitoneal pathology, pulmonary embolism, Guillain–Barré syndrome, myocardial infarction.

Investigations

- FBC, ESR (and myeloma screen if raised), CRP, ALP, calcium and PSA (in men).
- Plain X-rays may reveal diagnosis but 'wear and tear' changes are very common and correlate poorly with pain.
- Bone scan is useful especially if there are multiple sites of pain.
- CT or MRI if cord compression suspected. Will usually be diagnostic for infective discitis and metastases.

Treatment

First, make a diagnosis to guide therapy. **Specific therapies** include:
- Bisphosphonates or calcitonin for osteoporotic collapse.
- Radiotherapy is very effective for metastatic deposits.
- Urgent surgery or radiotherapy should be considered for cord compression, with high dose intravenous steroids in the meantime.

General therapies for most diagnoses include:
- Standard analgesia ladder (p154).
- Physiotherapy is often helpful in improving pain and function or at least preventing deconditioning.
- Exercise and weight loss (if obese) are difficult to achieve but will help.
- Transcutaneous nerve stimulators can help some and are without side effects.
- Antispasmodics e.g. diazepam 2mg if muscular spasm is prominent.
- Consider referral to pain specialist for local injections e.g. facet joints or epidurals.
- Once serious pathology has been excluded a chiropractor/osteopath can sometimes help.

The painful shoulder

The shoulder joint has little bony articulation (and hence little arthritis) but lots of muscle and tendon which is prone to damage. Many conditions become chronic and if you examine elderly people you will find a high prevalence of pain and restricted movement. Patients compensate (e.g. by avoiding clothes that need to be pulled over head) and may not report symptoms.

Before diagnosing one of the conditions below, exclude systemic problems such as polymyalgia rheumatica (p518) and rheumatoid arthritis. Remember that neck problems, diaphragmatic pathology, apical lung cancer, and angina can also produce shoulder pain.

Frozen shoulder/adhesive capsulitis
- Usually idiopathic but sometimes follow trauma and stroke.
- Commoner in diabetics.
- Loss of rotation (internal and external) and abduction.
- Initially painful for weeks to months then stiff (frozen) for further 4–12 months.
- Mainstay of treatment is physiotherapy/exercise—avoid rest.
- Intra-articular steroids may help pain and improve tolerance to early mobilization.

Bicepital tendonitis
- Pain in specific area (anterior/lateral humeral head) aggravated by supination on the forearm while elbow held flexed against body.
- Treatment is rest and corticosteroid injection followed by gentle biceps stretching exercises.

Rotator cuff tendonitis
- Dull ache radiating to upper arm with 'painful arc' (pain between 60–120 degrees when abducting arm).
- Rest, occasionally with immobilization in a sling, and corticosteroid injection.
- Physiotherapy and exercises may help.
- Arthroscopic decompression can sometimes relieve pain.

Rotator cuff tear
- May occur following trauma
- Reduced range of active and passive movements of shoulder
- Ultrasound and MRI diagnostic
- Treat with rest and corticosteroid injection
- Physiotherapy and exercises may help
- Surgical repair possible in some cases.

Pressure injuries

Pressure sores *546*
Compression mononeuropathy *548*
Rhabdomyolysis *550*

Pressure sores

Areas of skin necrosis due to pressure-induced ischaemia found on sacrum, heels, over greater trochanters, shoulders etc. Also known as decubitus ulcers or bedsores. Incidence higher in hospital (new sores form during acute illness) but prevalence higher in long-stay community settings (healing takes months/years). Average hospital prevalence 5–10% despite drives to improve education and preventative strategies. The financial and staffing resource burden of pressure sores is huge.

Risk factors

Include age, immobility (esp. post-operative), low or high body weight, malnutrition, dehydration, incontinence, neurological damage (either neuropathy or decreased conscious level), sedative drugs, vascular impairment.

Several scoring systems (e.g. Waterlow score) combine these factors to stratify risk. They aid/prompt clinical judgement of individual patient risk.

Grading

0	Skin hyperaemia
I	Non-blanching erythema
II	Broken skin or blistering (epidermis ± dermis only)
III	Ulcer down to subcutaneous fat
IV	Ulcer down to bone, joint or tendon

▶▶ It only takes less than **2 hours** for an ulcer to develop and the causative insult often occurs just prior to or at the time of admission (on A+E trolleys, intra-operative, at home). There is considerable lag between the ischaemic insult and the resulting ulcer. Grade I erythema can progress to deep ulcers over days/weeks without further ischaemic insult.

Mechanisms

- **Pressure** Normal capillary pressure 24–34mmHg—pressures exceeding 35mmHg compress and cause ischemia. This pressure is easily exceeded on a simple foam mattress at pressure points such as heels.
- **Shear** Where skin is pulled away from fixed axial skeleton small blood vessels can be kinked or torn. When a patient is propped up in bed or dragged (e.g. during a lift or transfer) there is considerable shear on the sacrum.
- **Friction** Rubbing the skin decreases its integrity especially at moving extremities e.g. elbows, heels. Avoid crumbs, drip sets, and debris between patient and sheets. Massage of pressure areas no longer recommended.
- **Moisture** Sweat, urine, and faeces cause maceration and decrease skin integrity.

Management

- **Prevention** Demands awareness—NICE guidelines from Oct 2003 suggest all patients are risk assessed within 6 hours of admission (www.nice.org.uk). Regular reassessment during hospital admission should occur especially if condition of patient changes.
- **Turning and handling** There is no evidence to suggest how often immobile, high risk patients should be turned in bed. Two hourly turns are historically based and rarely achieved. Frequency should be judged individually. Modern mattresses decrease frequency but don't eradicate need for turns. Avoid friction and sheer by using correct manual handling devices. Consider limiting sitting out to 2 hours. Encourage early mobilization, optimize pain control, minimize sedative drugs.
- **Pressure relieving devices** Consider both beds and chairs. There is little RCT data to compare but most hospitals have access to (in order of increased pressure reduction and cost).
  - High specification foam mattresses
  - Alternating pressure mattresses (airpockets intermittently inflate and deflate) e.g. Nimbus
  - Airfluidized (warm air pumped through tiny spheres to produce a fluid-like cushion) or Waterbed mattresses
- **Promote healing environment**
  - Nutrition such as protein and calorie supplements. There is no evidence to support the use of vitamins (e.g. vit C) or minerals (e.g. zinc) but they are unlikely to do harm.
  - Manage incontinence (one of the few times that a geriatrician might recommend a catheter).
  - Good glycaemic control in diabetics.
  - Correct anaemia (normochromic/normocytic anaemia common).
- **Debridement** Dead tissue should be removed with scalpel (no anaesthetic required), maggots, or occasionally topical streptokinase (Varidase®) or suction. Some patients benefit from surgery e.g. debridement, skin grafting, or myocutaneous flaps.
- **Dressings** Enormous choice with little evidence to favour one type over another. Use gels to soften, hydrofibre/gels (often seaweed based) for cavities then a secondary dressing over the top.
- **Antibiotics** All ulcers are colonized (surface swabs positive 100%), only 1% at any given time have active infection causing illness. Look for surrounding cellulitis and signs of sepsis, check blood cultures or deep tissue biopsy for confirmation. Common organisms include mixed gram negatives (bacteroides) Gram positives (enterococci and staphylococci) and yeasts. If antibiotics indicated use wide spectrum antibiotics (e.g. ciprofloxacin/cefuroxime with metronidazole). Consider osteomyelitis where bone is exposed (p534). MRSA colonization is a growing problem, it is very difficult to eradicate and often leads to a patient having prolonged isolation which is detrimental to their psychological wellbeing and rehabilitation.

Compression mononeuropathy

- Where nerves are compressed against bone they can be damaged.
- This is usually a demyelination injury (neuropraxia) which resolves spontaneously in 2–12 weeks.
- Alcohol, diabetes, and malnutrition increase susceptibility.
- Any patient who has had a period of immobility on a hard surface is at risk, especially if they were unconscious.
- Such injuries can be misdiagnosed as strokes but are lower motor neurone in one nerve territory only.
- Nerve conduction studies are rarely required to confirm diagnosis.
- Treatment is supportive—many such patients are acutely unwell—but recognition becomes more important during rehabilitation.

Nerve damaged	Site/mechanism	Motor effects	Sensory effects
Radial	Upper arm—spiral groove on humerus	Wrist drop and finger extension weakness	Small area of numbness at base of thumb
Ulnar	Elbow—cubital groove	Little and ring finger flexors and finger abduction and adduction	Little and ring finger
Common peroneal	Knee—fibula head	Foot drop and failure of foot eversion and toe extension	Lateral calf and top of foot
Sciatic	Buttock or thigh	Knee flexors plus common peroneal as above	Posterior thigh plus common peroneal as above

Rhabdomyolysis

Following prolonged pressure (e.g. if patient cannot get up after a fall or stroke or after a period of unconciousness), muscle necrosis can occur which releases myoglobin. High levels are nephrotoxic, precipitating to cause tubule obstruction with acute renal failure, especially as these patients are usually dehydrated.

▶▶ Remember to check creatinine kinase (CK) and electrolytes in all patients who have been found on the floor after a 'long lie'. Many frail elderly patients with bruises after a fall will have raised CK levels without developing renal problems but ensuring good hydration (often with 24–48 hours of intravenous fluids) and repeating renal function in such patients is good practice.

Suspect the full rhabdomyolysis syndrome in any patient with
- Prolonged unconciousness
- Signs of acute pressure sores of the skin and
- CK levels at least five times normal.

Urine may be dark ('coca-cola' urine) and urinalysis is positive to haemoglobin but without red blood cells. Hyperkalaemia and hypocalcaemia can occur.

Treat with aggressive rehydration. Monitor urine output, electrolytes, and renal function closely—if renal failure occurs consider temporary dialysis. Prognosis is good if patient survives initial few days.

Other causes of rhabdomyolysis include drugs (especially statins), compartment syndrome, acute myositis, severe exertion e.g. seizures/rigors, heat stroke (p448), and neuroleptic malignant syndrome (p180).

Genitourinary medicine

The ageing genitourinary system *552*
Benign prostatic hyperplasia: presentation *554*
Benign prostatic hyperplasia: treatment *556*
Prostatic cancer: presentation *558*
Prostate specific antigen *560*
Prostatic cancer: treatment *562*
Postmenopausal vaginal bleeding *564*
Vaginal prolapse *566*
   How to… care for a vaginal pessary *567*
Vulval disorders *568*
Sexual function *570*

The ageing genitourinary system

Changes in women

Oestrogen levels fall following menopause (usually around age 50). This leads to vaginal epithelium atrophy, decreased vaginal lubrication, and acidification and greater vulnerability to vaginal and urinary infection. The uterus and ovaries atrophy and the vagina becomes smaller and less elastic.

Hormone replacement therapy (HRT) improves menopausal symptoms but has other serious adverse effects that severely limit its use (see p484).

Changes in men

There are gradual changes in anatomy and function, but no sudden change in fertility, and most older men remain fertile. Testicular mass and sperm production fall as does semen quality. The prostate gland enlarges and fibroses—benign prostatic hypertrophy—but the volume of ejaculate remains similar.

Erection becomes less sustained, less firm, and the refractory period between erections lengthens. However, severe erectile dysfunction, i.e. inability to sustain an erection sufficient to have sexual intercourse, is usually the result of pathology or drug treatment rather than ageing itself.

Testosterone levels remain stable or decrease slightly. In a minority, more severe falls are seen and hypogonadism may become symptomatic, manifesting as fatigue, weakness, muscle atrophy, and impaired cognition. Male HRT may have symptomatic benefit, but risks serious disease. There are no good quality long-term trials of replacement therapy.

Changes in both sexes

Cross-sectional studies show much reduced frequency of sexual behaviour of all kinds in older people. However, longitudinal studies show much smaller changes, suggesting that many changes are due to cohort effects e.g. changes in the prevailing social environment during early adulthood.

Other factors include physical and psychological illness (e.g. arthritis, depression), reduced potency, social changes (e.g. lack of a partner due to bereavement). Most of these factors are modifiable.

Benign prostatic hyperplasia: presentation

Benign prostatic hyperplasia (BPH) is characterized by non-malignant enlargement of the prostate gland and an increase in prostatic smooth muscle tone. The resulting bladder outlet obstruction leads to lower urinary tract symptoms (LUTS; 'prostatism').

Prostatism affects 25–50% of men over 65 years, although the histological changes of BPH are even more common—almost universal in those over 70. The natural history is variable—some deteriorate, some stay the same, and some improve, even without treatment.

Assessment

Symptoms

Lower urinary tract symptoms are variable, and may be mostly either:
- *Obstructive*. Weak stream, straining, hesitancy, nocturia, acute retention, or chronic retention with overflow incontinence.
- *Irritative*. Frequency, dysuria, urgency, and urge incontinence.

Other presentations include haematuria (the prostate is hypervascular), urinary tract infection and renal failure secondary to hydronephrosis. Obstructive symptoms may be worsened by drugs e.g. sedating antihistamines. Tricyclic antidepressants may improve irritative symptoms, but worsen obstruction.

Scoring systems (see box opposite) can help determine symptom severity, track progression and response to treatment.

Examination

Include the genitals (phimosis or meatal stenosis), abdomen (palpable bladder), neurological system, and digital rectal examination (DRE).

In BPH, the prostate is usually smooth, firm and enlarged. An irregular prostate can occur in BPH, calculi, infarction, or cancer.

Investigations

Tests may help confirm the diagnosis, exclude other pathology, and identify complications:
- **Urinary flow rate** confirms obstruction, but is rarely needed.
- **Blood glucose** to exclude diabetes, a common cause of urinary symptoms.
- **U,C+E** (renal failure).
- **Urinalysis** (infection, haematuria).
- **USS renal tract** (hydronephrosis, high residual volume (see p577)
- **PSA**. Consider this, especially if the prostate is irregular. However, testing is not mandatory, and in general should be guided by the patient's views, after a discussion of risks and benefits of further investigation and treatment (see p560 and p562).
- **Cystoscopy and USS**. If haematuria is detected, to exclude renal and bladder cancer.

International prostate symptom score (IPSS)

This is a well-validated, widely used assessment tool that can be either self-administered, or given as part of a structured assessment by a health professional. Aggregate scores from the seven questions to give a total score range of 0–35:

0–7   Mildly symptomatic
8–19   Moderately symptomatic
20–35 Severely symptomatic

	Not at all	Less than 1 time in 5	Less than half the time	About half the time	More than half the time	Almost always
Incomplete emptying. Over the past month, how often have you had a sensation of not emptying your bladder completely after you finish urinating?	0	1	2	3	4	5
Frequency. Over the past month, how often have you had to urinate again less than two hours after you finished urinating?	0	1	2	3	4	5
Intermittency. Over the past month, how often have you found you stopped and started again several times when you urinated?	0	1	2	3	4	5
Urgency. Over the past month, how difficult have you found it to postpone urination?	0	1	2	3	4	5
Weak stream. Over the past month, how often have you had a weak urinary stream?	0	1	2	3	4	5
Straining. Over the past month, how often have you had to push or strain to begin urination?	0	1	2	3	4	5

	None	1 time	2 times	3 times	4 times	5 times or more
Nocturia. Over the past month, many times did you most typically get up to urinate, from the time you went to bed until the time you got up in the morning?	0	1	2	3	4	5

Benign prostatic hyperplasia: treatment

Treatment choice is influenced by patient preference, severity of symptoms, presence of complications, and fitness for surgery.

Conservative measures. 'Watchful waiting' is reasonable if symptoms are mild or moderate and complications absent. Reassure the patient. Reassess clinically and check renal function at 6–12 month intervals. Advise reduction in evening fluid intake; stop unnecessary diuretics. The main risk is acute urine retention (1–2% per year).

Herbal preparations. These are widely used by patients, bought 'over-the-counter'; always ask about non-prescription remedies. The most widely used is saw palmetto (*Serenoa repens*) extract, and there is some evidence that it works, especially in milder disease, perhaps acting as a 5-alpha reductase inhibitor (see below). PSA levels may therefore be reduced.

Drugs. Suitable for mild, moderate or severe symptoms without complications, especially if patient preference is strong. Patients with more severe symptoms benefit most. Two drug classes may help:
- *Alpha-adrenergic blockers* ('alpha-blockers' e.g. doxazosin, terazosin, tamsulosin). They relax prostatic smooth muscle, increasing urine flow rates and reducing symptoms in days. Side effects are common: the most important are hypotension, especially orthostatic hypotension, and syncope. Use cautiously, starting with low dose (e.g. doxazosin 1mg od, increased in 1mg increments at 2-week intervals to 4mg). Exercise great caution if prescribed with diuretics or other vasodilators, if there is a past history of syncope, and in the frail. Tamsulosin (400mcg od; dose titration not possible) may be more prostate-selective than other alpha-blockers and may have fewer circulatory side effects.
- *5-alpha reductase inhibitors* (e.g. finasteride). These inhibit prostatic testosterone metabolism, reducing prostatic size. Benefit occurs slowly (months) and is most likely if the prostate is large (>40ml); those with mild enlargement benefit little or not at all. Side effects are uncommon but include erectile dysfunction (<5%), gynaecomastia and loss of libido. Given the absence of cardiovascular side effects, 5-alpha reductase inhibitors may be a better option in the frail older person. PSA levels fall by ~50%, so double the observed value to give an indication of prostate cancer risk.
- *Combination treatment*. There is no evidence that this is more effective than monotherapy. If there is no significant benefit with one drug class, switch to another, or consider surgery.

Alpha-blockers, prostatism, and hypertension

Many men have both symptoms of prostatism and are hypertensive. Alpha-blockers can be an attractive option as the one drug may treat both. However, the evidence for alpha-blockers in the treatment of hypertension is less good than for several other drug classes (e.g. ACE-inhibitors). Assess the impact on each problem separately, and consider prescribing the most appropriate treatment for each individual condition. See also p291.

Surgery. More effective than drugs or 'watchful waiting', but side effects are more common and usually irreversible. Indicated if:
* Symptoms are moderate or severe (with patient preference).
* There are complications (recurrent UTI or haematuria, renal failure).
* A trial of drug treatment has failed.

Transurethral resection of the prostate (TURP). The (gold-) standard procedure. Success rates are >90%. Adverse effects include retrograde ejaculation (most), erectile dysfunction (5–10%), incontinence (1%) and death (<1%). 10% need further surgery within a few years.

Newer procedures. Several have been developed. They are generally less invasive and probably have fewer adverse effects, but long term outcome data is less good. Local availability and expertise are limited. For example:
* *Transurethral incision of the prostate (TUIP)*. Effective in those with smaller prostate glands. Low incidence of side effects.
* *Transurethral microwave thermotherapy (TUMT) and transurethral needle ablation (TUNA)*. These newer systems are well tolerated, and require only local anaesthetic in an outpatient setting. However, some are time-consuming and difficult to learn, long-term results are less well known, and availability varies locally.

Open prostatectomy is reserved for very large glands and where other interventions are needed, e.g. removal of bladder stones. It is very effective, but comorbidity is higher.

Urinary catheterization

Long-term urinary catheterization is an option where:
* Symptoms are severe, or significant complications have occurred.
* Surgical mortality and morbidity would be high.
* Drug treatment has not been tolerated, or is unlikely to be effective.

The usual example is acute or chronic urine retention where other contributory causes (e.g. constipation) have been addressed, but the patient remains in retention and has failed a trial (or trials) without catheter.

Prostatic cancer: presentation

A very common cancer in men, much more so with age: median age at diagnosis is over 70. However:
- Most die *with* tumour rather than *because* of it.
- Most are asymptomatic, or have only obstructive symptoms.
- Many tumours do not progress, even without treatment.

This leads to difficult management decisions, especially in older people, where life expectancy for other reasons may be low, and expensive, unpleasant or risky treatments may not be worthwhile.

Assessment

Predictors of an adverse disease course (symptoms, local progression, metastases and death) include more advanced stage (TNM classification) and histological grade (e.g. Gleason score: see below).

Localized cancer Often detected when evaluating a man with lower tract symptoms due to BPH (by finding an elevated PSA), or incidentally e.g. at TURP for BPH. Tumour remains within the gland capsule; the tumour focus may be very small, and in no way responsible for symptoms. DRE may be normal. Prognosis is generally good, especially if grade is favourable. Cure may be possible, although for more indolent tumours, attempts at cure (surgery, radiotherapy) may be worse than the disease.

Locally advanced cancer without metastases Usually detected in patients with urinary symptoms, or at DRE performed for other reasons. A much larger group now that PSA testing is more common. The tumour has broken through the capsule, and prognosis is more adverse. Cure is not usually possible, but survival may be prolonged.

Metastatic cancer Up to half of newly diagnosed patients have metastatic disease. Many are asymptomatic. Features (decreasing frequency) include urinary symptoms, bone pain, constitutional symptoms (e.g. weight loss), renal failure, pathological fracture, and anaemia due to bone marrow infiltration. A minority have an indolent course, and with treatment may survive many years.

Gleason score

A histological grading system that correlates well with outcome and helps guide treatment choice. A composite of two scores (each range 1–5), therefore range 2–10:

2–4:   Well differentiated
5–7:   Moderately differentiated
8–10: Poorly differentiated

Screening

There is no good evidence that earlier detection through screening improves prognosis. This often requires careful explanation (see *Oxford Handbook of Clinical Medicine*, 6th edition, p499). Rectal examination is insensitive: tumours detected in this way are often large and locally advanced. PSA has its own drawbacks (see p560).

Tests

These should be selected advisedly, after considering the patient's wishes, the implications of a negative or positive result, and any risks of the test.

- **PSA.** See following page.
- **FBC.** Evidence of marrow infiltration.
- **Serum calcium, LFTs.** Evidence of metastases.
- **U,C+E.** Evidence of post-renal renal failure.
- **Transrectal USS and biopsy.** Provides tissue for histological diagnosis and grading. Risks haemorrhage and infection.
- **Bone scan or X-rays.** If there are symptoms, or bone biochemistry is suggestive. Metastasis to bone is common; appearance is sclerotic much more commonly than lytic.
- **CT/MRI scan.** For tumour staging where surgery is contemplated.

Prostate specific antigen

Prostate specific antigen (PSA) is made in the prostate and blood levels reflect prostatic synthesis.

It has two definite useful roles:
- In very early detection of localized prostate cancer when treatment may be curative.
- In tracking tumour progression: changes in PSA usually reflect changes in tumour mass.

However, PSA is produced by both benign and malignant prostatic tissue, and there is no single useful cutoff point that separates those with cancer from those without:
- Two thirds of men with a high PSA do not have prostate cancer.
- One fifth of men with prostate cancer have a normal PSA.

The higher the PSA level, the more likely is cancer. However, even at moderately high levels (>10µg/L) the positive predictive value is only 65%. Specificity is even less in older people as the benign causes of elevated PSA are more common.

Combining this with the limitations of treatment, any screening programme utilizing PSA yields:
- Many people with high PSA but no cancer found after further tests.
- Many people with locally advanced prostate cancer for whom early treatment is not known to improve prognosis.

Non-malignant causes of increased PSA

PSA increases with age and with:
- BPH
- Prostatitis
- Urinary tract infection
- Rectal examination (up to 7 days)
- Prostatic biopsy (6 weeks)
- Urethral catheterization
- Urethral instrumentation e.g. cystoscopy
- Vigorous exercise (48 hrs)
- Ejaculation (48 hrs).

(Figures in brackets are approximate durations of elevation.)

Age-specific PSA values

The following have been suggested as cut-off points to reduce unnecessary referral and investigation of patients with benign prostate disease.

50–59 years: ≥3.0µg/L
60–69 years: ≥4.0µg/L
≥70 years: ≥5.0µg/L

PSA reduces with some drug treatment (e.g. 5-alpha-reductase inhibitors; herbal remedies such as saw palmetto (*Serenoa repens*)), and may therefore reduce the above thresholds for referral.

Prostatic cancer: treatment

Localized cancer. There are several treatment options, including 'watchful waiting', hormonal treatment, radiotherapy, or surgery.

'Watchful waiting' Usually reserved for those with modest life expectancy (<10 years) and lower grade (Gleason score 2–6) localized tumours, where progression is rare within 10 years. Check PSA each 4–6 months. Start treatment (usually hormonal) if symptoms, or if PSA rises.

Hormone treatment (see below). There is great doubt whether early hormone treatment improves outcome compared to 'watchful waiting'.

Radiotherapy The most usual choice for high grade localized tumours. Probably as effective as surgery, but better tolerated. Side effects include erectile dysfunction, irritative urinary symptoms, and radiation proctitis.

Surgery Radical prostatectomy is a major procedure, usually indicated only for those with long life expectancy, high grade tumours, and in good health. Major side effects are incontinence, impotence and haemorrhage.

Locally advanced disease without metastases. Key treatments are radiotherapy (see above) and/or androgen deprivation (see below). The relative benefits are unclear. Surgery probably offers no benefit, other than TURP to relieve outflow symptoms.

Metastatic disease. Androgen deprivation ('hormone treatment') is the linchpin of treatment. This can be achieved by castration (bilateral orchidectomy, usually under local anaesthetic), but is usually chemical, largely for reasons of patient preference. Treatment should not be delayed, even if there are no symptoms. Luteinizing hormone releasing hormone (LHRH) agonists are used commonly and are usually effective for 12–18 months. If disease progresses despite LHRH agonists, patients occasionally respond to antiandrogens. Surgery offers no benefits.

LHRH agonists (e.g. goserelin (Zoladex®)). Given as injections or implants, these cause initial (2 weeks) stimulation and then sustained depression of testosterone release. The initial increase can cause tumour growth ('flare') with adverse effects e.g. urinary outflow obstruction, spinal cord compression, or bone pain. If anticipated, anti-androgens may help. Continuous therapy is not needed: survival appears similar if therapy is stopped when PSA levels are normal and restarted when they rise.

Antiandrogens (e.g. bicalutamide (Casodex®), flutamide). Useful in inhibiting tumour flare after LHRH agonist initiation, in tumour refractory to LHRH agonists, if LHRH agonists are not tolerated or accepted (e.g. because of erectile dysfunction) or where oral drugs are preferred. There is no evidence that combined antiandrogens and LHRH agonists are helpful.

Side effects of LHRH agonists and antiandrogens include hot flushes, erectile dysfunction and gynaecomastia.

Late stage prostate cancer

Eventually, prostate cancer may become resistant (refractory) to hormone treatment, manifesting as a rising PSA and/or worsening symptoms whilst on treatment. Other treatments (e.g. oestrogens) may be tried, but are rarely very effective. Death follows, often in months.

Common complications, usually in more advanced disease, include:

Bone pain. A major cause of reduced quality of life. Optimize oral analgesia: combinations of paracetamol, opiates and NSAIDs are effective. Local pain is helped by radiotherapy. Bisphosphonates or steroids may also help.

Pathological bone fracture. Usually requires surgical fixation.

Acute urine retention. Catheterize. Intensify anti-tumour treatment if appropriate (e.g. hormone treatment, radiotherapy). Consider TURP.

Post-renal renal failure. Determine site of obstruction by ultrasound.

Prostatic obstruction: catheter, TURP, intensify anti-tumour treatment.
Ureteric obstruction: stenting or nephrostomy.

Spinal cord compression. An emergency, as early decompression improves neurological outcome. Confirm with CT or MRI. Steroids, radiotherapy, or surgery help decompress the cord.

Postmenopausal vaginal bleeding

Defined as bleeding from the genital tract over one year after onset of menopausal amenorrhoea. The time criterion reflects the fact that menstruation is often irregular and infrequent around menopause, and investigations for sinister pathology are not then worthwhile.

Most cases are secondary to benign pathology, but treatment of the few cases of cancer (largely endometrial) is far more effective if identified early, so do not delay assessment. Malignancy is more likely if bleeding is significant and recurrent—investigate vigorously if no cause is apparent.

Assessment

History. Assess the amount and frequency of bleeding, if necessary by discussing with carers. Consider other possible sources of blood e.g. urinary, rectal. Take an accurate drug history.

Examine. Examine the genitalia, perineum, and rectum to exclude tumour, trauma, and bleeding from atrophic sites. Obesity or osteoarthritis may make examination difficult; the left or right lateral positions are usually more successful.

Investigation. FBC to exclude severe anaemia. Urine dipstick for haematuria is unlikely to be specific to blood of urinary tract origin, especially if bleeding is recurrent or ongoing.

Further tests are usually guided by expert gynaecological advice, but may include:
- Cervical smear.
- Vaginal USS to assess endometrial thickness (<5mm effectively excludes cancer and may prevent the need for more tests).
- Hysteroscopy—can be done under local or general anaesthetic.
- Dilatation and curettage.
- Consider investigation of urinary and GI tract (cystoscopy, sigmoidoscopy).

Treatment

Is directed to the underlying cause, e.g.:
- ***Atrophic vaginitis:*** topical oestrogens (see pp484–5). HRT if topical oestrogens fail.
- ***HRT:*** review the balance of risks and benefits and consider stopping the drug (see pp484–5). Consider change of preparation e.g. reduction of oestrogen dose, increase in progestogen dose.
- ***Endometrial carcinoma:*** total abdominal hysterectomy and bilateral salpingo-oophorectomy and/or radiotherapy are the usual interventions. In those unfit for surgery, progestogens (e.g. medroxyprogesterone) may control the tumour.

Causes of post-menopausal vaginal bleeding

In approximate order of frequency:

- *Atrophic vaginitis.* Inflammation results as the thinner, less cornified epithelium is exposed to a more alkaline vaginal environment colonized by a broad microbial flora.
- *Endometrial hyperplasia* secondary to:
  - Exogenous oestrogen (e.g. HRT)
  - Unopposed endogenous oestrogen (especially in older, obese women where peripheral conversion of steroid hormones to oestrogens by fat cells is higher).
- *Benign tumour* e.g. cervical or endometrial polyps.
- *Vaginal prolapse* and ulceration.
- *Vaginal infection.*
- *Carcinoma.*
  - Endometrial
  - Cervical
  - Vulval
  - Vaginal
  - Ovarian.

Other relatively common causes of 'vaginal' bleeding include haematuria and rectal bleeding.

After hysterectomy, bleeding is commonly due to atrophic vaginitis or overgrowth of post-surgical granulation tissue.

Drugs causing endometrial disease (hyperplasia, polyps and cancer) include:

- *HRT*
  - Cyclical replacement: investigate if bleed at unexpected times.
  - Continuous oestrogen and progestogen: investigate if irregular bleeding persists for >12 months after treatment initiation.
- *Tamoxifen* (via a paradoxical endometrial oestrogen-like effect).

Vaginal prolapse

A prolapse is a protrusion into the vagina by a pelvic organ (bladder, bowel, or uterus) caused by:
- Weakness of pelvic connective tissue and musculature due to cumulative effects of childbirth trauma, ageing, and oestrogen deficiency.
- Increased abdominal pressure e.g. constipation, obesity and coughing.

Depending on which structures are weak, the following may be seen:
- *Cystocoele:* the bladder protrudes through the anterior vaginal wall.
- *Rectocoele:* the rectum protrudes through the posterior vaginal wall.
- *Enterocoele:* herniation of peritoneum and small bowel (the pouch of Douglas), through the posterior vaginal wall.
- *Uterine prolapse:* descent of the cervix and uterus down the vagina.
  - 1st degree: cervix lies within the vagina.
  - 2nd degree: cervix protrudes from the vagina on standing/straining.
  - 3rd degree (procidentia): cervix lies outside the vagina.

Assessment

Often asymptomatic. Most commonly there is a sensation of heaviness, fullness or bearing down, a palpable mass or a dull pelvic or back ache. Symptoms may be abolished by lying down.
- *Cystocoele* may cause stress or overflow urinary incontinence, urinary tract infection, or bladder outflow obstruction.
- *Rectocoele* may cause faecal incontinence or difficulty in defaecation—manual evacuation or digital reduction of the prolapse may be needed.
- *Enterocoele* causes pelvic fullness and discomfort.
- *Third degree uterine prolapse* may cause ulceration and bleeding, and bladder symptoms e.g. difficulty in urinating.

Perform a pelvic examination, using a speculum if available. Severe prolapse will be immediately apparent. Asking the patient to bear down may reveal smaller degrees of prolapse. Some prolapses (e.g. rectocoele) are detected only by bimanual examination of rectum and vagina.

Treatment

This is dictated by symptoms, prolapse severity, the organs involved, general fitness, and patient preference. Urodynamic testing and imaging may be needed prior to treatment.
- Mild symptoms: topical oestrogen cream and pelvic floor exercises.
- Moderate or severe symptoms: pessary or surgery.

Surgery is now generally well tolerated and effective. Usually via a transvaginal approach, weakened structures of the pelvic floor are strengthened and fixed in place. Hysterectomy is sometimes necessary.

Pessaries. Fitting of a pessary is indicated for reasons of patient preference, when the risks of surgery are unfavourable, and as a temporary measure prior to surgery. They come in many shapes and sizes, but the most commonly used is the ring pessary. Other shapes may be used, commonly for severe disease, but can be difficult to insert and remove.

HOW TO... care for a vaginal pessary

Every 4–6 months:
- Remove and clean the pessary
- Examine the vagina for evidence of ulceration
- Replace a damaged pessary
- Reinsert if all is well.

Complications
- If vaginal ulceration occurs, the pessary should be removed for several weeks, until complete healing has occurred. Local oestrogen creams assist healing and may prevent recurrent ulceration. Try a different shape or size of pessary.
- Pessaries can embed in inflamed vaginal mucosa and become stuck. Topical oestrogens and treatment of infection (e.g. candida) may reduce inflammation and assist removal. If the pessary remains stuck, refer for specialist gynaecological assessment.

Vulval disorders

Most non-malignant vulval disorders are worsened by local irritants (e.g. soap, deodorant, perfume) and improve if avoided. Good perineal hygiene also helps e.g. wiping front-to-back after urination or defaecation, keeping the area dry and wearing loose-fitting non-synthetic clothing.

Vulvitis

Symptoms: itching, discharge, burning discomfort.

Causes. These include:

- Candida ('thrush'). The most common cause, especially in diabetes and obesity. Vaginal infection almost always coexists.
- Local dermatitis. Often exacerbated by soap and deodorants.
- Sexually transmitted pathogens. Uncommonly, e.g. chlamydia.

Treatment

- Treat candida with antifungal cream to the vulva (e.g. clotrimazole 1% cream) and pessaries or cream inserted high into the vagina (e.g. clotrimazole 200mg pessary daily for three days). Single dose pessaries (e.g. clotrimazole 500mg pessary once) are effective and may be better tolerated. Oral treatment is also effective, e.g. fluconazole 150mg once.
- Treat irritant dermatitis by removing the cause and regular application of topical steroid cream (e.g. hydrocortisone 1%) for 7–14 days.
- Recurrent candidal infection is common, especially in diabetes and in those receiving repeated antibiotics. Consider longer-term treatment, e.g. weekly clotrimazole (500mg pessary) or fluconazole (100mg p.o.).
- If vulval itch persists without obvious cause, see pp650–2 and consider:
  - Systemic disease e.g. iron deficiency, thyroid disorders.
  - Use emollients and low potency topical steroid to break the itch-scratch-itch cycle. Antihistamines are not effective.

Vulvodynia

A chronic pain syndrome manifesting as burning, pain or tenderness of the vulva. There are often psychological contributors. Infection, dermatitis, and epithelial disorders (neoplastic and non-neoplastic) should be excluded. Refer for specialist assessment, and consider treating depression and empirical treatment with topical steroids or oestrogens.

Non-neoplastic epithelial disorders

Lichen sclerosus. Common in middle aged and older women. Asymptomatic or else causes itching or soreness or dyspareunia. Seen as white or pink/purple macules or papules resembling thin parchment paper and often in a figure-of-eight distribution around the vulva. Biopsy to exclude neoplasia. Treat with potent topical steroids, tapering the potency and frequency as symptoms improve. Progression to carcinoma can occur. Long-term follow-up is sensible.

Squamous hyperplasia. Raised white keratinized lesions that may be very localized. Biopsy may be needed to exclude malignancy. Treat with medium potency topical steroids, tapering to a stop as symptoms improve.

Other disorders. e.g. psoriasis and chronic dermatitis can usually be diagnosed clinically, but biopsy permits more confident management.

Malignant epithelial disorders

Vulval cancer. Easily treated in its early stages and often preceded by a pre-malignant stage. Late presentation is more common with age. Commonly asymptomatic and an incidental finding, but may itch, discharge, bleed, or cause pain. Appearance is variable—may be raised or ulcerated, or else appear as white or coloured macules. If in any doubt that a lesion may be malignant or pre-malignant, then refer for biopsy.

Treatment depends on the size and invasiveness of the tumour, the presence or absence of metastases, and the condition of the patient. Options include topical cytotoxic creams, resection under local anaesthetic, wide local excision, or radical vulvectomy. Extensive vulval surgery is relatively well tolerated in older people.

▶▶ If any vulval lesion does not respond as expected to treatment, re-consider the possibility of malignancy.

Sexual function

Studies show that most older people desire some sexual contact. However, the frequency of sexual intercourse, both penetrative and non-penetrative, falls with age. This decline is multifactorial, including:

- Lack of partner e.g. death of spouse.
- Physiological changes of ageing e.g. decreased vaginal secretions, less sustained penile erections.
- Physical comorbidity and medication e.g. circulatory disease, beta-blockers.
- Psychological comorbidity e.g. low self esteem, depression.
- Societal expectations and judgements.
- Lack of privacy, especially in institutional care.

The clinical response to a patient's report of sexual dysfunction involves addressing each of these factors in a supportive and understanding way.

Erectile dysfunction

Erection requires intact neurological, circulatory, hormonal, and psychological processes. In older people, several factors more commonly contribute to erectile dysfunction (ED) or impotence. A solely psychological cause is uncommon. Common contributors are drugs, vascular disease (arterial > venous) and neurological disease (stroke, autonomic neuropathy, local surgery e.g. prostatectomy)

History. Assess onset and progression, circumstances, and associated psychological issues. ED is common, yet is rarely asked about. Older men may volunteer the symptom, but many will accept it as part of 'normal ageing'. Do not assume that an older man is not sexually active, and always warn about impotence as a potential side effect of relevant drugs.

Drugs causing erectile dysfunction. Along with vascular disease, drugs are the most common cause in older people:

- Antihypertensives (especially beta-blockers and diuretics. ACE-inhibitors less so)
- Alcohol
- Antiandrogens, LHRH agonists, oestrogens, progestogens
- Antidepressants (all classes, except trazodone)
- Less commonly: cimetidine, spironolactone.

Examination. Of mental state (depression, anxiety). Presence of secondary sexual characteristics. Vascular disease. Genitourinary examination. Neurological examination to include perineal and perianal sensation.

Investigation. Exclude systemic illness with FBC, U,C+E and glucose. Diagnostic tests to determine an underlying cause of erectile dysfunction (ED) do not often alter management and are rarely performed. Hypogonadism is an uncommon cause of ED, so checking testosterone level is not usually necessary. If libido (rather than ED) is the problem, then exclude hypogonadism by checking testosterone, LH, TSH, and prolactin.

Treatment—where possible, stop incriminated drugs. Treat underlying disease including anxiety/depression. Recently developed drug treatments re highly effective.

Phosphodiesterase type-5 inhibitors e.g. sildenafil (Viagra®) cause smooth muscle relaxation and increase blood flow, they are easily used take p.o. before intercourse), effective, and safe. Contraindications nclude patients on nitrates; exercise caution in those with coronary or erebro-vascular disease. Side effects are gastrointestinal and vascular flushing, headache).

Alprostadil (prostaglandin E1) is usually given as an intraurethral pellet, s absorbed locally and causes local smooth muscle relaxation, There is no significant systemic absorption, so systemic side effects are rare and ascular disease is not a contraindication.

Other options include intracavernosal injections (the most effective reatment) and non-drug options such as vacuum devices (effective, but often discontinued due to discomfort).

Incontinence

Urinary incontinence: causes *574*
Urinary incontinence: assessment *576*
Urinary incontinence: management *578*
Catheters *580*
   How to… manage urinary incontinence without
   a catheter *580*
   How to… minimize and treat catheter complications *581*
Faecal incontinence: causes *582*
Faecal incontinence: assessment *584*
Faecal incontinence: management *586*
   How to… treat 'overflow' faecal incontinence *587*

Urinary incontinence: causes

▶▶ Incontinence has a major adverse impact on quality of life and has significant associated morbidity (it may be the last straw leading to institutionalization). Even longstanding cases may be reversible so always explore continence issues even if everyone else is complacent.

It is very common (around 30% of elderly at home, 50% in care homes) but is not a natural consequence of ageing. Most incontinence in the elderly is multifactorial and can be divided as follows:

Age related changes
- Diminished total bladder capacity but increased residual volume.
- Diminished bladder contractile function.
- Increased frequency of uninhibited bladder contractions.
- Reduced ability to postpone voiding.
- Excretion of fluid later in the day with less concentrated night-time urine.
- Atrophy of vagina and urethra in females.
- Loss of pelvic floor and urethral sphincter musculature.
- Hypertrophy of the prostate in males.

Comorbidity
- Diminished mobility and manual dexterity.
- Prescribed medications affect lower urinary tract or conscious state.
- Increased constipation.
- Impaired cognition—confusion can cause inappropriate micturition or interfere with upper motor neurone input into continence pathways.

Reversible factors
- Urinary tract infection (pp680–3).
- Delirium.
- Drugs e.g. diuretics cause polyuria, anticholinergics such as tricyclics cause retention, sedatives can reduce awareness or mobility.
- Constipation—may cause voiding difficulty and increased residual volumes in both sexes.
- Polyuria (e.g. poorly controlled diabetes, hypercalcaemia, oedema resorption at night can cause nocturnal polyuria, psychogenic polydipsia).
- Urethral irritability (e.g. atrophic vaginitis, candida infection).
- Bladder stones and tumours.

Irreversible (but treatable) factors
- In males, prostatic hypertrophy or carcinoma causes outflow obstruction, an unstable bladder or 'overflow' incontinence.
- Overactive bladder syndrome (symptom diagnosis)/detrusor overactivity (urodynamic diagnosis)—spontaneous contractions of the bladder muscle causes urgency and frequency ± incontinence.
- In females, outlet incompetence (stress incontinence)—usually due to pelvic muscle and ligament laxity (which supports the urethra) following childbirth—any rise in intrabdominal pressure causes small leaks e.g. with cough.
- Mixed symptoms—suggesting the presence of both overactivity and stress incontinence.

Urinary incontinence: assessment

Much is made in the literature of the different symptoms in different diagnostic groups.

- **Urgency symptoms** Frequent and precipitant voiding—inability to 'hold on' with passage of urine before toilet is reached. Nocturnal incontinence common. Urge symptoms are common with detrusor overactivity where residual volume small, but can occur in obstruction.
- **Stress symptoms** Small volume leaks during coughing, laughing etc. Often coexist with urge symptoms in women.
- **Obstructive symptoms** in men.

The elderly are often unable to give precise descriptions and the different symptom complexes can overlap. Even where a 'pure' symptom complex exists you may get the diagnosis wrong e.g. prostatic outflow symptoms where incontinence is actually detrusor overactivity or symptoms of urgency as a presentation for retention with overflow.

A more pragmatic approach is often required.

1. *Take a history.* A bladder or voiding diary can help, especially if you are relying on carers for information.
2. *Examination* Include vaginal, rectal, and neurological examination.
3. *Exclude a significant residual volume* See box opposite.
4. *Investigations* Urinalysis and MSU, general screening blood tests, cytology, and cystoscopy if haematuria. Urodynamics can be helpful if patient's incontinence cannot be explained or they are not responding to treatment and essential if surgical intervention is contemplated.

Residual volume

Normal young people have only a few ml of urine post-micturition but normal elderly can have up to 100ml.

Causes of raised residual volume include
- Prostatic hypertrophy, carcinoma
- Urethral stricture
- Bladder diverticulum
- Large urinary cystocoele (females)
- Hypocontractile detrusor
- Spinal cord disease
- Bladder tumour.

Acute retention is usually painful but can present atypically with delirium, renal failure etc.

Chronic bladder distention is usually painless, presenting with infection, abdominal distension/mass or incontinence (continuous dribbling due to overflow or urge incontinence due to detrusor instability).

Persistently elevated residual volume increases the risk of infection.

If pressure is elevated this can cause dilation of the urinary tract and eventually hydronephrosis and renal failure.

Residual volume can easily be estimated using a simple ultrasound bladder scan or a diagnostic (in/out) catheterization.

Urinary incontinence: management

- Depends on cause so try to make a diagnosis first.
- Incontinence is multifactorial in most elderly so combining treatments may be necessary e.g. a man with obstructive prostatic symptoms and detrusor hyperactivity may benefit from an alpha-blocker and an anti-muscarinic (e.g. tolterodine).

Treatment	Indication	Notes
Bladder retraining (gradually increasing time between voiding)	Overactive bladder syndrome/detrusor over activity	
Regular toileting (taking to toilet every 2–4 hours)	Dementia Overactive bladder syndrome	Decreases likelihood of incontinence episodes
Pelvic floor exercises	Stress incontinence	Effect wears off when exercises stop
Bladder stabilizing drugs Tolterodine 2mg bd–4mg od Solifenacin 5–10mg od Trospium chloride 20mg bd Oxybutynin 2.5mg bd–5mg tds	Overactive bladder syndrome/detrusor overactivity	May precipitate urinary retention—monitor carefully Side effects of dry mouth, constipation, postural hypotension may limit effectiveness. Titrate dose up slowly. Use for 6 weeks before maximal effect.
Surgery —female	For stress incontinence—tension-free vaginal tape (TVT) is promising new procedure Colposuspension—gold standard operation	Refer for urodynamics to prior to surgery
—male	For outflow tract obstruction TURP (transurethral prostatectomy)	
Anti-androgens Finasteride 5mg od	For prostatic hyperplasia Improves flow and obstructive symptoms	Slow onset of action Decreased libido/impotence

Table contd.

Treatment	Indication	Notes
Alpha-blockers Doxazosin 1mg–4mg od Tamsulosin 400mcg od	Smooth muscle relaxant for BPH—improves flow and obstructive symptoms	Titrate dose slowly—watch for hypotension (especially postural) and syncope/falls Useful for co-treatment of hypertension
Double micturition (ask patient to repeat voiding)	Sometimes helps reduce large residual volumes and decrease UTI	
Intermittent catheterization	Atonic/hypotonic bladder—removing residual volumes daily can aid continence and reduce renal damage and infection. Also used to dilate stenotic urethras.	Surprisingly well tolerated in 'flexible' elderly
Synthetic vasopressin either oral or intranasal	Useful for nocturnal frequency	Main troublesome side effect is dilutional hyponatraemia—unlicensed for over 65s in UK Caution in patients with co-morbid conditions likely to be exacerbated

Catheters

A catheter is indicated for:
- Symptomatic urinary retention.
- Obstructed outflow associated with deteriorating renal function or hydronephrosis.
- Acute renal failure for accurate urine output monitoring.
- Intensive care settings.
- Sacral pressure sores with incontinence.
- Where other methods of bladder management cause undue distress to a frail older person.

A catheter is NOT usually indicated for:
- Immobility—even from stroke.
- Heart failure—just because you are giving furosemide.
- Monitoring fluid balance in a continent patient.
- Convenience of nursing—at home or in hospital (see box below).
- Asymptomatic chronic retention—refer to urology for assessment.

HOW TO... **manage urinary incontinence without a catheter**

Assuming you have first made a diagnosis, and investigated and treated any reversible causes there will still be patients who will be permanently or intermittently incontinent of urine.

▶▶ An indwelling catheter is not always the best solution. They have been shown to increase morbidity (infection, stones, urethral erosion) and even mortality.

Suggesting that catheters are removed is one of a geriatrician's most important jobs in post-acute care. If in doubt involve a specialist continence nurse/team.

Other options for continence management include:
- *Environmental modifications*: urinals/commodes by the bed, easy access clothing etc can minimize or prevent accidents.
- *Regular or individualized toileting programmes*: this can be very successful in patients with dementia but is labour intensive.
- *Pad and pants*: can be very effective but is quite labour intensive for very immobile patients.
- *A drainage sheath* (Conveen is a manufacturer) for men: like a catheter but held onto the penis with a plastic sheath like a condom. Particularly useful for isolated nocturnal incontinence as it can be removed by day. Main problem is displacement and leakage which can be a problem with small or unusually-shaped penises.
- *Intermittent catheterization*: for those with obstruction or atonic bladders. Consider in agile, cognitively intact patients. Can be supported by district nursing services.

HOW TO... minimize and treat catheter complications

General
- Long term catheters should be either silicone, silastic or silver impregnated (expensive)—fewer blockages and infections.
- Catheters should be changed at least every 3 months.
- Encourage good oral intake of fluid.
- Consider the use of a catheter valve (like a beer keg tap) rather than a drainage bag.

Blocked catheters
- Consider possibility of stones, infection, or bladder tumour.
- Renew catheter, maintain good fluid intake, regular Suby G® catheter maintenance solution can be used for short periods.

'Bypassing'
- Catheters can irritate bladder causing contractions—resulting leak of urine past catheter can render them useless and occasionally causes very painful spasms.
- This is particularly common where detrusor overactivity was cause of incontinence.
- Can be induced or aggravated by infection.
- First exclude catheter blockage (which presents with identical spasms and leaks).
- If no residual volume try reducing catheter diameter and balloon size.
- Anti-muscarinic drugs can sometimes help.

Catheter infections
- All catheters become colonized after a few days, all catheter urine will dipstick positive, and all CSU specimens will grow bacteria.
- ▶▶ This alone is not an indication for antibiotics
- Bad smelling, dark coloured, and cloudy urine is more commonly due to dehydration and is not an indication for antibiotics per se.
- There are now some trials of cranberry juice/capsules that suggest there is a minor effect on reducing recurrent infections.
- Only treat clinically significant infections (fever, malaise, delirium, pain, abnormal inflammatory markers etc) or you will just promote resistant organisms.
- If you believe a catheter is a source of significant infection:
  - Send a CSU to guide antibiotic choice.
  - Remove the catheter where possible (even if only for 48 hours). If not possible change catheter with a single shot of IM gentamicin 80–120mg.
  - Ensure adequate hydration.
  - Choose a narrow spectrum antibiotic if sensitivities allow.
- For repeated significant infection consider if the catheter is really necessary. Low dose continuous antibiotic prophylaxis are advocated by some but there is little evidence.

Faecal incontinence: causes

Defined as the involuntary passage of faeces in inappropriate circumstances. The importance of situational factors mean there is potential for anyone to be incontinent in some circumstances.

- Incontinence of faeces is always abnormal, and nearly always curable.
- It is much less common than urinary incontinence, but more distressing.
- There is gross under-referral for diagnosis and treatment.
- Prevalence—10% of care home residents incontinent at least once per week

Continence mechanisms

- **The sigmo-rectal 'sphincter'** The rectum is usually empty. Passage of faeces into the rectum initiates rectal contraction (and anal relaxation), normally temporarily inhibited. The acute angle in the pelvic loop of the sigmoid may be important in causing temporary holdup.
- **The ano-rectal angle** The pubo-rectalis sling maintains an acute angle between rectum and anus, preventing passage of stool into the anal canal.
- **The anal sphincters** The external sphincter (striated, voluntary muscle), the internal sphincter (smooth muscle) and the anal vascular cushions which complete the seal.
- **Ano-rectal sensation** Sensation in the anus and rectum is usually sufficiently accurate to distinguish gas from faeces, permitting the passage of flatus without incontinence. Good sensation may be particularly important when diarrhoea is present.

Causes of faecal incontinence

- Disorders of the anal sphincter and lower rectum: sphincter laxity (from many causes), severe haemorrhoids, rectal prolapse, tumours, constipation.
- Any cause of faecal urgency (occasionally associated with reduced mobility): constipation (with spurious diarrhoea), any cause of diarrhoea (inflammatory bowel disease, drugs etc).
- Disorders of the neurological control of the ano-rectal muscle and sphincter: lower motor neurone lesions (neuropathic incontinence), spinal cord lesions, cognitive impairment (neurogenic incontinence).

The commonest cause (>50%) is faecal impaction. This is important because 95% are curable. The second commonest cause is neurogenic incontinence where the cure rate is still around 75%.

Faecal incontinence: assessment

Most patients can be helped by asking a few questions and performing a rectal examination.

Effective treatment is directed at the underlying cause so adequate assessment is vital.

History

- The duration of symptoms is not helpful: impaction is just as common in those who have been incontinent for more than three months as in those in whom the incontinence is recent.
- Having the bowels open regularly (e.g. every day) is usual in elderly patients with impaction.
- Complete constipation (not having the bowels open at all) is unusual in impaction.
- A feeling of rectal fullness with constant seepage of semi-liquid faeces is almost diagnostic of impaction, but rectal carcinoma may also present in this way.
- The combination of urinary and faecal incontinence strongly suggests impaction as the cause of both.
- Soiling without the patient being aware of it suggests neuropathy.

Examination

- **Inspect the anus** and ask the patient to strain as if at stool. Look for inflammation, deformities, large haemorrhoids (internal or external), and prolapse.
- **Rectal examination** Assess anal tone by the pressure on the finger after asking the patient 'tighten', feel for faeces and tumour, it is easy to miss even large internal haemorrhoids unless proctoscopy is performed.
- **Abdominal examination** Feel for the descending colon. Work proximally to assess colonic faecal loading (this may be misleading, see below).
- **Neurological examination** Look for signs of a peripheral neuropathy, and other neurological damage. Check perianal sensation (sacral dermatomes). Include a mental status assessment if you think neurogenic incontinence is likely.

Investigation

A plain abdominal radiograph may be necessary to detect proximal faecal loading of the colon (see p586). Investigation of the anal sphincter tone and neurological control of rectum and anus is in the province of the proctologist and may occasionally be needed for neuropathic incontinence.

Faecal incontinence: management

The two common treatments in old age are for constipation and neurogenic incontinence. In addition specialist proctology clinics can perform ano-rectal physiology assessment prior to the use of biofeedback techniques and surgery (even colostomy).

Treatment of constipation

Faecal impaction, faecal retention, faecal loading.

▶▶ In hospitalized older people, constipation is by far the commonest cause of incontinence; assume that any incontinent patient is constipated until proved otherwise and do not exclude it until after an adequate therapeutic trial of enemas for high faecal impaction.

See pp396–7 for definition, diagnosis, causes, prevention, and treatment of constipation. The box opposite shows how to treat 'overflow' incontinence.

Mechanism

Passage of faeces from the sigmoid into the rectum (often soon after a meal—the gastro-colic reflex) produces a sensation of rectal fullness, and a desire to defaecate. If this is ignored, the sensation gradually habituates and the rectum fills up with progressively harder faeces. At this stage some leakage past the anal sphincter (incontinence) is almost inevitable. Impaction of hard faecal material produces partial obstruction, stasis, irritation of the mucosa with excessive mucus production, and spurious diarrhoea. Emptying the colon of faeces has two main effects: it prevents spurious diarrhoea and therefore urgency and it permits normal colonic motility and habit to be restored.

Treatment of neurogenic faecal incontinence

Loss of control of the intrinsic rectal contraction caused by passage of normal faecal material from the sigmoid into the rectum results in the involuntary passage of a normal, formed stool at infrequent intervals, and usually at a timing characteristic of that patient (typically after breakfast).

It is a syndrome analogous with the uninhibited neurogenic bladder, and usually only occurs in the context of severe dementia. However, note that incontinence in demented patients is commonly due to constipation. The diagnosis is therefore usually made in a severely demented patient with a characteristic history after excluding the other common causes.

Since the diagnosis is usually one of exclusion, it is reasonable to treat most patients as though they have impaction, particularly if you cannot exclude high impaction by radiology. Once impaction has been excluded there are three strategies:

- In patients with a regular habit, toileting at the appropriate time (perhaps with the aid of a suppository) may be successful. This requires an attendant who knows the patient well.
- Arrange for a planned evacuation to suit the carers, by administering a constipating agent (e.g. loperamide 2mg od) combined with a phosphate enema two or three times weekly.
- If the patient has no regular habit and refuses enemas, the situation may have to be accepted and suitable protective clothing provided.

HOW TO... treat 'overflow' faecal incontinence

- **General** Rehydration (possibly intravenous), regular meals, and help with toileting are important.
- **Enemas** e.g. phosphate enema (120ml sodium phosphate (27%)) given once or (occasionally) twice daily. Continue until there is no result, the rectum is found to be empty on digital examination and the colon is impalpable abdominally. This may take a week or more.
- **Complete colonic washout** e.g. using bowel prep such as Picolax®. This is rather an extreme method but is sometimes required. Ensure the patient is well hydrated before you start.
- **Manual evacuation of faeces** Can cause further damage to the anal sphincters and is almost never necessary.
- **Laxatives** Generally less effective than enemas but can be used in addition, for milder cases and in the very frail. If the stool is hard use a stool softening laxative such as lactulose (20ml/day)—stimulant laxatives (e.g. senna) may produce severe pain. Stimulant laxatives or suppositories may be appropriate for those with soft faecal over-loading. A combination of stool softener and stimulant are some-times used. While extra fibre is useful in prophylaxis, stool bulking agents such as methylcellulose (Fybogel®) are of limited value in treating constipation as they increase the volume of stool being passed and may increase your problems.

▶▶ After treatment, think prevention (see p397).

If, despite the above measures, a patient becomes impacted for a second time (without an obvious and removable cause) then regular (say once or twice weekly) enemas should be prescribed. Progress can only be satisfactorily monitored by examining the patient abdominally and rectally.

Ears

Deafness and the ageing ear 590
  How to... assess hearing 592
Audiology 594
  How to... communicate with a deaf person 595
Hearing aids 596
  How to... use a hearing aid 597
Tinnitus 598
Vertigo 600
Vertigo: assessment 602
  How to... examine the vestibular system 603
Vertigo: management 604
  How to... perform Epley's manoeuvre 605

Deafness and the ageing ear

Deafness is a common, debilitating complaint, that increases with age. 6% of adults, 33% of retired people, and 80% of octogenarians in the UK have impaired hearing. Often ignored ('part of getting older') yet it prevents communication, causes social isolation, anxiety, depression, and can contribute to functional decline.

Around half could be helped by a hearing aid, yet less than a quarter has one.

▶▶ Be alert to hearing loss. A quick assessment directs appropriate referral to audiology or ENT when necessary.

Normal ageing

Presbyacusis

- Describes the decline in hearing that commonly occurs with age— 'degenerative deafness'.
- Males > females.
- Usually detectable from age 60–65.
- Both the sensory peripheral (cochlea) and central (neural) components of the auditory system are affected with peripheral degeneration being accountable for at least two thirds of the clinical features of presbyacusis.
- A variety of possible mechanisms exist—cellular degeneration gives rise to a reduction in the numbers of hair cells particularly at the basal end of the cochlea (the part responsible for high frequency sound appreciation). Circulatory changes such as atherosclerosis, micro-angiopathy and atrophy of the stria vascularis contribute.
- The relative contributions of 'normal ageing' and cumulative exposure to noxious stimuli (noise, toxins, oxidative stresses, otological disease, poor diet, vascular disease) are unclear, but not all older people have hearing problems.
- The high frequencies are lost first—usually noticed when high-pitched female voices become hard to hear. As consonants are high frequency, the patient can often hear noise, but not understand, feeling that everyone is 'mumbling' (loss of discrimination).
- 'Recruitment' is a common problem, where the thresholds for hearing and discomfort are very close ('Speak up…. don't shout').
- Busy, noisy environments make hearing harder, so patients may avoid social situations.
- There is no treatment to halt progression, but hearing aids may help.

Other ear changes with age include:

- Thinner walls to the external auditory canal, with fewer glands, making it drier, causing itching.
- Drier wax due to decreased sweat gland activity, making accumulation (a cause of reversible hearing impairment) more common.
- Degenerative changes of the inner ear and vestibular system contributing to increase in deafness, vertigo, and tinnitus.

Classifying deafness

Conductive

A disturbance in the mechanical attenuation of sound waves in outer/middle ear, preventing sound from reaching the inner ear.

- It can be caused by outer ear obstruction (e.g. wax, foreign body, otitis externa), some types of tympanic membrane perforation, tympanosclerosis, or middle ear problems (effusion, otosclerosis, ossicular erosion secondary to infection or cholesteatoma).
- It may be surgically correctable, and can be helped by a hearing aid.

Sensorineural

A problem with the cochlea or auditory nerve so impulses are not transmitted to the auditory cortex.

- Caused by genetic or perinatal factors in children.
- In adults may be traumatic, infective (viral, chronic otitis media, meningitis, syphilis), noise induced, degenerative (presbyacusis), ototoxic (e.g. aminoglycosides, cytotoxics), neoplastic (acoustic neuroma), or others such as Meniere's disease.
- Usually irreversible.
- The appropriate hearing aid can be helpful.

Mixed combination of both conductive and sensorineural.

HOW TO... assess hearing

General

Conversation will give an informal idea of hearing ability.

Clarify by performing free field speech tests by asking the patient to repeat words spoken in a whispered voice, conversation voice and shouted at 60cm from the ear. The non-test ear is masked by pressing the tragus backwards and rotating it with the index finger. Sit the patient next to you so that lip reading is not possible.

History

- Rate of onset and progression (witnesses will often be more accurate than patients).
- Unilateral or bilateral.
- History of trauma, noise exposure, or ear surgery.
- Family history of hearing problems or hearing aid use.
- Drug history of ototoxic drugs e.g. aminoglycoside antibiotics (gentamicin, streptomycin etc.) and high-dose furosemide.
- Associated symptoms (pain, discharge, tinnitus, vertigo).

Examination

- External ear and canal (looking for wax, inflammation, discharge, blood, abnormal growths etc.).
- Drum (perforations, myringitis, retraction, bulging of drum etc.).
- Tuning fork tests (with a 512kHz fork) may be helpful. Both are based on the principle of improved bone conduction perception with a conductive hearing loss.
  - **Rinne's**. Compares air and bone conduction. Hold tuning fork in front of ear then place on mastoid, to compare air and bone conduction. Air > bone is normal. Bone > air implies defective middle and outer ear function.
  - **Weber's**. Assesses bone conduction only. Hold tuning fork at vertex of the head and ask which ear hears the sound most loudly. With conductive deafness, it is heard loudest in the deafer ear; with sensorineural deafness it is heard most loudly in the normal ear.

Who to refer?

Patients with sinister features should be referred to an ENT surgeon:
- Recent or abrupt hearing loss
- Unilateral hearing loss or tinnitus
- Variable hearing loss
- Ear pain.

▶▶ Sudden onset sensorineural deafness is an ENT emergency, and requires urgent referral (causes include infection, vascular event, tumour, leaking canals etc.).

ALL other patients with suspected hearing loss should be referred to an audiologist for a full assessment, further testing and management.

Audiology

The majority of patients with hearing impairment are managed by audiologists and hearing therapists. They do the following:

Specialized hearing tests

- **Audiometry:** quantifies the degree and pattern of loss. May be 'pure tone' (using signals at varying frequencies and intensities) or 'speech' (discriminating spoken words at differing intensities). The hearing thresholds are charted on an audiogram and interpreted by the audiologist (indicates conduction or sensorineural deafness, which frequency and which ear).
- **Impedance tympanometry:** indirectly measures the compliance of the middle ear, identifying infection and effusion in the middle ear and Eustachian tube dysfunction.
- **Evoked response audiometry:** measures action potentials produced by sound. No conscious response is required by the patient and so tests are less open to bias. (Before MRI, this was the main diagnostic test for acoustic neuromas.)

Recommend and fit hearing aids

Many types. Help patients to have realistic expectations about their hearing aids (rarely a 'miracle cure') and train them how to use them optimally (e.g. minimizing background noise).

Offer practical advice about assistive listening devices such as:

- **Alternative signals:** buzzers and flashing lights instead of doorbell or telephone ring; vibrating devices that attach to the wrist and alert the wearer to environmental noises.
- **Television:** subtitles, or devices that connect to the hearing aid allowing the television signal to be amplified.
- **Telephones:** with high/low volume control and 'T' settings that amplify the telephone noise without the background noise.
- **Transmitter and receiver devices** (infrared or FM radio wave): for use in theatres etc. with transmission from the sound source. The listener can adjust the volume in their receiver.
- Advise about better **communication**: see box opposite.

Run aural rehabilitation programmes

Age matched group sessions that help with adjustment to the sudden reintroduction of noise with a hearing aid (after what is usually a gradual hearing loss), teach skills (e.g. blocking out background noise, lip reading) and share practical tips (e.g. eating in a booth at a restaurant to limit background noise).

Other

- Train people to **lip read**.
- Help manage **tinnitus**.
- **Counsel** about psychosocial implications of hearing impairment.

HOW TO... **communicate with a deaf person**

- Ensure hearing aids are inserted correctly, turned on and have working batteries.
- Speak clearly and at a normal rate.
- Use sentences, not one word answers—this gives contextual cues to lip readers.
- Increase volume, but do not shout.
- Lower the pitch of the voice.
- Minimize background noise.
- Maximize face-to-face visual contact—look straight at the person, and ensure there are not bright lights behind you that will dazzle.
- Use visual cues when talking (e.g. hand gestures).
- Be patient—repeat things if asked, changing the sentence slightly if possible.
- If confusion arises, write things down—do not give up.

Hearing aids

What do hearing aids do?

All consist of a microphone that gathers sound, an amplifier that increases the volume and a receiver that transmits the amplified sound to the ear.

Whom do they help?

- Help many to some degree, but not all.
- Does not restore normal hearing—the wearer needs to learn to interpret the new auditory input efficiently.
- Conductive hearing loss is helped more than sensorineural loss.

What are the different types?

Smaller sized units (e.g. completely-in-the-canal devices) are cosmetically more appealing and give good reception for mild—moderate hearing loss, but are fiddly and expensive. **Medium sized units** (e.g. in-the-ear devices) are more visible, and have more feedback, but can be used for worse hearing loss. **Larger sized units** (e.g. behind-the-ear) provide the most amplification and are easier to handle, but suffer from feedback if the ear mould deforms.

Analogue devices

- Cheapest, with least processing of sound.
- Set to hearing loss at the time of fitting.
- Audiologist adjusts amplification and tonality settings at time of fitting, but these are then fixed.
- Patient can adjust the volume manually (turn the device volume up when the noise is quiet, and down when it is loud).

Digitally programmable devices

- More expensive, with moderate sound processing.
- Analogue circuit that can be adjusted at the time of fitting by a computer programme to best fit the patients needs.
- Automatic volume control.

Digital devices

- Most health authorities have projects underway to fit digital hearing aids for all new referrals and exchange of old analogue aids (the 'Beacon Site project').
- Most expensive, most advanced, with the highest amount of sound processing.
- Programmable with flexible digital circuits that manipulate each sound according to pitch and volume to give the clearest sound for that individual.
- Higher clarity of sound, less circuit noise, faster processing, and automatic volume control.
- As with all hearing aids, will not help everyone, so should not be advised unless benefit is not obtained from a cheaper device.

Disposable devices

- 'One size fits all'—actually fit around 70% of patients.
- Instantly available.
- Not individual, so less good.
- No need for battery changes, low breakdown costs.
- Last about 40 days, so expensive in the long term.

HOW TO... use a hearing aid

To check a hearing aid
- Put a new battery in.
- Turn to the 'M' setting.
- Turn the volume up as far as it will go.
- A working hearing aid will whistle.

Putting it in
- The audiologist will take an impression of the ear to make a snugly fitting ear mould.
- This should be inserted so that it fits correctly and comfortably.

Turning it on
- Most hearing aids have three settings: 'O' = off; 'M' = microphone (use this setting for normal conversation); 'T' = telecoil (use this setting with listening equipment, such as loop devices. These transfer sound direct to the hearing aid and cut out background noise).
- In addition, there will often be a volume wheel, which can be adjusted as needed.

What to do if there is no sound
- Check the hearing aid is not switched to 'O' or 'T'.
- Check the batteries are not dead, or put in upside down.
- Check the mould is not clogged with wax.
- Check the tubing is not wet (dry with hairdryer) or twisted.

What to do if there is a whistling or squealing noise (feedback)
- Occurs when the earmould is not snug, allowing sound to escape into the microphone.
- Worse at high volumes.
- Check that the earmould is a good fit (return to audiologist if not), and is inserted correctly.
- Ensure there is not excess earwax impeding fit.
- Try turning the volume down.

Maintaining the hearing aid
- Handle carefully.
- Keep the hearing aid dry, away from strong heat or light.
- Use a clean dry tissue to clean, never a damp cloth.
- Use wax remover on a regular basis.

If the earmould is separate (e.g. behind-the-ear) then periodically remove and wash with warm soapy water, ensuring it is totally dry before reconnecting it.

Tinnitus

The perception of a sound in one or both ears, without an external stimulus. Intermittent or continuous. Varying kinds of noises (ringing, humming, buzzing, occasionally other noises) and at varying pitches. Large spectrum of disease. More common in men than women and incidence rises with age. Up to a quarter of older people may experience intermittent symptoms. About a sixth of these will find it bothersome, and one in twenty will be disabled by it. A quarter of patients will get worsening symptoms with time.

Tinnitus can be due to actual sounds that are generated by local structures:
- **Vascular structures** (aneurysmal vessels, vascular tumours etc.— generate a pulsatile or humming noise that may worsen with exercise).
- **Muscle spasms** (palatal or middle ear muscles—generate a clicking noise. Usually indicates underlying neurological disease).
- **Eustachian tube** may be patulous (can occur after dramatic weight loss) resulting in a roaring sound.
- **Joints** (e.g. temperomandibular joint, cervical spine joints).

More commonly, the noise is generated from somewhere within the auditory pathway (cochlear organ, nerve, brain stem or auditory cortex) after some sort of damage or injury. The following are associated with tinnitus:
- **Hearing loss:** a very common cause in older people. Mechanism unclear—may be akin to phantom limb pain. Note tinnitus may precede deafness. May be associated with conductive (e.g. wax accumulation) or more commonly sensorineural deafness (including presbyacusis). Treatment of deafness (with hearing aid or occasionally cochlear implant) often results in improvement of tinnitus.
- **Drugs:** many commonly prescribed drugs in older people can either cause or exacerbate tinnitus. (See box opposite.)
- **Vascular disease:** microvascular damage to the auditory system, or a stroke affecting the auditory cortex. Modify vascular risk factors to limit progression.
- **Infection:** e.g. chronic otitis media. Treat the cause, but may have residual problems.
- **Other:** Meniere's disease, diabetes, thyroid disease, Paget's disease, brain tumour (intracanalicular and cerebello-pontine), trauma and autoimmune disease. Treat underlying cause.

History
- Obtain a description of tinnitus. This may indicate cause e.g. pulsatile noise is often vascular; clicking noise is often due to palatal muscle spasms; high pitched continuous noise is usually due to sensorineural hearing loss; low pitched continuous noise is more commonly seen (but not exclusive to) Meniere's disease.
- Screen for possible causes (drug history, ear disease, noise exposure, injury etc.).

Examination
Should include full head and neck examination, cranial nerve examination, auscultation for bruits and inspection of the auditory canal.

Investigation

- Check FBC, glucose and thyroid function.
- Refer to specialist for full audiometric assessment and possible imaging especially if unilateral (MRI ± angiography).

Treatment

- Difficult and frustrating—often best done in specialist clinics with multidisciplinary team support.
- Stop all ototoxic medication and avoid in future.
- Assess whether caffeine, aspartame sweetener, alcohol, nicotine, and marijuana worsen tinnitus and avoid if so.
- Treat the cause wherever possible.
- Strong association with insomnia and depression, both of which worsen the suffering and should be treated. Some evidence to suggest that antidepressants (SSRIs) may help even when there is no overt depression.
- Many other treatments have been tried (e.g. lignocaine, magnetic and ultrasonic stimulation, melatonin, Ginkgo biloba, niacin, and zinc) but limited evidence they work and adverse effects common.
- Hearing aids are useful if hearing loss—the increased awareness of the background sound tends to make the noise less apparent.
- Masking techniques involve wearing a 'white noise' generator, rather like a hearing aid that aims to distract the patient from the tinnitus by reducing the contrast between the tinnitus signal and background noise, improving the plasticity of the central auditory cortex and thereby facilitating a reduction in perception of the sound.
- Mainstay of treatment is aimed at adjusting patients' perception of the tinnitus, trying to habituate them to the noise and limiting the negative emotions it generates. Includes tinnitus retraining therapy, biofeedback, stress reduction techniques and cognitive and behavioural therapy.
- Tinnitus support groups can be helpful (www.tinnitus.org.uk).

Drugs causing, or exacerbating, tinnitus

Aspirin (high dose)
Other non-steroidal anti-inflammatories
Loop diuretics
ACE inhibitors
Calcium channel-blockers
Doxazosin
Aminoglycoside antibiotics
Clarithromycin
Quinine and chloroquine
Carbamazepine
Tricyclic antidepressants
Benzodiazepines
Proton pump inhibitors
Some chemotherapy agents

Vertigo

Definition

Vertigo is the hallucination of movement. Either a sensation of rotatory motion either of the patient with respect to the environment ('its like being on a roundabout'), or the environment with respect to the patient ('the room is spinning'). The key element is a feeling of motion, without which a clinical diagnosis of vertigo should not be made.

Understanding vertigo

The vestibular system comprises the temporal bone labyrinths (composed of the semicircular canals, the saccule, and the utricle), the vestibular nerve and the central vestibular structures in the brainstem. Normally, there is a constant input from both ears updating the central structures on head position. In the brainstem they are integrated with inputs from the visual cortex and from proprioceptive receptors (most important are neck and ankles).

Any interruption of this signal leads to an excess of information from the good side, and so an acute feeling of dizziness and nausea (vertigo) along with disruption of the vestibuloocular reflex (which will cause nystagmus). This situation continues until either input is restored, or the vestibular system adapts to the altered balance of signals.

Adaptation means that:

- Vertigo is not a chronic condition. Multiple recurrences may occur, but a complaint of longstanding continuous dizziness is not vertigo.
- Vertigo rarely occurs with slowly progressive conditions (e.g. acoustic neuroma) as adaptation occurs along the way.
- All vertigo is made worse by head movement—if not, then seek an alternative diagnosis.
- The use of vestibular sedatives (see p604) should be limited to the acute phase for symptom relief only—prolonged use will delay adaptation.
- ▶▶There is no indication for long-term use of Stemetil® in vertigo.

Causes

- Around half of all patients complaining of dizziness will have vertigo (see p126).
- Over all ages, 80% of vertigo arises from peripheral structures (the ears) and 20% from central structures (the brain).
- Peripheral vertigo is due to benign positional paroxysmal vertigo in up to 50%.
- Central vertigo is usually due to stroke.
- The proportion of central vertigo increases with age, because of the increased incidence of stroke.

Common causes of vertigo

Condition	Features	Cause	Treatment
Benign paroxysmal positional vertigo (BPPV)	Mild episodes lasting less than a minute, recurring frequently over weeks to months	Calcium debris in semicircular canal Usually idiopathic May be preceded by minor head trauma	Resolves spontaneously but may recur Epley's manoeuvre may help (see p605)
Acute vestibular failure (labyrinthitis)	Acute onset of severe vertigo, lasting hours to days Associated nausea, vomiting and postural instability Patient in bed, refuses to move head	Ischaemia of vestibular apparatus, often preceded by a viral respiratory tract infection	High dose steroids acutely may speed recovery Treat with vestibular sedatives only whilst vomiting, then allow adaptation to occur May have recurrent (milder) episodes
Meniere's disease	Recurrent episodes of violent vertigo, vomiting, tinnitus, ear fullness (lasting up to 12 hours) and fluctuating hearing loss	Dilation of endolymphatic space in the canals—primary cause still unknown	Symptomatic treatment of acute attacks Betahistine is a labyrinthine vasodilator Diuretics may lessen attack frequency Surgical options include grommet insertion, transtympanic gentamicin, endolymphatic decompression and vestibular nerve sectioning
Vertebrobasilar stroke	TIAs cause stuttering symptoms (see also vertebrobasilar insufficiency p128). Stroke will cause abrupt onset, prolonged symptoms. Vertigo is most common symptom, usually associated with other neurology (e.g. ataxia, diplopia, visual loss, slurred speech, motor or sensory impairment) Cerebellar stroke can cause vertigo alone		After stroke, slow improvement is normal, but often residual defects Modify vascular risk factors (pp324–5) to prevent recurrence

Vertigo: assessment

History

- This is the most important diagnostic tool in vertigo, and should consist of open questions with clarification.
- Describe the dizziness—is it a sensation of movement of self or the room (likely vertigo) or a light-headed feeling (less likely vertigo)? A non-specific description does not exclude vertigo.
- Establish if likely peripheral (abrupt onset and cessation with nausea, vomiting and tinnitus) or central (more prolonged, less severe, less positional episodes. Usually with other neurological symptoms and signs).
- Ask about onset, severity, duration, progression and recurrence to narrow down cause (see table on previous page).
- Ask about provoking factors—may be spontaneous, or brought on by changes in middle ear pressure (sneezing, coughing) or head/neck position (question carefully to distinguish this from orthostatic symptoms).
- Ask about associated symptoms e.g. tinnitus and hearing loss (is it worse during an attack?).
- Ask about predisposing factors e.g. vascular risk factors, recent infections, headache, ototoxic drugs, ear discharge, deafness, tinnitus etc.
- Ask about psychiatric symptoms (e.g. low mood)—these are rarely offered spontaneously.

Examination

- General examination (including cardiovascular examination)
- Postural blood pressure measurements
- Neurological examination
- Head and neck examination including otoscopy
- Gait assessment
- Hearing test (see p592)
- Vestibular assessment (see box opposite).

HOW TO... **examine the vestibular system**

Hard to do directly—largely relies on testing the integrity of the vestibuloocular reflex.

- Test eye movements with the head still, looking for nystagmus (the eyes drift slowly *towards* the bad side, and the rapid correction phase is towards the good side). Visual fixation will suppress a peripheral nystagmus, but not a central. Peripheral lesions cause horizontal nystagmus in both eyes; central lesions cause nystagmus in any direction that is more prolonged and severe.
- Try to provoke vertigo and nystagmus by flexing, extending, rotating and laterally bending the cervical spine.
- Check visual acuity with a Snellen chart both with the head still, and with the patient slowly shaking their head. If acuity is >4 lines worse with head shaking this suggests impairment
- Ask the patient to fix gaze on a distant point, whilst the examiner turns the head rapidly. The patient should be able to keep gaze fixed—if the gaze drifts, there is impairment.
- Ask the patient to shake their head, and then check for nystagmus—if it is present, this implies impairment.

Hallpike manoeuvre

- Tests for BPPV (50–80% sensitive).
- Sit the patient up and stand behind them.
- Hold their head turned 45 degrees to one side.
- Keep holding the head at this angle and rapidly lie the patient down so the head is 30 degrees below the level of the couch, looking down to the floor (steps 1 and 2 of the Epley's manoeuvre, p605).
- Ask about symptoms, whilst watching for nystagmus (towards the floor).
- BPPV can be diagnosed confidently when the nystagmus is **latent** (occurs after a few seconds), **transient** (stops after less than 30 seconds), and **fatiguable** (lessens with repeat testing).
- If any of these features are absent, the vertigo is likely to be due to another cause.
- Repeat with the head turned in the other direction.

Vertigo: management

Some specific treatments depending on cause (see table on p601).

Symptomatic relief in the short term can be done with vestibula sedatives:

- Anticholinergics (e.g. hyoscine patch 1mg/24 hours).
- Antihistamines (e.g. cyclizine 50mg tds, cinnarizine 30mg tds).
- Phenothiazines—usually sedating (e.g. prochlorperazine (Stemetil®) 10mg tds).
- Benzodiazepines (e.g. diazepam) if unable to take anticholinergics.

May also benefit from antiemetics (e.g. metoclopramide, domperidone).

These drugs are not for long-term use, and rarely beneficial in BPPV a attacks are so short lived. Most vertigo will resolve with vestibular adap tation, leaving only brief feelings of imbalance on rapid head turns.

Some however, will develop chronic dysfunction, in which case man agement is directed towards facilitating adaptation and development c coping strategies—**'vestibular rehabilitation'**. This is done by physio therapists or ENT specialist nurses and adopts a holistic approach. I involves a series of habituating exercises performed regularly to enabl adaptation via compensation to occur. In addition to vestibular rehabilita tion, consider spectacles to improve visual acuity, exercise to improv muscle strength, and a walking stick to aid peripheral balance.

Specific manoeuvres (Epley's manoeuvre—see Figs.21.1–21.7) an exercises are used for BPPV.

HOW TO... perform Epley's manoeuvre

- Aims to clear debris from the posterior semicircular canal.
- Requires the patient to be fairly flexible.
- Premedication with a vestibular sedative is advised in severely affected patients.
- Stand behind the patient, firmly holding the head between your hands.
- Make movements quickly and smoothly, holding each position for at least 30 seconds.
- The procedure takes approximately 3–5 minutes.
- See Figs. 21.1–6 on pp606–7.

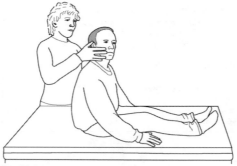

Fig. 21.1 With the patient upright, turn the head 45 degrees to the affected side

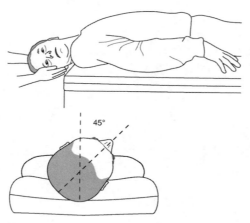

Fig. 21.2 Lie the patient down, with the head still turned until they are reclined beyond the horizontal (as in the Hallpike manoeuvre).

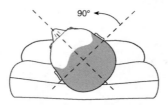

Fig. 21.3 With the patient still reclined beyond horizontal, rotate the head through 90 degrees, with the face upwards.

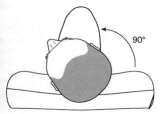

Fig. 21.4 Keeping the head still, ask the patient to roll on to their side.

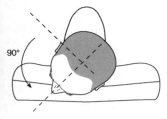

Fig. 21.5 Rotate the head so the patient is facing downwards.

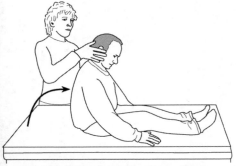

Fig. 21.6 Keep the head at this angle, and raise the patient to sitting position. Finally, rotate the head so it faces the midline with the neck flexed (looking forward, and downwards).

Eyes

The ageing eye 610
Visual impairment 612
  How to... optimize vision 613
Blind registration 614
Cataract 616
Glaucoma 618
Age-related macular degeneration 620
  How to... use an Amsler Grid to detect macular
  pathology 621
The eye and systemic disease 622
Visual hallucinations 624
Drugs and the eye 626
Eyelid disorders 628

The ageing eye

Vision is a complex activity which involves eye function, cognition, reasoning, and memory.

With increasing age the chance of visual impairment increases because of:
- Changes due to senescence
- Changes due to cumulative exposure to environmental toxins
- Changes in associated functions (cognition, hearing etc.)
- Increasing incidence of many eye diseases.

It is not inevitable—there is considerable diversity both in visual decline and in compensatory adaptations. There is a tendency for patients to blame failing vision on age, and so ignore it. Some changes may be age related, but there may be corrective action available (e.g. glasses) or it may herald the onset of disease. Many eye disorders can be slowed or even stopped with prompt identification and treatment and these actions may make all the difference between independence and dependence. Distinguishing what is 'normal' and when to refer to a specialist is key.

Changes in vision with age

Visual acuity often decreases
- Multifactorial—changes in macula, lens and cornea.
- May be corrected (e.g. glasses).
- Consider eye disease if deterioration is rapid.

Visual fields—peripheral vision less sensitive
- Although formal field-testing normal—consider cerebrovascular disease if distinct homonymous field defect.
- Multifactorial—pupil smaller, lens cloudier and peripheral retina less sensitive.

Near vision decreases
- Accommodative power diminishes due to increasingly rigid lens.
- Presbyopia (long sightedness) is part of normal ageing, beginning in middle age and can be corrected with glasses.

Colour vision
- Retinal receptors unchanged.
- Alterations in colour perception may relate to yellowing of the lens altering the light reaching the retina.

Light adaptation slower
- Rods and cones may be slower to react to changes in illumination, and the pupil may let in less light requiring more light for good vision.
- Causes difficulty with night driving in particular.
- Glare may be a problem as the lens, cornea and vitreous become less clear, and minute particles scatter light.

Contrast sensitivity decreases
Due to changes in cornea, lens and retina.

Floaters
- Due to aggregation of collagen fibrils in vitreous.
- Usually normal, but if sudden onset, or large quantity, may indicate retinal detachment or vitreous haemorrhage.

Visual impairment

2.5% of the UK population has visual impairment not amenable to correction by glasses alone. Considerable social and psychological impact, yet underreported and optimal help often not delivered.

Causes (from blind registration data):
- Macular degeneration (49%)
- Glaucoma (15%)
- Diabetes (6%)
- Cardiovascular disease (5%).

▶▶ 83% of registrations are over 65 years old.

Low vision clinics are available in most hospitals.
Interventions include:
- Change glasses prescription (benefits 10–20%).
- Explain disease (may NOT cause total blindness e.g. with macular degeneration, improve understanding of future).
- Psychological support (often combined with hearing loss in older people—beware social withdrawal. Acknowledge problem and discuss fears).
- Discuss blind registration.
- In some cases, consider guide dogs and learning braille.
- Take specific history of certain activities and provide practical advice:
  - **Reading**. What do they actually need to read? Advise about using good light, magnifiers, large print books, photocopy recipes etc. to larger size.
  - **Writing**. Use black pen on white paper, consider Millard writing frame or bold line paper, discuss specific tasks such as cheques and pension books.
  - **Television**. Sitting closer, black and white sets may improve contrast; closed circuit TV improves magnification and contrast.
  - **Telling the time**. Talking watches and clocks.
  - **Cooking**. Improving lighting in kitchen by removing net curtains, tactile markers for cookers, electronic fullness indicators on cups.
  - **Telephoning**. Large button telephones.
  - **Social interaction**. Sit with back to the window to improve light on visitor's face, discuss accessible holidays.

HOW TO... optimize vision

Bigger
- Magnifiers (glasses or contacts, hand magnifiers, stand magnifiers, illuminated magnifiers, reading telescopes). Consider portability, cosmetic aspects, and posture required to use.
- Larger print (books, enlarge frequently used items with photocopier).

Bolder
- Contrasting colours e.g. black on white.
- Use to emphasize written word, door handles, stair edges etc.
- Use white cups for dark drinks.
- Put contrasting strips round light fittings.

Brighter
- Remove net curtains.
- Use higher power bulbs (e.g. 150W rather than 60W).
- Use directable light sources (e.g. angle poise lamps).

Blind registration

Done by ophthalmologists. Copy of the form goes to social services, GP and the office for national statistics.

Generally under-registration—probably due to stigma and a sense that this is the end of the fight, rather than the start of new help and opportunity.

Definitions
- Partially sighted <6/60 in both eyes or reduced fields (e.g. homonymous hemianopia).
- Blind need not mean no vision. Statutory definition is that the person should be 'so blind as to be unable to perform any work for which eyesight is essential'. Pragmatically it is vision <3/60 or very diminished fields.

Benefits to individual
- Financial—personal income tax allowance, disability living allowance or attendance allowance, income support or pension credit, extra housing or council tax benefits, incapacity benefit, help towards care home fees, free NHS sight test, free NHS prescriptions, lower TV licence fee, car parking and public transport concessions, exemption from directory enquiries fees.
- Easier access to help from social services.
- Loan of cassette recorder and talking books and newspapers (also available without registration).

Further information
Royal National Institute for the Blind: www.rnib.org.uk
SENSE: www.sense.org.uk

Cataract

Term used to describe any lens opacity. Commonest cause of treatable blindness worldwide. In the UK it is largely a disease of the older population: 65% of people in their 50s and everyone over 80 have some opacification. This is probably caused by cumulative exposure to causative agents rather than senescence per se.

Causes

- Exposure to environmental agents (e.g. UV light, smoke, blood sugar)—more exposure with increasing age.
- Ocular conditions (trauma, uveitis, previous intraocular surgery).
- Systemic conditions (e.g. diabetes, hypocalcaemia, Down's syndrome).
- Drugs (especially steroids—ocular and systemic).

Symptoms

- Painless visual loss which varies depending on whether unilateral/bilateral and severity/position of the opacity.
- Commonly begins with difficulty in reading, recognizing faces and watching television.
- May be worse in bright light, or be associated with glare around lights.

Signs

- Reduced visual acuity—usually gradual.
- Diminished red reflex on ophthalmoscopy.
- Change in the appearance of the lens (appears cloudy brown or white when viewed with direct light).
- Beware co-existing conditions: pupil responses are normal, and the patient should be able to point to the position of a light source.

Management

▶▶ New glasses prescription may delay need for surgery
- Optimizing visual conditions.
- Surgical removal of opacified lens.
- No effective medical treatment.

When to treat?

Individually tailored. Depends on visual requirements of patient, severity of cataract and presence of other ocular disease (worsens outcome from surgery). Roughly speaking <6/18 in both eyes is likely to benefit, but an elderly person who does not read much may be quite happy with this visual level. Conversely, someone who wishes to continue driving, or needs precise vision for his/her life may wish for surgery much sooner. Previously surgeons waited for the cataract to 'ripen' to aid extraction—this is no longer the case. Have a frank discussion about risks and benefits with each individual.

What the surgery involves

- Usually done as a day case under local anaesthesia.
- Patient must be able to lie flat and still—demented patients may need sedation or general anaesthetic (altering risk/benefit); consider also heart failure, respiratory disease and spinal deformity—can they lie flat?
- Generally safe and well-tolerated procedure.
- Phacoemulsification is most commonly used in the UK. (Small cut in eye to access lens that is then liquefied with an ultrasonic probe.) A replacement lens is then folded into the empty lens capsule. Sutures are not usually needed.
- Other methods (extracapsular and intracapsular extraction) are less commonly used.
- Post-operatively the patient will wear an eye shield (usually at night) for a period, and use steroid and antibiotic eye drops.

Outcome

With no ocular comorbidity, 85% have a visual acuity of >6/12 at discharge. Outcome is worse with other eye diseases e.g. glaucoma and in patients with diabetes and cerebrovascular disease.

As the replacement lens has a fixed focus and is usually chosen to allow clear distance vision, the patient will usually require glasses for reading still. A new prescription should be made up a few weeks after surgery once post-operative inflammation has settled.

Glaucoma

Third most common cause of blindness worldwide.

▶▶ Leading cause of preventable blindness in the UK.

Definition

Visual loss due to a combination of loss of visual fields and cupping of the optic disc. Usually associated with a rise in intraocular pressure sufficient to cause damage to the optic nerve fibres (either direct mechanical damage, or by inducing ischaemia).

Intraocular pressure

- Ciliary body (posterior) makes aqueous humour (fluid), which flows anteriorly through the pupil and drains via the trabecular network in the anterior chamber angle of the eye.
- Balance of production and drainage determines pressure.
- Wide range of pressures seen in normal adults (detected with tonometry)—average 15.5mmHg, normal <21mmHg.
- Probably individually determined at which pressure ocular damage ensues.
- Can develop glaucoma with 'normal' pressure—'normal tension glaucoma' (may be high for that person/other factors such as ischaemia may be relevant). More common in older patients. Fluctuating BP may be contributory.
- Can have 'high' pressures without glaucoma—'ocular hypertension'.
- Symptoms depend on rate and degree of rise in pressure. Generally asymptomatic unless advanced or acute.

Primary ('chronic') open angle glaucoma

- Most common.
- Failure of outflow of aqueous causes slow rise in pressure, allowing adaptation, so subtle symptoms.
- No pain, corneal cloudiness, or haloes.
- Slow loss of visual field, typically in an arc shape ('arcuate scotoma') with preservation of central vision (macula has more nerve cells so is relatively protected). Progresses to tunnel vision, and then blindness.

▶▶ Early detection can slow/halt progression.

Risk factors
- Age (1% in 5th decade, rising to 10% in 9th decade).
- African/Caribbean origin (four times risk).
- Blood relatives with glaucoma.

Screening
- Target those at higher risk.
- Combination of ophthalmoscopy (looking for disc 'cupping'), automated perimetry testing (for minor field defects) and tonometry (for intraocular pressure) is best.
- Most cases picked up by optometrists.
- Encourage regular eye tests, and include careful fundoscopy in physical examination.

Treatment

- Topical treatments (eye drops): beta-blockers e.g. timolol (decrease aqueous secretion. Can cause systemic beta-blockade); prostaglandin analogues e.g. latanoprost (improve drainage, may darken iris); alpha agonists (decrease aqueous production); carbonic anhydrase inhibitors e.g. dorzolamide (decrease aqueous secretion); parasympathomimetics e.g. pilocarpine (constrict pupil so will reduce visual field—not commonly used).
- Oral treatments: carbonic anhydrase inhibitors e.g. acetazolamide (very powerful, with many side effects including electrolyte imbalance and paraesthesia of extremities).
- Surgical treatment: trabeculectomy—operation to improve aqueous outflow. Argon laser trabeculoplasty (applied to the trabecular meshwork) may be effective. Cyclodiode laser to the ciliary body (decreases production) is used in refractory cases.
- Support groups: International Glaucoma Association. www.iga.org.uk.

Acute angle closure glaucoma

- Apposition of lens to the back of the iris prevents outflow of aqueous fluid with a rapid rise in pressure.
- Causes red, painful eye with vomiting, blurred vision, and haloes around lights (due to corneal oedema).
- May be precipitated by pupil dilation e.g. at dusk. Pupil constricts when asleep so episodes at night may be aborted by sleep.
- More common in older patients, women, and longsighted individuals— beware of the vomiting older woman with a red eye.
- On examination cornea is usually cloudy and visual acuity significantly reduced (e.g. counting fingers only).

▶▶ Emergency sight threatening condition—requires urgent referral and treatment.

- Treat with iv acetazolamide, topical glaucoma treatment and laser iridotomy to restore flow. Treat other eye prophylactically with laser iridotomy to prevent pupil block.

Age-related macular degeneration

Age-related macular degeneration (AMD) is the most common cause of adult blind registrations in UK and US.

▶▶New treatments for early stages make detection crucial.

Definition

As it sounds—age-related degenerative changes affecting the macula (central part of the retina responsible for clear central vision).

Two types:
- 90% **dry** with gradual onset of symptoms (drusen and atrophy of the retinal pigment epithelium).
- 10% **wet**, where symptoms relate to leaking vessels causing distortion or sudden loss of central vision due to sub-macular haemorrhage (choroidal neovascularisation—new vessels can leak, bleed and scar causing visual loss in a few months).

Prevalence

- Increases with age.
- 25–30 million worldwide.
- Up to 30% of over 75s may have early disease, and 7% late disease.

Risk factors

- Cause unknown.
- Age, smoking, family history are strongly associated.
- Female sex, Caucasian race, hypertension, blue eyes, other ocular conditions (lens opacities, aphakia) and low dietary antioxidants also possibly increase risk.

Symptoms

- Asymptomatic in early stages, progressing to loss of central vision.
- May also have decreased contrast and colour detection, flashing lights and hallucinations.
- Distortion of straight lines is a feature of wet AMD.
- Peripheral vision is normal in absence of other pathology.

Detection

- Regular ocular examination.
- Use of Amsler grid in high risk patients (see opposite).

Prognosis

- Dry progresses slowly and rarely causes blindness.
- Wet form may progress rapidly (blind in under 3 months) and accounts for 90% of AMD blind registrations. Sudden onset of distortion of central vision should prompt urgent referral.
- Bilateral disease—42% with wet AMD in one eye will get it in the other by 5 years.

Prevention
- Smoking is the most important modifiable risk factor.
- A diet rich in fruit and vegetables reduces the risk of development of AMD.
- A combination of beta-carotene, vitamins C and E, and zinc is effective in preventing severe visual loss in established moderate-severe AMD.

Treatment
- Appropriate for subset of wet AMD only. Halts progression so early treatment is desirable.
- Photodynamic therapy. This targets sub-foveal neovascular areas (whilst preserving normal retina) by using photosensitive drug (verteporfin) along with a non-thermal activating laser. Used in early disease, this therapy can slow or halt progression.
- Laser photocoagulation is sometimes used for extra-foveal lesions.

HOW TO... use an **Amsler Grid** to detect macular pathology

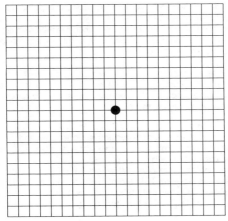

- Test one eye at a time.
- Usual reading glasses should be worn, and the grid held at comfortable reading distance.
- Ask the patient to look at the central spot, and not to look away.
- Assess the following:
  - Can all four corners of the grid be seen?
  - Are any of the lines missing, wavy, blurred or distorted?
  - Do all of the boxes appear the same size and shape?
- Any abnormalities may indicate macular pathology and should prompt referral to an ophthalmologist.

The eye and systemic disease

Two of the top four causes for blind registration are due to systemic disease—diabetes and vascular disease. Eye disease develops as a late complication of prolonged poor control in both cases, and the important message is to strive to prevent these problems in the first place.

Diabetes

Causes retinopathy, cataracts, and 'microvascular' cranial nerve palsies.

Retinopathy

- Associated with increasing duration of diabetes—at 20 years, 80% will have some retinopathy.
- All patients with diabetes require dilated annual screening (either photographic, or by appropriately trained professional). Direct ophthalmoscopy alone is inadequate.
- Appearance: microaneurysms, haemorrhages, (background retinopathy) progressing to cotton wool spots, blot haemorrhages and tortuous vessels (pre-proliferative retinopathy) then new vessels (proliferative retinopathy). Exudates and macular oedema are indicators of maculopathy.
- Early detection of problems (especially when near the macula) should prompt referral to an ophthalmologist. Sight threatening retinopathy requires laser treatment to limit progression.

▶▶ Remember a type two diabetic diagnosed at age 70 may well live 20 years, so tight control is desirable from the outset. (Meticulous control of diabetes and hypertension has been shown to reduce all complications including retinopathy.)

Vascular disease

- Affects the eye directly with hypertensive retinopathy, and more indirectly when cerebrovascular disease impacts on vision. Associated with 'microvascular' cranial nerve palsies.
- Early detection and control of risk factors for vascular disease will ameliorate this problem. Tight blood pressure control, smoking cessation, lipid lowering, diabetic control, and appropriate anti-platelet use should all be targeted at the older age group as aggressively as the younger patients.
- There is little in the way of treatment for the disease once it is established.
- Appearance: silver wiring, arteriovenous nipping, and arteriolar narrowing progressing to exudates, cotton wool spots, haemorrhages and papilloedema.

Giant cell arteritis

See p520.

Visual hallucinations

Management varies with the cause.

Organic brain disease

- Lewy body dementia (occur in 50–80%; usually well formed e.g. animals). Also occurs in dementia of Parkinson's disease. Can respond dramatically to cholinesterase inhibitors.
- Anoxia, migraine and delirium—treat the underlying cause.
- Focal neurological disease (especially occipital and temporal lobe—range from unformed lines and lights etc. to complex).
- Occipital lobe seizures—treat with anticonvulsants.

Drugs

- Common with dopamine agonists and anticonvulsants (usually mild and unformed). Try reducing the dose, watching for rebound in symptoms.
- Overdose of anticholinergic drugs such as antihistamines or tricyclic antidepressants.
- Use of amphetamines and LSD.
- Alcohol withdrawal.

Psychiatric disease

Visual hallucinations occasionally occur with schizophrenia (auditory more common).

Charles Bonnet's syndrome

- Diagnosis of exclusion.
- No other psychiatric symptoms or diseases present.
- Occurs with bilateral visual loss (typically secondary to cataracts or glaucoma) as a 'release phenomenon'.
- These are usually well-formed, vivid and occur in clear consciousness.
- Insight is usually present.
- Duration is usually seconds to a minute or so.
- May be simple (flashes, shapes) or complex (recognizable images).
- Non-threatening—the patient's reaction is often one of curiosity or amusement.
- Probably under-estimated as patients reluctant to tell doctors for fear of being labelled as 'mad'.
- Not related to psychiatric problems.
- Reassurance is often all that is required, but symptoms may be improved by enhancing vision.

Drugs and the eye

Many drugs that are frequently used in the older patient can cause ocular side effects. Older people are more vulnerable to developing side effects, but are least likely to report them (attributing it to part of getting older).

Direct toxicity

- Chloroquine and hydroxychloroquine (used in treatment of rheumatoid arthritis and other connective tissue diseases as well as malaria) cause a toxic maculopathy in large prolonged doses.
- Phenothiazines used for a long time (to treat psychosis) may cause retinal damage.
- Tamoxifen (for breast cancer treatment) may cause maculopathy.
- Amiodarone (for arrhythmias) may cause cataracts.
- Ethambutol (anti-tuberculous) can cause optic neuritis and red/green colour blindness.

Altering accommodation

Causes blurred vision.
- Antihistamines
- Some antihypertensives.

Decreasing pupil size

Causes less light accommodation.
- Opiates
- Miotic drops used for glaucoma.

Steroids

- Oral steroids over time can cause cataracts.
- Topical and oral steroids may raise the intraocular pressure.

Eyelid disorders

Eyelids provide physical protection to the eyes and ensure normal tear film and drainage. Disorders are common in older people, are often uncomfortable and yet are under-recognised and treated.

Entropion

In-turning of the (usually) lower lid. Occurs as orbicularis muscle weakens with age (or with conjunctival scarring distorting the lid). Lashes irritate the eye and may abrade the cornea, causing red eye. Lubricants and taping of the eye may relieve symptoms. Surgery (under local anaesthesia) provides definitive correction.

Ectropion

Eversion of the eyelid. Occurs with orbicularis weakness, scarring of the periorbital skin or 7th nerve palsy. Distortion prevents correct drainage of tears and correct tear film, leading to watery eye with conjunctival dryness. Treat with ointment to protect conjunctiva. Surgery (local anaesthesia) corrects.

Ptosis

Drooping of upper eyelid. When severe can cover pupil and impair vision. Causes: aponeurotic (defects in levator aponeurosis), mechanical (lid lesion, lid oedema), neurological (3rd nerve palsy—look for pupil and eye movement problems, Horner's syndrome), myogenic (congenital levator dystrophy, muscular dystrophies, myasthenia gravis, chronic progressive external ophthalmoplegia).

▶▶ Do not ignore ptosis in older people—may not be longstanding. Look for signs of underlying disease.

Dry eye

Common in elderly as tear secretion diminishes. Eye feels gritty, but is not red. Diuretics may exacerbate. Most common cause is blepharitis (inflamed lid margins with blocked meibomian gland orifices and crusting). This is usually worse in those with rosacea, eczema and psoriasis. Treat blepharitis with hot compresses (5 min bd), lid massage (upwards towards lid margin lower lid, downwards towards lid margin upper lid, eyelid cleaning targeting the base of eyelashes at the lid margin (warm water ± baby shampoo on a cotton wool bud). Antibiotic ointment not usually required unless staphylococcal infection suspected.

Treat dry eye with artificial tears or ointment (gives considerable relief).

Eyelid tumours

Commonest (90%) is basal cell carcinoma. Slow growing, non-metastasizing but locally invasive. Often ignored by patient. More common in fairer skins after chronic sun exposure. Waxy nodule with telangiectatic vessels on surface and pearly rolled border (rodent ulcer) is usual appearance. Treatment is with surgical excision (Moh's micrographic surgery preserves most tissue and may be appropriate in some) or radiotherapy.

Herpes zoster infection

Facial shingles. Involvement of the ophthalmic division of the trigeminal nerve will cause vesicles and crusting periorbitally (see pp686–7).

Skin

The ageing skin 630
Photoageing 632
Cellulitis 634
Other bacterial skin infections 636
Fungal skin infections 638
Intertrigo 640
Leg ulcers 642
Chronic venous insufficiency 644
Management of venous leg ulcers 646
Pruritus 648
Pruritus: treatment 650
Pruritic conditions 652
   How to… recognize and manage scabies 653
Blistering diseases 654
Skin cancers and pre-cancers 656
Other skin lesions 658

The ageing skin

Skin changes with age are universal, but many changes we associate with ageing are actually due to cumulative sun exposure (photoageing), and could be largely prevented by protecting the skin from the sun (compare an older person's facial skin to their buttock skin).

Intrinsic ageing does occur however (see table below) and there are several skin diseases that are age related (e.g. pruritus, pemphigoid, lichen sclerosus).

Age-related change	Clinical implications
Epidermis thins, with flattening of the dermo-epidermal junction, limiting transfer of nutrients and making separation of layers easier	Increased tendency to blistering
	Increased skin tearing
Slower cell turnover	Slower healing of wounds
Less melanocyte activity, with slower DNA repair	Increased photosensitivity, with increased tendency to skin malignancy
Altered epidermal protein binding	Dry, rough, and flaky skin more common
	Abnormal skin barrier, so more prone to irritant contact dermatitis
Altered connective tissue structure and function	Reduced elasticity and strength of skin
Decreased blood flow through dermal vascular beds	Skin appears cooler and paler
	Thermoregulation is less efficient
	Hair and gland growth and function slows
Subcutaneous fat decreases in volume and is distributed differently (e.g. more abdominal fat)	Thermoregulation is less efficient
	Protection against pressure injury lessens
Number of cutaneous nerve endings decreases	Cutaneous sensation blunts (e.g. fine touch, temperature, proprioception)
	Pain threshold increases
Fewer cutaneous glands	Thermoregulation is less efficient
Nail bed function decreases	Nails become thick, dry, brittle and yellow, with longitudinal ridges
The immune functioning of the skin decreases	Increased propensity to skin infections and malignancies

Hair changes

- 50% of the over 50s will have grey hair, as melanocyte numbers drop.
- Male pattern baldness (affecting the vertex and temples) starts in the late teens and progresses—80% of male pensioners are balding. Women may be affected after the menopause, but it is rarely as severe.
- Diffuse hair loss occurs in both sexes with advancing age (consider checking for iron deficiency, thyroid dysfunction, renal impairment, hypoproteinaemia, inflammatory skin conditions, use of antimetabolite drugs etc.).
- As hair follicles age, their function may be disrupted, leading to longer, tougher hairs growing in eyebrows, ears and noses of both sexes.
- Post-menopausal hormone changes may cause women to develop hair in the beard area and upper lip.

Photoageing

The dermis thickens with tangled elastic fibres; the epidermis is variable in thickness with regions of both hypertrophy and atrophy—leading to considerable skin changes:

- The skin becomes wrinkled (coarse and fine), rough, yellowed, and irregularly pigmented—these changes are all exacerbated by smoking.
- The skin may develop actinic (solar) elastosis—thickened, yellow skin with rhomboid pattern and senile comedones.
- Actinic (solar) purpura is a non-palpable rash often on the forearms, due to red cell extravasation from sun-damaged vessels (the platelet count is normal).
- Lesions include brown macules, multiple telangiectasia, actinic (solar) keratoses (scaly, rough hyperkeratotic areas on sun-exposed skin), as well as a tendency to skin tumours.

Prevention is better than cure for these changes, but topical retinoids may reduce the appearance of wrinkles and pigment, and certain plastic surgery techniques are employed (e.g. chemical peels and injections of collagen and botulinum toxin).

Sun protection

- Avoid unnecessary sun exposure.
- Stay out of the sun during the hottest time of the day (11am–3pm).
- Wear appropriate factor sun screen (increasing sun protection factor for fairer skins).
- Areas that are often forgotten include balding heads (wear a hat) and the tops of ears (apply sun screen).

Cellulitis

Deep infection of the skin and subcutaneous tissues with oedema, often on the lower leg. More common with increasing age, immunocompromise (e.g. diabetes) and with a predisposing skin condition (leg ulcer, pressure sore, lymphoedema, toe web intertrigo, traumatic wounds etc.).

Organisms

Usually streptococcus (Group A, commonly *S.pyogenes*) and/or staphylococcus. With leg ulcers, pressure sores and lymphoedema colonization is broader so infecting organisms may be more diverse, including highly resistant bacteria, such as MRSA (see p670).

Clinical features

- Red, hot, tender, raised area with poorly demarcated margins.
- Portal of entry for bacteria often evident (e.g. trauma).
- Systemic upset may follow (fever, malaise).
- Spread can cause lymphangitis with tender nodes in the inguinal region.
- Risk of bacteraemia (up to 80% in nursing home residents with pressure sores—need aggressive treatment as mortality is as much as 50%).

Investigations

- FBC: elevated white cell count in around 50%.
- Blood cultures: should be taken in all before antibiotics commenced (positive in 25%).
- Local culture: e.g. wound swab, injection and aspiration of saline in the dermis, skin biopsy. Rarely needed as empirical treatment often works.

Treatment

- If the cellulitis is mild, and the patient well, then oral therapy can be used to start. Oral options include penicillin V + flucloxacillin, erythromycin alone or co-amoxiclav.
- Draw around the cellulitis with a water-resistant pen to allow accurate subsequent assessments and arrange early review (at 24–48 hours).
- Elevate the limb—oedema with blistering may cause ulceration.
- If more extensive, with systemic upset, lymphangitis or worsening on oral therapy, then hospital admission for rest, elevation and parenteral therapy is needed.
- Options include benzylpenicillin + flucloxacillin or co-amoxiclav for 48 hours (or until the erythema starts to recede), then an oral course.
- Total treatment should be for 10–14 days.
- If cellulitis complicates ulcers, pressure sores or lymphoedema then broader spectrum antibiotics are needed at outset.
- Look for and treat toe web intertrigo in all (with topical antifungals).
- Cellulitis can be painful—ensure that the patient has adequate analgesia.
- Older patients will often become dehydrated with bacteraemia—assess clinically (pulse, blood pressure, general condition) and biochemically (urea, creatinine, and electrolytes) giving intravenous fluids in the acute phase if needed.

Other bacterial skin infections

Erysipelas

- Type of cellulitis that is common in older patients.
- Caused by *Streptococcus pyogenes* infection of the dermis and hypodermis.
- Occurs on face (bridge of nose and across cheeks), and less commonly on legs, arms and trunk.
- Flu-like prodrome.
- Well demarcated edge with erythema, oedema and pain.
- Progresses to vesicles that rupture and crust.
- Portal of entry may be unclear, especially with facial erysipelas.
- Bacteraemia in 55%; mortality of 10% without treatment.
- Requires parenteral therapy unless very mild—48 hours of iv benzylpenicillin followed by 12 days or oral penicillin V.
- Recurs in 30% at some point.

Necrotizing fasciitis

- Rare and serious infection.
- Affects soft tissues (usually arm and leg), and spreads rapidly along fascial planes.
- Commonly due to *Streptococcus pyogenes*, but polymicrobial infection also occurs (e.g. *Staphylococci*, *Pseudomonas*, *Bacteroides*, diphtheroids, coliforms).
- Patient feels and looks unwell with a high fever.
- Area of swelling, redness and tenderness enlarges rapidly and becomes purple and discoloured. Haemorrhagic bullae develop followed by necrosis.
- Prompt parenteral antibiotics and early aggressive surgical debridement are essential.

▶▶ Key to management is early recognition. Review a patient with cellulitis frequently if they are unwell, looking for rapid spread beyond the drawn margin (see p636).

Fungal skin infections

There are two main groups of fungi that cause infection in man:

Dermatophytes e.g. *Tinea* species ('ringworm')

- Infect the feet, groin, body, hands, nails, and scalp.
- Suspect if there is a distinct edge to an itchy lesion.
- Confirm diagnosis with skin scrapings, or trial treatment.
- Topical imidazoles e.g. clotrimazole (Canesten® cream) are effective. Terbinafine (Lamasil® cream) is more effective, but more expensive.
- Oral terbinafine will work for more resistant infection but should only be used if topical treatment fails and the diagnosis confirmed.

Yeasts e.g. *Candida albicans* ('thrush')

- Normal commensal of mouth and GI tract.
- Produces infection in certain circumstances e.g. moist skin folds, poor hygiene, diabetes, and use of broad-spectrum antibiotics—many of these commonly occurring in older patients.
- Common sites include genital (associated with catheter use), intertrigo (see p642), around the nail (chronic paronychia) and oral thrush (especially if dentures fit poorly).
- Topical imidazoles e.g. clotrimazole (Canesten® cream) are effective for skin infection.
- Nystatin, amphotericin, or miconazole lozenges, suspension, or gel can be used for oral infection.
- More widespread infection (e.g. oesophageal candidiasis) or in severe immunodeficiency may require systemic therapy—fluconazole 50–100mg daily is effective.

Seborrhoeic dermatitis

- Chronic inflammatory condition with erythematous scaly eruptions.
- Possibly due to a hypersensitivity to pityrosporum—a yeast skin commensal.
- Classic distribution—face (eyebrows, eyelids, nasolabial folds, postauricular, beard area), scalp (dandruff), central chest, central back and in older patients only, flexural (axillae, groins, submammary).
- May cause otitis externa or blepharitis.
- Increased prevalence and severity in older patients, exacerbated by poor skin care.
- Associated with Parkinsonism and HIV.
- Scalps are treated with ketoconazole shampoo.
- Elsewhere, use ketoconazole shampoo as a wash and apply miconazole combined with 1% hydrocortisone cream.
- Blepharitis is treated with warm compresses, cleaning eyelids with cotton buds and diluted baby shampoo, and steroid eye cream.
- Difficult to treat—recurrence is common, and repeated treatments are often required. Aim to control, not cure.

Intertrigo

- Common complaint, almost exclusively in older patients when superficial inflammation of skin surfaces that are in contact occurs e.g. flexures of limbs, groins, axillae, submammary.
- Due to friction in a continually warm, moist environment.
- May be underlying skin disease (e.g. seborrhoeic dermatitis, seborrhoeic eczema, irritant contact eczema (urine, faeces), psoriasis).
- Secondary infection with yeast is common.

Treatment
- Improve hygiene.
- Wash carefully and always dry the skin thoroughly.
- Use talcum powder to keep areas dry.
- Apply topical antifungal (e.g. clotrimazole cream plus 1% hydrocortisone cream).
- Separate skin surfaces where possible.

Leg ulcers

Common condition, afflicting 1% of adult population at any time.

50% are venous ulcers, 10% arterial, 25% mixed venous and arterial, and the remainder due to other causes (diabetes, infection, malignancy, blood disorders, vasculitis, drug eruptions etc.).

Cause a large amount of morbidity and health care expenditure.

Clinical features of common ulcers

Venous ulcers

- Occur on the medial ankle, along the course of the saphenous vein.
- Shallow and tender with irregular edges that are not undermined.
- The base is usually red, but may be sloughy.
- Associated skin features of chronic venous insufficiency.

Arterial ulcers

- Occur at sites of trauma or pressure—commonly the malleoli, toes, ball of foot, heel and base of 5th metatarsal.
- Deep, punched out, and painful with regular edges.
- Associated features of peripheral arterial disease (decreased pulses, slow capillary refill, pale, cool, hairless skin, see p320).

Diabetic ulcers

- Occur at pressure points.
- Painless (due to diabetic neuropathy).
- Often infected with undermined edges.

Malignant ulcers

- Painless with a raised edge.
- Be suspicious if an ulcer fails to heal, or has an atypical appearance.

A general approach to leg ulcers

- Establish cause—usually possible on clinical grounds. May need to consider doppler ultrasound (looking for deep venous occlusion, valvular incompetence and venous pressures), ABPI (diagnoses arterial disease), biopsy (looking for malignancy, or for tissue culture if infection suspected) or blood tests (FBC, glucose, ESR, CRP, autoantibody screen).
- Treat cause where possible e.g. compression bandaging for venous disease (p649), revascularization for arterial disease (p285).
- Keep ulcer clean and avoid irritant topical applications. Many available products will cause a contact dermatitis. Keep it simple.
- Ensure there is adequate pain relief.
- Re-evaluate regularly. If the ulcer is not healing then reassess the original diagnosis.
- Avoid antibiotics unless there is cellulitis or osteomyelitis. Colonization is inevitable, and swabs usually unhelpful.
- Patch test any patient with a longstanding ulcer to exclude an allergic contact dermatitis.

Chronic venous insufficiency

Common, ranging from minor cosmetic problems to debilitating leg ulcers.

More common after phlebitis or deep vein thrombosis (25% with a history of DVT will develop venous insufficiency at 20 years, 4% will eventually develop leg ulcers), after leg injury, in obese patients, and with advancing age. Probably more common in women, although female longevity may account for apparent difference.

Pathogenesis

Due to failure of the venous pump in the legs. Commonly caused by deep vein occlusion (although only half will show signs of this on venography). Retrograde blood flow in the deep veins, valvular incompetence and progressive pericapillary fibrin deposition also contribute to the process.

Clinical changes

Varicose veins

- Initially there may be no symptoms, just venous dilation (starts with submalleolar venous flares and progresses to dilated, tortuous, palpable varicose veins).
- Problems may include itch, ache, thrombophlebitis, or bleeding from varicosities. Treatment at this stage is largely cosmetic and includes surgical stripping of superficial veins (not where there is a history of deep vein occlusion). Ache may be relieved by use of support hosiery.

Oedema

- May initially be unilateral and wax and wane with position (classically occurring at the end of a day of standing up).
- A feeling of leg heaviness is common.
- Low dose thiazide diuretics (e.g. bendroflumethiazide 2.5mg od) may help, but as the patient is not fluid overloaded, beware of volume depletion.

Skin changes

- Haemosiderin pigmentation due to red cell extravasation.
- Telangiectasia.
- Lacey white scars.
- Eczematous changes with itchy, weepy skin exacerbated by many topical treatments—improve with topical steroid application.
- Lipodermatosclerosis occurs when fibrosis of the tissues leads to induration. May become circumferential and girdle the lower leg causing an inverted champagne bottle appearance.

Venous ulcers

Venous ulcers arise in the context of these skin changes, often precipitated by minor trauma (see pp648–9).

Management of venous leg ulcers

Chronic and debilitating condition, with serious psychological and social implications. Median duration is 9 months, although 25% will still be present at 5 years. Correctly treated, 70% can be healed within 3 months, but 75% are recurrent.

General measures

- Encourage mobility—this strengthens the muscle pump and helps prevent deep vein occlusion. If bed-bound, then exercises such as toe and ankle wiggling and quadriceps movements can help.
- Stop smoking.

Limb elevation

- Raising the legs above the level of the heart improves venous return, reduces oedema, and assists healing of venous ulcers.
- Unfortunately, this is rarely practical—many older patients cannot tolerate such a position owing to co morbidity (cardiac failure, COPD, arthritic hips, obesity etc.) and even if they can, it is difficult to sustain.
- Balance benefits against risks of immobility and complications (thrombosis, deconditioning)—usually only used for very resistant ulcers.
- Elevating the foot of the bed mattress at night is helpful (easiest with electronic hospital beds, otherwise use a wedge under the mattress).
- During the day, sitting with the feet on a stool is better than nothing, although it fails to raise the legs high enough.
- Elevation should *not* be used with peripheral arterial disease—check pedal pulses and ABPI (see p321) first.

Ulcer care

- Clean the ulcer by irrigation with saline.
- Debridement of dead tissue may improve healing (no trial evidence):
  - Scalpel (local EMLA cream may make this less uncomfortable).
  - Maggots (consume only dead tissue, leaving behind the healthy).
  - Facilitating the body's own system by creating a moist environment.
  - Chemical agents are not recommended (as they also harm healing tissue).
- No single wound dressing has been shown to improve healing.
- An ideal dressing keeps the wound moist with exudate, but not macerated, at an ideal temperature and pH for healing without irritants, excessive slough, or infection.
- Simple, low-adherent and low-cost dressings are the mainstay.
- Impregnated dressings (e.g. with antiseptic, antibiotic, debriding enzymes, growth factors or silver sulfadiazine) can cause contact allergic or irritant dermatitis (up to 85% of patients), worsening the ulcer, so avoid in routine use.
- Occlusive or semi occlusive dressings can aid with pain relief.
- Gel and hydrocolloid dressings can be useful to remove exudates.
- Metronidazole or charcoal dressings can be used for odour control.

Compression bandaging

- Mainstay of treatment for venous ulcers—when correctly applied, leads to healing for 70% in 3 months.
- Ensure that the ABPI is >0.8.
- When mixed aetiology ulcers are present, some compression is often required, but this has to be carefully moderated to compensate for the arterial insufficiency.
- Provides an active counter-pressure to venous blood pressure, and enhances the function of the muscle pump.
- Graduated four-layer compression from the ankle to the knee (wool bandage, crepe bandage, elasticated bandage and finally a self-adhesive elasticated bandage (e.g. Coban™).
- Should be comfortable, allow the patient to continue with daily life (e.g. wear shoes as usual) and last a week (unless highly exudative).
- Should be applied by an experienced practitioner, as incorrect bandaging can cause more harm than good.

Oral agents

- **Aspirin.** May improve ulcer healing time, but studies have been small.
- **Pentoxifylline**. 400mg tds may improve circulation and improve healing when used as an adjunct to bandaging, but again evidence is limited by small study size (see Further reading, below)
- **Antibiotics**. Most ulcers are permanently colonized (commonly staphylococci, streptococci, *E. coli*, *Proteus* and *Pseudomonas*) and routine use of oral antibiotics will only promote resistance. Wound swabs will only grow these colonizing organisms and are not indicated. Treat with systemic antibiotics only if there is evidence of spreading infection (rapidly increasing size, increased pain, surrounding erythema, tracking up lymphatics system or systemic upset).

Surgery

- Skin grafts may be helpful. Pinch or punch skin grafts may stimulate healing.
- Surgical correction of deep vein incompetence is considered where bandaging has failed. Involves ligation of superficial veins and valvuloplasty.

Further reading

Royal College of Nursing guidelines (in conjunction with NICE)
www.rcn.org.uk/publications/pdf/guidelines/venous_leg_ulcers.pdf

DA Simon et al. (2004). Clinical review: Management of venous leg ulcers. *BMJ* **328**: 1358–1362.

Pruritus

Intense itching. Common condition in older patients, often causing considerable distress. Threshold for itch affected by neurological and psychological factors—exacerbated by social isolation, sensory impairment (blind, deaf) and depression. Often ignored, yet simple measures can make a big difference.

Causes

Often associated with **dry skin** (xerosis), common with ageing, and frequently worst on lower legs, forearms and hands. Skin is dry, scaly and may develop inflamed fissures when severe (asteatotic dermatitis).

Contact dermatitis may show few skin changes if mild, yet cause troublesome itching. Limited to areas exposed to allergen (e.g. under clothing if due to washing power).

Systemic disease causes up to half of pruritus in the elderly, including:
- Liver failure (may be mild jaundice—itch caused by bile salts).
- Chronic renal failure.
- Iron deficiency—even before anaemic.
- Haematological disorders (lymphoma, polycythaemia—itch may be exacerbated by water).
- Infections (including fungal infection, scabies and lice infestations, GI parasite infections).
- Metabolic disorders (including: thyroid disease—affects 10% of hyperthyroid patients, and many hypothyroid patients because of dry skin; diabetes mellitus).
- Malignancy.

Many **drugs** can cause a pruritic rash as an adverse drug reaction (usually allergic) but some cause itch without a rash (e.g. morphine, allopurinol and benzodiazepines) or because of cholestasis.

Assessment

- **History** should include full systems enquiry looking for underlying disease, drug history and specific enquiries about possible irritants (e.g. biological washing powder, new bath products). Ask if anyone else is itching.
- **Examination** should include inspection of all skin and thorough general examination (looking for e.g. burrows or other signs of scabies, lymphadenopathy, hepatosplenomegaly, thyroid enlargement etc.).
- **Investigations** should include: FBC, iron and ferritin, ESR, U, C+E, LFT, TFT, and blood glucose. May include other tests, guided by history e.g. stool examination for ova, cysts and parasites, abdominal ultrasound if organomegaly felt etc.

Pruritus: treatment

- Treat the underlying cause wherever possible.
- Iron supplements if stores low (even if FBC normal).
- Stop any drugs that may be causing or exacerbating the condition.
- Apply emollients—light preparations such as aqueous cream can help itch even if the skin does not appear dry, and may be mixed with 0.5% menthol, which has a cooling and antiseptic action. Greasier preparations e.g. 50:50 liquid paraffin, white soft paraffin are useful when the dryness is more severe.
- Urea containing emollients are used where the skin is scaly, and are often useful in the elderly (e.g. Balneum® plus, E45® itch relief cream etc.).
- Avoid excessive bathing and use preparations such as aqueous cream or emulsifying ointments instead of soap. Emollient bath additives can be added to the water. Brand names such as Oilatum® and E45® make both ointments and bath oils, but there are very many alternatives.
- Avoid exacerbating factors, such as heat (especially hot baths), alcohol, hot drinks and vasodilating drugs.
- Wear loose, cotton clothing.
- Keep nails short to limit skin damage from scratching.
- Consider short-term bandaging where excoriation severe to allow healing.
- Antihistamines may be useful—sedating preparations such as hydroxyzine hydrochloride (Atarax®), 25mg at night can help sleep. Non sedating agents can be used during the day (e.g. cetirizine 5mg bd, loratidine 10mg daily).
- Colestyramine (4–8g daily) is used to decrease itch in biliary obstruction and primary biliary cirrhosis.
- Light therapy (phototherapy) may help—normal sunlight, or a course of UVB therapy can be arranged.

Pruritic conditions

Lichen simplex

- Local patch of pruritus, that is scratched leading to skin damage with thickening, discolouration, and excoriation.
- Worse in times of emotional stress.
- Treat with steroids (topical or intralesional) and avoidance of scratching (bandaging may help). Capsaicin cream may decrease itching by decreasing substance P in the skin.

Pruritus ani

- Common complaint.
- Occasionally due to infection (streptococci, candidiasis).
- Exclude allergic contact dermatitis, seborrhoeic dermatitis or psoriasis.
- Usually due to soiling of the perianal skin, which is worse with loose stool and difficulty in wiping effectively (e.g. with arthritis).
- Mainstay of treatment is improving hygiene after bowel movement (assist with wiping if physically difficult, consider wiping with a damp cloth etc.).
- Use aqueous cream as a soap substitute.
- Once developed, the itch may be self perpetuating—break the cycle with steroids ± topical antifungals or antiseptics.
- Patch test to exclude allergy.

HOW TO... **recognize and manage scabies**

▶▶ Thinking of this diagnosis is the first step.
- Caused by *Sarcoptes scabiei* mite.
- Spread by skin-to-skin contact.
- Outbreaks can occur within institutions (e.g. nursing homes, hospital wards).
- Occasionally serious, even fatal.

Symptoms and signs
- Intense itch (worse at night).
- Widespread excoriation.
- Examine the patient carefully for burrows and/or erythematous papules that are found:
  - Between fingers and toes
  - On the wrist flexor surface
  - Around the nipples and umbilicus
  - In the axillae and groin.

Treatment
- Isolate the patient (gloves, aprons).
- Apply topical pesticidal lotions or creams e.g. permethrin 5%, malathion 0.5%.
- Apply to whole body including the scalp, neck and face. Ensure the interdigital webs are well covered.
- Treat all household members (or all others in close contact in an institution) simultaneously, including asymptomatic contacts.
- Wash clothes and bedding.
- Repeat treatment after a week.
- Prescribe 30–60mg of cream and 100ml of lotion for each application.
- Applying after a hot bath is no longer recommended.
- Antibiotics may be needed for secondary infection.
- Itch may persist for weeks after treatment has eradicated the mite, but should slowly diminish. Topical steroids and sedating antihistamines to aid sleep can be helpful.
- Persistent itch may indicate treatment failure.

'Norwegian scabies' occurs in immunosuppressed and frail older patients. A heavy load of mites produces hyperkeratotic lesions. Highly contagious. May require additional oral treatment (e.g. ivermectin— not licensed).

Blistering diseases

There are many disorders causing skin blistering in older people—see box opposite for a differential. Common causes include blistering secondary to cellulitis or rapid onset **oedema**. Bullous pemphigoid is significant in that it occurs almost exclusively in the elderly population.

Bullous pemphigoid

Chronic autoimmune bullous eruption.

Clinical features
- Patient is systemically well.
- Skin becomes erythematous and itchy.
- Large, tense blisters then appear, usually on the limbs, trunk and flexures (rarely mucous membranes).
- Blisters then heal without scarring.
- May appear in normal looking skin, or at the site of previous skin damage (e.g. ulcer, trauma).
- Chronic and recurrent condition.

Diagnosis
- Confirmed by skin biopsy, that shows linear IgG deposited at the basement membrane.
- Circulating autoantibody (anti-BPAg1 and anti-BPAg2) is found in the serum of up to half of patients.

Treatment
- Responds well to steroids.
- Mild, local disease can be treated with strong topical steroids.
- More widespread disease requires oral prednisolone (40–60mg daily initially, reducing fairly rapidly to 10mg within a few weeks).
- Topical or intralesional steroids are used for resistant lesions.
- Remember to monitor for and protect against steroid side effects (pp156–7).
- Consider steroid sparing agents for longer treatment courses (e.g. azathioprine).

Prognosis
- 50% have self-limiting disease.
- The majority will be off medication within 2 years.

Causes of blistered skin

Blistering disorder	Clinical features
Blisters secondary to cellulitis	Features of cellulitis present (see p636)
Blisters secondary to oedema	Occurs when onset is rapid
Traumatic blisters	Due to friction, pressure, or knocks to skin
	Localized to site of insult e.g. heel blister with ill fitting shoes
Pressure blisters	Due to prolonged pressure that causes skin ischaemia
	Can occur after 2 hours of immobility
	Risk factors include advancing age, immobility, dehydration, extremes of body size
	May progress to pressure sore (pp546–7)
Fixed drug eruption	Itch, erythema, and blistering that appears and reappears at the same site after ingestion of a drug (e.g. furosemide)
	Reaction usually within 6 hours
Eczema	Blisters may occur in eczema, especially if there is secondary infection (e.g. eczema herpeticum, staphylococcal infection)
Infections	Herpes simplex—usually cause blisters on the face or genitals
	Herpes zoster—shingles is common in older patients (p686)
	Staphylococci and streptococci may cause primary infections (e.g. impetigo—facial blisters that rupture to leave a yellow crust; erysipelas—well defined area of redness and swelling that later blisters, usually on face or lower leg) or secondary infection of e.g. a leg ulcer or wound. Either may result in blistering.
Bullous pemphigoid	See opposite page
Pemphigus vulgaris	Serious autoimmune blistering disease
	Rare disorder, mainly affecting young or middle aged patients
	Widespread flaccid, superficial blisters that rupture early
	Patients are systemically unwell
Dermatitis herpetiformis	Symmetrical extensor surface tense blisters, associated with coeliac disease
	Rare, with peak incidence in the 4th decade

Skin cancers and pre-cancers

All the following increase in frequency with increasing age and sun exposure. They are most common on sun-exposed areas, especially the head and neck and are diagnosed by biopsy. Any suspicious skin lesion should be referred to a dermatologist for consideration of this after discussion with the patient.

Actinic keratoses

- Rough, scaly patches.
- Vary from skin coloured to red, brown, yellow, and black (often patchy).
- Pre-malignant, with a small risk of becoming squamous cell carcinoma over years. Some resolve spontaneously. Treat established lesions.
- Removal with cryotherapy, topical 5 fluorouracil (5 FU—applied bd for 4–6 weeks, causes erythema, burning, ulceration and then healing) or topical diclofenac (Solaraze®: treat for 60–90 days; therapeutic effect may occur up to 30 days after stopping).

Bowen's disease

- Intraepidermal carcinoma, with small risk of transformation into squamous cell carcinoma.
- Typically occurs on the lower leg of elderly women.
- Caused by sun exposure, arsenic exposure, or human papilloma virus infection.
- Pink or reddish scaly plaques with well-defined edges.
- Histology should be confirmed.
- Watchful waiting may be appropriate, but most lesions are removed by cryotherapy, topical 5FU, curettage, or excision.

Lentigo maligna

- Irregular pigmented macules that can be brown, black, red, or white.
- Usually over 1cm in size, they occur in areas of sun exposure.
- 1–2% become invasive with time.
- Excision is required.

Basal cell carcinoma

- Commonest, accounting for 75% of all skin cancers.
- Other risk factors include irradiation, arsenic ingestion, or chronic scarring.
- Slow growing and usually only locally invasive (metastasis virtually unknown), but facial tumours left untreated can cause erosion of cartilage and bone with significant disfigurement.
- Begins as a pearly papule, that then ulcerates, characteristically with a rolled everted edge and surface telangiectasia (so called rodent ulcer).
- Most lesions need excision with a 5mm margin; Moh's microsurgical method involves inspecting histology during the procedure to limit tissue loss; radiotherapy can be used where surgery is not an option, or in cases of recurrence. Intralesional interferon or photodynamic therapies are newer options.
- Recurrence in 5% at 5 years, so follow-up is required.

Squamous cell carcinoma

- Second most common skin cancer.
- Other risk factors include irradiation, chronic ulceration or scarring, (►► May develop in the edge of a leg ulcer.) smoking or exposure to industrial carcinogens.
- 5–10% will metastasize, usually to local lymph nodes initially.
- Begins as an erythematous, indurated area that becomes hyperkeratotic and scaly, and may then ulcerate.
- Removal is by surgical excision with 5mm margins. Radiotherapy can be used for recurrence, or in older patients if excision would be hard (e.g. on the face).

Malignant melanoma

- Most lethal of skin tumours, readily metastasizing.
- Different subtypes include superficial spreading melanoma (most common; plaque with irregular border and uneven pigmentation), nodular melanoma (dark pigmented nodule), lentigo maligna melanoma and acral lentiginous melanoma (pigmented macule in nail beds, palms and soles).
- Suspect if a pigmented lesion has changed in size or colour, become irregular in shape, bleeds, itches or looks inflamed.
- Early detection is key as the thicker the lesion the worse the outlook and once metastasized, the disease is fatal—older men often ignore suspicious looking skin lesions.
- Removal is by surgical excision with wide margins.

Other skin lesions

Campbell de Morgan spots

- Small bright red papules on the trunk.
- Benign capillary proliferations.
- Occur from middle age onwards, almost universal by old age in caucasians.

Skin tags

- Pedunculated, benign fibroepithelial polyps.
- Occur in older patients.
- Benign, usually multiple, cause unknown.
- Removal for cosmetic reasons by snipping the stalk with scissors, or cryotherapy (liquid nitrogen).

Seborrhoeic warts

- Also called basal cell papilloma.
- Not infectious.
- Oval papules (1–6 cm diameter) occurring on the face and trunk of older patients.
- Initially yellow, become darker and more warty in appearance.
- Seem to be 'stuck-on', usually multiple.
- Removal can be done (usually for cosmetic reasons) by cryotherapy or curettage.
- Where concerns exist about more serious pathology, excision biopsy is performed.

Infection and immunity

The ageing immune system 660
Overview of infection in older people 662
   How to... accurately diagnose infection in
   an older patient 663
Antibiotic use in older patients 664
Methicillin-resistant *Staphylococcus aureus* 666
MRSA disease 668
   How to... control MRSA 669
Clostridium difficile-associated diarrhoea 670
   How to... manage *Clostridium difficile* infection 672
Near patient urine tests 674
   How to... sample urine for dipstick, microscopy,
   and culture 675
Asymptomatic bacteriuria 676
Urinary tract infection 678
Urinary tract infection: treatment 680
Recurrent urinary tract infection 682
Varicella zoster infection 684

The ageing immune system

The immune system ages in a complex manner:
- Some activities increase (e.g. production of memory T lymphocytes, IgA and autoantibodies).
- Other activities diminish (e.g. production of some interleukins, antibodies in response to foreign antigens, macrophage clearance of antigens and complement during acute infection).
- Overall, immune responses become less efficient, less appropriate and occasionally harmful with age.
- The immune system does not wear out—it becomes dysfunctional.
- This is an insidious process, often unnoticed until times of physiological stress (e.g. acute illness).
- It is more marked in older people with chronic disease, multiple comorbidities, and significant genetic and environmental factors.

This immune dysfunction alters the response to infection in older people:
- Infectious disease is a more significant cause of morbidity and mortality in older people (up to ten times more likely to be the cause of death).
- Impaired cellular immunity predisposes older people to reactivation of certain diseases e.g.:
  - Shingles (p686)
  - Tuberculosis (p358).
- Altered antibody production increases fatality from pneumonia, influenza, bacterial endocarditis, and hospital-acquired infections.
- Decreased levels of lymphokines increase susceptibility to parasitic infections.
- Age related immune dysfunction probably has a negative impact of the course of AIDS in older patients.
  ▶▶ Investigations may not show characteristic changes associated with infection, or these changes may develop more slowly (e.g. rise in white cell count, CRP and complement).

It also has other clinical consequences:
- Increased autoantibody production does not lead to an increase in autoimmune disease (this peaks in middle age), but may contribute to degenerative diseases.
- Response to vaccination may be less good.
- Falling immune surveillance may contribute to the rising incidence of cancer.
- T-lymphocyte dysfunction may contribute to the increasing incidence of monoclonal gammopathy with age (see p504).
- IgE-mediated hypersensitivity reactions are less frequent, so allergic symptoms tend to improve with age.

Further reading

Evans J E et al. eds (2003). Immunity and ageing (section 4.3) in *Oxford Textbook of Geriatric Medicine*. Oxford: Oxford University Press.

Overview of infection in older people

Infectious disease causes significant morbidity and mortality in older people.

Susceptibility to infection is increased by:
- Immune senescence (see p662).
- Altered skin and mucosal barriers.

Response to established infection might be compromised by:
- Decreased cardiac adaptation to stress.
- Comorbid conditions and frailty.
- Decreased lean body mass or even malnutrition.
- Multiple previous hospital admissions or residence in a long-term care facility.

Presentation
- Frequently atypical e.g. global deterioration, non-specific functional decline, delirium, falls, incontinence.
- May initially give no clue to the site of sepsis e.g. chest infections may present with falls, rather than cough.
- Fever is often absent, reduced or delayed (due to senescent hypothalamic responses).
- Often indolent with a slow deterioration over several days.

▶▶ By the time sepsis is obvious, the patient may be very unwell.

Investigation
Obtaining samples can be difficult e.g. delirious uncooperative patient, urinary or faecal incontinence, inability to expectorate sputum etc.
Misleading results are common:
- Positive urine dipstick does not necessarily indicate urine infection (see p676).
- Urine samples from a catheterised patient will often be heavily colonized, making dipsticks positive and culture results difficult to interpret.
- Ulcers will usually be colonized and swab results should be interpreted with caution (see p644).
- Abdominal ultrasound scan will often reveal gall stones in older patients—these are usually asymptomatic and do not necessarily imply biliary sepsis.
- Classic markers of infection (leucocytosis, elevated CRP, increased complement) may be absent or delayed in older patients.

Treatment
Because of the difficulties in making an accurate diagnosis:
- Therapy is often empirical.
- Antibiotic failures are more common.
- Antibiotic resistance frequently develops.

In addition, treatment may be difficult to administer in delirious patients.

HOW TO... accurately diagnose infection in an older patient

Making an accurate diagnosis with evidence to support it is important to allow tailored antibiotic therapy. Have a low threshold for considering sepsis as a cause for decline of any sort, but conversely do not assume that all problems stem from infection.

Investigations

- Full blood count: white cell count may be elevated, suppressed (poor prognostic indicator) or be unchanged.
- ESR, CRP: often become elevated early on in infection, but this is very non-specific and they may take 24–48 hours to rise or remain normal. Serial measurements advised.
- U,C +E: septic older patients are prone to renal impairment.
- Blood and urine cultures: sent **before** antibiotics are started.
- CXR: a patch of consolidation on an X-ray may be the first indicator that a global deterioration is due to pneumonia.
- Consider stool culture (if diarrhoea) and sputum culture (if cough).

If the source remains unclear, repeat basic tests, then consider:

- **Skin**: check carefully for cellulitis and/or ulceration (p636).
- **Bones**: osteomyelitis (particularly vertebral, after joint replacement or where there is chronic deep ulceration of skin) may present indolently. Check for boney tenderness and consider X-rays, bone scans, or MRI (see pp534–5).
- **Heart valves**: bacterial endocarditis can be very hard to diagnose. Consider in all with a murmur, and actively exclude in those with prosthetic heart valves (See *OHCM* 6th edn for more details).
- **Biliary tree**: asymtomatic gallstones are common in older patients, but if an ultrasound also shows dilation of the gall bladder or biliary system with a thickened, oedematous wall, then infection is likely. There is usually (but not always) abdominal pain. Send blood cultures. ERCP may be needed to remove any obstruction.
- **Abdomen**: diverticular disease is common, and abscesses may present atypically. Examine for masses and consider abdominal ultrasound or CT if there is a history of diverticula or abdominal pain.
- **Brain**: meningitis, brain abscess, and encephalitis may present indolently in older patients, and the usual warning signs (confusion, drowsiness) may be misinterpreted. Headache and photophobia may be late or absent. Consider CT head followed by analysis of cerebrospinal fluid if a septic patient has focal neurology, headache, photophobia or bizarre behavioural change.
- **Tuberculosis**: may reactivate in older people and cause chronic infection. If there is known previous TB (clinical or CXR evidence) then look very carefully for reactivation. Consider early morning urines, sputum culture (induced if necessary), bronchoscopy, or biopsy of any abnormal tissue (e.g. enlarged lymph nodes).

▶▶ Remember that fever and raised inflammatory markers can also be due to non-infectious conditions (e.g. malignancy, vasculitis etc.)

Antibiotic use in older patients

Antibiotics are among the most frequently prescribed drugs, and their widespread use is promoting increasing antibiotic resistance.

This is a particular problem in older patients where infections are more common, yet accurate diagnosis can be more difficult (see p664).

Antibiotic resistance

This occurs when a bacterium encounters an antibiotic and is not eradicated fully, the selection pressure being for antibiotic resistance. The resistant strain can then be transmitted to other patients. Resistance is encouraged by:

- 'Blind' antibiotic therapy (where likely microbe and sensitivities are not known).
- Inappropriate antibiotic therapy (e.g. for viral respiratory tract infections).
- Inadequate treatment courses.
- Poor concordance with therapy.
- Transmission of resistant strains within healthcare settings.

Sensible antibiotic prescribing

Helps to limit the problem. Applies to all ages, but may be more of a challenge in older patients:

- Make a diagnosis—identify the source of sepsis (and so possible pathogens), which will guide therapy before microbiological confirmation is obtained.
- Avoid antibiotics for infections that are likely to be viral e.g. pharyngitis, upper respiratory tract infection.
- Always send samples for culture and sensitivity before initiating antibiotics.
- Local variations (e.g. diagnostic mix, local sensitivities) should be considered. Use guidelines from the local microbiological department.
- Choose the dose based on patient (allergies, age, weight, renal function etc), and the severity of the infection. Inadequate doses promote resistance.
- Choose the route—aim for oral wherever possible, and convert intravenous therapy to oral as soon as feasible. Intramuscular antibiotic therapy can be useful in certain circumstances (e.g. demented patients who refuse oral medication because of added delirium) but are uncomfortable.
- Choose the duration based on the type of infection e.g. simple urinary tract infection can be adequately treated in 3 days, whereas bacterial endocarditis can require many weeks of therapy. Unnecessarily long treatment courses will promote resistance, increase the risk of side effects and increase cost.
- Empirical broad-spectrum antibiotics should be changed to narrow spectrum alternatives as soon as sensitivities are known.

Further reading

British National Formulary Section 5.1 Antibacterial drugs www.bnf.org

Methicillin-resistant *Staphylococcus aureus*

Methicillin was introduced in the 1960s to treat staphylococcal infection. It was used widely (including spraying solutions into the air on wards) and initially successfully. Methicillin has now been discontinued and replaced by flucloxacillin but the term 'methicillin resistant *Staphylococcus aureus*' (MRSA) persists.

Resistance to methicillin gradually emerged—firstly small numbers within hospitals, but the problem slowly increased and spread into the community, until globally dispersed epidemic strains have emerged.

All staphylococci are easily transmissible, virulent (capacity to cause disease) and have capacity to develop further antibiotic resistance.

The problem today

- Varies enormously e.g. > 30% of hospitalized patients in Spain and France are colonized, compared with <1% in Scandinavia. Recent UK figures suggest levels close to those seen in Spain and France.
- MRSA accounts for > 40% of all staphylococcal bacteraemia (compulsory reporting in the UK). There were 3519 cases in England from April–September 2004, and 3574 cases over the same period in 2003.
- The National Audit Office estimated that MRSA caused 5000 deaths and cost the NHS £1 billion in 2002.
- MRSA reduction has become a political target in the UK (see www.doh.gov.uk).

Contamination and transmission

- Anything coming into contact with an MRSA source can become contaminated ie MRSA will exist for a short time on that surface.
- Transient carriage on the gloves or hands of healthcare workers is likely to represent the main mode of transmission to other patients.
- Up to 35% of environmental surfaces in a room being used by an MRSA patient will culture positive (role in transmission is unclear).
- Decontamination involves cleaning. Good hand hygiene and the use of alcohol hand gel after patient contact reduce transmission significantly.

Colonization

- This is asymptomatic carriage of MRSA.
- Common sites are anterior nares, perineum, hands, axillae, wounds, ulcers, sputum, throat, urine, venous access sites, and catheters.
- Duration of colonization varies from days to years.
- Transmission from a colonized person is more likely if there is a heavy bacterial load with abnormal skin (e.g. ulcers, eczema), devices (e.g. catheters, cannulae) or sinusitis/respiratory tract infection.
- Many healthcare workers are colonized (usually nasal) and are a potential reservoir for MRSA, but usually colonization is short-lived.
- Eradication of MRSA in healthcare workers and patients is sometimes done during large outbreaks. This is done by applying topical mupirocin to the nose, using antimicrobial soap and oral antibiotics (e.g. fusidic acid, rifampicin).

MRSA disease

MRSA does not cause a specific disease but the most common sites of infection are:
- Wounds—commonest cause of post-operative wound infections.
- Intravenous lines—often leading to bacteraemia.
- Ulcers—including pressure, diabetic and venous ulcers.
- Deep abscesses—infection can seed to many sites e.g. lungs, kidneys, bones, liver and spleen.
- Bacteraemia—there is compulsory reporting of this.

30–60% of hospital patients colonized with MRSA will go on to develop infection. This is more likely if there has been:
- Recent prior hospitalization.
- Surgery or wound debridement.
- Invasive procedures (including venepuncture and venous cannulation).

Infections due to MRSA cause increased morbidity and mortality, longer hospital stays and increased cost compared with a susceptible organism.

Management

Infection control measures to reduce the reservoir and lower the rate of transmission are crucial (see box opposite).

Antibiotic treatment is necessary when there is active infection—do not use for colonization, as this will promote drug resistance. Opposing responsibility to the patient (use the best drug available) and the community (do not promote antibiotic resistance) must be weighed up. The choice of drug will depend on local resistance patterns and the severity of the infection. Where possible, wait for sensitivities from microbiology. Options include:
- **Glycopeptide antibiotics** (e.g. vancomycin, teicoplanin): must be given intravenously; resistance is emerging.
- **Co-trimoxazole**: useful for susceptible skin, soft tissue and infections.
- **Fusidic acid, rifampicin and doxycycline**: can be effective, usually given in combination.
- **Clindamycin**: used for deeper infections, but most UK strains are resistant.
- **Fluoroquinolones**: e.g. ciprofloxacin. Resistance is rapidly emerging.
- **Linezolid**: a new oxazolidinone antibiotic with equivalent potency to vancomycin. Can be given orally or intravenously. Use with caution because of high cost and uncertain side effect profile (bone marrow toxicity common, especially with prolonged use).

HOW TO... **control MRSA**

Identify the MRSA type
During an outbreak, the microbiology laboratory will be able to determine if this is a cluster of unrelated cases, or a series of infections by a single strain—the latter indicating either high transmission rates or an ongoing reservoir.

Identify the reservoir
- Commonly a patient with a heavily colonized or infected wound.
- Healthcare workers may also act as reservoirs.
- During an epidemic, it is usual to attempt to eradicate MRSA from likely reservoir sources (using nasal mupirocin, antimicrobial soap, and oral antibiotics).

Reduce transmission rates
Transmission usually occurs from patient to patient via a healthcare worker. This is often when hands or gloves are transiently contaminated.
- **Hand hygiene** is the single most important factor in infection control. Good hand washing technique and bedside alcohol-based hand gels should be used by staff, visitors, patients, therapists, volunteers, and service personnel after touching a patient.
- Known MRSA patients should be **isolated** where possible.
- **Gloves** should be worn on entering the room, and removed before leaving.
- **Gowns/aprons** should be used if contact with the patient or environment is anticipated, or if the wound is open.
- **Masks** may reduce nasal acquisition by healthcare workers.
- Patients should be **moved about the hospital as little as possible.** Radiological investigations should be done at the end of a list to allow cleaning after the test.
- Minimize the use of **foreign devices** (e.g. catheters, nasogastric tubes).
- Use **dedicated equipment** (e.g. stethoscopes, blood pressure cuffs, thermometers) or clean carefully after use.
- **Active surveillance** for MRSA colonization allows these procedures to be put in place earlier.

▶▶ By following these guidelines, it is estimated that 70% of transmission can be prevented

Problems in geriatric care:
- Isolation can cause problems with depression and lack of social stimulation.
- Patients may feel stigmatized or scared by the diagnosis.
- Rehabilitation may be restricted (e.g. if the patient is confined to a side room and cannot visit the physiotherapy gym or practise mobilizing about the ward).
- It may be difficult to enforce isolation in patients with dementia.
- Moving to nursing homes or community facilities may be delayed (e.g. whilst waiting for a side room).

Clostridium difficile-associated diarrhoea

Clostridium difficile (CD) is a Gram positive, spore forming, anaerobic bacillus. It was rarely described before the late 1970s but is now a major cause of hospital acquired infection on geriatric wards. *Clostridium difficile* associated diarrhoea (CDAD) is a major problem, causing a huge burden of morbidity, mortality and cost to the NHS.

Pathogenesis
- Asymptomatic CD carriage occurs in less than 5% of population.
- Spores persist for months to years in the environment and are resistant to many traditional cleaning fluids. Vegetative forms and spores can be transmitted from patient to patient.
- Gastrointestinal carriage is increased in the hospital population, with advancing age, other bowel disease, cytotoxic drug use and debility (e.g. recent surgery, chronic renal impairment, cancer).
- Most antibiotics reduce the colonisation resistance of the colon to CD.
- CDAD occurs when toxins (A and B) elaborated by CD bind to the colonic mucosa causing inflammation.
- Outbreaks in hospital can occur from cross-infection and can affect patients never exposed to antibiotics.

Features
There is a wide range of manifestations from asymptomatic carriage to fulminant colitis. Most commonly presents with:
- Foul-smelling watery diarrhoea (mucous common but rarely blood)
- Abdominal pain and distension
- Fever.

In severe cases can mimic an 'acute abdomen'. Occasionally causes chronic diarrhoea.

▶▶ Beware that an acute decline in a patient's condition (e.g. fever, delirium, metabolic disturbance) can precede the diarrhoea; have a low threshold of suspicion in patients with multiple risk factors.

Investigations
- Raised white cell count and inflammatory markers (following treatment of an infection, differential diagnosis includes relapse of original infection).
- CD toxin detection by ELISA is both sensitive and specific for colitis. Can remain positive for weeks after resolution so NOT useful in diagnosing recurrence.
- Stool culture may be positive in asymptomatic patients but is rarely done.
- Abdominal X-ray or CT may show distended, thick walled large bowel.
- Sigmoidoscopy is often normal in mild disease or where colitis affects proximal bowel. Characteristic colitis with pseudomembrane formation is present in more severe cases (also known as pseudomembranous colitis).

Complications

Rarely occur, and include toxic megacolon, paralytic ileus, perforation, and bacteraemia. Older patients requiring surgery have at least 50% mortality.

Relapse

Defined as a second event within 2 months, occurring in around 20%. Rarely due to antibiotic resistance, but can be difficult to treat. Vancomycin, given orally, is an alternative to repeating the metronidazole course.

Patients with recurrence are then more prone to further repeated infection.

For repeated infection and recalcitrant CDAD, options include:

Further oral antibiotics e.g. metronidazole, vancomycin, bacitracin.

Adjuvant therapy with colestyramine.

Probiotics such as yeast or lactobacillus have also been shown to help induce and maintain remission.

Intravenous immunoglobulins and steroids have been used in severe recalcitrant colitis.

HOW TO... manage *Clostridium difficile* infection

Prevention

Use antibiotics wisely (p666):

- Only when good evidence of infection. Always try to obtain a microbiological diagnosis and only treat where you have diagnosed infection or if the patient is gravely ill and conservative management is judged unsafe.
- Use smallest number of antibiotics with narrowest spectrum possible. Some antibiotics are less likely to cause CD e.g. ceftriaxone or ciprofloxacin are better than cefuroxime.
- Use the shortest course possible. Three days for a simple urinary infection, seven for bronchitis, ten days or longer only for septicaemia, abscess etc.

In the future vaccines against CD might be available.

Treatment

▶▶ Have a high index of suspicion—if the patient is ill commence treatment without waiting for confirmatory tests.

- Stop antibiotics unless there is very good evidence they need a longer course.
- Aggressive rehydration—patients can become very hypovolaemic even before they start to get diarrhoea.
- Metronidazole 400mg tds po (for metronidazole intolerance, failure to respond or recurrence use vancomycin 125mcg qds po). Both drugs must be enteral to obtain high intraluminal levels. If unable to swallow consider nasogastric tube or metronidazole PR 1g bd. IV therapy may be added if septicaemia is suspected.
- Continue 7–10 days or until a formed stool.
- Stool chart will indicate if diarrhoea frequency is improving.
- Use of loperamide (2mg with each loose stool) is controversial—it may mask response to treatment and increase chances of complications. However, proponents suggest if the diagnosis is secure and treatment initiated it can reduce debilitating symptoms and speed recovery.
- Surgical complications may require colectomy.

Infection control

- Nurse in side room where possible.
- Use gloves and aprons for all contact.
- Clean the environment thoroughly, especially after patient has left.

Patients are much less infectious once diarrhoea has resolved, so avoid moving the patient between wards until 48 hours after the last loose stool.

Near patient urine tests

Urinary tract infection (UTI) is a common problem in older people, but there is an even higher prevalence of asymptomatic bacteruria and positive urinalysis without infection. In general, UTI is over diagnosed.

▶▶ It is important to know how to diagnose a UTI correctly, and when to initiate treatment appropriately.

Near patient urine tests (dipsticks)

Quick, cheap test that is commonly performed. Should only be done on urine that is collected as described in box opposite.

Urinary nitrite
- Positive result has a high predictive value for UTI.
- Many bacteria causing UTI convert urinary nitrate to nitrite, which is detected on dipstick.
- False negatives occur with dilute urine.
- Certain bacteria (e.g. *Pseudomonas, Staphylococcus, Enterococcus*) may not convert urinary nitrate, so the dipstick will be negative.

Leucocyte esterase
- Positive result has a high predictive value for UTI.
- Lysed white cells release esterase, which is detected on dipstick.
- Corresponds to significant pyuria—may not detect low levels.
- False negative results also occur when there is glucose, albumin, ketones, or antibiotic in the urine.
- False positives ('sterile pyuria') occur with vaginal contamination, chronic interstitial nephritis, nephrolithiasis and uroepithelial tumours. 'Sterile' pyuria can indicate renal tuberculosis and sexually transmitted diseases (e.g. *Chlamydia*)—consider testing if history suggestive.

'Blood'
- Positive result for blood has a low predictive value for infection.
- Dipstick does not distinguish red cells from haemoglobin or myoglobin.
- Detects red blood cells (blood in the renal tract), haemoglobin (after haemolysis) and myoglobin (rhabdomyolysis).
- Causes of a positive 'blood' dipstick are varied and may be pre-renal (e.g. haemolysis), renal (e.g. tumours, glomerulonephritis), ureteric (e.g. stones), bladder (e.g. tumours, occasionally infection), urethral (e.g. trauma) or contamination (e.g. bleeding from the vaginal vault).
- Always repeat to ensure the haematuria has resolved with treatment.
- Management of persistent isolated dipstick haematuria without apparent cause is difficult. In a fitter patient, referral for renal tract investigation by a urologist may be appropriate.

Protein
- Positive result has a low predictive value for infection.
- Commercial dipsticks generally only detect albumin, and a positive result implies proteinuric renal disease.
- False positives occur in very concentrated or contaminated urine.

▶▶ The combination of nitrites and leucocyte esterases on urine dipstick has the highest positive predictive value for infection. If these are negative and clinical suspicion is high, proceed to urinary microscopy and culture.

HOW TO... sample urine for dipstick, microscopy, and culture

Do not sample
- Stale urine.
- Urine that has been contaminated with faeces.
- Urine from a catheter bag.

Mid-stream urine sample
- Ideal sampling method, but may be hard in confused or immobile patients.
- The external genitalia should be cleaned, a small amount of urine voided, then the middle portion caught cleanly in a sterile container.
- Analysis should be performed whilst the urine is fresh.

In-out catheter sample
- Carries a small risk of introducing infection (around 1%).
- Often well-tolerated by older patients.
- Discard the first urine, and sample the middle portion drained.

Suprapubic aspiration of urine
- Rarely done, but will provide a clean specimen.
- Clean the skin, and percuss to identify the bladder.
- Aspirate with a green needle and 10ml syringe in the midline.

Samples from catheterized patients
- These should only be sent if the patient is symptomatic, as the prevalence of positive dipstick is almost universal, and bacterial colonization of urine is common.
- Clamp the catheter for a period, then collect a mid-stream sample directly from the draining tube sampling port.
- Do not use stale urine that has collected in the bag.

Asymptomatic bacteriuria

Defined as a positive urine culture in the absence of symptoms of urinary tract disease.
- It becomes more common with increasing age (5% of community dwelling females under the age of 60, rising to 30% over the age of 80).
- It is less common in men but again increases with age (<1% of those under 60, rising to 10% over the age of 80).
- Up to 50% of frail institutionalized patients and almost all catheterized patients will have bacteria in their urine (see p581).
- Other risk factors are as for urinary tract infection (see p680).
- Associated diseases include renal stones, diabetes, and chronic prostatitis in men.

What does it mean?
- Probably represents **urinary colonization** rather than infection.
- No increase in mortality directly associated with asymptomatic bacteriuria.
- Seems to be transient in most—only 6% will grow the same organism over three sequential cultures, however it is estimated that around 16% will go on to develop symptomatic urinary tract infection.

Treatment
No treatment is required for isolated bacteriuria, and the use of antibiotics:
- Does not impact on morbidity and mortality.
- Does not improve continence.
- Promotes antibiotic resistance.
- Recurrence after antibiotic treatment is common.
- ▶▶ Avoid treating patients unless they have symptoms.

Urinary tract infection

Major cause of morbidity and mortality in the older population. UTIs account for a quarter of infections in healthy older patients, and are the most common hospital-acquired infection. They are the most frequent cause of bacteraemia in older patients. The annual incidence is up to 10% for older adults (but many are recurrent).

Risk factors

- Advancing age.
- Female sex (although the gap narrows with age).
- Atrophic vaginitis and urethritis in women.
- Incomplete emptying (e.g. urethral strictures, prostatic hypertrophy or carcinoma, neuropathy).
- Abnormalities of the renal tract (e.g. tumours, fistulae, surgery).
- Foreign bodies (e.g. catheter, stones).
- Chronic infection (e.g. renal abscess, prostatitis).

Organisms

- *Escherichia coli* is the most common, as in younger adults.
- Older patients are more prone to UTI caused by other pathogens, including other Gram-negative organisms (e.g. *Proteus, Pseudomonas*) and some Gram-positive organisms (e.g. group B *Streptococcus*, MRSA).
- Catheter-related urinary tract infection is often polymicrobial and antibiotic resistant.

Presentation

The presence of symptoms is essential to make the diagnosis. Urinary frequency, dysuria (stinging or burning sensation on urinating) and new urinary incontinence are clear indications of urinary infection, but symptoms may be vague or atypical, including:

- Fever and general malaise.
- Nausea and vomiting.
- Confusion or delirium.
- Deterioration in physical or functional ability.

Infection may be:

- Uncomplicated UTI (normal renal tract and function).
- Complicated UTI (abnormal renal tract, patient debility, virulent organism, development of complications such as impaired renal function, bacteraemia, pyelonephritis, perinephric or prostatic abscess).
- Recurrent UTI (p684).
- Catheter associated UTI (p581).

Investigations

- Urinalysis: collect sample (p677), perform dipstick (p676) and send for microscopy and culture.
  ▶▶ A negative dipstick does not exclude the diagnosis if the clinical suspicion is high. Always send for culture.
- If the patient is unwell, consider checking blood tests, including renal function (risk of impairment), blood cultures (risk of bacteraemia), full blood count, and inflammatory markers.

Urinary tract infection: treatment

Treatment involves more than just antibiotics. Consider the following:
- Adequate hydration (oral often sufficient, sicker or more confused patients may require intravenous fluid).
- Medication review (consider suspending diuretics or drugs that are potentially nephrotoxic, such as non-steroidals or ACE inhibitors).
- Management of any symptoms (e.g. confusion or decreased mobility may necessitate temporary increase in care at home, or even admission to hospital).
- Assessment for complications (e.g. pyelonephritis, bacteraemia, abscess formation). Older patients are at high risk of dehydration and renal impairment. Consider admission for intravenous antibiotics and hydration if they are unwell.
- Prevention of recurrence with measures such as ensuring good fluid intake and avoiding catheters if possible. Topical oestrogens (vaginally) may be useful in postmenopausal women.

Antibiotic choice

Be guided by local sensitivity patterns—the local microbiology department is likely to have guidelines for UTI management.

Uncomplicated UTI can be treated empirically as follows:
- Trimethoprim 200mg bd (if local resistance is <20%)
- *or* nitrofurantoin 50mg qds
- *or* co-amoxiclav 375mg tds
- Ciprofloxacin 500mg bd is effective, but concerns about emerging resistance mean that it should be reserved for resistant or complicated infection.

Duration of treatment

- Younger females with uncomplicated UTI can be successfully treated with a short course of antibiotics (3 days, or perhaps even a single dose).
- There is limited evidence for the duration required in older patients, but it is likely that a longer course (5–10 days) is needed.

Treatment failure

Incorrect diagnosis

- Delirium and a positive urine dipstick may be misleading.
- Could the patient have another pathology?

Resistant organisms

- Review the results of the urine culture and pathogen sensitivities (ideally sent before empirical antibiotics started).
- *E. coli* is resistant to ampicillin, resistance to sulphonamides is widespread, and trimethoprim resistance is increasing. Most are susceptible to nitrofurantoin and fluoroquinolones (e.g. ciprofloxacin) at present, although fluoroquinolone resistance is increasing.
- Pathogens are more varied in older patients and these may not be susceptible to empirical treatment (e.g. nitrofurantoin is inactive against *Proteus* and *Klebsiella*).
- MRSA UTI may occur in older patients (especially with indwelling catheters), which may require intravenous therapy (e.g. vancomycin).
- *Candida* may cause UTI in the frail, catheterized older patient (identified on microscopy).
- If no culture result is available, and the diagnosis is secure, try an empirical second-line agent such as co-amoxiclav or ciprofloxacin.

Recurrent urinary tract infection

Defined as >3 symptomatic UTIs in a year, or >2 in 6 months. May represent either a relapse (recurrent infection caused by original infecting organism) or a reinfection (infection with different species or strain). Urinary culture is indicated.

Recurrent infection may be due to
- An ongoing source of infection (e.g. chronic prostatitis, renal abscess).
- Urological abnormality (e.g. stones, tumour, residual volume > 50ml, cystocoele).
- Catheterization.
- Poor hygiene (e.g. faecal soiling).
- Impaired immunity (e.g. diabetes, chronic disease).
- Genetic susceptibility.

Managing recurrent infection
- Repeat treatment with up to a week of antibiotics.
- Remove catheter if possible (see p580).
- General measures include increasing fluid intake, treating constipation etc.
- Arrange renal tract ultrasound to look for residual volume and any urological abnormalities (lower threshold of investigation for males).
- Consider blood tests (e.g. glucose, renal function, full blood count, serum electrophoresis, PSA in men).
- Prophylactic antibiotics are rarely indicated (examples include multiple recurrences despite general measures or significant renal damage). Trimethoprim is well studied. Nitrofurantoin is effective but carries a risk of pulmonary fibrosis with prolonged use.
- Pre-emptive treatment can be useful in cognitively intact patients. A short course of antibiotics is held in reserve by the patient, to be taken when symptomatic.

Varicella zoster infection

Initial exposure usually occurs in childhood, causing chicken pox in susceptible individuals. The virus lies dormant in the sensory dorsal root ganglia of the spinal cord and can be reactivated later in life to cause shingles.

Shingles is a painful, self-limiting, unilateral eruption of vesicles in a dermatomal distribution. It occurs in 20% of the population at some time but is most common in older people (probably due to a decline in cell-mediated immunity with age).

Clinical presentation

- Prodrome of fever, malaise, headache, and sensory symptoms (pain, tenderness or paraesthesia) in the dermatome to be affected.
- Rash follows after a few days, initially with a cluster of vesicles that spread across the dermatome and then become pustular.
- 50% affect thoracic dermatomes (T5–T12), 16% lumbosacral, and 15–20% cranial nerve distribution.
- Usually affects single dermatome, but may involve several adjacent.
- Acute herpetic pain is often a feature—may precede the rash by days, and often described as sharp.
- Crusting occurs after about a week, then the patient is no longer infectious (prior to this, susceptible individuals may catch chickenpox).
- Healing generally occurs within a month, but may leave scars.
- Recurrence in around 5%.

Treatment

- **General measures** include adequate oral fluid intake, simple analgesia (e.g. paracetamol) and topical agents such as calamine lotion.
- **Antiviral therapy** (e.g. aciclovir 800mg 5 times a day, famciclovir 250mg tds, valaciclovir 1g tds) should be given within 72 hours of rash onset to all patients over 50 years old, for a week, and has been shown to reduce the severity of the attack, promote rash healing and reduce the incidence of postherpetic neuralgia.
- **Prednisolone** (e.g. 40mg tailing down over a week) can be given with antiviral therapy to reduce the severity of the attack, but has limited value and possible drawbacks (e.g. increasing bacterial superinfection, causing significant side effects) and should only be used where the infection is severe.
- **Analgesia for neuralgia** should be given early where indicated.

Ophthalmic shingles

- More common in older patients.
- Occurs when the ophthalmic division of the trigeminal nerve is involved, resulting in a rash on the forehead and around the eye.
- Ocular involvement commonly occurs, causing a red painful eye. Inflammation of the iris and cornea can cause vision loss, and topical steroid eye drops are used to limit the inflammatory response.
- Prompt use of antivirals may limit the disease.

Ramsay Hunt syndrome

- Shingles of several adjacent cranial nerves cause vesicles in the ear canal, ear pain, and a lower motor neurone facial droop.
- May also cause vertigo, deafness and disturbance of taste and lacrimation.
- ➤➤ Always look in the ears for vesicles when a patient present with a facial palsy.
- Facial paralysis is less likely to fully recover than in Bell's palsy.
- Treat with antivirals as described opposite.

Post-herpetic neuralgia

- Occurs in up to 10% of cases.
- More common with older patients (up to a third of over 60s) who have sensory symptoms at prodrome and a more severe initial infection.
- Defined as sensory symptoms continuing >4 months beyond the onset of rash.
- Subsides in the majority by a year; may become chronic and disabling.
- Usually a deep steady burning sensation, sometimes exacerbated by movement or touch. Occasionally paroxysmal and stabbing.
- Can cause significant psychological symptoms (low mood, poor sleep, loss of appetite etc).
- Treatment is with tricyclic antidepressants (e.g. amitriptyline 10–150mg nocte), opioids (e.g. codeine 60mg qds, tramadol 50–100mg qds) or anticonvulsants (e.g. gabapentin, carbamazepine, phenytoin).
- Topical treatments with lidocaine or capsaicin are also effective.
- Other options can be used in specialist pain clinics, such as intravenous lidocaine, intrathecal steroids or local nerve blocks.

Other complications

All more common in older patients:

- **Bacterial superinfection** (around 2%, can delay rash healing. Treat with topical antiseptic or antibiotic initially—more severe cases require systemic treatment).
- **Motor neuropathy** (occurs when virus spreads to the anterior horn; symptoms depend on segment affected, e.g. C5/6 may cause diaphragmatic paralysis. Majority will recover spontaneously).
- **Meningeal irritation** (causes headache; occurs in up to 40%; the CSF shows reactive changes—lymphocytosis and elevated protein).
- **Meningitis and encephalitis** (rare; diagnosis enhanced by MRI imaging and CSF PCR. Usually occur with the rash, but may be up to 6 months later).
- **Transverse myelitis** (rare; occurs with thoracic shingles).
- **Stroke** (rare and serious; due to cerebral angiitis).

Malignancy

Malignancy in older people 688
An approach to malignancy 690
    How to… describe performance status 691
Presentation of malignancy 692
    How to… screen for malignancy 693
Treating malignancy in older people 694
    How to… manage symptomatic hypercalcaemia 695
Cancer with an unknown primary 696

Malignancy in older people

Cancer is a disease of the elderly population, being relatively rare in people under 35 years of age, and increasing in incidence with each decade.

Why is there more cancer in older people?

- As more people avoid death from infection and vascular events, so they remain alive to develop cancer.
- Some cancers are caused by cumulative exposure to environmental agents. A good example would be sunlight and skin cancer, or smoke and lung cancer, but dietary factors and exposure to other carcinogens are also likely to contribute over time.
- The process of cell replication may senesce, increasing the chance of malignant change.

Is cancer different in older people?

- Development of metastases may appear to be slower, the cancer overall having a more indolent course, possibly due to altered immune or hormonal responses.
- In contrast, some cancers appear to be more aggressive in older people (e.g. acute myeloid leukaemia, Hodgkin's disease, ovarian carcinoma).
- Overall, age itself has limited influence over disease progression and prognosis—factors such as co-morbidity and functional status are more important.
- The impact of cancer may be different in an older person. Non-cancer deaths are common in the frail elderly with malignancy, so cancer control by non-invasive means (e.g. tamoxifen for breast cancer) may be a better option than cancer cure by more unpleasant treatments (e.g. surgery).
- Never underestimate the psychological impact of a cancer diagnosis, whatever the age. Heart failure carries a worse prognosis than many cancers, yet news of its diagnosis rarely has such an impact. Whatever your assessment of a person's quality of life, they may see things very differently—you will not know until you ask. The adverse reaction to the diagnosis is often tied up with fears about a slow and painful death (rather than death itself) and careful explanation about symptom control measures may allay some concerns.

An approach to malignancy

Make the diagnosis

- Even if no curative treatment is possible, a diagnosis allows targeted symptom control and gives an idea about the likely course of the disease and the expected prognosis.
- Many people find 'not knowing what is wrong' very hard, and may find a diagnosis a relief, as it allows the future to be planned.
- Sometimes a frail patient is obviously dying, and investigations can be an additional burden, without hope of finding reversible pathology. In this case, blind palliation of symptoms is the best course. This should be combined with careful explanation to the patient and family.
- There are many shades of grey in between these two extremes. In some cases, finding multiple metastases on a scan may be enough to plan management. In others, a histological diagnosis by biopsy is required to fully balance risks and benefits of treatment. Each individual should have benefits of diagnosis weighed up against discomfort (and cost) of investigation.

Once diagnosis is made, attempt to stage the disease

This allows accurate prognostication and gives the patient better information on which to base treatment decisions. Again, there are exceptions to this (e.g. the very frail who are likely to die from other causes) and each individual should be considered separately.

Assess patient factors that will influence outcome

▶▶ Age is not one of these factors.

Co-morbidity will adversely affect both disease prognosis and tolerance to treatment. Functional status is the other main predictor—is the patient active and asymptomatic, active but with symptoms, slowed down by symptoms or incapacitated by them? Oncologists use 'performance status' as an indicator of functional ability (see box opposite) and a score of 3 or less correlates with a median survival of 3 months. Co-morbid conditions and poorer functional status will be more common in older people, but not universal, so purely age related treatment decisions are unwise.

Utilize a specialist multi-disciplinary approach

Cancer care changes rapidly, and it is hard for the generalist to keep up to date, so specialist referral is needed. Many different specialists can provide cancer treatments and they should work together to decide the best option for that individual. Specialist nurses often perform a co-ordinating role in the patient's journey through the system, providing consistent, non-threatening support, allowing fears to be discussed and providing practical help (e.g. arranging additional help at home).

Discuss decisions carefully with the patient wherever possible

Some patients who have led a long and healthy life (and so would potentially do well from therapy) may wish to simply die without being 'messed about'. Other patients with multiple problems and poorer outlook may take any chance at a prolongation of life whatever the cost.

HOW TO... describe performance status

0   Active, no limitations
1   Active, but unable to carry out strenuous or heavy physical work
2   Active, spending less than half the day in bed or resting
3   Spend over half the day in bed or resting, but still able to get up
4   Bedridden.

Presentation of malignancy

In a cognitively intact and physically fit older patient with a malignancy, presentation is often typical—a breast lump, a thyroid nodule, altered bowel habit with an iron deficiency anaemia etc. In these cases, there is little dilemma—management is as for all patients with such a complaint.

In the frailer elderly, the presentation is often less clear. Cancer may be found incidentally (e.g. a mass on a routine chest X-ray) or there may be a highly suggestive clinical scenario. Judging how hard to look and to what end is a common challenge in geriatric practice.

Common presenting scenarios include:

Weight loss without apparent cause

- Always check a dietary history, measure thyroid function, screen for depression and assess cognitive state.
- If there are no localizing symptoms or signs on careful history or examination, then check screening investigations (see box opposite).
- If these are normal, then malignancy is relatively unlikely, and dietary support with reassement at an interval may be appropriate (see p386).
- Following-up hints offered in a systems enquiry (e.g. admits to occasional loose stool) will depend on the individual patient—whether they would tolerate bowel investigation, whether they would be fit for treatment if malignancy is found and, crucially, what they wish to do.

Elevated inflammatory markers (ESR, CRP)

- This is a relatively common scenario.
- Begin with the screening history, examination, and investigations.
- The main differential diagnosis is sepsis, and this should be actively sought with cultures.
- Consider giving the patient a thermometer and temperature chart to fill in.
- Look at joints and bones as a possible source (gout, septic arthritis, osteomyelitis etc.).
- Remember diverticular abscesses.
- Have a low threshold for thinking of endocarditis (see p664).
- Vasculitides (especially giant cell arteritis, see p520) should be considered and a trial of steroids may be appropriate, even if the history is not convincing, but remember to check response and rethink the diagnosis if the blood results do not normalize.
- A CT scan of the thorax, abdomen and pelvis (looking for lymphadenopathy) may be justified if the patient is otherwise fit and has significantly elevated tests.
- Chasing mildly elevated markers in the frailer elderly is often unrewarding, and can be very distressing for the patient. If initial assessment is unhelpful, watchful waiting is a valid approach.

Anaemia

- Iron deficiency anaemia should always raise the query of gastrointestinal malignancy, and investigation tailored to the individual situation (see p492).
- A normochromic normocytic anaemia with normal haematinics is rather more difficult—it may represent anything from mild myelofibrosis or renal failure to disseminated malignancy.
- Screening history, examination and tests should be performed. If normal, then a decision about suitability for bone marrow biopsy needs to be made on an individual patient basis. Does the patient have a reasonable life expectancy? Would they be a candidate for treatments (e.g. chemotherapy) if haematological malignancy is confirmed?

HOW TO... screen for malignancy

History

Should include:
- Dietary history
- Mood assessment
- History of fevers and night sweats
- Travel history
- HIV risk factor assessment (if appropriate)
- Full systems enquiry (especially meticulous enquiry into gastrointestinal symptoms and post menopausal bleeding).

Examination

Full examination required, including:
- Lymphadenopathy
- Skin nodules or rashes (expose the patient fully)
- ENT examination
- Male external genitalia (testicular masses)
- Female breast and pelvic examination
- Rectal examination
- Thyroid examination.

Investigations

- Full blood count with film
- Haematinics
- Urea and electrolytes
- Liver function tests
- Calcium and phosphate
- Glucose
- Thyroid function tests
- ESR and CRP
- Urine and blood electrophoresis
- Urinalysis (dipstick for blood)
- Chest X-ray
- Faecal occult bloods (if anaemic)
- PSA in men.

Treating malignancy in older people

Overall, the response to treatment is as good in the fit elderly as in younger patients. Frailty and co-morbidity will alter tolerance to treatments more than age. Guidelines promote the development of specialist multi-disciplinary teams for cancer care that should help to ensure that the most appropriate treatment modalities are considered. Any treatment should be discussed (where possible) with the patient, outlining benefits, potential harm and practical considerations (such as travelling daily to the hospital for a course of treatment, or supplying support for activities of daily living when weakened by therapy).

▶▶ Decisions about cancer treatment should not be based on chronological age, rather on biological age, functional status and the presence of co-morbid conditions.

The patient should be at the centre of the decision making process—decisions are rarely clear-cut and require a balancing of the side effects of therapy against potential benefits. Frank discussion of what to expect should facilitate patient-led decisions, and there will be a wide variety of choices. Some older people will wish to avoid any 'messing about' whilst others will accept a high level of discomfort for the chance of a few extra months of life. You will not know which your patient wants until you ask!

- **Surgery** can be well-tolerated if the patient is pre-selected and receives optimal attention before, during, and after operation. Curative operations should always be considered regardless of age and even palliative surgery may be appropriate e.g. defunctioning colostomy for a sigmoid tumour may be preferable to constant diarrhoea that is causing skin break down in a frail octogenarian.
- **Radiotherapy** is well-tolerated by fit elderly, and side effects may be acceptable to even the more frail if the benefits are sufficient. It is often details such as daily travel to the hospital for a six-week course of treatment that is the hardest for an older person. They may have to rely on hospital transport which usually entails an early start and long trip picking up other patients in an uncomfortable mini-bus. This daily journey may be far worse than the treatment itself. These problems should be discussed prior to treatment and psychosocial support offered where possible.
- **Hormonal therapy** is often very useful in older people, being well-tolerated. It forms the mainstay of treatment for postmenopausal women with breast cancer and for men with prostate cancer. Its role is in disease control, not cure, but is often provides very effective palliation until they die from another cause.
- **Chemotherapy agents** are improving all the time, being better tolerated and more effective. Cardiac co-morbidity can cause problems with the amount of fluid that is required. Social isolation can make transport to and from treatments difficult and managing the side effects difficult. Recognition of this and provision of support is essential if treatment is considered.

HOW TO... manage symptomatic hypercalcaemia

Older patients often present with acute confusion and constipation, the classical symptoms of thirst, itch, and bone pain may be less prominent.

▶▶ Important to check serum calcium for any unexplained confusion or constipation.

▶▶ Beware hypoalbuminaemia which can mask a high calcium—always check the corrected calcium level

If corrected calcium is high send off a parathyroid hormone level and screen for tumours. Commonest malignant causes include myeloma and carcinomatosis with bone secondaries (e.g. prostate or breast) and squamous Ca lung (where calcitonin-like substances are excreted). Commonest benign cause is hyperparathyroidism.

Management

1. Rehydration with intravenous fluids—aim for 3 or 4 litres/day (but more cautious in heart failure).
2. Once patient is rehydrated, add frusemide 20–40mg per bag as this promotes calcium excretion in the urine and prevents fluid overload.
3. Monitor calcium daily and adjust treatment.

In **malignant disease**, consider:
- Intravenous bisphosphonates e.g. pamidronate.
- Steroids e.g. prednisolone 30mg/day or dexamethasone 2–4g/day. Work by slowing tumour turnover but can aggravate confusion. Watch for hyperglycaemia.
- Specific tumour therapy (e.g. antiandrogens for Ca prostate, radiotherapy for myeloma) but localized therapies seldom influence serum calcium levels.
- There is a group of patients with malignant hypercalcaemia who respond to treatment but relapse as soon as iv fluids are stopped. If all avenues of treatment have been tried a palliative approach is sometimes appropriate in which the calcium is allowed to rise and symptoms only are treated.

In **hyperparathyroidism**, consider parathyroidectomy.

Management of the **confused hypercalcaemic patient**:
- Can be particularly difficult especially as patients often pull out iv cannulae.
- Consider opiate analgesia (there may be bone pain which the patient cannot tell you about).
- Benzodiazepine sedation may be required.

Cancer with an unknown primary

Cancer with an unknown primary (CUP) makes up around 2% of all malignancy diagnoses, but this proportion increases with age because older patients may have less specific and less aggressive presentation. They also tend to seek medical attention less promptly. Presentation is with metastases, usually in liver, lungs, bones, or lymph nodes.

Finding metastases during investigation for vague symptoms or when looking into more specific problems (such as bone pain, abnormal liver function tests, breathlessness, enlarged lymph nodes etc.) is a commonly encountered problem in geriatric practice, and a structured approach to management is essential.

Aetiology

- After biopsy, 70% of CUP is found to be adenocarcinoma, 15–20% poorly differentiated carcinomas, and 10% poorly differentiated adeno-carcinoma.
- The primary becomes clear in only 20% after investigation (see below).
- At postmortem, 40–50% are found to be pancreatic, hepatobiliary or lung, and most of the remainder are from the GI tract while 20–30% still do not have a primary identified.

Approach to investigation

Sometimes, once metastatic cancer is identified, no further investigations are appropriate—for example if the patient is frail and asymptomatic, or if death is very near. In most cases however there is something to be gained by determining the primary and extent of metastases—ranging from (very rare) cure, through prolongation of life (e.g. for hormonally sensitive tumours), to the targeted palliation of symptoms.

Treatment has been greatly advanced by obtaining biopsy samples and using immunohistochemical techniques to improve diagnosis and recognizing clinical syndromes that can predict responses to certain chemotherapy combinations (see p699).

Arrange the following:

- Careful history and examination (including thyroid, breast, pelvis in women and a rectal examination) looking for hints of the primary.
- Blood tests, including FBC, U,C&E, LFT, calcium, phosphate, LDH, and PSA.
- Tumour markers (CEA, CA 15-3, CA 19-9, CA125, AFP, HCG) are not useful in diagnosis or prognosis, but may be used to monitor response to any treatment.
- Urinalysis.
- Faecal occult bloods (x3).
- CXR.
- Consider thyroid ultrasound.
- Consider mammogram (in women).
- Abdominal CT scan—identifies the primary site in 10–35% and shows additional metastatic sites.

▶▶ Further radiological or endoscopic investigation is rarely helpful, often uncomfortable, and a poor use of resources.

Biopsy specimens

- Should usually be obtained if possible (radiology may show the best site). Information from biopsy assists greatly in further management.
- Occasionally there will be histological hints as to the primary source (e.g. signet rings in the glandular cells indicating gastric cancer), but more commonly there is not enough differentiation to allow diagnosis.
- Immunohistochemical stains have helped considerably, and there are specific stains for prostate, thyroid and bronchogenic adenocarcinoma and stains highly suggestive of a breast primary.
- Combinations of stains (e.g. CEA, CA 19-9, CA 125, cytokeratins or breast cancer antigen) may reveal patterns that suggest the primary but these are less specific.

Prognosis is better with:

- Fewer metastases.
- Metastases only in lymph nodes and soft tissues, poorer if bones or liver involved.
- Certain histological sub-types.
- Female patient, with few co-morbidities and a good performance status.
- Normal serum lactate dehydrogenase level.
- ▶▶ It is unrelated to age.

Treatment options

Women with peritoneal metastases

- Usually ovarian or other gynaecological cancer.
- Some show extremely good response to chemotherapy, with 15–20% long term remission in papillary serous carcinoma.

Women with axillary lymph node metastases

- Usually breast cancer.
- Investigate with mammogram and MRI breasts if negative.
- Even if no breast lesion found, treat as breast cancer in the standard way.
- Involvement of axillary nodes only means potentially curable disease (by mastectomy, node clearance and radiotherapy).

Bone metastases

- In men these are usually from prostate cancer (especially if sclerotic or blastic metastases) and elevated PSA confirms this. Standard hormonal treatment for prostate cancer often provides effective palliation.
- Lung cancer is the other common cause, with liver, kidney, thyroid, and colon being rarer primary sources.

Single metastatic focus in brain, lung, adrenal, liver, bone, or lymph node

- Occasionally actually an unusual primary.
- Usually will metastasize to other sites fairly quickly.
- Consider surgical resection.
- Radiotherapy for a solitary brain metastasis can occasionally produce long-term survival.

None of the above
- Empirical chemotherapy (based on histology and clinical syndrome) produces some response in around 40%, and a good response in around 10%.
- Overall, there is up to 20% 3-year survival with treatment (median survival around 10 months).

Death and dying

Breaking bad news 700
   How to... break bad news 701
Bereavement 702
   How to... promote a 'healthy bereavement' 703
Palliative care 704
Symptom control in the terminally ill 706
   How to... prescribe a subcutaneous infusion for
      palliative care 708
Documentation after death 710
The coroner 712
Other issues after death 714

Breaking bad news

Geriatricians frequently break bad news. No matter how old and frail the patient, the news can always come as a devastating blow. Equally, news that may seem bad may be taken well—someone who has felt unwell for ages may welcome an explanation, even if it means a terminal diagnosis. Sometimes they will have been expecting worse ('I've had a stroke? Thank God it isn't cancer').

▶▶ Each case needs to be considered individually and carefully modified as reactions become apparent.

Who should be told bad news?

- Information about a patient's diagnosis and prognosis belong to the patient, and that individual has a right to know. The paternalistic tendency to 'protect' a patient or their relatives from bad news is now largely obsolete, but some patients and relatives still believe this exists and this may need to be corrected.
- Very often, fears that an older person will not cope with bad news are unfounded. They may not have asked questions because they are not culturally used to quizzing doctors, but will often have an idea that something is wrong. Anxieties about remaining family members (particularly spouses) can be addressed once everyone knows a patient's diagnosis and management plan. Open dialogue may ease distress.
- Equally, there are some older people who simply do not wish to know details about diagnosis and prognosis, preferring to trust others to make decisions for them. It is inappropriate to force information on such patients and crucial to identify them. Approaches range from blunt questioning—'If you turn out to have something serious, are you the sort of person who likes to know exactly what is going on?' to a more subtle line—'We have some test results back, and your daughter is keen to talk to me about them. Would you like to know about them too?' The response to this is usually informative—either 'Yes, of course I want to know' or 'Oh, well I'd rather let my daughter deal with all that'.
- Well-meaning relatives (usually children, who are more used to challenging authority) may be more proactive in seeking information than the patient, and then try to shield their relative from the truth, believing that they would not be able to cope. In such situations, try to avoid giving information to relatives first—explain that you cannot discuss it with them without the patient's permission. Be sympathetic—these wishes are usually born from genuine concern. Explore why they don't want news told, and encourage reality—the patient knows that they are unwell and must have had thoughts about what is wrong. Point out that it becomes almost impossible to continue to hide a diagnosis from a patient in a deteriorating condition and that such an approach can set up major conflicts between family and carers. Be open—tell the relative that you are going to talk to the patient, and promise discretion (i.e. you will not force unwanted information). A joint meeting can be valuable if the patient agrees. They may be right, and the patient does not want to be told, but establish this for yourself first and always get permission from the patient before disclosing details to anyone else.

HOW TO... break bad news

1. Make an appointment and ensure that there will be no interruptions.
2. Ensure that you are up-to-date on all the latest information—about the disease itself and the latest patient condition. (Have you seen them that morning?).
3. Talk in pleasant, homely surroundings away from busy clinical areas.
4. Ensure that you are appropriately dressed (e.g. not covered in blood from a failed resuscitation attempt).
5. Suggest that family members or friends come along to support.
6. Invite other members of the multi-disciplinary team (usually a nurse) who are involved in the patient's care.
7. Begin with introductions and context ('I am Dr Brown, the doctor in charge of your mother's care since arriving in the hospital. This is staff nurse Green. I already know Mrs. Jones but perhaps I could also know who everyone else is?'). It is sometimes useful to make some 'ice-breaking' non-medical comments, but do not be flippant ('how was the journey down?').
8. Establish what is already known ('a lot has happened here today—perhaps you could begin by telling me what you already know?' or in a non-acute setting 'when did you last speak to a doctor?').
9. Set the scene and give a 'warning shot'. ('Your mother has been unwell for some time now, and when she came in today she had become much more seriously ill' or 'I'm afraid I have some bad news').
10. Use simple jargon-free language to describe events, giving 'bite-sized' chunks of information, gauging comprehension and response as you go.
11. Avoid euphemisms—say 'dead' or 'cancer' if that is what you mean.
12. Allow time for the news to sink in—long silences may be necessary; try not to fill them because you are uncomfortable.
13. Allow time for emotional reactions, and reassure in verbal and non-verbal ways that this is an acceptable and normal response.
14. Encourage questions.
15. Do not be afraid to show your own emotions, whilst maintaining professionalism—strive for genuine empathy.
16. Summarize and clarify understanding if possible. If you feel that the message has been lost or misinterpreted, ask them to summarize what they have been told, allowing reinforcement and correction. Complex medical terms are usefully written down to take away and show to relatives or look up.
17. Someone should stay for as long as is needed, and offer opportunity for further meeting to clarify questions that will come up later.
18. Document your meeting carefully in the medical notes.

Bereavement

Common experience in older people—causes huge psychological morbidity. A quarter of older widowers/widows develop clinical anxiety and/or depression in the first year.

▶▶ The grieving process is amenable to positive and negative influences so awareness of those at risk can help target care.

Normal stages of grief

Not linear—often go back and forth between stages.

- **Shock/denial**: lasts from minutes to days. Longer if unexpected death. Resolves as reality is accepted.
- **Pining/searching**: feel sad, angry, guilty, vulnerable; urge to look back and search for the dead person; restless, irritable and tearful. Loss of appetite and weight. Poor short-term memory and concentration. Resolved by feeling pain and expressing sadness. May be hampered by social or cultural pressures to behave in a certain way.
- **Disorganization/despair**: feel life has no meaning. Tend to relive events and try to put it right. Common to experience hallucinations of the deceased when falling asleep (reassure that this is normal). Resolves as adjust to the new reality without the deceased.
- **Reorganization**: begin to look forward and explore a new life without the deceased. Find things to carry forward into the future from the past. May feel guilt and need reassurance. Period of adjustment.
- **Recurrence**: grief may recur on anniversaries, birthdays etc.

Abnormal grief

Hard to define as everyone is different (both individual and cultural variability) and the process cannot be prescribed. In general, weight is re gained by 3–4 months, interest is regained after several more months and the beginnings of recovery have usually been recognized by 2 years.

Risk factors for abnormal grief include:

- Sudden or unexpected loss
- Low self esteem
- Low social support
- Prior mental illness (especially depression)
- Multiple prior bereavements
- Ambivalent or dependent relationship with the deceased
- Having cared for the deceased in their final illness for more than 6 months
- Having fewer opportunities for developing new interests and relationships after the death.

Although older people are generally more accepting of death than younger people, they commonly have a number of these risk factors (e.g. an 80-year-old man who has cared for his demented wife for 3 years prior to her death, is likely to have had an ambivalent relationship as well as being her carer. He may have limited social support and opportunity for alternative social contacts).

▶▶ Elderly widowers have the highest rate of suicide amongst all groups of bereaved persons.

HOW TO... **promote a 'healthy bereavement'**

- Identify those at risk of abnormal grief (see list opposite).
- Encourage seeing the body after death if wished.
- Encourage involvement in funeral arrangements.
- A visit by the GP after death to answer questions, or a meeting with the hospital team can be very helpful.
- Good social support initially is crucial and professional/voluntary groups (e.g. CRUSE at www.crusebereavementcare.org.uk) or counsellors can be helpful if family/friends are not present.
- There needs to be permission for 'time out' and reassurance that they are experiencing a normal reaction.
- As time goes on, setting small goals for progressive change can structure recovery.

For the **confused, older patient**, repeated explanations, supported involvement in the funeral and visiting the grave has been shown to reduce repetitive questioning about the whereabouts of the deceased.

Palliative care

Death is inevitable and physicians should acknowledge their limitation not seeing each death as a personal failure. Society has a misperceptic that medical technology can always postpone death—this should b addressed, and death portrayed as a natural end.

Palliative care is concerned with holistic management of a patient whom death is likely to be soon, where curative treatments are n longer possible. It aims to help the patient (and relatives) come to term with death whilst optimizing the time left. It involves a multi-disciplinal team approach, with attention to relief of physical symptoms, socia psychological, spiritual, and family support.

Traditionally used in cases of incurable cancer (where a diagnosis ha often been made and a prognosis given) the approach is valuable in mal other situations. Death from e.g. end-stage heart failure is as predictabl as death from cancer, yet application of palliative care measures is infr quent. Discussing impending death with a patient may be hard for docte and patient alike, but it allows the goals to shift from hopeless (patie cure) to realistic and achievable (planning a good death). With the cor plexity of illness in older people, deciding when death is inevitable can b hard (see p733) but the rewards to patient and carers are many.

General principles of palliative care

- All symptoms should be evaluated and a diagnosis made, based on probability and pattern recognition.
- Explanation of cause and treatment planned empowers the patient an keeps expectations realistic.
- Treatment involves correcting what can be corrected (e.g. treating or candida that is contributing to anorexia), counselling to help patients accept the limitations imposed by the disease (e.g. a patient with COPD may never be able to walk in the garden, but supplying a wheelchair will allow them to be taken), and drugs to control symptoms.
- Treatment is planned for each individual with meticulous attention to detail and impact is monitored closely, and discontinued if ineffective.

At the very end

- Basic care should be always be continued (warmth, comfort, shelter, freedom from pain, cleanliness, symptom control, offer of oral nutrition, and hydration).
- 'Artificial' nutrition and hydration (i.e. that which bypasses swallowing is considered by many to be a treatment, and as such may be withhel
- Simplify medications. Use subcutaneous routes where appropriate.
- Communication with the patient and family becomes even more important—continue regular visits, even if there is no apparent chang
- Ask nurses and family about concerns they have (e.g. pain on turning)
- Enlist help from palliative care nurses if available.
- A proactive, positive approach at this time can transform the experience of losing a relative.

The principle of double effect

Sometimes treatments given to relieve symptoms can worsen the underlying disease e.g. opiates given for pain also cause respiratory depression.

Remember it is not a duty of the physician to prolong life at all costs. Good communication with family and other members of the team ensure that everyone understands the rationale behind a treatment plan.

The British Medical Association states: 'A single act having two possible foreseen effects, one good and one harmful, it is not always morally prohibited if the harmful effect is not intended.' In other words, if the primary aim of the morphine is to relieve pain, and a secondary (foreseen) consequence of this is respiratory depression and death, then the primary aim justifies the secondary consequence.

Symptom control in the terminally ill

Pain

- Use the analgesia ladder, starting with non-opioids (paracetamol, NSAIDs).
- Next, add weak opioids (codeine, dihydrocodeine, tramadol), escalate the dose then replace with strong opioids (e.g. morphine slow release (MST)). Give regularly and treat all side effects (nausea, constipation).
- Aim to give orally if possible, but consider subcutaneous bolus/infusion, transdermal or rectal routes if necessary.
- Identify likely cause(s)—may be different pains with different causes in one individual—and target treatment to cause.
- Neuropathic pain is often opioid responsive, but antidepressants and anticonvulsants can be added.
- Treat muscle spasm with physiotherapy, heat, antispasmodics and benzodiazepines and nerve compression pain with steroids.

Nausea and vomiting

- Identify cause—is it reversible? (E.g. medication, hypercalcaemia, bowel obstruction.)
- Give small portions of palatable food, avoid strong smells.
- Use regular antiemetics:
  - Metoclopramide is indicated when there is gastritis, stasis and functional bowel obstruction.
  - Cyclizine is used with raised intracranial pressure and functional bowel obstruction.
  - Haloperidol treats chemical causes such as hypercalcaemia.

Constipation

- Start with a stimulant laxative (e.g. senna) or stool softener if not on opiates depending on stool characteristics.
- Opiates cause decreased peristalsis so a stimulant laxative is needed.
- Danthron-containing stimulant laxatives are banned in all but terminal care, as they may be carcinogenic. Also cause skin burns so do not use with incontinent patients. Suppositories, enemas or digital evacuation may be needed.

Anorexia

- Normal in advanced cancer, and other conditions as death approaches.
- Family concerns may be the main problem—they may feel their relative is giving up.
- Deal with this directly—eating more will not alter the outlook and pressurising the patient can make them miserable.
- Decrease medications that cause nausea or anorexia (opiates, SSRIs).
- Give good mouth care.
- Help with feeding if weak.
- Offer frequent small meals.
- Prokinetics (e.g. metoclopramide) or steroids (prednisolone, medroxyprogesterone) may help.

Dyspnoea
- Treat cause (transfuse for anaemia, drain effusion etc.).
- A terrifying symptom—plan approach for how to deal with an attack without panicking.
- Oxygen can help, as can an anxiolytic or opiates.

Confusion
- Identify cause (infection, drugs, withdrawal from alcohol, electrolyte imbalances).
- Nurse in calm, well-lit environment. Relatives can often help with reorientation.
- Drugs (e.g. risperidone, benzodiazepines) can be used as a last resort.

Dehydration
- Dying patients drink less (weakness, nausea, decreased level of consciousness) and when this is chronic the body slowly adapts and thirst is not felt.
- Good mouth-care is all that is required where the decreased intake is part of the dying process.
- Reassure relatives (and nursing staff) that it is the disease that is killing the patient, not the dehydration.

'Death rattle'
- The patient is usually unaware. Reassure the family of this.
- If excess secretion is causing distress or discomfort to the patient or the family, use hyoscine butylbromide, hyoscine hydrobromide, or glycopyronium (available subcutaneously or as patches).

Further reading
British National Formulary. Prescribing in palliative care section. www.bnf.org

HOW TO... prescribe a subcutaneous infusion for palliative care

Is the subcutaneous route appropriate?
Use regular oral route where possible

Consider when:
- Vomiting/nausea/malabsorption
- Difficulty swallowing e.g. near the end or if semi-conscious

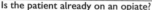

Is the patient already on an opiate?
- Calculate the current total dose given per 24 hours (including prn administration)
    - Has this been adequate? (Ask nurses, family, and patient)
- Convert the oral opiate dose to an equivalent parental dose (see *BNF*).
    - e.g. MST 20mg bd is equivalent to diamorphine 15mg s/c per 24 hours
- If starting diamorphine de novo, start low (e.g. 1 mg/hour with allowances on the prn side for breakthrough pain)
- Morphine is cheaper and more readily available, but diamorphine is more soluble so can be given in a smaller infusion volume and is less likely to precipitate with multiple other drugs. Morphine has about two-thirds potency of diamorphine

Are there any other symptoms?
Other agents can be added to the pump

e.g. Metoclopramide for nausea (30–60mg/24hr)
Hyoscine hydrobromide for respiratory secretions (0.6–2.4mg/24hr)
Haloperidol for nausea, restlessness and agitation (5–15mg/24hr)
Midazolam for sedation (10–60mg/24hr)

Write the prescription
- How large are the infusion pumps on the ward? (Usually 10ml or 50 ml)
- Are the components compatible with each other, and water for injection e.g. diamorphine 30mg + haloperidol 5mg made up to 10ml with water for injection, run in s/c syringe driver over 24 hours

Reassess every 4–6 hours
Do not wait for 24 hours
- Check whether there has been good symptom control—if not, increase the dose
- Check for side effects (e.g. drowsiness)—consider decreasing the opiate or benzodiazepine dose
- Check whether any prn doses have been used—add these to the next total dose you prescribe

Documentation after death

Verification of death

This is the confirmation that death has occurred and may be performed by any doctor, trained nurse, or paramedic before a body can be moved to the mortuary. It is recommended that you look for:

- Absence of response to pain/stimulation.
- Fixed dilated pupils.
- Absence of a pulse (check for at least 30 seconds).
- Absence of heart sounds (check for at least 30 seconds).
- Absence of respiratory movements (check for at least 30 seconds).
- Absence of breath sounds (check for at least 30 seconds).

Some of these tests can be done simultaneously to save time. Always record your findings in full along with the time of death and the time of verification (if different).

Certification of death

This is writing a death certificate. It is an important duty and legal requirement of the doctor that has recently been looking after the patient—it allows the family to arrange a funeral and provides very important statistics for disease surveillance and public health.

- Inexperienced doctors tend to record the mechanism of death rather than the underlying cause, which may lead to under-representation of the real pathology in national statistics. Patients die of dementia and stroke although their complications e.g. aspiration pneumonia may be the last thing that was treated.
- Always record as much information as possible, for example:

Ia	Aspiration pneumonia
Ib	Left total anterior circulation infarction
Ic	Non-insulin dependant diabetes, Atrial fibrillation
II	Parkinson's disease, peripheral vascular disease

  is more informative than:

Ia	Pneumonia
Ib	Stroke

- Old age is an acceptable cause of death in the very elderly person who has had a non-specific decline.
- Avoid using 'septicaemia' or cardiac/renal/liver 'failure' unless you can qualify it with a more precise cause (e.g. heart failure due to ischaemic heart disease).
- Use section II to record other diagnoses, which are often multiple in older people.
- You must have seen the patient alive during their recent illness (usually in the last 2 weeks) to write a certificate—sometimes the GP writes a certificate for a hospital patient and vice versa if the patient has recently moved between sites.

Cremation forms

There are two parts to a cremation form, completed by different doctors who should not be related or work on the same team. You must have looked after the patient in their terminal illness to complete Part I. If you do not know the patient well examine the body, the chest X-ray, and the ECG for evidence of a pacemaker.

In contrast, a Part II doctor should not have known the patient and is required by law to be an impartial examiner of the case before the evidence (the body) is cremated. You must be a senior doctor (two years post MRCP/FRCS) to complete Part II. Ensure you have seen the medical notes and personally questioned the Part I doctor and one other person who knew the deceased (another doctor, nurse or relative). If there are problems with the certificate or the Part I they can be corrected or re-issued. Sometimes you may need to suggest the case is discussed with the Coroner.

The Coroner

Coroners are officers appointed by the Council to investigate any sudden or unexplained death. They are independent of both local and central Government. The police, a doctor, or the registrar may report a death to the coroner. The registrar must await the outcome of the coroner's enquiries before registering the death, so families should delay making funeral arrangements.

Under UK law the following must be reported to the coroner:
• Death occurred in police custody or in prison.
• No doctor has treated the deceased during the last illness.
• The attending doctor did not see the patient within 14 days of death.
• Death occurred during an operation or before recovery from an anaesthetic.
• Death was sudden and unexplained or in suspicious circumstances.
• Death may be due to an industrial injury or disease, or to accident, violence, neglect or abortion, or to any kind of poisoning.
• Some coroners also like to be informed when death occurred less than 24 hours after admission to hospital but this is not a legal requirement.

Although there is an obligation to report such deaths, the Coroner might be happy to issue a 'Part A' certificate, which permits the doctor to write a death certificate. Only a minority of deaths that are reported will end up with a coroner's post-mortem or an inquest.

Consider discussing:
• Cases of pressure sores or severe malnutrition at home (neglect is possible).
• Postoperative cases.
• Mesothelioma and occupational disease (compensation may rely on a post mortem).
• Have a low threshold for reporting deaths when relatives are unhappy/litiginous.

The Coroner's officers can advise you about acceptable causes of death on a certificate but are not medically qualified. A 'Part A' certificate records that you have discussed the case with him/her but more commonly informal telephone advice is given—if you feel the case is at all contentious ensure that a 'Part A' is issued to protect you.

▶▶ If in doubt, discuss your case with the coroner.

Following the Shipman murders (a GP who was a serial killer) the documentation after death and the role of the Coroner is likely to be substantially revised by Parliament.

▶▶ The above information applies to the UK only—local guidance should be sought in other countries.

Other issues after death

Bereavement services

- Most hospitals now have a bereavement office that coordinate the paperwork required after a death and provide the family with information about registration and funeral arrangements.
- They provide a friendly, easily accessible interface between the hospital and relatives and can refer to voluntary bereavement support groups.
- If no family comes forward or if they are incapable/unwilling to arrange a funeral, the hospital (usually via the bereavement office) will arrange and pay for a low-cost cremation.

Post-mortems

- The coroner may initiate a post-mortem for legal reasons or where no doctor is able to write a certificate—family cannot veto this.
- Consented hospital post-mortems (which are at the family discretion) are good for education and audit especially in unusual/interesting cases.
- Unfortunately, the rate of hospital post-mortems is declining. If you take time and explain the procedure compassionately to relatives, you may be surprised how often they consent. A limited examination (e.g. restricted to torso or one organ) may be more acceptable.
- Since the Alder Hey scandal (retention and disposal of organs from children without parental consent; Liverpool, UK 1990s) new laws require a separate, explicit consent for retention of tissue for examination/teaching.

The registrar

- The registrar is responsible for recording all births and deaths.
- The relatives have to register the death within 5 working days and this usually involves making an appointment.
- The death must be registered before funeral arrangements can be made.
- If there is a mistake or omission on the death certificate they can refuse to register the death and will refer the case back to the certifying doctor.

Chapter 27

Ethics

Competency 716
  How to... assess competence 717
Making financial decisions 718
Making medical decisions 720
Making social decisions 722
  How to... manage a patient insisting on returning home
  against advice 723
Advance directives 724
  How to... assess whether an AD is valid and
  applicable 725
Cardiopulmonary resuscitation 726
The process of DNAR decisions 728
  How to... manage DNAR decisions 729
Diagnosing dying and estimating when treatment is
  without hope 730
Rationing and ageism 732
Elder abuse 734
  How to... manage suspected elder abuse 736

Competency

- A competent patient is intellectually able to make a decision for themselves.
- *Capacity is the equivalent legal term for competence.*
- It is a fundamental human right and a basic ethical principle that individuals can make autonomous decisions. However, society also accepts that some of its members e.g. children and adults with severe cognitive problems, do not have the ability to make decisions for themselves and mechanisms are in place to protect them.
- Older people and ill patients (matched for age) have much higher rates of incompetence than the general population and it is important that a geriatrician should be familiar with competence and its assessment.

▶▶ Always remember that in declaring someone incompetent you may be robbing them of the ability to be involved in important decisions about their health and lifestyle—however benevolent your motives, such decisions should never be taken lightly or inexpertly.

Assessing competence

Competence is decision-specific. Questions which are more complex and/or more important demand a higher level of competence.	Assess competence for each relevant question individually. Global tests e.g. mental test scores are not a substitute and can be misleading.
Competence is assumed for adults.	The burden of responsibility is with the assessor to prove incompetence.
Competency levels may fluctuate. Some types of dementia and delirium can cause transient reversible incompetence.	Ensure the patient is functioning at their best before assessing competence. If in doubt repeat the assessment later.
Ignorance is not the same as incompetence.	Patients should be educated about a subject before being asked to make a decision (just as you would expect a surgeon to explain an operation before asking you to sign a consent form).
A competent patient may make an unwise or unconventional decision.	Competent patients can make decisions which lead to illness, discomfort, danger or even death. Carers/relatives often need education and support when the patient chooses an unwise option.

The British Medical Society (www.bma.org.uk) and the General Medical Council (www.gmc-uk.org) provide extensive guidance on consent and competence. Legal precedent suggests that a competent patient should:
- Be able to comprehend and retain information relevant to the decision.
- Believe this information in relation to him/herself.
- Be able to weigh the information, balancing the risks and benefits in order to make a choice.

HOW TO... assess competence

- **Trigger:** doctors should be alert to the possibility of incompetence but it is often people closer to the patient (relatives/carers) who highlight a problem. In real life a competency assessment is usually only employed where there is conflict or where an important step (such as a will or enduring power of attorney) is being attempted. Previous assessments of competency for other decisions or at other times are not a substitute for the latest assessment.
- **Education:** the patient should be given ample time to absorb and discuss the facts/advice. Several education sessions may be needed. Encourage other health professionals and relatives to discuss the topic with the patient as well.
- **Assessment:** probe the patient to assess retention, understanding and reasoning. In borderline or contentious cases employ a second opinion (often from a psychogeriatrician).
- **Action:** document the results of the assessment using observations and patient quotes (see opposite). If the patient is incompetent, state how the substituted decision will be made e.g. medical decision in best interests, involvement of carers, case conference etc.

Further reading
Molloy DW, Darzins P and Strang D. (1999) *Capacity to Decide*. Troy, ontario: New Grange Press.

Making financial decisions

Power of attorney (POA)

This is a simple legal document that allows an adult to nominate another person to conduct financial affairs on their behalf. It is only valid while the person donating the attorney remains competent to do so.

Enduring power of attorney (EPOA)

• This continues to be valid even when a patient is incompetent.
• It is sensible for older people to make an EPOA in favour of a trusted family member or solicitor while they are competent, particularly if there is an illness, which might herald future incompetence.
• Once a patient becomes incompetent the EPOA should be registered with the public guardianship office (http://www.guardianship.gov.uk) who have the mandate to monitor how it is managed.
• In practice most EPOAs are never registered and the court of protection tend to only get involved where there are complaints of mismanagement of funds.
• A copy of an EPOA form can be purchased from the internet at www.hmso.gov.uk/
• An EPOA/POA does not cover anything other than financial decisions.

Lasting power of attorney (LPA)

This was introduced in the Mental Incapacity Act in April 2005 and is due to be implemented in April 2007. It is very similar to an EPOA but also allows for appointment of a proxy for health and welfare decisions.

Incompetent patients

• An EPOA/LPA cannot be made once the patient is incompetent to understand the principles of the document (although it is not necessary for them to be fully competent to run their financial affairs).
• If an EPOA is not available for incompetent patients then sometimes the finances can be managed informally e.g. the pension can be paid out and joint bank accounts can continue.
• To formally take over financial management in these circumstances (especially for large estates or where conflict exists) an application to the court of protection must be made.
• Since the new incapacity act (2005) this court can appoint deputies to manage financial, health and welfare decisions.

Testamentary capacity

This refers to the specific capacity to make a will. Solicitors and financial advisors can help draw up a will and occasionally request a doctor's opinion about competence. Legal guidelines are well established.

Signing an EPOA

Patients should avoid making an EPOA/LPA whilst unwell or in hospital as this would make it harder to prove that the patient was competent if the validity of the document was ever challenged. If a competency assessment is required then check that the patient understands that:

- The EPOA/LPA allows the attorney complete financial control.
- This power extends into the future even if they become incompetent.
- They will be unable to revoke the power if they are incompetent.

Document carefully as shown below:

Assessment of competence to complete an EPOA

I interviewed Mrs Jones today. She indicated she wished to make an EPOA in the favour of her husband and did not appear to be under duress from another person. She explained her health was deteriorating and she wanted her husband to manage the 'bills and things' if she did not feel up to it in the future. She was able to tell me that she owned a current account, savings account some premium bonds and that the mortgage had been paid off on their house. She understood that an EPOA would allow her husband to do as he wished with her money without necessarily consulting her both now and in the future. She knew that this power would continue even if she was too ill to be consulted. She confirmed that 'he has always sorted that sort of thing out and I don't want him to be stopped from doing it because I can't sign my cheques—I trust him to do the right thing'.

I believe Mrs Jones is competent to give enduring power of attorney to her husband. Dated 12.2.06 Signed

An EPOA/LPA must be witnessed by an independent person (often a friend or in hospital by an administrator or manager). If a doctor is asked to witness the signature of a patient then there is assumption that they believe the patient is competent.

▶▶ Refuse to witness a signature if you have doubts about competency.

Making medical decisions

Patients who are clearly incompetent:

- Unless a valid LPA is available in the UK no one can make a decision about medical treatment for another incompetent adult.
- Doctors are expected to make decisions in the 'best interests' of their incompetent patients.
- In the USA a hierarchy of next of kin can legally make substitute decisions. Relatives are often surprised and occasionally angry to find that they have few rights in the UK.
- In practice, doctors should routinely consult next of kin where important or contentious medical decisions are made for incompetent patients. The human rights legislation, through its support of 'family life' as a basic human right will reinforce the social shift towards increasing power for relatives. Relatives can help doctors to decide what the patient might have wanted under the circumstances.
- It is always worth enquiring if a LPA is completed or if there is a written or verbal advance directive made by the patient prior to them becoming incompetent (p720).
- If there is conflict between the medical team and relatives about what is in the best interests of the patient that cannot be resolved the doctor involved may wish to seek a second medical opinion or refer to the courts.
- The new LPA legislation (2005) may help by legally appointing a proxy medical decision-maker but it is likely that a tiny minority of incompetent patients will have such a document, at least in the near future.

Patients who may be competent:

- Patients' views should always be sought about medical treatments.
- Often these views will concur with those of the medical professional, or they are happy to be guided by the doctor.
- Rarely, a patient will express a view at odds with either the medical team or their family, in which case a careful assessment of capacity to make their own decision is required.
- Assess competence in line with the principals outlined previously and document meticulously in the notes (see example in box opposite).

Assessment of patient refusing a colectomy for cancer

Miss Joseph has told me she will not consent to a colectomy. She explains that in view of her age and lack of current symptoms she would rather not put herself through a major operation. She said 'I am 89 years old and I don't want to be mucked around'. She understands that by refusing surgery she might be shortening her life and that she may become ill in the future as the tumour grows but feels that this is a 'lesser evil' than an operation at the moment. I believe she is making a competent decision and we have agreed to discuss it again in two weeks time during an outpatient appointment after she has spoken to her family.

Dated 12.2.06 Signed

Cardiopulmonary resuscitation

Cardiopulmonary resuscitation (CPR) was first described in 1967 and is now widely applied both in and out of hospital. Around 20% of those who die in hospital in the UK will have at least one attempt at CPR during their terminal admission. Although the principles of CPR decisions are the same as for other medical decisions they demand special attention because:

- The urgent and unpredictable nature of CPR requires decisions to be made in advance.
- There is an assumption that all patients will receive CPR in hospital—unlike most treatments consent is required to withhold it.
- CPR is a highly emotive subject and there have been several media scandals where do not attempt resuscitation (DNAR) orders were made without patient consent.

CPR is undoubtedly a life-saving procedure (in hospital around 20% will recover a pulse and half of these patients will survive to leave hospital). Those who survive CPR have a reasonable life expectancy but a small percentage (1–2%) will be left with permanent hypoxic brain damage.

Predicting outcome for CPR

- Highest success rates are obtained treating arrests due to cardiac arrhythmia on coronary care units, lowest on general medical wards in frail patients with multiple pathologies.
- Older patients have lower survival rates but this is probably a feature of their multiple pathology and a good outcome is possible if older patients are carefully selected.
- Individual pre-arrest factors are not sensitive or specific enough to be useful in predicting outcome. Morbidity scores combine several variables to attempt to predict outcome of CPR more accurately but are not in common use.

Factors that predict outcome after CPR

	Worse survival rate	Better survival rate
Pre-arrest	Hypotension	Myocardial infarction
	Uraemia	
	Malignancy	
	Heart failure	
	Pneumonia	
	Homebound life style	
Peri- arrest	Out-of-hospital arrest	In hospital arrest
	Unwitnessed arrest	Witnessed arrest
	Asystole or EMD	Ventricular fibrillation
Post-arrest	Long duration of CPR	Short duration arrest
	Slow to waken	Quick to regain consciousness

The process of DNAR decisions

Until recently resuscitation status was determined informally and often unilaterally by doctors (ie a doctor would record DNAR based on medical futility without discussing it).

Fuelled by a social shift towards increasing patient education and autonomy there is now a requirement for more formal and open DNAR decisions. All hospitals are required to have a policy and most are based on the BMA's guidelines (www.bma.org.uk), which were updated in 2001 in line with the European Human Rights legislation.

Apart from reinforcing the right of a competent patient to reject CPR (contemporaneously or in an advance directive) the guidelines list three situations in which it is appropriate to consider a DNAR order:

● Where attempting CPR will not restart the patient's heart and breathing (medical futility).
● Where there is no benefit in restarting the patient's heart and breathing (quality or length of life).
● Where the expected benefit is outweighed by the burdens of CPR.

There is a rejection of a paternalistic medical-led model based on survival statistics to one in which potential for survival is only a part of a patient-led decision. The guidelines suggest that 'the appropriate course of action may be very different in apparently similar circumstances, because the wishes and preferences of the patient are an essential element of the decision' and 'doctors should, where possible, respect patients' wishes to receive treatment which carries only a very small chance of success'.

Furthermore a DNAR decision may not be recorded against the wishes of a competent patient even if this is against the advice of the health care team.

Occasionally a doctor may choose not to involve a competent patient in a DNAR order if they feel it would cause undue distress to the patient but this would be an exceptional case and there would have to be good evidence that distress would be likely.

For incompetent patients it is good practice to consult relatives who might be able to determine what the patient would have wanted but remember they have no legal right to make surrogate decisions (p720).

Further reading

British Medical Association (BMA) March 2001, Decisions relating to CPR. A joint statement from the BMA the Resuscitation Council (UK) and the Royal College of Nursing

Stewart K, Spice C, Rai GS (2003). Where now with DNAR Decisions? *Age and Ageing* **32**: 143–148.

Ebrahim S. (2000). Do Not Resuscitate Decisions: Flogging dead horses or a dignified death? (Editorial) *British Medical Journal* **320**: 1155–1156.

HOW TO... manage **DNAR decisions**

Busy physicians need to make time for DNAR decisions, although they often prove to be easier than anticipated:

- Although it could take 30min to get an elderly patient to make a fully informed decision (many have not even heard of CPR) you can often get a fairly accurate idea from a competent patient with a few quick questions like 'are you the kind of person that wants everything done/nature to take its course'.
- Never ignore a patient cue like 'I don't suppose I will come out of this?' or 'I've had my time'—these are ideal times to discuss end-of-life issues and the patient is relieved to have a policy recorded.

In reality, the majority of DNAR decisions on geriatric wards will not involve the patient (because of incompetence) so lengthy meetings with relatives may ensue:

- When sensitively handled there is rarely conflict and many are relieved to be consulted or happy to be guided by the doctors opinion.
- Try to use the time to discuss general management (emphasizing positive management steps first—even if that is just maintaining dignity and comfort) so that the family doesn't perceive the only medical priority is avoiding CPR.
- Where conflict does arise it is best to leave the patient for CPR and re-address the question later. Remember, CPR is only a small fraction of the patient's care and it may not be worth spending a huge amount of time on. Whilst this might lead to a rise in unsuccessful CPR attempts (with consequent reduction in morale of resuscitation teams and resource implications) it does protect patient autonomy and doctors from complaint/litigation.
- No doctor or nurse can be forced to provide a treatment which they feel is inappropriate so if there is conscientious objection to providing CPR consider moving the patient to a different doctor or ward.

Recording a DNAR decision

- Write the decision prominently in the medical notes.
- Sign and date clearly.
- Document the rationale for the decision and the names of those consulted in making the decision.
- If the patient was not consulted the reason should be listed.
- The responsible consultant should endorse a DNAR order made by a junior doctor as soon as possible.

▶▶ Ensure that the nurses are aware as soon as a DNAR order is made.

Diagnosing dying and estimating when treatment is without hope

A high percentage of elderly patients admitted to hospital are destined to die despite best medical care. A great deal of financial and manpower resources and most importantly patient suffering could be avoided if this death was predictable. The art of applying treatment aggressively when appropriate but backing off compassionately in other circumstances is one of the commonest and most challenging tasks in geriatric medicine.

There has been a lot of discussion about DNAR orders but decisions about less dramatic life-saving technologies are just as hard (e.g. whether to admit a patient from a nursing home for iv antibiotics and fluids or selecting patients for renal replacement therapy (see 422–4) or when to initiate artificial nutrition (see p384).

Unfortunately predicting futile treatment is fraught with difficulty—experienced doctors never underestimate the power of some older people to make a miraculous recovery. The following tips may help:

• Attempt to make a diagnosis (which usually requires some investigations and minor procedures) before estimating prognosis.
• Consider a trial of treatment but constantly monitor the clinical response and be willing to up or down regulate how aggressively to treat.
• Sometimes it is helpful to define limits at the onset of treatment (e.g. oral but not iv therapy, a 2 week trial of nasogastric feeding in a stroke patient, a 20 unit maximum transfusion for acute GI bleeding)
• Decide about each intervention separately—every procedure will have different risk/benefit and tolerability ratios.
• If there is doubt or disagreement about the appropriateness of treatment seek a second medical opinion.
• Remember that medical decisions are not made in isolation—relatives, nurses, therapists, and community carers are ultimately affected by such decisions and open dialogue will help everyone.

The patients' wishes are paramount but many severely ill patients are incompetent to make decisions. Beware patients who reject treatment out of ignorance, misconceptions, or fear. Likewise patients or relatives who continue to demand treatment which is clearly not working (or inappropriate) require education and support.

Deciding that treatment is futile is not the same as 'giving up'—a positive decision for terminal care allows a change in the therapeutic goal from 'cure' to 'keeping comfortable' and ensuring a dignified death. Whilst in some branches of medicine this shift can involve a change in environment (e.g. to hospice) and medical team (to community or palliative care team) in geriatric medicine the line is often blurred. See p706 for more practical advice.

Further reading

Withholding and Withdrawing Life-prolonging Medical Treatment. Guidance for decision making British Medical Association BMJ Books 2001 or www.bmjpg.com/withwith/ww.htm

Rationing and ageism

Rationing

- This has been present in the NHS since its inception in 1948 but the ever increasing cost of modern specialized, technological and pharmacological medicine, along with the growing sophistication of patients has meant that recently rationing has become more explicit and contentious.
- No UK government has ever openly admitted to rationing although 'cost-efficiency' and 'budgeting' are thinly disguised ways of handling difficult rationing decisions.
- The level at which rationing decisions are made has gradually moved up from physicians themselves (which led to considerable inequality), to hospital managers (which did not remove regional inequality). The introduction of NICE (National Institute for Clinical Excellence) in 1999 was designed to help make rationing decisions at a national level by setting guidelines.
- Unfortunately NICE recommendations that treatments should not be funded (e.g. beta interferon in MS) has been very controversial and where funding has been advised (e.g. donepezil in dementia or glycoprotein IIb/IIIa inhibitors in acute coronary syndromes) this has not led to widespread implementation.
- So called 'postcode prescribing' refers to the variable availability of drugs/services depending on health authority or GP boundaries.

Ageism

This is rationing applied by age criteria. Although the UK National Service Framework (see p32) has banned explicit rationing (standard 1 states 'NHS services will be provided, regardless of age, on the basis of clinical need alone') it is still widespread.

It is accepted that some medical interventions e.g. ITU may be less effective when applied to older people but remember:

- Some older people are physiologically younger (i.e. chronological age does not correlate well with biological age). Age is not a good guide to frailty.
- Some treatments (e.g. thrombolysis in myocardial infarction) save more lives in an older age group (number needed to treat is lower because untreated death rate is higher than in younger groups).

Disability and dependence costs the state dearly; preventing strokes, operating on severely osteoarthritic hips etc are highly cost efficient interventions if they enable patients to stay at home rather than go into costly institutional care (quite apart from the benefit to the patient). There is good evidence that the average patient uses the majority of health care resources in the last year of their life but it is rarely possible to predict prospectively when patients are entering their terminal year, nor is there evidence that voluntary restriction of medical treatment by advance directives (see p726) has any cost-cutting effect.

There is a more fundamental ideological principle that sectors of the population who are perceived to have less social worth, are less likely to complain and are largely politically inactive should not be discriminated against—whether those sectors are defined by age, sex, or race. The commonly quoted 'fair innings' argument suggests that after a certain age you have had your 'share' of world resources and younger patients should therefore take precedence. Older people commonly hold to this philosophy. This method of rationing assumes that everyone uses equal resources and enjoys equal quality of life up until the point that it 'runs out'. The logical consequence is that high users of resources (e.g. diabetics) should have had their fair innings at a much younger age. In reality society accepts that some of it members will take more than they give to the system—it is prejudice that allows us to accept rationing for older patients but not for a child with cerebral palsy.

Further reading

www.nice.org.uk
www.doh.gov.uk/nsf/olderpeople
The rationing debate (1997). *BMJ* **314**: 820 (case for) and 820 (case against).

Elder abuse

Defined as any act, or lack of action that causes harm or distress to an older person. Under recognized, with few prevalence studies. One estimated around 5% of community dwelling older people have suffered verbal abuse, and 2% physical abuse. Probably more prevalent within care homes, but precise extent unknown.

Different types of abuse include:

Psychological
- Bullying, shouting, swearing, blaming etc.
- Look for signs of fear, helplessness, emotional lability, ambivalence toward caregiver, withdrawal etc.

Physical
- Hitting, slapping, pushing, restraining etc.
- May also include inappropriate sedation with medication.
- Look for injuries that are unexplained, especially if they are different ages, evidence of restraint, excess sedation, broken glasses etc.

Financial
- Inappropriate use of an older person's financial assets.
- Includes using cheques, withdrawing money from an account, transferring assets, taking jewellery or other valuables, failing to pay bills, altering wills etc.

Sexual
- Forcing an older person to participate in a sexual act against their will.
- Look for genital bruising or bleeding, or sexual disinhibition.

Neglect
- Deprivation of food, heat, clothing, basic care.
- Occurs in situations where an older person is dependant.
- Look for malnutrition, poor personal hygiene, and poor skin condition. Easier to spot in situations where a certain standard of care is anticipated (e.g. patients from care homes being admitted to hospital who are unkempt, dirty, or inappropriately dressed may raise concerns).

Who abuses?
- Commonly someone in a care-giver role.
- Often arises because of carer anger, frustration, and lack of support, training or facilities along with social isolation.
- Relationship difficulties between carer and recipient, and carer mental illness or substance misuse (e.g. alcohol) exacerbate the situation.
- Sleep deprivation or dealing with faecal incontinence may also precipitate abuse.

▶▶ Most are under extreme stress ('at the end of my tether') and extremely remorseful afterwards.

HOW TO... **manage suspected elder abuse**

In the UK, there is no established legal framework. A standardized approach to elder abuse is evolving following a UK government inquiry, 'No Secrets' document and plans to protect vulnerable adults (www.dh.gov.uk). Local protocols should be in place, but often are not. The following act as a guide:

- An individual does not have to prove abuse to take action, only have a strong suspicion that it is occurring.
- The first step is to involve other agencies—this may include social services, involved agencies (e.g. home carers), the general practitioner, the local health authority, and (rarely at first) the police.
- Assessment of the carer and recipient should be detailed, multi-agency, and individually tailored
- As abuse is usually as a result of care-giver stress, a common approach is to attempt to relieve that stress (e.g. providing home care, day care, respite care, health support, advice about sleep or continence, financial help, rehousing etc.) whilst maintaining the patient at home.
- Close multidisciplinary supervision is essential until the situation improves.
- Removal of the patient from an abusive situation may occasionally be done using laws designed primarily for other purposes e.g. the Mental Health Act (provision to act in the best interests of patients with mental illness).
- Police involvement may occasionally be necessary where there are no remediable factors or a very high risk of future harm.

Further information is available from the UK charity Action on Elder Abuse www.elderabuse.org.uk

Benefits

Many pensioners are poor—in 2000, a third of UK pensioner households lived below the poverty line. Despite this, many do not claim all the benefits they are entitled to, usually because they are not aware of them, perceived stigma about 'hand-outs' (that can often be diminished by a few well-judged words from a doctor) or are daunted by application forms.

Care managers can help ensure all benefits are claimed, as can professional welfare rights advisors (working for Citizens Advice Bureaux, Age Concern, social services departments etc.). Some charity volunteers will also assist with filling in forms (e.g. Help the Aged).

Benefits vary with changes in government, and from country to country. The following describes the situation in the UK in 2005:

Benefits for low-income households
Pension credits
Given to over 60s, to top income up to a set amount (guarantee credit). This does not depend on national insurance contributions. In 2005, a single person was topped up to £109.45 per week. This amount may be more in certain circumstances e.g. severe disability.

Housing benefit
Help towards rent and service charges for low-income households.

Council tax benefit
Allows low-income households to pay less council tax, depending on income and savings.

The Social Fund
Provides lump sum payments, grants and loans.
- Community care grants can be given to help with exceptional expenses, such as home adaptations for disability.
- Funeral payments can be made to low-income households if needed.
- Cold weather payments are made to low-income households to help with heating costs when the temperature is below zero degrees for a week.
- Budgeting loans available to low income households to cover one-off expenses (e.g. clothing, household equipment). Repaid (interest free) from weekly allowance.
- Crisis loans are available to all income households, if there is an immediate difficulty in paying for something in an emergency. Repaid without interest.

Attendance allowance
Given to over 65s who need help with personal care because of an illness or disability (equivalent to Disability Living Allowance which is paid to younger people, but no account taken of mobility). Eligibility based on *need* for help or supervision, so even if a spouse is already providing this care, the benefit is still awarded.

Carers allowance
Paid to low-income carers of people receiving Attendance Allowance or Disability Living Allowance.

Healthcare assistance

- Free prescriptions for all over the age of 60.
- Low-income households can apply for free dental treatment, wigs, travel to hospital, eye tests, and get assistance with paying for glasses.

Travel assistance

- Free or reduced fare bus travel for over 60s.
- Reduced train fares with an appropriate rail card for pensioners.
- Free renewal of drivers licence over 70, subject to filling a medical questionnaire regarding fitness to drive every 3 years. A report from a doctor is not routinely required.

Other benefits

- Free television licence for over 75s.
- Winter fuel payments made to all households where there is a person over 60 years old.

Many of these are available regardless of income and savings, to reflect the additional costs of disability. Often older people (and the professionals caring for them) assume that they will not be entitled because they are not poor.

Further information

www.dwp.gov.uk/lifeevent/benefits/
www.ageconcern.org.uk

Taxation

- Most income received by older people in the UK is taxed.
- The allowance of tax-free income rises with age—in 2005, people under 65 could have an income of £4745 per anum without paying tax, whereas this figure rose to £6830 between the ages of 65 and 74.
- Some income is not taxed e.g. attendance allowance, pension credit, winter fuel payments, council tax, housing benefit and war pensions
- Some lump sums are also not taxed, for example from certain private pension schemes. Good financial advice will help to optimize an older persons resources.
- The rate of tax then depends on the total income, ranging from 10% at lower incomes up to 40% for incomes over £31,401 per anum.

Appendix

Barthel index 746
Geriatric depression scale 748
Abbreviated Mental Test Score 750
Mini-mental state examination 752
Clock drawing and the Mini-Cog 754
Glasgow coma score 756

Mini-mental state examination

The mini-mental state examination (MMSE) is a widely applicable and well-validated test of cognitive function.

It is a 30 point test, takes 10–15 minutes to complete, and covers a broader range of cognitive domains than the AMTS. It is therefore less useful as a brief screening test in general medical or geriatric practice, but is very useful in:

- Confirming the nature and magnitude of deficits identified by clinical suspicion, or by the AMTS.
- Tracking change, for example following the introduction of cholinesterase inhibitors in dementia.

The MMSE is widely used. Its copyright is now being robustly defended, and permission to publish it has not been granted. It is however widely available in older texts.

It is possible that the robust defence of copyright will result in a rapid decline in the use of what has been a useful clinical tool, to be replaced by other well-validated instruments such as the clock-drawing test.

bereavement services 714
beta-blockers 291, 311, 477
bicipital tendonitis 544
biguanides 458
blind registration 614
blistering diseases 654–5
  causes 655
blood test abnormalities
  76–7
  false negatives 76
  false positives 77
  reference ranges 76
bowel obstruction 408
Bowen's disease 656
bradycardia 127, 302–3
  causes 302
  management 302–3
  permanent pacemakers
    303
  presentation 302
brain, ageing 164
breaking bad news 700–1
bronchial carcinoma 354
bronchitis 334
bronchodilators 366
B-type natriuretic peptide
  315
bullous pemphigoid 654
bundle branch block 304–5
bunion 536

C

calcium channel blockers
  291
Campbell de Morgan spots
  658
cancer with unknown
    primary 696–8
  aetiology 696
  approach to investigation
    696
  biopsy specimens 697
  prognosis 697
  treatment 698
candidiasis
  oesophageal 389
  oral 377
carbimazole 476
cardiac failure
  acute 308
  assessment 306–7
  chronic 310–11
  diastolic 314–15
  terminal care 312
cardiac rehabilitation 287
cardiopulmonary resuscitation 726
cardiovascular system
  277–326
  effects of ageing 278–9
  see also individual conditions

careers in geriatric medicine
  56
  consultant career pathway
    56
  non-consultant career
    grade pathway 56
  overseas doctors 56
  primary care physicians
    56
care homes 40–1
  care home medicine 40
  funding 42
  management of diabetes
    in 459
  patients with dementia 40
  staffing 40
  standards 42
care management 108
carers allowance 742
carotid sinus massage 133
carotid sinus syndrome
  122, 132–3
cataract 156, 616–17
  causes 616
  management 618
  outcome 617
  signs 616
  surgery 617
  symptoms 616
  when to treat 616
catheters 213, 547, 557,
  580–1, 678, 680, 682
cause of death 8
cell mitosis, abnormal
  control 4
cellulitis 634
  clinical features 634
  investigations 634
  organisms 634
  treatment 634
cervical spondylosis 530–1
Charcot's joint 536
Charles Bonnet's syndrome
  624
chest medicine 327–72
chest pain 280–1
  examination 280–1
  history 280
  investigations 281
cholinesterase inhibitors
  240–1
chronic disease managment
  52–3
chronic lymphocytic
  leukaemia 502
chronic obstructive pulmonary disease
  assessment 364–5
  drug treatment 340,
    366–7
  non-drug treatment 368
chronic renal failure
  418–19

complications 420
chronic venous insufficiency
  644
  clinical changes 644
  pathogenesis 644
circadian rhythm disorders
  190
cirrhosis 394
claw toes 536
clinical assessment 15–58
clock-drawing tests 754
clopidogrel 325
Clostridium difficile
  diarrhoea 670–2
  management 672
cognition 88
cognitive ageing 220
cognitive function
  impairment 222
cognitive impairment 270
cognitive impairment no
  dementia 222
community care assessment
  46
community hospitals 36–7
  patient groups 37
community nurses 114
competency 260, 716–17
  assessment of 716, 717
complete heart block
  304–5
complex discharge 95
comprehensive geriatric
  assessment 78
compression bandaging
  647
compression mononeuro-
  pathy 548
compulsory detention/
  treatment 248–9
  common law 248
  Mental Health Act 248
  National Assistance Act
    (1948) 249
confusion in terminally ill
  patients 707
constipation 396–7
  terminally ill patients 706
consultation skills 60–1
  appointments 60–1
  environment 61
  giving advice 61
  rapport 60
contractures 532
coronary angiography 285
coronary artery bypass
  grafting 285
coronary syndromes 284–5
Coroner 712
corticosteroids 366
cough, chronic 352
cremation forms 711
crutches 98

D

ay centres 50
ay hospitals 26
history and evolution 26
eafness 590–2
classification of 591
communicating with deaf
people 595
eath certificate 710
eath and dying 699–714
bereavement 702–3
bereavement services 714
breaking bad news 700–1
certification of death 710
Coroner 712
cremation forms 711
diagnosis of death 730
palliative care 704–5
post-mortems 714
registrar 714
verification of death
710–12
eath rattle 707
ehydration 432–4
subcutaneous fluid
administration 434
terminally ill patients 707
elayed discharge 44
elirium
causes 254–5
clinical assessment 256–8
diagnosis 252–3
drugs causing 255
drug treatment 264–5
non-drug management 262
treatment 260
versus dementia 258
ementia 224–6
Alzheimer's disease 228,
229
behavioural problems
244–5
cholinesterase inhibitors
240–1
drivers with 237
and drugs/toxins 232
frontotemporal 232
history 224
and infection 232
Lewy body 174–5, 230
memantine 242
mental state 225, 226
non-drug management
236–7
and Parkinsonism 230
patients in care homes 40
physical examination 225
prevention 246
rehabilitation 92
risk management and
abuse 238

vascular 228, 229
vasculitis 233
versus delirium 258
depression 88
assessment 271
clinical features 270–1
drug treatments 274–5
non-drug management
272
presentation 268–9
versus depressive pseu-
dodementia 269
diabetes mellitus 454–5
complications 462–3
diagnosis 455
emergencies 464–6
insulin treatment 460–1
oral drug treatment
458–9
secondary 454
in terminally ill patients
466
treatment 456–7
type 1 vs type 2 454
diabetic retinopathy 624
dialysis 422–3
diarrhoea 402–3
Clostridium difficile 672–4
diastolic heart failure
314–15
dieticians 110
digoxin 299, 311
Diogenes syndrome 266
diploma in geriatric medicine 58
candidates 58
examination structure 58
syllabus 58
dipstick tests 674–5
dipyridamole 325
disease-specific scales 89
diverticular disease 398
dizziness 126–7
causes 126
domiciliary (home) visits
38–9
do not resuscitate decisions
728–30
how to make 729
driving regulations
cerebrovascular disease
214
dementia 224–6
epilepsy 177
drop attacks 129
drug-induced delirium 255
drugs 135–62
adverse reactions 148–9
history 144–7
in older patients 136
rules of prescribing 138–9
sensitivity 142–3

summary sheet 147
dry eye 628
dysequilibrium 124–5
dysphagia 390–1
dyspnoea in terminally ill
patients 707

E

early walking aids 99
ears 589–610
deafness 590–592
hearing aids 594, 596–7
hearing assessment 592
tinnitus 598–9
ectropion 628
elder abuse 734–5
abusers 734
management 735
types of 734
elderly foot 536–7
management 538
electroconvulsive therapy
272
emergency department
20
endocrinology 451–86
enduring power of attorney
718, 719
enteral feeding 380–2
entropion 628
epilepsy 176–7
driving regulations 177
drug treatment 178
Epley's manoeuvre 605
erectile dysfunction 570–1
erysipelas 636
erythrocyte sedimentation
rate 488
ethical issues 717–38
artificial feeding 384–6
do not resuscitate
decisions 728–9
medical decisions 720–1
eyelid disorders 628
eyelid tumours 628
eyes 609–28
ageing 610
age-related macular
degeneration 620–1
drug effects 626
glaucoma 618–20
visual hallucinations 624
visual impairment 612–13

F

facial pain 376
faecal incontinence 582
assessment 584

management 586–7
falls 33, 116
  assessment following 118
  banned terms 117
  drugs associated with 118
  examination 119
  frequency 116
  prevention 120–1
  severity 116
  tests 119
falls clinics 134
fertility 8
finances 737–44
  benefits 742–3
  making a will 738
  pensions 740–1
  taxation 744
financial decisions 718–19
  enduring power of attorney 718, 719
  incompetent patients 719
  lasting power of attorney 718, 719
  power of attorney 718
  testamentary capacity 718
first degree heart block 304–5
flecainide 295
frames 98
frontotemporal dementia 232
frozen shoulder 544
fungal infections 638
funny turns 05

G

gallbladder 375, 394
gallstones 394
gangrene 322
  dry 322
  wet 322
gastroenterology 373–408
gastro-oesophageal reflux disease 388
genitourinary medicine 551–72
  age-related changes 552
geriatric depression scale 748
geriatric services 02, 18
  acute problems 16
  chronic problems 17
  integration 22–3
  sub-acute problems 16
  use of 16–18
Glasgow Coma Score 196–7, 756
glaucoma 618–19
  acute angle closure 619
  definition 618

intraocular pressure 618
  primary open angle 618–19
glomerular filtration rate 419
glomerulonephritis 428
glucose metabolism, effects of ageing 452
gout 526–7, 536
GP contract 55
Grave's disease 472

H

haematology 487–508
haematopoietic system, ageing 488
haemoglobin 488
Haemophilus influenzae 335
hair changes 631
Hallpike manoeuvre 601
hammer toes 536
Heaf test 361
healthcare assistance 743
health visitors 114
hearing aids 594, 596–7
  how to use 597
  types of 596
hearing assessment 592
heat-related illness 448–9
herpes zoster 628
hiatus hernia 388
hip
  fracture 540
  osteoarthritis 540
  pain 540
history taking 64
  banned terms 65
  cognitive impairment 64
  information sources 66–7
  patient interview 64
  sensory impairment 64
holiday support 50
home care 46–7
  community care assessment 46
  costs 47
  problems of 47
homeostasis 431–50
hormone replacement therapy 484–5
hypercalcaemia, management 445
hypernatraemia 442
hyperosmolar non-ketotic coma 464–5
hypersomnolence 190
hypertension 156, 288–9
  assessment 288
  definitions 288

treatment 290–1
  treatment thresholds and goals 289
hyperthyroidism
  diagnosis 472–3
  drug treatment 476–7
  investigation 474
  non-drug treatment 478
  sub-clinical 477
hypoglycaemia 465
hyponatraemia
  assessment 436
  treatment 438–9, 439
hypotension, orthostatic (postural) 130–1
hypothermia
  diagnosis 444–5
  management 446
hypothyroidism
  diagnosis 468–9
  treatment 470–1

I

illness in older people 12–13
  features of 12
  investigation 12
  treatment 13
immune system, ageing 66
impedance tympanometry 594
incontinence 573–88
infection 662
  diagnosis 663
inferior vena cava filter 34
inflammatory bowel disease 400–1
influenza 332–3
  treatment 333
  vaccination 340
informal carers 48–9
information sources 66–7
  ambulance crew 66
  family 66
  general practitioner and community nurse 66
  neighbours/friends 66
  nursing and residential homes 67
  old medical notes 67
  professional carers 66
inpatient rehabilitation 90, 91
insomnia 188–9
integrated care 22–3
intermediate care 30–1
intertrigo 642
investigations 74–5
  toleration of 75
iron deficiency anaemia
  diagnosis 492–3

investigation 493
treatment 494
ron therapy 494
irritable bowel syndrome 404
ischaemia, acute 322
ischaemic colitis 404

K

kidney, ageing 410–11
blunted fluid and electrolyte homeostasis 410–11
falling renal reserve 410
structural changes 411
kyphosis 127

L

large intestine 375
lasting power of attorney 718, 719
Legionella pneumophila 335
lentigo maligna 656
leukaemia, chronic lymphocytic 502
Lewy body dementia 174–5, 230
lichen sclerosus 568
lichen simplex 652
life expectancy 6–7, 10
liver 375, 394
loop diuretics 311
lung, ageing 328
lung cancer 356–7
non-small cell 357
palliative interventions 357
small cell 357

M

macrocytic anaemia 496
malabsorption 402
malignancy 687–98
cancer with unknown primary 696–9
diagnosis 690, 691
in older people 688
presentation 692–3
screening for 693
treatment 694–5
see also individual cancer types
malignant melanoma 657
malignant otitis externa 535
Mantoux test 361
medical decisions 720–1

competent patients 720–1
incompetent patients 720
megaloblastic anaemia 496
memantine, dementia 242
menopause 484–5
mental health 33
mesothelioma 354
methicillin-resistant Staphylococcus aureus 666
control of 669
disease 696–8
microscopic colitis 404
Mini-Cog 754
minimal cognitive impairment 222
mini-mental state examination 752
mirtazipine 275
mitral regurgitation 317
mitral stenosis 317
mobility 88
monoamine oxidase inhibitors 275
monoclonal gammopathy of undetermined significance 504
morbidity 10
motor neurone disease 182
mouth 374, 376–7
mouth ulcers 377
multi-disciplinary meetings 93, 94
multiple myeloma 506
multiple pathology 62
multi-system atrophy 174
musculoskeletal system 509–44
myelodysplasia 500–1
myelodysplastic syndrome 500–1
myocardial infarction 286–7
myxoedema coma 473

N

nails 536
national service framework 32–3
age discrimination 32
falls 32
general hospital care 32
intermediate care 32
mental health 33
person-centered care 32
promotion of health and active life 33
stroke 32
nausea and vomiting 393
terminally ill patients 706
necrotizing fasciitis 636
nephrotic syndrome 426
neuralgia 168

neuroleptic malignant syndrome 180
neurology 163–90
ageing effects 164
epilepsy 176–7, 178
motor neurone disease 182
neuralgia 168
neuroleptic malignant syndrome 180
Parkinson's disease 170–2
peripheral neuropathies 184–5
sleep disorders 190
sleep and insomnia 188–9
subdural haematoma 186–7
tremor 166–7, 175
neuropathic foot 536
NIH stroke scale 196–7
nocturnal polyuria 319
normal pressure hydrocephalus 234
NSAIDs 154
nutrition 378
nutritional support 378

O

occupational therapy 100
assessments 102
components of personal ability 100
interventions 102–3
role of occupational therapist 100
skills vs habits 100
training 100
oedema 644
peripheral 318–19
oesophageal disease 388–9
oesophagus 374
ophthalmic shingles 684
opioids 154
orthostatic (postural) hypotension 130–1
osteoarthritis 127, 510, 536
hip 540
management 512
osteomyelitis 534–5
osteoporosis 120, 156, 514–15
management 516–17
oxidative damage 4
oxygen therapy 370–1

P

Paget's disease 524–5
palliative care 704–5

principle of double effect 705
subcutaneous infusion 708
pancreas 375
paraproteinaemias 504
parenteral feeding 381
Parkinson's disease 170–2
and dementia 230
diseases masquerading as 174–5
Parkinson's-Plus syndromes 174
parotitis 376
peak expiratory flow rate 364–5
pensions 740–1
occupational pensions 740
personal pensions 740
UK State pension 740
war pensions 741
pentoxyfylline 647
peptic ulcer disease 392–4
peripheral neuropathies 184–5
peripheral oedema 318–19
peripheral vascular disease 320–1
gangrene in 322
permanent pacemakers 303
pernicious anaemia 496
pet schemes 50
pharmacology 140–1
absorption 140
distribution 140
hepatic metabolism8 140
renal excretion 141
pharmacy 112
photoageing 632
physical examination 70
general advice 70
systems 72–3
physical slowness 270
physiotherapy 96–7
range of interventions 96–7
role of physiotherapist 96
training 96
pleural effusions 346–7
chronic 346
fluid aspiration 347
pleural plaques 354
pneumonia 334, 335
aspiration 380–1
CURB-65 score 336
hospital-acquired 337
treatment 336–8, 449
vaccination 340
polymyalgia rheumatica 518
population age structure 8–9

population 'pyramids' 8–9
post-herpetic neuralgia 168, 687
post-mortems 714
postprandial hypotension 131
postural blood pressure 131
power of attorney 718
predicted date of discharge 84
presbyacusis 590
prescribing 138–9
breaking the rules 162
pressure areas 88
pressure injuries 545–50
pressure sores 88
presyncope 122–3
primary care 54–5
problem lists 68–9
progressive supranuclear palsy 174
propylthiouracil 476
prostate specific antigen 560
prostatic cancer 558–9
Gleason score 558
treatment 562–3
protein modification 4
pruritic conditions 652–3
pruritus 648
assessment 648
causes 648
treatment 650
pruritus ani 652
pseudogout 528
psychiatry 219–76
psychosis 250
psychotherapy 272
ptosis 628
pulmonary aspiration 350
pulmonary embolism 348–9
pulmonary fibrosis 342

R

radioiodine 478
Ramsay Hunt syndrome 685
rationing 732
re-feeding syndrome 380–1
registrar 714
rehabilitation 80–1
aims and objectives 84
doctors in team 104
inpatient 90, 91
measurement instruments 88–9
measurement tools 86
nurses in team 106
occupational therapy 100

patients unlikely to benefit from 92–5
physiotherapy 96–7
predicted date of discharge 84
process of 82
setting 80
speech and language therapy 110
walking aids 98–9
WHO classification 81
renal artery stenosis 430
renal failure see acute renal failure; chronic renal failure
renal medicine 409–30
renal replacement therapy dialysis 422–3
transplantation 424
renal transplantation 424
respiratory infections 330
lower respiratory tract 334–5
upper respiratory tract 330
respite care 49
restless legs syndrome 190
revascularization 285
rhabdomyolysis 550
rib fractures 344
rotator cuff
tear 544
tendonitis 544

S

scabies 655
seborrhoeic dermatitis 440
seborrhoeic warts 658
second degree heart block 304–5
selective serotonin reuptake inhibitors 274
self-harm 270
senescence 2
senile self-neglect 266
serotonin and noradrena-line reuptake inhibitors 275
serotonin syndrome 180
sexual function 570–1
shoulder pain 544
sick euthyroid syndrome 452
sick sinus syndrome 304–5
single assessment process 34
sinoatrial block 304–5
sinus bradycardia 304–5

kin 629–58
  ageing 630–1
  bacterial infections 636
  fungal infections 638
  photoageing 632
kin cancers/pre-cancers
    656–7
kin tags 658
leep 188–9
leep apnoea 190
leep disorders 190
leep disturbance 270
mall intestine 374
social clubs 50
social decisions 723, 732–3
Social Fund 742
social work 108
omatization 271
pecialty clinics 28–9
speech and language
    therapy 110
pirometry 364–5
pironolactone 311
qualor syndrome 266
squamous cell carcinoma
    657
statins 325
steroids 156–7
sticks/canes 98
stomach 374
Streptococcus pneumoniae
    335
stroke 32, 181–218
  acute assessment
    196–7, 202
  acute management
    200–2
  complications 212–13
  definition and classifica-
    tion 192–3, 193
  and epilepsy 177
  investigations 198
  long-term issues 214–15
  ongoing management
    208–10
  predisposing factors 194
  prognosis 205
  secondary prevention
    210
  thrombolysis 206
stroke units 204–5
subcutaneous fluid
    administration 434
subdural haematoma
    186–7
suicidal ideation 270, 276
sulphonylureas 458
supraventricular ectopic
    beats 304–5
syncope 122–3
  causes 122
  examination 123
  history 122–3

  investigation 123
  treatment 123
syndrome of inappropriate
    ADH 440–1

T

tachybrady syndrome
    304–5
taste 374
taxation 746
teeth 374–5
temperature monitoring
    448
temporal arteritis 520–2
terminally ill patients,
    symptom control 706–8
theophylline 366
thiazide diuretics 291, 311
thiazolidinediones 458
thrombolysis 206, 349
thyroid function 452
thyroid function tests 474
thyroid storm 473
tinnitus 598–9
  drugs causing 599
  examination 598
  history 598
  investigation 599
  treatment 599
tongue, sore 376
toxic nodular goitre 472
transient ischaemic attack
    clinics 216–17
transient ischaemic
    attacks 192
  see also stroke
travel assistance 745
tremor 166–7, 175
tricyclic antidepressants
    274
trigeminal neuralgia 168
tuberculosis
  investigations 360–1
  presentation 358
  treatment 362
  tuberculin skin test 361

U

urinary catheterization
    557
urinary incontinence 574
  assessment 576
  management 578–9, 601
  residual volume 577
urinary tract infection 682
  investigations 678
  organisms 678
  presentation 678
  recurrent 682

  risk factors 678
  treatment 680–1
urine tests, near patient
    674–5

V

vaginal bleeding, post-
    menopausal 564–5
vaginal prolapse 566–7
valvular heart disease
    316–17, 317
varicella zoster 684–5
varicose veins 644
vascular dementia 228, 229
vascular disease, effects on
    eye 622
vascular secondary
    prevention 324–5
vasovagal syncope 122
venous leg ulcers 642
  management 646–7
verapamil 295
vertebrobasilar insufficiency
    128–9
vertigo 600–1
  assessment 602–3
  causes 600, 601
  definition 600
  examination of vestibular
    system 603
  management 604–10
  understanding 600
visual hallucinations 624
  Charles Bonnet's
    syndrome 624
  drugs 624
  organic brain disease 624
  psychiatric disease 624
visual impairment 612–13
volume depletion 432–4
vulval cancer 569
vulval disorders 568–9
vulvitis 568
vulvodynia 568

W

walkers/rollators 99
walking aids 98–9
warfarin 158–60, 301, 311
wear and tear 4
weight loss 270, 386
wills 738
  testamentary capacity
    738

X

xerostomia 377